A Perfect Knowledge of Mind-Body from the Abhidhamma (Dhātukathā)

The third book of Abhidhamma Piṭaka

P. B. Tan

A Perfect Knowledge of Mind-Body from the Abhidhamma (Dhātukathā)
: The third book of Abhidhamma Piṭaka

Copyright © 2017 by P.B. Tan

First Edition: March 2017
Republication: August 2019

Published by KDP

All Rights Reserved. No part of this book may be reproduced, stored in a retrieval system, or transmitted in the modes of electronic copy, photocopying, reproducing, or used in any manner whatsoever without the prior written permission of the author and publisher except for the use of brief quotations in a book review or scholarly journals.

ISBN: 978-1687647290

DEDICATED TO

all sentient beings,

living and dead.

Table of Contents

Abbreviations used vii
Introduction 1
Structural formulation of text 8
I. Aggrouping and Ungrouping 11
   Analysis of 371 states from 170 catechism *11*
      105 internal states of enquiry 14
         1. Aggregates (*Khandho*) 14
         2. Bases (*Āyatanaṃ*) 18
         3. Elements (*Dhātu*) 22
         4. Truths (*Saccaṃ*) 26
         5. Faculties (*Indriyaṃ*) 29
         6. Dependent Origination, etc. (*Paṭiccasamuppādādi*) ... 35
   66 states of enquiry from Dhammasaṅgaṇīmātikā triads *46*
         7. Triads (*Tikaṃ*) 46
   200 states of enquiry from Dhammasaṅgaṇīmātikā dyads *61*
         8. Dyads (*Dukaṃ*) 61
            Root Causes (*Hetū*) 61
            Short dyads (*Cūḷantara*) 64
            Defilement (*Āsava*) 67
            Fetter (*Saṃyojana*) 70
            Bond (*Gantha*) 71
            Raging current (*Ogha*) 72
            Yoke (*Yoga*) 72
            Hindrance (*Nīvaraṇa*) 73
            Attachment (*Parāmāsa*) 74
            Intermediate dyads (*Mahatara*) 77
            Clinging (*Upādāna*) 83
            Corruption (*Kilesa*) 85
            Final dyads (*Piṭṭhi*) 87
II. Aggrouped and Ungrouped 96
   Analysis of 42 states from 8 catechism *96*
      20 states of enquiry from 10 gross bases, 10 gross elements ... 98
      7 states of enquiry from consciousness elements 99

    15 other states of enquiry from matter aggregate **101**
III. Ungrouped and Aggrouped 105
    Analysis of 90 states from 12 catechism *105*
        53 internal states of enquiry *106*
        2 states of enquiry from Dhammasaṅgaṇīmātikā triads *113*
        35 states of enquiry from Dhammasaṅgaṇīmātikā dyads *113*
IV. Aggrouped and Aggrouped 119
    Analysis of 69 states from 2 catechism *119*
        39 internal states of enquiry *121*
        30 states of enquiry from Dhammasaṅgaṇīmātikā dyads *125*
V. Ungrouped and Ungrouped 129
    Analysis of 257 states from 35 catechism *129*
        99 internal states of enquiry *130*
        43 states of enquiry from Dhammasaṅgaṇīmātikā triads *144*
        115 states of enquiry from Dhammasaṅgaṇīmātikā dyads *152*
VI. Association and Dissociation 172
    Analysis of 250 states from 78 catechism *172*
        92 internal states of enquiry *174*
        47 states of enquiry from Dhammasaṅgaṇīmātikā triads *187*
        111 states of enquiry from Dhammasaṅgaṇīmātikā dyads *195*
VII. Associated and Dissociated 211
    Analysis of 37 states from 11 catechism *211*
        24 internal states of enquiry *212*
        3 states of enquiry from Dhammasaṅgaṇīmātikā triads *216*
        10 states of enquiry from Dhammasaṅgaṇīmātikā dyads *217*
VIII. Dissociated and Associated 220
    Analysis of 324 states from 2 catechism *220*
IX. Associated and Associated 225
    Analysis of 120 states from 34 catechism *225*
        56 internal states of enquiry *226*
        8 states of enquiry from Dhammasaṅgaṇīmātikā triads *233*
        56 states of enquiry from Dhammasaṅgaṇīmātikā dyads *235*
X. Dissociated and Dissociated 243

    Analysis of 250 states from 56 catechism 243
    92 internal states of enquiry 243
    47 states of enquiry from Dhammasaṅgaṇīmātikā triads 253
    111 states of enquiry from Dhammasaṅgaṇīmātikā dyads 264
XI. Associated and Dissociated from the Aggrouped 279
    Analysis of 69 states from 8 catechism 279
    39 internal states of enquiry 280
    30 states of enquiry from Dhammasaṅgaṇīmātikā dyads 286
XII. Aggrouped and Ungrouped from Associated 290
    Analysis of 120 states from 31 catechism 290
    56 internal states of enquiry 290
    8 states of enquiry from Dhammasaṅgaṇīmātikā triads 300
    56 states of enquiry from Dhammasaṅgaṇīmātikā dyads 301
XIII. Associated and Dissociated from Ungrouped 309
    Analysis of 130 states from 8 catechism 309
    16 internal states of enquiry 310
    41 states of enquiry from Dhammasaṅgaṇīmātikā triads 313
    73 states of enquiry from Dhammasaṅgaṇīmātikā dyads 319
XIV. Aggrouped and Ungrouped from Dissociated 328
    Analysis of 324 states from 63 catechism 328
    97 internal states of enquiry 329
    64 states of enquiry from Dhammasaṅgaṇīmātikā triads 341
    163 states of enquiry from Dhammasaṅgaṇīmātikā dyads 353
Conclusion 376
Appendix I: 28 Types of Material Phenomena 377
Appendix II: 89 States of Consciousness 378
Appendix III: Summarised tables of the 89 (121) cittas 382
Appendix IV: 52 Mental Factors (*Cetasikā*) 383
Appendix V. 52 cetasikas in relation to the 89 (or 121) cittas 384
Appendix VI. Other classifications by types 392
Bibliography 418
About The Author 419

Abbreviations used

AN	Aṅguttara-Nikāya
Dhs	Dhammasaṅgaṇi
DhsA	Atthasālinī (Dhammasaṅgaṇi-Aṭṭhakathā)
DN	Dīgha-Nikāya
KN	Khuddaka-Nikāya
MN	Majjhima-Nikāya
Pug	Puggalapaññatti
PañkA	Pañcappakaraṇa-Aṭṭhakathā
SN	Saṃyutta-Nikāya
Vibh	Vibhaṅga

A Perfect Knowledge of Mind-Body from the Abhidhamma (Dhātukathā)

Introduction

The Buddha through his course of teaching, had to expound the same things in many different ways, at different places, in different times in order to suit the different intellects of his audience. But then, his underlying intention has always been the same, which is to exhort us on the realities of unsatisfactoriness and suffering, impermanence and emptiness, delusion and non-substantiality, and the need for our discontinuity from the round of existence. This whole book about five aggregates, twelve bases, and eighteen elements are the integral part of the Buddha's teachings, but it has to use fourteen methods with the different combinations of 371 states of mind in well over 2400 states of enquiry, to tell us just the very same thing. It may be a little difficult for some to fully comprehend this book if they had not studied previously the first two books, Dhammasaṅgaṇī, and the first thirteen chapters of Vibhaṅga or at least its first three chapters.

The original title of the scripture should in fact not be solely the name 'Dāthukathā' for the reason the five aggregates and twelve bases are also the other two subject matters of study which are of comparable importance. A noticeable contrast in Dāthukathā being the catechism written in this scripture is different from the catechism written in the other books of Abhidhamma, in that all the answers that are provided with Dāthukathā come in the form of whole numbers, in terms of aggregates, bases, and elements. Apart from this difficulty which would require readers to have more groundwork and fact-finding as to what might be the possible answers, there are also intentional use of thought-inducing words in phrases throughout the 518 subject matters of enquiry. For example, intricate words of "this state", "that state", "these states", "those states", and the second "these states" are used in all the catechism. These alone, are enough to keep the otherwise might-be-interested readers away. From what I have just mentioned, it is easy to understand why Dāthukathā has always been amongst the least read of dhamma and Abhidhamma books in Buddhist libraries.

The translated English copy of Dāthukathā by U Nārada, Mūla Paṭṭhāna Sayadaw with the title "Discourse on Elements", was published by PTS in 1962. This book gives a good analysis of the 371 states of enquiry in the first chapter by providing some charts. The detailed analytical work provided in that first chapter has laid out the preliminary groundwork to facilitate readers in their examination of all other states of enquiry in the remaining thirteen chapters. The only drawback with this translated book is that it does not provide the breakdown answers for all the states of enquiry in the fourteen methods, except for only a predetermined list of enquiring states. This book is also found to have a few mistakes in terms of omitted translation from Pāli text, and error in Pāli words.

As we all know, the bulk of the Buddha's teaching and his intention, are concurred at the same centre-stage as perfecting our knowledge in respect of five aggregates, twelve bases, and eighteen elements. Having known how important the objective of this third book of Abhidhamma is weighed, most of us can not

1

Introduction

understand why all the answers in the catechism are given as plain whole numbers in terms of aggregates, bases, and elements. If the original intention in compiling the Dāthukathā was meant only for monks and ardent truth-seekers to explore beyond numeric answers, it would be a great loss for thousands others in the past two and half millenniums who otherwise might seriously study it had Dāthukathā been written with breakdown answers. The psycho-philosophical content of this book is a perfect gift to mankind regardless of their religious beliefs. Our comprehension of what this book teaches us would go a long way in helping us to apply our knowledge and understanding to all extents and levels of meditation, to every intolerable state of affairs around us, to every confusing and misguiding circumstances that we are faced with, to all sorts of enticements, covetousness and aversion in our daily life, for the perfectly right answers. And those reasons, had made me believe that a reproduction of this book with analytical details and breakdown answers for all these states of enquiry is somehow needed. The thoughts of a wearisome task lying ahead for an exhaustive work of this nature has not unnerve and hold me back, despite of having some health problems. My plan is to construct a chart for every subject matter of enquiry, each of them is to be followed by analysis and breakdown answers. The charts at the same time will also provide the well-versed readers in similar field of interest, who may opt not to read the descriptive form of answers, but who can comprehend from simply quick glance at the charts. For some, it can be a tremendous time-saving and convenience. Different kinds of classification given in tables and charts are provided in the appendixes as references for this book, and also intended as a supplementary guide to readers who might be interested in using them for further analysis, or for their additional knowledge. At the completion point of this book, Appendix VI alone have been included with 29 charts. My work by no means would be free of mistakes, given the challenging nature of this book which commands breakdown details and explanations from numeric values. Equal attention is dedicated to every state of enquiry, and meticulous in every single detail.

The treatment of this book follows the same fourteen chapters as in the original scripture. These fourteen chapters represent fourteen different methods used to enquire the states in question, based on the four principles of interrogation — classification or included (as aggrouped) and unclassification or not included (as ungrouped) under the three schemata of aggregates, bases, and elements; association (*sampayutta*) and dissociation (*vipayutta*) between states of enquiry and states of comparison. These fourteen methods examine the different combinations of states based on the 371 states of enquiry as given in Chapter 1, which comprise of 105 internal states of enquiry and 266 external states of enquiry. The internal states of enquiry consist of five aggregates, twelve bases, eighteen elements, four truths, twenty-two faculties, dependent originations (12 factors and 17 kinds), four foundations of mindfulness, four right strivings, four basis of psychic accomplishment, jhānas, Illimitables, five faculties, five powers, seven enlightenment-factors, noble eightfold path, and

A Perfect Knowledge of Mind-Body from the Abhidhamma (Dhātukathā)

contact-group of 7. The external states of enquiry consist of 22 triads and 100 dyads which are exactly the dhammasaṅgaṇī mātikā.

Chapter 1 is rewritten more than the content of the original text to give supplementary details of the 371 subject matters of enquiry, which are useful to guide study through the successive thirteen chapters. With regard to the internal states, the catechism in this chapter includes unary, twofold, up to fivefold enquiry of states for the five aggregates, and includes unary and twofold enquiry of states for the other remaining internal states. The catechism deals with 63 states of enquiry from the triads and 143 states of enquiry from the dyads, either in single or combined states, instead of the total 266 states. Those subject matters in question are measured by whether, and in which distribution they are aggrouped (or classified) and ungrouped (or not classified) under the three categories, namely, under how many aggregates, how many bases, and how many elements. Technical details as to inter-linkages of the five aggregates, twelve bases, and eighteen elements are formulated in a chart placed at the beginning of Chapter 1 to give the necessary familiarisation before going further.

Chapter 2 deals with the method which stipulates that each of the states of enquiry can be aggrouped (i.e. classified, or included) with its remaining states under the same aggregate, but they may not be classified under the same base and under the same element. In other examples, they can be classified both under the same aggregate and under the same base, but not under the same element. In this regard, matter aggregate as the subject matter pf enquiry can not include mental aggregates as its remaining states, because they can not be aggrouped under the same aggregate. Since the states of enquiry are from either aggregates, or bases, or elements, the remaining states must also be from the same category. The remaining states are then measured as ungrouped under the categories of bases and elements, or taken as ungrouped only under elements depending on situations. Finally, those other states, which are not part of the subject matter of enquiry in the same category, are taken as ungrouped under the three categories. This chapter deals with 42 states of enquiry, of which 35 belong to matter aggregate and remaining 7 belong to consciousness aggregate.

Chapter 3 deals with the method when the states of enquiry are dealt with the remaining states from the same category, those states can be included as under the same base and under same element, albeit not included as under the same aggregate. In this respect, only the 3 aggregates of feeling, perception and volitive formation, including also subtle matters and *Nibbāna*, are considered under analysis. Gross matters and consciousness aggregate are excluded from being states of enquiry. For gross matter is classified under 10 gross bases and 10 gross elements which can not be aggrouped with one or all of the other 3 aggregates under the same base and same element. Similarly for consciousness aggregate, which is classified under mind-base and 7 consciousness elements, is not aggrouped with one or all of the other 3 aggregates under the same base and same element. For the first part of answers, when each state of enquiry is dealt with its remaining states, they are taken as ungrouped under the same aggregate(s)

Introduction

as the subject matter of enquiry. The second part of answers are formed by those remaining states which are therefore taken as aggrouped under different aggregates, but are included under the same base (ideation-base) and under the same element (ideation-element). There are 90 states of enquiry out of the total 371, which form the subject matter of this chapter.

Chapter 4 provides twofold analysis to the 69 states of enquiry based on the principle that the subject matters of enquiry and their remaining states which are required to be from the similar category, they as a whole must be included under the same aggregate, under same base, and under same element. This is the first classification which gives the first aggrouped answers. Because the states of enquiry and their remaining states are on the same comparison level with reference to the three categories, these states are thus comparable and interchangeable. It is on this basis those remaining states can in turn be classified with these states of enquiry in order to give the second aggrouped answers. The exception rule in this chapter follows the same as described in Chapter 3, that states from gross matters and consciousness aggregate are not to be included in the states of enquiry. For if they were to be included, they contain 2 different aggregates, 11 different bases and 17 different elements which, in any way, can not be classified under the same aggregate, under the same base, and under the same element which is a prerequisite condition set for this fourth method.

Chapter 5 deals two cases of ungrouping on the predetermined condition that those states under comparison can not be included as under the same aggregate, under the same base, and under the same element. This chapter introduces the fundamental criterion of co-adjunct states and possible states of the subject matters of enquiry, which delimit what are to constitute the remaining states. The first case of unclassification is comparing the states of enquiry with their remaining states, either with or without co-adjunct states depending on each state of enquiry. The second case of unclassification works on the same prescribed principle that those remaining states can not be included with the respective states of enquiry, either with or without their associated possible states depending on each state of enquiry.

States which are connate with both consciousness aggregate and subtle matters, and states which consist of all five aggregates, are excluded from being states of enquiry. Consciousness aggregate and subtle matters, together with their co-adjunct states and possible states, encompass all five aggregates. States which embrace five aggregates leave no more aggregates to be taken as states of comparison. For this reason, 114 of the total 371 states are excluded from this chapter. A total of 257 states of enquiry are being examined, of which 99 are interior states while 158 states are taken from triads and dyads.

Chapter 6 discusses states which are in association with, and dissociation from other states according to aggregates, bases, and elements. Association is divided into total association and partial association. The same is applied to dissociation. Association in the Abhidhamma context is reserved only to mental phenomena in any single moment of thought. Consciousness is associated with

A Perfect Knowledge of Mind-Body from the Abhidhamma (Dhātukathā)

feeling, perception and volitive formation in only a single thought-moment (*cittakhaṇa*). A total of 250 states of enquiry form the subject matter of this chapter, of which 92 are internal states while 158 belong the external states of enquiry from triads and dyads.

Total association between different states is only possible if they commonly share these 4 characteristics — arise together, dissolve together, share common object, and are comparable. There are four kinds of dissociation in the states of comparison, namely, dissociation by spheres, by classes, by times, and by continuity. The 4 mental aggregates are mutually associated with one another, the same association condition is also explained in Patthāna. States which are both mentality-materiality are neither associated, nor partially associated with other the three categories, but having only dissociated states. States which are either matter aggregate or *Nibbāna* are neither in associations, nor any partial associations with the three categories. When the 4 mental aggregates are the subject matters of enquiry, they have no associated states, but sometimes have partially associated states. When states which are both materiality and *Nibbāna*, or the 4 mental aggregates and *Nibbāna* are dealt with, there are no associated states nor partially associated states.

States which are at all times in dissociation are between 28 Matters and 4 mental aggregates, *Nibbāna* and 4 mental aggregates, 4 mental aggregates and materiality, 4 mental aggregates and *Nibbāna*. In other word, when matter aggregate, or all 4 mental aggregates, or *Nibbāna* is enquired with, there are no associated states nor partially associated states, but having only dissociated states. Similarly, when materiality is dealt with materiality, consciousness is dealt with consciousness, etc., they are neither associated nor dissociated. Whenever materiality is dealt with *Nibbāna*, the state of *Nibbāna* is ignored because they are neither associated nor dissociated. Whenever one or all mental aggregates are the states of enquiry, 16 subtle matters and *Nibbāna* are always the partially dissociated states. Though, like cittas and cetasikas, *Nibbāna* belongs to mentality, it is related to the 4 mental aggregates only by way of dissociation.

In Chapter 7, it first demonstrates the association of states when subject matters of enquiry are dealt with. These states, taken together, are then determined for their dissociated states. The latter, those dissociated states, are in turn determined for their own dissociated states as well as their partially dissociated states. States which have no associations with other states are disregarded from this chapter. Materiality, *Nibbāna*, are the two of them. In this regard, only those states which have both associations, and dissociations from the three categories of states can be considered as states of enquiry. Also, those associated states must have dissociations. Therefore, the subject matters of enquiry in this chapter are confined to mental aggregates, mental factors, and those pure forms of consciousness excluding those states such as the 4 truths, etc. Total 37 states of enquiry are dealt with in this chapter, of which 24 are internal states, 13 are from triads and dyads.

Introduction

    Chapter 8 deals with 324 states which are also the same states discussed under Chapter 14. These 324 states are from 28 matters, one or more of the 4 mental aggregates, *Nibbāna*, and states which belong to both mentality and materiality but which are dissociated. All of them fall in with the four kinds of dissociation which are mentioned in Chapter 6. In this chapter, each subject matter is first enquired for its dissociated states. Those dissociated states are in turn associated with no other states. The answer as 'none' applies similarly to all the 324 states. For example, matter aggregate is dissociated from the 4 mental aggregates, but the latter are not associated with any other states. Similarly, consciousness aggregate is dissociated from matter aggregate and *Nibbāna*, but neither 28 matters nor *Nibbāna* are each associated with any other states. Of these 324 states, 97 are internal states while 227 are made up from triads and clusters of dyads. There are 47 states excluded from this chapter.

    Chapter 9 discusses two cases of association. First, the subject matters of enquiry are dealt with to find out the associated states of comparison, and subsequently those associated states exchange in similar association with the subject matters of enquiry. Those associated states and those states of enquiry are then taken as aggrouped under the aggregates, bases, and elements. In this chapter, states which are pure materiality, *Nibbāna*, and those which possess materiality-mentality such as vitality-faculty, birth, ageing, and death, are excluded from discussion. Only states from the mental aggregates are considered. Total 120 states are being analysed, of which 56 are from interior states, and 64 are from triads and dyad-clusters.

    Chapter 10 deals with two cases of dissociated states, taking into account 250 states of enquiry. The dissociation conditions and answers for these 250 states of enquiry can also be found in Chapter 6 which has the same number of states under discussion. All five aggregates and state of *Nibbāna* are taken into consideration in this chapter. Firstly, the states of enquiry are dealt with to determine the dissociated states of comparison by the 4 kinds of dissociations (by spheres, by class, by times and by continuity, whichever is applicable) and relate them to dissociations by category (aggregates, bases, and elements, whichever is applicable). Thereafter, those dissociated states of comparison are further enquired to find out all the other possible states in both dissociations and partial dissociations. In the latter case, there may not necessarily be direct dissociations and partial dissociations from all the aggregates, bases, and elements if all the other possible states had already been included in the earlier dissociations. Of these 250 states of enquiry 92 are the interior states, 158 are from triads and dyads.

    Chapter 11 examines the same 69 states of enquiry as previously discussed in Chapter 4, which requires the states of enquiry to be classified with the remaining states of comparison under the same same aggregate, under same base, and under same element. Such condition can not be applied when gross matters and consciousness aggregate become the states of comparison. For this reason, gross matters and consciousness aggregate are not included as the states of comparison. The next step is to apply the methods of association/partial association and dissociation/partial dissociation under the aggregates, bases, and elements as discussed in Chapter 6. Of these 69 states, 39 are internal states, 30 are from the dyads.

In Chapter 12, we find the same 120 states of enquiry that are examined in Chapter 9. The method in this chapter first ascertains the associated states which are inclusive of the partially associated states, as the basis for classification and unclassification as was first examined in Chapter 1. The answers to these 120 states of enquiry can also be found in Chapter 9. States which are matters and *Nibbāna* are excluded from being the subject matters of enquiry in this chapter because the two have no associated states. 56 from internal states, 64 from triads and dyads, made up the 120 states of enquiry.

Chapter 13 handles a total of 130 states which are drawn from the 257 in Chapter 5. The method here deals with association/partial association and dissociation/partial dissociation, drawing from the remaining states of comparison which are not classified with the states of enquiry including those classifiable possible states, to form as aggrouped under the same aggregate, under same base, and under same element. The classification method which takes into account of co-adjunct states and possible states to the states of enquiry are the same as described in Chapter 5. However, additional details as to aggrouping the unclassified states of enquiry under the three categories before dealing with association and dissociation, are included for all these 130 states. There are 16 internal states, and 114 from triads and dyads which form the total 130. States which are left out from this chapter include states which have many different states of comparison which can not be included in the same fashion of classification. Those states include gross matters, 4 mental aggregates, 7 consciousness elements, and states which contain all five aggregates like truth of the origin of suffering, four noble truths, and so on.

The 324 states of enquiry in Chapter 14 are the same as in Chapter 8. In this chapter, the states of enquiry are dealt with in four parts, to determine (i) dissociation, (ii) association, which are similarly associated with none for all the 324 states. Those dissociated states are then determined for (iii) classification, and (iv) unclassification. The classification and unclassification under the three categories follow the same as in Chapter 1. The dissociation follows the four kinds of dissociation as explained in Chapter 6. No exclusion of states are specified for this chapter which includes all materiality, one or all of the 4 mental aggregates, *Nibbāna*, and states which belong to mentality-materiality are always in dissociation.

p. b. tan

March, 2017
Kuching

I pay homage to the Blessed One, the Worthy One, the Fully Enlightened One.

Structural formulation of text

1. The 14 methods (*Nayamātikā*)

I. including/aggrouping, not including/ungrouping (*saṅgaho asaṅgaho*)
II. included/aggrouped, not included/ungrouped (*saṅgahitena asaṅgahitaṃ*)
III. not included/ungrouped, included/aggrouped (*asaṅgahitena saṅgahitaṃ*)
IV. aggrouped and aggrouped (*saṅgahitena saṅgahitaṃ*)
V. ungrouped and ungrouped (*asaṅgahitena asaṅgahitaṃ*)
VI. association and dissociation (*sampayogo vippayogo*)
VII. associated and dissociated (*sampayuttena vippayuttaṃ*)
VIII. dissociated and associated (*vippayuttena sampayuttaṃ*)
IX. associated and associated (*sampayuttena sampayuttaṃ*)
X. dissociated and dissociated (*vippayuttena vippayuttaṃ*)
XI. associated and dissociated concerning the aggrouped (*saṅgahitena sampayuttaṃ vippayuttaṃ*)
XII. aggrouped and ungrouped concerning the associated (*sampayuttena saṅgahitaṃ asaṅgahitaṃ*)
XIII. associated and dissociated concerning the ungrouped (*asaṅgahitena sampayuttaṃ vippayuttaṃ*)
XIV. aggrouped and ungrouped concerning the dissociated (*vippayuttena saṅgahitaṃ asaṅgahitaṃ*)

2. The 105 Interior states of enquiry (*Abbhantaramātikā*)

(5) Five Aggregates (*pañcakkhandhā*)
(12) Twelve Bases (*dvādasāyatanāni*)
(18) Eighteen Elements (*aṭṭhārasa dhātuyo*)
(4) Four Truths (*cattāri saccāni*)
(22) Twenty-two Faculties (*bāvīsatindriyāni*)
(28) Twenty-eight Dependent Origination (*paṭiccasamuppādo*) : 12 Factors (*aṅga*), 17 Kinds (*bheda*)
(1) Four Foundations of Mindfulness (*cattāro satipaṭṭhānā*)
(1) Four Right Strivings (*cattāro sammappadhānā*)
(1) Four Basis of Psychic Accomplishment (*cattāro iddhipādā*)
(1) Four Jhānas (*cattāri jhānāni*)
(1) Four Illimitable States (*catasso appamaññāyo*)
(1) Five Faculties (*pañcindriyāni*)
(1) Five Powers (*pañca balāni*)

A Perfect Knowledge of Mind-Body from the Abhidhamma (Dhātukathā)

(1) Seven Enlightenment-Factors (*satta bojjhaṅgā*)
(1) Noble Eightfold Path (*ariyo aṭṭhaṅgiko maggo*)
(7) The Contact-Group of 7:
   i. contact (*phasso*)
   ii. feeling (*vedanā*)
   iii. perception (*saññā*)
   iv. volition (*cetanā*), or sometimes interpreted as 'thought' which carries the qualifying ingredient of intention
   v. consciousness (*cittaṃ*)
   vi. decision (*adhimokkho*)
   vii. attention (*manasikāro*)

Above are 105 interior states of enquiry in total. If we count by their number of phenomenal states, it comprises total 142 phenomena.

3. Four principles of the methods (*Nayamukhamātikā*)

i. 3 aggrouping (under aggregates, bases, and elements)
ii. 3 ungrouping (under aggregates, bases, and elements)
iii. 4 association (therewith the 4 mental aggregates)
iv. 4 dissociation (therefrom the 4 mental aggregates)

4. Two attributes of the methods (*Lakkhaṇamātikā*)

i. common (*sabhāgo*) — complying with the principles of aggrouping, ungrouping, association and dissociation.
ii. uncommon (*visabhāgo*) — not complying with the principles of aggrouping, ungrouping, association and dissociation.

5. External states of enquiry (*Bāhiramātikā*)

i. 22 triads of the dhammasaṅgaṇī mātikā
ii. 100 dyads of the dhammasaṅgaṇī mātikā

Structural formulation of text

In Dhātukathā, we examine a total of 371 states of enquiry, of which 105 are interior states, 266 are external because they are states from the dhammasaṅgaṇī mātikā (22 triads x 3 and 100 dyads x 2, thus giving us 66+200=266). These 371 states are first expounded in Chapter 1 by use of tables which give short analysis of each interior and external states. These tables of the interior and external states form the basis on which further states of enquiries in different methods from the subsequent 13 chapters are based. Therefore, a full comprehension of the contents in Chapter 1 is essentially important before one should proceed further to the other chapters.

In Chapter 1, each state is aggrouped under certain aggregates, bases, and elements. The remainder from each aggrouped state are then categorised as "ungrouping" in terms of aggregates, bases and elements. Chart 1 provided at the beginning of Chapter 1 clarifies how these three groupings as aggregates, bases, and elements, are integrated with the four classifications of ultimate realities according to Abhidhamma. The information guide in Chart 1 is so essential that analysis of all the states of enquiries in this book are based entirely on it.

To further assist readers with better understanding in the analysis of states, charts and tables by the various types of classification are provided in the five appendixes. Charts or diagrams will also be constructed for every unit or combined group of enquiries, follow by analytical exposition throughout the 14 Chapters. Without these additional works, it is an uphill task or almost impossible for us to fully comprehend all these states in which the catechetical text summarises the answers only in absolute numbers under the three categories of aggregates, bases and elements.

A Perfect Knowledge of Mind-Body from the Abhidhamma (Dhātukathā)

CHAPTER 1

I. Aggrouping and Ungrouping
(*Saṅgahāsaṅgaha*)

Analysis of 371 states from 170 catechism

Chart 1. The three groupings as aggregates, bases, and elements in relation to the four classifications of ultimate realities

The 4 Ultimate Realities		5 Aggregates		12 Bases		18 Elements
1	28 Matters	Gross Matters (12)	Sensitive eye (1)	1	Eye-Base	1	Eye-Element
			Sensitive ear (1)	2	Ear-Base	2	Ear-Element
			Sensitive nose (1)	3	Nose-Base	3	Nose-Element
			Sensitive tongue (1)	4	Tongue-Base	4	Tongue-Element
			Sensitive body (1)	5	Body-Base	5	Body-Element
			Vision (1)	6	Vision-Base	6	Vision-Element
			Sound (1)	7	Sound-Base	7	Sound-Element
			Odour (1)	8	Odour-Base	8	Odour-Element
			Taste (1)	9	Taste-Base	9	Taste-Element
			Tangibility:	10	Tangible-Base	10	Tangible-Element
			- earth (1)		- earth		- earth
			- heat (1)		- heat		- heat
			- air (1)		- air		- air
			*Subtle Matters (16)				
2	Cetasikas		Feeling Aggregate. (1)	11	Ideation-Base (or mind-object base)	11	Ideation-Element (or mind-object element)
3			Perception Aggregate (1)				
4			Volitive formation Aggregate (50)				
	**Nibbāna (1)						
5	89 Consciousness	Consciousness Agr.	2 Eye-Consciousness (2)	12	Mind-Base	12	Eye-Cons. Element
			2 Ear-Consciousness (2)			13	Ear-Cons. Element
			2 Nose-Consciousness (2)			14	Nose-Cons. Element
			2 Tongue-Consciousness (2)			15	Tongue-Cons. Element
			2 Body-Consciousness (2)			16	Body-Cons. Element
			5-Door advertence (1), Receiving (2)			17	Mind-Element
			76 remaining consciousness			18	Mind-Cons. Element

* for the 16 classes of subtle matters, please refer to the table in Appendix I.
** the unconditioned *Nibbāna*, is not a part of 5 aggregates, but is ideational.

I. Aggrouping and Ungrouping

Chart 1 above depicts the basis and kernel of the Abhidhamma teaching, and essentially guides the readers in the analysis of all the states of enquiry throughout this book. Chart 1 is to be referred to necessarily when analysing the method used not only in Chapter 1, but also for the subsequent 13 methods from the 13 chapters. Therefore, this chart must be fully comprehended. Chart 1 shows classification of the four ultimate realities (28 types of material phenomena, 52 mental concomitants, 89 states of consciousness, and *Nibbāna*), and demonstrates how they are aligned to the specific components of the 5 aggregates, 12 bases, and 18 elements. The 28 types of material phenomena are made up of 12 gross matters and 16 subtle matters. The 12 gross matters correspond with 10 bases and 10 elements respectively. More detail of these 28 types of materiality is illustrated in Appendix I.

The 52 mental concomitants (*cetasikā*) are composed of feeling aggregate, perception aggregate, and volitive formation aggregate. The 52 mental concomitants 16 subtle matters, and *Nibbāna* are the 69 states (52+16+1=69) which are contained by ideation-base. In this respect, *Nibbāna*, which is the unconditioned element, does not belong to the grouping of 5 aggregates although it comes under mentality.

Above are only the direct explanation from the chart regarding its structural layout. More understanding on the co-relations between the different aspects of dhamma in Chart 1 is vital, so that readers can easily correlate the analysis and answers given for all subject matters of enquiry with Chart 1. Below elaborates in more details regarding the co-relations between the three categories and the four ultimate realities from Chart 1.

The 5 sense-bases function independently of each other, with mind-base playing the central role of communicating with each of them. These 5 sense-bases and mind-base form the '6 subjective bases'. Ideation-base, which is also called 'mind-object base', together with the 5 sense-object bases, they form the '6 object-bases'. These '6 object-bases' are stimuli, each impinges on the corresponding subjective base, which acts as a support for the element. The memory of an unpleasant past, for instance, forms as ideation-base (or mind-object base) which impinges on mind-base, therefrom arises mind-consciousness. The coinciding meeting point of these three phenomena is called 'contact', which occurs in the same way for the other 5 types of contacts. Because of contact, feelings arise; what is being felt brings about how it would be perceived; what is being perceived occasions volitive formation which are mental factors containing intentive thinking; because of intentive thought, there is unsettled aversion, restlessness and diffusedness; because of that, diffused perceptive mental impressions of the past, future, and present cognisable by mind-consciousness arises, and carry on with the person.

In Abhidhamma context, mind-base and the 32 types of resultant consciousness (from the three mundane spheres) function interdependently.

A Perfect Knowledge of Mind-Body from the Abhidhamma (Dhātukathā)

Mind-base conditions the 32 resultant consciousness which, in turn, also condition mind-base. Mind-base includes 89 cittas and 7 consciousness elements.

The 5 sense-elements and mind-element, together form the '6 subjective elements'. Mind-element consist of one 'five-doors advertence' consciousness, and the 2 types of receiving consciousness. Ideation-element, also called 'mind-object element' or "element of the mental-concomitants" according to dhammasaṅgaṇi, together with the 5 object-elements, they form the 6 object-elements. Ideation-element consists of 69 states (52 cetasikas, 16 subtle matters, and *Nibbāna*). The 7 consciousness-elements excluding mind-element, are called the '6 intellectual elements'. The 89 cittas excluding the fivefold pair of sensory cognitions (i.e. the 10 viññāṇas) and 3 mind-elements, are the remaining 76 consciousness which constitute mind-consciousness element. These 76 consciousness can be identified from the chart in Appendix II.

What are the differences between bases and elements? The base functions as a basis and support for the elements. For example, mind-base is the support base for the 7 consciousness elements. Ideation-base, or called the mind-object base, contains the three mental aggregates, an unconditioned element, and subtle matters such as male and female faculties, vitality faculty, the two intimations, etc., and which deals with mind-base. It is a support base for ideation-element, but not the other way. Ideation-element, according to the second book of Vibhaṅga, functions as very short-lived and imperceptible ten-steps of mental processes, occur immediately after the arising and cessation of each of the five sensory consciousness elements or the first advertence in all these five consciousness elements, thereafter giving rise to mind-element (*tajjāmanodhātu*). The latter, goes through the same infinitesimal ten mental processes, to emerge as mind-consciousness element. As for the ten gross bases, they support the ten gross elements which can be further sub-divided by internal, external, and by other properties. Elements can not contain bases which support them.

Greed, hate, and delusion as unwholesome mental factors, are included under volitive formation, ideation-base, and ideation-element. The 12 unwholesome states of consciousness (8 greed-rooted, 2 hatred-rooted, and 2 delusion-rooted) are among the 76 types of the remainder of 89 states of consciousness. The 10 sensory cognitions experiencing sense objects are in 5 pairs, is because each pair has one wholesome resultant citta and one unwholesome resultant citta.

Consciousness is never arisen by itself. As you will discover later in the chapter, that the 52 mental factors are either conjoined with, arising together with, or arising successively with consciousness. Consciousness in turn reinforces, modifies, and recreates mental factors and 17 mind-produced matters. So, consciousness is the primary reason which shapes our characters, behavioural proclivities, actions, future destinies, and is the same factor which explains whether one lapses into crimes or becomes a successful and respectful person.

How *nāma-rūpa* can be interpreted from Chart 1? *Nāma* (mind) comprises the three mental aggregates of feeling, perception, and volitive formation which is made up of the remaining 50 mental factors. Mind-base belongs to *nāma*. *Rūpa*

I. Aggrouping and Ungrouping

has shades of interpretation given as 'form, body, corporeality, materiality, matter', etc., but we should note that *rūpa* also contain energy. Light orbs, ghosts, for example, are energy belong to *rūpa*. In abhidhamma, 'matter' is the more accurate rendering for *rūpa*, which is composed of 4 great elements and 24 derived matters, and categorised in terms of 12 gross matters and 16 subtle matters, and has 4 conditions or causes as kamma-produced, consciousness-produced, temperature-produced, and nutriment-produced. The 10 gross bases are *rūpa* which consist of the 6 subjective bases as 'internal', and the 6 object bases as 'external'. In quantum physics, *rūpa* is equated with finer materials as particles and anti-particles, interacting with each other at infinitesimal intervals which the Buddhists refer to them as 17 thought-moments (*ksaṇā*), and which appear and perish almost instantaneously, and happens incessantly. *Nāma-rūpa* refers to those states which are embedded with the quality of mentality-materiality such as rebirth-becoming, states which are indeterminate, states without *vitakka* and *vicāra*, etc. Ideation-base belongs to *nāma-rūpa*. Consciousness conditions both mind and matter (*nāma-rūpa*) in the sensuous sphere and fine-material sphere, whereas it conditions only mind (*nāma*) in the immaterial sphere. But we should note that as in dependent origination, only consciousness and *nāma*, as well as consciousness and *nāma-rūpa* are coexistent and conditioning each other (*aññamaññapaccaya*). Herein, consciousness is referred to the 32 resultant cittas (*vipākacittāni*) and the 19 types of rebirth-linking consciousness (*paṭisandhi-viññāṇa*). Rebirth-linking consciousness happens soon after the death-moment consciousness or *cuti-viññāṇa*. (Previously I mentioned that it arises when it first appeared in the mother's womb is not correct). It arises at the thought moment of conception of next bhava rebirth — is conditioned by some or all of the 32 unconsumed kamma vipaka cittas and which generate the "life-forming" kamma-produced matters. Of these 32 resultant cittas, only the 8 great resultant cittas (*mahāvipakacittāni*) along with the 2 receiving cittas (*upekkhā-sampaṭicchanacittāni*) from the sensuous sphere, come to be reborn as normal humans, or deities and brahmas into the two upper spheres. The other 9 sublime resultant cittas (4+5=9 *mahaggata vipākacittāni*) function as rebirth-linking consciousness for beings who have already been born in the respective two sublime spheres as a result of previously practicing and attaining rūpajhānas and arūpajhānas. As such, the 8 *mahāvipakacittāni* and 2 *upekkhā-sampaṭicchanacittāni* from sensuous sphere (8+2=10), and 9 *mahaggata vipākacittāni* from fine-material and immaterial spheres, they first condition rebirth-linking consciousness, and continue to condition both the life-continuum and life-flux throughout the existence of the beings in current lifespan, and finally which condition the last dying moment of consciousness.

105 internal states of enquiry

1. Aggregates (*Khandho*)

A Perfect Knowledge of Mind-Body from the Abhidhamma (Dhātukathā)

The table below supplements the information on aggregates in Chart 1.

Table 1.1. Interior States of Enquiry - 5 Aggregates (*pañcakkhandhā*)

	Aggregates:	Equivalent states :	Aggregates	Bases	Elements
1	Matter (*rūpa*)	28 types of materiality	1	11	11
2	Feeling (*vedanā*)	feeling mental concomitant	1	1	1
3	Perception (*saññā*)	perception mental concomitant	1	1	1
4	Volitive formation (*saṅkhāra*)	remaining 50 mental concomitants	1	1	1
5	Consciousness (*viññāṇa*)	89 states of consciousness	1	1	7
	Non-aggregate: Emancipated (*vimutto*)	*Nibbāna* — unconditioned element	-	1	1

The following states of enquiry nos. 6 to 21 are to be referred to preceding Table 1.1 and Chart 1.

Chart 1.1. Aggrouping and Ungrouping of Aggregates

	By units :	Aggrouped Agr	Base	Ele
6.	Matter aggregate. It is aggrouped under 1 aggregate (matter), 11 bases (10 gross bases, ideation-base), and 11 elements (10 gross elements, ideation-element). It is ungrouped under 4 aggregates (4 mental aggregates), 1 base (mind-base), and 7 elements (7 consciousness elements).	1	11	11
7.	Feeling aggregate. It is aggrouped under 1 aggregate (feeling), 1 base (ideation-base), and 1 element (ideation-element). It is ungrouped under 4 aggregates (matter, perception, volitive formation, consciousness), 11 bases (10 gross bases, mind-base), and 17 elements (10 gross elements, 7 consciousness elements).	1	1	1
8.	Perception aggregate. It is aggrouped under 1 aggregate (perception), 1 base (ideation-base), and 1 element (ideation-element). It is ungrouped under 4 aggregates (matter, feeling, volitive formation, consciousness), 11 bases (10 gross bases, mind-base), and 17 elements (10 gross elements, 7 consciousness elements).	1	1	1

I. Aggrouping and Ungrouping

9. Volitive formation aggregate. | 1 | 1 | 1
It is aggrouped under 1 aggregate (volitive formation), 1 base (ideation-base), and 1 element (ideation-element).
It is ungrouped under 4 aggregates (matter, feeling, perception, consciousness), 11 bases (10 gross bases, mind-base), and 17 elements (10 gross elements, 7 consciousness elements).

10. Consciousness aggregate. | 1 | 1 | 7
It is aggrouped under 1 aggregate (consciousness), 1 base (mind-base), and 7 elements (7 consciousness elements).
It is ungrouped under 4 aggregates (matter, feeling, perception, volitive formation), 11 bases (10 gross bases, ideation-base), and 11 elements (10 gross elements, ideation-element).

Emancipated (*vimutto*), i.e. the unconditioned element of *Nibbāna* (non-aggregate), is aggrouped under 1 base (ideation-base), and 1 element (ideation-element). | - | 1 | 1
It is ungrouped under 5 aggregates (matter, feeling, perception, volitive formation, consciousness), 11 bases (10 gross bases, mind-base), and 17 elements (10 gross elements, 7 consciousness elements).

	Aggrouped		
By pairs :	Agr	Base	Ele
11. Matter and Feeling aggregates.	2	11	11

They are aggrouped under 2 aggregates (matter, feeling), 11 bases (10 gross bases, ideation-base), and 11 elements (10 gross elements, ideation-element).
They are ungrouped under 3 aggregates (perception, volitive formation, consciousness), 1 base (mind-base), and 7 elements (7 consciousness elements).

12. Matter and Perception aggregates. | 2 | 11 | 11
They are aggrouped under 2 aggregates (matter, perception), 11 bases (10 gross bases, ideation-base), and 11 elements (10 gross elements, ideation-element).
They are ungrouped under 3 aggregates (feeling, volitive formation, consciousness), 1 base (mind-base), and 7 elements (7 consciousness elements).

13. Matter and Volitive Formation aggregates. | 2 | 11 | 11
They are aggrouped under aggregates (matter, volitive formation), 11 bases (10 gross bases, ideation-base), and 11 elements (10 gross elements, ideation-element).
They are ungrouped under 3 aggregates (feeling, volitive formation, consciousness), 1 base (mind-base), and 7 elements (7 consciousness elements).

A Perfect Knowledge of Mind-Body from the Abhidhamma (Dhātukathā)

14. **Matter and Consciousness aggregates.**   2   12   18
    They are aggrouped under aggregates (matter, consciousness), 12 bases (10 gross bases, ideation-base, mind-base), and 18 elements (10 gross elements, ideation-element, 7 consciousness elements).
    They are ungrouped under 3 aggregates. Nothing is ungrouped under any bases and any elements.

	Aggrouped		
By triads :	Agr	Base	Ele

15. **Matter, Feeling, and Perception aggregates.**   3   11   11
    They are aggrouped under 3 aggregates (matter, feeling, perception), 11 bases (10 gross bases, ideation-base), and 11 elements (10 gross elements, ideation-element).
    They are ungrouped under 2 aggregates (volitive formation, consciousness), 1 base (mind-base), and 7 elements (7 consciousness elements).

16. **Matter, Feeling, and Volitive Formation aggregates.**   3   11   11
    They are aggrouped under 3 aggregates (matter, feeling, volitive formation), 11 bases (10 gross bases, ideation-base), and 11 elements (10 gross elements, ideation-element).
    They are ungrouped under 2 aggregates (perception, consciousness), 1 base (mind-base), and 7 elements (7 consciousness elements).

17. **Matter, Feeling, and Consciousness aggregates.**   3   12   18
    They are aggrouped under 3 aggregates (matter, feeling, consciousness), 12 bases (10 gross bases, ideation-base, mind-base), and 18 elements (10 gross elements, ideation-element, 7 consciousness elements).
    They are ungrouped under 2 aggregates (perception, volitive formation). Nothing is ungrouped under bases and elements.

	Aggrouped		
By tetrads :	Agr	Base	Ele

18. **Matter, Feeling, Perception, and Volitive Formation aggregates.**   4   11   11
    They are aggrouped under 4 aggregates (matter, feeling, perception, volitive formation), 11 bases (10 gross bases, ideation-base), and 11 elements (10 gross elements, ideation-element).
    They are ungrouped under 1 aggregate (consciousness), 1 base (mind-base), and 7 elements (7 consciousness elements).

I. Aggrouping and Ungrouping

19. Matter, Feeling, Perception, and Consciousness aggregates. | 4 12 18
    They are aggrouped under 4 aggregates (matter, feeling, perception, consciousness), 12 bases (10 gross bases, ideation-base, mind-base), and 18 elements (10 gross elements, ideation-element, 7 consciousness elements).
    They are ungrouped under 1 aggregate (volitive formation).
    None is ungrouped under any bases and any elements.

	Aggrouped
By pentads:	Agr Base Ele

20. Matter, Feeling, Perception, Volitive Formation, and Consciousness aggregates. | 5 12 18
    They are aggrouped under 5 aggregates (matter, feeling, perception, volitive formation, consciousness aggregates), 12 bases (10 gross bases, ideation-base, mind-base), and 18 elements (10 gross elements, ideation-element, 7 consciousness elements).
    The five aggregates have nothing in ungrouping under any aggregates, under any bases, under any elements.

21. Same as in the aforesaid (20). | 5 12 18

2. Bases (*Āyatanaṃ*)

The table below supplements the information on Bases in Chart 1.

Table 1.2. Interior States of Enquiry - 12 Bases (*dvādasāyatanāni*)

	Primary bases:	Equivalent states:	Aggregates	Bases	Elements
1	Eye-base (*cakkhāyatanaṃ*)	sensitive eye	1	1	1
2	Ear-base (*sotāyatanaṃ*)	sensitive ear	1	1	1
3	Nose-base (*ghānāyatanaṃ*)	sensitive nose	1	1	1
4	Tongue-base (*jivhāyatanaṃ*)	sensitive tongue	1	1	1
5	Body-base (*kāyāyatanaṃ*)	sensitive body	1	1	1
6	Vision-base (*rūpāyatanaṃ*)	visible object	1	1	1
7	Sound-base (*saddāyatanaṃ*)	audible object	1	1	1
8	Odour-base (*gandhāyatanaṃ*)	olfactory object	1	1	1
9	Taste-base (*rasāyatanaṃ*)	gustatory object	1	1	1
10	Touch-base (*phoṭṭhabbāyatanaṃ*)	tactile object	1	1	1
11	Mind-base (*manāyatanaṃ*)	89 states of consciousness	1	1	7
12	Ideation-base (*dhammāyatanaṃ*)	16 subtle matter, 52 cetasikas,	4	1	1

	and *Nibbāna*		

Below states of enquiry nos. 22 to 30 are to be referred to Table 1.2 & Chart 1.

Chart 1.2. Aggrouping and Ungrouping of Bases

By units:	Aggrouped Agr	Base	Ele
22. Eye-base.	1	1	1

It is aggrouped under 1 aggregate (matter), 1 base (eye-base), and 1 element (eye-element).

It is ungrouped under 4 aggregates (4 mental aggregates), 11 bases (the remaining 9 gross bases, ideation-base, mind-base), and 17 elements (the remaining 9 gross elements, ideation-element, 7 consciousness elements).

23. Ear-base.	1	1	1
Nose-base.	1	1	1
Tongue-base.	1	1	1
Body-base.	1	1	1
Vision-base.	1	1	1
Sound-base.	1	1	1
Odour-base.	1	1	1
Taste-base.	1	1	1
Touch-base.	1	1	1

Each of these 9 gross bases are aggrouped under 1 aggregate (matter), 1 base (respective gross base), and 1 element (respective gross element).

Each of them is ungrouped under 4 aggregates (4 mental aggregates), 11 bases (remaining 9 gross bases, ideation-base, mind-base), and 17 elements (remaining 9 gross elements, ideation-element, 7 consciousness elements).

24. Mind-base.	1	1	7

It is aggrouped under 1 aggregate (consciousness), 1 base (mind-base), and 7 elements (7 consciousness elements).

It is ungrouped under 4 aggregates (matter, feeling, perception, volitive formation), 11 bases (10 gross bases, ideation-base), and 11 elements (10 gross elements, ideation-element).

25. Ideation-base.	4	1	1

It is aggrouped under 4 aggregates (matter, feeling, perception, volitive formation), 1 base (ideation-base), and 1 element (ideation-element).

I. Aggrouping and Ungrouping

It is ungrouped under 1 aggregate (consciousness), 11 bases (10 gross bases, mind-base), and 17 elements (10 gross elements, 7 consciousness elements).

			Aggrouped	
By pairs:		Agr	Base	Ele
26. Eye-base and ear-base.		1	2	2

They are aggrouped under 1 aggregate (matter), 2 bases (eye-base, ear-base), and 2 elements (eye-element, ear-element).

They are ungrouped under 4 aggregates (4 mental aggregates), 10 bases (remaining 8 gross bases, ideation-base, mind-base), and 16 elements (remaining 8 gross elements, ideation-element, 7 consciousness elements).

	Agr	Base	Ele
27. Eye-base and nose-base	1	2	2
Eye-base and tongue-base.	1	2	2
Eye-base and body-base.	1	2	2
Eye-base and vision-base.	1	2	2
Eye-base and sound-base.	1	2	2
Eye-base and odour-base.	1	2	2
Eye-base and taste-base.	1	2	2
Eye-base and tangible-base.	1	2	2

Each of these 8 pairs of gross bases are aggrouped under 1 aggregate (matter), 2 bases (eye-base and the respective gross base in question), and 2 elements (eye-element and the respective gross element in question).

Each pair is ungrouped under 4 aggregates (4 mental aggregates), 10 bases (remaining 8 gross bases from each respective pair; ideation-base and mind-base), and 16 elements (remaining 8 gross elements from each respective pair; ideation-element and 7 consciousness elements).

	Agr	Base	Ele
28. Eye-base and mind-base.	2	2	8

They are aggrouped under 2 aggregates (matter and consciousness), 2 bases (eye-base, mind-base), and 8 elements (eye-element, 7 consciousness elements).

They are ungrouped under 3 aggregates (feeling, perception, volitive formation), 10 bases (remaining 9 gross bases, ideation-base), and 10 elements (remaining 9 gross elements, ideation- element).

	Agr	Base	Ele
29. Eye-base and ideation-base.	4	2	2

They are aggrouped under 4 aggregates excluding *Nibbāna* (matter, feeling, perception, volitive formation), 2 bases (eye-base, ideation-base), and 2 elements (eye-element, ideation-element).

A Perfect Knowledge of Mind-Body from the Abhidhamma (Dhātukathā)

They are ungrouped under 1 aggregate (consciousness), 10 bases (remaining 9 gross bases, mind-base), and 16 elements (remaining 9 gross elements, 7 consciousness elements).

By twelve :

30. The 12 bases.

They are aggrouped under 5 aggregates excluding *Nibbāna* (matter, feeling, perception, volitive formation, consciousness aggregates), 12 bases (10 gross bases, ideation-base, mind-base), and 18 elements (10 gross elements, ideation-element, 7 consciousness elements).
The 12 bases have no ungrouping.

Aggrouped		
Agr	Base	Ele
5	12	18

I. Aggrouping and Ungrouping

3. Elements (*Dhātu*)

This table supplements the information on Elements in Chart 1

Table 1.3. Interior States of Enquiry - 18 Elements (*aṭṭhārasa dhātuyo*)

#	Elements:	Equivalent states:	Aggregates	Bases	Elements
1	eye-element (*cakkhudhātu*)	sensitive eye	1	1	1
2	vision-element (*rūpadhātu*)	visible object	1	1	1
3	eye-consciousness element (*cakkhuviññāṇadhātu*)	eye-consciousness (2)	1	1	1
4	ear-element (*sotadhātu*)	sensitive ear	1	1	1
5	sound-element (*saddadhātu*)	audible object	1	1	1
6	ear-consciousness element (*sotaviññāṇadhātu*)	ear-consciousness (2)	1	1	1
7	nose-element (*ghānadhātu*)	sensitive nose	1	1	1
8	odour-element (*gandhadhātu*)	olfactory object	1	1	1
9	nose-consciousness element (*ghānaviññāṇadhātu*)	nose-consciousness (2)	1	1	1
10	tongue-element (*jivhādhātu*)	sensitive tongue	1	1	1
11	taste-element (*rasadhātu*)	gustatory object	1	1	1
12	tongue-consciousness element (*jivhāviññāṇadhātu*)	tongue-consciousness (2)	1	1	1
13	body-element (*kāyadhātu*)	sensitive body	1	1	1
14	touch-element (*phoṭṭhabbadhātu*)	tactile object	1	1	1
15	body-consciousness element (*kāyaviññāṇadhātu*)	body-consciousness (2)	1	1	1
16	mind-element (*manodhātu*)	5-doors advertence (1), Receiving (2)	1	1	1
17	ideation-element (*dhammadhātu*)	16 subtle matter, 52 *cetasikā*, and *Nibbāna*	4	1	1
18	mind-consciousness element (*manoviññāṇadhātu*)	remaining 76 of the 89 states of consciousness	1	1	1

The following states of enquiry from nos. 31 to 39 are to be referred to Table 1.3 and Chart 1.

A Perfect Knowledge of Mind-Body from the Abhidhamma (Dhātukathā)

Chart 1.3. Aggrouping and Ungrouping of Elements

By units :	Aggrouped		
	Agr	Base	Ele
31. Eye-element.	1	1	1

It is aggrouped under 1 aggregate (matter), 1 base (eye-base), and 1 element (eye-element).

It is ungrouped under 4 aggregates (4 mental aggregates), 11 bases (remaining 9 gross bases, ideation-base, mind-base), and 17 elements (remaining 9 gross elements, ideation-element, 7 consciousness elements).

	Agr	Base	Ele
32. Ear-element.	1	1	1
Nose-element.	1	1	1
Tongue-element.	1	1	1
Body-element.	1	1	1
Vision-element.	1	1	1
Sound-element.	1	1	1
Odour-element.	1	1	1
Taste-element.	1	1	1
Touch-element.	1	1	1
Eye-consciousness element.	1	1	1
Ear-consciousness element.	1	1	1
Nose-consciousness element.	1	1	1
Tongue-consciousness element.	1	1	1
Body- consciousness element.	1	1	1
Mind-element.	1	1	1
Mind-consciousness element.	1	1	1

These are the 9 gross elements (10 excluding eye-element) and the 7 consciousness elements. Each of these 9 gross elements are aggrouped under 1 aggregate (matter), 1 base (respective gross base), and 1 element (respective gross element). Each of these 7 consciousness elements are aggrouped under 1 aggregate (consciousness), 1 base (mind-base), and 1 element (respective consciousness element).

Each of the 9 gross elements is ungrouped under 4 aggregates (4 mental aggregates), 11 bases (remaining 9 gross bases, ideation-base, mind-base), and 17 elements (remaining 9 gross elements, ideation-element, 7 consciousness elements). Each of the 7 consciousness elements is ungrouped under 4 aggregates (matter, feeling, perception, volitive formation), 11 bases (10 gross bases, ideation-base), and 17 elements (10 gross elements, ideation-element, remaining 6 consciousness elements).

I. Aggrouping and Ungrouping

	Aggrouped		
	Agr	Base	Ele
33. Ideation-element.	4	1	1

It is aggrouped under 4 aggregates (matter, feeling, perception, volitive formation), 1 base (ideation-base), and 1 element (ideation-element).

It is ungrouped under 1 aggregate (consciousness), 11 bases (10 gross bases, mind-base), and 17 elements (10 gross elements, 7 consciousness elements).

By pairs :

34. Eye-element and ear-element.	1	2	2

They are aggrouped under 1 aggregate (matter), 2 bases (eye-base, ear-base), and 2 elements (eye-element, ear-element).

They are ungrouped under 4 aggregates (4 mental aggregates), 10 bases (remaining 8 gross bases, ideation-base, mind-base), and 16 elements (remaining 8 gross elements, ideation-element, 7 consciousness elements).

35. Eye-element and nose-element.	1	2	2
Eye-element and tongue-element.	1	2	2
Eye-element and body-element.	1	2	2
Eye-element and vision-element.	1	2	2
Eye-element and sound-element.	1	2	2
Eye-element and odour-element.	1	2	2
Eye-element and taste-element.	1	2	2
Eye-element and tangible-element.	1	2	2

Each of these 8 pairs of gross elements is aggrouped under 1 aggregate (matter), 2 bases (eye-base, and each respective gross base of the 8 types), and 2 elements (eye-element and each respective gross element of the 8 types).

Each pair is ungrouped under 4 aggregates (4 mental aggregates), 10 bases (remaining 8 gross bases from each respective pair; ideation-base; mind-base), and 16 elements (remaining 8 gross elements from each respective pair; ideation-element; 7 consciousness elements).

36. Eye-element and eye-consciousness element.	2	2	2

They are aggrouped under 2 aggregates (matter and consciousness), 2 bases (eye-base, mind-base), and 2 elements (eye-element, eye-consciousness element).

They are ungrouped under 3 aggregates (feeling, perception, volitive formation), 10 bases (remaining 9 gross bases, ideation-base), and 16 elements (remaining 9 gross elements, ideation-element, remaining 6 consciousness elements).

A Perfect Knowledge of Mind-Body from the Abhidhamma (Dhātukathā)

	Aggrouped		
	Agr	Base	Ele
37. Eye-element and ear-consciousness element.	2	2	2
Eye-element and nose-consciousness element.	2	2	2
Eye-element and tongue-consciousness element.	2	2	2
Eye-element and body-consciousness element.	2	2	2
Eye-element and mind-element.	2	2	2
Eye-element and mind-consciousness element.	2	2	2

Each of these 6 pairs of consciousness-elements is aggrouped under 2 aggregates (matter, consciousness), 2 bases (eye-base, mind-base), and 2 elements (eye-element, the one consciousness element in question).

Each pair is ungrouped under 3 aggregates (feeling, perception, volitive formation), 10 bases (remaining 9 gross bases, ideation-base), and 16 elements (remaining 9 gross elements, ideation-element, the remaining 6 consciousness elements in question).

| 38. Eye-element and ideation-element. | 4 | 2 | 2 |

They are aggrouped under 4 aggregates excluding *Nibbāna* (matter, feeling, perception, volitive formation), 2 bases (eye-base, ideation-base), and 2 elements (eye-element, ideation-element).

They are ungrouped under 1 aggregate (consciousness), 10 bases (remaining 9 gross bases, mind-base), and 16 elements (remaining 9 gross elements, 7 consciousness elements).

By eighteen :

| 39. The 18 elements. | 5 | 12 | 18 |

They are aggrouped under 5 aggregates excluding *Nibbāna* (matter, feeling, perception, volitive formation, consciousness aggregates), 12 bases (10 gross bases, ideation-base, mind-base), and 18 elements (10 gross elements, ideation-element, 7 consciousness elements).

The 18 elements have no ungrouping.

I. Aggrouping and Ungrouping

4. Truths (*Saccaṃ*)

The table below supplements the information given in Chart 1.

Table 1.4. Interior States of Enquiry – the Four Truths (*cattāri saccāni*)

	Truth components:	Equivalent states :	Aggregates	Bases	Elements
1	Suffering (*dukkhaṃ*)	28 matters, 51 cetasikas (excluded greed-factor), 81 mundane cittas.	5	12	18
2	The origin of suffering (Origin-truth). (*dukkhasamudayaṃ*)	Greed-*cetasika* arises with the 8 greed-rooted unwholesome cittas.	1	1	1
3	The cessation of suffering (*dukkhanirodhaṃ*)	*Nibbāna*.	-	1	1
4	Path leading to the cessation of suffering (Path-truth) (*dukkhanirodhagāminī magga*)	Noble Eightfold Path.	1	1	1

Below states of enquiry nos. 40 to 49 are facilitated by Table 1.4 and Chart 1.

Chart 1.4. Aggrouping and Ungrouping of Truths

	Aggrouped		
By units :	Agr	Base	Ele

40. The truth of suffering.   5   12   18
    It is aggrouped under 5 aggregates excluding *Nibbāna* (matter, feeling, perception, volitive formation, consciousness), 12 bases (10 gross bases, ideation-base, mind-base), and 18 elements (10 gross elements, ideation-element, 7 consciousness elements).
    It has no ungrouping.

41. The origin of suffering (Origin-truth) and the path leading to the cessation of suffering (Path-truth).   1   1   1
    Each of these two truths is aggrouped under 1 aggregate (volitive formation), 1 base (ideation-base), and 1 element (ideation-element).
    Each is ungrouped under 4 aggregates (matter, feeling, perception, consciousness), 11 bases (10 gross bases, mind-base), and 17 elements (10 gross elements, 7 consciousness elements).

A Perfect Knowledge of Mind-Body from the Abhidhamma (Dhātukathā)

		Aggrouped	
	Agr	Base	Ele

42. The cessation of suffering (Cessation-truth) comes under the state of *Nibbāna*. | - | 1 | 1

It is aggrouped under 1 base (ideation-base), and 1 element (ideation-element). It is not aggrouped under aggregate because *Nibbāna* is not aggregate. It is ungrouped under 5 aggregates (matter, feeling, perception, volitive formation, consciousness), 11 bases (10 gross bases, mind-base), and 17 elements (10 gross elements, 7 consciousness elements).

By pairs :

43. The truth of suffering and origin of suffering. | 5 | 12 | 18

The pair is aggrouped under 5 aggregates excluding *Nibbāna* (matter, feeling, perception, volitive formation, consciousness), 12 bases (10 gross bases, ideation-base, mind-base), and 18 elements (10 gross elements, ideation-element, 7 consciousness elements).

The pair has no ungrouping.

44. The truth of suffering and path leading to the cessation of suffering. | 5 | 12 | 18

Answers for the aggrouping and ungrouping are the same as in no. 43.

45. The truth of suffering and the cessation of suffering. | 5 | 12 | 18

Answers for the aggrouping and ungrouping are the same as in no. 43.

By triads :

46. The truth of suffering, the origin of suffering, and the path leading to the cessation of suffering. | 5 | 12 | 18

The triad is aggrouped under 5 aggregates excluding *Nibbāna* (matter, feeling, perception, volitive formation, consciousness), 12 bases (10 gross bases, ideation-base, mind-base), and 18 elements (10 gross elements, ideation-element, 7 consciousness elements).

47. The truth of suffering, the origin of suffering, and the cessation of suffering. | 5 | 12 | 18

Answers for aggrouping and ungrouping are the same as in no. 46 above.

I. Aggrouping and Ungrouping

	Aggrouped		
By tetrads :	Agr	Base	Ele
48. The truth of suffering, the origin of suffering, the cessation of suffering, and the path leading to the cessation of suffering.	5	12	18

The tetrad is aggrouped under 5 aggregates excluding *Nibbāna* (matter, feeling, perception, volitive formation, consciousness), 12 bases (10 gross bases, ideation-base, mind-base), and 18 elements (10 gross elements, ideation-element, 7 consciousness elements).

The tetrad of truths does not have any ungrouping.

49. The Four Noble Truths. They are the same as in aforesaid no. 48.	5	12	18

A Perfect Knowledge of Mind-Body from the Abhidhamma (Dhātukathā)

5. Faculties (*Indriyaṃ*)

The table below supplements the information given in Chart 1.

Table 1.5. Interior States of Enquiry – the 22 Faculties (*bāvīsatindriyāni*)

	Controlling Faculties:		Equivalent states:	Elements	Bases	Aggregates
1	Vision-faculty (*cakkhundriyaṃ*)	Sense-based	eye-faculty, sensitive eye	1	1	1
2	Hearing-faculty (*sotindriyaṃ*)		ear-faculty, sensitive ear	1	1	1
3	Smell-faculty (*ghānindriyaṃ*)		nose-faculty, sensitive nose	1	1	1
4	Taste-faculty (*jivhindriyaṃ*)		tongue-faculty, sensitive tongue	1	1	1
5	Touch-faculty (*kāyindriyaṃ*)		body-faculty, sensitive body	1	1	1
6	Mind-faculty (*manindriyaṃ*)		89 states of consciousness	1	1	7
7	Femininity-faculty (*itthindriyaṃ*)	Physical	born properties of a female	1	1	1
8	Masculinity-faculty (*purisindriyaṃ*)		born properties of a male	1	1	1
9	Vitality-faculty (*jīvitindriyaṃ*)		life faculty *cetasika* : physical as subtle matter, psychical as volition	2	1	1
10	Carnal pleasure-faculty (*sukhindriyaṃ*)	Feeling-based	feeling-*cetasika*, arises with the pleasurable body-consciousness	1	1	1
11	Carnal displeasure-faculty (*dukkhindriyaṃ*)		feeling-*cetasika*, arises with the painful body-consciousness	1	1	1
12	Joy-faculty (*somanassindriyaṃ*)		feeling-*cetasika*, arises with the 62 types of cittas accompanied by joy	1	1	1
13	Melancholy-faculty (*domanassindriyaṃ*)		feeling-*cetasika*, arises with the 2 hatred-root cittas of unwholesome consciousness	1	1	1
14	Equanimity-faculty (*upekkhindriyaṃ*)		feeling-*cetasika*, arises with the 55 types of cittas accompanied by equanimity	1	1	1

I. Aggrouping and Ungrouping

			A.	B.	E.
15	Confidence-faculty (*saddhindriyaṃ*)	faith-*cetasika*, arises with the 59 beautiful types of cittas [1]	1	1	1
16	Effort-faculty (*vīriyindriyaṃ*)	energy-*cetasika*, arises with 73 cittas (89 excluding the fivefold pairs of resultant sense-consciousness, 3 investigating cittas, 3 mind-elements. i.e. 89-16 = 73)	1	1	1
17	Mindfulness-faculty (*satindriyaṃ*)	mindfulness-*cetasika*, accompanies the 59 beautiful cittas [1]	1	1	1
18	Concentration-faculty (*samādhindriyaṃ*)	one-pointedness-*cetasika*, arises with 72 cittas (89 excluding the 2 pairs of 5 resultant sense-consciousness, 3 investigating cittas, 3 mind-elements, 1 delusion-rooted citta with doubt. i.e. 89-17=72)	1	1	1
19	Wisdom-faculty (*paññindriyaṃ*)	wisdom-*cetasika*, arises with the 39 mundane cittas associated with knowledge [2]	1	1	1
20	I-shall-comprehend-the-unknown faculty (Initial enlightenment) (*anaññātaññassāmīti indriyaṃ*)	wisdom-*cetasika*, arises with the 'Stream-Winning' path-citta. (*sotāpattimagge paññā*)	1	1	1
21	The higher knowledge faculty (Intermediate enlightenment) (*aññindriyaṃ*)	wisdom-*cetasika*, arises with the 3 path-cittas of the 'Once-Returning', 'Non-Returning', 'Arhantship'; and 3 fruition-consciousness of the 'Stream-Winning', 'Once-Returning', 'Non-Returning'.	1	1	1
22	The "final knower" faculty (Final enlightenment) (*aññātāvindriyaṃ*)	wisdom-*cetasika*, arises with the *Arahatta* fruition-citta	1	1	1

Items 15–19 are grouped as Spiritual; items 20–22 are grouped as Knowledge-based.

---

[1] The 59 beautiful cittas (*sobhanāññasamāna cittāni*), namely: those cittas excluding that which are from the 12 unwholesome states, 8 resultants of wholesome but without root (*kusala-ahetuka*), 7 resultants of unwholesome and without root, 3 functional states without root. (89–12-8–7-3=55). See Appendix II, and Chart 2 Appendix VI.

[2] 39 mundane states of consciousness associated with knowledge: 4 of the active wholesome, 4 of the resultant 'beautiful' states with root, and 4 of the functional 'beautiful' states with root in the sensuous sphere; 15 of the fine-material sphere; 12 of the immaterial sphere. (4+4+4+15+12 = 39). See Appendix II.

A Perfect Knowledge of Mind-Body from the Abhidhamma (Dhātukathā)

The following states of enquiry nos. 50 to 60 are made easier by referring to preceding Table 1.5 and Chart 1.

Chart 1.5. Aggrouping and Ungrouping of Faculties

By units :	Aggrouped Agr	Base	Ele
50. Vision-faculty.	1	1	1

It is aggrouped under 1 aggregate (matter), 1 base (eye-base), and 1 element (eye-element).

It is ungrouped under 4 aggregates (4 mental aggregates), 11 bases (remaining 9 gross bases, ideation-base, mind-base), and 17 elements (remaining 9 gross elements, ideation-element, 7 consciousness elements).

51. Hearing-faculty.	1	1	1
Smell-faculty.	1	1	1
Taste-faculty.	1	1	1
Touch-faculty.	1	1	1
Femininity-faculty.	1	1	1
Masculinity-faculty.	1	1	1

The first 4 faculties are each aggrouped under 1 aggregate (matter), 1 base (the respective gross base), and 1 element (the respective gross element). Each is ungrouped under 4 aggregates (4 mental aggregates), 11 bases (remaining 9 gross bases, ideation-base, mind-base), and 17 elements (remaining 9 gross elements, ideation-element, 7 consciousness elements).

Both femininity-faculty and masculinity-faculty come under subtle matters, are aggrouped under 1 aggregate (matter), 1 base (ideation-base), and 1 element (ideation-element). Each is ungrouped under 4 aggregates (4 mental aggregates), 11 bases (10 gross bases, mind-base), and 17 elements (10 gross elements, 7 consciousness elements).

52. Mind-faculty.	1	1	7

It is aggrouped under 1 aggregate (consciousness), 1 base (mind-base), and 7 elements (7 consciousness elements).

It is ungrouped under 4 aggregates (matter, feeling, perception, volitive formation), 11 bases (10 gross bases, ideation-base), and 11 elements (10 gross elements, ideation-element).

53. Vitality-faculty.	2	1	1

In physical life, it belongs to subtle matter. Psychically, it is volitive formation. So, vitality-faculty is aggrouped under 2

I. Aggrouping and Ungrouping

aggregates (matter, volitive formation), 1 base (ideation-base), and 1 element (ideation-element).
It is ungrouped under 3 aggregates (feeling, perception, consciousness), 11 bases (10 gross bases, mind-base), and 17 elements (10 gross elements, 7 consciousness elements).

	Aggrouped		
	Agr	Base	Ele
54. Faculty of the carnal pleasure.	1	1	1
Faculty of the carnal displeasure.	1	1	1
Faculty of joy (mental).	1	1	1
Faculty of melancholy.	1	1	1
Faculty of equanimity.	1	1	1
Faculty of confidence.	1	1	1
Faculty of effort.	1	1	1
Faculty of mindfulness	1	1	1
Faculty of concentration.	1	1	1
Faculty of wisdom.	1	1	1
Faculty of the "I-shall-comprehend-the-unknown".	1	1	1
Faculty of the higher knowledge.	1	1	1
Faculty of the "final knower".	1	1	1

The faculties of carnal pleasure, carnal displeasure, mental joy, melancholy, and equanimity are the five feeling faculties. Each of these five is aggrouped under 1 aggregate (feeling), 1 base (ideation-base), and 1 element (ideation-element). Each is ungrouped under 4 aggregates (matter, perception, volitive formation, consciousness), 11 bases (10 gross bases, mind-base), and 17 elements (10 gross elements, 7 consciousness elements).

The other eight faculties beling to volitive formation. Thus, each of them is aggrouped under 1 aggregate (volitive formation), 1 base (ideation-base), and 1 element (ideation-element). Each is ungrouped under 4 aggregates (matter, feeling, perception, consciousness), 11 bases (10 gross bases, mind-base), and 17 elements (10 gross elements, 7 consciousness elements).

By pairs :

55. Vision-faculty and hearing-faculty.   1   2   2

The pair is aggrouped under 1 aggregate (matter), 2 bases (eye-base, ear-base), and 2 elements (eye-element, ear-element).
The pair is ungrouped under 4 aggregates (4 mental aggregates), 10 bases (remaining 8 gross bases, ideation-base, mind-base), and 16 elements (remaining 8 gross elements, ideation-element, 7 consciousness elements).

A Perfect Knowledge of Mind-Body from the Abhidhamma (Dhātukathā)

		Aggrouped		
		Agr	Base	Ele
56.	Vision-faculty and smell-faculty.	1	2	2

The pair is aggrouped under 1 aggregate (matter), 2 bases (eye-base, nose-base), and 2 elements (eye-element, nose-element).

The pair is ungrouped under 4 aggregates (4 mental aggregates), 10 bases (remaining 8 gross bases, ideation-base, mind-base), and 16 elements (remaining 8 gross elements, ideation-element, 7 consciousness elements).

| 57. | Vision-faculty and mind-faculty. | 2 | 2 | 8 |

The pair is aggrouped under 2 aggregates (matter, consciousness), 2 bases (eye-base, mind-base), and 8 elements (eye-element, 7 consciousness elements).

The pair is ungrouped under 3 aggregates, 10 bases, and 10 elements.

| 58. | Vision-faculty and vitality-faculty. | 2 | 2 | 2 |

As vitality-faculty possesses both the characteristics of subtle matter and volitive formation, the pair of faculties is aggrouped under 2 aggregates (matter, volitive formation), 2 bases (eye-base, ideation-base), and 2 elements (eye-element, ideation-element).

The pair is ungrouped under 3 aggregates (feeling, perception, consciousness), 10 bases (remaining 9 gross bases, mind-base), and 16 elements (remaining 9 gross elements, 7 consciousness elements).

59.	Vision-faculty and carnal pleasure faculty.	2	2	2
	Vision-faculty and carnal displeasure faculty.	2	2	2
	Vision-faculty and joy-faculty.	2	2	2
	Vision-faculty and melancholy-faculty.	2	2	2
	Vision-faculty and equanimity-faculty.	2	2	2
	Vision-faculty and confidence-faculty.	2	2	2
	Vision-faculty and energy-faculty.	2	2	2
	Vision-faculty and mindfulness-faculty.	2	2	2
	Vision-faculty and concentration-faculty.	2	2	2
	Vision-faculty and wisdom-faculty.	2	2	2
	Vision-faculty and "I-shall-comprehend-the-unknown" faculty	2	2	2
	Vision-faculty and the "higher knowledge" faculty.	2	2	2
	Vision-faculty and the "final knower" faculty.	2	2	2

Because the first five pairs include the 5 feeling faculties, each of these first five pairs is aggrouped under 2 aggregates

I. Aggrouping and Ungrouping

(matter, feeling), 2 bases (eye-base, ideation-base), and 2 elements (eye-element, ideation-element). Each of these first five pairs is ungrouped under 3 aggregates (perception, volitive formation, consciousness), 10 bases (remaining 9 gross bases, mind-base), and 16 elements (remaining 9 gross elements, 7 consciousness elements).

The other eight pairs of faculties include volitive formation. Thus, each of these pairs is aggrouped under 2 aggregates (matter, volitive formation), 2 bases (eye-base, ideation-base), and 2 elements (eye-element, ideation-element). Each pair is ungrouped under 3 aggregates (feeling, perception, consciousness), 10 bases (remaining 9 gross bases, mind-base), and 16 elements (remaining 9 elements, 7 consciousness elements).

By twenty-twos :

60. The 22 faculties.

These 22 controlling faculties are aggrouped under 4 aggregates (matter, feeling, volitive formation, consciousness), 7 bases (eye-base, ear-base, nose-base, tongue-base, body-base, ideation-base, and mind-base), 13 elements (eye-element, ear-element, nose-element, tongue-element, body-element, ideation-element, and 7 consciousness elements).

These 22 controlling faculties are ungrouped under 1 aggregate (perception), 5 bases (visible object base, audible object base, olfactory object base, gustatory object base, tactile object base), and 5 elements (vision-element, sound-element, odour-element, taste-element, touch-element).

	Aggrouped	
Agr	Base	Ele
4	7	13

6. Dependent Origination, etc. (*Paṭiccasamuppādādi*)

The table below supplements the information given in Chart 1.

Table 1.6a. Interior States of Enquiry — Dependent Origination (12 Factors, 16 Kinds), 37 Requisites of Awakening (*sattatiṁsā bodhipakkhiyadhammā*) and so on

	12 factors & 16 kinds of dependent origination:	Equivalent states :	Elements	Bases	Aggregates
1	Ignorance (*avijjā*)	Corresponds to delusion-*cetasika*, it arises with the 2 delusion-root states of unwholesome cittas.	1	1	1
2	Conditioned by ignorance, is *volitive formation* (*saṅkhāra*)	Corresponds to volition-*cetasika* (it is also among the 7 common non-beautiful mental factors), volition arises with the active 17 mundane wholesome cittas, active 12 mundane unwholesome cittas.	1	1	1
3	Conditioned by volitive formation, is *consciousness* (*viññāṇa*)	States of consciousness are classified under 89 cittas.	1	1	7
4	Conditioned by consciousness, is *mentality-corporeality* (*nāmarūpa*)	Mind-matter correspond to 52 mental concomitants and 28 matters.	4	11	11
5	Conditioned by mentality-corporeality, are *six bases* (*saḷāyatana*)	Six bases correspond to the 5 sense organs, mind (mind-base), and 89 cittas.	2	6	12
6	Conditioned by six bases, is *contact* (*phassa*)	Contact-*cetasika* is among the 7 common-universal non-beautiful mental factors. It arises with 89 cittas.	1	1	1
7	Conditioned by contact, is *feeling* (*vedanā*)	Feeling-*cetasika* is among the 7 common-universal non-beautiful mental factors, it arises also with 89 cittas.	1	1	1
8	Conditioned by feeling, is *craving* (*taṇhā*)	Synonymous with greed-*cetasika* in the 10 unwholesome-occasionals, craving accompanies the 8 greed-rooted unwholesome cittas.	1	1	1

I. Aggrouping and Ungrouping

			A.	B.	E.
9	Conditioned by craving, is *clinging* (*upādāna*)	Synonymous with the two *cetasikā* of greed and wrong view (*diṭṭhi*), clinging accompanies, respectively, (i) the 8 greed-rooted unwholesome cittas, (ii) 4 of these 8 greed-rooted cittas associated with fallacy.	1	1	1
10	Conditioned by clinging, is *becoming* (*bhava*)	*Becoming* (*bhava*) has twofold division, viz. *kammabhava* (the active rebirth-producing, action-process of becoming) and *upapattibhava* (the rebirth process of becoming). Essentially, the 29 kammically wholesome and unwholesome cittas (together with mental concomitants which follow) constitute *kammabhava* process and which conditions the 32 types of kamma-resultants in the *upapattibhava* process.	1	1	1
i	Action-becoming (*kamma bhava*)	*Kammabhava* corresponds to volition-*cetasika*. Action-becoming arises with the active 17 whomesome cittas and active 12 unwhomesome cittas.	1	1	1
ii	Resultant-becoming (*upapatti bhava*), or sometimes called *rebirth-becoming*	Belongs to mentality-materiality, it consists of 20 kamma-produced matters [3], 32 kamma resultants, 35 cetasikas (i.e. 13 common non-beautiful factors, and 22 common-beautiful factors excluded the 3 Abstinence factors, i.e. 13+(25-3)=35).	5	11	17
	Resultant-becoming is further sub-divided into the following 9 kinds of becoming :				
iii	Sensuous becoming (*kāma-bhava*)	Belongs to mentality-materiality. It consists of 20 kamma-produced matters, 23 sensuous resultants, 33 cetasikas (38 excluded 3 Abstinences and 2 Illimitables).	5	11	17
iv	Fine-material becoming (*rūpa-bhava*)	Belongs to mentality-materiality, it consists of 5 resultant cittas, 2 eye-cittas, 2 ear-cittas, 2 receiving-cittas, 2 investigating-cittas, and 15 kamma-produced matters (20 excluding femininity, masculinity, nose, tongue, and body, i.e. 20-5=15), and 35 cetasikas (13+[25-3]=35).	5	5	8

---

[3] 20 types of matter produced by kamma: the 28 types of matter excluding sound, 5 vikāra matters, decay, and impermanence. These 20 matters are also present at the moment of rebirth consciousness. (See Appendix VI, Chart 13)

A Perfect Knowledge of Mind-Body from the Abhidhamma (Dhātukathā)

			A.	B.	E.
v	Immaterial becoming (arūpa-bhava)	Belongs to mentality-materiality excluding gross matter. It corresponds to 4 immaterial resultants, and 30 cetasikas (13 excluding vitakka, vicāra, and pīti; 25 excluding the 3 virati and 2 appamaññā, i.e. 10+20=30) arisen with the fifth-jhānas.	4	2	2
vi	Perception-becoming (saññā-bhava)	It is mentality-materiality, consists of 31 resultants, namely, 32 resultants excluding neither-perception-nor-nonperception immaterial resultant citta. (32-1=31).	5	11	17
vii	Non-perception becoming (asaññā-bhava)	Corresponds to the ninefold vitality-group [4]	1	2	2
viii	Neither perception nor non-perception becoming (nevasaññā nāsaññā-bhava)	Belongs to mentality-materiality but excluding gross matter. It corresponds to neither-perception-nor-nonperception immaterial resultant citta, and the 30 cetasikas as in aforesaid (v).	4	2	2
ix	Single-aggregate becoming (ekavokāra-bhava)	Same as non-perception becoming.	1	2	2
x	Four-aggregate becoming (catuvokāra-bhava)	Same as immaterial becoming, it belongs to mentality-materiality excluding gross matter.	4	2	2
xi	Five-aggregate becoming (pañcavokāra-bhava)	Corresponds to becomings in the 26 planes of existence (excluding single-aggregate becoming, and the fourfold four-aggregate becomings). It is mentality-materiality, consists of 20 kamma-produced matters, 23 sense-sphere resultants, 5 immaterial resultants, and 35 cetasikas (13+[25-3]=35).	5	11	17
11	Becoming conditions birth (jāti)	The 'birth' of materiality is ascribed to the occurrence of the 18 concretely produced matters; the 'birth' of mentality is ascribed to the occurrence of the 4 mental aggregates.	2	1	1

---

[4] ninefold vitality-group — eye-decad, ear-decad, nose-decad, tongue-decad, body-decad, femininity-decad, masculinity-decad, heart-decad, vitality-nonad (each decad, except the vitality-nonad, consists of 8 inseparable matters + vitality + the respective individual rūpa of the aforesaid 9 material qualities).

I. Aggrouping and Ungrouping

			A.	B.	E.
	The inevitable results of birth :				
12	Birth conditions the inevitable 'ageing and death' (*jarāmaraṇa*)	The 'ageing' of materiality corresponds to the agedness of the 18 concretely produced matters. The 'ageing' of mentality corresponds to the agedness of the 4 mental aggregates.	2	1	1
		The 'death' of materiality corresponds to the worn-out and dissolution of the 18 concretely produced matters. The 'death' of mentality corresponds to the worn-out and dissolution of the 4 mental aggregates.	2	1	1
	The 5 evitable, separate, and incidental consequences of birth :				
xii	Sorrow (*soko*)	It is grievous feeling which sprung from the 2 hatred-rooted cittas, accompanied by hatred-*cetasika*.	1	1	1
xiii	Lamentation (*parideva*)	It is audible object of passionate grief due to wailing.	1	1	1
xiv	Suffering/ Painfulness (*dukkha*)	It is grievous feeling born of body-consciousness associated with suffering.	1	1	1
xv	Melancholy (*domanassa*)	It is grievous feeling sprung from the 2 hatred-rooted cittas, accompanied by hatred-*cetasika*.	1	1	1
xvi	Despair (*upāyāsa*)	Corresponds to the occasional hatred-*cetasika* which accompanies the 2 hatred-rooted cittas.	1	1	1

The following states of enquiry nos. 61 to 72 are made easier by referring to preceding Table 1.6a and Chart 1.

Chart 1.6a. Aggrouping and Ungrouping of Dependent Origination

By units :

Aggrouped
Agr Base Ele

61. Ignorance.
    It is aggrouped under 1 aggregate (volitive formation), 1 base (ideation-base), and 1 element (ideation-element).   1   1   1
    It is ungrouped under 4 aggregates (matter, feeling, perception, consciousness), 11 bases (10 gross bases, mind-base), and 17 elements (10 gross elements, 7 consciousness elements).

A Perfect Knowledge of Mind-Body from the Abhidhamma (Dhātukathā)

	Aggrouped		
	Agr	Base	Ele

62. Conditioned by Ignorance, is Volitive Formation.   1   1   1
    Volitive Formation is aggrouped under 1 aggregate (volitive formation), 1 base (ideation-base), and 1 element (ideation-element).
    Volitive Formation is ungrouped under 4 aggregates (matter, feeling, perception, consciousness), 11 bases (10 gross bases, mind-base), and 17 elements (10 gross elements, 7 consciousness elements).

63. Conditioned by Volitive Formation, is Consciousness.   1   1   7
    Consciousness is aggrouped under 1 aggregate (consciousness), 1 base (mind-base), and 7 elements (7 consciousness elements).
    Consciousness is ungrouped under 4 aggregates (matter, feeling, perception, volitive formation), 11 bases (10 gross bases, ideation-base), and 11 elements (10 gross elements, ideation-element).

64. Conditioned by Consciousness, is Mentality-Materiality.   4   11   11
    Mentality-Materiality is the equivalent of 52 mental factors and 28 matters. Thus, mentality-materiality (or mind-matter) are aggrouped under 4 aggregates (matter, feeling, perception, volitive formation), 11 bases (10 gross bases, ideation-base), and 11 elements (10 gross elements, ideation-element).
    Mentality-Materiality are ungrouped under 1 aggregate (consciousness), 1 base (mind-base), and 7 elements (7 consciousness elements).

65. Conditioned by Mentality-Materiality, are the Six Bases.   2   6   12
    Six Bases are the 5 sense-organs and mind. Thus, six bases are aggrouped under 2 aggregates (matter, consciousness), 6 bases (eye-base, ear-base, nose-base, tongue-base, body-base, mind-base), and 12 elements (eye-element, ear-element, nose-element, tongue-element, body-element, and 7 consciousness elements).
    Six Bases are ungrouped under 3 aggregates (feeling, perception, volitive formation), 6 bases (visible object base, audible object base, olfactory object base, gustatory object base, tactile object base, ideation-base), 6 elements (vision-element, sound-element, odour-element, taste-element, touch-element, ideation-element).

I. Aggrouping and Ungrouping

	Aggrouped		
	Agr	Base	Ele
66. Because of Six bases, there is Contact; because of Contact, there is Feeling; because of Feeling, there is Craving; because of Craving, there is Clinging; because of Clinging, there is Becoming (starting with Action-Becoming).	1	1	1

Contact, Feeling, Craving, Clinging, Becoming — with the exception of Feeling which belongs to feeling aggregate, each of the other four factors of dependent origination is aggrouped under 1 aggregate (volitive formation), 1 base (ideation-base), and 1 element (ideation-element). Feeling is aggrouped under 1 aggregate (feeling), 1 base (ideation-base), and 1 element (ideation-element).

Feeling is ungrouped under 4 aggregates (matter, perception, volitive formation, consciousness), 11 bases (10 gross bases, mind-base), and 17 elements (10 gross elements, 7 consciousness elements).

Each of the other four factors of dependent origination is ungrouped under 4 aggregates (matter, feeling, perception, consciousness), 11 bases (10 gross bases, mind-base), and 17 elements (10 gross elements, 7 consciousness elements).

67. Resultant-becoming (or Rebirth-becoming), Sensuous becoming, Perception-becoming, Five-Aggregate becoming.	5	11	17

These four kinds of becoming belong to mentality-materiality, are bound up with 20 kamma-produced matters, eye-cons. element, ear-cons. element, nose-cons. element, tongue-cons. element, body-cons. element, mind-element, and mind-cons. element.

Each is aggrouped under 5 aggregates excluding *Nibbāna* (matter, feeling, perception, volitive formation, consciousness), 11 bases (10 gross bases, mind-base), and 17 elements (10 gross elements, 7 consciousness elements).

Each is ungrouped under 1 base (ideation-base) and 1 element (ideation-element).

68. Fine-material becoming.	5	5	8

It belongs to mentality-materiality, which are dissociated from sensitive nose, sensitive tongue, sensitive body, femininity and masculinity. Thus, it is aggrouped under 5 aggregates excluding *Nibbāna* (matter, feeling, perception, volitive formation, consciousness), 5 bases (eye-base, ear-base, visible object base, audible object base, mind-base), and 8 elements (eye-element, ear- element, visible object element,

A Perfect Knowledge of Mind-Body from the Abhidhamma (Dhātukathā)

audible object element, eye-cons. element, ear-cons. element, mind-element, mind-cons. element).

It is ungrouped under 7 bases (remaining 6 gross bases, ideation-base) and 10 elements (remaining 6 gross elements, nose-cons. element, tongue-cons. element, body-cons. element, and ideation-element)

	Aggrouped		
	Agr	Base	Ele

69. Immaterial becoming, Neither perception nor non-perception becoming, and Four-Aggregate becoming. [4 2 2]

These three kinds of becoming belong to mentality-materiality but excluding gross matter. The three becomings are aggrouped under 4 aggregates (the 4 mental aggregates), 2 bases (ideation-base, mind-base), and 2 elements (ideation-element, mind-consciousness element).

The three kinds of becoming are ungrouped under 1 aggregate (matter), 10 bases (10 gross bases), and 16 elements (10 gross, the remaining 6 consciousness elements).

70. Non-perception becoming, and One-aggregate becoming. [1 2 2]

These two becomings belong to visible object associated with the ninefold vitality group. Thus, they are aggrouped under 1 aggregate (matter), 2 bases (eye-base, ideation-base), and 2 elements (eye-element, ideation-element).

These two becoming are ungrouped under 4 aggregates (4 mental aggregates), 10 bases (remaining 9 gross bases, mind-base) and 16 elements (remaining 9 gross elements, 7 consciousness elements).

71. Birth; Ageing; Death. [2 1 1]

Birth, Ageing, and Death belong to matters and volitive formation. Each of them is ungrouped under 2 aggregates (matter, volitive formation), 1 base (ideation-base), and 1 element (ideation-element).

Birth, Ageing and Death are ungrouped under 3 aggregates (feeling, perception, consciousnes), 11 bases (10 gross bases, mind-base), and 17 elements (10 gross elements, 7 consciousness elements).

72. The five evitable and incidental consequences of birth, namely, sorrow, lamentation, painfulness, melancholy, and despair. [1 1 1]

Sorrow, lamentation, painfulness, and melancholy belong to feeling. The three are aggrouped under 1 aggregate (feeling), 1 base (ideation-base), and 1 element (ideation-element). They are ungrouped under 4 aggregates (matter, perception, volitive formation, consciousness), 11 bases (10 gross bases,

I. Aggrouping and Ungrouping

mind-base), and 17 elements (10 gross elements, 7 consciousness elements).

Despair belongs to volitive formation, and is aggrouped under 1 aggregate (volitive formation), 1 base (ideation-base), and 1 element (ideation-element). It is ungrouped under 4 aggregates (matter, feeling, perception, consciousness), 11 bases (10 gross bases, mind-base), and 17 elements (10 gross elements, 7 consciousness elements).

The table below supplements the information given in Chart 1.

Table 1.6b. Interior States of Enquiry - the 37 Requisites of Awakening (*sattatiṁsā bodhipakkhiyadhammā*) and 7 Contact-Group

	Methods :	Constituent states :	Aggregates	Bases	Elements
1	The 4 Foundations/ Application of Mindfulness (*cattāro satipaṭṭhānā*)	Associate with mindfulness-*cetasika*, accompanying the 8 supramundane cittas.	1	1	1
2	The 4 Right Strivings (*cattāro sammappadhānā*)	Associate with effort-*cetasika*, follows the 8 supramundane cittas.	1	1	1
3	The 4 Basis of Psychic Accomplishment (*cattāro iddhipādā*)	Associate with the cetasikas of *viriya*, *chanda*, and *amoha*, present at the 8 x 5 supramundane cittas, accompanied by 33 cetasikas (13 commons excluding *viriya*, *chanda*, and 25 beautifuls excluding 2 Illimitables and *amoha*).	2	2	2
4	The 4 or 5 Jhānas (*cattāri jhānāni*)	Associate with initial application, sustained application, zest, happiness, and one-pointedness of mind. The 4 or 5 jhānas belong to the 27 sublime cittas and 8 x 5 supramunndane cittas, accompanied by the varied cetasikas. (See Appendix VI, Chart 11).	2	1	1
5	The 4 Illimitable States (*catasso appamaññāyo*)	Associate with the cetasikas of compassion (*Karunā*), altruistic joy (*Muditā*), benevolence (*Mettā* is implied in *Adosa* as greedlessness), and equanimity (*Upekkhā* is implied in *Tatramajjhattatā* as the neutrality of mind presents at the 5th *jhāna*).	1	1	1

A Perfect Knowledge of Mind-Body from the Abhidhamma (Dhātukathā)

			A.	B.	E.
6	The 5 Faculties (*pañcindriyāni*)	Associate with the respective cetasikas of faith, effort, mindfulness, one-pointedness, non-delusion (wisdom), accompanying the 8 supramundane cittas.	1	1	1
7	The 5 Powers (*pañca balāni*)	Same as that of the 5 Faculties.	1	1	1
8	The 7 Factors of Enlightenment (*satta bojjhaṅgā*) [5]	Associate with the cetasikas of mindfulness, non-delusion (*amoha* as implied in *dhammavicaya*), effort, zest, calmness (*passaddhi* applicable to body and mind), one-pointedness, and equanimity, accompanying the 8 supramundane cittas.	1	1	1
9	The Noble Eightfold Path (*ariyo aṭṭhaṅgiko maggo*) [6]	Associate with the respective cetasikas of non-delusion (wisdom), sustained application, 3 abstinences, effort, mindfulness, and one-pointedness, accompanying the 4 supramundane path-consciousness.	1	1	1
	The 7 Contact-Group				
	i. Contact (*10*) (*phasso*)	Contact-*cetasika*, occur at 89 cittas.	1	1	1
	ii. Feeling (*11*) (*vedanā*)	Feeling-*cetasika*, occur at 89 cittas.	1	1	1
	iii. Perception (*12*) (*saññā*)	Perception-*cetasika*, occur at 89 cittas.	1	1	1
	iv. Volition (*13*) (*cetanā*)	Volition-*cetasika*, occur at 89 cittas.	1	1	1
	v. State of consciousness (*14*) (*citta*)	All 89 cittas.	1	1	7
	vi. Decision (*15*) (*adhimokkho*)	Decision-*cetasika*, requires for the 78 cittas having excluded the 5 pairs of sense-door resultant cittas and unwholesome cittas associated with doubt. i.e. (89-10-1=78)	1	1	1
	vi. Attention (*16*) (*manasikāro*)	Attention-*cetasika*, requires for the 89 cittas.	1	1	1

---

[5] the 7 Enlightenment-Factors (*satta sambojjhaṅgā*) :1. mindfulness (*sati*), 2. truth-investigation (*dhammavicaya*), 3. effort (*vīriya*), 4. zest (*pīti*), 5. calmness (*passaddhi*), 6. concentration (*samādhi*), 7. equanimity (*upekkhā*).

[6] Noble Eightfold Path (*ariya-aṭṭhangikamagga*): right view (*sammādiṭṭhi*), right thought (*sammāsaṅkappa*), right speech (*sammāvācā*), right action (*sammākammanta*), right livelihood (*sammā-ājīva*), right effort (*sammāvāyāma*), right mindfulness (*sammāsati*), right concentration (*sammāsamādhi*)

I. Aggrouping and Ungrouping

The following states of enquiry nos. 72 to 76 can be better comprehended by referring to preceding Table 1.6b and Chart 1.

Chart 1.6b. Aggrouping and Ungrouping of the 37 Requisites of Awakening and the 7 Contact-Group

By units :	Aggrouped Agr	Base	Ele
* The following continues from preceding nos. 72.			
The four Foundations of Mindfulness and four Right Strivings. These two methods of practice belong to volitive formation. They are aggrouped under 1 aggregate (volitive formation), 1 base (ideation-base), and 1 element (ideation-element). They are ungrouped under 4 aggregates (matter, feeling, perception, consciousness), 11 bases (10 gross bases, mind-base), and 17 elements (10 gross elements, 7 consciousness elements).	1	1	1
73. The (four) Basis of Psychic Accomplishment. This basis of practice consists of supramundane cittas, comes under consciousness (partially associated with volitive formation). They are aggrouped under 2 aggregates (volitive formation, consciousness), 2 bases (ideation-base, mind-base), and 2 elements (ideation-element, mind-consciousness element). The practice is ungrouped under 3 aggregates (matter, feeling, perception), 10 bases (10 gross bases), and 16 elements (10 gross elements, remaining 6 consciousness elements).	2	2	2
74. The 4 or 5 Jhānas. *Jhānas* belong to feeling (partially associated with volitive formation). They are aggrouped under 2 aggregates (feeling, volitive formation), 1 base (ideation-base), and 1 element (ideation-element). They are ungrouped under 3 aggregates (matter, perception, consciousness), 11 bases (10 gross bases, mind-base), and 17 elements (10 gross elements, 7 consciousness elements).	2	1	1
75. The 4 Illimitable States.	1	1	1
The 5 Faculties.	1	1	1
The 5 Powers.	1	1	1
The 7 Factors of Enlightenment.	1	1	1
The 8 constituents of the Noble Path.	1	1	1

A Perfect Knowledge of Mind-Body from the Abhidhamma (Dhātukathā)

	Aggrouped		
	Agr	Base	Ele

The 6 constituents of the Contact-Group (Contact, Feeling, Perception, Volition, Decision, and Attention). | 1 | 1 | 1

The states of 4 Illimitables, 5 Faculties, 5 Powers, 7 Factors of Enlightenment, 8 constituents of the noble Path, contact, volition, decision, and attention belong to volitive formation.

Each of those states is aggrouped under 1 aggregate (volitive formation), 1 base (ideation-base), and 1 element (ideation-element). Each is ungrouped under 4 aggregates (matter, feeling, perception, consciousness), 11 bases (10 gross bases, mind-base), and 17 elements (10 gross elements, 7 consciousness elements).

Feeling is aggrouped under 1 aggregate (feeling), 1 base (ideation-base), and 1 element (ideation-element). It is ungrouped under 4 aggregates (matter, perception, volitive formation, consciousness), 11 bases (10 gross bases, mind-base), and 17 elements (10 gross elements, 7 consciousness elements).

Perception is aggrouped under 1 aggregate (perception), 1 base (ideation-base), and 1 element (ideation-element). It is ungrouped under 4 aggregates (matter, feeling, volitive formation, consciousness), 11 bases (10 gross bases, mind-base), and 17 elements (10 gross elements, 7 consciousness elements).

76. State of consciousness. | 1 | 1 | 7
    A constituent of the Contact group of 7, it is aggrouped under 1 aggregate (consciousness), 1 base (mind-base), and 7 elements (7 consciousness elements).
    It is ungrouped under 4 aggregates (matter, feeling, perception, volitive formation), 11 bases (10 gross bases, ideation-base), and 11 elements (10 gross elements, ideation-element).

I. Aggrouping and Ungrouping

66 states of enquiry from Dhammasaṅgaṇīmātikā triads

7. Triads (*Tikaṃ*)

Table 1.7. External Enquiry of States — Dhammasaṅgaṇīmātikā 22 Triads

	States of enquiry :	Compositional states :	Aggregates	Bases	Elements
1	Wholesome states (*kusalā dhammā*). (Dhs 985, 1384)	active 21 mundane wholesome cittas, 38 cetasikas (13 common non-beautiful factors and 25 beautiful factors). (13+25=38).	4	2	2
	Unwholesome states (*akusalā dhammā*). (Dhs 986, 1385)	active 12 unwholesome cittas, 27 cetasikas (13 common non-beautiful factors and 14 unwholesome factors). (13+14=27).	4	2	2
	Indeterminate states (*abyākatā dhammā*). (Dhs 987, 1386)	36 resultant cittas, 20 functional cittas, 38 cetasikas, 28 matters, and *Nibbāna*.	5	12	18
2	States associated with happy or pleasurable feeling. (Dhs 988, 1387)	63 cittas (accompanied by joy and by happiness), 46 cetasikas (52 excluding feeling, hatred, envy, avarice, worry, doubt. i.e. 52-6=46).	3	2	3
	States associated with feeling of pain or suffering. (Dhs 989, 1388)	3 cittas accompanied by displeasure (2 hatred-rooted cittas, 1 resultant of body-*viññāṇa*), 21 cetasikas (27 excluding feeling, zest, greed, wrong view, conceit, doubt, i.e. 27-6=21).	3	2	3
	States associated with neither happy feeling nor painful feeling/suffering feeling. (Dhs 990, 1389)	55 cittas accompanied by equanimity (see Chart 16 in Appendix VI); 46 cetasikas (52 excluding feeling, zest, hatred, envy, avarice, worry. i.e. 52-6=46).	3	2	7
3	Resultant states. (Dhs 991, 1390)	36 resultants, 38 cetasikas. (13+25=38)	4	2	8
	States which caused resultants (Dhs 992, 1391)	active 21 wholesome cittas, active 12 unwholesome cittas, 52 cetasikas.	4	2	2
	States which neither are resultants nor are causing resultants. (Dhs 993, 1392)	20 functional cittas, 35 cetasikas (38 excluding the 3 Abstinences, namely, 13+(25-3)=35), 28 matters, *Nibbāna*.	5	12	13

A Perfect Knowledge of Mind-Body from the Abhidhamma (Dhātukathā)

			A.	B.	E.
4	States which are the result of clinging, and are favourable to clinging. (Dhs 994, 1393)	20 kamma-produced matters [3], 32 mundane resultant cittas, 35 cetasikas (38 excluding the 3 Abstinences, i.e. 13+(25-3)=35).	5	11	17
	States which are not the result of clinging but are favourable to clinging. (Dhs 995, 1394)	49 cittas (comprised of 17 wholesome cittas, 12 unwholesome cittas, 20 functional cittas); 52 cetasikas; 17 mind-produced matters, 15 temperature-produced matters, and 14 nutriment-produced matters.	5	7	8
	States which neither are the result of clinging nor are favourable to clinging. (Dhs 996, 1395)	8 supramundane cittas, 36 cetasikas (13+(25-2 Illimitables)=36), and *Nibbāna*.	4	2	2
5	States which are corrupted and are favourable to corruptions. (Dhs 997, 1396)	12 unwholesome cittas; 27 cetasikas (13 common non-beautiful factors and 14 unwholesome factors). (13+14=27).	4	2	2
	States which are not corrupted but are favourable to corruptions. (Dhs 998, 1397)	69 cittas (17 mundane wholesome cittas; 32 mundane resultant cittas; 20 functional cittas); 38 cetasikas (13+25=38); 28 matters.	5	12	18
	States which neither are corrupted nor are favourable to corruptions. (Dhs 999, 1398)	8 supramundane cittas, 36 cetasikas (13+(25-2 Illimitables)=36), and *Nibbāna*.	4	2	2
6	States with initial application and sustained application (*savitakka savicārā*). (Dhs 1000, 1399)	55 cittas (see Appendix V, and Chart 7 in Appendix VI), 50 cetasikas (52 excluding *vitakka*, *vicāra*).	4	2	3
	States without initial application but with sustained application. (Dhs 1001, 1400)	11 Second-*Jhāna* cittas (8+3=11), 66 cittas with sustained application, 36 cetasikas (38 excluding *vitakka*, *vicāra*, i.e. (13+25)-2=36).	4	2	2
	States without both initial application and sustained application. (Dhs 1002, 1401)	11 Second-*Jhāna* cittas (8+3=11), 55 cittas (dissociated from *vitakka* and *vicāra*), 36 cetasikas (38 excluding vitakka, vicāra), 28 matters; *Nibbāna*.	5	12	17

I. Aggrouping and Ungrouping

			A.	B.	E.
	States accompanied by zest (*pīti*). (Dhs 1003, 1402)	51 cittas accompanied by zest; 46 cetasikas (52 excluding zest, hatred, envy, avarice, worry, and doubt, i.e. 52-6=46).	4	2	2
7	States accompanied by pleasure/happiness (*sukha*). (Dhs 1004, 1403)	63 cittas (accompanied both by joy and happiness), 46 cetasikas (52 excluding feeling, hatred, envy, avarice, worry, doubt. i.e. 52-6=46).	3	2	3
	States accompanied by equanimity, i.e. indifference to happiness (*upekkhā*). (Dhs 1005, 1404)	55 cittas accompanied by equanimity (see Chart 18 in Appendix VI); 46 cetasikas (52 excluding feeling, zest, hatred, envy, avarice, worry. 52-6=46)	3	2	7
	States eliminated by the first Path, *Sotāpattimagga*. (Dhs 1006, 1405)	5 cittas (4 greed-rooted cittas associated with wrong view, 1 delusion-rooted citta with doubt), arisen with 22 cetasikas.	4	2	2
8	States eliminated by the higher three paths. (Dhs 1011, 1406)	4 greed-rooted cittas dissociated from wrong view, 2 hatred-rooted cittas, 1 delusion-rooted citta accompanied by restlessness [7]; 25 cetasikas by the second and third Paths (27 excluding wrong view and doubt); 21 cetasikas (by the final Path).	4	2	2
	States eliminated neither by the first Path nor by the higher three Paths. (Dhs 1012, 1407)	77 mundane cittas (21+36+20 =77), 38 cetasikas (13+25=38), 28 matters, and *Nibbāna*.	5	12	18

---

[7] Of the 12 three-evils-rooted unwholesome cittas, the first Path (*Sotāpattimagga*) eliminated the 4 greed-rooted cittas associated with wrong view, and 1 delusion-rooted citta associated with doubt (or the 3 Fetters of *sakkāyadiṭṭhi, vicikicchā, sīlabbataparāmāsa*). The Second Path (*Sakadāgāmimagga*) only attenuated the remaining 7 active unwholesome cittas. The Third Path (*Anāgāmimagga*) eliminated the 2 hatred-rooted cittas with aversion. The Final Path (*Arahattamagga*) eliminated remaining 4 greed-rooted cittas dissociated from wrong view, and 1 delusion-rooted citta associated with restlessness. In other word, the first Path eradicated the 3 Fetters (*sakkāyadiṭṭhi, vicikicchā, sīlabbataparāmāsa*); the Second Path only attenuated the remaining of the 10 Fetters; the Third Path eradicated the Five fetters of the 'Lower region' (*sakkāyadiṭṭhi, sīlabbataparāmāsa, vicikicchā, kāmarāga*—attenuated from *kāmacchandā*, and *paṭigha*—attenuated from *byāpāda*); the Fourth Path eradicated the Five Fetters of the 'upper region' (*rūparāga, arūparāga, māna, uddhacca*, and *avijjā*). *Cf.* Pp: nos. 36-40, 209.

A Perfect Knowledge of Mind-Body from the Abhidhamma (Dhātukathā)

			A.	B.	E.
9	States with root causes eliminated by *Sotāpattimagga*. (Dhs 1013, 1408)	5 cittas (4 greed-rooted cittas associated with wrong view, 1 delusion-rooted citta with doubt [7]), arisen with 22 cetasikas.	4	2	2
	States with root causes eliminated by the higher three paths. (Dhs 1018, 1409)	4 greed-rooted cittas dissociated from wrong view, 2 hatred-rooted cittas, 1 delusion-rooted citta with restlessness [7], 25 cetasikas (27 excluding wrong view and doubt).	4	2	2
	States with root causes eliminated neither by the first Path nor by the higher three paths. (Dhs 1019, 1410)	77 mundane cittas (21+36+20 =77), 38 cetasikas (13+25=38), delusion from the 2 delusion-rooted cittas, 28 matters, and *Nibbāna*.	5	12	18
10	States which make for the continuity of rebirth and death. (Dhs 1020, 1411)	the active 17 mundane wholesome cittas, 12 unwholesome cittas, 52 cetasikas.	4	2	2
	States which lead out (from round of rebirths and deaths) (Dhs 1021, 1412)	4 supramundane path-cittas; 36 cetasikas, i.e. (13+(25-2 Illimitables) =36).	4	2	2
	States which neither lead to round of deaths and rebirths nor to *Nibbāna*. (Dhs 1022, 1413)	36 resultant cittas, 20 functional cittas, 38 cetasikas (13+25=38), 28 matters, and *Nibbāna*.	5	12	18
11	States appertaining to Learners (*sekhā*). (Dhs 1023, 1414)	7 supramundane cittas excluded that of *Arahatta* fruition, arisen with 36 cetasikas (13+(25-2 Illimitables)=36).	4	2	2
	States appertaining to 'beyond-learner' or *Arahatta* (*asekhā*). (Dhs 1024, 1415)	*Arahatta* fruition-citta, 36 cetasikas (13+(25-2 Illimitables)=36).	4	2	2
	States appertaining to neither Learners nor *Arahatta*. (Dhs 1025, 1416)	81 mundane cittas, 52 cetasikas, 28 matters, and *Nibbāna*.	5	12	18
12	States which are limited. (Dhs 1026, 1417)	54 sensuous cittas, 52 cetasikas, 28 matters, and *Nibbāna*.	5	12	18
	States which are sublime. (Dhs 1027, 1418)	27 sublime cittas (*mahaggacittāni*), 35 cetasikas (38 excluding the 3 Abstinences, i.e. 13+(25-3)=35).	4	2	2
	States which are immeasurable/incomparable. (Dhs 1028, 1419)	supramundane 4 Path- and 4 fruition-cittas, 36 cetasikas (13+(25-2 Illimitables)=36), and *Nibbāna*.	4	2	2
13	States with limited objects. (Dhs 1029, 1420)	54 sensuous cittas, 52 cetasikas.	4	2	8

I. Aggrouping and Ungrouping

			A.	B.	E.
13	States with sublime objects. (*mahaggata-arammaṇa*). (Dhs 1030, 1421)	8 great wholesome cittas, 8 beautiful functional cittas, 1 mind-door advertence citta, 6 *jhāna* cittas of the immaterial sphere (viz. 3 cittas of Infinity and 3 cittas of neither-perception-nor-nonperception) as the 1st and 3rd cittas are taken as their respective 'concept objects'; 2 abhiññā powers attained from Fifth rūpajhānas; 47 cetasikas (52 excluding 3 Abstinences and 2 Illimitables, thus 52-3-2=47).	4	2	2
	States with immeasurable objects. (Dhs 1031, 1422)	4 great wholesome cittas associated with knowledge, 4 functional cittas associated with knowledge, 1 mind-door advertence citta (*manodvārāvajjana*), 2 of the 5 abhiññā powers attained from Fifth rūpajhānas, supramundane 4 path-cittas and 4 fruition-cittas, 36 cetasikas (13+(25-2 Illimitables)=36)	4	2	2
	Inferior states. (Dhs 1032, 1423)	12 unwholesome cittas, 27 cetasikas (13 common non-beautiful factors and 14 unwholesome factors).	4	2	2
14	States of medium worth. (Dhs 1033, 1424)	the 17 mundane wholesome cittas, 32 resultant cittas, 20 functional cittas, 38 cetasikas (13+25=38), 28 Matters.	5	12	18
	Superior states. (Dhs 1034, 1425)	supramundane 4 path- and 4 fruition-cittas, 36 cetasikas (13+(25-2 Illimitables)=36), and *Nibbāna*.	4	2	2
15	States fixed as to their destinies or consequences due to wrong views. (Dhs 1035, 1426)	7th sensuous *javana* (impulsion) present at the 4 greed-rooted cittas associated with wrong view and at the 2 hatred-rooted cittas; 25 cetasikas (27 excluding conceit and doubt).	4	2	2
	States with fixed destinies as a result of right views. (Dhs 1036, 1427)	supramundane 4 path-cittas (excluding 4 fruition-cittas), 36 cetasikas (13+(25-2 Illimitables)=36).	4	2	2
	States which do not entail fixed destinies. (Dhs 1037, 1428)	4 greed-rooted cittas dissociated from wrong view, 2 delusion-rooted cittas, 17 mundane wholesome cittas, 32 resultant cittas, 20 functional cittas, 52 cetasikas, 28 Matters, *Nibbāna*.	5	12	18

A Perfect Knowledge of Mind-Body from the Abhidhamma (Dhātukathā)

			A.	B.	E.
16	States having Path as its object. (Dhs 1038, 1429)	4 great wholesome cittas associated with knowledge, 4 great functional cittas associated with knowledge, 1 mind-door advertence citta (*manodvārāvajjana*), 2 of the 5 abhiññā powers attained from Fifth rūpajhānas, 33 cetasikas (25 beautiful factors excluding 3 Abstinences and 2 Illimitables (13+(25-3-2)=33).	4	2	2
	States which are conditioned by Path. (Dhs 1039, 1429)	the supramundane 4 path-cittas (excluding the 4 fruition-cittas), 36 cetasikas (38 excluding the 2 Illimitables).	4	2	2
	States which have Path as their predominant factor. (Dhs 1040, 1429)	4 great wholesome cittas associated with knowledge, 4 functional cittas associated with knowledge, 4 supramundane path-cittas, 36 cetasikas (38-2 Illimitables =36).	4	2	2
17	States arisen. (Dhs 1041, 1430)	all 89 cittas, 52 cetasikas, all that is corporeality.	5	12	18
	States not arisen. (Dhs 1042, 1430)	53 cittas which have not occurred (consist of 12 unwholesome, 21 wholesome, 20 functionals), 52 cetasikas, 17 rupas of kammaja-kalāpā, 15 utuja-kalāpā, and 14 āhāraja-kalāpā.	5	7	8
	States bound to arise. (Dhs 1043, 1430)	future states from 36 resultant cittas that have not yet occurred; 38 cetasikas (13+25=38); 20 kamma-produced matters.	5	11	17
18	Past states. (Dhs 1044, 1431)	any of the 89 cittas which have already occurred, 52 cetasikas, and all that is corporeality.	5	12	18
	Future states. (Dhs 1045, 1431)	any of the 89 cittas which have not yet occurred, 52 cetasikas, and all that is corporeality.	5	12	18
	Present states. (Dhs 1046, 1431)	any current states of the 89 cittas, 52 cetasikas, and all that is corporeality.	5	12	18

I. Aggrouping and Ungrouping

			A.	B.	E.
19	States having past object (Dhs 1047, 1432)	1 mind-door advertence citta (*manodvārāvajjana*), 29 sensuous javanas (active 17 kusala and 12 akusala cittas, that of *kammabhava*), 11 Registering cittas (3 Investigating cittas and 8 mahāvipākas), 2 of the 5 abhiññā powers attained from Fifth rūpajhānas, 6 *jhāna* cittas of immaterial sphere (3 cittas of Infinity, 3 cittas of neither-perception-nor-nonperception), 47 cetasikas (52 excluding 3 Abstinences and 2 Illimitables, i.e. 52-3-2=47).	4	2	2
	States having future object. (Dhs 1048, 1433)	1 mind-door advertence citta, 29 sensuous javanas, 11 Registering cittas, 2 of the 5 abhiññā powers attained from Fifth rūpajhānas, 50 cetasikas without the 2 Illimitables (52-2=50).	4	2	2
	States having present object. (Dhs 1049, 1434)	43 cittas (from 10 Viññāṇa cittas, 3 mind-elements, 1 mind-door advertence citta, 29 sensuous javanas); 11 Registering cittas; 2 of 5 abhiññā powers; 50 cetasikas without the 2 Illimitables (52-2=50).	4	2	8
20	Internal states. (Dhs 1050, 1435)	89 cittas, 52 cetasikas, all that is corporeality.	5	12	18
	External states. (Dhs 1051, 1435)	89 cittas, 52 cetasikas, all that is corporeality, and *Nibbāna*.	5	12	18
	States which are both internal and external. (Dhs 1052, 1435)	89 cittas, 52 cetasikas, all that is corporeality.	5	12	18
21	States with internal object. (Dhs 1053, 1436)	54 sensuous cittas, 3 Fifth rūpajhānas (2 abhiññā powers), 3 arūpajhānas of the base of neither-perception-nor-nonperception, 49 cetasikas (52 excluding env and 2 Illimitables).	4	2	8
	States with external object. (Dhs 1054, 1437)	54 sensuous cittas, 15 rūpajhāna cittas excluding 3 Fifth jhānas (with 2 of 5 abhiññā powers), 3 arūpajhāna cittas on the base of Infinity, supramundane 4 Path- and 4 fruition-cittas, 51 cetasikas (52 excluding avarice).	4	2	8

A Perfect Knowledge of Mind-Body from the Abhidhamma (Dhātukathā)

			A.	B.	E.
22	States with both internal and external objects. (Dhs 1055, 1437)	54 sensuous cittas, 15 rūpajhānas, 48 cetasikas (52 excluding envy, avarice, the 2 Illimitables. i.e. 52-2-2=48).	4	2	8
	States which are visible and impinging. (Dhs 1056, 1438)	2 eye-consciousness, and visible object.	1	1	1
	States which are not visible but impinging. (Dhs 1057, 1439)	11 gross matters (12 excluding visible object).	1	9	9
	States not visible and not impinging. (Dhs 1058, 1440)	89 cittas, 52 cetasikas, 16 subtle matters, and *Nibbāna*.	5	2	8

The following states of enquiry, nos. 77 to 110, are to be referred to preceding Table 1.7 and Chart 1.

Chart 1.7. Aggrouping and Ungrouping of the 22 Triads

	Aggrouped		
By units :	Agr	Base	Ele
77. States which are wholesome. States which are unwholesome. Each of these two states is aggrouped under 4 aggregates (4 mental aggregates), 2 bases (ideation-base, mind-base), and 2 elements (ideation-element, mind-consciousness element). Each is ungrouped under 1 aggregate (matter), 10 bases (10 gross bases), and 16 elements (10 gross elements, remaining 6 consciousness elements).	4	2	2
78. Indeterminate states. Indeterminate states belong to mentality-materiality, are aggrouped under 5 aggregates excluding *Nibbāna* (matter, feeling, perception, volitive formation, consciousness), 12 bases (10 gross bases, ideation-base, mind-base), and 18 elements (10 gross elements, ideation-element, 7 consciousness elements). There are no ungrouped states.	5	12	18

I. Aggrouping and Ungrouping

		Aggrouped		
		Agr	Base	Ele
79.	States with happy or pleasurable feeling.	3	2	3
	States with painful feeling.	3	2	3
	Each of these two states are aggrouped under 3 aggregates (perception, volitive formation, consciousness), 2 bases (ideation-base, mind-base), and 3 elements (body-consciousness element, ideation-element, and mind-consciousness element).			
	Each of them is ungrouped under 2 aggregates (matter, feeling), 10 bases (10 gross bases), and 15 elements (10 gross elements, remaining 5 consciousness elements).			
80.	States with neither pleasurable feeling nor painful feeling.	3	2	7
	They are aggrouped under 3 aggregates (perception, volitive formation, consciousness), 2 bases (ideation-base, mind-base), and 7 elements (eye-cons. element, ear-cons. element, nose-cons. element, tongue-cons. element, mind-element, ideation-element, mind-cons. element).			
	They are ungrouped under 2 aggregates (matter, feeling), 10 bases (10 gross bases), and 11 elements (10 gross elements, body-cons. element).			
81.	Resultant states.	4	2	8
	They are aggrouped under 4 aggregates (4 mental aggregates), 2 bases (ideation-base, mind-base), and 8 elements (ideation-element, 7 consciousness elements).			
	They are ungrouped under 1 aggregate (matter), 10 bases (10 gross bases), and 10 elements (10 gross elements).			
82.	States which are resultant-producing (*vipākadhamma dhammā*);	4	2	2
	States which are corrupted as well as are objects of corruptions (*saṃkiliṭṭhasaṃkilesikā*).	4	2	2
	Each of these two states is aggrouped under 4 aggregates (4 mental aggregates), 2 bases (ideation-base, mind-base), 2 elements (ideation-element, mind-consciousness element).			
	They are ungrouped under 1 aggregate (matter), 10 bases (10 gross bases), and 16 elements (10 gross elements, remaining 6 consciousness elements).			
83.	States which neither are resultants, nor are resultant-producing states (*nevavipākanavipākadhammadhamma*).	5	12	13
	These states belong to mentality-materiality, are aggrouped under 5 aggregates excluding *Nibbāna* (matter, feeling, perception, volitive formation, consciousness), 12 bases (10			

A Perfect Knowledge of Mind-Body from the Abhidhamma (Dhātukathā)

Agr	Base	Ele

gross bases, ideation-base, mind-base), and 13 elements (10 gross elements, mind-element of the functional *manodvārāvajjana* consciousness (mind-door advertence), ideation-element, and mind-consciousness element).
They are ungrouped under 5 elements (eye-cons. element, ear-cons. element, nose-cons. element, tongue-cons. element, body-cons. element). They have no ungrouping under aggregates and bases.

84. States which are the result of clinging as well as are objects of clinging (*upādinnupādāniyā*).   5   11   17
These states belong to mentality-materiality, are aggrouped under 5 aggregates excluding *Nibbāna* (matter, feeling, perception, volitive formation, consciousness), 11 bases (9 gross bases excluded sound-base; ideation-base; mind-base), and 17 elements (9 gross elements excluded sound-element; ideation-element; 7 consciousness elements).
They are ungrouped under 1 base (sound-base) and 1 element (sound-element). There is no ungrouping under aggregate.

85. States which are not the result of clinging but are objects of clinging (*anupādinnupādāniyā*)   5   7   8
These states belong to mentality-materiality, are aggrouped under 5 aggregates excluding *Nibbāna* (matter, feeling, perception, volitive formation, consciousness), 7 bases (vision-base, sound-base, odour-base, taste-base, touch-base, ideation-base, mind-base), and 8 elements (vision-element, sound-element, odour-element, taste-element, touch-element, mind-element, ideation-element, mind-consciousness element).
They are ungrouped under 5 bases (remaining 5 gross sense-bases) and 10 elements (remaining 5 gross sense-elements, remaining 5 consciousness elements). There is no ungrouping under aggregate.

86. States which neither are the result of clinging nor are objects of clinging (*anupādinna-anupādāniyā*).   4   2   2
States which are not corrupted as well as are not objects of corruptions (*asaṃkiliṭṭha-asaṃkilesikā*), excluding the unconditioned element (*asaṅkhatadhātu*), i.e. *Nibbāna*.   4   2   2
Each of these two states is aggrouped under 4 aggregates (4 mental aggregates), 2 bases (ideation-base, mind-base), and 2 elements (ideation-element, mind-consciousness element).
They are ungrouped under 1 aggregate (matter), 10 bases (10 gross bases), and 16 elements (10 gross elements, remaining 6 consciousness elements).

I. Aggrouping and Ungrouping

	Agr	Base	Ele
87. States which are not corrupted but are objects of corruptions (*asaṃkiliṭṭhasaṃkilesikā*).	5	12	18

They belong to mentality-materiality, are aggrouped under 5 aggregates excluding *Nibbāna* (matter, feeling, perception, volitive formation, consciousness), 12 bases (10 gross bases, ideation-base, mind-base), and 18 elements (10 gross elements, ideation-element, 7 consciousness elements). There are no ungrouped states.

	Agr	Base	Ele
88. States with both initial application and sustained application.	4	2	3

They are aggrouped under 4 aggregates (4 mental aggregates), 2 bases (ideation-base, mind-base), 3 elements (mind-element, ideation-element, mind-consciousness element).

They are ungrouped under 1 aggregate (matter), 10 bases (10 gross bases), and 15 elements (10 gross elements, remaining 5 consciousness elements).

	Agr	Base	Ele
89. States without initial application but with sustained application.	4	2	2
States accompanied by zest.	4	2	2

Each of these two states is aggrouped under 4 aggregates (4 mental aggregates), 2 bases (ideation-base, mind-base), 2 elements (ideation-element, mind-consciousness element).

They are ungrouped under 1 aggregate (matter), 10 bases (10 gross bases), and 16 elements (10 gross bases, remaining 6 consciousness elements).

	Agr	Base	Ele
90. States without initial application and sustained application.	5	12	17

They are mentality-materiality, are aggrouped under 5 aggregates excluding *Nibbāna* (matter, feeling, perception, volitive formation, consciousness), 12 bases (10 gross bases, ideation-base, mind-base), and 17 elements (10 gross elements, ideation-element, 6 consciousness elements excluded mind-element).

They are ungrouped under 1 element (mind-element). There is no ungrouping under aggregate and base.

	Agr	Base	Ele
91. States accompanied by happiness.	3	2	3

They are aggrouped under 3 aggregates (perception, volitive formation, consciousness), 2 bases (ideation-base, mind-base), 3 elements (body-consciousness element, ideation-element, mind-consciousness element).

They are all ungrouped under 2 aggregates (matter, feeling), 10 bases (10 gross bases), and 15 elements (10 gross elements, remaining 5 consciousness elements).

A Perfect Knowledge of Mind-Body from the Abhidhamma (Dhātukathā)

	Agr	Base	Ele
92. States accompanied by equanimity.	3	2	7

They are aggrouped under 3 aggregates (perception, volitive formation, consciousness), 2 bases (ideation-base, mind-base), 7 elements (eye-cons. element, ear-cons. element, nose-cons. element, tongue-cons. element, mind-element, ideation-element, mind-cons. element).

They are ungrouped under 2 aggregates (matter, feeling), 10 bases (10 gross bases), and 11 elements (10 gross elements, body-cons. element).

	Agr	Base	Ele
93. States eliminated by the first Path.	4	2	2
States eliminated by the higher three Paths.	4	2	2
States with root causes eliminated by the first Path.	4	2	2
States with root causes eliminated by the Higher three Paths.	4	2	2
States leading to round of deaths and rebirths.	4	2	2
States leading to liberation from round of deaths and rebirths.	4	2	2
States appertaining to Learners (*sekhā*).	4	2	2
States appertaining to *Arahatta* (*asekhā*).	4	2	2
States which are sublime (27 *mahaggatācittāni*)	4	2	2

Each of these nine states of enquiry is aggrouped under 4 aggregates (4 mental aggregates), 2 bases (ideation-base, mind-base), and 2 elements (ideation-element, mind-consciousness element).

Each is ungrouped under 1 aggregate (matter), 10 bases (10 gross bases), and 16 elements (10 gross bases, remaining 6 consciousness elements).

	Agr	Base	Ele
94. States which are eliminated neither by the first Path nor by the higher three Paths.	5	12	18
States with root causes eliminated neither by the first Path, nor by the higher three Paths.	5	12	18
States which neither are leading to round of rebirths and death, nor to *Nibbāna*;	5	12	18
States appertaining to neither Learners (*sekhā*) nor *Arahatta* (*asekhā*).	5	12	18

These four states of enquiry all belong to mentality-materiality, are aggrouped under 5 aggregates excluding *Nibbāna* (matter, feeling, perception, volitive formation, consciousness), 12 bases (10 gross bases, ideation-base, mind-base), and 18 elements (10 gross elements, ideation-element, 7 consciousness elements). There are no ungrouped states.

I. Aggrouping and Ungrouping

		Agr	Base	Ele
95.	States which are limited.	5	12	18

These states are mentality-materiality, are aggrouped under 5 aggregates excluding *Nibbāna* (matter, feeling, perception, volitive formation, consciousness), 12 bases (10 gross bases, ideation-base, mind-base), and 18 elements (10 gross elements, ideation-element, 7 consciousness elements). There are no ungrouped states.

		Agr	Base	Ele
96.	States which are immeasurable/incomparable.	4	2	2
	States which are superior.	4	2	2

Each of these states is aggrouped under 4 aggregates (4 mental aggregates), 2 bases (ideation-base, mind-base), and 2 elements (ideation-element, mind-consciousness element).

Each is ungrouped under 1 aggregate (matter), 10 bases (10 gross bases), and 16 elements (10 gross bases, remaining 6 consciousness elements).

		Agr	Base	Ele
97.	States with limited objects.	4	2	8

They are aggrouped under 4 aggregates (4 mental aggregates), 2 bases (ideation-base, mind-base), and 8 elements (ideation-element, 7 consciousness elements).

They are ungrouped under 1 aggregate (matter), 10 bases (10 gross bases), and 10 elements (10 gross elements).

		Agr	Base	Ele
98.	States with sublime objects.	4	2	2
	States with immeasurable objects.	4	2	2
	Inferior states;	4	2	2
	States fixed as to their future destinies due to wrong views.	4	2	2
	States fixed as to their future destinies due to right views.	4	2	2
	States having Path as its object.	4	2	2
	States which are conditioned by the Path.	4	2	2
	States having Path as their predominant factor.	4	2	2

Each of these states is aggrouped under 4 aggregates (4 mental aggregates), 2 bases (ideation-base, mind-base), and 2 elements (ideation-element, mind-consciousness element).

Each of them is ungrouped under 1 aggregate (matter), 10 bases (10 gross bases), and 16 elements (10 gross bases, remaining 6 consciousness elements).

		Agr	Base	Ele
99.	States of medium worth.	5	12	18
100.	States which do not entail fixed future destinies.	5	12	18
101.	States arisen.	5	12	18

A Perfect Knowledge of Mind-Body from the Abhidhamma (Dhātukathā)

	Agr	Base	Ele
These three states are mentality-materiality, are each aggrouped under 5 aggregates excluding *Nibbāna* (matter, feeling, perception, volitive formation, consciousness), 12 bases (10 gross bases, ideation-base, mind-base), and 18 elements (10 gross elements, ideation-element, 7 consciousness elements). There are no ungrouped states.			
102. States not arisen.	5	7	8

They are mentality-materiality, are aggrouped under 5 aggregates excluding *Nibbāna* (matter, feeling, perception, volitive formation, consciousness), 7 bases (vision-base, sound-base, odour-base, taste-base, touch-base, ideation-base, mind-base), and 8 elements (vision-element, sound-element, odour-element, taste-element, touch-element, mind-element (of the functional *manodvārāvajjanacittaṃ*), ideation-element, and mind-consciousness element).
They are ungrouped under 5 bases (remaining 5 gross sense-bases) and 10 elements (remaining 5 gross sense-elements, remaining 5 consciousness elements). There is no ungrouping under aggregate.

103. States which are bound to arise.	5	11	17

They are mentality-materiality, are aggrouped under 5 aggregates excluding *Nibbāna* (matter, feeling, perception, volitive formation, consciousness), 11 bases (9 gross bases excluded sound-base; ideation-base; mind-base), and 17 elements (10 gross elements excluded sound-element; ideation-element; 7 consciousness elements). Herein the mind-element belongs to the 2 Receiving cittas accompanied by equanimity.
They are ungrouped under 1 base (sound-base) and 1 element (sound-element). There is no ungrouping under aggregate.

104. Past states; Future states; Present states; Internal states; States which are both internal and external.	5	12	18
105. External states.	5	12	18

All these six states are mentality-materiality. Each of them is aggrouped under 5 aggregates excluding *Nibbāna* (matter, feeling, perception, volitive formation, consciousness), 12 bases (10 gross bases, ideation-base, mind-base), and 18 elements (10 gross elements, ideation-element, 7 consciousness elements). There are no ungrouped states.

I. Aggrouping and Ungrouping

	Agr	Base	Ele
106. States with past object;	4	2	2
States with future object.	4	2	2

These states are each aggrouped under 4 aggregates (4 mental aggregates), 2 bases (ideation-base, mind-base), and 2 elements (ideation-element, mind-consciousness element).

Each of them is ungrouped under 1 aggregate (matter), 10 bases (10 gross bases), and 16 elements (10 gross elements, remaining 6 consciousness elements).

	Agr	Base	Ele
107. States with present object.	4	2	8

They are aggrouped under 4 aggregates (4 mental aggregates), 2 bases (ideation-base, mind-base), and 8 elements (ideation-element, 7 consciousness elements).

They are ungrouped under 1 aggregate (matter), 10 bases (10 gross bases), and 10 elements (10 gross elements).

	Agr	Base	Ele
108. States which are visible and impinging.	1	1	1

They are aggrouped under 1 aggregate (matter), 1 base (visible object base), and 1 element (visible object element).

They are ungrouped under 4 aggregates (4 mental aggregates), 11 bases (remaining 9 gross bases, ideation-base, mind-base), and 17 elements (remaining 9 gross elements, ideation-element, 7 consciousness elements).

	Agr	Base	Ele
109. States which are not visible but impinging.	1	9	9

These states consist of 11 gross matters having excluded gross visible object. They are aggrouped under 1 aggregate (matter), 9 bases (10 gross bases excluding visible object base), and 9 elements (10 gross elements excluding visible object element).

These states are ungrouped under 4 aggregates (4 mental aggregates), 3 bases (visible object base, ideation-base, mind-base), and 9 elements (visible object element, ideation-element, 7 consciousness elements).

	Agr	Base	Ele
110. States not visible and not impinging.	5	2	8

These states belong to mentality-materiality, are aggrouped under 5 aggregates excluding *Nibbāna* (16 subtle matters, feeling, perception, volitive formation, consciousness), 2 bases (ideation-base, mind-base), and 8 elements (ideation-element, 7 consciousness elements).

These states are ungrouped under 10 bases (10 gross bases) and 10 elements (10 gross elements). There is no ungrouping under aggregate.

A Perfect Knowledge of Mind-Body from the Abhidhamma (Dhātukathā)

200 states of enquiry from Dhammasaṅgaṇīmātikā dyads

8. Dyads (*Dukaṃ*)

The following tables supplements the information provided in Chart 1

Table 1.8.1. 6 dyads on Root Causes

	Cluster of 6 Dyads in relation to Root Causes (*Hetū*)		Aggregates	Bases	Elements
	States of enquiry :	Compositional states :			
1	States which are root causes. (Dhs 1077, 1441)	6 states of roots causes — greed, hatred, delusion, absence of greed, absence of hatred, absence of delusion.	1	1	1
	States which are not root causes. (Dhs 1078, 1442)	89 cittas; 46 cetasikas (52 excluding the above 6 root causes, i.e. 52-6=46); 28 matters; *Nibbāna*.	5	12	18
2	States which have root causes (i.e. accompanied by root causes). (*sahetukā*) (Dhs 1079, 1443)	71 cittas which have associated roots, 50 cetasikas (52 excluding the delusion, non-delusion, i.e. 52-2=50).	4	2	2
	States which have no root causes (i.e. not accompanied by root causes). (Dhs 1080, 1444)	18 cittas without roots; 12 cetasikas (13 common, non-beautiful cetasikas excluding *vicikicchā* present at the 2 delusion-rooted cittas; 28 matters, and *Nibbāna*.	5	12	18
3	States which are associated with root causes. (Dhs 1081, 1445)	71 cittas which have associated roots, 50 cetasikas (52 excluding the delusion, non-delusion, i.e. 52-2=50).	4	2	2
	States which are dissociated from root causes. (Dhs 1082, 1446)	18 cittas without roots; 12 cetasikas (13 common, non-beautiful cetasikas excluding *vicikicchā* present at the 2 delusion-rooted cittas; 28 matters, and *Nibbāna*.	5	12	18
4	States which are root causes, and also having root causes. (Dhs 1083, 1447)	6 roots causes (excluding delusion present at the 2 delusion-rooted cittas).	1	1	1

I. Aggrouping and Ungrouping

			A.	B.	E.
5	States which have associated root causes but are not root causes per se. (*sahetukā ceva na ca hetū*) (Dhs 1084, 1448)	71 cittas which have associated roots, 46 cetasikas (52 excluding the 6 roots causes, i.e. 52-6=46).	4	2	2
	States which are root causes as well as are associated with them. (Dhs 1085, 1449)	6 roots causes (excluding delusion present at the 2 delusion-rooted cittas).	1	1	1
	States which are not root causes but are associated with root causes. (Dhs 1086, 1450)	71 cittas which have associated roots, 46 cetasikas (52 excluding the 6 roots causes, i.e. 52-6=46).	4	2	2
6	States which are not root causes but have associated root causes. (*na hetū kho pana sahetukā pi*) (Dhs 1087, 1451)	71 cittas which have associated roots, 46 cetasikas (52 excluding the 6 roots causes, i.e. 52-6=46).	4	2	2
	States which are neither root causes nor having root causes. (Dhs 1088, 1452)	same as in 2 (2nd) above as to states which have no root causes.	5	12	18

The following states of enquiry, nos. 111 to 113, are to be referred to preceding Table 1.8.1 and Chart 1.

Chart 1.8.1 Aggrouping and Ungrouping of the dyads on Root Causes

	Aggrouped		
By units :	Agr	Base	Ele
111. States which are root causes.			
States which have root causes (i.e. accompanied by root causes) and are root causes.	1	1	1
These states are each aggrouped under 1 aggregate (volitive formation), 1 base (ideation-base), and 1 element (ideation-element).			
They are each ungrouped under 4 aggregates (matter, feeling, perception, consciousness), 11 bases (10 gross bases, mind-base), and 17 elements (10 gross elements, 7 consciousness elements).			
112. States which are not root causes.	5	12	18
States which have no root causes (i.e. not accompanied by root causes).	5	12	18
States which are dissociated from root causes.	5	12	18

A Perfect Knowledge of Mind-Body from the Abhidhamma (Dhātukathā)

	Agr	Base	Ele
States which are neither root causes nor having root causes, excluding *Nibbāna*.	5	12	18

All these states are mentality-materiality. Each of them is aggrouped under 5 aggregates excluding Nibbāna (matter, feeling, perception, volitive formation, consciousness), 12 bases (10 gross bases, ideation-base, mind-base), and 18 elements (10 gross elements, ideation-element, 7 consciousness elements). There are no ungrouped states.

	Agr	Base	Ele
113. States which have root causes (accompanied by root causes).	4	2	2
States which are associated with root causes.	4	2	2
States which have root causes, but are not root causes per se.	4	2	2
States which are associated with root causes, but are not root causes.	4	2	2
States which are not root causes but having root causes.	4	2	2

These states are each aggrouped under 4 aggregates (feeling, perception, volitive formation, consciousness), 2 bases (ideation-base, mind-base), and 2 elements (ideation-element, mind-consciousness element).

These states are each ungrouped under 1 aggregate (matter), 10 bases (10 gross bases), and 16 elements (10 gross elements, eye-consciousness element, ear-consciousness element, nose-consciousness element, tongue-consciousness element, body-consciousness element, mind-element).

I. Aggrouping and Ungrouping

Table 1.8.2. the shorter 7 dyads (*cūḷantara duka*)

	The short 7 non-interrelated dyads (*Cūḷantara*)		Aggregates	Bases	Elements
	States of enquiry :	Compositional states :			
7	States arisen from causes. (Dhs 1089, 1453)	89 cittas, 52 cetasikas, all that is corporeality.	5	12	18
	States not arisen from causes. (Dhs 1090, 1454)	*Nibbāna*.	-	1	1
8	States which are conditioned by causes. (Dhs 1091, 1455)	89 cittas, 52 cetasikas, all that is corporeality.	5	12	18
	States which are not conditioned by causes. (Dhs 1092, 1456)	*Nibbāna*.	-	1	1
9	States with visibility. (Dhs 1093, 1457)	2 eye-consciousness; the visible object.	1	1	1
	States without visibility. (Dhs 1094, 1458)	89 cittas, 52 cetasikas, 27 Matters (28 less visible object), *Nibbāna*.	5	11	17
10	States with impinging. (Dhs 1095, 1459)	12 gross matters.	1	10	10
	States without impinging. (Dhs 1096, 1460)	89 cittas, 52 cetasikas, 16 subtle matters, and *Nibbāna*.	5	2	8
11	States with physical change. (Dhs 1097, 1461)	all that is corporeality.	1	11	11
	States with no physical change. (Dhs 1098, 1462)	89 cittas, 52 cetasikas, *Nibbāna*.	4	2	8
12	Mundane states. (Dhs 1099, 1463)	81 *lokiya* cittas, 52 cetasikas, all that is corporeality.	5	12	18
	Supramundane states. (Dhs 1100, 1464)	8 supramundane cittas; 36 cetasikas (38 excluding 2 Illimitables, i.e. 13+(25-2)=36), and *Nibbāna*.	4	2	2
13	States cognisable by certain kind of sense-consciousness. (Dhs 1101, 1464)	89 cittas, 52 cetasikas, all that is corporeality, *Nibbāna*.	5	12	18
	States not cognisable by certain sense-consciousness. (Dhs 1101, 1464)	same as aforesaid.	5	12	18

A Perfect Knowledge of Mind-Body from the Abhidhamma (Dhātukathā)

States of enquiry, nos.114 to 124 below are to refer Table 1.8.2 and Chart 1.

Chart 1.8.2 Aggrouping and Ungrouping of the shorter 7 dyads

By units :	Aggrouped		
	Agr	Base	Ele
114. States arisen from causes (*sappaccayā*).	5	12	18
States which are conditioned by causes (*saṅkhatā*).	5	12	18

These states are mentality-materiality, are each aggrouped under 5 aggregates excluding *Nibbāna* (matter, feeling, perception, volitive formation, consciousness), 12 bases (10 gross bases, ideation-base, mind-base), and 18 elements (10 gross elements, ideation-element, 7 consciousness elements). There are no ungrouped states.

115. States not arisen from causes.	-	1	1
States which are unconditioned by causes.	-	1	1

These states are the same as those states unconditioned by causes, namely, *Nibbāna*. They are each aggrouped under 1 base (ideation-base), and 1 element (ideation-element). Because *Nibbāna* is non-aggregate, there are no ungrouped states under aggregate.

These states are ungrouped under 5 aggregates (matter and 4 mental aggregates), 11 bases (10 gross bases, mind-base), and 17 elements (10 gross elements, 7 consciousness elements).

116. States with visibility.	1	1	1

These are visible gross matters. They are aggrouped under 1 aggregate (matter), 1 base (visible object base), and 1 element (visible object element).
They are ungrouped under 4 aggregates (4 mental aggregates), 11 bases (remaining 9 gross bases, ideation-base, mind-base), and 17 elements (remaining 9 gross elements, ideation-element, 7 consciousness elements).

117. States without visibility, excluding *Nibbāna*.	5	11	17

These states consist of 89 cittas, 52 cetasikas, and the remaining 27 matter having excluded visible object. They are aggrouped under 5 aggregates, 11 bases (remaining 9 gross bases, ideation-base, mind-base), and 17 elements (remaining 9 gross elements, ideation-element, 7 cons. elements).
They are ungrouped under 1 base (vision-base) and 1 element (vision-element). There is no ungrouping under aggregate.

I. Aggrouping and Ungrouping

		Agr	Base	Ele
118.	**States with impinging.** These are the 12 gross matters. They are aggrouped under 1 aggregate (matter), 10 bases (10 gross bases), and 10 elements (10 gross elements). They are ungrouped under 4 aggregates, 2 bases, and 8 elements.	1	10	10
119.	**States without impinging, excluding *Nibbāna*.** These states consist of 16 subtle matters, 89 cittas, 52 cetasikas. Thus, they are mentality-materiality, are aggrouped under 5 aggregates excluding *Nibbāna*, 2 bases (ideation-base, mind-base), and 8 elements (ideation-element, 7 consciousness elements). They are ungrouped under 10 bases (10 gross bases), and 10 elements (10 gross elements). There is no ungrouping under aggregate.	5	2	8
120.	**States which have physical change.** They refer to all 28 matters, are aggrouped under 1 aggregate (matter), 11 bases (10 gross bases, ideation-base), and 10 elements (10 gross elements, ideation-element). They are ungrouped under 4 aggregates (4 mental aggregates), 1 base (mind-base), and 7 elements (7 consciousness elements).	1	11	11
121.	**States which have no physical change, excluding *Nibbāna*.** These are non-matters. They are aggrouped under 4 aggregates (4 mental aggregates), 2 bases (ideation-base, mind-base), and 8 elements (ideation-element, 7 consciousness elements). They are ungrouped under 1 aggregate (matter), 10 bases (10 gross bases), and 10 elements (10 gross elements).	4	2	8
122.	**States which are mundane.** They are mentality-materiality, are each aggrouped under 5 aggregates excluding *Nibbāna* (matter, feeling, perception, volitive formation, consciousness), 12 bases (10 gross bases, ideation-base, mind-base), and 18 elements (10 gross elements, ideation-element, 7 consciousness elements). There are no ungrouped states.	5	12	18

A Perfect Knowledge of Mind-Body from the Abhidhamma (Dhātukathā)

	Agr	Base	Ele
123. States which are supramundane (excluding *Nibbāna*). They are aggrouped under 4 aggregates (4 mental aggregates), 2 bases (ideation-base, mind-base), and 2 elements (ideation-element, mind-consciousness element). They are ungrouped under 1 aggregate (matter), 10 bases (10 gross bases), and 16 elements (10 gross bases, eye consciousness element, ear-consciousness element, nose-consciousness element, tongue-consciousness element, body-consciousness element, mind-element).	4	2	2
124. States cognisable by certain kind of sense-consciousness.	5	12	18
States not cognisable by certain sense-consciousness. These states are mentality-materiality, are each aggrouped under 5 aggregates excluding *Nibbāna* (matter, feeling, perception, volitive formation, consciousness), 12 bases (10 gross bases, ideation-base, mind-base), and 18 elements (10 gross elements, ideation-element, 7 consciousness elements). There are no ungrouped states.	5	12	18

Table 1.8.3. 6 dyads on Defilement

	States of enquiry :	Compositional states :	Aggregates	Bases	Elements
	Cluster of 6 Dyads on 'Outflow' or Defilement (*Āsava*)				
14	States which are defilement. (Dhs 1102, 1465)	3 factors, namely, greed (or sensual desire), wrong view, and delusion.	1	1	1
	States which are not defilement. (Dhs 1103, 1466)	89 cittas, 49 cetasikas (52 excluding the 3 defilement factors, i.e. 52-3=49), 28 matters, and *Nibbāna*.	5	12	18
15	States which are objects of defilement. (Dhs 1104, 1467)	81 mundane cittas, 52 cetasikas, all that is materiality.	5	12	18
	States which are not objects of defilement. (Dhs 1105, 1468)	8 supramundane cittas, 36 cetasikas (38 excluding 2 Illimitables, i.e. 13+(25-2)=36), and *Nibbāna*.	4	2	2
16	States which are associated with defilement. (Dhs 1106, 1469)	12 unwholesome cittas; 26 cetasikas (27 excluding delusion-*cetasika* present at the 2 hate-rooted cittas and 2 delusion-rooted cittas).	4	2	2

I. Aggrouping and Ungrouping

			A.	B.	E.
	States which are dissociated from defilement. (Dhs 1107, 1470)	77 cittas (21 mundane wholesome cittas, 36 resultant cittas, and 20 functional cittas), 38 cetasikas (13+25=38), delusion present at the 2 hate-rooted cittas and 2 delusion-rooted cittas, 28 matters, *Nibbāna*.	5	12	18
17	States which are both defilement and objects of defilement. (Dhs 1108, 1471)	3 factors of defilement as greed (or sensual desire), wrong view, and delusion.	1	1	1
	States which are objects of defilement but are not defilement. (Dhs 1109, 1472)	81 mundane cittas; 49 cetasikas (52 excluding the 3 defilement factors of greed, wrong view and delusion), 28 matters.	5	12	18
18	States which are both defilement and associated with defilement. (Dhs 1110, 1473)	3 defilement factors of (or sensual desire), wrong view, and delusion.	1	1	1
	States which are associated with defilement but are not defilement. (Dhs 1111, 1474)	12 unwholesome cittas, 24 cetasikas (27 excluding the 3 defilement factors, i.e. (13+14)-3=24).	4	2	2
19	States which are dissociated from defilement but still are objects of defilement. (Dhs 1112, 1475)	69 mundane cittas (17 wholesome cittas, 32 resultant cittas; 20 functional cittas), delusion present at the 2 delusion-rooted cittas and 2 hatred-rooted cittas, 38 cetasikas (13+25=38), 28 matters.	5	12	18
	States which are both dissociated from defilement and not objects of defilement. (Dhs 1113, 1476)	8 supramundane cittas; 36 cetasikas (38 excluding 2 Illimitables, and *Nibbāna*.	4	2	2

A Perfect Knowledge of Mind-Body from the Abhidhamma (Dhātukathā)

The following states of enquiry, nos. 125 to 129, are to be referred to Table 1.8.3 and Chart 1.

Chart 1.8.3 Aggrouping and Ungrouping of the dyads on Defilement

By units :	Agr	Aggrouped Base	Ele
125. States which are defilement.	1	1	1
States which are defilement and are objects of defilement.	1	1	1
States which are defilement and associated with defilement.	1	1	1
These states are each aggrouped under 1 aggregate (volitive formation), 1 base (ideation-base), and 1 element (ideation-element).			
They are ungrouped under 4 aggregates (matter, feeling, perception, consciousness), 11 bases (10 gross bases, mind-base), and 17 elements (10 gross elements, 7 consciousness elements).			
126. States which are not defilement.	5	12	18
States dissociated from defilement, excluding *Nibbāna*.	5	12	18
These states are mentality-materiality, are each aggrouped under 5 aggregates, 12 base, and 18 elements. There are no ungrouped states.			
127. States which are objects of defilement.	5	12	18
States which are objects of defilement but are not defilement.	5	12	18
Answers are the same as in nos. 126 above.			
128. States which are not objects of defilement.	4	2	2
States which are dissociated from defilement and are not objects of defilement, excluding *Nibbāna*.	4	2	2
These states are each aggrouped under 4 aggregates (4 mental aggregates), 2 bases (ideation-base, mind-base), and 2 elements (ideation-element, mind-consciousness element).			
They are ungrouped under 1 aggregate (matter), 10 bases (10 gross bases), and 16 elements (10 gross elements, eye-consciousness element, ear-consciousness element, nose-consciousness element, tongue-consciousness element, body-consciousness element, mind-element).			
129. States which are associated with defilement.	4	2	2
States which are associated with defilement but are not defilement.	4	2	2
Answers are the same as in nos. 128 above.			

I. Aggrouping and Ungrouping

Table 1.8.4. 6 dyads on Fetter

Cluster of 6 Dyads relating to Fetter (*Saṃyojana*)

	States of enquiry :	Compositional states :	Aggregates	Bases	Elements
20	States which are fetters. (Dhs 1118-1128, 1477)	states related to the 8 or 10 types of fetters — attachment to sensual pleasures, ill-will, conceit, wrong view, skeptical doubt, adherence to rites and ceremonial practices, lust for becoming or existence, envy, avarice, ignorance. [8]	1	1	1
	States which are not fetters. (Dhs 1129, 1478)	89 cittas, 44 cetasikas (52 excluding the 8 fetters, i.e. 52-8=44), 28 matters, *Nibbāna*.	5	12	18
21	States which are objects of fetters. (Dhs 1130, 1479)	81 mundane cittas, 52 cetasikas, 28 matters.	5	12	18
	States which are not objects of fetters. (Dhs 1131, 1480)	8 supramundane cittas; 36 cetasikas (38 excluding the 2 Illimitables (13+(25-2)=36), and *Nibbāna*.	4	2	2
22	States which are associated with fetters. (Dhs 1132, 1481)	12 unwholesome cittas, 26 cetasikas (27 excluding restlessness, i.e. (13+14)-1=26).	4	2	2
	States which are dissociated from fetters. (Dhs 1133, 1482)	77 cittas (21 wholesome cittas, 36 resultant cittas, 20 functional cittas), 38 cetasikas (13+25=38), 1 delusion-rooted citta associated with restlessness, 28 matters, *Nibbāna*.	5	12	18
23	States which are both fetters and objects of fetters. (Dhs 1134, 1482)	the 8 types of fetters as in nos. 20 above.	1	1	1
	States which are objects of fetters but are not fetters. (Dhs 1135, 1484)	81 mundane cittas, 44 cetasikas (52 exclude the 8 fetters, i.e 52-8=44), and 28 matters.	5	12	18

[8] 10 types of fetters (*dasa saṃyojanāni*): *kāmarāga, paṭigha, māna, diṭṭhi, vicikicchā, sīlabbataparāmāsa, bhavarāga, issā, macchariya, avijjā.* *Cf.* Dhs 1118-1128. Herein they are reduced to 8 types of fetters present at the 14 unwholesome cetasikas because *sīlabbataparāmāsa* is grouped under *diṭṭhi* (wrong view), and *bhavarāga* is grouped under *lobha cetasika*.

	States of enquiry	Compositional states	Elements	Bases	Aggregates
24	States which are both fetters and associated with fetters. (Dhs 1136, 1485)	the 8 types of fetters, excluding delusion present at one delusion-rooted citta associated with restlessness.	1	1	1
	States which are associated with fetters but are not fetters. (Dhs 1137, 1486)	12 unwholesome cittas, 19 cetasikas (27 excluding 8 states of fetters, i.e. 27-8=19).	4	2	2
25	States which are dissociated from fetters but still are objects of fetters. (Dhs 1138, 1487)	69 cittas (17 mundane wholesome cittas, 32 resultant cittas, 20 functional cittas), 1 delusion-rooted citta associated with restlessness, 38 cetasikas, 28 matters.	5	12	18
	States which are dissociated from fetters and are not objects of fetters. (Dhs 1139, 1488)	8 supramundane cittas; 36 cetasikas (38 excluding 2 Illimitables, i.e. 13+(25-2)=36), and *Nibbāna*.	4	2	2

Table 1.8.5. 6 dyads on Bond

	Cluster of 6 Dyads relating to Bond (*Gantha*)		Elements	Bases	Aggregates
	States of enquiry :	Compositional states :			
26	States which are bonds. (Dhs 1140, 1489)	3 types of bonds — greed, hatred, wrong view.	1	1	1
	States which are not bonds. (Dhs 1145, 1490)	89 cittas, 49 cetasikas (52 excluding factors related to the 3 states of bonds, i.e. 52-3=49), 28 matters, and *Nibbāna*.	5	12	18
27	States which are objects of bonds. (Dhs 1146, 1491)	81 mundane cittas, 52 cetasikas, 28 matters.	5	12	18
	States which are not objects of bonds. (Dhs 1147, 1492)	8 supramundane cittas; 36 cetasikas (38 excluding 2 Illimitables, and *Nibbāna*.	4	2	2
28	States which are associated with bonds. (Dhs 1148, 1493)	8 greed-rooted cittas, 2 hatred-rooted cittas, 25 cetasikas (27 excluding greed-*cetasika* present at the 4 greed-rooted cittas dissociated from wrong view, and hate-*cetasika* present at the 2 hate-rooted cittas) excluding doubt.	4	2	2

I. Aggrouping and Ungrouping

			A.	B.	E.
29	States which are dissociated from bonds. (Dhs 1149, 1494)	2 delusion-rooted cittas, 21 wholesome cittas, 36 resultant cittas, 20 functional cittas, 43 cetasikas (52 excluding greed, hatred, wrong view, conceit, envy, avarice, worry, sloth, and torpor, i.e. 52-9=43), greed from 4 greed-rooted cittas dissociated from wrong view, hate from 2 hate-rooted cittas, 28 matters, *Nibbāna*.	5	12	18
	States which are both bonds and objects of bonds. (Dhs 1150, 1495)	the 3 types of bonds.	1	1	1
	States which are objects of bonds but are not bonds. (Dhs 1151, 1496)	81 mundane cittas, 49 cetasikas (52 excluding the 3 states of bonds, i.e. 52-3=49), and 28 matters	5	12	18
30	States which are both bonds and associated with bonds. (Dhs 1152, 1497)	2 states of bonds, viz. greed and wrong view; greed and wrong views present at 4 greed-rooted cittas associated with wrong view.	1	1	1
	States which are associated with bonds but are not bonds. (Dhs 1153, 1498)	8 greed-rooted cittas, 2 hatred-rooted cittas, 23 cetasikas (27 excluding 3 states of bonds and doubt, i.e. 27-3-1=23).	4	2	2
31	States which are dissociated from bonds but are objects of bonds. (Dhs 1154, 1499)	2 delusion-rooted cittas, 69 cittas (17 wholesome cittas, 32 resultant cittas, 20 functional cittas), greed from 4 greed-rooted cittas dissociated from wrong view, hate from 2 hate-rooted cittas, 43 cetasikas (52 excluding greed, hatred, wrong view, conceit, envy, avarice, worry, sloth, and torpor, i.e. 52-9=43), 28 matters.	5	12	18
	States which are both dissociated from bonds and not objects of bonds. (Dhs 1155, 1500)	8 supramundane cittas; 36 cetasikas (38 excluding the 2 Illimitables, and *Nibbāna*.	4	2	2

The next two clusters, **Ogha** and **Yoga**, are identical to the 6-dyad clusters of 'Outflow' or Defilement (*Āsava*) :

- Cluster of 6 Dyads relating to Raging Current (*Ogha*)
- Cluster of 6 Dyads relating to Yoke (*Yoga*)

Table 1.8.6. 6 dyads on Hindrance

	Cluster of 6 Dyads relating to Hindrance (*Nīvaraṇa*)		Aggregates	Bases	Elements
	States of enquiry :	Compositional states :			
44	States which are hindrances (to the attainment of jhānas, Path, and Fruition cittas). (Dhs 1158-1168, 1503)	states related to the 8 types of hindrances — restlessness, greed, hatred, delusion, worry, doubt, sloth, and torpor.	1	1	1
	States which are not hindrances. (Dhs 1169, 1504)	89 cittas, 44 cetasikas (52 excluding factors related to the 8 states of hindrances, i.e. 52-8=44), 28 matters, *Nibbāna*.	5	12	18
45	States which are objects of hindrances (Dhs 1170, 1505)	81 mundane cittas, 52 cetasikas, 28 matters.	5	12	18
	States which are not objects of hindrances (Dhs 1171, 1506)	8 supramundane cittas; 36 cetasikas (38 excluding the 2 Illimitables (13+(25-2)=36), and *Nibbāna*.	4	2	2
46	States which are associated with hindrances. (Dhs 1172, 1507)	12 unwholesome cittas, 27 cetasikas, i.e. (13+14=27).	4	2	2
	States which are dissociated from hindrances. (Dhs 1173, 1508)	77 cittas (21 mundane wholesome cittas, 36 resultant cittas, 20 functional cittas), 38 cetasikas (13+25=38), 28 matters, *Nibbāna*.	5	12	18
47	States which are both hindrances and objects of hindrances. (Dhs 1174, 1509)	the 8 states of hindrances.	1	1	1
	States which are objects of hindrances but are not hindrances. (Dhs 1175, 1510)	81 mundane cittas, 44 cetasikas (52 excluding factors related to the 8 states of hindrances, i.e. 52-8=44), and 28 types of matters.	5	12	18
48	States which are both hindrances and associated with hindrances. (Dhs 1176, 1511)	the 8 states of hindrances.	1	1	1
	States which are associated with hindrances but are not hindrances. (Dhs 1177, 1512)	12 unwholesome cittas, 19 cetasikas (27 excluding the 8 states of hindrances, i.e. 27-8=19).	4	2	2
49	States which are dissociated from hindrances but are objects of hindrances. (Dhs 1178, 1513)	69 cittas (17 mundane wholesome cittas, 32 resultant cittas, 20 functional cittas), 38 cetasikas (13+25=38), 28 matters.	5	12	18

I. Aggrouping and Ungrouping

	States which are both dissociated from hindrances and not objects of hindrances. (Dhs 1179, 1514)	4 Paths and 4 Fruitions of the supramundane cittas, 36 cetasikas, (i.e. (13+25) excluding 2 Illimitables=36), and *Nibbāna*.	4	2	2

Table 1.8.7. 6 dyads on Attachment

	Cluster of 5 Dyads on Attachment (*Parāmāsa*) [9]		Elements	Bases	Aggregates
	States of enquiry :	Compositional states :			
50	States which are attachment. (Dhs 1180-81, 1515)	a person's persistent attachment to something desirable is because of misapprehension which originates from holding on to 'wrong view'.	1	1	1
	States which are not attachment. (Dhs 1182, 1516)	89 cittas, 51 cetasikas (52 excluding wrong view), 28 matters, *Nibbāna*.	5	12	18
51	States which are objects of attachment. (Dhs 1183, 1517)	81 mundane cittas, 52 cetasikas, and 28 matters.	5	12	18
	States which are not objects of attachment. (Dhs 1184, 1518)	8 supramundane cittas; 36 cetasikas (38 excluding 2 Illimitables, i.e. 38-2=36), and *Nibbāna*.	4	2	2
52	States which are associated with attachment. (Dhs 1185, 1519)	the 4 greed-rooted cittas associated with wrong view, 20 cetasikas (27 excluding wrong view, conceit hatred, envy, avarice, worry, doubt, i.e. 27-7=20).	4	2	2
	States which are dissociated from attachment. (Dhs 1186, 1520)	77 cittas (21 wholesome cittas, 36 resultant cittas, 20 functional cittas), 4 greed-rooted cittas dissociated from wrong view, 2 hatred-rooted cittas, 2 delusion-rooted cittas, 51 cetasikas (52 excluding wrong view), 28 matters, and *Nibbāna*.	5	12	18
53	States which are both attachment and objects of attachment. (Dhs 1187, 1521)	states originate from holding on to 'wrong view', arisen with *diṭṭhi-cetasika*.	1	1	1

---

[9] The term *parāmāsa*, was interpreted as 'seizing, grasping, attached to, touching, contagion' in the PTS Pali-English dictionary. In the Buddhist Dictionary: Manual of Buddhist Terms & Doctrines, Nyanaponika Thera interprets *parāmāsa* as 'adherence, attachment, misapprehension'. The rendering as 'attachment' ascribed to one's wrong view seems a better fitting.

A Perfect Knowledge of Mind-Body from the Abhidhamma (Dhātukathā)

			A.	B.	E.
54	States which are objects of attachment but are not attachment. (Dhs 1188, 1522)	81 mundane cittas, 51 cetasikas (52 excluding wrong view), and 28 matters.	5	12	18
	States which are dissociated from attachment but are objects of attachment. (Dhs 1189, 1523)	77 cittas (21 wholesome cittas, 36 resultant cittas, 20 functional cittas), 4 greed-rooted cittas dissociated from wrong view, 2 hatred-rooted cittas, 2 delusion-rooted cittas, 51 cetasikas (52 excluding wrong view), 28 matters (without *Nibbāna*)	5	12	18
	States which are both dissociated from attachment and not objects of attachment. Dhs 1190, 1524)	4 Paths and 4 Fruitions of the supramundane cittas, 36 cetasikas (i.e. (13+25) excluding 2 Illimitables=36), and *Nibbāna*.	4	2	2

The following states of enquiry, nos. 130 to 134, are based on preceding Table 1.8.4 to Table 1.8.7, and also to be referred to Chart 1.

Chart 1.8.4. Aggrouping and Ungrouping of the dyads of Fetter, Bond, Raging Current, Yoke, Hindrance, and Attachment.

	Aggrouped		
By units :	<u>Agr</u>	<u>Base</u>	<u>Ele</u>
130. States which are fetters.	1	1	1
States which are bonds.	1	1	1
States which are raging current.	1	1	1
States which are yokes.	1	1	1
States which are hindrances.	1	1	1
States which are attachment.	1	1	1
States which are both attachment and objects of attachment.	1	1	1

These states are each aggrouped under 1 aggregate (volitive formation), 1 base (ideation-base), and 1 element (ideation-element).

They are ungrouped under 4 aggregates (matter, feeling, perception, consciousness), 11 bases (10 gross bases, mind-base), and 17 elements (10 gross elements, 7 consciousness elements).

* *Examples nos. 131 to 134 below on Attachment-dyads are to be repeated in the same manner for the dyads of Fetter, Bond, Raging Current, Yoke, and Hindrance.*

I. Aggrouping and Ungrouping

		Agr	Base	Ele
131.	States which are not attachment.	5	12	18
	States which are dissociated from attachment, excluding *Nibbāna*.	5	12	18

These states belong to mentality-materiality, are each aggrouped under 5 aggregates, 12 base, and 18 elements. There are no ungrouped states.

		Agr	Base	Ele
132.	States which are objects of attachment.	5	12	18
	States which are objects of attachment but are not attachment.	5	12	18
	States which are dissociated from attachment but are objects of attachment.	5	12	18

Answers are same as in nos. 131 above.

		Agr	Base	Ele
133.	States which are not objects of attachment.	4	2	2
	States which are both dissociated from attachment and not objects of attachment, excluding *Nibbāna*.	4	2	2

These states are each aggrouped under 4 aggregates (4 mental aggregates), 2 bases (ideation-base, mind-base), and 2 elements (ideation-element, mind-consciousness element).

They are ungrouped under 1 aggregate (matter), 10 bases (10 gross bases), and 16 elements (10 gross elements, remaining 6 consciousness elements).

		Agr	Base	Ele
134.	States which are associated with attachment.	4	2	2

Answers are same as in nos. 133 above.

A Perfect Knowledge of Mind-Body from the Abhidhamma (Dhātukathā)

Table 1.8.8. the intermediate 14 dyads (*mahatara duka*)

	Intermediate 14 non-interrelated dyads (*Mahatara*)		Aggregates	Bases	Elements
	States of enquiry :	Compositional states :			
55	States which attend to objects (or which have objects). (Dhs 1191, 1525)	all 89 cittas and 52 cetasikas.	4	2	8
	States which do not attend to objects (or have no objects). (Dhs 1192, 1526)	28 matters and *Nibbāna*.	1	11	11
56	States which are consciousness (or mind). (Dhs 1193, 1527)	89 cittas.	1	1	7
	States which are not consciousness. (Dhs 1194, 1528)	28 matters and *Nibbāna*.	4	11	11
57	States which are mental concomitants (Dhs 1195, 1529)	52 cetasikas.	3	1	1
	States which are not mental concomitants. (Dhs 1196, 1530)	89 cittas, 28 matters, *Nibbāna*.	2	12	18
58	States which are associated with consciousness. (Dhs 1197, 1531)	52 cetasikas.	3	1	1
	States which are dissociated from consciousness. (Dhs 1198, 1532)	28 matters and *Nibbāna*.	1	11	11
59	States which are conjoined with consciousness. (Dhs 1199, 1533)	52 cetasikas.	3	1	1
	States which are not conjoined with consciousness. (Dhs 1200, 1534)	28 matters and *Nibbāna*.	1	11	11
60	States which are produced by consciousness. (Dhs 1201, 1535)	52 cetasikas, 17 mind-produced matters (*cittajarūpā*).	4	6	6
	States which are not produced by consciousness. (Dhs 1202, 1536)	89 cittas, 20 kamma-produced matters (*kammajarūpā*), 15 temperature-produced matters (*utujarūpā*), 14 nutriment-produced matters (*āhajarūpā*), and *Nibbāna*.	2	12	18
61	States which arise together with consciousness. (Dhs 1203, 1537)	52 cetasikas, intimation 2 *viññatti-rūpā* (bodily intimation, vocal intimation).	4	1	1

I. Aggrouping and Ungrouping

			A.	B.	E.
	States which do not arise concurrently with consciousness. (Dhs 1204, 1538)	89 cittas, 26 matters (28 excluding the 2 *viññatti-rūpā*), and *Nibbāna*.	2	12	18
62	States which arise successively with consciousness. the (Dhs 1205, 1539)	52 cetasikas, intimation 2 *viññatti-rūpā* (bodily intimation, vocal intimation).	4	1	1
	States which do not arise successively with consciousness. (Dhs 1206, 1540)	89 cittas, 26 matters (28 excluding the 2 *viññatti-rūpā*).	2	12	18
63	States which are both conjoined with consciousness, and originated from consciousness. (Dhs 1207, 1541)	52 cetasikas.	3	1	1
	States which neither are conjoined with consciousness, nor are originated from consciousness. (Dhs 1208, 1542)	89 cittas, 28 matters, and *Nibbāna*.	2	12	18
64	States which are conjoined with, originated from, and arise concurrently with consciousness. (Dhs 1209, 1543)	52 cetasikas.	3	1	1
	States which are not conjoined with, not originated from, and not arise together with consciousness. (Dhs 1210, 1544)	89 cittas, 28 matters, and *Nibbāna*.	2	12	18
65	States which are conjoined with, originated from, and arise consecutively with consciousness. (Dhs 1211, 1545)	52 cetasikas.	3	1	1
	States which are not conjoined with, not originated from, and not arise consecutively with consciousness. (Dhs 1212, 1546)	89 cittas, 28 matters, and *Nibbāna*.	2	12	18
66	States which are internal. (Dhs 1213, 1547)	89 cittas, 5 sensitive organs (*pasāda-rūpā*)	2	6	12
	States which are external. (Dhs 1214, 1548)	52 cetasikas, 23 matters (28 excluding 5 *pasāda-rūpā*, i.e. 28-5=23), and *Nibbāna*	4	6	6
67	States which are derived. (Dhs 1215, 1549)	24 derived matters (28 matters excluding the 4 Great Elements).	1	10	10
	States which are not derived. (Dhs 1216, 1550)	89 cittas, 52 cetasikas, 4 Great Elements and *Nibbāna*.	5	3	9

A Perfect Knowledge of Mind-Body from the Abhidhamma (Dhātukathā)

			A.	B.	E.
68	States which are the result of clinging by the 5 aggregates (i.e. which are acquired by clinging). (Dhs 1217, 1551)	32 mundane resultant cittas (excluded 4 fruition-cittas), 35 cetasikas (38 excluding the 3 Abstinences, i.e. 38-3=35), and 20 kammajarūpa.	5	11	17
	States which are not the result of clinging by the 5 aggregates. (*Anupādiṇṇā dhammā*) (Dhs 1218, 1552)	57 cittas (21 mundane wholesome cittas, 12 mundane unwholesome cittas, 20 functional cittas, 4 supramundane fruition-cittas), 52 cetasikas, 17 *cittajarūpa*, 15 *utujarūpa*, 14 *āhajarūpa*, and Nibbāna.	5	7	8

The following states of enquiry, nos. 135 to 152 are to be referred to Table 1.8.8 and Chart 1.

Chart 1.8.5. Aggrouping and Ungrouping of the intermediate 14 dyads

	Aggrouped		
By units :	Agr	Base	Ele
135. States which attend to objects (or which have objects).	4	2	8

These are non-matters. They are aggrouped under 4 aggregates (4 mental aggregates), 2 bases (ideation-base, mind-base), and 8 elements (ideation-element, 7 consciousness elements).

They are ungrouped under 1 aggregate (matter), 10 bases (10 gross bases), and 10 elements (10 gross elements).

136. States which do not attend to objects, excluding *Nibbāna*.	1	11	11

These states refer to materiality, are aggrouped under 1 aggregate (matter), 11 bases (10 gross bases, ideation-base), and 10 elements (10 gross elements, ideation-element).

They are ungrouped under 4 aggregates (4 mental aggregates), 1 base (mind-base), and 7 elements (7 consciousness elements).

137. States which are consciousness.	1	1	7

They are aggrouped under 1 aggregate (consciousness), 1 base (mind-base), and 7 elements (7 consciousness elements).

They are ungrouped under 4 aggregates (matter, feeling, perception, volitive formation), 11 bases (10 gross bases, ideation-base), and 11 elements (10 gross elements, ideation-element).

I. Aggrouping and Ungrouping

		Agr	Base	Ele
138.	States which are not consciousness, excluding *Nibbāna*.	4	11	11

They are aggrouped under 4 aggregate (matter and the remaining 3 mental aggregates), 11 bases (10 gross bases, ideation-base), and 10 elements (10 gross elements, ideation-element).

They are ungrouped under 1 aggregate (consciousness), 1 base (mind-base), and 7 elements (7 consciousness elements).

		Agr	Base	Ele
139.	States which are mental concomitants.	3	1	1

States which are associated with consciousness.
States which are conjoined with consciousness.

All these states are cetasikas, are aggrouped under 3 aggregates (feeling, perception, volitive formation), 1 base (ideation-base), and 1 element (ideation-element).

They are ungrouped under 2 aggregates (matter and consciousness), 11 bases (10 gross bases, mind-base), and 17 elements (10 gross elements, 7 consciousness elements).

		Agr	Base	Ele
140.	States which are not mental concomitants, excluding *Nibbāna*.	2	12	18

They are referring to states other than the 52 cetasikas. They are aggrouped under 2 aggregates (matter, consciousness), 12 bases, and 18 elements.

They are ungrouped under 3 aggregates (feeling, perception and volitive formation). There is no ungrouping under bases and elements.

		Agr	Base	Ele
141.	States which are dissociated from consciousness.	1	11	11

States which are not conjoined with consciousness, excluding *Nibbāna*.

These states are materiality. They are each aggrouped under 1 aggregate (matter), 11 bases (10 gross bases, ideation-base), and 10 elements (10 gross elements, ideation-element).

They are ungrouped under 1 aggregate (consciousness), 1 base (mind-base), and 7 elements (7 consciousness elements).

		Agr	Base	Ele
142.	States which are produced by consciousness.	4	6	6

These states consist of 52 cetasikas and 17 mind-produced matters. They are aggrouped under 4 aggregates (matter, feeling, perception, volitive formation), 6 bases (vision-base, sound-base, odour-base, taste-base, touch-base, ideation-base), 6 elements (vision-element, sound-element, odour-element, taste-element, touch-element, ideation-element.

They are ungrouped under 1 aggregate (consciousness), 6 bases (remaining 5 gross bases, mind-base), and 12 elements (remaining 5 gross elements, 7 consciousness elements).

A Perfect Knowledge of Mind-Body from the Abhidhamma (Dhātukathā)

	Agr	Base	Ele

143. States which are not produced by consciousness.   2   12   18
States which do not arise concurrently with consciousness.   2   12   18
States which do not arise successively with consciousness, excluding *Nibbāna*.   2   12   18

These states refer to the 20 action-produced matters, 15 temperature-produced matters, 14 nutriment-produced matters, and 89 cittas. They belong to matters and consciousness. Answers are the same in nos. 140 above.

144. States which arise concurrently with consciousness.   4   1   1
States which arise successively with consciousness.   4   1   1

These states consist of 52 cetasikas, and 2 non-concrete mattes of body intimation and vocal intimation (2 *viññatti rupā*). They are aggrouped under 4 aggregates (matter, feeling, perception, volitive formation), 1 base (ideation-base), and 1 element (ideation-element).

They are ungrouped under 1 aggregates (consciousness), 11 bases (10 gross bases, mind-base), and 17 elements (10 gross elements, 7 consciousness elements).

145. States which are both conjoined with and are originated from consciousness.   3   1   1
States which are conjoined with, originated from, and arise concurrently with consciousness.   3   1   1
States which are conjoined with, originated from, and arise successively with consciousness.   3   1   1

These states are all cetasikas. Answers are the same in nos. 139 above.

146. States which neither are conjoined with, nor originated from consciousness.   2   12   18
States which are not conjoined with, not originated from, and not arise together with consciousness.   2   12   18
States which are not conjoined with, not originated from, and not arise successively with consciousness, excluding *Nibbāna*.   2   12   18

These states consist of matters and consciousness. Answers are the same in nos. 140 above.

147. States which are internal.   2   6   12

These states are referred to the 5 sensitive organs and 89 cittas, are aggrouped under 2 aggregates (matter, consciousness), 6 bases (eye-base, ear-base, nose-base, tongue-base, body-base, mind-base), and 12 elements (eye-element, ear-

I. Aggrouping and Ungrouping

	Agr	Base	Ele

element, nose-element, tongue-element, body-element, mind-element, 7 consciousness elements).
They are ungrouped under 3 aggregates (feeling, perception, volitive formation), 6 bases (remaining 5 gross object bases, ideation-base), and 6 elements (remaining 5 gross object elements, ideation-element).

148. States which are external, excluding *Nibbāna*.   4   6   6
These states refer to the remaining 23 matters (28 excluding the 5 sensitive organs) and 52 cetasikas. They are aggrouped under 4 aggregates (matter, feeling, perception, volitive formation), 6 bases (vision-base, sound-base, odour-base, taste-base, touch-base, ideation-base), 6 elements (vision-element, sound-element, odour-element, taste-element, touch-element, ideation-element).
The ungrouped answers are the same as in nos. 142 above.

149. States which are derived.   1   10   10
These are the 24 derived matters. They are aggrouped under 1 aggregate (matter), 10 bases (10 gross bases), and 10 elements (10 gross elements).
They are ungrouped under 4 aggregates (4 mental aggregates), 2 bases (ideation-base, mind-base), and 8 elements (ideation-element, 7 consciousness elements).

150. States which are not derived, excluding *Nibbāna*.   5   3   9
These states are referred to the 4 great elements, 89 cittas, and 52 cetasikas. They are aggrouped under 5 aggregates, 3 bases (tangibility-base, ideation-base, mind-base), and 9 elements (tangibility-element, ideation-element, 7 consciousness elements).
They are ungrouped under 9 bases (remaining 9 gross bases) and 9 elements (remaining 9 gross elements). They are not ungrouped under aggregates.

151. States which are the result of clinging by the 5 aggregates   5   11   17
(*upādinnā dhammā pañcahi khandhehi*).
These states consist of 20 kamma-produced matters and 4 mental aggregates. Sound-base is excluded. These states are aggrouped under 5 aggregates, 11 bases (12 bases excluding sound-base), 17 elements (18 elements excluding sound-element).
They are ungrouped under 1 base (sound-base) and 1 element (sound-element). They are not ungrouped under aggregates.

A Perfect Knowledge of Mind-Body from the Abhidhamma (Dhātukathā)

	Agr	Base	Ele
152. States which are not the result of clinging by 5 aggregates, excluding *Nibbāna*.	5	7	8

These states consist of 17 mind-produced matters, 15 temperature-produced matters, 14 nutriment-produced matters, and the 4 mentalities. They are aggrouped under 5 aggregates, 7 bases (vision-base, sound-base, odour-base, taste-base, touch-base, ideation-base, mind-base), 8 elements (vision-element, sound-element, odour-element, taste-element, touch-element, mind-element, ideation-element, mind-consciousness element).

They are ungrouped under 5 bases (remaining 5 gross bases) and 10 elements (remaining 5 gross elements, remaining 5 cons. elements). They are not ungrouped under aggregates.

Subsequent states of enquiry, nos. 153 to 157, are based on the dyads-cluster of Clinging and Corruption. They will be analysed after Table 1.8.10.

Table 1.8.9. 6 dyads on Clinging

	Cluster of 6 Dyads relating to Clinging (*Upādāna*)		Aggregates	Bases	Elements
	States of enquiry :	Compositional states :			
69	States which are clinging. (Dhs 1219-1223, 1553)	states related to the 2 or 4 kinds of clinging — *kāma* (sensual desire), *diṭṭhi* (wrong view), *sīlabbata* (ceremonial observances), *attavāda* (theory of the mind and matter as soul). Herein it is treated as 2 kinds (*sīlabbata* and *attavāda* are considered as under *diṭṭhi*).	1	1	1
	States which are not clinging. (Dhs 1224, 1554)	89 cittas, 50 cetasikas (52 less greed and wrong view, i.e. 52-2=50), 28 matters, and *Nibbāna*.	5	12	18
70	States which are objects of clinging. (Dhs 1225, 1555)	81 mundane cittas, 52 cetasikas, 28 matters.	5	12	18
	States which are not objects of clinging. (Dhs 1226, 1556)	supramundane 4 path-cittas and 4 Fruitions-cittas, 36 cetasikas (38 excluding 2 Illimitables), *Nibbāna*.	4	2	2

I. Aggrouping and Ungrouping

			A.	B.	E.
71	States which are associated with clinging. (Dhs 1227, 1557)	8 greed-rooted cittas, 22 cetasikas (27 excluding hatred, envy, avarice, worry, doubt, i.e. (13+14)-5=22), and and greed present at the 4 greed-rooted cittas dissociated from wrong view.	4	2	2
	States which are dissociated from clinging. (Dhs 1228, 1558)	81 cittas (2 hatred-rooted cittas, 2 delusion-rooted cittas, 21 wholesome cittas, 36 resultant cittas, 20 functional cittas), 4 greed-rooted cittas dissociated from wrong view, 49 cetasikas (52 excluding greed, wrong view, conceit), 28 matters, and *Nibbāna*.	5	12	18
72	States which are both clinging and objects of clinging. (Dhs 1229, 1559)	2 states of clinging as greed and wrong view (present at the 4 greed-rooted cittas accompanied by greed and associated with wrong view).	1	1	1
	States which are objects of clinging but are not clinging. (Dhs 1230, 1560)	81 mundane cittas, 50 cetasikas (52 excluding greed and wrong view), and 28 matters.	5	12	18
73	States which are both clinging and associated with clinging. (Dhs 1231, 1561)	2 states of clinging as greed and wrong view (present at the 4 greed-rooted cittas accompanied by greed and associated with wrong view).	1	1	1
	States which are associated with clinging but are not clinging. (Dhs 1232, 1562)	8 greed-rooted cittas, 20 cetasikas (27 excluding hatred, envy, avarice, worry, doubt, and 2 states of clinging, i.e. (13+14)-5-2=20).	4	2	2
74	States which are dissociated from clinging but are objects of clinging. (Dhs 1233, 1563)	73 cittas (2 hatred-rooted cittas, 2 delusion-rooted cittas, 17 mundane wholesome cittas, 32 resultant cittas, 20 functional cittas), greed present at the 4 greed-rooted cittas dissociated from wrong view, 49 cetasikas (52 excluding greed, wrong view, and conceit, i.e. 52-3=49), and 28 matters.	5	12	18
	States which are both dissociated from clinging and not objects of clinging. (Dhs 1234, 1564)	4 Paths and 4 Fruitions of the supramundane cittas, 36 cetasikas (13+(25-2 Illimitables)=36), and *Nibbāna*.	4	2	2

Table 1.8.10. 8 dyads on Corruption

	Cluster of 8 Dyads relating to Corruption (*Kilesa*)		Aggregates	Bases	Elements
	States of enquiry :	Compositional states :			
75	States which are corruptions. (Dhs 1235-1245, 1565)	states related to the 10 kinds of corruptions — greed, hatred, delusion, conceit, wrong view, doubt, sloth, restlessness, shamelessness, guiltlessness of conscience [10].	1	1	1
	States which are not corruptions. (Dhs 1246, 1566)	89 cittas, 42 cetasikas (52 excluding these 10 factors of corruptions, i.e. 52-10=42), 28 matters, and *Nibbāna*.	5	12	18
76	States which are objects of corruption. (Dhs 1247, 1567)	81 mundane cittas, 52 cetasikas, and 28 matters.	5	12	18
	States which are not objects of corruption. (Dhs 1248, 1568)	supramundane 4 path- and 4 fruition-cittas, 36 cetasikas (38 excluding 2 Illimitables, *Nibbāna*.	4	2	2
77	States which are corrupted. (Dhs 1249, 1569)	12 mundane unwholesome cittas, 27 cetasikas (13+14=27).	4	2	2
	States which are not corrupted. (Dhs 1250, 1570)	77 cittas (21 mundane wholesome cittas, 36 resultant cittas, 20 functional cittas), 38 cetasikas (13+25), 28 matters, and *Nibbāna*.	5	12	18
78	States which are associated with corruptions. (Dhs 1251, 1571)	12 mundane unwholesome cittas, 27 cetasikas (13+14=27).	4	2	2
	States which are dissociated from corruptions. (Dhs 1252, 1572)	77 cittas (21 mundane wholesome cittas, 36 resultant cittas, 20 functional cittas), 38 cetasikas (13+25), 28 matters, and *Nibbāna*.	5	12	18
79	States which are both corruptions and objects of corruption. (Dhs 1253, 1573)	the 10 kinds of corruptions.	1	1	1
	States which are not corruptions but are objects of corruption. (Dhs 1254, 1574)	81 mundane cittas, 42 cetasikas (52 excluding 10 states of corruptions, i.e. 52-10=42), and 28 matters.	5	12	18

---

[10] 10 kinds of corruptions (*dasa kilesavatthūni*) : lobho, doso, moho, māno, diṭṭhi, vicikicchā, thinaṃ, uddhaccaṃ, ahirikaṃ, anottappaṃ.

I. Aggrouping and Ungrouping

			A.	B.	E.
80	States which are both corruptions and corrupted. (Dhs 1255, 1575)	the 10 kinds of corruptions.	1	1	1
	States which are corrupted but are not corruptions. (Dhs 1256, 1576)	12 unwholesome cittas, 17 cetasikas (27 excluding the 10 factors of corruptions. i.e. (13+14)-10=17).	4	2	2
81	States both are corruptions and associated with corruptions. (Dhs 1257, 1577)	the 10 kinds of corruptions.	1	1	1
	States which are associated with corruptions but are not corruptions. (Dhs 1258, 1578)	12 unwholesome cittas, 17 cetasikas (27 excluding the 10 factors of corruptions).	4	2	2
82	States which are dissociated from corruptions but are objects of corruption. (Dhs 1259, 1579)	69 cittas (active 17 mundane wholesome cittas, 32 resultant cittas, 20 functional cittas), 38 cetasikas (13+25), 28 matters.	5	12	18
	States which are both dissociated from corruptions and not objects of corruption. (Dhs 1260, 1580)	4 Paths and 4 Fruitions of the supramundane cittas, 36 cetasikas (i.e. (13+25) excluding 2 Illimitables), and *Nibbāna*.	4	2	2

The following states of enquiry from nos. 153 to 157 are to be referred to Table 1.8.9, 1.8.10, and Chart 1.

Chart 1.8.6. Aggrouping and Ungrouping of the dyads on Clinging and Corruption

	Aggrouped		
By units :	Agr	Base	Ele
153. States which are clinging.	1	1	1
States which are corruptions.	1	1	1
States which are clinging and are objects of clinging.	1	1	1
States which are corruptions and are objects of corruption.	1	1	1
States which are both corruptions and are corrupted.	1	1	1
States which are both clinging and associated with clinging.	1	1	1
States which are corruptions and associated with corruption.	1	1	1
These seven states are each aggrouped under 1 aggregate (volitive formation), 1 base (ideation-base), 1 element (ideation-element).			
They are each ungrouped under 4 aggregates (remaining aggregates), 11 bases (12 excluding ideation-base), and 17 elements (18 excluding ideation-element).			

A Perfect Knowledge of Mind-Body from the Abhidhamma (Dhātukathā)

	Agr	Base	Ele
154. States which are not clinging.	5	12	18
States which are not corruptions.	5	12	18
States which are not corrupted.	5	12	18
States which are dissociated from clinging.	5	12	18
States which are dissociated from corruptions, excluding *Nibbāna*.	5	12	18

These are all states of mentality-materiality, are each aggrouped under 5 aggregates, 12 bases, and 18 elements.

	Agr	Base	Ele
155. States which are objects of clinging.	5	12	18
States which are objects of corruption.	5	12	18
States which are objects of clinging but are not clinging.	5	12	18
States which are objects of corruption but are not corruption.	5	12	18
States dissociated from clinging but are objects of clinging.	5	12	18
States dissociated from corruption but are objects of corruption.	5	12	18

All of these states are mentality-materiality, are each aggrouped under 5 aggregates, 12 bases, and 18 elements.

	Agr	Base	Ele
156. States which are not the objects of clinging.	4	2	2
States which are not the objects of corruption.	4	2	2
States which are both dissociated from clinging and not objects of clinging.	4	2	2
States which are both dissociated from corruption and not objects of corruption, excluding *Nibbāna*.	4	2	2

These states are each aggrouped under 4 aggregates (4 mental aggregates), 2 bases (ideation-base, mind-base), and 2 elements (ideation-element, mind-consciousness element). They are each ungrouped under 1 aggregate (matter), 10 bases (10 gross bases), and 16 elements (10 gross elements, remaining 6 consciousness elements).

	Agr	Base	Ele
157. States which are corrupted.	4	2	2
States which are associated with clinging.	4	2	2
States which are associated with corruptions.	4	2	2
States which are corrupted but are not corruptions.	4	2	2
States associated with clinging but are not clinging.	4	2	2
States associated with corruptions but are not corruptions.	4	2	2

All these states belong to 4 mental aggregates. Answers are the same as in nos. 156 above.

I. Aggrouping and Ungrouping

Table 1.8.11. the last 18 dyads

Final 18 non-interrelated dyads (*Piṭṭhi*)

		States of enquiry :	Compositional states :	Aggregates	Bases	Elements
83		States eliminated by the first Path (*dassanena pahātabbā*), namely, Sotāpattimagga. (Dhs 1261-1264, 1581)	eliminated are 3 fetters [11], [7] — wrong view as ignoring the five khandhas or mind-matter as a theory of soul; doubt or perplexity; wrong view as to the observances of rites and rituals. Herein the associated states eradicated are the 4 greed-rooted cittas associated with wrong view, 1 delusion-rooted citta associated with doubt, 22 cetasikas.	4	2	2
		States not eliminated by the first Path. (Dhs 1265, 1582)	4 greed-rooted cittas dissociated from wrong view, 2 hatred-rooted cittas, 1 delusion-rooted citta with restlessness, 77 cittas (21 wholesome cittas, 36 resultant cittas, 20 functional cittas), 50 cetasikas (52 excluding wrong view and doubt), 28 matters, and *Nibbāna*.	5	12	18
84		States eliminated by the higher three Paths. (Dhs 1266, 1583)	4 greed-rooted cittas dissociated from wrong view, 2 hatred-rooted cittas, 1 delusion-rooted citta with restlessness, 25 cetasikas (27 excluding wrong view and doubt), or 21 cetasikas (completely eradicated by *Arahatta*).	4	2	2
		States not eliminated by the higher three Paths. (Dhs 1267, 1584)	5 cittas which are already eliminated by the first Path, 77 cittas (21 wholesome cittas, 36 resultant cittas, 20 functional cittas), 38 cetasikas, 28 matters, *Nibbāna*.	5	12	18
	85	States with root causes eliminated by first Path. (Dhs 1268-1271, 1585)	4 greed-rooted cittas associated with wrong view, 1 delusion-rooted citta associated with doubt, 22 cetasikas.	4	2	2

---

[11] Tīṇi saṃyojanāni – *sakkāyadiṭṭhi, vicikicchā, sīlabbataparāmāso*.
 Also, (83-86) in Table 1.8 are cross-referenced to (8) in Table 1.7 which are all mentioned in Dhs 1261-1274.

A Perfect Knowledge of Mind-Body from the Abhidhamma (Dhātukathā)

			A.	B.	E.
86	States with root causes not eliminated by first Path. (Dhs 1272, 1586)	4 greed-rooted cittas dissociated from wrong view, 2 hatred-rooted cittas, 1 delusion-rooted citta associated with restlessness, 77 cittas (21 wholesome cittas, 36 resultant cittas, 20 functional cittas), 50 cetasikas (52 excluding wrong view and doubt), 28 matters, and *Nibbāna*.	5	12	18
	States with root causes eliminated by the higher three Paths. (Dhs 1273, 1587)	4 greed-rooted cittas dissociated from wrong view, 2 hatred-rooted cittas, 1 delusion-rooted citta associated with restlessness, 25 cetasikas (27 excluding wrong view and doubt).	4	2	2
	States with root causes not eliminated by the higher three Paths. (Dhs 1274, 1588)	the 5 akusala cittas which are already eliminated by the first Path, 21 mundane wholesome cittas, 36 resultant cittas, 20 functional cittas, 38 cetasikas, 28 matters, *Nibbāna*.	5	12	18
87	States with initial application (*savitakkā*). (Dhs 1275, 1589)	55 cittas (see Appendix V, and Chart 7 in Appendix VI), 51 cetasikas (52 excluding *vitakka*).	4	2	3
	States without initial application. (Dhs 1276, 1590)	66 cittas without *vitakka* (see Chart 7 in Appendix VI), 37 cetasikas (13+25 exclude *vitakka*), 28 matters, *Nibbāna*.	5	12	17
88	States with sustained application (*savicārā*). (Dhs 1277, 1591)	66 cittas with *vicāra* (see Chart 7 in Appendix VI), 51 cetasikas *(52 excluding vicāra)*.	4	2	3
	States without sustained application. (Dhs 1278, 1592)	55 cittas without *vicāra* (see Chart 7 in Appendix VI), 36 cetasikas (13+25 excluding both *vitakka-vicāra*), 28 matters, and *Nibbāna*.	5	12	17
89	States with zest (*sappītikā*). (Dhs 1279, 1593)	51 associated cittas (see Chart 7 in Appendix VI), 46 cetasikas (52 excluding zest, hatred, envy, avarice, worry, and doubt, i.e. 52-6=46).	4	2	2
	States without zest. (Dhs 1280, 1594)	70 dissociated cittas (see Chart 7 in Appendix VI), 51 cetasikas (52 excluding zest connate with the 51 associated cittas), 28 matters, *Nibbāna*.	5	12	18
90	States which are accompanied by zest. (*pītisahagatā*). (Dhs 1281, 1595)	same as nos. 89 (1st) above.	4	2	2

I. Aggrouping and Ungrouping

			A.	B.	E.
91	States which are not accompanied by zest. (Dhs 1282, 1596)	same as nos. 89 (2nd) above.	5	12	18
	States which are accompanied by happiness (*sukhasahagatā*) (Dhs 1283, 1597)	63 cittas (62+1) with *pīti* and *sukha* (see Chart 18 in Appendix VI), 46 cetasikas (52 excluding feeling, hatred, envy, avarice, worry, doubt, i.e. 52-6=46).	3	2	3
	States which are not accompanied by happiness. (Dhs 1284, 1598)	3 types of cittas accompanied by pain (*domanassa* and *dukha*), 55 cittas accompanied by equanimity (see Chart 18 in Appendix VI), 51 cetasikas (52 excluding feeling connate with the 63 cittas accompanied by pleasure/happiness), 28 matters, and *Nibbāna*	5	12	18
92	States which are accompanied by equanimity, i.e. indifference to happiness. (*upekkhāsahagatā*). (Dhs 1285, 1599)	55 cittas accompanied by equanimity (see Chart 18 in Appendix VI), 46 cetasikas (52 excluding feeling, zest, hatred, envy, avarice, and worry, i.e. 52-6=46)	3	2	7
	States which are not accompanied by equanimity. (Dhs 1286, 1600)	63 cittas accompanied by joy and by pleasure, 3 types of cittas accompanied by displeasure and pain, 51 cetasikas (52 excluding doubt), 55 feeling of indifference connate with the 55 cittas accompanied by equanimity, 28 matters, and *Nibbāna*.	5	12	13
93	States characteristic of sensuous sphere. (Dhs 1287, 1601)	54 sensuous cittas, 52 cetasikas, and all that is corporeality.	5	12	18
	States which are not characteristic of sensuous sphere. (Dhs 1288, 1602)	27 *Mahaggatacittāni* (See the first table in Appendix III), 4 Paths and 4 Fruitions of the supramundane cittas, 38 cetasikas (13 common + 25 beautiful factors), and *Nibbāna*.	4	2	2
94	States which are characteristic of form sphere. (Dhs 1289, 1603)	15 fine-material cittas, 35 cetasikas (38 excluding the 3 Abstinences), i.e. 13+(25-3)=35.	4	2	2
	States which are not characteristic of form sphere. (Dhs 1290, 1604)	54 sensuous cittas, 12 formless cittas, 8 supramundane cittas, 52 cetasikas, 28 matters, and *Nibbāna*.	5	12	18

A Perfect Knowledge of Mind-Body from the Abhidhamma (Dhātukathā)

			A.	B.	E.
95	States which are characteristic of immaterial sphere. (Dhs 1291, 1605)	12 formless sublime cittas, 30 cetasikas (13 non-beautiful factors excluding *vitakka*, *vicāra*, and *pīti*; 25 beautiful excluding the 3 *viratī* and 2 *appamaññā*, i.e. (13-3)+(25-3-2)=30).	4	2	2
	States which are not characteristic of immaterial sphere. (Dhs 1292, 1606)	54 sensuous cittas, 15 fine-material cittas, 8 supramundane cittas, 52 cetasikas, 28 matters, and *Nibbāna*.	5	12	18
96	States which are included (in round of rebirths). (Dhs 1293, 1607)	81 mundane cittas, 52 cetasikas, 28 matters.	5	12	18
	States which are not included (in round of rebirths). (Dhs 1294, 1608)	4 Paths and 4 Fruitions of the supramundane cittas, 36 cetasikas (38 excluding the 2 Illimitables, i.e. 13+(25-2)=36), and *Nibbāna*.	4	2	2
97	States which lead out (from round of existence). (Dhs 1295, 1609)	4 supramundane path-cittas, 36 cetasikas (38 excluding 2 Illimitables, i.e. 13+(25-2)=36).	4	2	2
	States which do not lead out (from round of existence). (Dhs 1296, 1610)	remaining 85 cittas (4 Fruition supramundane cittas, 81 mundane cittas), 52 cetasikas, 28 matters, and *Nibbāna*. (Note that supramundane 4 fruition-cittas & *Nibbāna* are not paths)	5	12	18
98	States which are fixed as to their future destinies. (Dhs 1297, 1611)	4 supramundane path-cittas arisen with 36 cetasikas (38 excluding the 2 Illimitables); 7th sensuous *javana* (impulsion) present at the 4 greed-rooted cittas associated with wrong view and at the 2 delusion-rooted cittas, arisen with 25 cetasikas (27 excluding conceit and doubt).	4	2	2
	States which are not fixed as to their future destinies. (Dhs 1298, 1612)	79 cittas (17 wholesome cittas, 36 resultant cittas, 20 functional cittas, 7th sensuous *javana* connate with the 4 greed-rooted cittas associated with wrong view and with the 2 delusion-rooted cittas), 52 cetasikas, 28 matters, *Nibbāna*.	5	12	18
99	States which are surpassable (*sauttara*). (Dhs 1299, 1613)	81 mundane cittas, 52 cetasikas, 28 matters.	5	12	18

I. Aggrouping and Ungrouping

			A.	B.	E.
100	States which are unsurpassable/ incomparable (*anuttarā*). (Dhs 1300, 1614)	4 Paths and 4 Fruitions of the supramundane cittas, 36 cetasikas (38 excluding 2 Illimitables (i.e. 13+(25-2)=36), and *Nibbāna*.	4	2	2
	States which are at odds (*saraṇā*) (with the supramundane Path). (Dhs 1301, 1615)	12 mundane unwholesome cittas, 27 cetasikas, i.e. (13+14=27).	4	2	2
	States which are not at odds (*araṇā*) (with the supramundane Path). (Dhs 1302, 1616)	77 cittas (21 mundane wholesome cittas, 36 resultant cittas, 20 functional cittas), 38 cetasikas (13+25=38), 28 matters, and *Nibbāna*.	5	12	18

Below states of enquiry nos. 158 to 170 are to be referred to Table 1.8.11 and Chart 1.

Chart 1.8.7. Aggrouping and Ungrouping of the final 18 dyads

	Aggrouped		
By units :	Agr	Base	Ele
158. States eliminated by the first Path.	4	2	2
States eliminated by the higher three Paths.	4	2	2
States with root causes eliminated by the first Path.	4	2	2
States with root causes eliminated by the higher three Paths.	4	2	2

These states are each aggrouped under 4 aggregates (4 mental aggregates), 2 bases (ideation-base, mind-base), and 2 elements (ideation-element, mind-consciousness element). They are each ungrouped under 1 aggregate (matter), 10 bases (10 gross bases), and 16 elements (10 gross elements, remaining 6 consciousness elements).

159. States not eliminated by the first Path.	5	12	18
States not eliminated by the higher three Paths.	5	12	18
States with root causes not eliminated by first Path.	5	12	18
States with root causes not eliminated by the higher three Paths, excluding *Nibbāna*.	5	12	18

These four states belong to mentality-materiality, are each aggrouped under 5 aggregates, 12 bases, and 18 elements.

160. States with initial application.	4	2	3
States with sustained application.	4	2	3

A Perfect Knowledge of Mind-Body from the Abhidhamma (Dhātukathā)

They belong to mentalities, are each aggrouped under 4 aggregates (4 mental aggregates), 2 bases (ideation-base, mind-base), and 2 elements (mind-element, ideation-element, mind-consciousness element).

They are ungrouped under 1 aggregate (matter), 10 bases (10 gross bases), and 15 elements (10 gross elements, remaining 5 consciousness elements).

	Agr	Base	Ele
161. States without initial application.	5	12	17
States without sustained application, excluding *Nibbāna*.	5	12	17

These states belong to mentality-materiality and excluded mind-element. They are each aggrouped under 5 aggregates, 12 bases, and 17 elements (18 excluding mind-element).

They are ungrouped under 1 element (mind-element). They are not ungrouped under aggregates and bases.

	Agr	Base	Ele
162. States with zest.	4	2	2
States which are accompanied by zest.	4	2	2

They belong to 4 mental aggregates, are each aggrouped under 4 aggregates (4 mental aggregates), 2 bases (ideation-base, mind-base), and 2 elements (ideation-element, mind-consciousness element).

They are each ungrouped under 1 aggregate (matter), 10 bases (10 gross bases), and 16 elements (10 gross elements, remaining 6 consciousness elements).

	Agr	Base	Ele
163. States without zest.	5	12	18
States which are not accompanied by zest.	5	12	18
States which are not accompanied by happiness, excluding *Nibbāna*.	5	12	18

These three states belong to mentality-materiality, are each aggrouped under 5 aggregates, 12 bases, and 18 elements.

	Agr	Base	Ele
164. States which are accompanied by happiness.	3	2	3

These states are closely bound up with body-consciousness element. They are aggrouped under 3 aggregates (perception, volitive perception, consciousness), 2 bases (ideation-base, mind-base), and 3 elements (body-consciousness element, ideation-element, and mind-consciousness element).

They are ungrouped under 2 aggregates (matter, feeling), 10 bases (10 gross bases), and 15 elements (10 gross elements, eye-consciousness element, ear-consciousness element, nose-consciousness element, tongue-consciousness element, and mind-element).

I. Aggrouping and Ungrouping

	Agr	Base	Ele
165. States which are accompanied by equanimity.	3	2	7

These states are dissociated from body-consciousness element. They are aggrouped under 3 aggregates (perception, volitive perception, consciousness), 2 bases (ideation-base, mind-base), and 7 elements (eye-consciousness element, ear-consciousness element, nose-consciousness element, tongue-consciousness element, mind-element, ideation-element, mind-consciousness element).

They are ungrouped under 2 aggregates (matter, feeling), 10 bases (10 gross bases), and 11 elements (10 gross elements, body-consciousness element).

	Agr	Base	Ele
166. States which are not accompanied by equanimity, excluding *Nibbāna*.	5	12	13

These states are mentality-materiality, are dissociated from eye-consciousness element, ear-consciousness element, nose-consciousness element, tongue-consciousness element, and mind-element. They are aggrouped under 5 aggregates, 12 bases, and 13 elements (10 gross elements, ideation-element, body-consciousness element, mind-consciousness element).

They are ungrouped under 5 elements (eye-consciousness element, ear-consciousness element, nose-consciousness element, tongue-consciousness element, and mind-element). They are not ungrouped under aggregates and bases.

	Agr	Base	Ele
167. States which are characteristic of sensuous sphere.	5	12	18
States which are included (in round of deaths and rebirths).	5	12	18
States which are surpassable.	5	12	18

These states are mentality-materiality, are each aggrouped under 5 aggregates, 12 bases, and 18 elements.

	Agr	Base	Ele
168. States which are not characteristic of sensuous sphere.	4	2	2
States which are not included (in round of deaths and rebirths).	4	2	2
States which are unsurpassable/incomparable, excluding *Nibbāna*.	4	2	2

They belong to 4 mental aggregates, are each aggrouped under 4 aggregates (4 mental aggregates), 2 bases (ideation-base, mind-base), and 2 elements (ideation-element, mind-consciousness element).

They are each ungrouped under 1 aggregate (matter), 10 bases (10 gross bases), and 16 elements (10 gross elements, remaining 6 consciousness elements).

A Perfect Knowledge of Mind-Body from the Abhidhamma (Dhātukathā)

	Agr	Base	Ele
169. States which are characteristic of the form sphere.	4	2	2
States which are characteristic of the formless sphere.	4	2	2
States which lead out (from round of existence).	4	2	2
States which are fixed as to future destinies.	4	2	2
States which are at odds (with supramundane Path).	4	2	2
Aggrouped and ungrouped answers are the same as in nos. 162 and 168.			
170. States which are not characteristic of the form sphere.	5	12	18
States which are not characteristic of the formless sphere.	5	12	18
States which do not lead out (from round of existence).	5	12	18
States which are not fixed as to future destinies.	5	12	18
States which are not at odds (with supramundane Path), excluding *Nibbāna*.	5	12	18
These states are mentality-materiality, are each aggrouped under 5 aggregates, 12 bases, and 18 elements.			

CHAPTER 2

II. Aggrouped and Ungrouped
(*Saṅgahitenāsaṅgahita*)

Analysis of 42 states from 8 catechism

This Chapter deals with 42 states of enquiry, of which 35 of them belong to matter aggregate while the remaining 7 belong to consciousness aggregate. The method in this chapter follows the rule that each of the states of enquiry can be aggrouped (or classified, included) with the respective remaining states under the same aggregate (i.e. all of them must be from the same aggregate), but they may not be classified either under the same base or under the same element. In other cases, they can be classified both under the same aggregate and under the same base, but not under the same element. Take for instance, the eye-base in nos. 171 can be classified with the remaining 27 states of matter aggregate (taken as *these* states) as aggrouped under the same aggregate, but not under the same base and not under the same element. In the case of the 7 consciousness-elements in nos. 172, each of which can be classified with the remaining 6 states of enquiry under the same aggregate and under the same base, but not under the same element.

According to nos. 171 in the text,

> "Eye-base is aggrouped with "*these states*" ... Tangible object base is aggrouped with "*these states*" ... eye-element ... tangible object element, each of which is aggrouped with "*these states*" under the same aggregate, but are not aggrouped under the same base, and under the same element". *Those* states are not aggrouped under 4 aggregates, under 2 bases and under 8 elements."

To better understand the differences between *these* states and *those* states from this paragraph and similarly from the rest, it would be useful to first illustrate with a simple flow diagram as in below. The initial classification in process A is possible on a comparable basis of the same aggregate, thus giving aggrouped answers. In process B, classification can not happen between *those* non-SOE states and these SOE under the same aggregate (because *those* non-SOE states belong to mental aggregates). Therefore, process B gives answers of the not-aggrouped (i.e. ungrouped).

A Perfect Knowledge of Mind-Body from the Abhidhamma (Dhātukathā)

Diagram 2.1. Classified between SOE and *these* states as aggrouped, and unclassified between *those* states and SOE as ungrouped

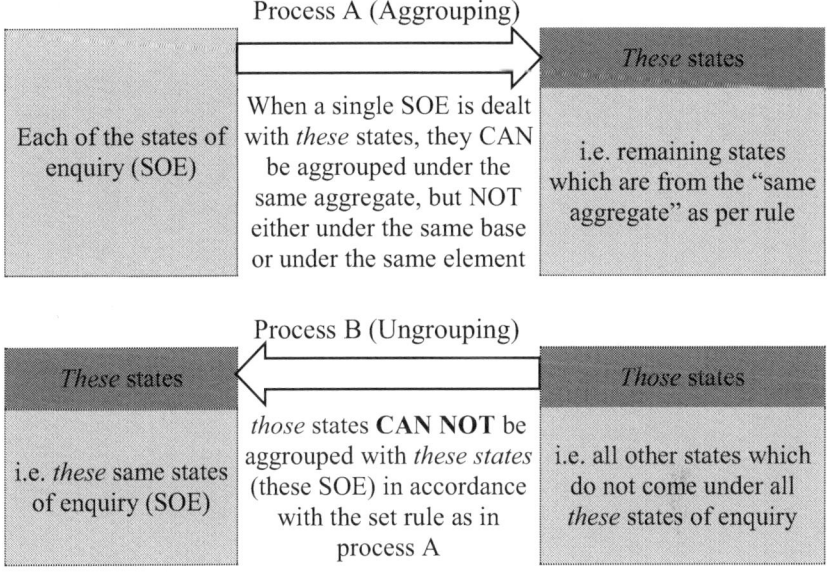

The following abbreviations, whichever are applicable, are used throughout Chapter 2, presented in the form of charts which are composed from the 8 catechism from nos. 171 to 178. To ascertain under how many aggregates, under how many bases, and under how many elements each state of enquiry form as aggrouped, and those non-SOE states form as ungrouped, it is useful that readers refer to the internal and external tables in Chapter 1, and also Chart 1.

Abbreviations

Agr	: Aggregates
Bse	: Bases
Cons	: Consciousness
El	: Elements
Gr	: Gross matters
Sb	: Subtle matters
Mat	: Matters
SOE	: States of Enquiry

II. Aggrouped and Ungrouped

20 states of enquiry from 10 gross bases, 10 gross elements

Chart 2.1. States of enquiry from a group of 10 bases and 10 elements

					(Aggrouped)	(Ungrouped)	(Ungrouped)	*Those* other states (Ungrouped)		
	These state of enquiry (SOE) :		Type of aggregates: Gross matters/Subtle matters: *These* remaining physical states:		Agr	Bse	El.	Agr	Bse	El.
171	1.	Eye-base	Matter	Gr	27	1	1	1		
	2.	Ear-base	Matter	Gr	27	1	1	1		
	3.	Nose-base	Matter	Gr	27	1	1	1		
	4.	Tongue-base	Matter	Gr	27	1	1	1		
	5.	Body-base	Matter	Gr	27	1	1	1		
	6.	Vision-base	Matter	Gr	27	1	1	1		
	7.	Sound-base	Matter	Gr	27	1	1	1		
	8.	Odour-base	Matter	Gr	27	1	1	1		
	9.	Taste-base	Matter	Gr	27	1	1	1	all with the same answer		
	10.	Tangibility-base	Matter	Gr	25	1	1	1	4	2	8
	11.	Eye-element	Matter	Gr	27	1	1	1			
	12.	Ear-element	Matter	Gr	27	1	1	1			
	13	Nose-element	Matter	Gr	27	1	1	1			
	14	Tongue-element	Matter	Gr	27	1	1	1			
	15	Body-element	Matter	Gr	27	1	1	1			
	16	Vision-element	Matter	Gr	27	1	1	1			
	17	Sound-element	Matter	Gr	27	1	1	1			
	18	Odour-element	Matter	Gr	27	1	1	1			
	19	Taste-element	Matter	Gr	27	1	1	1			
	20	Tangibility-element	Matter	Gr	25	1	1	1			

These 20 states of enquiry in chart 2.1 above belong to matter aggregate. Because the 10 bases contain also the 5 sensitive organs, 5 sense-objects, and 5 elements (for example, eye-base is also the sensitive eye, visible object, and eye-element), and the 10 elements contain also the 5 sensitive organs, 5 sense-bases, and 5 sense-objects (for example, the eye-element is also the sensitive eye, eye-base, and visible object). Thus these 20 states of enquiry fall under the category of 12 physical gross matters.

When one of these physical states of enquiry is taken into account, its remaining physical states are the 27 matters, except for the tangibility-base and tangibility-element in which each consists of the 3 great elements of earth, heat, and wind (air), thereby their remaining physical states are 25 matters (28-3=25). It is only in this way that the SOE can be classifiable with their remaining states.

A Perfect Knowledge of Mind-Body from the Abhidhamma (Dhātukathā)

Each state of enquiry is aggrouped with the remaining 25 or 27 physical states under the same matter aggregate, but they can not be aggrouped under the same object base and under the same object element. For example, the eye-base is aggrouped with the remaining 27 physical states under 1 matter aggregate. But eye-base and its remaining 27 physical states can not be aggrouped under the same base and under the same element because they come under different bases and different elements. Eye-base is 1 base, eye-element is 1 element, both are declared as ungrouped. The rest of the SOE are to be dealt with in similar manner.

Those states which are not part of the SOE, do not conform to this rule. They thus come as ungrouped and form under 4 aggregates (feeling, perception, volitive formation, consciousness), under 2 bases (ideation-base, mind-base), and under 8 elements (ideation-element, 7 consciousness-elements).

7 states of enquiry from consciousness elements

Chart 2.2. States of enquiry from group of 7 consciousness elements

These states of enquiry:	These remaining consciousness elements: Type of aggregates:	(Aggrouped) Agr	(Aggrouped) Bse	(Ungrouped) El	Those other states (Ungrouped) Agr Bse El
172 1. Eye-cons. element	consciousness	6	1	1	1
2. Ear-cons. element	consciousness	6	1	1	1
3. Nose-cons. element	consciousness	6	1	1	1	all with the same answer 4 11 12
4. Tongue-cons. element	consciousness	6	1	1	1
5. Body-cons. element	consciousness	6	1	1	1
6. Mind-element	consciousness	6	1	1	1
7. Mind-cons. element	consciousness	6	1	1	1

These states of enquiry belong to the group of 7 consciousness elements, come under consciousness aggregate. When each of these SOE is taken into account, the 6 consciousness elements become the remaining states. Each SOE can be classified with these remaining states under the same aggregate (consciousness) and under the same base (mind-base), but they can not be aggrouped under the same element. Each SOE can not classify with itself either.

For example, when eye-consciousness element is enquired with the remaining 6 consciousness elements, they are aggrouped under 1 aggregate (consciousness) and under 1 base (mind-base). Eye-consciousness element is declared as ungrouped under 1 element (eye-consciousness element) because it can not be included with its remaining 6 consciousness elements as aggrouping under a single same element.

II. Aggrouped and Ungrouped

Those other states are taken as ungrouped under 4 aggregates (matter, feeling, perception, and volitive formation), 11 bases (12 excluding mind-base), and 12 elements (5 sense-elements, 5 sense-object elements, ideation-element, and eye-consciousness element). The rest of the SOE are to be dealt with in similar manner as explained.

Chart 2.3. States of enquiry from a group of 7 faculties

	State of enquiry:	*These* remaining physical states: Gross matter or subtle matter: Type of aggregates:			Agr (Aggrouped)	Bse (Ungrouped)	El (Ungrouped)	*Those* other states (Ungrouped) Agr Bse El
173	1. Vision-faculty	Matter	Gr	27	1	1	1	
	2. Hearing-faculty	Matter	Gr	27	1	1	1	
	3. Smell-faculty	Matter	Gr	27	1	1	1	all with the
	4. Taste-faculty	Matter	Gr	27	1	1	1	same answer
	5. Touch-faculty	Matter	Gr	27	1	1	1	4 2 8
	6. Femininity-faculty	Matter	Sb	12 Gr	1	1	1	
	7. Masculinity-faculty	Matter	Sb	12 Gr	1	1	1	

Because the vision-faculty, hearing-faculty, smell-faculty, taste-faculty, and touch-faculty are also, respectively, the sensitive eye, eye-element and visible object; sensitive ear, ear-element and audible object, etc ... , thus these 5 controlling faculties are included in the 12 physical gross matters. When one of these 5 gross physical faculties is taken as a subject matter of enquiry, its remaining physical states are 27 matters. Because femininity-faculty and masculinity-faculty are subtle matters, the 12 gross matters become their remaining states (28-16=12).

When each of these sense-based faculties is taken as a state of enquiry, it is aggrouped with the remaining 27 physical states under the same matter aggregate, but they can not be aggrouped under the same object base and the same object element. It follows the same way as has been explained in nos. 171 above.

When either of the femininity and masculinity faculties (which come under subtle matters and ideation-base) is enquired with the remaining 12 gross matters, each is aggrouped under 1 physical aggregate, but not under the same base and under the same element. Also, because both ideation-base and ideation-element can not classify with itself, femininity faculty and masculinity faculty are each formed as ungrouped under 1 base (ideation-base) and under 1 element (ideation-element).

Those states which are not part of the SOE are treated as not-included and formed as ungrouped under 4 aggregates (feeling, perception, volitive formation, consciousness aggregates), under 2 bases (ideation-base, mind-base), and under 8 elements (ideation-element, 7 consciousness-elements).

Chart 2.4. States of enquiry from a group of 2 becomings

				(Aggrouped)	(Ungrouped)	(Ungrouped)	Those other states (Ungrouped)		
State of enquiry :				Agr	Bse	El	Agr	Bse	El
174 1. Non-perception becoming	Matter	Gr	11 Gr	1	-	-	4	3	9
2. One-aggregate becoming	Matter	Gr	11 Gr	1	-	-	4	3	9

These remaining physical states: Gross matter or subtle matter: Type of aggregates:

The non-perception becoming and the single-aggregate becoming are identical. The 2 becomings consist of visible object base (which is gross matter) and ideation-base (which includes subtle matters). Therefore, the remaining physical states have to be the 11 gross physical matters.

Each SOE can be classified with these remaining 11 gross matters under the same aggregate (matter) but they can not be aggrouped under the same base, and under the same element. In other word, vision-base with ideation-base, and similarly vision-element with ideation-element also can not be taken as ungrouped under one base and under one element.

Therefore, those non-SOE states are taken as ungrouped under 4 aggregates (4 mental aggregates), under 3 bases (vision-base, ideation-base, and mind-base), and under 9 elements (vision-element, ideation-element, 7 consciousness-elements).

15 other states of enquiry from matter aggregate

Chart 2.5. States of enquiry from a group of two

				(Aggrouped)	(Ungrouped)	(Ungrouped)	Those other states Ungrouped)		
States of enquiry :				Agr	Bse	El	Agr	Bse	El
175 1. Lamentation	Mat	Gr	27	1	1	1	4	2	8
2. States both visible and impinging	Mat	Gr	27	1	1	1	4	2	8

These remaining physical states: Gross matter or subtle matter: Type of aggregates:

These two states of enquiry both belong to matter aggregate. The state of lamentation is taken as audible object base as a result of wailing. States which are both visible and impinging correspond to visible object base. So, the remaining physical states for each SOE are the 27 physical matters.

Each SOE is aggrouped with these remaining 27 physical states under the same matter aggregate, but they can not be aggrouped under the same object base and under the same object element. Each is aggrouped under 1 aggregate (matter).

II. Aggrouped and Ungrouped

Sound-base and vision-base are each taken as ungrouped under 1 base (sound-base and vision-base, respectively), and under 1 element (sound-element and vision-element, respectively). Those non-SOE states are thereby ungrouped under 4 aggregates (4 mental aggregates), 2 bases (ideation-base and mind-base), and 8 elements (ideation-element and the 7 consciousness-elements).

Chart 2.6. States of enquiry from that which are invisible but impinging

States of enquiry (SOE)		*These* remaining physical states: Gross matter or subtle matter: Type of aggregates:			(Aggrouped) Agr	(Ungrouped) Bse	(Ungrouped) El	*Those* other states (Ungrouped) Agr Bse El
176	States which are invisible but impinging	Mat	11 Gr	16 Subtle matters and visible object base	1	9	9	4 10 16

States which are invisible but impinging indicate the absence of visible object base from the 10 gross bases, and the absence of sensitive eye from the 12 gross matters (i.e. the other 9 gross bases and 11 gross matters are still impinging). So, visible object base and 16 subtle matters become the remaining states. Subtle matters also come under ideation-base and ideation-element.

These states of enquiry can be classified with the remaining physical states under 1 aggregate, but all these physical states can not be classified in this manner under the same base and under same element. SOE is thereby taken as ungrouped under 9 bases (9 gross bases without vision-base), and under 9 elements (9 gross elements without vision-element).

Those other states are taken ungrouped come under 4 aggregates (the 4 mental aggregates), under 10 bases (10 gross bases excluding vision-base; mind-base), and under 16 elements (10 gross elements excluding vision-element; 7 consciousness-elements).

Chart 2.7. States of enquiry from that which are visible

State of enquiry (SOE)		*These* remaining physical states: Gross matter or subtle matter: Type of aggregates:			(Aggrouped) Agr	(Ungrouped) Bse	(Ungrouped) El	*Those* other states (Ungrouped) Agr Bse El
177	States with visibility	Matter	Gross	27	1	1	1	4 2 8

A Perfect Knowledge of Mind-Body from the Abhidhamma (Dhātukathā)

States which are visible meaning the presence of sensitive eye, visible object base and visible object element. Therefore, the remaining physical states are 27 matters. When these states are dealt with the remaining 27 matters, they can be aggrouped under matter aggregate, but not under the same object base and under same object element. The SOE is taken as ungrouped under 1 base (visible object base) and 1 element (visible object element). On the other hand, those other states (other than these physical states) can not be aggrouped under the same aggregate, same object base, and same object element. Those states are ungrouped under 4 aggregates, 2 bases, and 8 elements similar to that in nos. 171, 173 and 175.

Chart 2.8. States of enquiry from that which are impinging, and that which are derived

These remaining physical states: Gross matter or subtle matter: Type of aggregates:				(Aggrouped)	(Ungrouped)	(Ungrouped)	*Those* other states (Ungrouped)		
States of enquiry :				Agr	Bse	El	Agr	Bse	El
178. 1. States which are impinging	Mat	Gr	16 Sb	1	10	10	4	11	17
2. States which are derived	Mat	Gr	Earth, Heat, Wind	1	10*	10*	4	11	17

States which are impinging belong to 10 gross matters, thereby 16 subtle matters are taken as the remaining physical states. When SOE is dealt with these remaining 16 subtle matters (which also come under ideation-base and ideation-element), these physical states are aggrouped under 1 aggregate (matter) but they can not be aggrouped under the same base and under the same element. The 10 gross bases and 10 gross elements are placed at ungrouped.

The 4 Great Elements are the primary non-derived physical matters. But, because only earth, heat, and wind (air) are treated as under the sphere of tangibility, thereby water-element is excluded. Water as the element of cohesion can not be physically sensed, for which it can only be known inferentially. Earth, heat, and wind (air) are taken as the remaining physical states excluding water. All these physical states excluding the 3 great elements, can only be aggrouped under 1 matter aggregate, and can not be aggrouped under the same base and under the same element. Thus, the 10* bases (9 gross bases excluded touch-base but includes ideation-base) and 10* elements (9 gross elements excluded touch-element but includes ideation-element) are taken as ungrouped.

Those other states which are not aggrouped are taken as under 4 aggregates (4 mental aggregates), under 11 bases (10 gross bases excluding tangibility-base; ideation-base; mind-base), and under 17 elements (10 gross elements excluding tangibility-element; ideation-element; 7 consciousness-elements).

II. Aggrouped and Ungrouped

Key points from the text :

10 gross bases, 17 elements, 7 faculties,
non-perception becoming, one-aggregate becoming,
lamentation, states both are visible and impinging,
invisible states but impinging,
visible states, impinging states

Chart 2.9. Summary of the 42 states of enquiry (by their remaining states)

	(Ungrouped)			remaining 27 physical states	remaining 25 physical states	remaining 6 cons. elements	remaining 12 gross matters	remaining 11 gross matters	remaining: 16 subtle matters + visible object	remaining states : 16 subtle matters	remaining states : Earth, heat, and wind (air)	Number of states
	Agr	Bse	El									
171.	4	2	8	18	2							20
172.	4	11	12			7						7
173.	4	2	8	5			2					7
174.	4	3	9					2				2
175.	4	2	8	2								2
176.	4	10	16						1			1
177.	4	2	8	1								1
178.	4	11	17							1	1	2
Number of states :				26	2	7	2	2	1	1	1	42

From the groups of enquiry, nos. 171 to 178, we can draw conclusion from the associated charts that there are 8 different kinds of those remaining states to the 42 states of enquiry (See the names from the top 8 header rows). The chart above summarises the number of states appertaining to these 8 groups of enquiry.

If we look at the answers from remaining states by ungrouped in Chart 2.9, we notice that there are 30 number of states ungrouped under the 4 aggregates, under 2 bases, and under 8 elements (i.e. 20+7+2+1=30) with the remainder as the other 12 kinds (i.e. 7+2+1+2=12).

Of the 42 states of enquiry as being the subject matter of this Chapter, there are 5 which belong to the external sources (dhammasaṅgaṇī mātikā) — viz. states both are visible and impinging; states which are invisible but impinging; states which are visible; states which are impinging; states which are derived. The remaining are the 37 internal states of enquiry.

CHAPTER 3

III. Ungrouped and Aggrouped
(*Asaṅgahitenasaṅgahita*)

Analysis of 90 states from 12 catechism

The 90 states of enquiry form the subject matter of this chapter, all of which come exclusively under ideation-base. The rule which applies in these states of enquiry is that, these are the states which — whether they come from a group of enquiry or from a single enquiry but having both mentality-materiality qualities — are classifiable under the same base and under the same element (i.e. under ideation-base and ideation-element). These states can not be classified under the same aggregate because they belong to different aggregates. In this chapter, states from the matter aggregate (i.e. gross matters, apart from subtle matters) and consciousness aggregate are excluded, because they belong to the different bases and different elements which fall outside the rule to be observed.

The following abbreviations are used in all the charts throughout Chapter 3, appertaining to nos. 179 to 190. From time to time, it may be necessary to refer to preceding internal and external tables of enquiry and also to Chart 1 when examining these states under discussion.

Abbreviations

Agr	: Aggregates
Bse	: Bases
El.	: Elements
SOE	: States of Enquiry
Gr	: Gross matters
Sb	: Subtle matters

First, let's clarify what constitutes *these* states and *those* states (and "*they*") which are mentioned throughout the chapter. For instance, according to nos. 179 in the text,

> "Feeling aggregate is not aggrouped with *these* states; Perception aggregate; Volitive formation aggregate; Origin-truth; Path-truth is not aggrouped with *these* states under the same aggregate, but are aggrouped under the same base and under the same element. *Those* states ... they, excluding *Nibbāna* from the aggregates, are aggrouped under 3 aggregates, under 1 base, and under 1 element."

III. Ungrouped and Aggrouped

A simple diagram below illustrates the difference between *these* states and *those* states.

Diagram 3.1. Ungrouped between *these* states and *those* states, and aggrouped between *those* states and *these* states

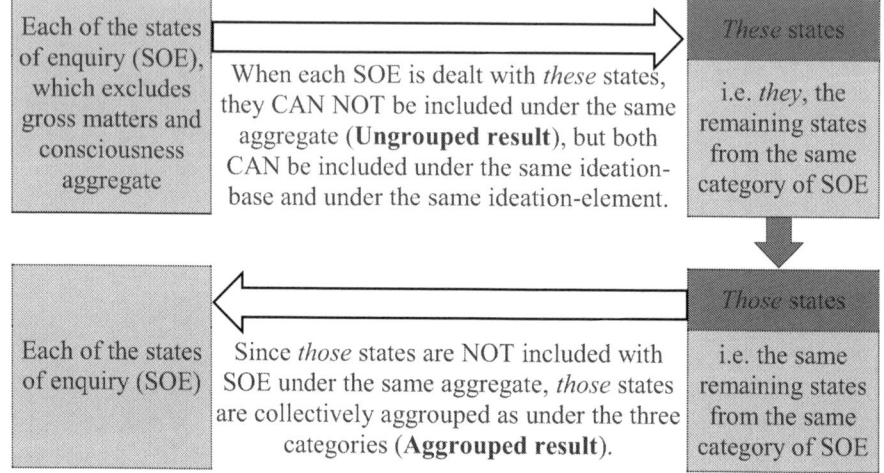

53 internal states of enquiry

Chart 3.1. States of enquiry from 3 mental aggregates and 2 truths

		These remaining states :				SOE (Ungrouped)			*Those* states (Aggrouped)		
States of enquiry (SOE):	Subtle matters	Feeling	Perception	Volitive formation	Nibbāna	Agr	Bse	El.	Agr	Bse	El.
1. Feeling aggregate	16		1	1	1	1	-	-	3	1	1
2. Perception aggregate	16	1		1	1	1	-	-	3	1	1
3. Volitive formation aggregate	16	1	1		1	1	-	-	3	1	1
4. Origin-truth (of suffering)	16	1	1		1	1	-	-	3	1	1
5. Path-truth (leading out)	16	1	1		1	1	-	-	3	1	1

According to the text, "feeling aggregate, perception aggregate, volitive formation aggregate, Origin-truth, Path-truth, are all not aggrouped with "*these states*" under the same aggregate, but are aggrouped under the same base, and

A Perfect Knowledge of Mind-Body from the Abhidhamma (Dhātukathā)

under the same element". *"These states"* are referring to the remaining states of the subjects matters of enquiry. The phrase *"these states"* should be understood in the same context in all the subsequent charts.

All these five states of enquiry indicated in Chart 3.1 above come under ideation-base and ideation-element. If you would refer back to Chart 1, you will notice that it encompasses 4 aggregates (16 subtle matters of matter aggregate, feeling aggregate, perception aggregate, and volitive formation aggregate), and *Nibbāna*. When each subject matter of enquiry is taken into account, the other 4 states become its remaining states. *Nibbāna* is only part of these remaining states but not an aggregate. Because these five states of enquiry come under the 3 different aggregates, they can not be aggrouped with their respective remaining states under the same aggregate. But the five states of enquiry can be aggrouped under the same base (ideation-base) and under same element (ideation-element).

Take for instance, when feeling aggregate is dealt with *those* states (i.e. the remaining 4 states of subtle matters, perception, volitive formation, and *Nibbāna*), they can not be aggrouped under the same aggregate but they can be aggrouped under ideation-base and under ideation-element. Thus, feeling aggregate is taken as ungrouped under 1 aggregate (feeling), while *those* states, which are the remaining states, are aggrouped under 3 aggregates excluding *Nibbāna* (matter, perception, and volitive formation), under 1 base (ideation-base), and under 1 element (ideation-element). The remaining 4 subject matters of enquiry are to be dealt with in the same manner with the similar results for the ungrouped and the aggrouped.

Gross matters and consciousness aggregate are excluded because if they were to be included, they encompass 11 different bases (10 gross bases, mind-base) and 17 different elements (10 gross elements, 7 consciousness-elements) which fall outside the set rule for this chapter.

Chart 3.2. States of enquiry from truth as regards cessation of suffering

States of enquiry (SOE) :	Subtle matters:	Feeling:	Perception:	Volitive formation:	Nibbāna:	SOE (Ungrouped) Agr Bse El.	Those states (Aggrouped) Agr Bse El.
180 1. the truth of the cessation of suffering	16	1	1	1		0 - -	4 1 1

The truth concerning the cessation of suffering comes under *Nibbāna* which comes under ideation-base and ideation-element. The latter in turn encompasses 4 aggregates (16 subtle matters, feeling aggregate, perception aggregate, volitive

III. Ungrouped and Aggrouped

formation aggregate). Because this subject matter of enquiry comes under different aggregates, they can not be aggrouped under the same aggregate, but can be aggrouped under the same base and under the same element.

When cessation-truth is dealt with its remaining 4 states (16 subtle matters, feeling aggregate, perception aggregate, volitive formation aggregate), SOE is taken as ungrouped under no aggregate (marked as zero) for *Nibbāna* not being an aggregate, is excluded. Those remaining states are then taken as aggrouped under 4 aggregates (matter, feeling, perception, volitive formation), under 1 base (ideation-base), and under 1 element (ideation-element).

Chart 3.3. States of enquiry from vitality-faculty

States of enquiry (SOE):	Subtle matters:	Feeling:	Perception:	Volitive formation:	Nibbāna:	SOE (Ungrouped) Agr	Bse	El.	Those states (Aggrouped) Agr	Bse	El.
181 1. Vitality-faculty		1		1		1	2	–	–	2	1	1

Herein we have a subject matter of enquiry which is imbedded with connate qualities of dual aggregates. Vitality-faculty, which embraces both physical life and mental life, comes under subtle matters and the aggregate of volitive formation, are both bound by ideation-base and ideation-element. The latter encompasses 4 aggregates and *Nibbāna*. Because the state of enquiry belongs to two different aggregates, and furthermore it can not be aggrouped with its remaining states (feeling, perception) under the same aggregate (excluding *Nibbāna*), but they can be aggrouped under ideation-base and under ideation-element. *Nibbāna*, being only a part of the remaining states, does not belong to the aggregates.

Thus, when vitality-faculty is enquired with its remaining 2 states, it is taken as ungrouped under 2 aggregates (subtle matters and volitive formation aggregate). The reason is the same as was explained in the previous example nos. 179. Those remaining states from the same category of aggregate, are then taken as aggrouped under 2 aggregates excluding *Nibbāna* (matter and volitive formation), under 1 base (ideation-base) and under 1 element (ideation-element).

A Perfect Knowledge of Mind-Body from the Abhidhamma (Dhātukathā)

Chart 3.4 States of enquiry from 15 faculties and dependent origination

States of enquiry (SOE):	Subtle matters:	Feeling:	Perception:	Volitive formation:	*These* remaining states: Nibbāna:	SOE (Ungrouped) Agr	Bse	El.	Those states (Aggrouped) Agr	Bse	El.
1. Femininity-faculty		1	1	1	1	1	-	-			
2. Masculinity-faculty		1	1	1	1	1	-	-			
3. Carnal pleasure-faculty	16		1	1	1	1	-	-			
4. Carnal pain-faculty	16		1	1	1	1	-	-			
5. Joy-faculty	16		1	1	1	1	-	-			
6. Melancholy-faculty	16		1	1	1	1	-	-			
7. Equanimity-faculty	16		1	1	1	1	-	-			
8. Confidence-faculty	16	1	1		1	1	-	-			
9. Effort-faculty-faculty	16	1	1		1	1	-	-			
10. Mindfulness-faculty	16	1	1		1	1	-	-			
11. Concentration-faculty	16	1	1		1	1	-	-			
12. Wisdom-faculty	16	1	1		1	1	-	-			
13. "I-shall-comprehend-the-unknown" faculty	16	1	1		1	1	-	-			
14. The "higher knowledge" faculty	16	1	1		1	1	-	-	all with the same answer 3	1	1
15. The "Final Knower" faculty	16	1	1		1	1	-	-			
16. Ignorance	16	1	1		1	1	-	-			
17. Conditioned by Ignorance, Volitive formation….	16	1	1		1	1	-	-			
18. Conditioned by Six bases, Contact	16	1	1		1	1	-	-			
19. Conditioned by Contact, Feeling	16		1	1	1	1	-	-			
20. Conditioned by Feeling, Craving	16	1	1		1	1	-	-			
21. Conditioned by Craving, Clinging	16	1	1		1	1	-	-			
22. Action-becoming	16	1	1		1	1	-	-			

III. Ungrouped and Aggrouped

Of these states of enquiry, femininity-faculty and masculinity-faculty are subtle matters, feeling and the 5 feeling faculties belong to feeling aggregate, the rest belong to volitive formation aggregate. Because each of these states of enquiry come under different aggregates, it can not be aggrouped with its remaining states under the same aggregate, but they can be aggrouped under the same base and under the same element.

Let's take femininity-faculty for an example. When it is dealt with the remaining 4 states, they can not be aggrouped under the same aggregate, but they can be included under the same base (ideation-base) and same element (ideation-element). The SOE is thus placed as ungrouped under 1 aggregate (matter). Those remaining states from the same category as the SOE are taken as aggrouped under 3 aggregates excluding *Nibbāna* (feeling, perception, and volitive formation), 1 base (ideation-base) and 1 element (ideation-element).

Taking another example, the carnal pleasure-faculty. For similar reason, the subject matter is taken as ungrouped under the same aggregate (feeling) while aggrouped under the same base and same element. Reason is the same as in the aforesaid. Those remaining states are aggrouped under 3 aggregates excluding *Nibbāna* (matter, perception, and volitive formation), 1 base (ideation-base) and 1 element (ideation-element). The rest of the subject matters of enquiry are to be dealt with in similar manner with the same number of states as ungrouped and aggrouped answers under the three categories.

Chart 3.5. States of enquiry from birth, ageing, death, and Jhāna

States of enquiry (SOE):	Matters:	Feeling:	Perception:	Volitive formation:	Nibbāna:	SOE (Ungrouped) Agr	Bse	El.	Those states (Aggrouped) Agr	Bse	El.
183 1. Birth	Gr	1	1		1	2	-	-	2	1	1
2. Ageing, and	Gr	1	1		1	2	-	-	2	1	1
3. Death	Gr	1	1		1	2	-	-	2	1	1
4. Jhāna	28		1		1	2	-	-	2	1	1

The states of birth, ageing, and death contain subtle matters, and volitive formation. Thus, birth, ageing, and death are connate with dual characteristics of mentality-materiality. Note that gross matters are herein taken as among those remaining states.

Jhāna is the same case as in nos. 181 in which the subject matter of enquiry belongs to 2 out of the 5 states. *Jhāna* is classified as aggrouped under 2 aggregates (feeling and volitive formation). This, 28 matters, perception aggregate, and *Nibbāna* are taken as those remaining states.

When each of these states of enquiry is dealt with its remaining states, they can not be aggrouped under the same aggregate, but they can be aggrouped under the same base (ideation-base) and under the same element (ideation-element). The 4 subject matters of enquiry are all contained by ideation-base and ideation-element.

The first *Jhāna* must have the presence of 5 factors — initial application, sustained application, zest, happiness, and one-pointedness. Zest and happiness belong to feeling aggregate, while the other 3 factors belong to aggregate of the volitive formation. Therefore, *Jhāna* has its remaining 3 states as subtle matters, perception, and *Nibbāna*. When *jhāna* is dealt with its remaining 3 states, they can not be classified under the same 2 aggregates as *jhāna*. So, *Jjāna* SOE is placed as ungrouped under 2 aggregates (feeling, volitive formation). Those remaining states are then taken as aggrouped under 2 aggregates excluding *Nibbāna* (subtle matters and perception), 1 base (ideation-base) and 1 element (ideation-element).

The other 11 different bases (10 gross bases and mind-base) and 17 different elements (10 gross elements and the 7 consciousness-elements) are excluded because they belong to matter aggregate and consciousness aggregate which can not be conjoined under same base and same element. The other 3 states are to be enquired in similar manner with the same number of states as ungrouped and aggrouped answers under the three categories.

Chart 3.6. States of enquiry from miscellaneous (17) and cluster of root causes (3)

States of enquiry (SOE) :	Subtle matters:	Feeling:	Perception:	Volitive formation:	Nibbāna:	SOE (Ungrouped) Agr Bse El.	Those states (Aggrouped) Agr Bse El.
184 1. Sorrow	16	1	1	1		1 - -	
2. Suffering	16	1	1	1		1 - -	
3. Melancholy	16	1	1	1		1 - -	
4. Despair	16	1	1	1		1 - -	all with the same answer
5. Application of Mindfulness	16	1	1		1	1 - -	
6. The Right Striving	16	1	1		1	1 - -	3 1 1
7. The Illimitables	16	1	1		1	1 - -	
8. 5 Faculties	16	1	1		1	1 - -	
9. 5 Powers	16	1	1		1	1 - -	

III. Ungrouped and Aggrouped

10. 7 Enlightenment-Factors	16	1	1		1	1	-	-
11. Noble Eightfold Path	16	1	1		1	1	-	-
12. Contact	16	1	1		1	1	-	-
13. Feeling	16		1	1	1	1	-	-
14. Perception	16	1		1	1	1	-	-
15. Volition	16	1	1		1	1	-	-
16. Decision	16	1	1		1	1	-	-
17. Attention	16	1	1		1	1	-	-
18. States which are root causes	16	1	1		1	1	-	-
19. States which are both root causes and accompanied by root causes.	16	1	1		1	1	-	-
20. States which are both root causes and associated with root causes.	16	1	1		1	1	-	-

These 20 subject matters of enquiry all belong to 1 out of the 5 states. For example, regarding sorrow, suffering and melancholy, their remaining states are subtle matters, perception, volitive formation, and *Nibbāna* (because gross matters and consciousness aggregate are excluded as per guideline). When one of these 3 SOE is enquired with these remaining 4 states, they can not be classified under the same aggregate, but can be all included under ideation-base and ideation-element. Thus, each of them is taken as ungrouped under 1 aggregate (feeling). Those remaining states are in turn taken as aggrouped under 3 aggregates excluding *Nibbāna* (subtle matters, perception, volitive formation), under 1 base (ideation-base), and under 1 element (ideation-element).

Take another example, the 20th state of enquiry, i.e. "states which are root causes and also associated with root causes", which is volitive formation. When it is dealt with its remaining 4 states, they can not be classified under the same aggregate. So, the SOE is taken as ungrouped under 1 aggregate (volitive formation). Those remaining states are in turn taken as aggrouped under 3 aggregates excluding *Nibbāna* (subtle matters, feeling, and perception), under 1 base (ideation-base) and under 1 element (ideation-element). The rest of the subject matters of enquiry are to be dealt with in the same manner with similar ungrouped and aggrouped number of states.

Note that the other 11 bases (10 gross bases and mind-base) and 17 different elements (10 gross elements and the 7 consciousness-elements) are excluded because they include the whole of materiality and consciousness aggregate which can not be classified under the same base and under the same element.

A Perfect Knowledge of Mind-Body from the Abhidhamma (Dhātukathā)

2 states of enquiry from Dhammasaṅgaṇīmātikā triads

Chart 3.7. State of enquiry regarding causes

		These remaining states: Nibbāna: Volitive formation: Perception: Feeling: Subtle matters:				SOE (Ungrouped) Agr Bse El.			Those states (Aggrouped) Agr Bse El.		
	States of enquiry (SOE):										
185	1. States not arisen from causes.	16	1	1	1	0	-	-	4	1	1
	2. States unconditioned by causes.	16	1	1	1	0	-	-	4	1	1

These 2 subject matters of enquiry are identical to that in nos. 180 wherein *Nibbāna* is the only state of enquiry. The 4 different aggregates (matter, feeling, perception, volitive formation) thus become the remaining states. Taking each of these subject matters of enquiry with the remaining states, they can not be classified under the same aggregate, but can be aggrouped under the same base and under the same element. So, SOE is taken as ungrouped under no aggregate (marked as zero) because *Nibbāna* which is not an aggregate, is being excluded.

Those remaining states from the same category as the state of *Nibbāna*, are then taken as aggrouped under 4 aggregates (matter, feeling, perception, volitive formation), under 1 base (ideation-base), and under 1 element (ideation-element).

35 states of enquiry from Dhammasaṅgaṇīmātikā dyads

Chart 3.8. State of enquiry from the cluster of defilements

	These remaining states: Nibbāna: Volitive formation: Perception: Feeling: Subtle matters:					SOE (Ungrouped) Agr Bse El.			Those states (Aggrouped) Agr Bse El.		
States of enquiry (SOE):											
186. States which are defilement; States which are both defilement and objects of defilement; States which are both defilement and associated with defilement (3)		16	1	1		1	all have same answer 1	-	-	all with the same answer 3	1	1

113

III. Ungrouped and Aggrouped

The 3 states of enquiry belong to the aggregate of volitive formation which comes under ideation-base and ideation-element. The 4 different aggregates (matter, feeling, perception, volitive formation) thus are the remaining states. When each SOE is dealt with the remaining 4 states, they can not be classified under the same aggregate, but can be classified under the same base and under the same element. Each is thus taken as ungrouped under 1 aggregate (volitive formation). Those remaining states from the same category as SOE, are then taken as aggrouped under 3 aggregates excluding *Nibbāna* (subtle matters, feeling, and perception), 1 base (ideation-base) and 1 element (ideation-element).

Chart 3.9. State of enquiry from a group of 6 clusters

States of enquiry (SOE) :	Subtle matters	Feeling	Perception	Volitive formation	Nibbāna	SOE (Ungrouped) Agr Bse El.	Those states (Aggrouped) Agr Bse El.
187 States which are Fetters; States which are both Fetters and the objects of Fetters; States which are both Fetters and associated with Fetters (3); States which are Bonds; States which are both Bonds and the objects of Bonds; States which are both Bonds and associated with Bonds (3); States which are Raging current; States which are both Raging current and objects of Raging current; States which are both Raging current and associated with Raging current. (3); States which are Yokes; States which are both Yokes and the objects of Yokes; States which are both Yokes and associated with Yokes (3); States which are Hindrances; States which are both Hindrances and objects of Hindrances; States which are both Hindrances and associated with Hindrances. (3); States which are attachments; States which are attachment and objects of attachments. (2)	16	1	1		1	all with the same answer 1 - -	all with the same answer 3 1 1

The dyad-cluster of defilements in preceding nos. 186 continue here with a further 6 clusters, namely, fetters, bonds, raging current, yokes, and hindrances,

A Perfect Knowledge of Mind-Body from the Abhidhamma (Dhātukathā)

except for attachments with only 2 states of enquiry. Altogether there are 17 states of enquiry, all of which belong to the aggregate of volitive formation.

When each of these SOE is enquired with its remaining 4 states, they can not be classified under the same aggregate, but can be all included under ideation-base and ideation-element. Thus, each of the SOE is taken as ungrouped under 1 aggregate (volitive formation). Those remaining states are in turn taken as aggrouped under 3 aggregates excluding *Nibbāna* (matter, feeling, perception), under 1 base (ideation-base), and under 1 element (ideation-element).

Chart 3.10. State of enquiry from mental factors

States of enquiry (SOE) :	These remaining states : Subtle matters: Feeling: Perception: Volitive formation: Nibbāna:		SOE (Ungrouped) Agr Bse El.	Those states (Aggrouped) Agr Bse El.
188. States which are mental factors; States associated with cittas; States conjoined with cittas; States which are conjoined with and originated from cittas; States which are conjoined with, originated from, and arise concurrently with cittas; States which are conjoined with, originated from, and arise consecutively with cittas. (6)	16	1	all with the same answer 3 - -	all with the same answer 1 1 1

These 6 subject matters of enquiry correspond to cetasikas, encompass the 3 aggregates of feeling, perception and volitive formation out of the 5 states. All of them are included under ideation-base and ideation-element. So, subtle matters and *Nibbāna* are taken as the only remaining states. When each of the states of enquiry is dealt with these remaining states, they can not be classified under the same aggregate but can be classified under the same base (ideation-base) and under the same element (ideation-element). Thus, each SOE is placed as ungrouped under 3 aggregates excluding *Nibbāna* (feeling, perception, and volitive formation). Those remaining states from the same category, which can be classified under the same aggregate, same base, and same element, are aggrouped under 1 aggregate (matter), 1 base (ideation-base) and 1 element (ideation-element).

III. Ungrouped and Aggrouped

Chart 3.11. State of enquiry from a group of 2 cittas

States of enquiry (SOE)	Subtle matters:	Feeling:	Perception:	Volitive formation:	Nibbāna:	SOE (Ungrouped) Agr Bse El.	Those states (Aggrouped) Agr Bse El.
189. 1. States which arise concurrently with cittas.						1 4 - -	0 1 1
2. States which arise successively with cittas.						1 4 - -	0 1 1

These remaining states are shown above the Nibbāna row.

These SOE consist of 52 mental factors, bodily intimation and vocal intimation. (See Table 1.8.8). So, each SOE belongs to the 4 out of 5 states, making *Nibbāna* the only remaining state. When each of the SOE is dealt with the remaining states, these states are taken as ungrouped under 4 aggregates (matter, feeling, perception, and volitive formation) because they can not be included under the same aggregate. *Nibbāna* as the remaining state, is aggrouped under no aggregate (marked as zero) because it is not an aggregate. *Nibbāna* is aggrouped under 1 base (ideation-base) and under 1 element (ideation-element).

Chart 3.12. State of enquiry from a group of 2 clusters

States of enquiry (SOE)	Subtle matters:	Feeling:	Perception:	Volitive formation:	Nibbāna:	SOE (Ungrouped) Agr Bse El.	Those states (Aggrouped) Agr Bse El.
190 States which are clinging; States which are both clinging and objects of clinging; States which are both clinging and associated with clinging; States which are corruptions; States which are both corruptions and objects of corruptions; States which are corruptions and are corrupted; States which are both corruptions and associated with corruptions. (7)	16	1	1		1	all with the same answer 1 - -	all with the same answer 3 1 1

These remaining states are shown above the Nibbāna row.

A Perfect Knowledge of Mind-Body from the Abhidhamma (Dhātukathā)

These 7 states of enquiry are the same with nos. 187 concerning the 6 clusters of fetters, bonds, raging current, yokes, and hindrances, all of which belong to the aggregate of volitive formation. When either SOE is enquired with the remaining 4 states, they can not be aggrouped under the same aggregate. So, each SOE is taken as ungrouped under 1 aggregate (volitive formation). Those remaining states are then aggrouped under 3 aggregates (subtle matters, feeling, perception) excluding *Nibbāna*, 1 base (ideation-base), and 1 element (ideation-element).

Key points from the text :

3 aggregates (feeling, perception, volitive formation), truths, 16 faculties,
14 dependent originations, 14 miscellaneous,
30 kinds from the 10 clusters of dyads,
2 kinds from the shorter dyads, 8 kinds (cetasikas and cittas) from the intermediate dyads.

Chart 3.13. Summary of the 90 states of enquiry by kinds

	Aggrouped:			SOE: subtle matters	SOE: feeling	SOE: perception	SOE: volitive formation	SOE: *nibbāna*	SOE: feeling, volitive formation	SOE: feeling, perception, volitive formation	SOE: subtle matters, volitive formation	SOE: *subtle matters,* feeling, perception, volitive formation	
	Agr	Bse	El.										
179.	3	1	1		1	1	3						5
180.	4	1	1					1					1
181.	2	1	1								1		1
182.	3	1	1	2	6		14						22
183.	2	1	1						1		3		4
184.	3	1	1		1	1	15		3				20
185.	4	1	1					2					2
186.	3	1	1				3						3
187.	3	1	1				17						17
188.	1	1	1							6			6
189.	0	1	1									2	2
190.	3	1	1				7						7
Number of states :				*2*	*6*	*4*	*4*	*2*	*8*	*2*	*3*	*59*	*90*

III. Ungrouped and Aggrouped

Going through the subject matters from the 12 groups of enquiry (nos. 179. to 190.), we derive at total 90 states as shown in Chart 3.13 above. The names of the 9 row headers on top of the chart indicate the 9 kinds of states to which the subject matters of enquiry belong (instead of tabulating it by remaining states as I had done for summary at end of Chapter 2). Of these 90 states of enquiry, 50 kinds are internal states while 40 kinds are external states appertaining to dyads. The 30 kinds obtained from the ten cluster of dyads, 2 kinds obtained from the shorter dyads, 8 kinds which are the mental factors obtained from the intermediate dyads — together they form the 40 external states of enquiry (30+2+8=40). The rest are the 50 internal states of enquiry.

From this same chart, we can determine there are 5 kinds of the number of states if we gather them in terms of aggrouped answers as shown in chart 3.14 below. The numbers indicated in those brackets represent the number of enquiring states corresponding to the text's paragraph nos. placed besides them on the left. The bracketed numbers also correspond to the answers under aggregates, bases, and elements in the aggrouped columns on the right side. These bracketed numbers of enquiring states add up to the totals in the rightmost column which sum up to 90 states. The columns on the right contain the numbers of states taken as aggrouped under aggregates, bases and elements, are from "those remaining states" which correspond to the respective groups of states of enquiry (i.e. those bracketed numbers on the left).

Chart 3.14. 90 states of enquiry by aggrouped answers

	(Aggrouped)			
	Agr	Bse	El.	
179 (5), 182 (22), 184 (20), 186 (3), 187 (17), 190 (7)	3	1	1	*74*
180 (1), 185 (2)	4	1	1	*3*
181 (1), 183 (4)	2	1	1	*5*
188 (6)	1	1	1	*6*
189 (2)	0	1	1	*2*
	Number of states :			**90**

CHAPTER 4

IV. Aggrouped and Aggrouped
(*Saṅgahitenasaṅgahita*)

Analysis of 69 states from 2 catechism

This Chapter deals with 69 states of enquiry which are also mentioned in Chapter 3 showing the kind of their remaining states. To ascertain how many aggregates, bases and elements are aggrouped under each state of enquiry, it is useful that readers also refer to the relevant internal and external enquiry of states and Chart 1 in Chapter 1.

The twofold method of aggrouping in this Chapter follows the rule that both the subject matters of enquiry and their remaining states from similar category, must be included under the same aggregate, under same base, and under same element in order to have the first aggrouped answers. Because the states of enquiry and the remaining states from the same category, both belong to the same aggregate, same base and same element, these states can now be compared, reciprocated and interchanged permissibly. It is on this basis that *those* remaining states can be classified with *these* states of enquiry to give second aggrouped answers for the former. The same as in Chapter 3, states from the aggregates of gross matters and consciousness are excluded from being treated as states of enquiry because they consist of different bases and different elements. Either of which can not be classified under the same base and under the same element which falls outside the set rule for this fourth method.

For example, according to the nos. 191 in the text,

"Origin-truth is classified with "*these states*"; Path-truth is classified with "*these states*", both under the same aggregate, under the same base, and under the same element. "*Those states*" are classified with "*these states*" under the same aggregate, under the same base, and under the same element."

This kind of phrase describing "*these states*" and "*those states*" repeats throughout the rest of the chapters. Sometimes it is not easy to understand the differences. Hence, I provide a simple flow diagram below to illustrate how the initial classification and the reverse classification between the states of enquiry and the remaining states is possible only in two aggroupings because they both belong to the same aggregate, the same base, and the same element.

IV. Aggrouped and Aggrouped

Diagram 4.1. Flow process between SOE and the remaining states on comparable basis to give two-way aggrouped results

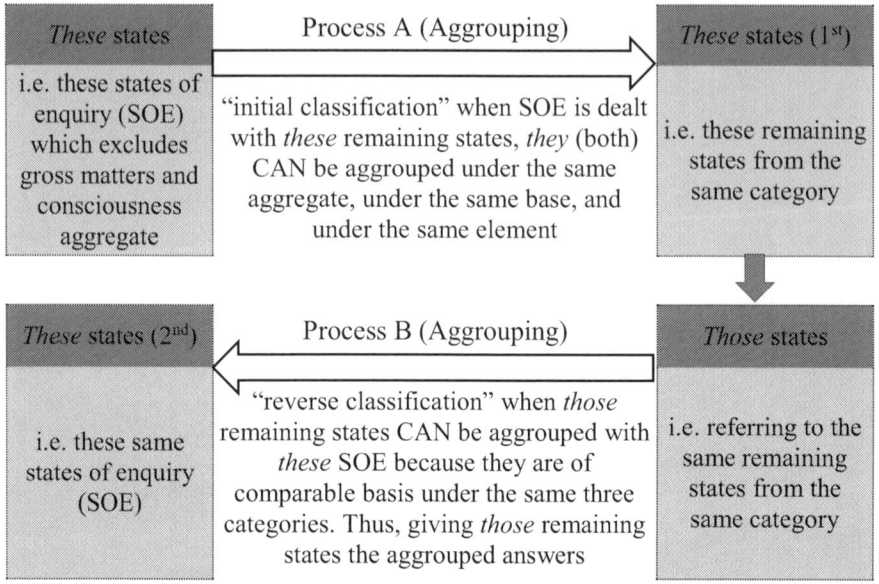

The following abbreviations are used in all the charts in Chapter 4.

Agr	: Aggregates
Bse	: Bases
El.	: Elements
SOE	: States of enquiry
M.	: Matters
Gr	: Gross matters
S.	: Subtle matters
F.	: Feeling aggregate
P.	: Perception aggregate
V.	: Volitive formation aggregate
N.	: *Nibbāna*
cons.	: consciousness

The symbol † used in all the following charts denotes that the states of enquiry (SOE) are classified with the remaining states under the same aggregate, under the same base, and under the same element.

A Perfect Knowledge of Mind-Body from the Abhidhamma (Dhātukathā)

39 internal states of enquiry

Chart 4.1. States of enquiry from 2 truths

	† *These* remaining states :			
	Nibbāna: Volitive formation: Perception: Feeling: Subtle matters:		(A) SOE classified with *These* remaining states (Aggrouped)	(B) "*Those*" remaining states classified with *these* SOE (Aggrouped)
These states of enquiry (SOE):			Agr Bse El.	Agr Bse El.
191 1. Origin-truth (of suffering)		49	1 1 1	1 1 1
2. Path-truth (leading out)		50	1 1 1	1 1 1

These 2 states of enquiry are also mentioned in Chapter 3. We know from preceding example nos. 179 that both Origin-truth (the cause of suffering) and Path-truth (the path leading to the cessation of suffering) belong to the aggregate of volitive formation. Origin-truth is bound by the greed mental factor. Path-truth corresponds to Noble Eightfold Path which consists of the 4 supramundane path-consciousness.

Let's take Origin-truth as an example. In Chart 4.1, the initial process designated as (A) means that when Origin-truth as the subject matter of enquiry is first dealt with *these* remaining 49 mental states from volitive formation aggregate (i.e. 50 excluding greed-*cetasika*), they both are aggrouped under the same aggregate (volitive formation), under the same base (ideation-base), and under the same element (ideation-element).

The reverse process designated as (B) means that *those* remaining 49 states (herein *these* remaining states and *those* remaining states are referring to the same states) are in turn dealt with *these* states of enquiry (the Origin-truth as SOE), and *those* remaining states are taken aggrouped under the same aggregate (volitive formation), under the same base (ideation-base), and under the same element (ideation-element). Because of a common basis of comparison in regard to the three categories, these states of enquiry and those remaining states can legitimately correlate and interchange.

As for Path-truth, 50 mental factors of the volitive formation aggregate become the remaining states, and which are conjoined and arisen with consciousness. The twofold classifications in this case are to be dealt with in similar manner as explained in Path-truth above, which gives the same twofold aggrouped results.

IV. Aggrouped and Aggrouped

Chart 4.2. States of enquiry from the 15 faculties

	† *These* remaining states: Nibbāna: Volitive formation: Perception: Feeling: Subtle matters:	(A) SOE classified with *These* remaining states (Aggrouped) Agr Bse El.	(B) *"Those"* remaining states classified with SOE (Aggrouped) Agr Bse El.
These states of enquiry (SOE):			
1. Femininity-faculty	15		
2. Masculinity-faculty	15		
3. Bodily pleasure-faculty	4		
4. Bodily pain-faculty	4		
5. Joy-faculty	4		
6. Melancholy-faculty	4		
7. Equanimity-faculty	4		
8. Confidence-faculty	49	all with the same answer 1 1 1	all with the same answer 1 1 1
9. Effort-faculty-faculty	49		
10. Mindfulness-faculty	49		
11. Concentration-faculty	49		
12. Wisdom-faculty	49		
13. "I-shall-comprehend-the-unknown" faculty	49		
14. The "higher knowledge" faculty	49		
15. The "final knower" faculty	49		

Referring to the above chart, each of the states of enquiry and their remaining states are classifiable to be aggrouped under the same aggregate, under the same base, and under the same element. How are the remaining states being derived?

Femininity-faculty and masculinity-faculty both belong to subtle matters, thus the 15 subtle matters are taken as the remaining physical states (16-1=15). It is for this reason the states of feeling aggregate, perception aggregate, volitive formation aggregate, and *Nibbāna* are not taken as the remaining states. This same rationale applies to the rest of the SOE.

The respective faculties of bodily pleasure, bodily pain, joy, melancholy, and equanimity, are taken as a fixed unit of 5 feeling faculties. So, when each of them is taken as a state of enquiry, the other 4 feeling faculties are correspondingly treated as the remaining 4 states.

These next 8 SOE all come under voilitive formation aggregate. Confidence faculty contains faith-*cetasika*; effort faculty contains energy-*cetasika*; mindfulness faculty contains mindfulness-*cetasika*; concentration faculty contains one-pointedness-*cetasika*; wisdom-faculty and the last three

A Perfect Knowledge of Mind-Body from the Abhidhamma (Dhātukathā)

knowledge-oriented faculties each contains wisdom-*cetasika*. Each of these last 8 SOE is accompanied by 49 cetasikas (50 excluding the respective *cetasika*).

When each of these states of enquiry is dealt with those remaining states on the initial classification, they are first aggrouped under 1 aggregate (matter), 1 base (ideation-base), and 1 element (ideation-element). Because of such comparable basis and interchangeability with respect to the three categories, reverse-classification is possible. Thus, those remaining states are classified with the corresponding SOE. Those remaining states are taken as aggrouped under 1 aggregate (matter), 1 base (ideation-base), and 1 element (ideation-element).

Chart 4.3. States of enquiry from 11 dependent originations, 11 others

	† *These* remaining states:				(A) SOE classified with *These* remaining states (Aggrouped)			(B) "*Those*" remaining states classified with SOE (Aggrouped)		
These states of enquiry (SOE):	Nibbāna:	Volitive formation:	Perception:	Feeling:	Matters:	Agr	Bse	El.	Agr	Bse	El.
192 16. Ignorance.					49						
17. Conditioned by ignorance, is Volitive Formation.					49						
18. Conditioned by six bases, is Contact.					49						
19. Conditioned by feeling, is Craving.					49						
20. Conditioned by craving, is Clinging.					48						
21. Action-becoming.					49						
22. Sorrow.				4	49						
23. Lamentation.		Gr									
24. Suffering.				4	49	all with the same answer 1 1 1			all with the same answer 1 1 1		
25. Melancholy.				4	49						
26. Despair.					49						
27. Application of Mindfulness.					49						
28. Right Striving.					49						
29. The Illimitables.					48						
30. The 5 Faculties.					45						
31. The 5 Powers.					45						
32. 7 Factors of Enlightenment.					43						
33. Noble Eightfold Path.					42						
34. Contact.					49						
35. Volition.					49						
36. Decision.					49						
37. Attention.					49						

IV. Aggrouped and Aggrouped

In the chart above, except for lamentation which is treated as audible object as a result of wailing and which belongs to gross matter, the other 21 SOE all belong to voilitive formation aggregate. Ignorance contains delusion-*cetasika*; volitive formation contains volition-*cetasika*; contact includes contact-*cetasika*; craving includes greed-*cetasika*; clinging includes two cetasikas of greed and wrong view; action-becoming (*kammabhava*) contains volition-*cetasika*; sorrow, suffering and melancholy belong to the group of 5 feeling faculties, each of which contains also hatred-*cetasika*; despair contains occasionally hatred-*cetasika*; the four foundation/application of mindfulness contain mindfulness-*cetasika*; the four right striving contain energy-*cetasika*; the four Illimitables contain the cetasikas of compassion (*karunā*) and altruistic joy (*muditā*); the 5 faculties contain 5 cetasikas of faith, effort, mindfulness, onepointedness, and non-delusion; the 5 powers contain the same 5 cetasikas as in the 5 faculties; the 7 factors of enlightenment contain the 7 cetasikas of mindfulness, non-delusion, effort, zest, calmness, one-pointedness, and equanimity; noble eightfold path includes the 8 cetasikas of mindfulness, non-delusion, 3 abstinences, effort, mindfulness, and one-pointedness; contact includes contact-*cetasika*, volition includes volition-*cetasika*; decision includes decision-*cetasika*; attention includes decision–*cetasika*. Their respective remaining states of mental factors are shown in the chart above under the column of volitive formation aggregate (i.e. by taking 50 cetasikas belonging to volitive formation aggregate, subtracts the respective number of cetasikas corresponding to each SOE).

The state of lamentation is taken as audible object, belongs to gross matter. In this regard, subtle matters, the three mental aggregates and *Nibbāna* can not be taken as its remaining states. The reason being these states are not aggroupable with SOE in conformity with the classification rule set for this chapter. Likewise, audible object base and audible object element can not be the remaining states because of homogeneity of the same kind. The other 2 audible objects — non-lamented audible object and temperature-born audible object— become its remaining states. When lamentation is dealt with these remaining states, they are taken as aggrouped under 1 aggregate (matter), under 1 base (audible object object), and under 1 element (audible object element). In turn, because of comparable basis, these remaining states can be classified with state of lamentation under same three categories, having similar aggrouped answers.

In the group of five feeling-faculties, sorrow and suffering belong to the bodily displeasure faculty, while melancholy belongs to melancholy-faculty. They are feeling faculties, and so the corresponding four member faculties are taken as the remaining 4 states. Alternatively, since sorrow, suffering and melancholy also contain hatred-*cetasika*, the remaining 49 states of mental factors also become the remaining states. When each of these states of enquiry is dealt with those remaining states, they are taken as aggrouped under 1 aggregate (feeling aggregate), under 1 base (ideation-base), and under 1 element

A Perfect Knowledge of Mind-Body from the Abhidhamma (Dhātukathā)

(ideation-element). Because of comparability, those remaining states are also aggrouped with each SOE under same three categories and having same answers.

For the rest of the 18 states of enquiry, each of them is dealt with its remaining states of mental factors and classified under the same aggregate (volitive formation), under the same base (ideation-base), and under the same element (ideation-element). Because of interchangeability under the same three categories, those remaining states are also classified with the corresponding SOE, and similarly taken as aggrouped under 1 aggregate (volitive formation), 1 base (ideation-base), and 1 element (ideation-element).

30 states of enquiry from Dhammasaṅgaṇīmātikā dyads

Chart 4.4. States of enquiry from 30 kinds of dyads (10 clusters)

192 *These* states of enquiry (SOE):	† *Those* remaining states (cetasikas in volitive formation aggregate)	(A) SOE classified with *These* remaining states (Aggrouped) Agr Bse El.	(B) "*Those*" remaining states classified with SOE (Aggrouped) Agr Bse El.
38. States which are root causes.	44		
39. States which are root causes and having root causes.	44		
40. States which are root causes and also associated with them.	44		
41. States which are *defilement*.	47		
42. States which are both defilement and objects of defilement.	47		
43. States which are both defilement and associated with defilement.	47		
44. States which are *fetters*.	42	all with the same answer 1 1 1	all with the same answer 1 1 1
45. States which are both fetters and objects of fetters.	42		
46. States which are both fetters and associated with fetters.	42		
47. States which are *bonds*.	47		
48. States which are both bonds and objects of bonds.	47		
49. States which are both bonds and associated with bonds.	48		
Repeats step 42, 43 & 44 for *Raging current* (3).	47,47,47		
Repeats step 42, 43 & 44 for *Yokes* (3).	47,47,47		

IV. Aggrouped and Aggrouped

Repeats step 42, 43 & 44 for *Hindrances* (3).	42,42,42
Repeats step 42 & 43 for *Attachment* (2).	49, 49
Repeats step 42, 43 & 44 for *Clinging* (3).	48,48,48
64. States which are corruptions.	40
65. States which are both corruptions and objects of corruptions.	40
66. States which are corruptions and are corrupted.	40
67. States which are both corruptions and associated with corruptions.	40

These 30 states of enquiry as shown in the chart above all belong to volitive formation aggregate. The following describes the respective cetasikas belong to each of these states, as well as listing out their remaining states of cetasikas.

38. States which are root causes — include the 6 cetasikas of greed, hatred, delusion, non-greed, non-hatred, non-delusion. Thus, the remaining states are the 44 states of mental factors (i.e. 50-6=44).
39. States which are root causes and having root causes — include the 6 roots causes (but excluding delusion present at the 2 delusion-rooted cittas). Thus, there are remaining 44 states of mental factors.
40. States which are root causes and are also associated with root causes — same as in nos. 39 above.
41. States which are defilement — include the 3 factors of greed (or sensual desire), wrong view, and delusion, present at the 12 unwholesome cittas. Thus, the other 47 mental factors become the remaining states (i.e. 50-3=47).
42. States which are both defilement and objects of defilement — same as in nos. 41 above.
43. States which are both defilement and associated with defilement — same as in nos. 41 above.
44. States which are fetters — include the 8 states of fetters (8 as in Dhammasaṅgaṇi), namely, greed, ill-will, conceit, wrong view, doubt, envy, avarice, ignorance. Thus, the other 42 cetasikas become the remaining states, i.e. (50-8=42).
45. States which are both fetters and objects of fetters — same as in 44. above.
46. States both are fetters and associated with fetters — same as in 44. above.
47. States which are bonds — include the 3 states of bonds, namely, greed, hatred, and wrong view. Thus, 47 cetasikas become the remaining states.
48. States which are bonds and are also objects of bonds — same as in 47. above.
49. States which are bonds and are also associated with bonds — include the 2 states of bonds; greed and wrong view present at the 4 greed-rooted cittas associated with wrong view. Thus, giving 48 cetasikas as the remaining states (i.e. 50-2=48).

A Perfect Knowledge of Mind-Body from the Abhidhamma (Dhātukathā)

50. States which are raging current — same as that of defilement in 41. above.
51. States which are both raging current and objects of raging current — same as that of defilement in nos. 42 above.
52. States which are both raging current and associated with raging current — same as that of defilement in nos. 43 above.
53. States which are yokes — same as that of defilement in nos. 41 above.
54. States which are both yokes and objects of yokes — same as that of defilement in nos. nos. 42 above.
55. States which are both yokes and associated with yokes — same as that of defilement in nos. 43 above.
56. States which are hindrances — include the 8 states of hindrances, namely, restlessness, greed, hatred, delusion, worry, doubt, sloth, and torpor. Thus, the other 42 cetasikas become the remaining states.
57. States which are both hindrances and objects of hindrances — same as in nos. 56 above.
58. States which are both hindrances and associated with hindrances — same as in nos. 56 above.
59. States which are attachment — include the wrong view *cetasika* (*diṭṭhi*) present at the 4 greed-rooted cittas associated with wrong view. Thus, giving 49 cetasikas as the remaining states.
60. States which are both attachment and objects of attachment — same as in nos. 59 above.
61. States which are clinging — include the 2 states of clinging (as in Dhammasaṅgaṇi), namely, *kāma* (sensual desire) and *diṭṭhi* (wrong view), identical to greed-*cetasika* and wrong view-*cetasika*. Thus, the other 48 cetasikas become the remaining states.
62. States which are both clinging and objects of clinging — same as in 61 above.
63. States which are both clinging and associated with clinging — same as in nos. 61 above.
64. States which are corruptions — include the 10 states of corruptions, namely, the 10 cetasikas of greed, hatred, delusion, conceit, wrong view, doubt, sloth, restlessness, shamelessness, and the guiltlessness of conscience. Thus, giving 40 remaining states.
65. States which are both corruptions and objects of corruptions — same as in nos. 64 above.
66. States which are corruptions and are corrupted — same as in nos. 64 above.
67. States which are both corruptions and associated with corruptions — same as in nos. 64 above.

These abovementioned remaining states of mental factors are shown in the chart above under the column of volitive formation aggregate, corresponding to each state matter of enquiry. When each of these SOE is enquired with its remaining states, they can be aggrouped under the same aggregate (volitive formation), under the same base (ideation-base), and under the same element

IV. Aggrouped and Aggrouped

(ideation-element). In turn, on a comparable basis and reciprocity, those remaining states are also taken as aggrouped with each SOE under the same aggregate (volitive formation), under the same base (ideation-base), and under the same element (ideation-element).

Key points from the text :

2 truths, 15 faculties, 11 dependent originations, next 11, 30 kinds from clusters

In the two table below, the number in the brackets represents the number of enquiries belong to the associated text paragraph nos.

Table 4.1 Summary of the 69 states of enquiry by subject matters

Text's paragraph nos.
(with numbers of enquiries):   Subject matter:

191 (2)	2	Truths
192 (15)	15	Faculties
192 (11)	11	Dependent Originations
192 (11)	11	Others
192 (30)	30	Ten dyad-clusters

Total = 69 states

Table 4.2 Summary of the 69 states of enquiry by answers

			† *These* remaining states				first aggrouped answers			second aggrouped answers		
			M.	S.	F.	P.	V.	Agr	Bse	El.	Agr	Bse	El.
1.	191 (1), 192 (25)	26					49	1	1	1	1	1	1
2.	191 (1)	1					50	1	1	1	1	1	1
3.	192 (6)	6					48	1	1	1	1	1	1
4.	192 (11)	11					47	1	1	1	1	1	1
5.	192 (2)	2					45	1	1	1	1	1	1
6.	192 (3)	3					44	1	1	1	1	1	1
7.	192 (1)	1					43	1	1	1	1	1	1
8.	192 (7)	7					42	1	1	1	1	1	1
9.	192 (4)	4					40	1	1	1	1	1	1
10.	192 (2)	2		15				1	1	1	1	1	1
11.	192 (5)	5			4			1	1	1	1	1	1
12.	192 (1)	1	Gr					1	1	1	1	1	1

Total 69 states in   **69**
12 kinds of answer

CHAPTER 5

V. Ungrouped and Ungrouped
(*Asaṅgahitenāsaṅgahita*)

Analysis of 257 states from 35 catechism

A total of 257 states of enquiry which come under 5 aggregates, form the subject matter of this Chapter. Of these 257 subject matters of enquiry, 99 are interior states while 158 belong to external states of enquiry. For all the analytical exercises in this Chapter, it is useful to refer to Chart 1 in Chapter 1.

The analytics to be observed when enquiring with these 257 states is that, these are states which can not be classified with their remaining states under the same aggregate, under the same base, and under the same element. Also, those remaining states are delimited not only by the states of enquiry, but also by their co-adjunct states and "possible states", all of them may be conforming with the classification requirement. The same rule applies to the twofold ungrouping. In this regard, states which are connate with the mentality-materiality quality of consciousness aggregate and subtle matters, or that which embrace the five aggregates, are ruled out from being states of enquiry. Consciousness aggregate and subtle matters, together with their co-adjunct states and possible states, encompass all five aggregates which downrightly invalidate the method of twofold ungrouping. For example, indeterminate states which come under five aggregates, leaves no more other aggregates to be taken as states of comparison. For this reason, the other 114 of the total 371 states are excluded.

The following abbreviations are used in all the charts throughout this Chapter. Those italicised letters in the charts denote the possible states for classification.

Agr : Aggregates
Bse : Bases
El. : Elements
Mat : Matters
Gr : Gross matters
Sb : Subtle matters
Cons. : Consciousness
SOE : States of enquiry

A flow diagram below demonstrates the relationship between *these* states (1st) and *those* states, *those* states and *these* states (2nd) which are the standard phrases used throughout this Chapter. This diagram demonstrates using two comparative processes, A and B, to distinguish their differences.

V. Ungrouped and Ungrouped

Diagram 5.1. SOE and remaining states on incomparable basis giving two ungrouped answers

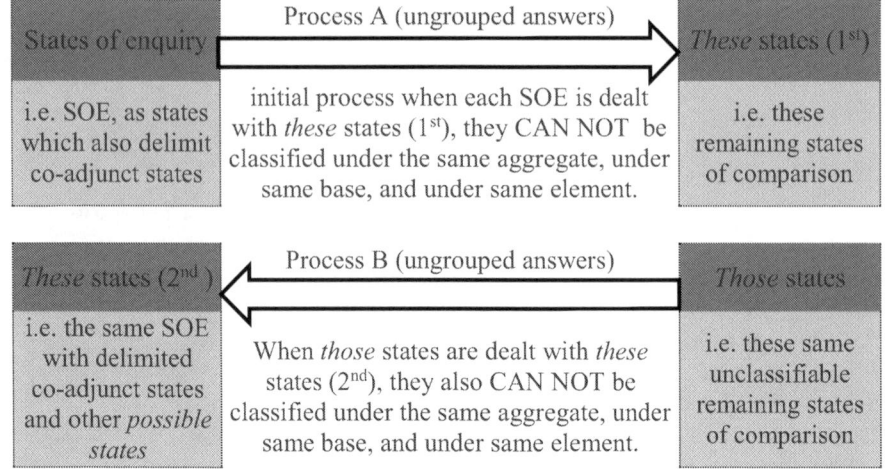

99 internal states of enquiry

Chart 5.1. States of enquiry from matter aggregate

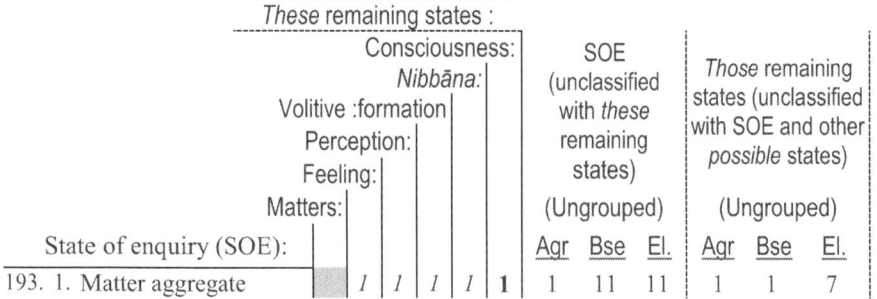

According to the text:

"Matter aggregate is not classified with "*these states*" under the same aggregate, under the same base, and under the same element. *Those states* are not classified with "*these states*" under the same aggregate, under the same base, and under the same element. *Those states* are not aggrouped under 1 aggregate, under 1 base, and under 7 elements".

Herein, matter aggregate as the state of enquiry has "delimiting" effect because it comes under 1 aggregate (12 gross matters + 16 subtle matters), 11 bases (10 gross bases + ideation base), 11 elements (10 gross elements + ideation element). I designate it as "delimiter" SOE because subtle matters as part of 28

A Perfect Knowledge of Mind-Body from the Abhidhamma (Dhātukathā)

matters, are contained by ideation-base and ideation-element, and they meet the classification condition. Ideation-base and ideation-element encompass aggregates of feeling, perception, and volitive formation, and which can so be classified by aggregates. In this respect, the "delimiter" SOE determines what forms the unclassifiable remaining states. Thus, the only unclassified remaining states turn to consciousness aggregate.

In the initial process, marked as (A) in diagram 5.1 above, matter aggregate (SOE, which has the effect of demarcating co-adjunct states) can not be classified with *these* states (consciousness aggregate as remaining states of comparison) under the same aggregate, under the same base, and under the same element. They are unclassified and thus the SOE is taken as ungrouped under 1 aggregate (matter), under 11 bases (10 gross bases, ideation-base), and under 11 elements (10 gross elements, ideation-element). Ideation-base and ideation-element are included because 16 subtle matters come under them.

In the second process, marked as (B) in diagram 5.1 above, *those* states (i.e. consciousness aggregate as unclassified remaining states) are in turn not classified with *these* states (i.e. 2nd *these* states in the text which are the same SOE but with its co-adjunct states and possible states) under the same aggregate, under the same base, and under the same element. Therefore, *those* unclassified remaining states (consciousness aggregate) are taken as ungrouped under 1 aggregate (consciousness), under 1 base (mind-base), and under 7 elements (7 consciousness-elements).

Diagram below demarcates the areas contained by 1st *these* states, 2nd *these* states, *those* states, co-adjuncts, possible states, and the two ungrouped answers.

Diagram 5.2. The 1st *these* states, *those* states, and 2nd *these* states

5 Aggregates		12 Bases	18 Elements
Matter aggregate as SOE	Gross matters	10 gross bases	10 gross elements
	Subtle matters	Ideation base	Ideation element
Feeling aggregate			
Perception aggregate			
Volitive formation aggregate			
Nibbāna (non-aggregate)			
Consciousness aggregate		Mind base	7 consciousness elements

- State of enquiry (SOE) = 2nd *these* states
- Co-adjunct states delimited by matter aggregate (can be classified)
- Possible states delimited by co-adjunct states (can be classified)
- Unclassified remaining states = 1st *these* states = *those* states
- Answers from first ungrouped
- Answers from second ungrouped

V. Ungrouped and Ungrouped

Subtle matters come under ideation-base and ideation-element, and so the latter become *co-adjunct states* of the 16 subtle matters. In turn, the three mental aggregates of feeling, perception and volitive formation, including *Nibbāna* are also contained by these *co-adjunct states* (ideation-base and ideation-element). Thus, these three mental aggregates and *Nibbāna* become the *possible states* of classification to matter aggregate.

Chart 5.2. States of enquiry from 3 mental aggregates

		These remaining states: Consciousness: *Nibbāna:* Volitive formation: Perception: Feeling: Matters:					SOE (unclassified with *these* remaining states) (Ungrouped)			*Those* remaining states (unclassified with SOE and other *possible* states) (Ungrouped)		
States of enquiry (SOE):							Agr	Bse	El.	Agr	Bse	El.
194. 1. Feeling aggregate.	Gr		*1*	*1*	*1*	1						
2. Perception aggregate.	Gr	*1*		*1*	*1*	1	1	1	1	2	11	17
3. Volitive Formation agr.	Gr	*1*	*1*		*1*	1						

These three aggregates are contained by ideation-base and ideation-element. Subtle matters, *Nibbāna*, and the other two mental aggregates are included as the possible states to each of these SOE. Thus, 12 gross matters and consciousness aggregate become the remaining states which, in a sense, is "delimited" by these possible states of classification.

When feeling aggregate is dealt with *these* remaining states, they can not be classified under the same aggregate, under the same base, and under the same element. Feeling aggregate is thus taken as ungrouped under 1 aggregate (feeling), under 1 base (ideation-base), and under 1 element (ideation-element).

Because *those* remaining states are not classified with feeling aggregate including its possible states, under the same aggregate, under the same base, and under the same element, *those* remaining states (12 gross matters and consciousness aggregate) are placed as ungrouped under 2 aggregates (matter, consciousness), under 11 bases (10 gross bases, mind-base), and under 17 elements (10 gross elements, 7 consciousness-elements). The other two states of enquiry are to be dealt with in the same manner with similar results.

A Perfect Knowledge of Mind-Body from the Abhidhamma (Dhātukathā)

Chart 5.3. States of enquiry from groups of consciousness aggregate

States of enquiry (SOE):	*These* remaining states: Consciousness: *Nibbāna:* Volitive formation; Perception: Feeling: Matters:					SOE (unclassified with *these* remaining states) (Ungrouped) Agr Bse El.	*Those* remaining states (unclassified with SOE and other *possible* states) (Ungrouped) Agr Bse El.
195. 1. Consciousness aggregate 2. Mind-base 3. Eye-cons. elements 4. Ear-cons. elements 5. Nose-cons. elements 6. Tongue-cons. elements 7. Body-cons. elements 8. Mind-element 9. Mind-cons. elements 10. Mind-faculty	28	1	1	1	1	all with the same answer 1 1 7	all with the same answer 4 11 11

These SOE form a mix group of 1 aggregate (consciousness), 1 base (mind-base), 7 elements (7 consciousness elements), and mind-faculty. They all come under consciousness aggregate associated with 89 cittas. All these states of enquiry are taken as consciousness aggregate so that comparison on the same basis as aggregates can be done. The 28 matters, aggregates of feeling, perception, volitive formation, and *Nibbāna* become the remaining states.

Let's take consciousness aggregate as an example. When consciousness aggregate is dealt with *these* remaining states, they can not be classified under the same aggregate, under the same base, and under the same element. Thus, consciousness aggregate is taken as ungrouped under 1 aggregate (consciousness), under 1 base (mind-base), and under 7 elements (7 consciousness elements).

As *those* remaining states are not classifiable with consciousness aggregate under the same aggregate, under the same base, and under the same element, *those* remaining states are placed as ungrouped under 4 aggregates excluding *Nibbāna* (matter, feeling, perception, volitive formation), under 11 bases (10 gross bases ideation-base), and under 17 elements (10 gross elements, ideation-element). The other states of enquiry are to be dealt with in this manner with similar answers.

V. Ungrouped and Ungrouped

Chart 5.4. States of enquiry from gross bases and gross elements

States of enquiry (SOE):	*These* remaining states: Consciousness: Nibbāna: Volitive formation: Perception: Feeling: Matters:						SOE (unclassified with *these* remaining states) (Ungrouped) Agr Bse El.	*Those* remaining states unclassified with SOE and other *possible* states (Ungrouped) Agr Bse El.
196. Eye-base; Ear-base; Nose-base; Tongue-base; Body-base; Vision-base; Sound-base; Odour-base; Taste-base; Tangible-base. (10) Eye-element; Ear-element; Nose-element; Tongue-element; Body-element; Vision-element; Sound-element; Odour-element; Taste-element; Tangible-element (10).	Sb	1	1	1	1	1	all with the same answer 1 1 1	all with the same answer 4 2 8

These 20 states of enquiry (10 gross bases and the 10 gross elements) belong to 12 gross matters. These gross bases and gross elements are also the sensitive organs and sensitive objects. The remaining states to each of these states of enquiry are the subtle matters, 4 mental aggregates, and *Nibbāna*. Herein subtle matters are taken co-adjunct states to these gross matters.

Let's take eye-base as an example. When eye-base as the state of enquiry is dealt with these remaining states, they can not be classified under the same aggregate, under the same base, and under the same element. The eye-base is thus taken as ungrouped under 1 aggregate (matter), 1 base (eye-base), and 1 elements (eye-element). Following the same manner of enquiry, ear-base is taken as ungrouped under 1 aggregate (matter), 1 base (ear-base), and 1 elements (ear-element). The rest of the subject matters of enquiry are to be dealt with the remaining states in the similar manner with the same answers as the first ungrouped

Those remaining states which are unclassified with eye-base under the same aggregate, under the same base, and under the same element, are taken as ungrouped under 4 aggregates excluding *Nibbāna* (feeling, perception, volitive formation, consciousness), under 2 bases (ideation-base, mind-base), and under 8 elements (ideation-element, 7 consciousness-elements). The rest of the subject matters of enquiry are to be dealt with in this manner with similar answer for the second ungrouped.

A Perfect Knowledge of Mind-Body from the Abhidhamma (Dhātukathā)

Chart 5.5. States of enquiry from a group of 5

						SOE (unclassified with *these* remaining states) (Ungrouped)			*Those* remaining states (unclassified with SOE and other *possible* states) (Ungrouped)		
							These remaining states: Consciousness: Nibbāna: Volitive formation: Perception: Feeling: Matters:				
States of enquiry (SOE):						Agr	Bse	El.	Agr	Bse	El.
197. 1. Ideation-base	Gr					1					
2. Ideation-element	Gr					1	all with same answer		all with same answer		
3. Femininity-faculty	Gr					1					
4. Masculinity-faculty	Gr					1	4	1	1	1	1	7
5. Vitality-faculty	Gr					1					

Both ideation-base and ideation-element include 16 subtle matters, *Nibbāna*, aggregates of feeling, perception, and volitive formation. Both male and female faculties belong to subtle matters. Vitality-faculty has both physical and mental life which comes under subtle matters and aggregate of volitive formation. But, the last 3 SOE are operating on ideation-base and ideation-element. Thus, leaving gross matters and consciousness aggregate as remaining states.

Take ideation-base for example. When ideation-base is dealt with mind-base, they can not be classified under the same aggregate, under the same base, and under the same element. Ideation-base and its co-adjuncts are taken as ungrouped under 4 aggregates excluding *Nibbāna* (matters, feeling, perception, volitive formation), under 1 base (ideation-base), and under 1 element (ideation-element). The same works out for the other states of enquiry. Those remaining states which are unclassified with each SOE including their co-adjuncts and those possible states, are taken as ungrouped under 1 aggregate (consciousness-aggregate), under 1 base (mind-base), and under 7 elements (7 consciousness-elements).

Chart 5.6. States of enquiry from 3 truths

							SOE (unclassified with *these* remaining states) (Ungrouped)			*Those* remaining states (unclassified with SOE and other *possible* states) (Ungrouped)		
							These remaining states: Consciousness: Nibbāna: Volitive formation: Perception: Feeling: Matters:					
States of enquiry (SOE):							Agr	Bse	El.	Agr	Bse	El.
198. 1. Origin-truth (suffering).	Gr	1	1		1	1	1	1	1			
2. Path-truth (leading out).	Gr	1	1		1	1	1	1	1	2	11	17
3. Cessation-truth.	Gr	1	1	1		1	0	1	1			

V. Ungrouped and Ungrouped

Origin-truth and Path-truth come under the aggregate of volitive formation (see nos. 179 and 191) while Cessation-truth comes under *Nibbāna* (see nos. 180). All three SOE are contained by ideation-base and ideation-element. In this case, subtle matters, feeling aggregate, perception aggregate, and *Nibbāna* (except for cessation-truth) are the possible states for classification. Thus, 12 gross matters and consciousness aggregate become the remaining states.

When origin-truth is enquired with these remaining states, it is not classified with these remaining states under the same aggregate, under the same base, and under the same element. Origin-truth is thus taken as ungrouped under 1 aggregate (volitive formation), under 1 base (ideation-base), and under 1 element (ideation-element).

Those remaining states are in turn not classified with origin-truth including those possible states under the same aggregate, under the same base, and under the same element. Therefore, those remaining states are taken as ungrouped under 2 aggregates (matter and consciousness), 11 bases (10 gross bases, mind-base), and 17 elements (10 gross elements, 7 consciousness-elements).

The rest of the subject matters of enquiry are to be dealt with in this manner with similar answers for the twofold ungrouped.

Chart 5.7. States of enquiry from 5 sense faculties

States of enquiry (SOE):	*These* remaining states: Matters:	Feeling:	Perception:	Volitive formation:	*Nibbāna*:	Consciousness:	SOE (unclassified with *these* remaining states) (Ungrouped) Agr	Bse	El.	*Those* remaining states (unclassified with SOE and other *possible* states) (Ungrouped) Agr	Bse	El.
199. Vision-faculty; Hearing-faculty; Smell-faculty; Taste-faculty; Touch-faculty. (5)		1	1	1	1	1	1	1	1	4	2	8

The 5 faculties are also the 5 sensitive organs, 5 sense elements, which are gross matters. Subtle matters become the co-adjuncts to these gross physical states. The remaining states thus turn to 4 mental aggregates and *Nibbāna*. The analysis and answers for the twofold ungrouped are to follow the same as in preceding nos. 196.

A Perfect Knowledge of Mind-Body from the Abhidhamma (Dhātukathā)

Chart 5.8. States of enquiry from next 13 faculties, etc

		These remaining states:					SOE (unclassified with *these* remaining states) (Ungrouped)			*Those* remaining states (unclassified with SOF and other *possible* states) (Ungrouped)		
States of enquiry (SOE):	Matters:	Feeling:	Perception:	Volitive formation:	Nibbāna:	Consciousness:	Agr	Bse	El.	Agr	Bse	El.
200. 1. Carnal pleasure-faculty.	Gr		*1*	*1*	*1*	1						
2. Carnal pain-faculty.	Gr		*1*	*1*	*1*	1						
3. Joy-faculty.	Gr		*1*	*1*	*1*	1						
4. Melancholy-faculty.	Gr		*1*	*1*	*1*	1						
5. Equanimity-faculty.	Gr		*1*	*1*	*1*	1						
6. Confidence-faculty.	Gr	*1*	*1*		*1*	1						
7. Effort-faculty-faculty.	Gr	*1*	*1*		*1*	1						
8. Mindfulness-faculty.	Gr	*1*	*1*		*1*	1	all with the same answer 1 1 1			all with the same answer 2 11 17		
9. Concentration-faculty.	Gr	*1*	*1*		*1*	1						
10. Wisdom-faculty.	Gr	*1*	*1*		*1*	1						
11. "I-shall-comprehend-the-unknown" faculty.	Gr	*1*	*1*		*1*	1						
12. The "higher knowledge" faculty.	Gr	*1*	*1*		*1*	1						
13. "Final Knower" faculty.	Gr	*1*	*1*		*1*	1						
14. Ignorance.	Gr	*1*	*1*		*1*	1						
15. Ignorance conditions Volitive formation.	Gr	*1*	*1*		*1*	1						

The italicised *1* in the chart above denote the possible states for classification.

The first 5 feeling faculties belong to feeling aggregate, are all contained by ideation-base and ideation-element (giving subtle matters, *Nibbāna*, perception and volitive formation aggregates as possible states for classification). The remaining states are gross matters and consciousness aggregate. The next 10 (8 faculties, 2 dependent origination factors) belong to volitive formation, leaving subtle matters, *Nibbāna*, feeling and perception aggregates are possible states.

Each of first 5 SOE is not classified with these remaining states under the same aggregate, under the same base, and under the same element. So, each of them is taken as ungrouped under 1 aggregate (feeling), 1 base (ideation-base), and 1 element (ideation-element). The same analysis applies to other 10 SOE.

Those remaining states are also not classified with the SOE including those possible states, and are taken as ungrouped under 2 aggregates (matter and consciousness), under 11 bases (10 gross bases, mind-base), and under 17 elements (10 gross elements, 7 consciousness elements).

V. Ungrouped and Ungrouped

Chart 5.9. States of enquiry from Consciousness factor

	These remaining states:					SOE (unclassified with *these* remaining states)			*Those* remaining states (unclassified with SOE and other *possible* states)		
	Consciousness: Nibbāna: Volitive formation: Perception: Feeling: Matters:										
States of enquiry (SOE):						(Ungrouped)			(Ungrouped)		
						Agr	Bse	El.	Agr	Bse	El.
201. 1. Consciousness, is conditioned by volitive formation.	28	1	1	1	1	1	1	7	4	11	11

The remaining states are the aggregates of matters, feeling, perception, volitive formation, also *Nibbāna*. Either way, the state of enquiry and these remaining states can not be classified under the same aggregate, under the same base, and under the same element. The SOE is placed as ungrouped under 1 aggregate (consciousness), 1 base (mind-base) and 7 elements (7 consciousness-elements). Those remaining states are taken as ungrouped under 4 aggregates (matter, feeling, perception, volitive formation), under 11 bases (10 gross bases, ideation-base), and under 11 elements (10 gross elements, ideation-element).

Chart 5.10. States of enquiry from Mind-Matter factor

	These remaining states:	SOE (unclassified with *these* remaining states)			*Those* remaining states (unclassified with SOE and other *possible* states)		
	Consciousness: Nibbāna: Volitive formation: Perception: Feeling: Matters:						
States of enquiry (SOE):		(Ungrouped)			(Ungrouped)		
		Agr	Bse	El.	Agr	Bse	El.
202. 1. Mind-Matter, conditioned by consciousness.	1	4	11	11	1	1	7

Mind-matter are bound by 28 matters and 3 mental aggregates (i.e. 52 cetasikas). Consciousness aggregate is the remaining state. Either way, mind-matter and consciousness aggregate are not classified under the same aggregate, under the same base, and under the same element. Mind-matter are thus taken as ungrouped under 4 aggregates (28 matters, feeling, perception, volitive formation), under 11 bases (10 gross bases, ideation-base), and under 11 elements (10 gross elements, ideation-element). Consciousness as remaining states is placed as ungrouped under 1 aggregate (consciousness), 1 base (mind-base), and 7 elements (7 consciousness-elements).

Chart 5.11. States of enquiry from the Six Bases

	These remaining states: Consciousness: *Nibbāna:* Volitive formation Perception: Feeling: Matters:					SOE (unclassified with *these* remaining states) (Ungrouped)			*Those* remaining states (unclassified with SOE and other *possible* states) (Ungrouped)		
States of enquiry (SOE):						Agr	Bse	El.	Agr	Bse	El.
203. 1. Six bases, conditioned by Mind-Matter.	Sb	1	1	1	1	2	6	12	3	1	1

The Six Bases are bound by the aggregates of gross matters (sensory organs) and consciousness aggregate. The remaining states are thus the 3 aggregates of feeling, perception and volitive formation, subtle matters and *Nibbāna*.

When the six bases are dealt with these remaining states, they can not be classified under the same aggregate, under the same base, and under the same element. The Six Bases are taken as ungrouped under 2 aggregates (gross matters and consciousness), 6 bases (5 gross sense-bases and mind-base), and 12 elements (5 gross sense-elements, 7 consciousness-elements). Those remaining states are in turn taken as ungrouped under 3 aggregates (feeling, perception, volitive formation), under 1 base (ideation-base), and under 1 element (ideation-element).

Chart 5.12. States of enquiry from 5 dependent origination factors

	These remaining states: Consciousness: *Nibbāna:* Volitive formation: Perception: Feeling: Matters:					SOE (unclassified with *these* remaining states) (Ungrouped)			*Those* remaining states unclassified with SOE and other *possible* states (Ungrouped)		
States of enquiry (SOE):						Agr	Bse	El.	Agr	Bse	El.
204. 1. conditioned by Six Bases, is Contact.	Gr	1	1		1	1						
2. conditioned by Contact, is Feeling.	Gr		1	1	1	1	all with the same answer 1 1 1			all with the same answer 2 11 17		
3. conditioned by Feeling is Craving.	Gr	1	1		1	1						
4. conditioned by Craving, is Clinging.	Gr	1	1		1	1						
5. Action-becoming.	Gr	1	1		1	1						

V. Ungrouped and Ungrouped

The italicised *I* in the chart above denote the possible states for classification. Let's take the second example. Conditioned by contact, is feeling which comes under ideation-base and ideation-element. Feeling as states of enquiry also include the aggregates of perception and volitive formation, subtle matters and *Nibbāna* as other possible states in terms of classification. Remaining states, therefore, are 12 gross matters, *Nibbāna*, and consciousness aggregate.

When feeling is taken as a state of enquiry with these remaining states, they can not be classified under the same aggregate, under the same base, and under the same element. So, feeling is taken as ungrouped under 1 aggregate (feeling), 1 base (ideation-base), and 1 element (ideation-element). Those remaining states are also not classified with the feeling and those other possible states. Those remaining states are thus taken as ungrouped under 2 aggregates (matter and consciousness), under 11 bases (10 gross bases and mind-base), under 17 elements (10 gross elements and 7 consciousness-elements).

The answers for Craving, Clinging, and Kamma-becoming are the same, are to be followed in the same manner as explained.

Chart 5.13. States of enquiry from 4 Becomings

These remaining states:
Consciousness:
Nibbāna:
Volitive formation:
Perception:
Feeling:
Matters:

States of enquiry (SOE):		SOE (unclassified with *these* remaining states) (Ungrouped) Agr Bse El.	*Those* remaining states (unclassified with SOE and other *possible* states) (Ungrouped) Agr Bse El.
205. 1. Immaterial-becoming.	Gr		
2. Neither perception nor non-perception becoming.	Gr	all with the same answer 4 2 2	all with the same answer 1 10 10
3. Four-aggregate becoming.	Gr		
4. Four Basis of Psychic Accomplishment.	Gr		

These 4 states of enquiry are bound by subtle matters, 4 aggregates of, feeling, perception, volitive formation, and consciousness, and *Nibbāna*. In this case, 12 gross matters become the remaining states. When each of these states is enquired with gross matters, they can not be classified under the same aggregate, under the same base, and under the same element. Each of these states of enquiry is taken as ungrouped under 4 aggregates excluding *Nibbāna* (feeling, perception, volitive formation, consciousness), under 2 bases (ideation-base and mind-base), and under 2 elements (ideation-element, and mind-consciousness element). The

A Perfect Knowledge of Mind-Body from the Abhidhamma (Dhātukathā)

12 gross matters as remaining states are unclassified with the states of enquiry, are taken as ungrouped under 1 aggregate (matter), under 10 bases (10 gross bases), and under 10 elements (10 gross elements). Each of the subject matters of enquiry is to be dealt with in this manner as explained.

Chart 5.14. States of enquiry from 2 Becomings and 3 Inescapables

States of enquiry (SOE):	*These* remaining states: Consciousness: *Nibbāna:* Volitive formation: Perception: Feeling: Matters:						SOE (unclassified with *these* remaining states) (Ungrouped) Agr Bse El.	*Those* remaining states (unclassified with SOE and other *possible* states) (Ungrouped) Agr Bse El.
206. 1. Non-perception becoming.		*1*	*1*	*1*	**1**	**1**		
2. Single aggregate becoming.		*1*	*1*	*1*	**1**	**1**	all with the same answer	all with the same answer
3. Birth.		*1*	*1*	*1*	**1**	**1**	1 2 2	1 1 7
4. Ageing, and		*1*	*1*	*1*	**1**	**1**		
5. Death.		*1*	*1*	*1*	**1**	**1**		

The italicised *Sb* and *1* in the chart above are referring to those possible states in terms of classification.

In these subject matters of enquiry, non-perception becoming and single-aggregate becoming are identical. These first 2 states of enquiry belong to gross visible object, are associated with the ninefold vitality-group. Vitality consists of subtle matters and volitive formation, which is contained by ideation-base and ideation-element.

Birth contains concretely produced subtle matters. Ageing, and death involve volitive formation. Birth, ageing, and death all come under gross visible object.

Therefore, possible states for classification consist of feeling aggregate, perception aggregate, volitive formation aggregate, and *Nibbāna* which can be classified. Subtle matters are part of materiality under classification. Thus, consciousness aggregate becomes the sole remaining states.

When each of these states of enquiry is dealt with consciousness aggregate as remaining states, they can not be classified under the same aggregate, under the same base, and under the same element. Each of these SOE is taken as ungrouped under 1 aggregate (matter), under 2 bases (eye-base, visible object base), and under 2 elements (eye-element, visible object element). Those remaining states are not classified with each SOE including those possible states, are likewise taken as ungrouped under 1 aggregate (consciousness), under 1 base (mind-base), and under 7 elements (7 consciousness-elements).

V. Ungrouped and Ungrouped

Chart 5.12. States of enquiry from Lamentation

States of enquiry (SOE):	*These* remaining states : Consciousness; *Nibbāna;* Volitive formation; Perception; Feeling; Matters;					SOE (unclassified with *these* remaining states) (Ungrouped) Agr Bse El.	*Those* remaining states (unclassified with SOE and other *possible* states) (Ungrouped) Agr Bse El.
207. 1. Lamentation.	1	1	1	1	1	1 1 1	4 2 8

The state of lamentation is taken as sound as a result of wailing, and belongs to matter aggregate. The 4 mental aggregates and *Nibbāna* thus become the remaining states.

Lamentation is not classified with these remaining states under the same aggregate, under the same base, and under the same element. Thus, it is taken as ungrouped under 1 aggregate (matter), under 1 base (audible object base), and under 1 element (audible object element). Those remaining states which are not classified with lamentation are placed as ungrouped under 4 mental aggregates, under 2 bases (ideation-base, mind-base), and under 8 elements (ideation-element, 7 consciousness-elements).

Chart 5.12. States of enquiry from miscellaneous (18)

States of enquiry (SOE):	*These* remaining states : Consciousness; *Nibbāna;* Volitive formation; Perception; Feeling; Matters;			SOE (unclassified with *these* remaining states) (Ungrouped) Agr Bse El.	*Those* remaining states (unclassified with SOE and other *possible* states) (Ungrouped) Agr Bse El.
208. Sorrow; Suffering; Melancholy; Despair; Application of mindfulness; Right striving; *Jhāna;* Illimitables; 5 Faculties; 5 Powers; 7 Enlightenment-Factors; Noble Eightfold Path; Contact; Feeling; Perception; Volition; Decision; Attention. (18)	28	Refers to nos. 183 and 184	1	all with the same answer 1 1 1	all with the same answer 2 11 17

A Perfect Knowledge of Mind-Body from the Abhidhamma (Dhātukathā)

These 18 subject matters of enquiry belong to the different mental aggregates of feeling, perception, and volitive formation. The remaining states are therefore the 28 matters and consciousness aggregate.

Sorrow, suffering, and melancholy belong to feeling aggregate. Feeling comes under feeling aggregate. Perception comes under perception aggregate. The remaining 13 states of enquiry belong to volitive formation aggregate. Neither of these states of enquiry can be classified with the remaining states under the same aggregate, under the same base, and under the same element. Thus, sorrow, suffering, and melancholy are ungrouped under 1 aggregate (feeling), under 1 base (ideation-base), and under 1 element (ideation-element). The rest 15 SOE are ungrouped under 1 aggregate (either perception or volitive formation depending on which SOE), under 1 base (ideation-base), and under 1 element (ideation-element).

Those remaining states can not be classified with each of these SOE including those possible states, are taken as ungrouped under 2 aggregates (matter and consciousness), under 11 bases (10 gross bases and mind-base), under 17 elements (10 gross elements and 7 consciousness-elements).

Chart 5.12. States of enquiry from Consciousness

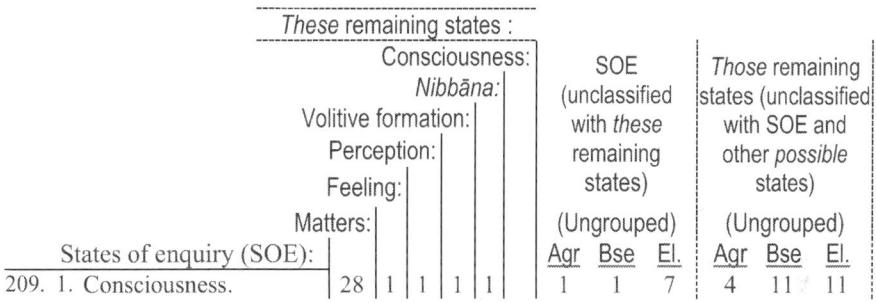

Consciousness consists of 89 cittas, belongs to consciousness aggregate. The remaining states are the 28 matters, feeling, perception, volitive formation, and *Nibbāna*. Consciousness is not classified with remaining states under the same aggregate, under the same base, and under the same element. And so, consciousness is taken as ungrouped under 1 aggregate (consciousness), under 1 base (mind-base), and under 7 elements (7 consciousness-elements). Those remaining states also can not be classified in this manner, are taken as ungrouped under 4 aggregates excluding *Nibbāna* (28 matters, feeling, perception, and volitive formation), 11 bases (10 gross bases and ideation-base), and 11 elements (10 gross elements and ideation-element).

V. Ungrouped and Ungrouped

43 states of enquiry from Dhammasaṅgaṇīmātikā triads

Chart 5.13. States of enquiry from 43 triads

210. *These* states of enquiry (SOE):	*These* Remaining states — Consciousness: Nibbāna: Volitive formation Perception: Feeling: Matters:				SOE (unclassified with *these* remaining states) (Ungrouped)			*Those* remaining states (unclassified with SOE and other *possible* states) (Ungrouped)		
					Agr	Bse	El	Agr	Bse	El
1. Wholesome states.	28			1	4	2	2			
2. Unwholesome states.	28			1	4	2	2			
3. States associated with happy feeling.	28	*1*		1	3	2	3			
4. States associated with painful feeling.	28	*1*		1	3	2	3			
5. States associated with neither happy feeling nor painful feeling.	28	*1*		1	3	2	7			
6. Resultant states.	28			1	4	2	8			
7. States which caused resultants.	28			1	4	2	2			
8. States which neither are the result of clinging nor are favourable to clinging.	12			1	4	2	2			
9. States which are corrupted and are objects of corruptions.	28			1	4	2	2			
10. States which neither are corrupted nor are objects of corruptions.	28				4	2	2			
11. States with initial application and sustained application.	28			1	4	2	3			
12. States without initial application but with sustained application.	28			1	4	2	2	all with the same answer		
13. States accompanied by zest.	28			1	4	2	2	1	10	10
14. States accompanied by happiness.	28	*1*		1	3	2	3			
15. States accompanied by equanimity.	28	*1*		1	3	2	7			
16. States eliminated by *Sotāpattimagga*.	28			1	4	2	2			
17. States eliminated by higher three Paths.	28			1	4	2	2			
18. States with root causes eliminated by first Path (*Sotāpattimagga*).	28			1	4	2	2			
19. States with root causes eliminated by the higher three Paths.	28			1	4	2	2			
20. States which make for the continuance of death and rebirth.	28			1	4	2	2			
21. States which make for the undoing of death and rebirth (leading to *Nibbāna*).	28			1	4	2	2			
22. States appertaining to learners (*sekhā*).	28			1	4	2	2			
23. States of "completed training", Arahatta (*Asekhā*).	28			1	4	2	2			

A Perfect Knowledge of Mind-Body from the Abhidhamma (Dhātukathā)

	M.	F.	P.	V.	N.	C.	Agr	Bse	El.	Agr	Bse	El.
24. States which are sublime.	28					1	4	2	2			
25. States which are immeasurable.	28					1	4	2	2			
26. States with limited object.	28					1	4	2	8			
27. States with sublime object.	28					1	4	2	2			
28. States with immeasurable object.	28					1	4	2	2			
29. Inferior states.	28					1	4	2	2			
30. Superior states.	28					1	4	2	2			
31. States fixed as to destinies due to wrong views.	28					1	4	2	2			
32. States with fixed destinies as a result of right views.	28					1	4	2	2	all with the same answer		
33. States with Path as its object.	28					1	4	2	2	1	10	10
34. States conditioned by the Path.	28					1	4	2	2			
35. States dominated by Path.	28					1	4	2	2			
36. States with past object.	28					1	4	2	2			
37. States with future object.	28					1	4	2	2			
38. States with present object.	28					1	4	2	8			
39. States with internal object.	28					1	4	2	8			
40. States with external object.	28					1	4	2	8			
41. States with both internal and external object.	28					1	4	2	8			

The italicised *1* in the chart above denote the possible states for classification.

Below are the explanatory notes with reference to these 41 states of enquiry.

1. Wholesome states consist of 21 cittas and 38 cetasikas (13+25=38), are classified under 4 mental aggregates. So, matters and *Nibbāna* are the remaining states. Either way, SOE and remaining states are unclassified as per set rule. Therefore, SOE is placed as ungrouped under 4 aggregates (feeling, perception, volitive formation, consciousness), 2 bases (ideation-base, mind-base), and 2 elements (ideation-element, mind-consciousness element). The remaining states are placed as ungrouped under 1 aggregate excluding *Nibbāna* (matter), under 10 bases (10 gross bases), under 10 elements (10 gross elements).

2. Unwholesome states consist of 12 cittas and 27 cetasikas (13+14=27), are classified under 4 mental aggregates. The two ungrouped answers are the same as in nos. 1 above.

3. States associated with happy or pleasurable feeling are the 63 cittas (accompanied by joy+pleasure), arisen with 46 cetasikas (52 excluding feeling, hatred, envy, avarice, worry, doubt. i.e. 52-6=46). They are classified under the aggregates of perception, volitive formation, and consciousness. Feeling aggregate becomes the possible states. Matters and *Nibbāna* are the remaining

V. Ungrouped and Ungrouped

states. SOE is unclassified with remaining states under the same aggregate, same base, and same element. SOE is thus taken as ungrouped under 3 aggregates (perception, volitive formation, consciousness), 2 bases (ideation-base, mind-base), and 3 elements (body-consciousness element, ideation-element, mind-consciousness element). The remaining states can not be included with SOE and those possible states in the same manner as aforesaid, are taken as ungrouped under the three categories with similar answer as in nos. 1 above.

4. States associated with painful feeling are the 3 cittas (in the 2 hatred-rooted, 1 body-consciousness resultant), 21 cetasikas (27 excluding feeling, zest, greed, wrong view, conceit, doubt, i.e (13+14)-6=21). They are classified under the aggregates of perception, volitive formation, and consciousness. They have the same possible states, remaining states, and ungrouped answers as in nos. 3 above.

5. States associated with neither happiness feeling nor painful feeling are the 55 cittas accompanied by equanimity, and 46 cetasikas (52 excluding feeling, zest, hatred, envy, avarice, worry, i.e. 52-6=46). They have the same possible states and remaining states as in nos. 3 & 4 above. SOE is unclassified with remaining states under the same aggregate, same base, and same element. SOE is thus taken as ungrouped under 3 aggregates (perception, volitive formation, consciousness), 2 bases (ideation-base, mind-base), and 7 elements (eye-cons. element, ear-cons. element, nose-cons. element, tongue-cons. element, mind-element, ideation-element, and mind-consciousness element). Remaining states can not be included with SOE and those possible states in the same manner as aforesaid, are taken as ungrouped under the three categories with similar answer as in first SOE.

6. Resultant states are the 36 resultants, 38 cetasikas (13+25=38). They belong to feeling, perception, volitive formation, and consciousness. Matters and *Nibbāna* are the remaining states. Either way, SOE and remaining states are unclassified as per the predetermined condition. SOE is placed as ungrouped under 4 aggregates (feeling, perception, volitive formation, consciousness), under 2 bases (ideation-base, mind-base), and under 8 elements (ideation-element, 7 consciousness elements). The remaining states have the same ungrouped answers as the rest. (See the first SOE).

7. States which caused resultants are the 21 wholesome cittas, 12 unwholesome cittas, and 52 cetasikas. They belong to feeling, perception, volitive formation, and consciousness. Matters and *Nibbāna* are the remaining states. Either way, SOE and remaining states are unclassified as per the predetermined rule. SOE is placed as ungrouped under 4 aggregates (feeling, perception, volitive formation, consciousness), 2 bases (ideation-base and mind-base), and 2 elements (ideation-element and mind-consciousness element). The remaining states have the same ungrouped answers as the rest. (See the first SOE).

A Perfect Knowledge of Mind-Body from the Abhidhamma (Dhātukathā)

8. States which neither are the result of clinging nor are favourable to clinging correspond to the 49 cittas, 52 cetasikas, 17 *cittajarūpa*, 15 *utujarūpa*, and 14 *āhārajarūpa*. They belong to the 4 mental aggregates and subtle matters, so gross matters and *Nibbāna* are the remaining states. Either way, SOE and remaining states are unclassified as per set rule in the same manner as in preceding nos. 1, 2, and 7. The two ungrouped answers are the same.

9. States which are corrupted and are objects of corruptions are 12 unwholesome cittas and 27 cetasikas. (13+14=27). They belong to the 4 mental aggregates. Matters and *Nibbāna* becomes the remaining state. Either way, SOE and remaining states are unclassified as per predetermined rule in the same manner as in preceding nos. 1, 2, 7-8. The two ungrouped answers are also the same.

10. States which neither are corrupted nor are objects corruptions are the 8 supramundane cittas, 36 cetasikas (13+(25-2 Illimitables)=36), and *Nibbāna*. The states belong to 4 mental aggregates. They have the same remaining states, same ungrouped answers as in the preceding nos. 1, 2, 7-9.

11. States with initial application and sustained application are the 55 cittas, 50 cetasikas (52 less *vitakka* and *vicāra*). They belong to the 4 mental aggregates. Matters and *Nibbāna* are the remaining states. Either way, SOE and remaining states are unclassified as per the predetermined rule. Thus, SOE is placed as ungrouped under 4 aggregates excluding *Nibbāna* (feeling, perception, volitive formation, consciousness), 2 bases (ideation-base and mind-base), and 3 elements (mind-element, ideation-element, mind-consciousness element). The remaining states have the same ungrouped answers as the rest.

12. States without initial application but with sustained application are the 11 Second-*Jhāna* cittas (8+3=11), 66 cittas with *vicāra*, 36 cetasikas (38 excluding *vitakka*, *vicāra*, i.e. (13+25)-2=36). They belong to the 4 mental aggregates. They have the same remaining states, same twofold ungrouped answers as in nos. 1, 2, 7-10.

13. States accompanied by zest consist of 51 cittas with zest, 46 cetasikas (52 excluding zest, hatred, envy, avarice, worry, and doubt, i.e. 52-6=46). They have the same remaining states, same twofold ungrouped answers as in nos. 1, 2, 7-10, 12.

14. States accompanied by happiness are the 63 cittas accompanied by joy and by pleasure, 46 cetasikas (52 excluding feeling, hatred, envy, avarice, worry, doubt. i.e. 52-6=46). They have the same possible states, same remaining states, and same twofold ungrouped answers as in preceding nos. 3 & 4.

V. Ungrouped and Ungrouped

15. States accompanied by equanimity are the 55 cittas accompanied by equanimity, and 46 cetasikas (52 excluding feeling, zest, hatred, envy, avarice, worry. i.e. 52-6=46). They are classified under the aggregates of perception, volitive formation, and consciousness. Feeling aggregate becomes the possible states. Matters and *Nibbāna* become the remaining states. SOE is unclassified with remaining states as per the predetermined rule, is thus taken as ungrouped under 3 aggregates (perception, volitive formation, consciousness), 2 bases (ideation-base, mind-base), and 7 elements (eye-cons. element, ear-cons. element, nose-cons. element, tongue-cons. element, mind-element, ideation-element, mind-consciousness element). Remaining states can not be included with SOE and those possible states in the same manner as aforesaid, are taken as ungrouped under the three categories with similar answer as the rest.

16. States eliminated by *Sotāpattimagga* [7] are the 4 greed-rooted cittas associated with wrong view, 1 delusion-rooted citta with doubt, 27 cetasikas (13+14=27). They belong to 4 mental aggregates. Matters and *Nibbāna* are the remaining states. The explanation and twofold ungrouped answers are the same as in preceding nos. 1, 2, 7-10, 12-13.

17. States eliminated by the higher three Paths [7] are the 2 hatred-rooted cittas (by *anāgāmimagga*), 4 greed-rooted cittas dissociated from wrong view, and 1 delusion-rooted citta with restlessness (by *arahattamagga*); 25 cetasikas (27 excluding wrong view and doubt). They belong to 4 mental aggregates. Matters and *Nibbāna* are the remaining states. The explanation and twofold ungrouped answers are the same as in preceding nos. 1, 2, 7-10, 12-13, 16.

18. States with root causes eliminated by *Sotāpattimagga*. The explanation and twofold ungrouped answers are the same as in nos. 16.

19. States with root causes eliminated by the higher three Paths. The explanation and twofold ungrouped answers are the same as in nos. 17.

20. States which make for the continuance of rebirth and death are the 17 mundane wholesome cittas, 12 unwholesome cittas, and 52 cetasikas. They belong to the 4 mental aggregates. Matters and *Nibbāna* becomes the remaining state. The explanation and twofold ungrouped answers are the same as in preceding nos. 1, 2, 7-10, 12-13, 16-19.

21. States which make for the discontinuity of rebirth and death (*Nibbāna*) are 4 supramundane path-cittas, 36 cetasikas (13+(25-2 Illimitables)=36). They belong to the 4 mental aggregates. Matters and *Nibbāna* becomes the remaining state. The explanation and twofold ungrouped answers are the same as in preceding nos. 1, 2, 7-10, 12-13, 16-20.

A Perfect Knowledge of Mind-Body from the Abhidhamma (Dhātukathā)

22. States appertaining to Learners (*sekhā*) are the 7 supramundane cittas excluded the *Arahatta* fruition, 36 cetasikas (13+(25-2 Illimitables)=36). The explanation and twofold ungrouped answers are the same as in preceding nos. 1, 2, 7-10, 12-13, 16-21.

23. States of the *Arahatta* (*Asekhā*) are Arahat's fruition-citta, and 36 cetasikas (13+(25-2 Illimitables)=36). The explanation and twofold ungrouped answers are the same as in preceding nos. 1, 2, 7-10, 12-13, 16-22.

24. States which are sublime are the 27 *Mahaggatacittāni*, the 35 cetasikas (38 excluding the 3 Abstinences). The explanation and twofold ungrouped answers are the same as in preceding nos. 1, 2, 7-10, 12-13, 16-23.

25. States which are immeasurable are the 8 supramundane cittas, 36 cetasikas (13+(25-2 Illimitables), and *Nibbāna*. The explanation and twofold ungrouped answers are the same as in preceding nos. 1, 2, 7-10, 12-13, 16-24.

26. States with limited object are the 54 sensuous cittas, 52 cetasikas. They belong to feeling, perception, volitive formation, and consciousness. Matters and *Nibbāna* are the remaining states. Either way, SOE and remaining states are unclassified as per the predetermined condition. The explanation and twofold ungrouped answers are the same as in nos. 6, the resultant states.

27. States with sublime object are 2 abhiññā powers from fifth rūpajhānas, 6 arūpajhānas, 47 cetasikas (52 excluding 3 Abstinences and 2 Illimitables). The explanation and twofold ungrouped answers are the same as in preceding nos. 1, 2, 7-10, 12-13, 16-25.

28. States with immeasurable object are the 4 mundane wholesome cittas with knowledge, 4 functional cittas with knowledge, *manodvārāvajjana* mind-consciousness element, 2 of the 5 abhiññā powers from the fifth rūpajhānas, 36 cetasikas (13+(25-2 Illimitables)). The explanation and twofold ungrouped answers are the same as in preceding nos. 1, 2, 7-10, 12-13, 16-25, 27.

29. Inferior states are the 12 unwholesome cittas, 27 cetasikas (13+14). The explanation and twofold ungrouped answers are the same as in preceding nos. 1, 2, 7-10, 12-13, 16-25, 27-28.

30. Superior states are the 8 supramundane cittas, 36 cetasikas (13+(25-2 Illimitables), and *Nibbāna*. The explanation and twofold ungrouped answers are the same as in preceding nos. 1, 2, 7-10, 12-13, 16-25, 27-29.

V. Ungrouped and Ungrouped

31-32. States fixed as to destinies due to wrong views and right views, respectively. The explanation and twofold ungrouped answers are the same as in preceding nos. 1, 2, 7-10, 12-13, 16-25, 27-30.

33. States with Path as its object are the 4 mundane wholesome cittas and 4 functional cittas with knowledge, both associated with knowledge; *manodvārāvajjana*, 2 abhiññā powers from fifth rūpajhānas, 33 cetasikas (38 excluding 3 Abstinences and 2 Illimitables). The explanation and twofold ungrouped answers are the same as in preceding nos. 1, 2, 7-10, 12-13, 16-25, 27-32.

34. States conditioned by the Path are the 8 supramundane cittas, 36 cetasikas (38 excluding the 2 Illimitables). The explanation and twofold ungrouped answers are the same as in preceding nos. 1, 2, 7-10, 12-13, 16-25, 27-33.

35. States dominated by Path are the 4 mundane wholesome cittas with knowledge, 4 functional cittas with knowledge, 4 supramundane path-cittas, 36 cetasikas (38-2 Illimitables). The explanation and twofold ungrouped answers are the same as in preceding nos. 1, 2, 7-10, 12-13, 16-25, 27-34.

36. States with past object are *manodvārāvajjana*, 29 sensuous javanas, 11 Registering cittas, 2 abhiññā powers from the fifth rūpajhānas, 6 arūpajhānas, 47 cetasikas (52 - 3 Abstinences - 2 Illimitables states). The explanation and twofold ungrouped answers are the same as in preceding nos. 1, 2, 7-10, 12-13, 16-25, 27-35.

37. States with future object are the *manodvārāvajjana*, 29 sensuous javanas, 11 Registering cittas, 2 of the 5 abhiññā powers attained from fifth rūpajhānas, 50 cetasikas having excluded 2 Illimitbles. The explanation and twofold ungrouped answers are the same as in preceding nos. 1, 2, 7-10, 12-13, 16-25, 27-36.

38. States with present object are the 10 viññāṇas, 3 mind-elements, *manodvārāvajjana*, 29 sensuous javanas, 11 Registering cittas, 2 of the 5 abhiññā powers attained from fifth rūpajhānas, 50 cetasikas having excluded 2 Illimitbles. They belong to aggregates of feeling, perception, volitive formation, and consciousness. Matters and *Nibbāna* are thus the remaining states. The explanation and twofold ungrouped answers are the same as in nos. 6 & 26.

39. States with internal object are the 54 sensuous cittas, fifth rūpajhānas (with 2 of 5 *abhiññā* powers), 3 arūpajhānas of the base of neither-perception-nor-nonperception, 49 cetasikas (52 having excluded envy and 2 Illimitables The explanation and twofold ungrouped answers are the same as in nos. 6, 26, 38.

A Perfect Knowledge of Mind-Body from the Abhidhamma (Dhātukathā)

40. States with external object are the 54 sensuous cittas, 15 rūpajhānas excluding the 3 Fifth jhānas (with 2 *abhiññā* powers), 3 arūpajhāna cittas on the base of Infinity, supramundane 4 Path- and 4 fruition-cittas, 51 cetasikas having excluded avarice. The explanation and twofold ungrouped answers are the same as in nos. 6, 26, 38-39.

41. States with both internal and external object are the 54 sensuous cittas, 15 rūpajhānas, 48 cetasikas excluding envy, avarice, 2 Illimitables (52-2-2=48). The explanation and twofold ungrouped answers are the same as in nos. 6, 26, 38-40.

Chart 5.14. States of enquiry from visibility and impinging

	These remaining states : Consciousness, Nibbāna, Volitive formation, Perception, Feeling, Matters						SOE (unclassified with *these* remaining states) (Ungrouped)			Those remaining states unclassified with SOE and other *possible* states (Ungrouped)		
These states of enquiry							Agr	Bse	El.	Agr	Bse	El.
211. 1. States which are visible and impinging.	11 Gr	1	1	1	1	1	1	1	1	4	2	8
2. States not visible but impinging.	11 Gr	1	1	1	1	1	1	9	9	4	2	8

1. States which are visible and impinging are the gross visible object. So, the remaining states are the 11 gross matters, feeling, perception, volitive formation, consciousness, and *Nibbāna*. Either way, SOE and remaining states are unclassified as per the prescribed rule. Therefore, SOE is placed as ungrouped under 1 aggregate (matter), 1 base (visible object base), and 1 element (visible object element). The unclassified remaining states are taken as ungrouped under 4 aggregates excluding *Nibbāna* (feeling, perception, volitive formation, consciousness), under 2 bases (ideation-base and mind-base), and under 8 elements (ideation-element and 7 consciousness elements).

2. States which are invisible but impinging are the 11 gross matters having excluded visible object. So, the remaining states are 1 gross matter, feeling, perception, volitive formation, consciousness, and *Nibbāna*. Either way, SOE and remaining states are unclassified as per prescribed rule. Therefore, SOE is placed as ungrouped under 1 aggregate (matter), 9 bases (10 gross bases excluding visible object base), and 9 elements (10 gross elements excluding visible object element). The unclassified remaining states are ungrouped with the same answers as in aforesaid nos. 1.

V. Ungrouped and Ungrouped

115 states of enquiry from Dhammasaṅgaṇīmātikā dyads

Chart 5.15. States of enquiry from the group of *hetu duka*

212. *These* states of enquiry (SOE):	*These* Remaining states — Consciousness: Nibbāna: Volitive formation Perception: Feeling: Matters:						SOE (unclassified with *these* remaining states) (Ungrouped) Agr Bse El			*Those* remaining states unclassified with SOE and other *possible* states (Ungrouped) Agr Bse El		
1. States which are root causes.	Gr	*1*	*1*		*1*	1						
2. States which are root causes as well as having root causes.	Gr	*1*	*1*		*1*	1	1	1	1	2	11	17
3. States which are root causes as well as are associated with root causes.	Gr	*1*	*1*		*1*	1						

The italicised *1* in the chart above denote the possible states for classification.

States which are root causes are these 6 — greed, hatred, delusion, non-greed, non-hatred, non-delusion. They belong to volitive formation aggregate. The states of feeling aggregate, perception aggregate, subtle matters and *Nibbāna* become the possible states as they are contained by ideation-base and ideation-element. Hence, gross matters and consciousness aggregate become the remaining states. When each of the SOE is taken as a state of enquiry with these remaining states, they can not be classified under the same aggregate, under the same base, and under the same element. So, the SOE is taken as ungrouped under 1 aggregate (volitive formation), under 1 base (ideation-base), and under 1 element (ideation-element). Those remaining states likewise can not be classified with each SOE and those possible states, and are thus taken as ungrouped under 2 aggregates (matter and consciousness), under 11 bases (10 gross bases and mind-base), under 17 elements (10 gross elements and 7 consciousness-elements).

States which are root causes as well as having root causes (i.e. accompanied by root causes) are greed, non-greed, hatred and non-hatred. States which are root causes as well as are associated with root causes are the same as aforesaid. The explanation and two ungrouped answers for these two SOE are obtained in the same manner as the aforesaid first SOE.

A Perfect Knowledge of Mind-Body from the Abhidhamma (Dhātukathā)

Chart 5.16. States of enquiry from the group of *hetū duka*

	These Remaining states Consciousness: Nibbāna: Volitive formation Perception: Feeling: Matters:	SOE (unclassified with *these* remaining states) (Ungrouped) Agr Bse El	*Those* remaining states unclassified with SOE and other *possible* states (Ungrouped) Agr Bse El.
213. *These* states of enquiry (SOE):			
1. States which have root causes (i.e. accompanied by root causes).	28 1		
2. States associated with root causes.	28 1		
3. States which have root causes but are not root causes per se (*sahetukehi ceva na ca hetūhi*).	28 1	all with the same answer 4 2 2	all with the same answer 1 10 10
4. States which are associated with root causes but are not root causes.	28 1		
5. States which are not root causes but have root causes (*na hetusahetukehi*).	28 1		

The first 2 SOE correspond to 71 cittas with associated roots, and 50 cetasikas having excluded the 2 delusion-rooted cittas. The other 3 SOE are the 71 cittas with associated roots, and 46 cetasikas having excluded the 6 roots causes. The five subject matters of enquiry belong to the 4 mental aggregates. When each of the SOE is enquired with the remaining states, they can not be classified under the same aggregate, under the same base, and under the same element. SOE is thus placed as ungrouped under 4 aggregates (feeling, perception, volitive formation, consciousness), under 2 bases (ideation-base, mind-base), and under 2 elements (ideation-element, mind-consciousness element). Those unclassified remaining states are placed as ungrouped under 1 aggregate (matter), under 10 bases (10 gross bases), and under 10 elements (10 gross elements).

Chart 5.17. States of enquiry from the group of shorter 7 dyads

	These Remaining states Consciousness: Nibbāna: Volitive formation Perception: Feeling: Matters:	SOE (unclassified with *these* remaining states) (Ungrouped) Agr Bse El	*Those* remaining states unclassified with SOE and other *possible* states (Ungrouped) Agr Bse El.
214. *These* states of enquiry (SOE):			
1. States not arisen from causes.	Gr *1* *1* *1* 1	- 1 1	2 11 17
2. States unconditioned by causes.	Gr *1* *1* *1* 1	- 1 1	2 11 17

V. Ungrouped and Ungrouped

These above two SOE belong to *Nibbāna*. The aggregates of feeling, perception and volitive formation, including subtle matters, become the possible states as they are contained by ideation-base and ideation-element. Hence, gross matters and consciousness aggregate become the remaining states.

When each SOE is dealt with these remaining states, they can not be included under the same aggregate, under the same base, and under the same element. So, each SOE is taken as ungrouped under no aggregate, under 1 base (ideation-base), and under 1 element (ideation-element). Those remaining states likewise can not be classified with each SOE and those so-called possible states, are thus taken as ungrouped under 2 aggregates (matter, consciousness), under 11 bases (10 gross bases, mind-base), under 17 elements (10 gross elements, 7 consciousness-elements).

Chart 5.18. States of enquiry from the group of shorter 7 dyads

	These Remaining states						SOE (unclassified with *these* remaining states) (Ungrouped)			*Those* remaining states unclassified with SOE and other *possible* states (Ungrouped)		
	Consciousness: Nibbāna: Volitive formation Perception: Feeling: Matters:											
215. *These* states of enquiry:							Agr	Bse	El	Agr	Bse	El
1. States with visibility.	11 Gr, Sb	1	1	1	1	1	1	1	1	4	2	8
2. States with impinging.	Sb	1	1	1	1	1	1	10	10	4	2	8

States with visibility are visible gross matters. The other 11 gross matters and 16 subtle matters are co-adjunct states, while the 4 mental aggregates become the remaining states. Because SOE is unclassified with the remaining states under the same aggregate, under the same base, and under the same element, SOE is therefore taken as ungrouped under 1 aggregate (matter), under 1 base (visible object base), and under 1 element (visible object element). Those remaining states which are unclassified with SOE and its co-adjuncts in the same said manner, are taken as ungrouped under 4 aggregates excluding *Nibbāna* (feeling, perception, volitive formation, consciousness), under 2 bases (ideation-base, mind-base), under 8 elements (ideation-element, 7 consciousness-elements).

States with impinging belong to 12 gross matters. So the 4 mental aggregates become the remaining states. Since this SOE is unclassified in the same aforesaid condition, it is taken as ungrouped under 1 aggregate (matter), under 10 gross bases, and under 10 gross elements. Those unclassified remaining states are taken as ungrouped under 4 aggregates excluding *Nibbāna* (feeling, perception,

A Perfect Knowledge of Mind-Body from the Abhidhamma (Dhātukathā)

volitive formation, consciousness), under 2 bases (ideation-base, mind-base), under 8 elements (ideation-element, 7 consciousness-elements).

Chart 5.19. States of enquiry from the group of shorter 7 dyads

	These remaining states		SOE (unclassified with *these* remaining states)			*Those* remaining states (unclassified with SOE and other *possible* states)		
	Consciousness: Nibbāna: Volitive formation Perception: Feeling: Matters:		(Ungrouped)			(Ungrouped)		
216. *These* states of enquiry (SOE):			Agr	Bse	El	Agr	Bse	El
States with corporeal change.	Gr 1 1 1 1 1		1	11	11	1	1	7

States with corporeal change are materiality including the 16 subtle matters. Gross matters, *Nibbāna*, the aggregates feeling, perception, and volitive formation, thus become those possible states, while consciousness aggregate becomes the remaining states. SOE is not classified with consciousness aggregate according to the prescribed condition, is thus taken as ungrouped under 1 aggregate (matter), under 11 bases (10 gross bases, ideation-base), under 11 elements (10 gross elements, ideation-element). The remaining states are also not classified with SOE and those possible states in the same said manner, are thus taken as ungrouped under 1 aggregate (consciousness), under 1 base (mind base), under 7 elements (7 consciousness-elements).

Chart 5.20. States of enquiry from the group of shorter 7 dyads

	These remaining states	SOE (unclassified with *these* remaining states)			*Those* remaining states (unclassified with SOE and other *possible* states)		
	Consciousness: Nibbāna: Volitive formation Perception: Feeling: Matters:	(Ungrouped)			(Ungrouped)		
217. *These* states of enquiry (SOE):		Agr	Bse	El	Agr	Bse	El
1. States without corporeal change.	28	4	2	8	1	10	10
2. Supramundane states.	28	4	2	2	1	10	10

States without corporeal change correspond to 89 cittas, 52 cetasikas, and *Nibbāna*. Supramundane states are the 8 supramundane cittas, 36 cetasikas (38 having excluded the 2 Illimitables), and *Nibbāna*. These SOE belong to 4 mental aggregates and *Nibbāna*. So, matters become the remaining states. Either way,

V. Ungrouped and Ungrouped

each of these two SOE and materiality can not be included as under the same aggregate, under the same base, and under the same element.

The first unclassified SOE is thus placed as ungrouped under 4 aggregates excluding *Nibbāna* (feeling, perception, volitive formation, consciousness), under 2 bases (ideation-base, mind-base), under 8 elements (ideation-element, 7 consciousness-elements).

The second unclassified SOE is thus placed as ungrouped under 4 aggregates excluding *Nibbāna* (feeling, perception, volitive formation, consciousness), under 2 bases (ideation-base, mind-base), under 2 elements (ideation-element, mind-consciousness element).

In either SOE, materiality can not be included with as meeting the prescribed condition under the three categories, materiality is therefore taken as ungrouped under 1 aggregate (matter), under 10 bases (10 gross bases), and under 10 elements (10 gross elements).

Chart 5.21. States of enquiry from the group of *āsavā duka*

	These remaining states					SOE (unclassified with *these* remaining states) (Ungrouped)			*Those* remaining states unclassified with SOE and other *possible* states (Ungrouped)		
	Consciousness:	Nibbāna:	Volitive formation	Perception:	Feeling:						
	Matters:										
218. *These* states of enquiry (SOE):						Agr	Bse	El	Agr	Bse	El.
1. States which are defilement (*Āsavā*)	28	*1*	*1*		*1*	1					
2. States which are both defilement and objects of defilement.	28	*1*	*1*		*1*	1	1	1	1	2	11	17
3. States which are both defilement and associated with defilement.	28	*1*	*1*		*1*	1					

The three SOE consist of the 3 factors of greed (or sensual desire), wrong view, and delusion present at the 12 unwholesome cittas, and belong to volitive formation aggregate. Feeling aggregate, perception aggregate, and and *Nibbāna* become the possible states (marked in italicised "*1*") as they are contained by ideation-base and ideation-element. Matters, consciousness aggregate thus become the remaining states.

Each SOE can not be classified with the remaining states under the same aggregate, under the same base, and under the same element. Each SOE is therefore taken as ungrouped under 1 aggregate (volitive formation), under 1 base (ideation-base), and under 1 element (ideation-element). The remaining states also can not be included with each SOE and its other possible states in the same manner as in the aforesaid condition. They are thus taken as ungrouped under 2 aggregates (matter and consciousness), under 2 bases (10 gross bases and mind-base), under 17 elements (10 gross elements and the 7 consciousness-elements).

Chart 5.22. States of enquiry from the group of *āsavā duka*

219. *These* states of enquiry (SOE):	Matters:	Feeling:	Perception:	Volitive formation:	Nibbāna:	Consciousness:	SOE (unclassified with *these* remaining states) (Ungrouped) Agr Bse El	Those remaining states (unclassified with SOE and other *possible* states) (Ungrouped) Agr Bse El
1. States which are not objects of defilement.	28							
2. States associated with defilement.	28						*1*	all with the same answer
3. States associated with defilement but are not defilement.	28						*1*	all with the same answer
4. States which are both dissociated from defilement and not objects of defilement.	28						4 2 2	1 10 10

The 1st and 4th states of enquiry concur with the 8 supramundane cittas, 36 cetasikas (38 having excluded the 2 Illimitables), and *Nibbāna*.

States associated with defilement are 12 unwholesome cittas, 26 cetasikas (27 excluding delusion-*cetasika* present at the 2 hate-rooted cittas and 2 delusion-rooted cittas).

States which are associated with defilement but are not defilement are the 12 unwholesome cittas, 24 cetasikas (27 excluding the 3 defilement factors of greed (or sensual desire), wrong view, and delusion).

All SOE belong to 4 mental aggregates with the 1st and 4th SOE including *Nibbāna*. So, materiality becomes the remaining states.

Either way, each SOE and materiality are can not be classified under the same aggregate, under the same base, and under the same element. Each SOE is thus taken as ungrouped under 4 aggregates excluding *Nibbāna* (feeling, perception, volitive formation, consciousness), under 2 bases (ideation-base and mind-base), under 2 elements (ideation-element and mind-consciousness element). The unclassified remaining states are thus taken as ungrouped under 1 aggregate (matter), under 10 bases (10 gross bases), and under 10 elements (10 gross elements).

V. Ungrouped and Ungrouped

Chart 5.23. States of enquiry from *Saṃyojana, Gantha, Ogha, Yoga, Nīvaraṇa*, and *Parāmāsa duka*

	These Remaining states					SOE (unclassified with *these* remaining states) (Ungrouped)			*Those* remaining states (unclassified with SOE and other *possible* states) (Ungrouped)		
220 *These* states of enquiry (SOE):	Consciousness: Nibbāna: Volitive formation Perception: Feeling: Matters:					Agr	Bse	El	Agr	Bse	El.
Repeats the same from preceding *āsavā* cluster for Fetters, Bonds, Raging Current, Yokes, Hindrances, respectively, following nos. 218. Altogether 3 x 5 =15 (no. 1 to 15)	Gr	1	1	1	1	1	1	1	2	11	17
Repeats the same from preceding *āsavā* cluster for Fetters, Bonds, Raging Current, Yokes, Hindrances, respectively, following nos. 219. Altogether 4 x 5 =20 (no. 16 to 35)	refers to nos. 219 (with different remaining states)					4	2	2	1	10	10
36. States which are attachment (*Parāmāsa*)	Gr	1	1	1	1	1	1	1	2	11	17
37. States which are both attachment and objects of attachment.	Gr	1	1	1	1						

With reference to the above chart, all these 37 states belong to volitive formation aggregate. Feeling aggregate, perception aggregate and *Nibbāna* are the possible states (marked in italicised "*1*") as they are contained by ideation-base and ideation-element (except for no. 16,19; 20,23; 24,27; 28,31; 32,35 where *Nibbāna* is part of the qualities of these SOE). Gross matters and consciousness aggregate thus become the remaining states.

The analysis and answers to these 37 states of enquiry are to be obtained in the same manner as explained in preceding nos. 218 & 219.

A Perfect Knowledge of Mind-Body from the Abhidhamma (Dhātukathā)

Chart 5.24. States of enquiry from the group of *parāmāsa duka*, etc

221. *These* states of enquiry (SOE):	*These* Remaining states — Consciousness; Nibbāna; Volitive formation; Perception; Feeling; Matters:				SOE (unclassified with *these* remaining states) (Ungrouped) Agr Bse El	*Those* remaining states (unclassified with SOE and other *possible* states) (Ungrouped) Agr Bse El.
1. States which are not objects of attachment.	28					
2. States dissociated from attachment and are not objects of attachment.	28				all with the same answer 4 2 2	all with the same answer 1 10 10
3. States which are associated with attachment.	28			*1*		
4. States which attend to objects.	28			*1*		

The 1st and 2nd SOE consist of 8 supramundane cittas, 36 cetasikas (38-2 Illimitables=36), and *Nibbāna*. So, they belong to 4 mental aggregates and *Nibbāna*. There are no other possible states. Matters thus become the remaining states.

States which are associated with attachment are the 4 greed-rooted cittas with wrong view, and 20 cetasikas (27 excluding wrong view, conceit hatred, envy, avarice, worry, doubt, i.e. 27-7=20). They belong to 4 mental aggregates. *Nibbāna* becomes possible states as to classification. 28 matters thus become the remaining states.

States which attend to objects are all the 89 cittas, and 52 cetasikas. *Nibbāna* becomes possible states as to classification. The remaining states thus are the 28 matters.

When each of these subject matters of enquiry is dealt with their remaining states, they are can not be classified under the same aggregate, under the same base, and under the same element. Each SOE is therefore taken as ungrouped under 4 aggregates excluding *Nibbāna* (feeling, perception, volitive formation, consciousness), under 2 bases (ideation-base and mind-base), under 2 elements (ideation-element and mind-consciousness element).

The remaining states of 28 matters are likewise unclassified with each SOE and possible states in the same aforesaid condition, are thus taken as ungrouped under 1 aggregate (matter), under 10 bases (10 gross bases), and under 10 elements (10 gross elements).

V. Ungrouped and Ungrouped

Chart 5.25. States of enquiry from group of intermediate 14 dyads

	These Remaining states						SOE (unclassified with *these* remaining states) (Ungrouped)			*Those* remaining states unclassified with SOE and other *possible* states (Ungrouped)		
222. *These* states of enquiry (SOE):	Consciousness	Nibbāna	Volitive formation	Perception	Feeling	Matters	Agr	Bse	El	Agr	Bse	El
1. States which do not have objects.	*1*	*1*	*1*			**1**	1	11	11			
2. States which are not consciousness.						**1**	4	11	11			
3. States dissociated from consciousness.	*1*	*1*	*1*			**1**	1	11	11			
4. States not conjoined with consciousness	*1*	*1*	*1*			**1**	1	11	11	all with the same answer 1 1 7		
5. States produced by consciousness.					*1*	**1**	4	11	11			
6. States arise together with consciousness					*1*	**1**	4	11	11			
7. States which arise successively with consciousness.					*1*	**1**	4	11	11			
8. States which are external.	5				*1*	**1**	4	6	6			
9. States which are derived.	4	*1*	*1*	*1*	*1*	**1**	1	11	11			

Below are the explanatory notes and answers with reference to the above 9 states of enquiry. Those italicised *1* in the chart above denote possible states of SOE.

1. States which have no objects are the 28 matters and *Nibbāna*. The remaining states are consciousness aggregate while the other 3 mental aggregates are the possible states. The SOE is unclassified with remaining states as per the predetermined condition, is taken as ungrouped under 1 aggregate (matter), under 11 bases (10 gross bases, ideation-base), under 11 elements (10 gross elements, ideation-element).

2. States which are not consciousness are the 28 matters, 52 cetasikas, and *Nibbāna*. The remaining states are consciousness aggregate. The SOE is unclassified with remaining states as per the predetermined condition, is taken as ungrouped under 4 aggregates (4 mental aggregates), under 11 bases (10 gross bases, ideation-base), and under 11 elements (10 gross elements, ideation-element).

3. States which are dissociated from consciousness are 28 matters and *Nibbāna*. The remaining states are consciousness aggregate while the other 3 mental aggregates are the possible states. SOE is unclassified with remaining states in the same way as explained in nos. 1 above.

4. States which are not conjoined with consciousness are 28 matters and *Nibbāna*. The remaining states are consciousness aggregate while the other 3 mental aggregates are the possible states. SOE is unclassified with remaining states in the same way as explained in nos. 1 & 3 above.

5. States which are produced by consciousness are 52 cetasikas, and 17 mind-produced matters. *Nibbāna* is the possible state, while consciousness aggregate becomes remaining states. The SOE is unclassified with the remaining states as per the prescribed condition, is taken as ungrouped under 4 aggregates (4 mental aggregates), under 11 bases (10 gross bases, ideation-base), and under 11 elements (10 gross elements, ideation-element).
6. States which arise together with consciousness are 52 cetasikas, 2 viññatti-rūpas (bodily intimation and vocal intimation). *Nibbāna* is the possible state, while consciousness aggregate becomes remaining states. The explanation and ungrouped answer follow the same as in nos. 5 above
7. States which arise successively with consciousness are 52 cetasikas, and the 2 intimations. *Nibbāna* is the possible state, while consciousness aggregate are remaining states. The explanation and ungrouped answer follow the same as in nos. 5, 6 above.
8. States which are external are 52 cetasikas, and 23 matters (excluded 5 *pasāda-rūpā*). Remaining states are the 5 sensory corporealities and consciousness aggregate, while *Nibbāna* is possible, classifiable state. The SOE is unclassified with remaining states as per the predetermined condition, is taken as ungrouped under 4 aggregates (matter, feeling, perception, volitive formation), under 6 bases (vision-base, sound-base, odour-base, taste-base, touch-base, ideation-base), and under 6 elements (vision-element, sound-element, odour-element, taste-element, touch-element, ideation-element).
9. States which are derived are 24 derived matters (excluded 4 Great Elements). The remaining states are consciousness aggregate, leaving *Nibbāna* and the other 3 mental aggregates as possible states. SOE is unclassified with consciousness aggregate as per the predetermined condition, is taken as ungrouped under 1 aggregate (matter), under 11 bases (10 gross bases, ideation-base), under 11 elements (10 gross elements, ideation-element).

Those remaining states are not classified with the respective SOE, with or without their possible states depending on which SOE is being enquired at the time, are taken as ungrouped under 1 aggregate (consciousness), under 1 base (mind-base), and under 7 elements (7 consciousness-elements).

Chart 5.26. States of enquiry from group of intermediate 14 dyads

	These remaining states					SOE (unclassified with *these* remaining states)			Those remaining states (unclassified with SOE and other *possible* states)		
	Consciousness:	Nibbāna:	Volitive formation	Perception:	Feeling:	Matters:						
							(Ungrouped)			(Ungrouped)		
223. *These* states of enquiry (SOE):							Agr	Bse	El	Agr	Bse	El
1. States which are consciousness.	28	1	1	1	1		1	1	7	4	11	11

V. Ungrouped and Ungrouped

They are the 89 cittas belonging to consciousness aggregate which are not classified with those remaining states, are thus taken as ungrouped under 1 aggregate (consciousness), under 1 base (mind-base), and under 7 elements (7 consciousness-elements).

Those unclassified remaining states are taken as ungrouped under 4 aggregates excluding *Nibbāna* (matter, feeling, perception, and volitive formation), under 11 bases (10 gross bases and ideation-base), and under 11 elements (10 gross elements and ideation-element).

Chart 5.27. States of enquiry from group of intermediate 14 dyads

	These Remaining states: Consciousness: *Nibbāna:* Volitive formation Perception: Feeling: Matters:	SOE (unclassified with *these* remaining states) (Ungrouped)			*Those* remaining states unclassified with SOE and other *possible* states (Ungrouped)		
224. *These* states of enquiry (SOE):		Agr	Bse	El	Agr	Bse	El.
1. States which are mental factors.	28 / 1						
2. States associated with consciousness.	28 / 1						
3. States conjoined with consciousness.	28 / 1						
4. States both conjoined with cons. and originated from cons.	28 / 1	all with the same answer 3	1	1	all with the same answer 2	11	17
5. States conjoined with, originated from, and arise concurrently with cons.	28 / 1						
6. States conjoined with, originated from, and arise consecutively with cons.	28 / 1						

These 7 states of enquiry are all ascribed to the 52 mental concomitants. Materiality and consciousness aggregate are the remaining states. *Nibbāna* is the possible state as to classification. Either of the SOE can not be classified with these remaining states under the same aggregate, under the same base, and under the same element. Each of the SOE is then taken as ungrouped under 3 aggregates (feeling, perception, volitive formation), 1 base (ideation-base), and 1 element (ideation-element).

Those remaining states are unclassified with each SOE and those possible states, are ungrouped under 2 aggregates (matter and consciousness), under 11 bases (10 gross bases and mind-base), and under 17 elements (10 gross elements and the 7 consciousness-elements).

A Perfect Knowledge of Mind-Body from the Abhidhamma (Dhātukathā)

Chart 5.28. States of enquiry from group of intermediate 14 dyads

	These Remaining states: Consciousness: Nibbāna: Volitive formation Perception: Feeling: Matters:					SOE (unclassified with *these* remaining states) (Ungrouped) Agr Bse El			*Those* remaining states (unclassified with SOE and other *possible* states) (Ungrouped) Agr Bse El		
225. *These* states of enquiry (SOE):											
1. States which are internal.	1	1	1	1		2	6	12	3	1	1

Internal states are the 4 great elements and 89 cittas. The remaining states are *Nibbāna* and the aggregates of feeling, perception, and volitive formation. When the subject matter of enquiry is compared with these remaining states, this state can not be classified with those remaining states under the same aggregate, under the same base, and under the same element. The subject matter of enquiry is thus placed as ungrouped under 2 aggregates (matters and consciousness), under 6 bases (5 gross sense-bases and mind-base), and under 12 elements (5 gross sense-elements and 7 consciousness-elements). Those likewise unclassified remaining states are placed as ungrouped under 3 aggregates (feeling, perception, volitive formation), 1 base (ideation-base), and 1 element (ideation-element).

Chart 5.29. States of enquiry from *upādāna duka*

	These Remaining states: Consciousness: Nibbāna: Volitive formation Perception: Feeling: Matters:					SOE (unclassified with *these* remaining states) (Ungrouped) Agr Bse El			*Those* remaining states unclassified with SOE and other *possible* states (Ungrouped) Agr Bse El		
226. *These* states of enquiry (SOE):											
1. States which are clinging (*upādāna*)	28	1	1		1	1					
2. States which are both clinging and objects of clinging.	28	1	1		1	1	1	1	1	2	11	17
3. States which are both clinging and associated with clinging.	28	1	1		1	1						
4. States which are not objects of clinging.	28											
5. States dissociated from clinging as well as are not objects of clinging.	28					4	2	2	1	10	10
6. States associated with clinging.	28			1								
7. States associated with clinging but are not clinging.	28			1								

V. Ungrouped and Ungrouped

Continue from Chart 5.29 above.

	These Remaining states Consciousness: *Nibbāna:* Volitive formation Perception: Feeling: Matters:					SOE (unclassified with *these* remaining states) (Ungrouped)			*Those* remaining states unclassified with SOE and other *possible* states (Ungrouped)		
226. *These* states of enquiry (SOE):						Agr	Bse	El	Agr	Bse	El.
8. States which are corruptions (*kilesa*)	28	*1*	*1*		*1*	**1**						
9. States which are both corruptions and objects of corruptions.	28	*1*	*1*		*1*	**1**						
10. States which are corruptions and are corrupted.	28	*1*	*1*		*1*	**1**	1	1	1	2	11	17
11. States which are both corruptions and associated with corruptions.	28	*1*	*1*		*1*	**1**						

The states marked as italicised *1* in Chart 5.29 above indicate that they are the possible states of classification, with reference to individual SOE.

The 1st, 2nd, and 3rd SOE, are ascribed to sensual desires and wrong view, belong to volitive formation aggregate. *Nibbāna* and the aggregates of feeling and perception are the possible states. Materiality and consciousness aggregate thus become the remaining states. Each of these SOE can not be classified with the remaining states under the same aggregate, under the same base, and under the same element. Each is thus taken as ungrouped under 1 aggregate (volitive formation), under 1 base (ideation-base), and under 1 element (ideation-element). The remaining states are also not classified with each SOE and its other possible states in the same aforesaid manner. Remaining states are thus taken as ungrouped under 2 aggregates (matter, consciousness), under 2 bases (10 gross bases, mind-base), and under 17 elements (10 gross elements, 7 consciousness-elements).

The 4th and 5th SOE concur with the 8 supramundane cittas, 36 cetasikas (38 excluding the 2 Illimitables), and *Nibbāna*. They belong to 4 mental aggregates and *Nibbāna*. Thus, remaining states are matters.

The 6th SOE, states associated with clinging, consist of 8 greed-rooted cittas, 22 cetasikas (27 excluding hatred, envy, avarice, worry, doubt), and greed present at the 4 greed-rooted cittas dissociated from wrong view. They belong to 4 mental aggregates. Thus, matters are the remaining states, while *Nibbāna* is the possible state as to classification.

A Perfect Knowledge of Mind-Body from the Abhidhamma (Dhātukathā)

The 7th SOE, states which are associated with clinging but are not clinging, are the 8 greed-rooted cittas, accompanied by 20 cetasikas (27 excluding hatred, envy, avarice, worry, doubt, and the 2 states of clinging). They belong to 4 mental aggregates. Thus, matters are the remaining states, while *Nibbāna* is the possible state for classification.

Above 4th to 7th SOE are each unclassified with the remaining states according to the prescribed condition, are each taken as ungrouped under 4 aggregates excluding *Nibbāna* (feeling, perception, volitive formation, consciousness), under 2 bases (ideation-base, mind-base), under 2 elements (ideation-element, mind-consciousness element). The remaining states are also unclassified with each SOE and the possible states according to the prescribed condition, and are taken as ungrouped under 1 aggregate (matter), under 10 bases (10 gross bases), and under 10 elements (10 gross elements).

The 8th, 9th, 10th, and 11th SOE are attributed to the 10 kinds of corruptions — greed, hatred, delusion, conceit, wrong view, doubt, sloth, restlessness, shamelessness, guiltlessness of conscience — they belong to volitive formation aggregate. Feeling aggregate, perception aggregate, and *Nibbāna* which are bound by ideation-base and ideation-element, becomes those possible states. Materiality and consciousness aggregate therefore become the remaining states. Explanation and answers for the twofold unclassifications follow the same as in the 1st, 2nd, and 3rd SOE.

V. Ungrouped and Ungrouped

Chart 5.30. States of enquiry from *kilesa duka* and last 18 dyads

227. *These* states of enquiry (SOE):	Matters:	Feeling:	Perception:	Volitive formation	Consciousness: Nibbāna:	SOE (unclassified with *these* remaining states) (Ungrouped) Agr Bse El	*Those* remaining states unclassified with SOE and other *possible* states (Ungrouped) Agr Bse El.
1. States not the objects of corruptions.	28					4 2 2	
2. States which are corrupted.	28				*1*	4 2 2	
3. States associated with corruptions.	28				*1*	4 2 2	
4. States which are corrupted but are not corruptions.	28				*1*	4 2 2	
5. States associated with corruptions but are not corruptions.	28				*1*	4 2 2	
6. States both dissociated from corruptions and are not objects of corruption.	28					4 2 2	
7. States eliminated by first Path.	28				*1*	4 2 2	
8. States eliminated by the higher three Paths.	28				*1*	4 2 2	
9. States with root causes eliminated by the first Path.	28				*1*	4 2 2	
10. States with root causes eliminated by the higher three Paths.	28				*1*	4 2 2	all with the same answer
11. States with initial application.	28				*1*	4 2 3	1 10 10
12. States with sustained application.	28				*1*	4 2 3	
13. States with zest.	28				*1*	4 2 2	
14. States which are accompanied by zest.	28				*1*	4 2 2	
15. States accompanied by happiness.	28	*1*			*1*	3 2 3	
16. States accompanied by equanimity.	28	*1*			*1*	3 2 7	
17. States not characteristic of the sensuous sphere.	28					4 2 2	
18. States characteristic of form sphere.	28				*1*	4 2 2	
19. States characteristic of formless sphere	28				*1*	4 2 2	
20. States which are not included (in the round of death and rebirth).	28					4 2 2	
21. States which lead out to liberation.	28				*1*	4 2 2	
22. States which are fixed as to their future destinies.	28				*1*	4 2 2	
23. States which are unsurpassable.	28					4 2 2	
24. States which are at odds. (with supramundane Path)	28				*1*	4 2 2	

A Perfect Knowledge of Mind-Body from the Abhidhamma (Dhātukathā)

Below are explanatory notes and answers with reference to the above 24 SOE. Those marked as italicised *1* in the chart above denote the possible states in terms of classification.

1. States which are not objects of corruptions are the 8 supramundane cittas, 36 cetasikas, *Nibbāna*. They belong to 4 mental aggregates and *Nibbāna*. Thus, 28 matters become the remaining states. The SOE is unclassified with materiality in accordance with the prescribed condition, is thus taken as ungrouped under 4 aggregates excluding *Nibbāna* (feeling, perception, volitive formation, consciousness), under 2 bases (ideation-base, mind-base), and under 2 elements (ideation-element, mind-consciousness element).
2. States which are corrupted are the 12 mundane unwholesome cittas, and 27 cetasikas. They belong to 4 mental aggregates. Matters become the remaining states. *Nibbāna* becomes the possible state. The SOE is unclassified with materiality and *Nibbāna* as per the prescribed condition, is thus taken as ungrouped under 4 aggregates excluding *Nibbāna* (feeling, perception, volitive formation, consciousness), under 2 bases (ideation-base, mind-base), and under 2 elements (ideation-element, mind-consciousness element).
3. States which are associated with corruptions are the 12 mundane unwholesome cittas, and 27 cetasikas. They belong to 4 mental aggregates. Answers are same as in no. 2 above.
4. States which are corrupted but are not corruptions are the 12 mundane unwholesome cittas, 17 cetasikas. They belong to 4 mental aggregates. Answers are same as in no. 2 above.
5. States which are associated with corruptions but are not corruptions are the 12 mundane unwholesome cittas, 17 cetasikas. They belong to 4 mental aggregates. Answers are same as in no. 2 above.
6. States both dissociated from corruptions and are not objects of corruption are the 8 supramundane cittas, 36 cetasikas, *Nibbāna*. They belong to 4 mental aggregates. Answers are same as in no. 2 above.
7. States eliminated by the first Path are 4 greed-rooted cittas associated with wrong view, and 1 delusion-rooted citta associated with doubt (or the 3 Fetters of *sakkāyadiṭṭhi*, *vicikicchā*, *sīlabbataparāmāsa*). They belong to 4 mental aggregates. Answers are same as in no. 2 above.
8. States eliminated by the higher three Paths are 4 greed-rooted cittas dissociated from wrong view, 2 hatred-rooted cittas, 1 delusion-rooted citta with restlessness, 25 cetasikas. They belong to 4 mental aggregates. Answers are same as in no. 2 above.
9. States with root causes eliminated by the first Path are 4 greed-rooted cittas (with wrong view), 1 delusion-rooted citta (with doubt), 26 cetasika (27 excluding 1 delusion-rooted citta with doubt). They belong to 4 mental aggregates. Answers are same as in no. 2 above.

V. Ungrouped and Ungrouped

10. States with root causes eliminated by the higher three Paths are 4 greed-rooted cittas (dissociated from wrong view), 2 hatred-rooted cittas, 1 delusion-rooted citta (with restlessness), 25 cetasikas. They belong to 4 mental aggregates. Answers are same as in no. 2 above.
11. States with initial application are 55 cittas, 51 cetasikas. They belong to 4 mental aggregates. *Nibbāna* becomes the possible state. Matters are the remaining states. The SOE is unclassified with the remaining states in accordance with the prescribed condition, is thus taken as ungrouped under 4 aggregates (feeling, perception, volitive formation, consciousness), under 2 bases (ideation-base, mind-base), and under 3 elements (mind-element, ideation-element, mind-consciousness element).
12. States with sustained application are 66 cittas, 51 cetasikas. They belong to 4 mental aggregates. *Nibbāna* becomes the possible state. Matters are the remaining states. Ungrouped answers are same as in no. 11 above.
13. States with zest are 51 cittas and 46 cetasikas, belong to 4 mental aggregates. Answers are same as in no. 2 above.
14. States which are accompanied by zest 51 cittas, 46 cetasikas. They belong to 4 mental aggregates. Answers are same as in no. 2 above.
15. States which are accompanied by happiness are 63 cittas, 46 cetasikas. They belong to the aggregates of perception, volitive formation, and consciousness. Feeling aggregate and *Nibbāna* are the possible states, while matters are the remaining states. The SOE is unclassified with the remaining states in accordance with the prescribed condition, is thus taken as ungrouped under 3 aggregates (perception, volitive formation, and consciousness), under 2 bases (ideation-base and mind-base), and under 3 elements (body-consciousness element, ideation-element, and mind-consciousness element).
16. States which are accompanied by equanimity are 55 cittas, 46 cetasikas. They belong to the aggregates of perception, volitive formation, and consciousness. Feeling aggregate and *Nibbāna* become the possible states. Matters are the remaining states. The SOE is unclassified with the remaining states in accordance with the prescribed condition of the three categories, is thus taken as ungrouped under 3 aggregates (perception, volitive formation, consciousness), under 2 bases (ideation-base, mind-base), under 7 elements (eye-cons. element, ear-cons. element, nose-cons. element, tongue-cons. element, mind-element, ideation-element, mind-consciousness element).
17. States not characteristic of sensuous sphere are the 27 *Mahaggatacittāni*, 8 supramundane cittas, 38 cetasikas, and *Nibbāna*. Thus, 28 matters become the remaining states. Answers are same as in no. 1 above.
18. States characteristic of the form sphere are the 15 fine-material cittas, 35 cetasikas. They belong to 4 mental aggregates. Answers are same as in no. 2 above.
19. States characteristic of the immaterial sphere are 12 sublime cittas, 30 cetasikas. They belong to 4 mental aggregates. Answers are same as in no. 2 above.

A Perfect Knowledge of Mind-Body from the Abhidhamma (Dhātukathā)

20. States which are not included (in round of deaths and rebirths) are the 8 supramundane cittas, 36 cetasikas, *Nibbāna*. Answers are same as in no. 1 above.
21. States which lead out (to *Nibbāna*) are 4 supramundane path-cittas, 36 cetasikas. The 28 matters are the remaining states. Answers are same as in no. 2 above.
22. States which are fixed as regards their future destinies are the 4 supramundane path-cittas, 36 cetasikas; 7th sensuous *javana* present at the 4 greed-rooted cittas associated with wrong view and at the 2 delusion-rooted cittas. They belong to 4 mental aggregates. Answers are same as in no. 2 above.
23. States which are unsurpassable consist of the 8 supramundane cittas, 36 cetasikas (38 excluding the 2 Illimitables), and *Nibbāna*. Thus, they belong to 4 mental aggregates and *Nibbāna*. The remaining states are 28 matters. Answers are same as in no. 1 above.
24. States which are at odds (*saraṇā*) with supramundane Path consist of the 12 mundane unwholesome cittas, and 27 cetasikas. They belong to 4 mental aggregates. Answers are same as in no. 2 above.

Those remaining states are not classified with the respective SOE (with possible states from nos. 15 & 16) under the same aggregate, under the same base, and under the same element. Remaining states from each SOE are thus taken as ungrouped under 1 aggregate (matter), under 10 bases (10 gross bases), and under 10 elements (10 gross elements).

Key points from the text :

All 5 aggregates, all 12 bases, all 18 elements, 3 truths, all the faculties, 23 dependent originations, 16 miscellaneous, 43 triads, 72 clusters, 7 shorter dyads, 18 intermediate dyads, 18 kinds of the last 18 dyads (total 257 kinds of states).

Matter aggregate, ideation-base, ideation-element, femininity-faculty, masculinity-faculty, vitality-faculty, mentality-materiality; two becomings, birth, ageing, death, corporeal states, objectless states, non-consciousness, dissociated from consciousness; not conjoined with consciousness, produced by consciousness, arising together with consciousness, arising consecutively with consciousness; external states, derived states.

V. Ungrouped and Ungrouped

In the two summary tables below, the numbers in brackets represent the number of enquiries with reference to each of the text's paragraph's nos.

Chart 5.31. Summary table of the 257 states of enquiry by subject matters

Text paragraph nos. (with the numbers of enquiries) :		Subject matter:
193 (1), 194 (3), 195 (1), 201 (1), 209 (1)	7	Aggregates
196 (10), 197 (1)	11	Bases
195 (8), 196 (10), 197 (1)	19	Elements
198 (3)	3	Truths
195 (1), 197 (3), 199 (5), 200 (13)	22	Faculties
200 (2), 202 (1), 203 (1), 204 (5), 205 (4), 206 (5), 207 (1)	19	Dependent Originations
208 (18)	18	Others
210 (41), 211 (2)	43	Triads
218 (3), 219 (4), 220 (37), 221 (3), 226 (11), 227 (6)	64	30 kinds from the 10 clusters of dyad
212 (3), 213 (5),	8	Shorter dyads
214 (2), 215 (2), 216 (1), 217 (2)	7	Intermediate dyads
221 (1), 222 (9), 223 (1), 224 (6), 225 (1), 227 (18)	36	Last dyads

Total = 257

A Perfect Knowledge of Mind-Body from the Abhidhamma (Dhātukathā)

Chart 5.32. Summary table of the 257 states of enquiry by answers

	Text's paragraph nos. (with numbers of enquiries):		SOE (unclassified with *these* remaining states).			Those unclassified remaining states.		
			Ungrouped			Ungrouped		
			agr	bse	el.	agr	bse	el.
1.	193 (1), 216 (1), 222 (4)	6	1	11	11	1	1	7
	197 (5)	5	4	1	1	1	1	7
	202 (1), 222 (4)	5	4	11	11	1	1	7
	206 (5)	5	1	2	2	1	1	7
	222 (1)	1	4	6	6	1	1	7
2.	194 (3), 198 (2), 200 (15), 204 (5), 208 (18), 212 (3), 218 (3), 220 (17), 226 (7)	73	1	1	1	2	11	17
	198 (1), 214 (2)	3	0	1	1	2	11	17
	224 (6)	6	3	1	1	2	11	17
3.	195 (10), 201 (1), 209 (1), 223 (1)	13	1	1	7	4	11	11
4.	196 (20), 199 (5), 207 (1), 211 (1), 215 (1)	28	1	1	1	4	2	8
	211 (1)	1	1	9	9	4	2	8
	215 (1)	1	1	10	10	4	2	8
5.	203 (1), 225 (1)	2	2	6	12	3	1	1
6.	205 (4), 210 (28), 213 (5), 219 (4), 210 (1), 220 (20), 221 (4), 226 (4), 227 (20)	90	4	2	2	1	10	10
	227 (2), 210 (1)	3	4	2	3	1	10	10
	210 (6), 217 (2)	8	4	2	8	1	10	10
	210 (3), 227 (1)	4	3	2	3	1	10	10
	210 (2), 227 (1)	3	3	2	7	1	10	10
	Total 257 states in 18 kinds of answer	**257**						

CHAPTER 6

VI. Association and Dissociation
(*Sampayogavippayoga*)

Analysis of 250 states from 78 catechism

A total of 250 states of enquiry form the subject matter of this chapter, of which 92 are internal states, 158 belong the external states from triads and dyads. This chapter has the same topical layout as that in Chapter 1, except that in this chapter, it analyses by association and dissociation by the three categories instead of by classified and unclassified. Association is divided into total association and partial association. The same is for the dissociation of states. Association in this book is reserved only to the mental phenomena in a single moment of consciousness (*cittakhaṇa*). This chapter must be fully comprehended so that subsequent chapters can be understood without difficulty.

i. *Association* (total) — the association between the different states are based on the following 4 characteristics :

- they arise together
- they dissolve together
- they share the same object
- they are comparable on the same basis

The 4 mental aggregates are mutually associated with one another, which is also the association condition as explained in Patthāna.

ii. *Partial Association* — for example, feeling is mutually associated with the aggregates of perception and volitive formation, and because part of 4 mental aggregates come under ideation-base and ideation-element, feeling is said to be partially associated with ideation-base and ideation-element.

When the subject matters of enquiry belong to both mentality and materiality, these states are neither associated nor partially associated with the aggregates, bases, and elements. When either matter aggregate or *Nibbāna* becomes the subject matters of enquiry, there are always no associations, nor any partial association with the three categories. When the 4 mental aggregates are the subject matters of enquiry, they have no associated states, but may sometimes have partially associated states. However, in those states where materiality and *Nibbāna*, or the 4 mental aggregates and *Nibbāna* are the subject matters of enquiry, there are no associated states, nor partially associated states.

A Perfect Knowledge of Mind-Body from the Abhidhamma (Dhātukathā)

iii. *Dissociation* (total) — the different states to be compared are said to be in total dissociation when they do not comply with the 4 characteristics on which association of states is based. States which are at all times in dissociation are between 28 Matters and 4 mental aggregates, *Nibbāna* and 4 mental aggregates, 4 mental aggregates and materiality, 4 mental aggregates and *Nibbāna*.

How does *Nibbāna*, which is also mentality, related to 4 mental aggregates? How does materiality related to the 4 mental aggregates? They are related only by way of dissociation. There are 4 kinds of dissociation as follows:

- by spheres (the 3 mundane spheres and supramundane sphere)
- by classes (wholesome, unwholesome, resultant, functional, with root, without root, non-beautiful, etc.)
- by times (past, future, and present)
- by continuity (*santāna*) (states arise internally or arise externally)

iv. *Partial Dissociation* — for example, volitive formation is dissociated from matter aggregate, 10 gross bases, and 10 gross elements. But the 16 subtle matters form part of ideation-base and ideation-element. Thus, volitive formation is partially dissociated from ideation-base and ideation-element.

Below are summary of key points which need to be remembered.

- The 4 mental aggregates are dissociated from materiality and *Nibbāna*, and vice-versa.
- The 4 mental aggregates are mutually associated at any one time.
- When all 4 mental aggregates are the states of enquiry, they have no associated states.
- When matter aggregate, or *Nibbāna* becomes the states of enquiry, there are no associated nor partially associated states, only having dissociated states.
- When materiality is dealt with *Nibbāna*, the states of *Nibbāna* is ignored because they are neither associated nor dissociated.
- When materiality is enquired with mentalities, subtle matters as part of materiality are ignored.
- *Nibbāna* belongs to mentality but is not an aggregate.
- When the states to be compared are materiality and materiality, *Nibbāna* and *Nibbāna*, consciousness and consciousness, feeling and feeling, contact and contact, materiality and *Nibbāna*, indeterminate states and unwholesome states, etc., they are neither associated nor dissociated. Reason being that they do not comply with the all 4 characteristics of association.
- When one of the 4 mental aggregates is dealt with the remaining 3 mental aggregates, they must both comply with the aforesaid 4 characteristics of association. Otherwise they are dissociated from each other.

VI. Association and Dissociation

- When states of enquiry are the phenomenal mentality-materiality, they have no associations nor partial associations, but having only dissociated states.
- Whenever mental aggregates are the states of enquiry, the 16 subtle matters and *Nibbāna* are always delimited as partially dissociated states.

The following abbreviations are used in all the tables throughout this Chapter. It is also useful to refer the analysis and explanations for these tables to the internal and external tables, and Chart 1 in Chapter 1 for better comprehension.

SOE	: States of enquiry
cons.	: Consciousness
agr.	: aggregate
el.	: element
As	: Associated
Pas	: Partially associated
Ds	: Dissociated
Pds	: Partially dissociated

92 internal states of enquiry

1. Aggregates (*Khandho*)

Table 6.1. Internal states of enquiry from 5 Aggregates

Aggregates as SOE:	Aggregate				Base				Element			
	As	Pas	Ds	Pds	As	Pas	Ds	Pds	As	Pas	Ds	Pds
228. Matter	-	-	4	-	-	-	1	1	-	-	7	1
229. Feeling; Perception; Volitive formation	3	-	1	-	1	1	10	1	7	1	10	1
230. Consciousness	3	-	1	-	-	1	10	1	-	1	10	1

Regarding SOE nos. 228, matter aggregate can not deal with itself. There is neither association nor partial association. Materiality is dissociated from the remaining 4 mental aggregates (feeling, perception, volitive formation, consciousness), 1 base (mind-base), and 7 elements (the 7 consciousness-elements). The state of *Nibbāna* is ignored because when materiality is dealt with *Nibbāna*, they are neither associated nor dissociated. Because subtle matters and the three mental aggregates (feeling, perception, and volitive formation) are contained by ideation-base and ideation-element, and in deed materiality includes the 16 subtle matters, and so subtle matters also need not be considered as part of dissociation. It thus left with only 52 cetasikas (inclusive aggregates of feeling, perception, and volitive formation) that come under ideation-base and ideation-element. In that sense, materiality is totally dissociated from consciousness aggregate. Materiality is partially dissociated from 1 base (ideation-base), 1 element (ideation-element), and also 52 cetasikas. It is because, as mentioned above, the 52 mental factors form a part of ideation-base and ideation-element, and 52 mental factors are associated with consciousness aggregate.

In SOE nos. 229, each of the states of enquiry is mutually associated with the remaining 3 mental aggregates. The first SOE, feeling, is mutually associated with 3 aggregates (perception, volitive formation, consciousness), with 1 base (mind-base), with 7 elements (7 consciousness-elements). This is because as mentioned above, only the 52 cetasikas from aggregates are considered which form under ideation-base and ideation-element. But, herein is 51 cetasikas because feeling can not associate with itself (52-1=51). Thus, feeling is partially associated with 1 base (ideation-base), with 1 element (ideation-element), and with 51 cetasikas. Feeling, perception or volitive formation aggregate is dissociated from 1 aggregate (12 gross matters), 10 bases (10 gross bases), and 10 elements (10 gross elements). Though *Nibbāna* is also dissociated, it comes not under aggregate. Each of these three SOE is also partially dissociated from 1 base (ideation-base), 1 element (ideation-element), subtle matters, and *Nibbāna*.

As for SOE nos. 230, consciousness is mutually associated with the remaining 3 mental aggregates. Because consciousness aggregate can not associate with itself, it therefore also can not associate with its co-adjuncts of mind-base and the 7 consciousness-elements. Consciousness aggregate is partially associated with 1 base (ideation-base), with 1 element (ideation-element), and with 52 cetasikas which come under them. It is dissociated from 1 aggregate (12 gross matters), 10 bases (10 gross bases), and 10 elements (10 gross elements). It is partially dissociated from 1 base (ideation-base), from 1 element (ideation-element), from 16 subtle matters and *Nibbāna*. The reason is the same as mentioned earlier, that 16 subtle matters and *Nibbāna* are always the partially dissociated states whenever mental aggregates are the states of enquiry.

2. Bases (*Āyatanaṃ*)

Table 6.2. Internal states of enquiry from 10 gross bases

231. Bases as states of enquiry:	Aggregate				Base				Element			
	As	Pas	Ds	Pds	As	Pas	Ds	Pds	As	Pas	Ds	Pds
Eye-base; Ear-base; Nose-base; Tongue-base; Body-base; Visible object base; Sound-base; Odour-base; Taste-base; Touch-base. (10)	-	-	4	-	-	-	1	1	-	-	7	1

VI. Association and Dissociation

These 10 gross bases correspond to gross materiality, and therefore they are not in association nor in partial dissociation. Each of them is dissociated from 4 mental aggregates, mind base, and 7 consciousness-elements. Because 52 cetasikas are contained by ideation-base and ideation-element, each of these subject matters of enquiry is therefore partially dissociated from 1 base (ideation-base), 1 element (ideation-element), and 52 cetasikas. Subtle matters, being a part of materiality, is herein ignored.

3. Elements (*Dhātu*)

Table 6.3. Internal states of enquiry from Mind-base

	Aggregate				Base				Element			
States of enquiry (SOE):	As	Pas	Ds	Pds	As	Pas	Ds	Pds	As	Pas	Ds	Pds
232. Mind-base. (1)	3	-	1	-	-	1	10	1	-	1	10	1

Mind-base is viewed as under consciousness aggregate in order comparison with other aggregates can be made. Consciousness aggregate is mutually associated with the remaining 3 mental aggregates. Herein, mind-base can not associate with itself, nor with the corresponding 7 consciousness-elements. Since the 7 consciousness elements are also associated with the 7 common mental factors (see Chart 10 in Appendix VI), mind-base is partially associated with 1 base (ideation-base), with 1 element (ideation-element), and with 52 cetasikas. Mind-base is dissociated from 1 aggregate (matter), 10 bases (10 gross bases), and 10 elements (10 gross elements). It is partially dissociated from 1 base (ideation-base), 1 element (ideation-element), 16 subtle matters, and *Nibbāna*.

Table 6.4. Internal states of enquiry from 10 gross elements

	Aggregate				Base				Element			
States of enquiry (SOE):	As	Pas	Ds	Pds	As	Pas	Ds	Pds	As	Pas	Ds	Pds
233. Eye element, ear element, nose element, tongue element, body element, vision element, sound element, odour element, taste element, touch element. (10)	-	-	4	-	-	-	1	1	-	-	7	1

Because these 10 subject matters of enquiry belong to gross materiality, therefore there are no associated states, nor partially associated states. Each of these states is totally dissociated from 4 aggregates (4 mental aggregates), 1 base (mind-base), and 7 elements (7 consciousness-elements). Because 52 cetasikas come under ideation-base and ideation-element, each SOE is thus partially

A Perfect Knowledge of Mind-Body from the Abhidhamma (Dhātukathā)

dissociated from 1 base (ideation-base), 1 element (ideation-element), and 52 cetasikas. Subtle matters, being a part of materiality, is therefore ignored.

Table 6.5. Internal states of enquiry from 7 consciousness elements

States of enquiry (SOE):	Aggregate				Base				Element			
	As	Pas	Ds	Pds	As	Pas	Ds	Pds	As	Pas	Ds	Pds
234. Eye cons. element; ear cons. element; nose cons. element; tongue cons. element; body cons. element; mind-element; mind-cons. element. (7)	3	-	1	-	-	1	10	1	-	1	16	1

These 7 states of enquiry belong to the group of 7 consciousness-elements. They are included under consciousness and belong to consciousness aggregate. Take eye-consciousness element for example. Eye-consciousness element is thus taken as associated with 3 aggregates (feeling, perception, volitive formation) but has no association with mind-base and consciousness aggregate. For one can not associate with itself, in the same case as in consciousness aggregate in preceding nos. 230. Same like the 10 *viññāna* cittas, eye-consciousness element is accompanied by the 7 common-universal cetasikas (see Chart 10 in Appendix VI). Thus, it is partially associated with 1 base (ideation-base) and with 1 element (ideation-element), and therefore, also with 52 cetasikas

It is dissociated from 1 aggregate (matter), 10 bases (10 gross bases), and 16 elements (10 gross elements, and 6 consciousness-elements having excluded eye-consciousness element). It is partially dissociated from 1 base (ideation-base), 1 element (ideation-element), 16 subtle matters, and *Nibbāna*.

The other six kinds of consciousness-elements are to dealt with in the similar as explained for eye-consciousness element.

4. Truths, etc. (*Saccādi*)

Table 6.6. Internal states of enquiry from two truths

	Aggregate				Base				Element			
235. States of enquiry (SOE):	As	Pas	Ds	Pds	As	Pas	Ds	Pds	As	Pas	Ds	Pds
1. Origin-truth 2. Path-truth	3	1	1	-	1	1	10	1	1	1	16	1

Origin-truth contains greed-*cetasika* present at the 8 greed-rooted unwholesome cittas, and 21 cetasikas. Path-truth corresponds to Noble Eightfold Path and the 4 supramundane path-consciousness, accompanied by 36 cetasikas. The two truths belong to volitive formation, are bound up with mind-consciousness element. Each of these SOE is mutually associated with the

VI. Association and Dissociation

remaining 3 mental aggregates (feeling, perception, consciousness), with 1 base (mind-base), with 1 element (mind-consciousness element). Each of the two truths is partially associated with 1 aggregate (volitive formation), with 1 base (ideation-base), with 1 element (ideation-element), and with 21 or 36 cetasikas.

Each SOE is dissociated from 1 aggregate (matter), 10 bases (10 gross bases), and 16 elements (10 gross elements, and 6 consciousness-elements having excluded mind-consciousness element). It is partially dissociated from 1 base (ideation-base), 1 element (ideation-element), 16 subtle matters, and *Nibbāna*.

Table 6.7. Internal states of enquiry from Cessation-truth, 7 faculties

	Aggregate				Base				Element			
236. States of enquiry (SOE):	As	Pas	Ds	Pds	As	Pas	Ds	Pds	As	Pas	Ds	Pds
1. Cessation-truth (of suffering)												
2. Vision-faculty												
3. Hearing-faculty												
4. Smell-faculty	-	-	4	-	-	-	1	1	-	-	7	1
5. Taste-faculty												
6. Touch-faculty												
7. Femininity-faculty												
8. Masculinity-faculty												

Cessation-truth comes under *Nibbāna*, thus there are no associations, nor partial associations. The next 5 sense-faculties come under gross matters, while the female and male faculties come under subtle matters. As mentioned earlier, when either matter aggregate or *Nibbāna* is the state of enquiry, there are no associated states, nor partially associated states. In this case, each of these 7 faculties is dissociated from 4 aggregates (4 mental aggregates), from 1 base (mind-base), from 7 elements (7 consciousness-elements). Each is partially dissociated from 1 base (ideation-base), from 1 element (ideation-element), and from 52 cetasikas. *Nibbāna* is herein ignored because when materiality is enquired with *Nibbāna*, they are neither associated nor dissociated as mentioned earlier. Subtle matters are ignored for they are both part of materiality and 2 SOE.

Table 6.8. Internal states of enquiry from Mind-faculty

	Aggregate				Base				Element			
States of enquiry (SOE):	As	Pas	Ds	Pds	As	Pas	Ds	Pds	As	Pas	Ds	Pds
237. Mind-faculty. (1)	3	-	1	-	-	1	10	1	-	1	10	1

Mind-faculty is associated with 89 cittas under consciousness aggregate. So, it is associated with 3 mental aggregates (feeling, perception, volitive formation). It has no association with base and element for consciousness can not associate

A Perfect Knowledge of Mind-Body from the Abhidhamma (Dhātukathā)

with consciousness. It is partially associated with 1 base (ideation-base), with 1 element (ideation-element), and with 52 cetasikas which come under them.

It is dissociated from 1 aggregate (matter), 10 bases (10 gross bases), and 10 elements (10 gross elements). It is partially dissociated from 1 base (ideation-base), 1 element (ideation-element), 16 subtle matters, and *Nibbāna*.

Table 6.9. Internal states of enquiry from 4 feeling faculties

	Aggregate				Base				Element			
States of enquiry (SOE):	As	Pas	Ds	Pds	As	Pas	Ds	Pds	As	Pas	Ds	Pds
238. Carnal or bodily pleasure faculty; carnal displeasure faculty; mental joy faculty; melancholy faculty. (4)	3	-	1	-	1	1	10	1	1	1	16	1

These four are feeling faculties, come under feeling aggregate. Each of them is mutually associated with the remaining 3 mental aggregates (perception, volitive formation, and consciousness), with 1 base (mind-base), with 1 element (body-consciousness element). Each is partially associated with 1 base (ideation-base), with 1 element (ideation-element), and with 6 cetasikas (7 common non-beautiful mental factors excluding feeling).

Each is dissociated from 1 aggregate (matter), 10 bases (10 gross bases), and 16 elements (10 gross elements, and 6 consciousness-elements having excluded body-consciousness element). It is partially dissociated from 1 base (ideation-base), 1 element (ideation-element), 16 subtle matters, and *Nibbāna*.

Table 6.10. Internal states of enquiry from Equanimity-faculty

	Aggregate				Base				Element			
States of enquiry (SOE):	As	Pas	Ds	Pds	As	Pas	Ds	Pds	As	Pas	Ds	Pds
239. Equanimity-faculty. (1)	3	-	1	-	1	1	10	1	6	1	11	1

Equanimity-faculty, like the other four faculties in nos.238, comes under feeling aggregate, and is accompanied by 46 cetasikas (52 excluding feeling, zest, hatred, envy, avarice, worry, i.e. 52-6=46). It is mutually associated with the remaining 3 mental aggregates (perception, volitive formation, consciousness), with 1 base (mind-base), with 6 elements (7 consciousness-elements excluding body-consciousness element). It is partially associated with 1 base (ideation-base), with 1 element (ideation-element), and with 46 cetasikas.

Equanimity-faculty is dissociated from 1 aggregate (matter), 10 bases (10 gross bases), and 11 elements (10 gross elements and body-consciousness element). It is partially dissociated from 1 base (ideation-base), 1 element (ideation-element), 16 subtle matters, and *Nibbāna*.

VI. Association and Dissociation

Table 6.11. Internal states of enquiry from 8 volition-based faculties, and others

States of enquiry (SOE):	Aggregate				Base				Element			
	As	Pas	Ds	Pds	As	Pas	Ds	Pds	As	Pas	Ds	Pds
240. Confidence-faculty; effort-faculty; mindfulness-faculty; concentration-faculty; wisdom-faculty; "I-shall-comprehend-the-unknown" faculty; higher knowledge faculty; "final knower" faculty; ignorance; conditioned by ignorance, volitive formation (10)	3	1	1	-	1	1	10	1	1	1	16	1

These 10 sttes of enquiry belong to volitive formation aggregate. So, each of them is mutually associated with the remaining 3 mental aggregates (feeling, perception, consciousness), with 1 base (mind-base), with 1 element (mind-consciousness element). Each is partially associated with 1 base (ideation-base), with 1 element (ideation-element), and with 51 cetasikas (52 excluding, respectively, *saddhā, viriya, sati, ekaggata* for the first 4 faculties, *amoha* for the next 4 faculties, *moha* and *cetanā* for the last 2 factors of the dependent origination).

Each of them is dissociated from 1 aggregate (matter), 10 bases (10 gross bases), and 16 elements (10 gross elements, and 6 consciousness-elements having excluded mind-consciousness element). It is partially dissociated from 1 base (ideation-base), 1 element (ideation-element), 16 subtle matters, and *Nibbāna*.

Table 6.12. Internal states of enquiry from Consciousness

States of enquiry (SOE):	Aggregate				Base				Element			
	As	Pas	Ds	Pds	As	Pas	Ds	Pds	As	Pas	Ds	Pds
241. Conditioned by volitive formation, is Consciousness. (1)	3	-	1	-	-	1	10	1	-	1	10	1

Consciousness herein is under consciousness aggregate. Explanation and answers are the same as in nos. 230 above.

Table 6.13. Internal states of enquiry from Contact

States of enquiry (SOE):	Aggregate				Base				Element			
	As	Pas	Ds	Pds	As	Pas	Ds	Pds	As	Pas	Ds	Pds
242. Conditioned by the six bases, is Contact. (1)	3	1	1	-	1	1	10	1	7	1	10	1

A Perfect Knowledge of Mind-Body from the Abhidhamma (Dhātukathā)

Contact is one of the 7 common non-beautiful cetasikas, and it accompanies 89 cittas. It is included in volitive formation. Contact is associated with 3 aggregates (feeling, perception, consciousness), with 1 base (mind-base), with 7 elements (the 7 consciousness-elements). It is partially associated with 1 aggregate (volitive formation), with 1 base (ideation-base), with 1 element (ideation-element), and with 51 cetasikas (52 excluding contact-*cetasika*).

Contact is dissociated from 1 aggregate (matter), 10 bases (10 gross bases), and 10 elements (10 gross elements). It is partially dissociated from 1 base (ideation-base), 1 element (ideation-element), 16 subtle matters, and *Nibbāna*.

Table 6.14. Internal states of enquiry from Feeling

	Aggregate				Base				Element			
States of enquiry (SOE):	As	Pas	Ds	Pds	As	Pas	Ds	Pds	As	Pas	Ds	Pds
243. Conditioned by contact, is Feeling. (1)	3	-	1	-	1	1	10	1	7	1	10	1

Feeling is one of the 7 common non-beautiful cetasikas. It is present at 89 cittas, accompanied by 51 cetasikas (52 excluding feeling-*cetasika*). It comes under feeling aggregate. Therefore, it is associated with the remaining 3 mental aggregates (perception, volitive formation, consciousness), with 1 base (mind-base), with 7 elements (the 7 consciousness-elements). It is partially associated with 1 base (ideation-base), with 1 element (ideation-element), and with 51 cetasikas.

Feeling is dissociated from 1 aggregate (matter), 10 bases (10 gross bases), and 10 elements (10 gross elements). It is partially dissociated from 1 base (ideation-base), 1 element (ideation-element), 16 subtle matters, and *Nibbāna*.

Table 6.15. States of enquiry from Craving, Clinging, Action-becoming

	Aggregate				Base				Element			
States of enquiry (SOE):	As	Pas	Ds	Pds	As	Pas	Ds	Pds	As	Pas	Ds	Pds
244. Conditioned by feeling, Craving; Conditioned by craving, Clinging; Action-becoming (3)	3	1	1	-	1	1	10	1	1	1	16	1

Craving is accompanied by greed-*cetasika*, while clinging is accompanied by greed and wrong view cetasikas. These cetasikas are present at the 8 greed-rooted cittas. Kamma-becoming is accompanied by volition-*cetasika*, present at the 17 wholesome cittas and 12 unwholesome cittas. The three states of enquiry belong to volitive formation aggregate.

Each of them is mutually associated with the remaining 3 mental aggregates (feeling, perception, consciousness), with 1 base (mind-base), with 1 element

VI. Association and Dissociation

(mind-consciousness element). Each is partially associated with 1 aggregate (volitive formation), 1 base (ideation-base), with 1 element (ideation-element), and with 51 cetasikas, or 50 in the case of clinging.

Each is dissociated from 1 aggregate (matter), 10 bases (10 gross bases), and 16 elements (10 gross elements, and 6 consciousness-elements having excluded mind-consciousness element). It is partially dissociated from 1 base (ideation-base), 1 element (ideation-element), 16 subtle matters, and *Nibbāna*.

Table 6.16. Internal states of enquiry from Fine-material becoming

States of enquiry (SOE):	Aggregate				Base				Element			
	As	Pas	Ds	Pds	As	Pas	Ds	Pds	As	Pas	Ds	Pds
245. Fine-material becoming (1)	-	-	-	-	-	-	-	-	-	-	3	-

Fine-material becoming consists of 5 resultant cittas, 2 eye-cittas, 2 ear-cittas, 2 receiving-cittas, 2 investigating-cittas, 35 cetasikas (13+[25-3]=35), and 15 kamma-produced matters (20 excluding femininity, masculinity, nose, tongue, and body, i.e. 20-5=15). Because fine-material becoming belongs to mentality-materiality, it is therefore neither associated, nor partially associated.

Because beings born in the fine-material sphere are devoid of consciousness in respect of the three senses of nose, tongue, and body, fine-material becoming is therefore dissociated from 3 elements (nose-consciousness element, tongue-consciousness element, and body-consciousness element). It has no other partially dissociated states.

Table 6.17. Internal states of enquiry from Immaterial-becoming, etc.

States of enquiry (SOE):	Aggregate				Base				Element			
	As	Pas	Ds	Pds	As	Pas	Ds	Pds	As	Pas	Ds	Pds
246. Immaterial-becoming; Neither-perception-nor-non-perception becoming; Four-aggregate becoming (3)	-	-	1	-	-	-	10	1	-	-	16	1

Both neither-perception-nor-non-perception becoming and four-aggregate becoming are similar to immaterial-becoming. These three states of enquiry belong to subtle matters, 4 mental aggregates and *Nibbāna*, are closely bound up with mind-consciousness element. Since they are both mentality and materiality, they are neither associated nor partially associated.

Each of these three states is dissociated from 1 aggregate (matter), 10 bases (10 gross bases), and 16 elements (10 gross elements, and 6 consciousness-elements having excluded mind-consciousness element). It is partially

A Perfect Knowledge of Mind-Body from the Abhidhamma (Dhātukathā)

dissociated from 1 base (ideation-base), 1 element (ideation-element), 16 subtle matters, and *Nibbāna*.

Table 6.18. Internal states of enquiry from 2 becomings, Lamentation

States of enquiry (SOE):	Aggregate				Base				Element			
	As	Pas	Ds	Pds	As	Pas	Ds	Pds	As	Pas	Ds	Pds
247. Non-perception becoming; Single-aggregate becoming; Lamentation. (3)	-	-	4	-	-	-	1	1	-	-	7	1

Non-perception becoming and single-aggregate becoming are identical, both are bound up with visible object base. Lamentation is taken as sound base because of wailing, and belongs to matter aggregate. Since these three states are gross materiality, they have no association nor partial association. Each of these SOE is dissociated from the remaining 4 mental aggregates (feeling, perception, volitive formation, consciousness), 1 base (mind-base), and 7 elements (7 consciousness-elements). Each of them is partially dissociated from 1 base (ideation-base), 1 element (ideation-element), and 52 cetasikas. For the same reason as explained earlier in nos. 228, 231 & 233, subtle matters and *Nibbāna* are herein not being considered.

Table 6.19. States of enquiry from Sorrow, Suffering, Melancholy

States of enquiry (SOE):	Aggregate				Base				Element			
	As	Pas	Ds	Pds	As	Pas	Ds	Pds	As	Pas	Ds	Pds
248. Sorrow; suffering; melancholy. (3)	3	-	1	-	1	1	10	1	1	1	16	1

All of them are grievous feeling, belong to the feeling faculties. They are associated with the two hatred-rooted cittas. Each of them is associated with 3 aggregates (perception, volitive formation, consciousness), with 1 base (mind-base), with 1 element (body-consciousness element). Each is partially associated with 1 base (ideation-base), 1 element (ideation-element), and 51 cetasikas (excluded hatred-*cetasika*). Each is dissociated from 1 aggregate (matter), 10 bases (10 gross bases), and 16 elements (10 gross elements, and 6 consciousness-elements without body-consciousness element). It is also partially dissociated from 1 base (ideation-base), 1 element (ideation-element), 16 subtle matters, and *Nibbāna*.

Table 6.20. Internal states of enquiry from 4 others

States of enquiry (SOE):	Aggregate				Base				Element			
	As	Pas	Ds	Pds	As	Pas	Ds	Pds	As	Pas	Ds	Pds
249. Despair; Four Foundations of Mindfulness; Four Right Strivings. (3)	3	1	1	-	1	1	10	1	1	1	16	1

VI. Association and Dissociation

Despair is associated with occasional hatred-*cetasika*; Four Foundations of Mindfulness is associated with mindfulness-*cetasika*; Four Right Strivings is associated with energy-*cetasika*. The three belong to volitive formation aggregate. Thus, each of them is associated with remaining 3 mental aggregates (feeling, perception, consciousness), 1 base (mind-base), 1 element (mind-consciousness element). Each of these three states is partially associated with 1 base (ideation-base), 1 element (ideation-element), and 51 cetasikas (52 excluding respectively, *dosa, sati,* and *viriya* from each SOE).

Each is dissociated from 1 aggregate (matter), 10 bases (10 gross bases), and 16 elements (10 gross elements, and 6 consciousness-elements having excluded mind-consciousness element). It is partially dissociated from 1 base (ideation-base), 1 element (ideation-element), 16 subtle matters, and *Nibbāna*.

Table 6.21. States of enquiry from Basis of Psychic Accomplishment

States of enquiry (SOE):	Aggregate				Base				Element			
	As	Pas	Ds	Pds	As	Pas	Ds	Pds	As	Pas	Ds	Pds
250. Basis of Psychic Accomplishment. (1)	2	1	1	-	-	1	10	1	-	1	16	1

These states are the four Basis of Psychic Accomplishment, are followed by the mental factors of *viriya, chanda,* and *amoha* (effort, desire, and wisdom). The SOE are states associated with 8 x 5 supramundane cittas, accompanied by 33 cetasikas (i.e. 13 common cetasikas excluding effort and desire, and 25 beautiful cetasikas excluding 2 Illimitables and wisdom). These states belong to consciousness aggregate. So, the SOE is mutually associated with remaining 2 aggregates (feeling, perception). Ideation-base and ideation-element can not be associated directly because consciousness aggregate is included in the states of enquiry. The SOE is partially associated with 1 aggregate (volitive formation), with 1 base (ideation-base), 1 element (ideation-element), and 33 cetasikas present at the 40 kinds of supramundane jhānas (i.e. 8 x 5).

It is dissociated from 1 aggregate (matter), 10 bases (10 gross bases), and 16 elements (10 gross elements, and 6 consciousness-elements having excluded mind-consciousness element). It is partially dissociated from 1 base (ideation-base), 1 element (ideation-element), 16 subtle matters, and *Nibbāna*.

A Perfect Knowledge of Mind-Body from the Abhidhamma (Dhātukathā)

Table 6.22. Internal states of enquiry from Jhāna

States of enquiry (SOE):	Aggregate				Base				Element			
	As	Pas	Ds	Pds	As	Pas	Ds	Pds	As	Pas	Ds	Pds
251. Jhāna. (1)	2	1	1	-	1	1	10	1	1	1	16	1

Jhāna is present at the 27 sublime cittas from the two mundane spheres, accompanied by 33 cetasikas (38 excluding the 5 jhānic factors present at First *jhāna*). At the transcendental sphere, it belongs to the 8 supramundane Fifth-jhānas. *Jhāna* belongs to feeling aggregate. So, it is mutually associated with the remaining 2 aggregates (perception, consciousness), 1 base (mind-base), 1 element (mind-consciousness element), and 33 cetasikas (38 excluding 5 *jhāna*-factors). It is partially associated with 1 aggregate (volitive formation), 1 base (ideation-base), with 1 element (ideation-element), and also with 33 cetasikas (13 excluding *vitakka*, *vicāra*, *pīti*, and 25 excluding the 2 Illimitables) present at the 8 supramundane Fifth-jhānas.

Jhāna is dissociated from 1 aggregate (matter), 10 bases (10 gross bases), and 16 elements (10 gross elements, and 6 consciousness-elements having excluded mind-consciousness element). It is partially dissociated from 1 base (ideation-base), 1 element (ideation-element), 16 subtle matters, and *Nibbāna*.

Table 6.23. Internal states of enquiry from the Illimitables, etc

States of enquiry (SOE):	Aggregate				Base				Element			
	As	Pas	Ds	Pds	As	Pas	Ds	Pds	As	Pas	Ds	Pds
252. The Illimitables; 5 Faculties; 5 Powers; 7 Enlightenment-Factors; Noble Eightfold Path (5)	3	1	1	-	1	1	10	1	1	1	16	1

Each of these five subject matters of enquiry is associated with different cetasikas (see Table 1.6b), but all of them come under volitive formation aggregate. And so, each is associated with 3 aggregates (feeling, perception, consciousness), 1 base (mind-base), 1 element (mind-consciousness element). It is partially associated with 1 aggregate (volitive formation), 1 base (ideation-base), 1 element (ideation-element), and with its specific group of cetasikas.

Each of them is dissociated from 1 aggregate (matter), 10 bases (10 gross bases), and 16 elements (10 gross elements, and 6 consciousness-elements having excluded mind-consciousness element). It is partially dissociated from 1 base (ideation-base), 1 element (ideation-element), 16 subtle matters, and *Nibbāna*.

VI. Association and Dissociation

Table 6.24. Internal states of enquiry from Contact, Volition, Attention

States of enquiry (SOE):	Aggregate				Base				Element			
	As	Pas	Ds	Pds	As	Pas	Ds	Pds	As	Pas	Ds	Pds
253. Contact; Volition; Attention. (3)	3	1	1	-	1	1	10	1	7	1	10	1

Contact is accompanied by mental factor of *phasso*; Volition is accompanied by mental factor of *cetanā*; Attention is accompanied by mental factor of *manasikāra*. These three states of enquiry belong to volitive formation aggregate. Each of them is associated with 3 aggregates (feeling, perception, consciousness), 1 base (mind-base), 7 elements (the 7 consciousness-elements). Each is partially associated with 1 aggregate (volitive formation), 1 base (ideation-base), 1 element (ideation-element), and 51 cetasikas.

Each of them is dissociated from 1 aggregate (matter), 10 bases (10 gross bases), and 10 elements (10 gross elements). It is partially dissociated from 1 base (ideation-base), 1 element (ideation-element), 16 subtle matters, and *Nibbāna*.

Table 6.25. Internal states of enquiry from Feeling, Perception

States of enquiry (SOE):	Aggregate				Base				Element			
	As	Pas	Ds	Pds	As	Pas	Ds	Pds	As	Pas	Ds	Pds
254. Feeling; Perception. (2)	3	-	1	-	1	1	10	1	7	1	10	1

Feeling is accompanied by the mental factor of *vedanā*; Perception is accompanied by mental factor of *saññā*. The answers are the same as in nos. 229.

Table 6.26. Internal states of enquiry from Consciousness

States of enquiry (SOE):	Aggregate				Base				Element			
	As	Pas	Ds	Pds	As	Pas	Ds	Pds	As	Pas	Ds	Pds
255. Consciousness. (1)	3	-	1	-	-	1	10	1	-	1	10	1

Answers are the same as in nos. 230.

Table 6.27. Internal states of enquiry from Decision

States of enquiry (SOE):	Aggregate				Base				Element			
	As	Pas	Ds	Pds	As	Pas	Ds	Pds	As	Pas	Ds	Pds
256. Decision. (1)	3	1	1	-	1	1	10	1	2	1	15	1

Decision is accompanied by the mental factor of *adhimokkha*, belong to volitive formation. Decision is mutually associated with 3 aggregates (feeling, perception, consciousness), with 1 base (mind-base), with 2 elements (mind-element, and mind-consciousness element). It is partially associated with 1 aggregate (volitive formation), 1 base (ideation-base), 1 element (ideation-element), and 50 cetasikas (52 excluding doubt and decision).

Decision is dissociated from 1 aggregate (matter), 10 bases (10 gross bases), and 15 elements (10 gross elements and the remaining 5 sense consciousness elements). It is partially dissociated from 1 base (ideation-base), 1 element (ideation-element), 16 subtle matters, and *Nibbāna*.

47 states of enquiry from Dhammasaṅgaṇīmātikā triads

5. Triads (*Tikaṃ*)

	Aggregate				Base				Element			
States of enquiry (SOE):	As	Pas	Ds	Pds	As	Pas	Ds	Pds	As	Pas	Ds	Pds
257. Wholesome states; Unwholesome states. (2)	-	-	1	-	-	-	10	1	-	-	16	1

Both states belong to 4 mental aggregates, and so there are no associations. Each of them is dissociated from 1 aggregate (matter), 10 bases (10 gross bases), and 16 elements (10 gross elements, and 6 consciousness-elements having excluded mind-consciousness element). It is partially dissociated from 1 base (ideation-base), 1 element (ideation-element), 16 subtle matters, and *Nibbāna*.

	Aggregate				Base				Element			
States of enquiry (SOE):	As	Pas	Ds	Pds	As	Pas	Ds	Pds	As	Pas	Ds	Pds
258. States associated with happy feeling; States associated with painful feeling. (2)	1	-	1	-	-	1	10	1	-	1	15	1

States associated with happy feeling are consist of 63 cittas and accompanied by 46 cetasikas (52 excluding feeling, hatred, envy, avarice, worry, doubt). States associated with painful feeling consist of 3 cittas (2 hatred-rooted, 1 body-consciousness resultant), accompanied by 21 cetasikas (27 excluding feeling, zest, greed, wrong view, conceit, doubt. i.e. $(13+14)-6=21$). The two SOE are classified under the aggregates of perception, volitive formation and consciousness, are both bound up with body-consciousness element.

Each of them is thus associated with 1 aggregate (feeling). Although feeling aggregate can not associate with itself, but herein ideation-base and ideation-element also come under the aggregates of perception and volitive formation. Each of these two states is thereby partially associated with 1 base (ideation-base), 1 element (ideation-element), and 46 or 21 cetasikas depending on which SOE is being dealt with at the time.

VI. Association and Dissociation

Each of them is dissociated from 1 aggregate (matter), 10 bases (10 gross bases), and 15 elements (10 gross elements, and 5 consciousness-elements having excluded body-consciousness element and mind-consciousness element). It is partially dissociated from 1 base (ideation-base), 1 element (ideation-element), 16 subtle matters, and *Nibbāna*.

States of enquiry (SOE):	Aggregate				Base				Element			
	As	Pas	Ds	Pds	As	Pas	Ds	Pds	As	Pas	Ds	Pds
259. States associated with neither happy feeling nor painful feeling. (1)	1	-	1	-	-	1	10	1	-	1	11	1

These states correspond to 55 cittas accompanied by equanimity, and 46 cetasikas (52 excluding feeling, zest, hatred, envy, avarice, worry), are classified under the aggregates of perception, volitive formation and consciousness. The SOE is associated with 1 aggregate (feeling). Herein, ideation-base and ideation-element are excluded because they also come under the aggregates of perception and volitive formation. It is thus only partially associated with 1 base (ideation-base), 1 element (ideation-element), and 46 cetasikas.

The SOE is dissociated from 1 aggregate (matter), 10 bases (10 gross bases), and 11 elements (10 gross elements and body-consciousness element). It is also partially dissociated from 1 base (ideation-base), 1 element (ideation-element), 16 subtle matters, and *Nibbāna*.

States of enquiry (SOE):	Aggregate				Base				Element			
	As	Pas	Ds	Pds	As	Pas	Ds	Pds	As	Pas	Ds	Pds
260. Resultant states. (1)	-	-	1	-	-	-	10	1	-	-	10	1

Resultant states, namely the 36 resultants, are followed by 38 cetasikas (13 common and 25 beautiful factors). Resultant states consist of the 4 aggregates of feeling, perception, volitive formation, and consciousness. Thus, states of enquiry encompass 4 mental aggregates, and so they have no associations. They are in dissociation only from materiality. Resultant states are dissociated from 1 aggregate (matter), 10 bases (10 gross bases), and 10 elements (10 gross elements). They are partially dissociated from 1 base (ideation-base), 1 element (ideation-element), 16 subtle matters, and *Nibbāna*.

States of enquiry (SOE):	Aggregate				Base				Element			
	As	Pas	Ds	Pds	As	Pas	Ds	Pds	As	Pas	Ds	Pds
261. States which produce resultants; States which are both corrupted and favourable to corruption. (2)	-	-	1	-	-	-	10	1	-	-	16	1

A Perfect Knowledge of Mind-Body from the Abhidhamma (Dhātukathā)

States which produce resultants are 21 wholesome cittas, 12 unwholesome cittas, and 52 cetasikas. States which are both corrupted and favourable to corruption are 12 unwholesome cittas, and 27 cetasikas (13+14=27). Both states of enquiry belong to 4 mental aggregates. As such, there are no association. Each of the SOE is dissociated from 1 aggregate (matter), 10 bases (10 gross bases), and 16 elements (10 gross elements, and 6 consciousness-elements having excluded mind-consciousness element). Each is partially dissociated from 1 base (ideation-base), 1 element (ideation-element), 16 subtle matters, and *Nibbāna*.

States of enquiry (SOE):	Aggregate				Base				Element			
	As	Pas	Ds	Pds	As	Pas	Ds	Pds	As	Pas	Ds	Pds
262. States which neither are resultants nor producing resultants; States are not the result of clinging but are favourable to clinging. (2)	-	-	-	-	-	-	-	-	-	-	5	-

States which neither are resultants nor are causing resultants are associated with 20 functional cittas, 35 cetasikas (38 excluding the 3 abstinences), 28 matters, and *Nibbāna*. The second SOE is associated with 69 cittas, 52 cetasikas, 17 mind-produced matters, 15 temperature-produced matters, and 14 nutriment-produced matters. Because both SOE embrace the dual qualities of mentality and materiality, they therefore have no associations.

Because the two SOE consist of both materiality and functional states, therefore mind-element of the functional mind-door advertence, together with mind-consciousness element are to be excluded. Hence, each of the two SOE is in dissociation from 5 elements (eye-consciousness element, ear-consciousness element, nose-consciousness element, tongue-consciousness element, and body-consciousness element).

263. States of enquiry (SOE):	Aggregate				Base				Element			
	As	Pas	Ds	Pds	As	Pas	Ds	Pds	As	Pas	Ds	Pds
1. States neither are the result of clinging nor are favourable to clinging. (*anupādinna anupādāniyā*)	-	-	-	-	-	-	-	-	-	-	6	-
2. States which are not corrupted and not objects of corruptions. (*asaṃkiliṭṭha asaṃkilesikā*)												

These two states consist of 8 supramundane cittas, 36 cetasikas (38 excluding the 2 Illimitables), and *Nibbāna*. Because these states of enquiry belong to 4 mental aggregates and *Nibbāna*, there are no associated states, nor partially associated states. We may have earlier thought that *Nibbāna*, being the ultimate

VI. Association and Dissociation

objective of noble eightfold path and when we undertake persistent sanitisation of the subjective cetasikas and cittas for achieving that level of enlightenment, these three ambits of mentality must have been associated without doubt. We learned it here that, in fact, they are not. The three mentalities are related to each other only by dissociation condition which we shall discover in the later chapters. It is also mentioned in Paṭṭhāna.

These states are in dissociation from 6 consciousness elements (eye-consciousness element, ear-consciousness element, nose-consciousness element, tongue-consciousness element, body-consciousness element, and mind-element). There are no dissociations from aggregate and base, nor any partial dissociation.

States of enquiry (SOE):	Aggregate				Base				Element			
	As	Pas	Ds	Pds	As	Pas	Ds	Pds	As	Pas	Ds	Pds
264. States with initial application and sustained application. (1)	-	1	1	-	-	1	10	1	-	1	15	1

These states are associated with 55 cittas and 50 cetasikas, belong to 4 mental aggregates. Thus, there are no associations. Although volitive formation aggregate is herein excluded from direct association with initial application and sustained application, it is still partially associated because of the associated 50 cetasikas. Thereby these states have partial association with 1 aggregate (volitive formation), 1 base (ideation-base), 1 element (ideation-element), and 50 cetasikas.

They are dissociated from 1 aggregate (matter), 10 bases (10 gross bases), and 15 elements (10 gross elements, and 5 sensory consciousness elements having excluded mind-element and mind-consciousness element). They are partially dissociated from 1 base (ideation-base), 1 element (ideation-element), 16 subtle matters, and *Nibbāna*.

States of enquiry (SOE):	Aggregate				Base				Element			
	As	Pas	Ds	Pds	As	Pas	Ds	Pds	As	Pas	Ds	Pds
265. States without initial application but with sustained application; States accompanied by zest. (2)	-	1	1	-	-	1	10	1	-	1	16	1

States without initial application but with sustained application are the 11 Second-*Jhāna* cittas (8+3=11), 66 cittas with sustained application, and 36 cetasikas. States accompanied by zest are 51 associated cittas, 46 cetasikas (52 excluding zest, hatred, envy, avarice, worry, and doubt, i.e. 52-6=46). Both SOE belong to 4 mental aggregates, and thus there are no direct associations. Each of these SOE have partial association with 1 aggregate (volitive formation, which is at work with sustained application), with 1 base (ideation-base), with 1

A Perfect Knowledge of Mind-Body from the Abhidhamma (Dhātukathā)

element (ideation-element), and with 37 or 46 cetasikas depending on which SOE is being enquired at the time.

Each of these SOE is dissociated from 1 aggregate (matter), 10 bases (10 gross bases), and 16 elements (10 gross elements, and 6 consciousness-elements having excluded mind-consciousness element). Each is partially dissociated from 1 base (ideation-base), 1 element (ideation-element), 16 subtle matters, and *Nibbāna*.

	Aggregate				Base				Element			
States of enquiry (SOE):	As	Pas	Ds	Pds	As	Pas	Ds	Pds	As	Pas	Ds	Pds
266. States without initial application and without sustained application. (1)	-	-	-	-	-	-	-	-	-	-	1	-

These states consist of 11 Second-*Jhāna* cittas, 55 cittas dissociated from *vitakka* and *vicāra*, 36 cetasikas (13+25 excluding both *vitakka* and *vicāra*), 28 matters, and *Nibbāna*. Because materiality-mentality, and *Nibbāna* are the states of enquiry, there are neither associated nor partially associated states. The same is explained in preceding nos. 263. There are no dissociations from base and element. There is only 1 element (mind-element) in dissociation from these states.

	Aggregate				Base				Element			
States of enquiry (SOE):	As	Pas	Ds	Pds	As	Pas	Ds	Pds	As	Pas	Ds	Pds
267. States accompanied by happiness or pleasure. (1)	1	-	1	-	-	1	10	1	-	1	15	1

These states consist of 63 cittas, and 46 cetasikas. They belong to perception, volitive formation, and consciousness. These states are bound up with body-consciousness element. They are associated with 1 aggregate (feeling). There is no association with ideation-base and ideation-element because they also come under perception and volitive formation aggregates. These states are only partially associated with 1 base (ideation-base), 1 element (ideation-element), and 46 cetasikas.

These states are in dissociation from 1 aggregate (matter), 10 bases (10 gross bases), and 15 elements (10 gross elements, eye-cons. element., ear-cons. element, nose-cons. element, tongue-cons. element, and mind-element). They are partially dissociated from 1 base (ideation-base), 1 element (ideation-element), 16 subtle matters, and *Nibbāna*.

	Aggregate				Base				Element			
States of enquiry (SOE):	As	Pas	Ds	Pds	As	Pas	Ds	Pds	As	Pas	Ds	Pds
268. States accompanied by equanimity.	1	-	1	-	-	1	10	1	-	1	11	1

VI. Association and Dissociation

These are states which endure neither happy feeling nor painful feeling, consist of 55 cittas accompanied by equanimity, and 46 cetasikas (52 excluding feeling, zest, hatred, envy, avarice, worry). They belong to perception, volitive formation, and consciousness aggregates. These equanimous states are associated with 1 aggregate (feeling). There are no associations with bases and elements. These states are partially associated with 1 base (ideation-base), 1 element (ideation-element), and 46 cetasikas.

These states are dissociated from 1 aggregate (matter), 10 bases (10 gross bases), and 11 elements (10 gross elements, and body-consciousness element). They are partially dissociated from 1 base (ideation-base), 1 element (ideation-element), 16 subtle matters, and *Nibbāna*.

	Aggregate				Base				Element			
269. States of enquiry (SOE):	As	Pas	Ds	Pds	As	Pas	Ds	Pds	As	Pas	Ds	Pds
1. States eliminated by first Path.												
2. States eliminated by higher three Paths.												
3. States with root causes eliminated by first Path.												
4. States with root causes eliminated by higher three Paths.												
5. States which make for the continuance of death and rebirth. (*ācayagāmino*)	-	-	1	-	-	-	10	1	-	-	16	1
6. States which make for the discontinuity of rebirth, i.e. leading out to *Nibbāna* (*apacayagāmino*).												
7. States appertaining to Learners (*sekhā*).												
8. States appertaining to *Arahatta* (*asekhā*)												
9. Sublime states.												

These nine subject matters of enquiry are bound up with mind-consciousness element. They all belong to 4 mental aggregates, and so there are no associations. Each of these SOE is in dissociation from 1 aggregate (matter), 10 bases (10 gross bases), and 16 elements (10 gross elements, and 6 consciousness-elements having excluded mind-consciousness element). It is partially dissociated from 1 base (ideation-base), 1 element (ideation-element), 16 subtle matters, and *Nibbāna*. The answers are identical to that in nos. 261.

	Aggregate				Base				Element			
States of enquiry (SOE):	As	Pas	Ds	Pds	As	Pas	Ds	Pds	As	Pas	Ds	Pds
270. Immeasurable states; Superior states. (2)	-	-	-	-	-	-	-	-	-	-	6	-

A Perfect Knowledge of Mind-Body from the Abhidhamma (Dhātukathā)

Both immeasurable and superior states consist of 8 supramundane cittas, and 36 cetasikas (38 excluding 2 Illimitables), are bound up with mind-consciousness element. These two states belong to 4 mental aggregates. So, there are no associations. There are no dissociations from aggregate and base, except these two states are in dissociation from 6 consciousness elements (eye-cons. element, ear-cons. element, nose-cons. element, tongue-cons. element, body-cons. element, and mind-element).

States of enquiry (SOE):	Aggregate				Base				Element			
	As	Pas	Ds	Pds	As	Pas	Ds	Pds	As	Pas	Ds	Pds
271. States with limited objects.	-	-	1	-	-	-	10	1	-	-	10	1

States with limited object consist of 54 sensuous cittas and 52 cetasikas, are bound up with ideation-element and the 7 consciousness elements. They belong to 4 mental aggregates, and so there are no associations. They are dissociated from 1 aggregate (matter), 10 bases (10 gross bases), and 10 elements (10 gross elements). They are in partial dissociation from 1 base (ideation-base), 1 element (ideation-element), 16 subtle matters, and *Nibbāna*.

272. States of enquiry (SOE):	Aggregate				Base				Element			
	As	Pas	Ds	Pds	As	Pas	Ds	Pds	As	Pas	Ds	Pds
1. States with sublime objects.												
2. States with immeasurable objects.												
3. Inferior states.												
4. States fixed as to their future destinies due to wrong views.												
5. States with fixed future destinies due to right views.	-	-	1	-	-	-	10	1	-	-	16	1
6. States having Path as its object.												
7. States conditioned by the Path.												
8. States having Path as the most predominant factor.												

The eight subject matters of enquiry correspond to a diversity of cittas and cetasikas (See Table 1.7), are bound up with mind-consciousness element. All these states belong to 4 mental aggregates. As a result, there are no associations. Each of these SOE is in dissociation from 1 aggregate (matter), 10 bases (10 gross bases), and 16 elements (10 gross elements, and 6 consciousness-elements having excluded mind-consciousness element). It is partially dissociated from 1 base (ideation-base), 1 element (ideation-element), 16 subtle matters, and *Nibbāna*.

VI. Association and Dissociation

States of enquiry (SOE):	Aggregate				Base				Element			
	As	Pas	Ds	Pds	As	Pas	Ds	Pds	As	Pas	Ds	Pds
273. States not arisen. (1)	-	-	-	-	-	-	-	-	-	-	5	-

States not arisen consist of 53 cittas which have not yet occurred, namely, the 12 unwholesome cittas, 21 wholesome cittas, 20 functional cittas, 52 mental factors, 17 matters produced by action, 15 produced by temperature, and 14 produced by nutriment. These states are bound up with the 5 gross object elements, mind-element, ideation-element, and mind-consciousness element.

But since these SOE belong to materiality and 4 mental aggregates, they have no associations. There are no dissociations from aggregate and base. They are in dissociation from the remaining 5 sensory consciousness elements (eye-consciousness, element, ear-consciousness element, nose-consciousness element, tongue-consciousness element, and body-consciousness element).

	Aggregate				Base				Element			
274. States of enquiry (SOE):	As	Pas	Ds	Pds	As	Pas	Ds	Pds	As	Pas	Ds	Pds
1. States with past object.	-	-	1	-	-	-	10	1	-	-	16	1
2. States with future object.												

States with past object are accompanied by 47 cetasikas, while states with future object have 50 cetasikas. Each of them sometimes have 43 cittas, sometimes more. These states are bound up with mind-consciousness element.

But, because these states belong to 4 mental aggregates, there are no associations. Each of these states is in dissociation from 1 aggregate (matter), 10 bases (10 gross bases), and 16 elements (10 gross elements, and 6 consciousness-elements having excluded mind-consciousness element). Each is partially dissociated from 1 base (ideation-base), 1 element (ideation-element), 16 subtle matters, and *Nibbāna*.

	Aggregate				Base				Element			
States of enquiry (SOE):	As	Pas	Ds	Pds	As	Pas	Ds	Pds	As	Pas	Ds	Pds
275. States with present object; States with internal object; States with external object; States with both internal and external objects. (4)	-	-	1	-	-	-	10	1	-	-	10	1

States with present object consist of 43 cittas, 50 cetasikas. The rest three SOE consist of 54 sensuous cittas, different rūpajhānas and arūpajhānas, accompanied by 49 cetasikas, 51 cetasikas, and 48 cetasikas, respectively. These four states are bound up with ideation-element and the 7 consciousness elements. They all belong to 4 mental aggregates, and thus there are no associations.

A Perfect Knowledge of Mind-Body from the Abhidhamma (Dhātukathā)

Each of these four states is in dissociation from 1 aggregate (matter), 10 bases (10 gross bases), and 10 elements (10 gross elements). Each is partially dissociated from 1 base (ideation-base), 1 element (ideation-element), 16 subtle matters, and *Nibbāna*.

276. States of enquiry (SOE):	Aggregate				Base				Element			
	As	Pas	Ds	Pds	As	Pas	Ds	Pds	As	Pas	Ds	Pds
1. States which are visible and impinging.	-	-	4	-	-	-	1	1	-	-	7	1
2. States invisible but impinging.												

States which are visible and impinging consist of gross visible object. States invisible but impinging are the remaining 11 gross matters (12 excluding visible object). As both belong to materiality, there are no associations nor partial associations. Each of them is dissociated from the remaining 4 mental aggregates (feeling, perception, volitive formation, consciousness), 1 base (mind-base), and 7 elements (7 consciousness-elements). Each of them is partially dissociated from 1 base (ideation-base), 1 element (ideation-element), and 52 cetasikas. These two states are of the same scenario as in nos. 228, 231, 233, 236, 247.

111 states of enquiry from Dhammasaṅgaṇīmātikā dyads

6. Dyads (*Dukaṃ*)

277. States of enquiry (SOE):	Aggregate				Base				Element			
	As	Pas	Ds	Pds	As	Pas	Ds	Pds	As	Pas	Ds	Pds
1. States which are root causes.												
2. States which are root causes as well as having root causes.	3	1	1	-	1	1	10	1	1	1	16	1
3. States which are root causes as well as are associated with root causes.												

States which are root causes include the 6 roots of greed, hatred, delusion, non-greed, non-hatred, non-delusion. States which are root causes and also having root causes, together with states which are root causes as well as are associated with them, are bound up with the same 6 root causes and exclude greed present at the 2 delusion-rooted cittas. The three SOE belong to volitive formation aggregate.

Each of the SOE is associated with the remaining 3 mental aggregates (feeling, perception, consciousness), 1 base (mind-base), and 1 element (mind-consciousness element). Each is partially associated with 1 aggregate (volitive formation), 1 base (ideation-base), 1 element (ideation-element), and 46

VI. Association and Dissociation

cetasikas (52 excluding the 6 root-cause factors). The 6 root causes can not associate with themselves.

Each of them is in dissociation from 1 aggregate (matter), 10 bases (10 gross bases), and 16 elements (10 gross elements, and the remaining 6 consciousness-elements). Each is partially dissociated from 1 base (ideation-base), 1 element (ideation-element), 16 subtle matters, and *Nibbāna*.

States of enquiry (SOE):	Aggregate				Base				Element			
	As	Pas	Ds	Pds	As	Pas	Ds	Pds	As	Pas	Ds	Pds
278. States which have root causes (i.e. accompanied by root causes); States which are associated with root causes. (2)	-	-	1	-	-	-	10	1	-	-	16	1

Both states of enquiry include the 71 cittas and 50 cetasikas (51 excluding delusion and non-delusion), are bound up with mind-consciousness element. They both belong to 4 mental aggregates. Thus, there are no associations.

Each of these states is in dissociation from 1 aggregate (matter), 10 bases (10 gross bases), and 16 elements (10 gross elements, and 6 consciousness-elements having excluded mind-consciousness element). Each is partially dissociated from 1 base (ideation-base), 1 element (ideation-element), 16 subtle matters, and *Nibbāna*.

279. States of enquiry (SOE):	Aggregate				Base				Element			
	As	Pas	Ds	Pds	As	Pas	Ds	Pds	As	Pas	Ds	Pds
1. States which have root causes but are not root causes per se. (*sahetukehi ceva na ca hetūhi*).	-	1	1	-	-	1	10	1	-	1	16	1
2. States associated with root causes but are not root causes.												
3. States which are not root causes but have root causes (*na hetusahetukehi*).												

The three states of enquiry include 71 cittas and 46 cetasikas (52 excluding the 6 roots causes), are bound up with mind-consciousness element. All the three belong to 4 mental aggregates, and so there are no associations. But in these cases, because volitive formation exists as a result of states having associated root causes, the three SOE are associated only partly with 1 aggregate (volitive formation), with 1 base (ideation-base), with 1 element (ideation-element), and with 46 cetasikas.

Each of them is dissociated from 1 aggregate (matter), 10 bases (10 gross bases), and 16 elements (10 gross elements, and 6 consciousness-elements having excluded mind-consciousness element). Each is partially dissociated

A Perfect Knowledge of Mind-Body from the Abhidhamma (Dhātukathā)

from 1 base (ideation-base), 1 element (ideation-element), 16 subtle matters, and *Nibbāna*.

	Aggregate				Base				Element			
280. States of enquiry (SOE):	As	Pas	Ds	Pds	As	Pas	Ds	Pds	As	Pas	Ds	Pds
1. States not arisen from causes.												
2. States unconditioned by causes.												
3. States with visibility.	-	-	4	-	-	-	1	1	-	-	7	1
4. States with impinging.												
5. States with corporeal change.												

States which are not arisen from causes and not conditioned by causes belong to *Nibbāna*. States with visibility are first coming from gross visible object which causes eye-consciousness. States with impinging belong to 12 gross matters. States with corporeal change are the 28 matters. Thus, the first 2 belong to *Nibbāna*, the rest belong to materiality. Thus, there are no direct associations. Since *Nibbāna* is included, there are also no partial association.

The four of them are dissociated from 4 aggregates (4 mental aggregates), 1 base (mind-base), and 7 elements (7 consciousness-elements). They are partially dissociated from 1 base (ideation-base), 1 element (ideation-element), and 52 cetasikas. Subtle matters are herein ignored as being part of materiality.

	Aggregate				Base				Element			
States of enquiry (SOE):	As	Pas	Ds	Pds	As	Pas	Ds	Pds	As	Pas	Ds	Pds
281. Supramundane states. (1)	-	-	-	-	-	-	-	-	-	-	6	-

These states consist of 8 supramundane cittas, 36 cetasikas (38 excluding 2 Illimitables), and *Nibbāna*. They belong to 4 mental aggregates and *Nibbāna*, and so there are no associations. These states are essentially ideation-element and mind-consciousness element, which sometimes are either mundane or supramundane. They are thus dissociated from the remaining 6 consciousness elements (eye-cons. el., ear-cons. el., nose-cons. el., tongue-cons. el., body-cons. el., and mind-el.). There are no dissociations from aggregate and base.

	Aggregate				Base				Element			
282. States of enquiry (SOE):	As	Pas	Ds	Pds	As	Pas	Ds	Pds	As	Pas	Ds	Pds
1. States which are defilement (*Āsavā*).												
2. States which are both defilement and objects of defilement.	3	1	1	-	1	1	10	1	1	1	16	1
3. States which are both defilement and associated with defilement.												

VI. Association and Dissociation

These three states are ascribed to the three factors of defilement — greed or sensual desire, wrong view (instead of hatred), and delusion. They all belong to volitive formation aggregate. Each of them is associated with the remaining 3 mental aggregates (feeling, perception, consciousness), 1 base (mind-base), and 1 element (mind-consciousness element). Each is partially associated with 1 aggregate (volitive formation), 1 base (ideation-base), 1 element (ideation-element), and 27 cetasikas.

Each of them is in dissociation from 1 aggregate (matter), 10 bases (10 gross bases), and 16 elements (10 gross elements, and 6 consciousness-elements having excluded mind-consciousness element). It is partially dissociated from 1 base (ideation-base), 1 element (ideation-element), subtle matters, and *Nibbāna*.

	Aggregate				Base				Element			
283. States of enquiry (SOE):	As	Pas	Ds	Pds	As	Pas	Ds	Pds	As	Pas	Ds	Pds
1. States not the objects of defilement.												
2. States which are dissociated from defilement and are also not objects of defilement.	-	-	-	-	-	-	-	-	-	-	6	-

The two subject matters of enquiry concur with the 8 supramundane cittas accompanied by 36 cetasikas (38 excluding 2 Illimitables), and *Nibbāna*. These states belong to 4 mental aggregates. Also, since *Nibbāna* is also the state of enquiry, there are no associations nor partial associations. These are similar cases as in nos. 281, supramundane states, which are bound up with ideation-element and mind-consciousness element. Thus, these states are dissociated from the other 6 consciousness elements (eye-cons. el., ear-cons. el., nose-cons. el., tongue-cons. el., body-cons. el., and mind-el.). There are no dissociations from aggregate and base.

	Aggregate				Base				Element			
States of enquiry (SOE):	As	Pas	Ds	Pds	As	Pas	Ds	Pds	As	Pas	Ds	Pds
284. States associated with defilement.	-	-	1	-	-	-	10	1	-	-	16	1

These states are the 12 unwholesome cittas and 26 cetasikas (27 excluding delusion-*cetasika* present at the 2 hate-rooted cittas and 2 delusion-rooted cittas), and are bound up with mind-consciousness element. They belong to 4 mental aggregates, and so there are no associations.

They are dissociated from 1 aggregate (matter), 10 bases (10 gross bases), and 16 elements (10 gross elements, and the remaining 6 consciousness-elements). They are partially dissociated from 1 base (ideation-base), 1 element (ideation-element), 16 subtle matters, and *Nibbāna*. Note that they are not in partial dissociation from volitive formation aggregate for they may or may not be defilement per se.

A Perfect Knowledge of Mind-Body from the Abhidhamma (Dhātukathā)

States of enquiry (SOE):	Aggregate				Base				Element			
	As	Pas	Ds	Pds	As	Pas	Ds	Pds	As	Pas	Ds	Pds
285. States associated with defilement but are not defilement. (1)	-	1	1	-	-	1	10	1	-	1	16	1

These states include 12 unwholesome cittas, 24 cetasikas (27 excluding the 3 defilement factors of greed (or sensual desire), wrong view, and delusion). They are bound up with mind-consciousness element. As they belong to 4 mental aggregates, there are no direct associations. Because they are not defilement per se, they are also partially associated with 1 aggregate (volitive formation), 1 base (ideation-base), 1 element (ideation-element), and with 24 cetasikas.

They are in dissociation from 1 aggregate (matter), 10 bases (10 gross bases), and 16 elements (10 gross elements, and 6 consciousness-elements having excluded mind-consciousness element). Since they are not defilement, they are partially dissociated from 1 base (ideation-base), 1 element (ideation-element), 16 subtle matters, and *Nibbāna*.

286. States of enquiry (SOE):	Aggregate				Base				Element			
	As	Pas	Ds	Pds	As	Pas	Ds	Pds	As	Pas	Ds	Pds
Repeats the same from preceding Defilement cluster for Fetters, Bonds, Raging Current, Yokes, Hindrances, respectively, following nos. 282. Altogether 5 x 3 =15. (nos. 1 to 15)	3	1	1	-	1	1	10	1	1	1	16	1
Repeats the same from preceding Defilement cluster for Fetters, Bonds, Raging Current, Yokes, Hindrances, respectively, following nos. 283. Altogether 5 x 2 =10. (nos. 16 to 25)	-	-	-	-	-	-	-	-	-	-	6	-
Repeats the same from preceding Defilement cluster for Fetters, Bonds, Raging Current, Yokes, Hindrances, respectively, following nos. 284. Altogether 5 x 1 =5. (nos. 26 to 30)	-	-	1	-	-	-	10	1	-	-	16	1
Repeats the same from preceding Defilement cluster for Fetters, Bonds, Raging Current, Yokes, Hindrances, respectively, following nos. 285. Altogether 5 x 1 =5. (nos. 31 to 35)	-	1	1	-	-	1	10	1	-	1	16	1
36. States which are Attachment (*Parāmāsa*). 37. States which are both attachment and objects of attachment.	3	1	1	-	1	1	10	1	1	1	16	1

VI. Association and Dissociation

The answers for these 37 states of enquiry can be obtained in the same manner as explained in preceding nos. 282 to 285, and by referring to Table 1.8.4 to Table 1.8.6 as well as Chart 1. These five kinds of answers are also the same as in subsequent nos. 294.

	Aggregate				Base				Element			
287. States of enquiry (SOE):	As	Pas	Ds	Pds	As	Pas	Ds	Pds	As	Pas	Ds	Pds
1. States which are not objects of attachment. 2. States dissociated from attachment and are not objects of attachment.	-	-	-	-	-	-	-	-	-	-	6	-

Same as in nos. 283, both SOE belong to 8 supramundane cittas, 36 cetasikas (38 excluding 2 Illimitables), and *Nibbāna*. They belong to 4 mental aggregates and *Nibbāna*, and so there are no associations. Essentially, these states are bound up with ideation-element and mind-consciousness element. Thus, these states are dissociated from the other 6 consciousness elements (eye-cons. el., ear-cons. el., nose-cons. el., tongue-cons. el., body-cons. el., and mind-el.). There are no dissociations from aggregate and base.

	Aggregate				Base				Element			
States of enquiry (SOE):	As	Pas	Ds	Pds	As	Pas	Ds	Pds	As	Pas	Ds	Pds
288. States associated with attachment.	-	1	1	-	-	1	10	1	-	1	16	1

These states consist of 4 greed-rooted cittas associated with wrong view, arisen with 20 cetasikas (27 excluding wrong view, conceit hatred, envy, avarice, worry, doubt). They belong to 4 mental aggregates, and so there are no direct associations. They are partially associated with 1 aggregate (volitive formation), 1 base (ideation-base), 1 element (ideation-element), and 20 cetasikas.

They are in dissociation from 1 aggregate (matter), 10 bases (10 gross bases), and 16 elements (10 gross elements, and 6 consciousness-elements having excluded mind-consciousness element). They are partially dissociated from 1 base (ideation-base), 1 element (ideation-element), 16 subtle matters, and *Nibbāna*. They are not partially dissociated from volitive formation aggregate because they could be attachment per se.

A Perfect Knowledge of Mind-Body from the Abhidhamma (Dhātukathā)

States of enquiry (SOE):	Aggregate				Base				Element			
	As	Pas	Ds	Pds	As	Pas	Ds	Pds	As	Pas	Ds	Pds
289. States which attend to objects.	-	-	1	-	-	-	10	1	-	-	10	1

These states are all 89 cittas and 52 cetasikas. They belong to 4 mental aggregates, and so there are no associations. They are dissociated from 1 aggregate (matter), 10 bases (10 gross bases), and 10 elements (10 gross elements). They are partially dissociated from 1 base (ideation-base), 1 element (ideation-element), 16 subtle matters, and *Nibbāna*.

	Aggregate				Base				Element			
290. States of enquiry (SOE):	As	Pas	Ds	Pds	As	Pas	Ds	Pds	As	Pas	Ds	Pds
1. States which do not have objects.												
2. States dissociated from consciousness.	-	-	4	-	-	-	1	1	-	-	7	1
3. States not conjoined with consciousness												
4. States which are derived.												

The first 3 SOE include 28 matters and *Nibbāna*. We know that states which are not derived are the 89 cittas, 52 cetasikas, 4 Great Elements and *Nibbāna*. So, states which are derived are the 24 matters (28 excluding the 4 Great Elements). So, the 4th SOE belongs to materiality. In this case, all SOE have no associations.

Each of these states are dissociated from 4 mental aggregates, 1 base (mind-base), and 7 elements (7 consciousness-elements). Each is partially dissociated from 1 base (ideation-base), and 1 element (ideation-element). *Nibbāna* is ignored with reference to 4th SOE, because when materiality is dealt with *Nibbāna*, they are neither associated nor dissociated. Subtle matters is part of materiality, is ignored from partial dissociation.

States of enquiry (SOE):	Aggregate				Base				Element			
	As	Pas	Ds	Pds	As	Pas	Ds	Pds	As	Pas	Ds	Pds
291. States which are consciousness.	3	-	1	-	-	1	10	1	-	1	10	1

States of consciousness are mutually associated with the other 3 mental aggregates. Consciousness aggregate can not associate with itself, nor with mind-base and the 7 consciousness-elements. So, consciousness is partially associated with 1 base (ideation-base), 1 element (ideation-element), and 52 cetasikas.

States of consciousness are dissociated from 1 aggregate (matter), 10 bases (10 gross bases), and 10 elements (10 gross elements). Consciousness is partially dissociated from 1 base (ideation-base), 1 element (ideation-element), 16 subtle matters, and *Nibbāna*.

VI. Association and Dissociation

292. States of enquiry (SOE):	Aggregate				Base				Element			
	As	Pas	Ds	Pds	As	Pas	Ds	Pds	As	Pas	Ds	Pds
1. States which are mental factors.												
2. States associated with consciousness.												
3. States conjoined with consciousness.												
4. States both conjoined with and originated from consciousness.	1	-	1	-	1	-	10	1	7	-	10	1
5. States conjoined with, originated from, and arise concurrently with cons.												
6. States conjoined with, originated from, and arise consecutively with cons.												

All these states are referring to the 52 cetasikas. They belong to the aggregates of feeling, perception, and volitive formation. Each SOE is in association with 1 aggregate (consciousness), 1 base (mind-base), 7 elements (7 consciousness-elements). There are no partial association because 52 cetasikas are all included which are actually all those states of enquiry.

Each SOE is dissociated from 1 aggregate (matter), 10 bases (10 gross bases), and 10 elements (10 gross elements). Each is partially dissociated from 1 base (ideation-base), 1 element (ideation-element), 16 subtle matters, and *Nibbāna*.

States of enquiry (SOE):	Aggregate				Base				Element			
	As	Pas	Ds	Pds	As	Pas	Ds	Pds	As	Pas	Ds	Pds
293. States which are not the result of clinging (*anupādinnā dhammā*) (1)	-	-	-	-	-	-	-	-	-	-	5	-

States which are not the result of clinging consist of 57 cittas (comprised of 21 mundane wholesome cittas, 12 mundane unwholesome cittas, 20 functional cittas, 4 supramundane fruition-cittas), arisen with 52 cetasikas; 17 mind-produced matters, 15 temperature-produced matters, 14 nutriment-produced matters, and *Nibbāna*. They belong to materiality, 4 mental aggregates, and *Nibbāna*. As such, there are no associations. These states are dissociated from the 5 elements (eye- consciousness element, ear-consciousness element, nose-consciousness element, tongue-consciousness element, and body-consciousness element). There are no dissociations from aggregate and base, nor partial dissociations.

A Perfect Knowledge of Mind-Body from the Abhidhamma (Dhātukathā)

294. States of enquiry (SOE):	Aggregate				Base				Element			
	As	Pas	Ds	Pds	As	Pas	Ds	Pds	As	Pas	Ds	Pds
1. States which are clinging (*upādāna*)												
2. States which are both clinging and objects of clinging.	3	1	1	-	1	1	10	1	1	1	16	1
3. States which are both clinging and associated with clinging.												
4. States which are not objects of clinging.												
5. States dissociated from clinging as well as are not objects of clinging.	-	-	-	-	-	-	-	-	-	-	6	-
6. States associated with clinging.	-	-	1	-	-	-	10	1	-	-	16	1
7. States associated with clinging but are not clinging.	-	1	1	-	-	1	10	1	-	1	16	1
8. States which are corruptions (*kilesa*)												
9. States which are both corruptions and objects of corruptions.												
10. States which are both corruptions and are corrupted.	3	1	1	-	1	1	10	1	1	1	16	1
11. States which are both corruptions and associated with corruptions.												

The 1st, 2nd, 3rd SOE are ascribed to sensual desires, wrong view, and delusion, belong to volitive formation. Each of the SOE is associated with the remaining 3 mental aggregates (feeling, perception, consciousness), 1 base (mind-base), and 1 element (mind-consciousness element). Each is partially associated with 1 aggregate (volitive formation), 1 base (ideation-base), and 1 element (ideation-element). Each of them is dissociated from 1 aggregate (matter), 10 bases (10 gross bases), and 16 elements (10 gross elements, and 6 consciousness-elements having excluded mind-consciousness element). It is partially dissociated from 1 base (ideation-base), 1 element (ideation-element), including 16 subtle matters and *Nibbāna*.

The 4th and 5th SOE are the 8 supramundane cittas, 36 cetasikas (38 having excluded the 2 Illimitables). Each belong to 4 mental aggregates and *Nibbāna*, and so there are no associations. Essentially, these states are closely connected to mind-consciousness element. Therefore, each of them is dissociated from the remaining 6 consciousness elements (eye-cons. element, ear-cons. element, nose-cons. element, tongue-cons. element, body-cons. element, and mind-element). There are no dissociations from aggregate and base, nor are there partial dissociations.

The 6th SOE are the 8 greed-rooted cittas, accompanied by 22 cetasikas (27 excluding hatred, envy, avarice, worry, doubt). They belong to 4 mental aggregates, and so there are no associations. These states are dissociated from 1 aggregate (matter), 10 bases (10 gross bases), and 16 elements (10 gross elements, 6 consciousness-elements having excluded mind-consciousness

VI. Association and Dissociation

element). They are partially dissociated from 1 base (ideation-base), 1 element (ideation-element), 16 subtle matters, and *Nibbāna*. Note that they are not in partial dissociation from volitive formation aggregate for they may or may not be defilement per se.

The 7th SOE are the 8 greed-rooted cittas, accompanied by 20 cetasikas (27 excluding hatred, envy, avarice, worry, doubt, and the 2 states of clinging). They belong to 4 mental aggregates, and so there are no associations. They are partially associated with 1 aggregate (volitive formation), 1 base (ideation-base), 1 element (ideation-element), and 20 cetasikas. They are in dissociation from 1 aggregate (matter), 10 bases (10 gross bases), and 16 elements (10 gross elements, and 6 consciousness-elements having excluded mind-consciousness element). They are partially dissociated from 1 base (ideation-base), 1 element (ideation-element), 16 subtle matters, and *Nibbāna*. They are not partially dissociated from volitive formation aggregate because they are not clinging.

The 8th to 11th SOE are the 10 states of corruptions (the cetasikas of greed, hatred, delusion, conceit, wrong view, doubt, sloth, restlessness, shamelessness, guiltlessness of conscience). These four states belong to volitive formation. The answers are the same as the 1st, 2nd and 3rd SOE.

States of enquiry (SOE):	Aggregate				Base				Element			
	As	Pas	Ds	Pds	As	Pas	Ds	Pds	As	Pas	Ds	Pds
295. States which are not objects of corruptions; States dissociated from corruptions and are not objects of corruptions. (2)	-	-	-	-	-	-	-	-	-	-	6	-

Both states consist of 8 supramundane cittas, 36 cetasikas (38-2 Illimitables), and *Nibbāna*. Since they belong to 4 mental aggregates and *Nibbāna*, there are no associations. There are no dissociations from the aggregate and base. These states are dissociated from the 6 elements (eye-cons. el., ear-cons. el., nose-cons. el., tongue-cons. el., body-cons. el., and mind-el.).

States of enquiry (SOE):	Aggregate				Base				Element			
	As	Pas	Ds	Pds	As	Pas	Ds	Pds	As	Pas	Ds	Pds
296. States which are corrupted; States which are associated with corruptions. (2)	-	-	1	-	-	-	10	1	-	-	16	1

Both states correspond to the 12 mundane unwholesome cittas, and 27 cetasikas. These states are bound up with mind-consciousness element. Since they belong to 4 mental aggregates, there are no associations. And since they involve 14 unwholesome cetasikas, each of them is dissociated from 1 aggregate

A Perfect Knowledge of Mind-Body from the Abhidhamma (Dhātukathā)

(matter), 10 bases (10 gross bases), and 16 elements (10 gross elements, and 6 consciousness-elements having excluded mind-consciousness element). It is partially dissociated from 1 base (ideation-base), 1 element (ideation-element), subtle matters and *Nibbāna*.

States of enquiry (SOE):	Aggregate				Base				Element			
	As	Pas	Ds	Pds	As	Pas	Ds	Pds	As	Pas	Ds	Pds
297. States which are corrupted but are not corruptions; States which are associated with corruptions but are not corruptions. (2)	-	1	1	-	-	1	10	1	-	1	16	1

These states are sprung from 12 unwholesome cittas, arisen with 17 cetasikas. They are bound up with mind-consciousness element. Since they belong to 4 mental aggregates, they have no direct associations. Because each of them involve the two antithetical states, they are partially associated with 1 aggregate (volitive formation), 1 base (ideation-base), 1 element (ideation-element), and 17 cetasikas.

Each of these states is in dissociation from 1 aggregate (matter), 10 bases (10 gross bases), and 16 elements (10 gross elements, and 6 consciousness-elements having excluded mind-consciousness element). They are partially dissociated from 1 base (ideation-base), 1 element (ideation-element), 16 subtle matters, and *Nibbāna*.

	Aggregate				Base				Element			
298. States of enquiry (SOE):	As	Pas	Ds	Pds	As	Pas	Ds	Pds	As	Pas	Ds	Pds
1. States eliminated by first Path.												
2. States eliminated by the higher 3 Paths.												
3. States with root causes eliminated by the first Path.	-	-	1	-	-	-	10	1	-	-	16	1
4. States with root causes eliminated by the higher 3 Paths.												

All these states belong to 4 mental aggregates. So, there are no associations. Each of them is dissociated from 1 aggregate (matter), 10 bases (10 gross bases), and 16 elements (10 gross elements, and 6 consciousness-elements having excluded mind-consciousness element). Each is partially dissociated from 1 base (ideation-base), 1 element (ideation-element), subtle matters and *Nibbāna*.

States of enquiry (SOE):	Aggregate				Base				Element			
	As	Pas	Ds	Pds	As	Pas	Ds	Pds	As	Pas	Ds	Pds
299. States with initial application; States with sustained application. (2)	-	1	1	-	-	1	10	1	-	1	15	1

VI. Association and Dissociation

These two states consist of 55 cittas and 66 cittas respectively, accompanied by 51 cetasikas. (See Chart 7 in Appendix VI, referring to 121 cittas in total). These states are bound up with mind-element and mind-consciousness element. Since they belong to 4 mental aggregates, there are no associations. Because of the associated 50 cetasikas, each of these states is in partial association with 1 aggregate (volitive formation), 1 base (ideation-base), 1 element (ideation-element), and with 51 cetasikas.

They are dissociated from 1 aggregate (matter), 10 bases (10 gross bases), and 15 elements (10 gross elements, and the remaining 5 sensory consciousness elements). They are partially dissociated from 1 base (ideation-base), 1 element (ideation-element), 16 subtle matters, and *Nibbāna*.

	Aggregate				Base				Element			
States of enquiry (SOE):	As	Pas	Ds	Pds	As	Pas	Ds	Pds	As	Pas	Ds	Pds
300. States without initial application; States without sustained application. (2)	-	-	-	-	-	-	-	-	-	-	1	-

The 1st SOE consists of 66 cittas, accompanied by 37 cetasikas, 28 matters, and *Nibbāna*. The 2nd SOE consists of 55 cittas, accompanied by 36 cetasikas, 28 matters, and *Nibbāna*. The 66 cittas and 55 cittas can be referred to Chart 7 in Appendix VI.

Since materiality-mentality, and *Nibbāna* are the states of enquiry, there are no associated and partially associated states. Because 5 aggregates and 12 bases are included, there are no dissociations from base and element. Since these two states are classified under 17 elements, there is only 1 element (mind-element) in dissociation from these states.

	Aggregate				Base				Element			
States of enquiry (SOE):	As	Pas	Ds	Pds	As	Pas	Ds	Pds	As	Pas	Ds	Pds
301. States with zest; States accompanied by zest. (2)	-	1	1	-	-	1	10	1	-	1	16	1

Both states are from 51 cittas and 46 cetasikas (52 excluding zest, hatred, envy, avarice, worry, doubt. i.e. 52-6=46). Both belong to 4 mental aggregates, and so there are no associations. Each has partial association with 1 aggregate (volitive formation which is with zest), 1 base (ideation-base), 1 element (ideation-element), and 46 cetasikas. They are partially associated because the 46 cetasikas are associated with conssciousness aggregate.

Since these states are bound up with mind-consciousness element, each is in dissociation from 1 aggregate (matter), 10 bases (10 gross bases), and 16 elements (10 gross elements, and the remaining 6 consciousness-elements). Each

A Perfect Knowledge of Mind-Body from the Abhidhamma (Dhātukathā)

of them is in partial dissociation from 1 base (ideation-base), 1 element (ideation-element), 16 subtle matters, and *Nibbāna*.

States of enquiry (SOE):	Aggregate				Base				Element			
	As	Pas	Ds	Pds	As	Pas	Ds	Pds	As	Pas	Ds	Pds
302. States accompanied by happiness.	1	-	1	-	-	1	10	1	-	1	15	1

These states consist of 63 cittas, and 46 cetasikas. They belong to the aggregates of perception, volitive formation, and consciousness. These states are bound up with body-consciousness element. These are the same states as in preceding nos. 267, with similar answers.

States of enquiry (SOE):	Aggregate				Base				Element			
	As	Pas	Ds	Pds	As	Pas	Ds	Pds	As	Pas	Ds	Pds
303. States accompanied by equanimity (i.e. indifference to happiness).	1	-	1	-	-	1	10	1	-	1	11	1

These are states which endure neither happy feeling nor painful feeling, consist of 55 cittas accompanied by equanimity, and arisen 46 cetasikas (52 excluding feeling, zest, hatred, envy, avarice, worry). They belong to the aggregates of perception, volitive formation, and consciousness. These are the same states as in preceding nos. 268, with similar answers.

304. States of enquiry (SOE):	Aggregate				Base				Element			
	As	Pas	Ds	Pds	As	Pas	Ds	Pds	As	Pas	Ds	Pds
1. States not characteristic of the sensuous sphere.												
2. States which are not included (in round of rebirth).	-	-	-	-	-	-	-	-	-	-	6	-
3. States which are unsurpassable/incomparable.												

States not characteristic of the sensuous sphere comprise the 27 *Mahaggata* cittas (See the first table in Appendix III), 8 supramundane cittas, and 38 cetasikas. The other two states consist of 8 supramundane cittas, 36 cetasikas, and *Nibbāna*. All these states belong to 4 mental aggregates, and since *Nibbāna* is also the state of enquiry, there are no associations nor partial associations.

There are no dissociations from aggregate and base. Each of these states is in dissociation from the 6 consciousness elements (7 consciousness elements excluding mind-consciousness element).

VI. Association and Dissociation

305. States of enquiry (SOE):	Aggregate				Base				Element			
	As	Pas	Ds	Pds	As	Pas	Ds	Pds	As	Pas	Ds	Pds
1. States belong to form sphere.												
2. States belong to formless sphere.												
3. States which lead out (from cycle of rebirth).	-	-	1	-	-	-	10	1	-	-	16	1
4. States fixed as to their future destinies.												
5. States which are at odds with supramundane Path.												

The 1st SOE consists of the 15 fine-material cittas, and 35 cetasikas. The 2nd SOE consists of 12 immaterial sublime cittas, and 30 cetasikas. The 3rd SOE consists of the 4 supramundane path-cittas, and 36 cetasikas. The 4th SOE has the same as the 3rd but including also 7th sensuous *javana* present at the greed-rooted cittas with wrong view and at the 2 delusion-rooted cittas. The 5th SOE consists of 12 mundane unwholesome cittas, and 27 cetasikas. All these states of inquires belong to 4 mental aggregates, and so they have associations.

Each of these states is dissociated from 1 aggregate (matter), 10 bases (10 gross bases), and 16 elements (10 gross elements, and 6 consciousness-elements having excluded mind-consciousness element). It is partially dissociated from 1 base (ideation-base), 1 element (ideation-element), subtle matters and *Nibbāna*.

Key points from the text :

Ideation-base, ideation-element, origin-truth and path-truth, vitality-faculty, six bases, mentality-materiality, four greater becomings (fine-material becoming, immaterial-becoming, neither perception nor non-perception becoming, four-aggregate becoming), birth, ageing, death, 19 triplets included in 47 states of enquiry of tikas, 111 states of enquiry of dukas (50 groups, 6 from the shorter clusters, 13 from the intermediate dyads-cluster, and 19 from the last dyads-cluster).

There are 123 states not included in this chapter which include states not of the pure form of materiality and mentality (e.g. ideation-base), states which have included the full measure of the 3 categories (e.g. indeterminate states), states with include both materiality and consciousness aggregate (e.g. six bases), etc.

A Perfect Knowledge of Mind-Body from the Abhidhamma (Dhātukathā)

In the two summary tables below, the bracketed numbers indicate the number of enquiries to each of the text's paragraph's nos.

Table 6.27. Total 250 states of enquiry by subject matters

Text paragraph nos. (with the numbers of enquiries) :		Subject matter:
228 (1), 229 (3), 230 (1)	5	Aggregates
231 (10), 232 (1)	11	Bases
233 (10), 234 (7)	17	Elements
235 (2), 236 (1),	3	Truths
236 (7), 237 (1), 238 (4), 239 (1), 240 (8)	21	Faculties
240 (2), 241 (1), 242 (1), 243 (1), 244 (3), 245 (1), 246 (3), 247 (3), 248 (3), 249 (1)	19	Dependent Originations
249 (2), 250 (1), 251 (1), 252 (5), 253 (3), 254 (2), 255 (1), 256 (1)	16	Others
257 (2), 258 (2), 259 (1), 260 (1), 261 (2), 262 (2), 263 (2), 264 (1), 265 (2), 266 (1), 267 (1), 268 (1), 269 (9), 270 (2), 271 (1), 272 (8), 273 (1), 274 (2), 275 (4), 276 (2)	47	Triads
277 (3), 278 (2), 279 (3), 294 (11), 295 (2), 296 (2), 297 (2), 282 (3), 283 (2), 284 (1), 285 (1), 286 (37), 287 (2), 288 (1)	72	Dyad-clusters
280 (5), 281 (1),	6	Shorter dyads
289 (1), 290 (4), 291 (1), 292 (6), 293 (1)	13	Intermediate dyads
298 (4), 299 (2), 300 (2), 301 (2), 302 (1), 303 (1), 304 (3), 305 (5)	20	Last dyads

Total = 250 states

VI. Association and Dissociation

Table 6.28. Total 250 states of enquiry by answers

#	Text's paragraph nos. (with numbers of enquiries):		Aggregate				Base				Element			
			As	Pas	Ds	Pds	As	Pas	Ds	Pds	As	Pas	Ds	Pds
1.	228 (1), 231 (10), 233 (10), 236 (8), 247 (3), 276 (2), 280 (5), 290 (4)	43	-	-	4	-	-	-	1	1	-	-	7	1
2.	229 (3), 243 (1), 254 (2)	6	3	-	1	-	1	1	10	1	7	1	10	1
3.	230 (1), 232 (1), 237 (1), 241 (1), 255 (1), 291 (1)	6	3	-	1	-	-	1	10	1	-	1	10	1
4.	234 (7)	7	3	-	1	-	-	1	10	1	-	1	16	1
5.	235 (2), 240 (10), 244 (3), 249 (3), 252 (5), 277 (3), 282 (3), 286 (17), 294 (7)	53	3	1	1	-	1	1	10	1	1	1	16	1
6.	238 (4), 248 (3)	7	3	-	1	-	1	1	10	1	1	1	16	1
7.	239 (1)	1	3	-	1	-	1	1	10	1	6	1	11	1
8.	242 (1), 253 (3)	4	3	1	1	-	1	1	10	1	7	1	10	1
9.	245 (1)	1	-	-	-	-	-	-	-	-	-	-	3	-
10.	246 (3), 257 (2), 261 (2), 269 (9), 272 (8), 274 (2), 278 (2), 284 (1), 286 (5), 294 (1), 296 (2), 298 (4), 305 (5)	46	-	-	1	-	-	-	10	1	-	-	16	1
11.	250 (1)	1	2	1	1	-	-	1	10	1	-	1	16	1
12.	251 (1)	1	2	1	1	-	1	1	10	1	1	1	16	1
13.	256 (1)	1	3	1	1	-	1	1	10	1	2	1	15	1
14.	258 (2), 267 (1), 302 (1)	4	1	-	1	-	-	1	10	1	-	1	15	1
15.	259 (1), 268 (1), 303 (1)	3	1	-	1	-	-	1	10	1	-	1	11	1
16.	260 (1), 271 (1), 275 (4), 289 (1)	7	-	-	1	-	-	-	10	1	-	-	10	1
17.	262 (2), 273 (1), 293 (1)	4	-	-	-	-	-	-	-	-	-	-	5	-
18.	263 (2), 270 (2), 281 (1), 283 (2), 286 (10), 287 (2), 294 (2), 295 (2), 304 (3)	26	-	-	-	-	-	-	-	-	-	-	6	-
19.	264 (1), 299 (2)	3	-	1	1	-	-	1	10	1	-	1	15	1
20.	265 (2), 279 (3), 285 (1), 286 (5), 288 (1), 294 (1), 297 (2), 301 (2)	17	-	1	1	-	-	1	10	1	-	1	16	1
21.	266 (1), 300 (2)	3	-	-	-	-	-	-	-	-	-	-	1	-
22.	292 (6)	6	1	-	1	-	1	-	10	1	7	-	10	1
	250 states in 22 kind of answers	250												

CHAPTER 7

VII. Associated and Dissociated
(Sampayuttenavippayutta)

Analysis of 37 states from 11 catechism

Of these 37 states of enquiry from this chapter, 24 are interior states while 13 form the states of enquiry from Dhammasaṅgaṇīmātikā triads and dyads. This chapter follows the same association method as explained in Chapter 6 except that the dissociation method that is used in this chapter varies slightly from that in the previous chapter. The states of enquiry in this chapter are restricted to mental aggregates, mental factors, and those complete forms of consciousness excluding those such as the 4 truths, the 4 basis of psychic powers, and so on. Matters are excluded from being taken as the subject matters of enquiry in this chapter is because materiality has no association with any other states. The answers are obtained in terms of associated with, and dissociated from the aggregates, bases, and elements.

Again, because each catechetical text also uses the kind of intriguing words like those in the preceding chapters, such as *these* states and *these* states, *those* states and *these* states, an initial clarification is therefore needed.

For instance, according to the text nos. 307 which mentions that:

"Eye consciousness element; ... mind element; mind consciousness element is associated with *these* states. *Those* states are dissociated from *these* states ..."

The following simple diagram will give the readers a clearer picture as to *these* states, *those* states, and another *these* states. Diagrams will depict answers better than mere textual description, and is also a quicker way for readers to remember as and when they want to refer back to the chapters again at a later time. Using the same example in nos. 307, the diagram depicts two comparative steps to differentiate between *these* and '*these* states', '*those* states' and '*these* states'. The two steps are marked as (*a*) and (*b*) as shown in the diagram below.

VII. Associated and Dissociated

Diagram 7.1. Association between *these* states and *those* states, and dissociation between *those* states and *these* states

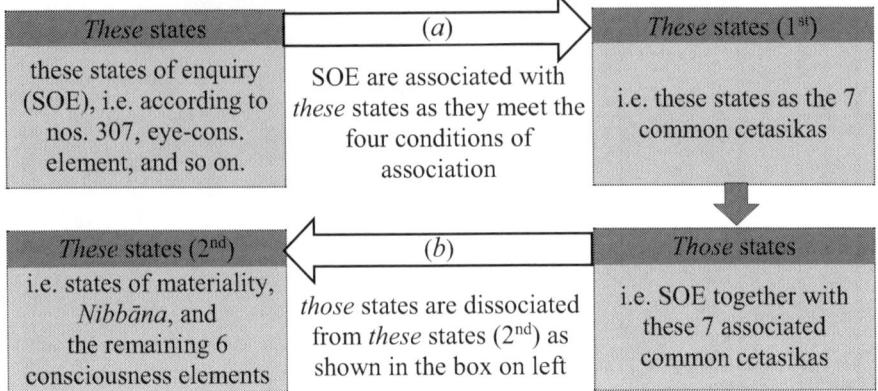

The following abbreviations are used in the charts throughout this Chapter.

SOE	: States of enquiry
cons.	: Consciousness
agr	: aggregate
bse	: base
el.	: element
As	: Associated
Pas	: Partially associated
Ds	: Dissociated
Pds	: Partially dissociated

24 internal states of enquiry

States of enquiry (SOE):	SOE associate with *these* states (A) :	SOE+(A) dissociate from (B):			These states, (B), Ds from:			These states, (B), Pds from:		
		agr	bse	el.	agr	bse	el.	agr	bse	el.
306. Feeling aggregate; Perception aggregate; Volitive formation aggregate; Consciousness aggregate; Mind-base (5)	89 cittas, 51 or 52 cetasikas depending on each SOE	1	10	10	4	1	7	-	1	1

A Perfect Knowledge of Mind-Body from the Abhidhamma (Dhātukathā)

These subject matters of enquiry are all associated with 89 cittas and cetasikas, and therefore each of them is associated with the remaining 3 mental aggregates. Take the first example, the aggregates of feeling, perception, and volitive formation are each associated with 89 cittas and 51 cetasikas (52 excluding the mental factor of *vedanā*, *saññā* or *cetanā*, respectively). The exception is consciousness aggregate which is accompanied by 52 cetasikas. For example, feeling aggregate, together with its associated remaining 3 mental aggregates, i.e. *these* states designated as SOE+(A), are dissociated from 1 aggregate (10 gross bases), 1 element (10 gross elements), and *Nibbāna*. Subtle matters are herein considered as already included in matter aggregate.

Materiality and *Nibbāna* are *those* states I designated them as (B) in the chart above. *Those* states, (B), are in turn dissociated from the 4 aggregates (4 mental aggregates), 1 base (mind-base), 7 elements (the 7 consciousness elements). *Those* states (B) are partially dissociated from 1 base (ideation-base), 1 element (ideation-element), and 52 cetasikas. Herein, ideation-base is always in partial dissociation, which is because the 52 mental factors (the 3 mental aggregates) are mutually associated with consciousness aggregate, and also, 52 mental factors together subtle matters and *Nibbāna,* are commonly sharing ideation-base.

Take another example, mind-base, which is taken as under consciousness aggregate in order that comparison and association can be made on the same basis (i.e. on aggregates), and consciousness aggregate, too, is associated with the remaining 3 mental aggregates. The answers are the same as aforesaid. The other SOE are to be analysed in the similar manner.

States of enquiry (SOE):	SOE associate with *these* states (A) :	SOE+(A) dissociate from (B):			*These* states, (B), Ds from:			*These* states, (B), Pds from:		
		agr	bse	el.	agr	bse	el.	agr	bse	el.
307. Eye-cons. element; Ear-cons. element; Nose-cons. element; Tongue-cons. element; Body-cons. element; Mind-element; Mind-cons. element. (7)	3 mental aggregates (excl cons.), 7 common non-beautiful mental factors	1	10	16	-	-	1	-	-	-

These states belong to the group of 7 consciousness-elements, are included under consciousness aggregate. Take the first example, when eye-consciousness element, treated as consciousness aggregate, is dealt with, it is associated with 3 aggregates (feeling, perception, volitive formation), accompanied by 7 common, non-beautiful mental factors. But then, eye-consciousness element has no direct association with other bases and elements. It is only partially associated with 1 base (ideation-base) and with 1 element (ideation-element). Eye-consciousness element, together with its associated 3 mental aggregates and 7 common mental factors, are dissociated from materiality (all 28 matters), *Nibbāna*, and the 6

VII. Associated and Dissociated

elements (7 excluding eye-consciousness element). The latter called (B). Thus, these states (B) are only left with dissociation from 1 element (eye-consciousness element). The rest SOE are to be interpreted in similar manner.

States of enquiry (SOE):	SOE associate with *these* states (A) :	SOE+(A) dissociate from (B):			These states, (B), Ds from:			These states, (B), Pds from:		
		agr	bse	el.	agr	bse	el.	agr	bse	el.
308. Mind-faculty	3 mental aggregates (feeling, perception, volitive formation)	1	10	10	4	1	7	-	1	1

Mind-faculty is associated with 89 cittas which come under consciousness aggregate. So, mind-faculty is taken as mutually associated with the other 3 mental aggregates. Mind-faculty, together with these associated states, are dissociated from matter aggregate, 10 gross bases, 10 gross elements, and *Nibbāna*. In turn, these states as (B), are in dissociation from 4 aggregates (4 mental aggregates), 1 base (mind-base), 7 elements (the 7 consciousness elements). They are also partially dissociated from 1 base (ideation-base), 1 element (ideation-element), and 52 cetasikas. There are no other aggregates left from which materiality and *Nibbāna* can become partially dissociated.

States of enquiry (SOE):	SOE associate with *these* states (A) :	SOE+(A) dissociate from (B):			These states, (B), Ds from:			These states, (B), Pds from:		
		agr	bse	el.	agr	bse	el.	agr	bse	el.
309. Equanimity-faculty	3 mental aggregates (perception, volitive formation, consciousness)	1	10	11	-	-	5	-	-	-

Equanimity-faculty consist of 55 cittas, accompanied by equanimity. It belongs to feeling aggregate. It is associated with 3 aggregates (remaining 3 mental aggregates), with 1 base (mind-base), with 6 elements (7 consciousness-elements excluding body-consciousness element). It is partially associated with 1 base (ideation-base), 1 element (ideation-element), and 46 cetasikas (52 excluding feeling, zest, hatred, envy, avarice, worry). Together these states, marked as (B), are dissociated from 1 aggregate (matter), 10 bases (10 gross bases), 11 elements (10 gross elements, and body-consciousness element), and *Nibbāna*. Dissociation from body-consciousness element includes indifferent feeling as to states of bodily pleasure, bodily pain, joy (mental), and melancholy.

These states (B) are in turn dissociated from 5 elements (eye-consciousness element, ear-consciousness element, nose-consciousness element, tongue-consciousness. element, and mind-element). There are no dissociations from

A Perfect Knowledge of Mind-Body from the Abhidhamma (Dhātukathā)

aggregates and bases, as well as no partial dissociations from the three categories, because those are already included in SOE+(A).

States of enquiry (SOE):	SOE associate with *these* states (A) :	SOE+(A) dissociate from (B):			These states, (B), Ds from:			These states, (B), Pds from:		
		agr	bse	el.	agr	bse	el.	agr	bse	el.
310. Volitive formation conditions Consciousness; six bases condition Contact; contact conditions Feeling; Contact; Feeling; Perception; Volition; Consciousness.; Attention (9)	89 cittas, 51 or 52 cetasikas depending on each SOE	1	10	10	4	1	7	-	1	1

These states consists of 89 cittas, and 51 cetasikas (52 excluding the cetasikas of *phassa*, *vedanā*, *saññā*, *cetanā* and *manasikāra*) with reference to the states of contact, feeling, perception, volition, and attention, respectively. Each of them is thus associated with its other remaining 3 mental aggregates. The exception is consciousness which is accompanied by 52 cetasikas.

Take for example, consciousness, together with its associated remaining 3 mental aggregates, they are dissociated from materiality (matter aggregate, 10 gross bases, and 10 gross elements) and *Nibbāna*. Materiality and *Nibbāna* are in turn dissociated from 4 aggregates (the 4 mental aggregates), 1 base (mind-base), and 7 elements (the 7 consciousness elements). They are also partially dissociated from 1 base (ideation-base), 1 element (ideation-element), and 52 cetasikas. The rest of the SOE are to be explained in the same manner.

States of enquiry:	SOE associate with *these* states (A) :	SOE+(A) dissociate from (B):			These states, (B), Ds from:			These states, (B), Pds from:		
		agr	bse	el.	agr	bse	el.	agr	bse	el.
311. Decision	78 cittas, 50 cetasikas (excl doubt, decision)	1	10	15	-	-	1	-	-	-

These states which are decision are associated with 78 cittas, and accompanied by 50 cetasikas (52 excluding *vicikicchā* and *adhimokkha*). Decision belongs to volitive formation. Therefore, decision is mutually associated with 3 aggregates (feeling, perception, consciousness), with 1 base (mind-base), with 2 elements (mind-element, and mind-consciousness element). Decision is partially associated with 1 aggregate (volitive formation), 1 base (ideation-base), 1 element (ideation-element), and 50 cetasikas.

Together, these states (A) are dissociated from 1 aggregate (matter), 10 bases (10 gross bases), 15 elements (10 gross elements, remaining 5 consciousness

VII. Associated and Dissociated

elements, namely, eye-cons. element, ear-cons. element, nose-cons. element, tongue-cons. element, and body-cons. element) and *Nibbāna*. Those states (B) are in turn dissociated from only 1 element (mind-element). There are no more possible dissociated states from the three categories.

3 states of enquiry from Dhammasaṅgaṇīmātikā triads

States of enquiry (SOE):	SOE associate with *these* states (A) :	SOE+(A) dissociate from (B):			These states, (B), Ds from:			*These* states, (B), Pds from:		
		agr	bse	el.	agr	bse	el.	agr	bse	el.
312. States associated with neither happy feeling nor painful feeling; States accompanied by equanimity. (2)	55 cittas accompanied by equanimity, and both have 46 cetasikas.	1	10	11	-	-	5	-	-	-

Both of these SOE consist of 55 cittas accompanied by equanimity, and both have 46 cetasikas. They belong to the aggregates of perception, volitive formation, and consciousness. Each SOE is in association with 1 aggregate (feeling). Each is partially associated with 1 base (ideation-base), with 1 element (ideation-element), and with 46 cetasikas. Together, each SOE and these associated states are dissociated from 1 aggregate (matter), 10 bases (10 gross bases), 11 elements (10 gross elements, body-consciousness element), and *Nibbāna*. Dissociation from body-consciousness element meaning indifference as to the states of bodily pleasure, bodily pain, mental joy, and melancholy.

These states (B) are in turn in dissociation only from 5 elements (7 consciousness elements excluding body-consciousness element and mind-consciousness element). There are no more possible dissociated states from the aggregates, bases and elements.

States of enquiry (SOE):	SOE associate with *these* states (A) :	SOE dissociate from (B):			These states, (B), Ds from:			*These* states, (B), Pds from:		
		agr	bse	el.	agr	bse	el.	agr	bse	el.
313. States with initial application and sustained application.	55 cittas, 50 cetasikas (excl. *vitakka* and *vicāra*)	1	10	15	-	-	1	-	-	-

States with initial application and sustained application are 55 cittas, accompanied by 50 cetasikas. But because they belong to 4 mental aggregates, there are no associations. Thus, these states, without states (A), are dissociated

A Perfect Knowledge of Mind-Body from the Abhidhamma (Dhātukathā)

from 1 aggregate (matter), 10 bases (10 gross bases), 15 elements (10 gross elements, and remaining 5 sensory consciousness elements having excluded mind-element and mind-consciousness element) and *Nibbāna*. Those states, marked as (B), in turn have no more dissociations from aggregates and bases, but have dissociation from 1 element (mind-element). There are no more partial dissociations.

10 states of enquiry from Dhammasaṅgaṇīmātikā dyads

	SOE associate with *these* states (A):	SOE+(A) dissociate from (B):			*These* states, (B), Ds from:			*These* states, (B),Pds from:		
314. States of enquiry (SOE):		agr	bse	el.	agr	bse	el.	agr	bse	el.
1. States which are consciousness;										
2. States which are mental factors.										
3. States associated with cons.										
4. States conjoined with cons.	All 52 cetasikas	1	10	10	4	1	7	-	1	1
5. States both conjoined with and originated from cons.										
6. States conjoined with, originated from, and arise concurrently with cons.										
7. States conjoined with, originated from, and arise consecutively with cons.										

States which are consciousness correspond to 89 cittas, and thus are associated with the aggregates of feeling, perception, and volitive formation. As consciousness aggregate can not associate with mind-base and the 7 consciousness-elements, it is partially associated with 1 base (ideation-base), 1 element (ideation-element), and 52 cetasikas.

The other 6 SOE are the 52 cetasikas, and so they are associated with consciousness aggregate. Each of these states is in association with 1 aggregate (consciousness), with 1 base (mind-base), 1 element (7 consciousness-elements). There are no partial association because 52 cetasikas are all included as the states of enquiry.

Take states which are consciousness as example. Together with its associated 3 mental aggregates, these states designated as SOE+(A), are dissociated from 1 aggregate (matter), 10 bases (10 gross bases), and 10 elements (10 gross elements) and *Nibbāna*. Subtle matters are already included in matter aggregate. These are dissociated states which are marked as (B).

In turn, those states (B) are in dissociation from 4 aggregates (feeling, perception, volitive formation, consciousness), 1 base (mind-base), 7 elements

VII. Associated and Dissociated

(the 7 consciousness elements). Those states (B) are also partially dissociated from 1 base (ideation-base), 1 element (ideation-element), and 52 cetasikas. The other six SOE are each to be analysed in the same manner.

315. States of enquiry (SOE):	SOE associate with *these* states (A) :	SOE+(A) dissociate from (B):			These states, (B), Ds from:			These states, (B), Pds from:		
		agr	bse	el.	agr	bse	el.	agr	bse	el.
1. States with initial application.	55 cittas, *vitakka* cetasika.	1	10	15	-	-	1	-	-	-
2. States with sustained application.	55 cittas, *vicāra* cetasika.									

Each of these states are bound by 55 cittas, and accompanied by 51 cetasikas. They are the same as in nos. 313.

States of enquiry (SOE):	SOE associate with *these* states (A) :	SOE+(A) dissociate from (B):			These states, (B), Ds from:			These states, (B), Pds from:		
		agr	bse	el.	agr	bse	el.	agr	bse	el.
316. States accompanied by equanimity.	55 cittas, 46 cetasikas	1	10	11	-	-	5	-	-	-

These states consist of 55 cittas accompanied by equanimity, and have 46 cetasikas. They belong to the aggregates of perception, volitive formation, and consciousness. The analysis and answers are the same as in nos. 312.

Key points from the text :

4 mental aggregates, 1 base; 7 consciousness elements, 2 faculties;
3 dependent originations; contact group of 7;
3 triads, 7 intermediate dyads; 2 initial application, 2 sustained application; decision associated with mind element;
3 states accompanied by equanimous feeling

There are 334 other states not included as subject matters of enquiry in this chapter, including matters.

A Perfect Knowledge of Mind-Body from the Abhidhamma (Dhātukathā)

In the two summary tables below, the number in the brackets represents the number of enquiries belong to the associated text paragraph nos.

Table 7.1. 37 states of enquiry by subject matter

Paragraph nos.
(with numbers of enquiries) :   Subject matter:

Paragraph nos. (with numbers of enquiries)		Subject matter
306 (4)	4	Aggregates
306 (1)	1	Bases
307 (7)	7	Elements
308 (1), 309 (1)	2	Faculties
310 (3)	3	Dependent originations
310 (6), 311 (1)	7	Contact group of 7
312 (2), 313 (1)	3	Triads
314 (7)	7	Intermediate dyads
315 (2), 316 (1)	3	Last dyads

Total = 37 states

Table 7.2 Summary of the 37 states of enquiry by answers

Text's paragraph nos. (with numbers of enquiries):		Dissociated from			Partially dissociated from		
		agr	bse	el.	agr	bse	el.
306 (5), 308 (1), 310 (9), 314 (7)	22	4	1	7	-	1	1
307 (7), 311 (1), 313 (1), 315 (2)	11	-	-	1	-	-	-
309 (1), 312 (2), 316 (1)	4	-	-	5	-	-	-

Total = 37 states in
3 kinds of answer

CHAPTER 8

VIII. Dissociated and Associated
(*Vippayuttenasampayutta*)

Analysis of 324 states from 2 catechism

There are a lengthy 324 states of enquiry from only two catechism in this chapter. It is because these 324 states are the same as in Chapter 14, and furthermore, all of them have the similar answers in this chapter. That is, those dissociated states from these states of enquiry are in turn associated with None.

Of these 324 states, 97 are internal states while 227 belong to triads and clusters of dyads. All these states of enquiries conform to the four kinds of dissociation condition as mentioned in Chapter 6 (by spheres, by classes, by times, and by continuity) which form the basis of these subject matters. When each subject matter of enquiry is dealt with, it asks for the dissociated states. Those dissociated states are in turn associated with no other states. The answer as 'none' applies invariably to all the 324 states of inquiry. The only thing you need to know regarding the analysis of dissociated and subsequent associated methods in this chapter is that, these states of inquiry belong to either 28 matters, or one of the 4 mental aggregates, or state of *Nibbāna*, or states which have both the characteristic of mentality and materiality but which are dissociated. For example, materiality and *Nibbāna*, either of which is always in dissociation with the four remaining mentalities. In turn, those dissociated 4 mental aggregates can not associated with themselves. The reason is because they simply do not comply with the 4 characteristics of association, i.e. they are neither associated nor dissociated. The answers thus become those dissociated states are associated with 'none'. There are 47 other states which are excluded from discussion.

Nos. States of enquiry :	dissociate from *these* states :	*These* states are associated with:
317. Matter aggregate (1)	*Nibbāna*, and aggregates of feeling, perception, volitive formation, and consciousness.	none

Nos. 318 contains 323 states as listed below which are the same as in Chapter 14. When each of these states is enquired with the dissociated states, those dissociated states are all similarly associated with no other states. In the meantime, I will leave the analysis for these 324 states of enquiry until the last chapter which will include columns on dissociated and associated, aggrouped, and ungrouped.

A Perfect Knowledge of Mind-Body from the Abhidhamma (Dhātukathā)

Nos. 318 contains the following states, identical to those in Chapter 14:

Nos. 456. Matter aggregate. (1)

Nos. 457. Feeling aggregate; Perception aggregate; Volitive formation aggregate; Consciousness aggregate; Mind-base, Mind-faculty. (6)

Nos. 458. Eye-base; Ear-base; Nose-base; Tongue-base; Body-base; Vision-base; Sound-base; Odour-base; Taste-base; Tangible-base; Eye-element; Ear-element; Nose-element; Tongue-element; Body-element; Vision-element; Sound-element; Odour-element; Taste-element; Tangible-element (20).

Nos. 459. Eye cons. element, ear cons. element, nose cons. element, tongue cons. element, body cons. element, mind-element, mind-cons. element. (7)

Nos. 460. The truth as to suffering. (1)

Nos. 461. Origin-truth; Path-truth. (2)

Nos. 462. Truth of the cessation of suffering; Vision-faculty; Hearing-faculty; Smell-faculty; Taste-faculty; Touch-faculty; Femininity-faculty; Masculinity-faculty. (8)

Nos. 463. Carnal pleasure faculty, carnal displeasure faculty, joy faculty, Melancholy faculty. (4)

Nos. 464. Equanimity-faculty. (1)

Nos. 465. Confidence-faculty; effort-faculty; mindfulness-faculty; concentration-faculty; wisdom-faculty; "I-shall-comprehend-the-unknown" faculty; higher knowledge faculty; "final knower" faculty; ignorance; conditioned by ignorance, volitive formation. (10)

Nos. 466. Conditioned by Volitive Formation, is Consciousness; conditioned by the six bases, is Contact; conditioned by contact, is Feeling. (3)

Nos. 467. Conditioned by feeling, Craving; Conditioned by craving, Clinging; Action-becoming. (3)

Nos. 468. Rebirth-becoming; Perception-becoming; Five-aggregate becoming. (3)

Nos. 469. Sensuous becoming. (1)

Nos. 470. Fine-material becoming; Non-perception becoming; Single-aggregate becoming; Lamentation. (4)

Nos. 471. Immaterial becoming; Neither perception nor non-perception becoming; Four-aggregate becoming; Sorrow; Suffering; Melancholy; Despair; Four Foundations of Mindfulness; Four Right Strivings; Basis of Psychic Accomplishment; Jhāna; The Illimitables; 5 Faculties; 5 Powers; 7 Enlightenment-Factors; Noble Eightfold Path. (16)

Nos. 472. Contact; Feeling; Perception; Volition; Consciousness; Attention. (6)

Nos. 473. Decision. (1)

Nos. 474. Wholesome states; Unwholesome states; States associated with happy feeling; States associated with painful feeling. (4)

Nos. 475. Indeterminate states. (1)

Nos. 476. States associated with neither happy feeling nor suffering feeling. (1)

VIII. Dissociated and Associated

Nos. 477. States which produce resultants; States which are corrupted and favourable to corruption. (2)

Nos. 478. States which neither are resultants nor causing resultants; States are not the result of clinging but are favourable to clinging; States neither are the result of clinging nor are favourable to clinging; States which neither are corrupted nor are favourable to corruptions (*asaṃkiliṭṭha asaṃkilesikā*). (4)

Nos. 479. States which are the result of clinging and favourable to clinging. (1)

Nos. 480. States which are not corrupted but are objects of corruptions (*asaṃkiliṭṭhasaṃkilesikehi dhammehi*) (1)

Nos. 481. States with initial application and sustained application. (1)

Nos. 482. States without initial application but with sustained application; States accompanied by zest; States accompanied by happiness. (3)

Nos. 483. States without initial application and without sustained application. (1)

Nos. 484. States accompanied by equanimity. (1)

Nos. 485. States eliminated by first Path; States eliminated by the higher three Paths; States with root causes eliminated by first Path; States with root causes eliminated by the higher three Paths; States which make for the continuance of death and rebirth. (*ācayagāmino*); States which make for the discontinuity of death and rebirth; States which lead out to *Nibbāna* (*apacayagāmino*); States appertaining to Learners (*sekhā*); States appertaining to *Arahatta* (*asekhā*); Sublime states. (9)

Nos. 486. States neither eliminated by the first Path nor by the higher three paths; States with root causes eliminated neither by first Path nor by the higher three Paths; States which neither lead to rebirth and death nor to *Nibbāna*; States appertaining to neither Learners nor *Arahatta*; States which are limited. (5)

Nos. 487. Immeasurable states; Superior states. (2)

Nos. 488. States with limited object. (1)

Nos. 489. States with sublime object; States with immeasurable object; States which are inferior; States fixed as to their destinies due to wrong views; States fixed as to their destinies due to right views; States having Path as its object; States conditioned by the Path; States having Path as predominant factor. (8)

Nos. 490. States of medium worth; States which do not entail fixed destiny. (2)

Nos. 491. States arisen; States not arisen; States bound to arise; Past states; Future states; Present states; Internal states; External states; States which are visible and impinging; States not visible but are impinging. (10)

Nos. 492. States having past object; States having future object; States having internal object; States having external object. (4)

Nos. 493. States having present object; States having both internal and external objects. (2)

Nos. 494. States which are root causes; States which have root causes (i.e. accompanied by root causes); States which are associated with root causes; States which are root causes and also having root causes; States which are not root causes but having root causes; States which are root causes and also associated with root causes; States which are not root causes but are associated

A Perfect Knowledge of Mind-Body from the Abhidhamma (Dhātukathā)

with root causes; States which are not root causes but have associated root causes. (8)

Nos. 495. States which have no root causes (i.e. not accompanied by root causes); States which dissociated from root causes; States which are neither root causes nor having root causes. (3)

Nos. 496. States not arisen from causes; States unconditioned by causes; States with visibility; States with impinging; States with physical change; States which are supramundane. (6)

Nos. 497. States which are mundane. (1)

Nos. 498. States which are defilement; States which are associated with defilement; States which are both defilement and objects of defilement; States which are both defilement and associated with defilement; States associated with defilement but are not defilement. (5)

Nos. 499. States which are objects of defilement; States which are dissociated from defilement; States which are objects of defilement but are not defilement; States which are dissociated from defilement but are objects of defilement. (4)

Nos. 500. States which are not objects of defilement; States which are dissociated from defilement as well as are not objects of defilement. (2)

Nos. 501. States which are fetters (*Saṃyojana*); States which are associated with fetters; States which are both fetters and objects of fetters; States which are both fetters and associated with fetters; States which are associated with fetters but are not fetters; States which are objects of fetters; States which are dissociated from fetters; States which are objects of fetters but are not fetters; States which are dissociated from fetters but are objects of fetters; States which are not objects of fetters; States which are dissociated from fetters as well as are not objects of fetters. (11) (repeat the same for *Gantha, Ogha, Yoga,* and *Nīvaraṇa,* i.e. 11 x 4 =44); States which are attachment (*Parāmāsa*); States associated with attachment; States which are both attachment and objects of attachment. (3). 11+44+3, thus total=(58).

Nos. 502. States which are not objects of attachment; States which are dissociated from attachment; States which are objects of attachment but are not attachment; States which are dissociated from attachment but are objects of attachment. (4)

Nos. 503. States which are not objects of attachment; States which are dissociated from attachment and are also not objects of attachment. (2)

Nos. 504. States which attend to objects; States which are consciousness; States which are mental factors; States associated with consciousness; States conjoined with consciousness; States both conjoined with and originated from consciousness; States conjoined with, originated from, and arise concurrently with consciousness; States conjoined with, originated from, and arise consecutively with consciousness. (8)

Nos. 505. States which do not have objects; States dissociated from consciousness; States not conjoined with consciousness; States which are derived; States which are not the result of clinging. (5)

VIII. Dissociated and Associated

Nos. 506. States which are the result of clinging (obtained by clinging). (1)

Nos. 507. States which are clinging (*upādānā*); States which are associated with clinging; States which are both clinging and objects of clinging; States which are both clinging and associated with clinging; States which are associated with clinging but are not clinging; States which are objects of clinging; States which are dissociated from clinging; States which are objects of clinging but are not clinging; States which are dissociated from clinging but are objects of clinging; States which are not objects of clinging; States which are dissociated from clinging as well as are not objects of clinging; States which are corruptions (*kilesa*); States which are corrupted; States which are associated with corruptions; States which are both corruptions and objects of corruptions; States which are both corruptions and are corrupted; States which are corrupted but are not corruptions; States which are both corruptions and associated with corruptions; States associated with corruptions but are not corruptions. (19)

Nos. 508. States which are objects of corruptions; States which are not corrupt; States dissociated from corruptions; States which are favourable to corruptions but are not corruptions; States dissociated from corruptions but are favourable to corruptions. (5)

Nos. 509. States which are not objects of corruptions; States dissociated from corruptions and are not objects of corruptions. (2)

Nos. 510. States eliminated by first Path; States eliminated by the higher three Paths; States with root causes eliminated by first Path; States with root causes eliminated by the higher three Paths. (4)

Nos. 511. States not eliminated by the first Path; States not eliminated by the higher three Paths; States with root causes not eliminated by the first Path; States with root causes not eliminated by the higher three Paths. (4)

Nos. 512. States with initial application; States with sustained application. (2)

Nos. 513. States with zest; States which are accompanied by zest; States accompanied by happiness. (3)

Nos. 514. States accompanied by equanimity. (1)

Nos. 515. States which are characteristic of the sensuous sphere; States which are included (in round of death and rebirth); States leading to liberation. (3)

Nos. 516. States not characteristic of the sensuous sphere; States which are not included (in round of death and rebirth); States which do not lead out to liberation. (3)

Nos. 517. States which are characteristic of the form sphere; States which are characteristic of the formless sphere; States which lead out to liberation; States which are fixed as to their destinies; States at odds (*saraṇā*) with supramundane Path. (5)

Nos. 518. States which are not characteristic of the form sphere; States which are not characteristic of the formless sphere; States which do not lead out to liberation; States which are not fixed as to their destinies; States which are not at odds (*araṇā*) with the supramundane Path. (5)

CHAPTER 9

IX. Associated and Associated
(*Sampayuttenasampayutta*)

Analysis of 120 states from 34 catechism

This chapter's analysis of states excludes pure materiality, state of *Nibbāna*, and those states which exhibit the characteristics of materiality and mentality such as vitality-faculty, kāma-becoming, birth, ageing, and death. Total 120 states of enquiry which belong to pure mentality, form the subject matter of this chapter. Of these, 56 are from interior states, and 64 are from the triads and dyad-clusters. The association conditions follow the same as explained at the beginning of Chapter 6 except that in this context, only the mental aggregates are being considered. Let's refresh our memory a little from Chapter 6. When one of the 4 mental aggregates is enquired with the remaining 3 mental aggregates, together they must both comply with the 4 characteristics of association (i.e. arise together, cease together, share the same object, and comparable on the same basis). Otherwise, they are excluded from this chapter.

According to the text, each of the states of enquiry is enquired to determine its remaining states with which each of them is directly associated and partially associated. The associated remaining states are taken as *these* states. *Those* states (same as *these* associated remaining states are associated with *these* states (i.e. the same states of enquiry). The original text does not mention the combined classification of *these* states and *those* states under the three categories, but I provide those answers taken as aggrouped under the three categories in the descriptive exposition even though those answers are not shown directly in all the charts in this chapter. The foregoing diagram 4.1 in Chapter 4 describes the similar relationship between *these* states (1st), *those* states, and *these* states (2nd).

The following abbreviations will be used in the charts and tables throughout this Chapter.

SOE : States of enquiry
cons. : Consciousness
agr. : aggregate
el. : element
Asc : Associated
Pasc : Partially associated

IX. Associated and Associated

56 internal states of enquiry

States of enquiry (SOE):	Aggregate		Base		Element	
	Asc	Pasc	Asc	Pasc	Asc	Pasc
319. Feeling aggregate; Perception aggregate; Volitive formation. (3)	3	-	1	1	7	1

These three subject matters of enquiry are all associated with 89 cittas and 51 cetasikas (i.e. 52 excluding the respective mental factor of *vedanā*, *saññā* or *cetanā*). Thus, each of them is associated with 3 aggregates (the respective remaining 3 mental aggregates), with 1 base (mind-base), and with 7 elements (the 7 consciousness elements). Each of them is partially associated with 1 base (ideation-base), with 1 element (ideation-element), and with 51 cetasikas. Those remaining states are taken as aggrouped under 3 aggregates (the remaining 3 mental aggregates excluding the individual SOE), 2 bases (ideation-base and mind-base), and 8 elements (ideation-element, 7 consciousness elements).

States of enquiry (SOE):	Aggregate		Base		Element	
	Asc	Pasc	Asc	Pasc	Asc	Pasc
320. Consciousness aggregate; Mind base; Eye-consciousness element, Ear-consciousness element; Nose-consciousness element; Tongue-consciousness element; Body-consciousness element; Mind element; Mind consciousness element. (9)	3	-	-	1	-	1

All these subject matters of enquiry come under the consciousness aggregate, are connected to 89 cittas, accompanied by 52 cetasikas. All these states are taken as under consciousness aggregate so that comparison is possible only on the same basis. As materiality is excluded from discussion, the aggregates of feeling, perception, and volitive formation become the remaining states. And as consciousness aggregate can not associate with its co-adjunct states of consciousness, each of these SOE is thus only associated with 3 mental aggregates (feeling, perception, volitive formation), and the 7 common, non-beautiful mental factors (contact, feeling, perception, volition, one-pointedness, vitality-faculty, attention).

Each of these SOE is partially associated with 1 base (ideation-base), 1 element (ideation-element), and the aforesaid 7 common cetasikas. Those remaining states are taken as aggrouped under 3 aggregates (feeling, perception, and volitive formation), 1 base (ideation-base), and 1 element (ideation-element).

A Perfect Knowledge of Mind-Body from the Abhidhamma (Dhātukathā)

States of enquiry (SOE):	Aggregate		Base		Element	
	Asc	Pasc	Asc	Pasc	Asc	Pasc
321. Origin-truth; Path-truth. (2)	3	1	1	1	1	1

Origin-truth consists of 8 greed-rooted cittas, accompanied by 21 cetasikas (27 excluding feeling, zest, greed, wrong view, conceit, doubt). Path-truth corresponds to Noble Eightfold Path with 4 supramundane path consciousness. Origin-truth and Path-truth both belong to volitive formation aggregate, are bound up with mind-consciousness element. Each of them is associated with 3 mental aggregates (feeling, perception, consciousness), 1 base (mind-base), and 1 element (mind-consciousness element). Each is partially associated with 1 aggregate (volitive formation), 1 base (ideation-base), and 1 element (ideation-element). For origin-truth, it is also partially associated with the 21 cetasikas. Those remaining states are taken as aggrouped under 4 aggregates (feeling, perception, volitive formation, consciousness), 2 bases (ideation-base, mind-base), and 2 elements (ideation-element, mind-consciousness element).

States of enquiry (SOE):	Aggregate		Base		Element	
	Asc	Pasc	Asc	Pasc	Asc	Pasc
322. Mind-faculty. (1)	3	-	-	1	-	1

Mind-faculty is bound with 89 cittas under consciousness aggregate. So, mind-faculty is associated with 3 aggregates (feeling, perception, volitive formation). It has no association with mind-base and cons. elements because consciousness can not associate with itself. It is partially associated with 1 base (ideation-base), with 1 element (ideation-element), and with 52 cetasikas. Those remaining states are taken as aggrouped under 3 aggregates (feeling, perception, volitive formation), 1 base (ideation-base), and 1 element (ideation-element).

States of enquiry (SOE):	Aggregate		Base		Element	
	Asc	Pasc	Asc	Pasc	Asc	Pasc
323. Carnal pleasure faculty, Carnal displeasure faculty, Joy faculty, Melancholy faculty. (4)	3	-	1	1	1	1

These four feeling faculties belong to feeling aggregate. So, each of them is associated with the remaining 3 mental aggregates. Each of them is associated with 3 aggregates (perception, volitive formation, consciousness), 1 base (mind-base), and 1 element (body-consciousness element). Each is partially associated with 1 base (ideation-base), with 1 element (ideation-element), and also with 6 cetasikas (7 common and non-beautiful mental factors excluding feeling). Those remaining states are taken as aggrouped under 3 aggregates (perception, volitive

IX. Associated and Associated

formation, consciousness), 2 bases (ideation-base, mind-base), and 2 elements (ideation-element, body-consciousness element).

States of enquiry (SOE):	Aggregate		Base		Element	
	Asc	Pasc	Asc	Pasc	Asc	Pasc
324. Equanimity-faculty. (1)	3	-	1	1	6	1

Equanimity-faculty, like the preceding four faculties, belong to feeling aggregate. It is associated with the remaining 3 mental aggregates (perception, volitive formation, consciousness), with 1 base (mind-base), with 6 elements (7 consciousness-elements having excluded body-consciousness element). It is partially associated with 1 base (ideation-base), with 1 element (ideation-element), and with 46 cetasikas (which accompany 55 cittas). Those remaining states are taken as aggrouped under 3 aggregates (perception, volitive formation, consciousness), 2 bases (ideation-base, mind-base), and 7 elements (ideation-element, 6 consciousness elements having excluded body-consciousness element).

States of enquiry (SOE):	Aggregate		Base		Element	
	Asc	Pasc	Asc	Pasc	Asc	Pasc
325. Confidence-faculty; effort-faculty; mindfulness-faculty; concentration-faculty; wisdom-faculty; "I-shall-comprehend-the-unknown" faculty; higher knowledge faculty; "final knower" faculty; ignorance; conditioned by ignorance, is volitive formation. (10)	3	1	1	1	1	1

These 10 States of enquiry are bound by volitive formation. So, each of them is associated with the remaining 3 mental aggregates (feeling, perception, consciousness), 1 base (mind-base), and 1 element (mind-consciousness element). Each of them is partially associated with 1 aggregate (volitive formation), 1 base (ideation-base), 1 element (ideation-element), and 51 cetasikas (52 excluding, respectively, *saddhā, viriya, sati, ekaggata* for the first 4 faculties, *amoha* for the next 4 faculties, *moha* and *cetanā* for the last 2 factors of the dependent origination). Those remaining states are taken as aggrouped under 4 aggregates (feeling, perception, volitive formation, consciousness), 2 bases (ideation-base and mind-base), and 2 elements (ideation-element and mind-consciousness element).

States of enquiry (SOE):	Aggregate		Base		Element	
	Asc	Pasc	Asc	Pasc	Asc	Pasc
326. Conditioned by volitive formations, is Consciousness (1)	3	-	-	1	-	1

A Perfect Knowledge of Mind-Body from the Abhidhamma (Dhātukathā)

Consciousness is 89 cittas which come under consciousness aggregate, and so it is associated with the remaining 3 mental aggregates (feeling, perception, volitive formation). There are no direct associations for base and element for consciousness aggregate can not associate with itself. It therefore can not associate with its co-adjunct mind-base and 7 consciousness-elements. Consciousness is partially associated with 1 base (ideation-base), 1 element (ideation-element), and 52 cetasikas. Those remaining states are taken as aggrouped under 3 aggregates (feeling, perception, volitive formation), 1 base (ideation-base), and 1 element (ideation-element).

States of enquiry (SOE):	Aggregate		Base		Element	
	Asc	Pasc	Asc	Pasc	Asc	Pasc
327. Conditioned by six bases, is Contact. (1)	3	1	1	1	7	1

Contact is amongst the 7 common non-beautiful cetasikas, accompanies 89 cittas. Contact belongs to volitive formation. It is thus associated with 3 aggregates (feeling, perception, consciousness), 1 base (mind-base), and 7 elements (the 7 consciousness-elements). It is partially associated with 1 aggregate (volitive formation), 1 base (ideation-base), 1 element (ideation-element), and 51 cetasikas (52 excluding contact-*cetasika*). Those remaining states are taken as aggrouped under 4 aggregates (feeling, perception, volitive formation, consciousness), 2 bases (ideation-base, mind-base), and 8 elements (ideation-element, 7 consciousness elements).

States of enquiry (SOE):	Aggregate		Base		Element	
	Asc	Pasc	Asc	Pasc	Asc	Pasc
328. Conditioned by contact, is Feeling. (1)	3	-	1	1	7	1

Feeling is one of the 7 common non-beautiful cetasikas which present at the 89 cittas, accompanied by 51 cetasikas (52 excluding feeling-*cetasika*). It comes under feeling aggregate. Thus, it is associated with the remaining 3 mental aggregates (perception, volitive formation, consciousness), 1 base (mind-base), and 7 elements (the 7 consciousness-elements). It is partially associated with 1 base (ideation-base), 1 element (ideation-element), and 51 cetasikas (52 excluding feeling-*cetasika*). Those remaining states are taken as aggrouped under 3 aggregates (perception, volitive formation, consciousness), 2 bases (ideation-base, mind-base), and 2 elements (ideation-element, 7 cons. elements).

States of enquiry (SOE):	Aggregate		Base		Element	
	Asc	Pasc	Asc	Pasc	Asc	Pasc
329. Conditioned by feeling, is Craving; conditioned by craving, is Clinging; Action-becoming. (3)	3	1	1	1	1	1

IX. Associated and Associated

Craving is accompanied by greed-*cetasika*, while clinging is accompanied by greed-*cetasika* and wrong view-*cetasika*. These two cetasikas are present at the 8 greed-rooted cittas. Kamma-becoming is accompanied by volition-*cetasika*, present at the 17 wholesome cittas and 12 unwholesome cittas. The three states of enquiry belong to volitive formation aggregate. Each of these states is associated with the remaining 3 mental aggregates (feeling, perception, consciousness), 1 base (mind-base), and 1 element (mind-consciousness element). Each of them is partially associated with 1 aggregate (volitive formation), 1 base (ideation-base), with 1 element (ideation-element), and 51 cetasikas (50 in the case of clinging). Those remaining states are taken as aggrouped under 4 aggregates (feeling, perception, volitive formation, consciousness), 2 bases (ideation-base, mind-base), and 2 elements (ideation-element, mind-consciousness element).

States of enquiry (SOE):	Aggregate		Base		Element	
	Asc	Pasc	Asc	Pasc	Asc	Pasc
330. Sorrow; Suffering; Melancholy. (3)	3	-	1	1	1	1

The three of them are grievous feeling, belong to feeling faculty and are associated with the two hatred-rooted cittas. Each of these SOE is associated with 3 aggregates (perception, volitive formation, consciousness), 1 base (mind-base), and 1 element (body-consciousness element). Each is partially associated with 1 base (ideation-base), 1 element (ideation-element), and 51 cetasikas (52 excluding hatred-*cetasika*). Those remaining states are taken as aggrouped under 3 aggregates (perception, volitive formation, consciousness), 2 bases (ideation-base, mind-base), and 2 elements (body-consciousness element, ideation-element).

States of enquiry (SOE):	Aggregate		Base		Element	
	Asc	Pasc	Asc	Pasc	Asc	Pasc
331. Despair; Foundations of mindfulness; Right strivings. (3)	3	1	1	1	1	1

Despair is occasionally accompanied by hatred-*cetasika*; application or the four foundation of mindfulness is associated with mindfulness-*cetasika*; right strivings are associated with energy-*cetasika*. The three belong to volitive formation. Thus, each of them is associated with 3 mental aggregates (feeling, perception, consciousness), 1 base (mind-base), 1 element (mind-consciousness element). Each is partially associated 1 aggregate (volitive formation), 1 base (ideation-base), 1 element (ideation-element), and 51 cetasikas (52 excluding, respectively, *dosa, sati,* and *viriya*, for each state of enquiry). Those remaining

A Perfect Knowledge of Mind-Body from the Abhidhamma (Dhātukathā)

states are taken as aggrouped under 4 aggregates (feeling, perception, volitive formation, consciousness), 2 bases (ideation-base mind-base), and 2 elements (ideation-element, mind-consciousness element).

States of enquiry (SOE):	Aggregate		Base		Element	
	Asc	Pasc	Asc	Pasc	Asc	Pasc
332. Basis of Psychic Accomplishment. (1)	2	1	-	1	-	1

These are the four means to psychic accomplishment, which are followed by three cetasikas of *viriya*, *chanda*, and *amoha*. These states belong to 8 x 5 supramundane cittas with 33 associated cetasikas (that is, 13 primary common cetasikas excluding *viriya*, *chanda*, and 25 beautiful cetasikas excluding 2 *appamaññā*, and *amoha*). These states belong to consciousness aggregate and is only partially associated with volitive formation. They are therefore mutually associated with 2 mental aggregates (feeling, perception). There are no associations with base and element for they can not associated with their respective co-adjunct bases and elements. The SOE is partially associated with 1 aggregate (volitive formation), 1 base (ideation-base), 1 element (ideation-element), and 33 cetasikas. Those remaining states are taken as aggrouped under 3 aggregates (feeling, perception, volitive formation), 1 base (ideation-base), and 1 element (ideation-element).

States of enquiry (SOE):	Aggregate		Base		Element	
	Asc	Pasc	Asc	Pasc	Asc	Pasc
333. *Jhāna*. (1)	2	1	1	1	1	1

Jhāna is present at the 27 sublime cittas (cittas in the fine-material and immaterial spheres) accompanied by the varied cetasikas (First-*jhāna* with 35 cetasikas, Second-*jhāna* with 34 cetasikas, Third-*jhāna* with 33 cetasikas, Fourth-*jhāna* with 32 cetasikas, Fifth-*jhāna* with 30 cetasikas), and also present at the 8 x 5 supramundane cittas accompanied by various different cetasikas. (See Appendix VI, Chart 11). *Jhāna* belongs to feeling, and only partially associated with volitive formation. So, it is directly associated with 2 aggregates (perception, consciousness), with 1 base (mind-base), and with 1 element (mind-consciousness element). *Jhāna* is partially associated with 1 aggregate (volitive formation), with 1 base (ideation-base), with 1 element (ideation-element), and with the respective cetasikas present at the 27 sublime cittas and 8 x 5 supramundane cittas. Those remaining states are taken as aggrouped under 3 aggregates (feeling, perception, volitive formation), 2 bases (ideation-base, mind-base), and 2 elements (ideation-element, and mind-consciousness element).

IX. Associated and Associated

States of enquiry (SOE):	Aggregate		Base		Element	
	Asc	Pasc	Asc	Pasc	Asc	Pasc
334. The Illimitables ; 5 Faculties ; 5 Powers ; 7 Enlightenment-Factors; Noble Eightfold Path (5)	3	1	1	1	1	1

Each of these five subject matters of enquiry is accompanied by the different cetasikas (See Table 1.6b), but all of them belong to volitive formation aggregate. Each of them is associated with 3 aggregates (feeling, perception, consciousness), 1 base (mind-base), and 1 element (mind-consciousness element). Each is partially associated with 1 aggregate (volitive formation), 1 base (ideation-base), 1 element (ideation-element), and with its specific group of cetasikas (See Table 1.6b). Those remaining states are taken as aggrouped under 4 aggregates (feeling, perception, volitive formation, consciousness), 2 bases (ideation-base, mind-base), and 2 elements (ideation-element, mind-consciousness element).

States of enquiry (SOE):	Aggregate		Base		Element	
	Asc	Pasc	Asc	Pasc	Asc	Pasc
335. Contact; Volition; Attention. (3)	3	1	1	1	7	1

Contact is accompanied by *phasso*-cetasika. Volition is accompanied by *cetanā*-cetasika. Attention is accompanied by *manasikāra*-cetasika. The three states of enquiry belong to volitive formation aggregate. Each of them is associated with 3 mental aggregates (feeling, perception, consciousness), 1 base (mind-base), and 7 elements (7 consciousness-elements). Each is partially associated with 1 aggregate (volitive formation), 1 base (ideation-base), 1 element (ideation-element), and 51 cetasikas. Those remaining states are taken as aggrouped under 4 aggregates (feeling, perception, volitive formation, consciousness), 2 bases (ideation-base, mind-base), and 8 elements (ideation-element, 7 consciousness elements).

States of enquiry (SOE):	Aggregate		Base		Element	
	Asc	Pasc	Asc	Pasc	Asc	Pasc
336. Feeling; Perception. (2)	3	-	1	1	7	1

Feeling is accompanied by *vedanā-cetasika*; Perception is accompanied by *saññā-cetasika*. Each of them arises with 89 cittas and 51cetasikas (i.e. 52 excluding the respective mental factor of *vedanā* and *saññā*). Thus, each of them is associated with 3 aggregates (either feeing or perception depending on which SOE is being dealt with; volitive formation; consciousness), with 1 base (mind-base), and with 7 elements (7 consciousness elements). Each is partially associated with 1 base (ideation-base), 1 element (ideation-element), and 51

A Perfect Knowledge of Mind-Body from the Abhidhamma (Dhātukathā)

cetasikas. Those remaining states are taken as aggrouped under 3 aggregates (the remaining 3 mental aggregates excluding the respective aggregate which is being enquired), 2 bases (ideation-base, mind-base), and 2 elements (ideation-element, 7 consciousness elements).

States of enquiry (SOE):	Aggregate		Base		Element	
	Asc	Pasc	Asc	Pasc	Asc	Pasc
337. Consciousness. (1)	3	-	-	1	-	1

Consciousness consists of 89 cittas, accompanied by 52 cetasikas. It is associated with remaining 3 aggregates (feeling, perception, volitive formation). It has no association with base and element because consciousness can not associate with itself. Consciousness is partially associated with 1 base (ideation-base), 1 element (ideation-element), and 52 cetasikas. Those remaining states are taken as aggrouped under 3 aggregates (feeling, perception, volitive formation), 1 base (ideation-base), and 1 element (ideation-element).

States of enquiry (SOE):	Aggregate		Base		Element	
	Asc	Pasc	Asc	Pasc	Asc	Pasc
338. Decision. (1)	3	1	1	1	2	1

Decision follows 78 cittas (see Appendix VI, Chart 7), is accompanied by 50 cetasikas (52 excluding two cetasikas of *vicikicchā* and *adhimokkha*). Decision belongs to volitive formation. Decision is thus mutually associated with 3 aggregates (feeling, perception, consciousness), 1 base (mind-base), and 2 elements (mind-element, mind-consciousness element). It is partially associated with 1 aggregate (volitive formation), 1 base (ideation-base), 1 element (ideation-element), and 50 cetasikas (doubt and decision are excluded). Those remaining states are taken as aggrouped under 4 aggregates (feeling, perception, volitive formation, consciousness), 2 bases (ideation-base, mind-base), and 3 elements (mind-element, ideation-element, mind-consciousness element).

8 states of enquiry from Dhammasaṅgaṇīmātikā triads

States of enquiry (SOE):	Aggregate		Base		Element	
	Asc	Pasc	Asc	Pasc	Asc	Pasc
339. States associated with happy feeling; States associated with painful feeling; States associated with neither happy feeling nor painful feeling. (3)	1	-	-	1	-	1

IX. Associated and Associated

States associated with happy feeling (include those with joy) belong to 63 cittas, accompanied by 46 cetasikas (52 excluding feeling, hatred, envy, avarice, worry, doubt). States associated with painful feeling (include those with displeasure) belong to 3 cittas (2 hatred-rooted, 1 body-consciousness resultant), accompanied by 21 cetasikas (27 excluding feeling, zest, greed, wrong view, conceit, doubt). States associated with neither happy feeling nor painful feeling belong to 55 cittas, accompanied by equanimity, and have 46 associated cetasikas (52 excluding feeling, zest, hatred, envy, avarice, worry). Readers can refer to Appendix VI, Chart 18 regarding the above-mentioned. All these SOE come under the aggregates of perception, volitive formation, and consciousness.

Each of them is associated with 1 mental aggregate (feeling). Herein, ideation-base and ideation-element are excluded because they are common co-adjuncts to both perception aggregate and volitive formation aggregate. Each is partially associated with 1 base (ideation-base), 1 element (ideation-element), and with 46, 21, or 55 cetasikas depending on which SOE is being enquired at the time. Those remaining states are taken as aggrouped under 1 aggregate (feeling), 1 base (ideation-base), and 1 element (ideation-element).

States of enquiry (SOE):	Aggregate		Base		Element	
	Asc	Pasc	Asc	Pasc	Asc	Pasc
340. States with initial application and sustained application; States without initial application but with sustained application; States accompanied by zest. (3)	-	1	-	1	-	1

The first SOE belongs to 55 cittas, accompanied by 50 cetasikas. The second SOE belongs to 11 Second-*Jhāna* cittas (see Appendix VI, Chart 5), 66 cittas with sustained application, and accompanied by 36 cetasikas (38 excluding *vitakka, vicāra*). States accompanied by zest belong to 51 cittas, accompanied by 46 cetasikas (52 excluding zest, hatred, envy, avarice, worry, and doubt). All these three states of enquiry belong to 4 mental aggregates, and so there are no direct associations. Although volitive formation aggregate is excluded from direct association, this mental aggregate contains the associated cetasikas as mentioned above. So, these states have partial association with 1 aggregate (volitive formation), 1 base (ideation-base), 1 element (ideation-element), and 50, 37, or 46 cetasikas depending on which SOE is being dealt with at the time. Those remaining states are taken as aggrouped under 1 aggregate (volitive formation), 1 base (ideation-base), and 1 element (ideation-element).

States of enquiry (SOE):	Aggregate		Base		Element	
	Asc	Pasc	Asc	Pasc	Asc	Pasc
341. States accompanied by happiness; States accompanied by equanimity. (2)	1	-	-	1	-	1

A Perfect Knowledge of Mind-Body from the Abhidhamma (Dhātukathā)

States accompanied by happiness consist of 63 cittas, accompanied by 46 cetasikas. States accompanied by equanimity are states which endure neither happy feeling nor painful feeling, and consist of 55 cittas accompanied by 46 cetasikas. (See Appendix VI, Chart 18). These two states belong to the aggregates of perception, volitive formation, and consciousness. Each of these SOE is associated with 1 aggregate (feeling). There is no association with ideation-base and ideation-element because they come under both feeling and perception aggregates. Each of these two states is partially associated with 1 base (ideation-base), 1 element (ideation-element), and 44 or 46 cetasikas depending on which SOE is being enquired at the time. Those remaining states are taken as aggrouped under 1 aggregate (feeling), 1 base (ideation-base), and 1 element (ideation-element).

56 states of enquiry from Dhammasaṅgaṇīmātikā dyads

States of enquiry (SOE):	Aggregate		Base		Element	
	Asc	Pasc	Asc	Pasc	Asc	Pasc
342. States which are root causes (*hetū*); States which are root causes and also having root causes; States which are root causes and also associated with root causes. (3)	3	1	1	1	1	1

States which are root causes are concerned with the 6 roots of greed, hatred, delusion, non-greed, non-hatred, and non-delusion. States which are root causes and also having root causes, together with states which are root causes as well as are associated with root causes — are bound up with the same 6 root causes, and excluding delusion present at the 2 delusion-rooted cittas. The three states belong to volitive formation. So, each of them is associated with 3 aggregates (feeling, perception, consciousness), 1 base (mind-base), and 1 element (mind-consciousness element). It is partially associated with 1 aggregate (volitive formation), 1 base (ideation-base), and 1 element (ideation-element). Those remaining states are taken as aggrouped under 4 aggregates (feeling, perception, volitive formation, consciousness), 2 bases (ideation-base, mind-base), and 2 elements (ideation-element, mind-consciousness element).

States of enquiry (SOE):	Aggregate		Base		Element	
	Asc	Pasc	Asc	Pasc	Asc	Pasc
343. States which are not root causes but having root causes; States which are not root causes but are associated with root causes; States which are not root causes but have associated root causes (*na hetusahetukehi*). (3)	-	1	-	1	-	1

235

IX. Associated and Associated

These three states of enquiry include 71 cittas, and accompanied by 46 cetasikas (52 excluding the 6 roots causes). These states, all of which are not root causes per se, belong to the 4 mental aggregates. Since the 4 mental aggregates are the states of enquiry, there are no direct associations. Thus, each of these three states are only partially associated with 1 aggregate (volitive formation), 1 base (ideation-base), 1 element (ideation-element), and 46 cetasikas. Those remaining states are taken as aggrouped under 1 aggregate (volitive formation), 1 base (ideation-base), and 1 element (ideation-element).

States of enquiry (SOE):	Aggregate Asc Pasc	Base Asc Pasc	Element Asc Pasc
344. States which are defilement (*āsavā*); States which are both defilement and objects of defilement; States which are defilement and also associated with defilement. (3)	3 1	1 1	1 1

These three states of enquiries contains the 3 defilement factors of greed (or sensual desire), wrong view, and delusion, They belong to volitive formation. Because the three states are defilement per se, are unwholesome states, they are bound up with mind-consciousness element. Each of them is thus associated with 3 mental aggregates (feeling, perception, consciousness), 1 base (mind-base), and 1 element (mind-consciousness element). Each of them is partially associated with 1 aggregate (volitive formation), 1 base (ideation-base), 1 element (ideation-element), and 52 or 26 cetasikas. (States which are objects of defilement contain 52 cetasikas, while states associated with defilement are followed by 26 cetasikas). Those remaining states are taken as aggrouped under 4 aggregates (feeling, perception, volitive formation, consciousness), 2 bases (ideation-base, mind-base), and 2 elements (ideation-element, mind-consciousness element).

States of enquiry (SOE):	Aggregate Asc Pasc	Base Asc Pasc	Element Asc Pasc
345. States which are associated with defilement but are not defilement. (1)	- 1	- 1	- 1

These states are included in the 12 mundane unwholesome cittas. As these states are not the defilement per se, they are therefore accompanied by 24 cetasikas (27 excluding the 3 defilement factors of greed or sensual desire, wrong view, and delusion, present at the 12 unwholesome cittas). The SOE belongs to 4 mental aggregates, and so there are no direct associations. The SOE is partially associated with 1 aggregate (volitive formation), 1 base (ideation-base), 1

A Perfect Knowledge of Mind-Body from the Abhidhamma (Dhātukathā)

element (ideation-element), and 24 cetasikas. Those remaining states are taken as aggrouped under 1 aggregate (volitive formation), 1 base (ideation-base), and 1 element (ideation-element).

346. States of enquiry (SOE):	Aggregate Asc Pasc	Base Asc Pasc	Element Asc Pasc
Repeats the same from preceding *āsava* cluster for the groups of Fetters, Bonds, Raging Current, Yokes, Hindrances (*Saṃyojana, Gantha, Ogha, Yoga, Nīvaraṇa*) respectively following nos. 344. Altogether 3 x 5 =15 (nos. 1. to 15.)	3 1	1 1	1 1
Repeats the same from preceding *āsava* cluster for the groups of Fetters, Bonds, Raging Current, Yokes, Hindrances (*Saṃyojana, Gantha, Ogha, Yoga, Nīvaraṇa*) respectively following nos. 345. Altogether 5 x 1 = 5 (nos. 16. to 20.)	- 1	- 1	- 1
21. States which are attachment (*parāmāsa*). 22. States which are both attachment and objects of attachment.	3 1	1 1	1 1

Those 17 states (nos. 1 to 15, 21, 22) have similar answers as in nos. 344, and they belong to volitive formation aggregate. The three states from each of the five clusters consist of different cetasikas. Each of these 17 states is mutually associated with the remaining 3 mental aggregates (feeling, perception, consciousness), 1 base (mind-base), and 1 element (mind-consciousness element). Each of them is partially associated with 1 aggregate (volitive formation), 1 base (ideation-base), 1 element (ideation-element), and associated cetasikas. (See Table 1.8.4 to Table 1.8.6). Those remaining states are taken as aggrouped under 4 aggregates (feeling, perception, volitive formation, consciousness), 2 bases (ideation-base, mind-base), and 2 elements (ideation-element, mind-consciousness element).

Those 5 states (nos. 16 to 20) follow the same answers as in nos. 345, they belong to 4 mental aggregates.

Those 5 states of enquiry (nos. 16 to 20) are from 12 mundane unwholesome cittas, and accompanied by different cetasikas. They belong to 4 mental aggregates. Analysis and answers are as follows:

i. States which are associated with Fetters but are not Fetters (nos. 16) — consist of the 12 unwholesome cittas, and 19 cetasikas (27 excluding the 8 states of fetters, viz. greed, ill-will, conceit, wrong view, doubt, adherence to rites and ceremonial practices, lust for becoming, envy, avarice, and

IX. Associated and Associated

ignorance). These states belong to 4 mental aggregates, and so there are no direct associations. They are partially associated with 1 aggregate (volitive formation), 1 base (ideation-base), 1 element (ideation-element), and with *19 cetasikas*. Those remaining states are taken as aggrouped under 1 aggregate (volitive formation), 1 base (ideation-base), 1 element (ideation-element).

ii. States which are associated with Bonds but are not Bonds (nos. 17) — consist of 8 greed-rooted cittas, 2 hatred-rooted cittas, 23 cetasikas (27 excluding 3 states of bonds and doubt). These states belong to 4 mental aggregates, and so there are no direct associations. They are partially associated with 1 aggregate (volitive formation), 1 base (ideation-base), 1 element (ideation-element), and *23 cetasikas*. Those remaining states are taken as aggrouped under 1 aggregate (volitive formation), 1 base (ideation-base), 1 element (ideation-element).

iii. States which are associated with Raging current but are not Raging current (nos. 18) — consist of 12 unwholesome cittas and *24 cetasikas*. Raging current (*Ogha*) cluster is the same as cluster of defilement (*Āsava*), and thus answer is the same as in nos. 345.

iv. States which are associated with Yokes but are not Yokes (nos. 19) — consist of 12 unwholesome cittas and *24 cetasikas*. Yokes (*Yoga*) cluster is the same as the cluster of defilement (*Āsava*), and thus answer is the same as in nos. 345.

v. States which are associated with Hindrances but are not Hindrances (nos. 20) — consist of 12 unwholesome cittas, and 19 cetasikas (27 excluding the 8 states of hindrances, viz. restlessness, greed, hatred, delusion, worry, doubt, sloth, and torpor). These states belong to 4 mental aggregates, and so there are no direct associations. They are partially associated with 1 aggregate (volitive formation), 1 base (ideation-base), 1 element (ideation-element), and *19 cetasikas*. Those remaining states are taken as aggrouped under 1 aggregate (volitive formation), 1 base (ideation-base), 1 element (ideation-element).

	Aggregate		Base		Element	
States of enquiry (SOE):	Asc	Pasc	Asc	Pasc	Asc	Pasc
347. States which are associated with attachment.	-	1	-	1	-	1

These states consist of 4 greed-rooted cittas associated with wrong view, and 20 cetasikas (27 excluding wrong view, conceit hatred, envy, avarice, worry, doubt). They belong to 4 mental aggregates, and so there are no direct associations. They are partially associated with 1 aggregate (volitive formation), 1 base (ideation-base), 1 element (ideation-element), and 20 cetasikas. Those remaining states are taken as aggrouped under 1 aggregate (volitive formation), 1 base (ideation-base), and 1 element (ideation-element).

A Perfect Knowledge of Mind-Body from the Abhidhamma (Dhātukathā)

States of enquiry (SOE):	Aggregate		Base		Element	
	Asc	Pasc	Asc	Pasc	Asc	Pasc
348. States which are consciousness.	3	-	-	1	-	1

States which are consciousness, belong to 89 cittas, are mutually associated with the remaining 3 mental aggregates (feeling, perception, volitive formation). Consciousness aggregate can not associate with its co-adjuncts of mind-base and consciousness-elements. So, consciousness is partially associated with 1 base (ideation-base), 1 element (ideation-element), and 52 cetasikas. Those remaining states are taken as aggrouped under 3 aggregates (feeling, perception, volitive formation), 1 base (ideation-base), and 1 element (ideation-element).

349. States of enquiry (SOE):	Aggregate		Base		Element	
	Asc	Pasc	Asc	Pasc	Asc	Pasc
1. States which are mental factors.						
2. States associated with consciousness.						
3. States conjoined with consciousness.						
4. States both conjoined with and originated from consciousness.	1	-	1	-	7	-
5. States conjoined with, originated from, and arise concurrently with consciousness.						
6. States conjoined with, originated from, and arise consecutively with consciousness.						

All these states of enquiry are referring to 52 cetasikas, in association with 89 cittas. These 6 states of enquiry come under the aggregates of feeling, perception, and volitive formation. Each of them is in association with 1 aggregate (consciousness), with 1 base (mind-base), and with 7 elements (7 consciousness-elements). There are no partial association because 52 cetasikas are all included which are actually states of enquiry. Those remaining states are taken as aggrouped under 1 aggregates (consciousness), 1 bases (mind-base), and 7 elements (7 consciousness elements).

IX. Associated and Associated

350. States of enquiry (SOE):	Aggregate		Base		Element	
	Asc	Pasc	Asc	Pasc	Asc	Pasc
1. States which are clinging (*upādāna*).						
2. States which are both clinging and objects of clinging.	3	1	1	1	1	1
3. States which are clinging and also associated with clinging.						
4. States which are associated with clinging but are not clinging.	-	1	-	1	-	1
5. States which are corruptions.						
6. States which are both corruptions and objects of corruptions.	3	1	1	1	1	1
7. States which are corruptions and are corrupted.						
8. States which are both corruptions and associated with corruptions.						

The 1st, 2nd, and 3rd SOE correspond to greed and wrong view (present at the 4 greed-rooted cittas accompanied by greed and associated with wrong view). These states belong to volitive formation. The 5th, 6th, 7th, and 8th SOE are the 10 states of corruptions (greed, hatred, delusion, conceit, wrong view, doubt, sloth, restlessness, shamelessness, guiltlessness of conscience), all of which belong to volitive formation. As they are either clingings or corruptions per se, are unwholesome states, are thus bound up with mind-consciousness element.

Each of these 7 SOE is associated with 3 mental aggregates (feeling, perception, consciousness), 1 base (mind-base), and 1 element (mind-consciousness element). Each is partially associated with 1 aggregate (volitive formation), 1 base (ideation-base), 1 element (ideation-element), with 52 or 22 cetasikas, and with 52 or 27 cetasikas. (See Table 1.8.9 and Table 1.8.10). Those remaining states are thus taken as aggrouped under 4 aggregates (feeling, perception, volitive formation, consciousness), 2 bases (ideation-base, mind-base), 2 elements (ideation-element, mind-consciousness element).

The 4th SOE consists of 8 greed-rooted cittas, accompanied by 20 cetasikas (27 excluding hatred, envy, avarice, worry, doubt, and the 2 states of clinging, i.e. sensual desire and wrong view) — it belongs to 4 mental aggregates. As such, there are no direct associations. They are partially associated with 1 aggregate (volitive formation), 1 base (ideation-base), 1 element (ideation-element), and 20 cetasikas. Those remaining states are taken as aggrouped under 1 aggregate (volitive formation), 1 base (ideation-base), and 1 element (ideation-element).

A Perfect Knowledge of Mind-Body from the Abhidhamma (Dhātukathā)

351. States of enquiry (SOE):	Aggregate		Base		Element	
	Asc	Pasc	Asc	Pasc	Asc	Pasc
1. States which are corrupted but are not corruptions (*saṃkiliṭṭha ceva no ca kilesa*).						
2. States which are associated with corruptions but are not corruptions.						
3. States with initial application.	-	1	-	1	-	1
4. States with sustained application.						
5. States with zest.						
6. States accompanied by zest.						

The 1st and 2nd SOE are included in the 12 unwholesome cittas, accompanied by 17 cetasikas (27 excluding the 10 factors of corruptions). The 3rd and 4th SOE consists of 55 cittas and 66 cittas respectively, accompanied by 51 cetasikas. The 5th and 6th SOE are from 51 cittas, and 46 cetasikas (52 excluding zest, hatred, envy, avarice, worry, doubt). All of these subject matters of enquiry belong to 4 mental aggregates, and thus there are no direct associations. Each of them is partially associated with 1 aggregate (volitive formation), 1 base (ideation-base), 1 element (ideation-element), and with 17, 51, or 46 cetasikas depending on which of the SOE is being enquired at the time. Those remaining states are taken as aggrouped under 1 aggregate (volitive formation), 1 base (ideation-base), and 1 element (ideation-element).

States of enquiry (SOE):	Aggregate		Base		Element	
	Asc	Pasc	Asc	Pasc	Asc	Pasc
352. States accompanied by happiness; States accompanied by equanimity. (2)	1	-	-	1	-	1

These states are the same as in preceding nos. 341.

Key points from the text :

4 mental aggregates (ideation-base and mind-base), 7 consciousness elements, 2 Truths, 14 faculties, 12 dependent originations, the next 17; 8 triads, 43 clusters, 7 intermediate dyads, 6 last dyads.

IX. Associated and Associated

Referring to the following two summary tables, the number in the brackets represents the number of enquiries belong to the associated text paragraph nos.

Table 9.1 Total 120 states of enquiry by subject matters

Subject matter:		Text's paragraph nos. (with the numbers of enquiries) :
Mental aggregates	3	319 (3)
Elements	9	320 (9)
Truths	2	321 (2)
Faculties	14	322 (1), 323 (4), 324 (1), 325 (8)
Dependent Originations	11	325 (2), 326 (1), 327 (1), 328 (1), 329 (3), 330 (3)
Miscellaneous	17	331 (3), 332 (1), 333 (1), 334 (5), 335 (3), 336 (2), 337 (1), 338 (1)
Triads	8	339 (3), 340 (3), 341 (2)
Dyad-clusters	41	342 (3), 343 (3), 344 (3), 345 (1), 346 (22), 347 (1), 350 (8)
Intermediate dyads	9	351 (2), 348 (1), 349 (6)
Last dyads	6	351 (4), 352 (2)

Total = 120 states

Table 9.2 Total 120 states of enquiry by answers

	Text's paragraph nos. (with numbers of enquiries):		Associated with			Partially associated with		
			agr	bse	el.	agr	bse	el.
1.	319 (3), 328 (1), 336 (2)	6	3	1	7	-	1	1
2.	320 (9), 322 (1), 326 (1), 337 (1), 348 (1)	13	3	-	-	-	1	1
3.	321 (2), 325 (10), 329 (3), 331 (3), 334 (5), 342 (3), 344 (3), 346 (15+2), 350 (7)	53	3	1	1	1	1	1
4.	323 (4), 330 (3)	7	3	1	1	-	1	1
5.	324 (1)	1	3	1	6	-	1	1
6.	327 (1), 335 (3)	4	3	1	7	1	1	1
7.	332 (1)	1	2	-	-	1	1	1
8.	333 (1)	1	2	1	1	1	1	1
9.	338 (1)	1	3	1	2	1	1	1
10.	339 (3), 341 (2), 352 (2)	7	1	-	-	-	1	1
11.	340 (3), 343 (3), 345 (1), 346 (5), 347 (1), 350 (1), 351 (6)	20	-	-	-	1	1	1
12.	349 (6)	6	1	1	7	-	-	-
	Total 120 states with 12 kinds of answer	120						

CHAPTER 10

X. Dissociated and Dissociated
(*Vippayuttenavippayutta*)

Analysis of 250 states from 56 catechism
92 internal states of enquiry

This chapter deals with two cases of dissociated states. Total 250 states of enquiry form the subject matter of this chapter, of which 92 are the interior states, 158 belong to external states from the triads and dyads. These 250 states are also mentioned in Chapter 6. The dissociation conditions and answers for these 250 states of enquiry in this chapter are also found in Chapter 6. All five aggregates are taken into account in this chapter. Similar guidelines must be followed, e.g. pure materiality and *Nibbāna* are always in dissociation from four mental aggregates; and whenever mentalities are the states of enquiry, subtle matters and *Nibbāna* are included as partially dissociated states; other possible states, etc.

Taking nos. 353, matter aggregate, as an example which says that:

"Matter aggregate is dissociated from *these* states. *Those* states are dissociated from *these* states ... *They* are dissociated from ... partially dissociated from ... "

The Diagram below depicts the dissociation relationships in nos. 353, as to *these* states (1st), *those* states, *these* states (2nd), and are "*they*" refer to.

Diagram 10.1 '*these* states', '*those* states', '*they*', used in Dissociation

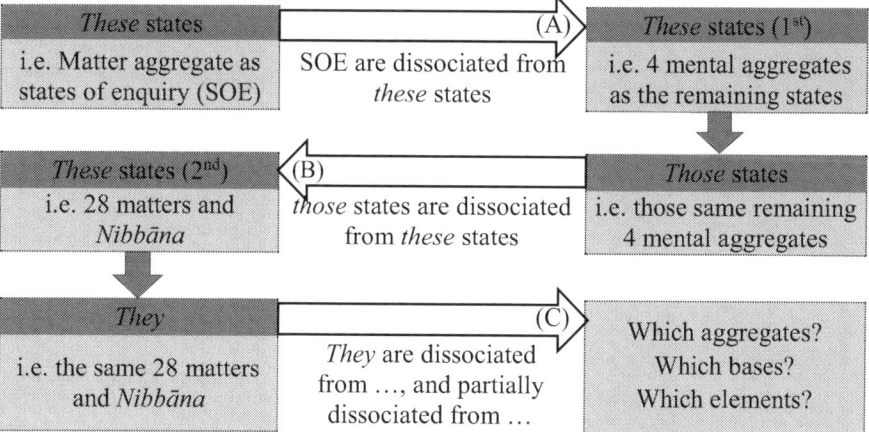

X. Dissociated and Dissociated

The following abbreviations will be used in the charts and tables throughout this Chapter.

SOE : States of enquiry
cons. : Consciousness
agr : aggregate
bse : base
el. : element

States of enquiry (SOE):	SOE dissociate from *these* states (A) :	*These* states (A) dissociate from (B):			*Those* states, (B), dissociate from:			*These* states, (B), partially dissociated from:		
		agr	bse	el.	agr	bse	el.	agr	bse	el.
353. Matter aggregate (1)	4 mental aggregates	1	10	10	4	1	7	-	1	1

Materiality is always dissociated from 4 mental aggregates (feeling, perception, volitive formation, consciousness). I called *these* states (1st) as dissociated states (A). These 4 mental aggregates are in turn dissociated from 1 aggregate (28 matters), 10 bases (10 gross bases), 10 elements (10 gross elements), and *Nibbāna*. I called *these* states (2nd) as dissociated states (B). So, *those* states (B) are dissociated from 4 aggregates (feeling, perception, volitive formation, consciousness), 1 base (mind-base), and 7 elements (7 consciousness-elements). *Those* states (B) are partially dissociated from 1 base (ideation-base), 1 element (ideation-element), and 52 cetasikas. I designated the final dissociation and partial dissociation under the aggregates, bases and elements as final states (C). The 52 mental factors are in partial dissociation because they are mutually associated with consciousness aggregate, and they encompass 3 mental aggregates which come under ideation-base, while the latter contains subtle matters and *Nibbāna*.

States of enquiry (SOE):	SOE dissociate from *these* states (A) :	*These* states (A) dissociate from (B):			*Those* states, (B), dissociate from:			*These* states, (B), partially dissociated from:		
		agr	bse	el.	agr	bse	el.	agr	bse	el.
354. Feeling aggregate; Perception aggregate; Volitive formation aggregate; Consciousness aggregate; Mind-base. (5)	28 matters, and *Nibbāna*	4	1	7	1	10	10	-	1	1

A Perfect Knowledge of Mind-Body from the Abhidhamma (Dhātukathā)

These five subject matters of enquiry are mentalities, which are always in dissociation from 28 matters and *Nibbāna*. I called the latter, dissociated states (A). These two states of pure materiality are in turn dissociated from 4 mental aggregates (feeling, perception, volitive formation, and consciousness), 1 base (mind-base), and 7 elements (7 consciousness-elements). The latter, I called them dissociated states (B). Those states (B) are dissociated from 1 aggregate (12 gross matters), 10 bases (10 gross bases), and 10 elements (10 gross elements). Those states (B) are partially dissociated from 1 base (ideation-base), 1 element (ideation-element), subtle matters, and *Nibbāna*.

States of enquiry (SOE):	SOE dissociate from *these* states (A) :	These states (A) dissociate from (B):			Those states, (B), dissociate from:			These states, (B), partially dissociated from:		
		agr	bse	el.	agr	bse	el.	agr	bse	el.
355. Eye-base; Ear-base; Nose-base; Tongue-base; Body-base; Vision-base; Sound-base; Odour-base; Taste-base; Tangible-base; Eye-element; Ear-element; Nose-element; Tongue-element; Body-element; Vision-element; Sound-element; Odour-element; Taste-element; Tangible-element (20).	4 mental aggregates	1	10	10	4	1	7	-	1	1

These states of enquiry are the 10 gross bases and 10 gross elements. These states of gross materiality, which have no associations, are directly dissociated from the 4 mental aggregates. The latter are in turn dissociated from 1 aggregate (12 gross matters), 10 bases (10 gross bases), 10 elements (10 gross elements), and *Nibbāna*. The latter, I designated them as dissociated states (B). Those states (B) are thereby in dissociation from 4 mental aggregates (feeling, perception, volitive formation, consciousness), 1 base (mind-base), 7 elements (7 consciousness-elements). Those states (B) are in partial dissociation from 1 base (ideation-base), 1 element (ideation-element), and 52 cetasikas.

X. Dissociated and Dissociated

States of enquiry (SOE):	SOE dissociate from *these* states (A) :	*These* states (A) dissociate from (B):			*Those* states, (B), dissociate from:			*These* states, (B), partially dissociated from:		
		agr	bse	el.	agr	bse	el.	agr	bse	el.
356. Eye cons. element; Ear cons. element; Nose cons. element; Tongue cons. element; Body cons. element; Mind-element; Mind-consciousness element; Origin-truth; Path-truth. (9)	28 matters, and *Nibbāna*	4	1	1	1	10	16	-	1	1

The first 7 states are members of the 7 consciousness-elements which come under consciousness aggregate. Like the 10 viññāṇas, these 7 consciousness-elements are associated with 7 common non-beautiful cetasikas.

Origin-truth consists of greed-*cetasika* present at the 8 greed-rooted cittas. Path-truth refers to Noble Eightfold Path with 4 supramundane path consciousness. These two truths belong to volitive formation, are associated with 3 mental aggregates (feeling, perception, consciousness), mind-base, and mind-consciousness element.

Each of these SOE is therefore dissociated from 28 matters and *Nibbāna*. The latter, as dissociated states (A), are in turn dissociated from 4 mental aggregates (feeling, perception, volitive formation, and consciousness), 1 base (mind-base), and 1 element (the respective state that is being enquired).

The latter, designated as those dissociated states (B), are in dissociation from 1 aggregate (28 matters), 10 bases (10 gross bases), and 16 elements (10 gross elements, and the remaining 6 consciousness-elements). Those dissociated states (B) are partially dissociated from 1 base (ideation-base), 1 element (ideation-element), subtle matters, and *Nibbāna*.

States of enquiry (SOE):	SOE dissociate from *these* states (A) :	*These* states (A) dissociate from (B):			*Those* states, (B), dissociate from:			*These* states, (B), partially dissociated from:		
		agr	bse	el.	agr	bse	el.	agr	bse	el.
357. Cessation-truth (of suffering); Vision-faculty; Hearing-faculty; Smell-faculty; Taste-faculty; Touch-faculty; Femininity-faculty; Masculinity-faculty. (8)	4 mental aggregates	1	10	10	4	1	7	-	1	1

A Perfect Knowledge of Mind-Body from the Abhidhamma (Dhātukathā)

Cessation-truth comes under *Nibbāna*, the 5 sense-faculties come under gross matters, while femininity-faculty and masculinity-faculty come under subtle matters. Thus, each SOE is totally dissociated from the 4 mental aggregates. The latter are in turn dissociated from 28 matters (taken as aggrouped under 1 aggregate, 10 gross bases, 10 gross elements) and *Nibbāna*. The latter, those dissociated (B), are dissociated from 4 mental aggregates (feeling, perception, volitive formation, and consciousness), 1 base (mind-base), and 7 elements (7 consciousness-elements). Those dissociated states (B) are partially dissociated from 1 base (ideation-base), 1 element (ideation-element), and 52 cetasikas.

States of enquiry (SOE):	SOE dissociate from *these* states (A) :	*These* states (A) dissociate from (B):			*Those* states, (B), dissociate from:			*These* states, (B), partially dissociated from:		
		agr	bse	el.	agr	bse	el.	agr	bse	el.
358. Mind-faculty. (1)	28 matters, and *Nibbāna*	4	1	7	1	10	10	-	1	1

Mind-faculty is concerned with 89 cittas, arisen with 52 cetasikas. Mind-faculty comes under consciousness aggregate which is mutually associated with the other 3 mental aggregates. Thus, it is dissociated from 28 matters and *Nibbāna*. The latter, states (A), are dissociated from 4 aggregates (4 mental aggregates), 1 base (mind-base), and 7 elements (7 consciousness-elements). The latter, those dissociated states (B), are in turn dissociated from 1 aggregate (matter), 10 bases (10 gross bases), and 10 elements (10 gross elements). Those states are also partially dissociated from 1 base (ideation-base), 1 element (ideation-element), subtle matters, and *Nibbāna*.

States of enquiry (SOE):	SOE dissociate from *these* states (A) :	*These* states (A) dissociate from (B):			*Those* states, (B), dissociate from:			*These* states, (B), partially dissociated from:		
		agr	bse	el.	agr	bse	el.	agr	bse	el.
359. Carnal or bodily pleasure faculty; carnal displeasure faculty; joy faculty; melancholy faculty. (4)	28 matters, and *Nibbāna*	4	1	1	1	10	16	-	1	1

These four feeling faculties belong to feeling aggregate, are mutually associated with the remaining 3 mental aggregates, mind-base and body-consciousness element, while partially associated with ideation-base, ideation-element, and 6 cetasikas (7 excluding feeling-*cetasika*). Thus, each of these feeling faculties is dissociated from materiality and *Nibbāna*. The latter, these

X. Dissociated and Dissociated

states (A), are dissociated from 4 aggregates (4 mental aggregates), 1 base (mind-base), and 1 element (body-consciousness element). The latter, those dissociated states (B), are in turn dissociated from 1 aggregate (matter), 10 bases (10 gross bases), and 16 elements (10 gross elements, and the remaining 6 consciousness-elements). Those states (B) are partially dissociated from 1 base (ideation-base), 1 element (ideation-element), subtle matters, and *Nibbāna*.

States of enquiry (SOE):	SOE is dissociated from body-consciousness element, and 51 cetasikas.	These states (A) dissociate from (B):			Those states, (B), dissociate from:			These states, (B), partially dissociated from:		
		agr	bse	el.	agr	bse	el.	agr	bse	el.
360. Equanimity-faculty. (1)	Also dissociated from 28 matters, and *Nibbāna*. The latter as states (A)	4	1	6	1	10	11	-	1	1

Equanimity-faculty, like the preceding four faculties, comes under feeling aggregate. Equanimity-faculty is dissociated from body-consciousness element (as regard carnal pleasure, carnal pain, joy, melancholy) and 51 cetasikas (52 excluding feeling-*cetasika*) by class. Equanimity-faculty is associated with the other 3 mental aggregates, mind-base, and 6 consciousness elements (7 excluding body-consciousness element) by category. And so, equanimity-faculty is dissociated from 28 matters, and *Nibbāna* The latter, these states (A), are dissociated from 4 aggregates (4 mental aggregates), 1 base (mind-base), and 6 elements (7 excluding body-consciousness element). The latter, those states (B), are in dissociation from 1 aggregate (matter), 10 bases (10 gross bases), and 11 elements (10 gross elements, body-consciousness element). They are also partially dissociated from 1 base (ideation-base), 1 element (ideation-element), subtle matters, and *Nibbāna*.

361. States of enquiry (SOE):	SOE dissociate from *these* states (A) :	These states (A) dissociate from (B):			Those states, (B), dissociate from:			These states, (B), partially dissociated from:		
		agr	bse	el.	agr	bse	el.	agr	bse	el.
Confidence-faculty; Effort-faculty; Mindfulness-faculty; Concentration-faculty; Wisdom-faculty; "I-shall-comprehend-the-unknown" faculty; Higher knowledge faculty; "Final knower" faculty; Ignorance; conditioned by ignorance, Volitive formation (10)	28 matters and *Nibbāna*	4	1	1	1	10	16	-	1	1

A Perfect Knowledge of Mind-Body from the Abhidhamma (Dhātukathā)

These 10 SOE belong to volitive formation aggregate, are accompanied by 51 cetasikas (52 excluding, respectively, *saddhā, viriya, sati, ekaggata* for the first 4 faculties, *amoha* for the next 4 faculties, *moha* and *cetanā* for the last 2 factors of dependent origination). Given that these states are mutually associated with the remaining 3 mental aggregates, mind-base, and mind-consciousness element, each SOE is thereby dissociated from materiality and *Nibbāna*. The latter, these states (A), are dissociated from 4 mental aggregates, 1 base (mind-base), and 1 element (mind-consciousness element). The latter, these dissociated states (B), are in turn dissociated from 1 aggregate (matter), 10 bases (10 gross bases), and 16 elements (10 gross elements, and 6 elements having excluded mind-consciousness element). They are partially dissociated from 1 base (ideation-base), 1 element (ideation-element), subtle matters, and *Nibbāna*.

States of enquiry (SOE):	SOE dissociate from *these* states (A) :	These states (A) dissociate from (B):			Those states, (B), dissociate from:			These states, (B), partially dissociated from:		
		agr	bse	el.	agr	bse	el.	agr	bse	el.
362. Conditioned by volition formation, is Consciousness; conditioned by the six bases, is Contact; conditioned by contact, is Feeling. (3)	28 matters and *Nibbāna*	4	1	7	1	10	10	-	1	1

Consciousness is under consciousness aggregate, accompanied by 52 cetasikas. Contact contains volition-*cetasika*, while feeling contains feeling-*cetasika*. Contact and feeling are amongst the 7 common non-beautiful cetasikas, accompanying 89 cittas. The three states of enquiry are mentalities, are directly dissociated from all materiality and *Nibbāna*. The latter, these states (A), are in turn dissociated from 4 mental aggregates, 1 base (mind-base), and 7 elements (7 consciousness-elements). The latter, those dissociated states (B), are in dissociation from 1 aggregate (matter), 10 bases (10 gross bases), and 10 elements (10 gross elements). Those dissociated states (B) are partially dissociated from 1 base (ideation-base), 1 element (ideation-element), subtle matters, and *Nibbāna*.

X. Dissociated and Dissociated

States of enquiry (SOE):	SOE dissociate from *these* states (A):	These states (A) dissociate from (B):			Those states, (B), dissociate from:			These states, (B), partially dissociated from:		
		agr	bse	el.	agr	bse	el.	agr	bse	el.
363. Conditioned by feeling, is Craving; Conditioned by craving, is Clinging; Action-becoming (3)	28 matters, and *Nibbāna*	4	1	1	1	10	16	-	1	1

Craving includes greed-*cetasika*, while clinging includes greed-*cetasika* and wrong view-*cetasika*. Both are present at the 8 greed-rooted cittas. Action-becoming (*kammabhava*) includes volition-*cetasika*, present at the 17 wholesome cittas and 12 unwholesome cittas. The three SOE belong to volitive formation. These three states are mutually associated with the remaining 3 mental aggregates, mind-base, and mind-consciousness element. And so, each of these states of enquiry is dissociated from all materiality and *Nibbāna*. The latter, these dissociated states (A), are dissociated from 4 aggregates (4 mental aggregates), 1 base (mind-base), 1 element (mind-consciousness element). The latter, those dissociated states (B), are dissociated from 1 aggregate (matter), 10 bases (10 gross bases), and 16 elements (10 gross elements, and remaining 6 consciousness elements). They are partially dissociated from 1 base (ideation-base), 1 element (ideation-element), subtle matters, and *Nibbāna*.

States of enquiry :	SOE dissociate from *these* states (A) :	These states (A) dissociate from (B):			Those states, (B), dissociate from:			These states, (B), partially dissociated from:		
		agr	bse	el.	agr	bse	el.	agr	bse	el.
364. Fine-material becoming (1)	wholesome cittas, unwholesome cittas, functional cittas, sensuous becoming, formless-becoming, fruition-cittas	-	-	4	-	-	3	-	-	-

Fine-material becoming consists of 5 resultant cittas, 2 eye-cittas, 2 ear-cittas, 2 receiving-cittas, 2 investigating-cittas, 35 cetasikas (38 excluding 3 Abstinences), and 15 kamma-produced matters (20 excluding femininity, masculinity, nose, tongue, and body, i.e. 20-5=15). It belongs to both mentality and materiality. It is dissociated from active wholesome cittas, unwholesome cittas, functional cittas, sensuous becoming, immaterial-becoming, and fruition cittas or *Nibbāna*. These dissociated states are in turn dissociated from fine-material becoming which form under 4 elements (eye-cons. element, ear-cons. element, mind-element, mind-cons. element). Because beings in the fine-

A Perfect Knowledge of Mind-Body from the Abhidhamma (Dhātukathā)

material sphere are without the consciousness of nose, tongue and body, thereby the latter, those dissociated states (B), are dissociated from 3 elements (nose-cons. element, tongue-cons. element, body-cons. element). There are no more possible dissociations from aggregates and bases, nor partial dissociations.

States of enquiry (SOE):	SOE dissociate from *these* states (A) :	These states (A) dissociate from (B):			Those states, (B), dissociate from:			These states, (B), partially dissociated from:		
		agr	bse	el.	agr	bse	el.	agr	bse	el.
365. Non-perception becoming; Single-aggregate becoming; Lamentation. (3)	4 mental aggregates	1	10	10	4	1	7	-	1	1

Non-perception becoming and single-aggregate becoming are identical, are both bound by visible object base. Lamentation is taken as audible object base because of wailing. These three states are gross materiality which have no associations. Each of them is dissociated from 4 mental aggregates. The latter are dissociated from 1 aggregate (matter), 10 bases (10 gross bases), and 10 elements (10 gross elements). The latter, those states (B), are in turn dissociated from 4 mental aggregates, 1 base (mind-base), and 7 elements (7 consciousness-elements). They are partially dissociated from 1 base (ideation-base), 1 element (ideation-element), 16 subtle matters, and *Nibbāna*.

States of enquiry (SOE):	SOE dissociate from *these* states (A) :	These states (A) dissociate from (B):			Those states, (B), dissociate from:			These states, (B), partially dissociated from:		
		agr	bse	el.	agr	bse	el.	agr	bse	el.
366. Immaterial-becoming; Neither perception nor non-perception becoming; Four-aggregate becoming; Sorrow; Suffering; Melancholy; Despair; Foundations of mindfulness; Right strivings; Basis of psychic accomplishment; *Jhāna*, Illimitables; 5 Faculties; 5 Powers; 7 Enlightenment-Factors; Noble Eightfold Path. (16)	materiality	4	1	1	1	10	16	-	1	1

X. Dissociated and Dissociated

Neither perception nor non-perception becoming and four-aggregate becoming are similar to immaterial-becoming, which consists of immaterial resultants, accompanied by 30 cetasikas. These three becomings belong to the subtle matters, 4 mental aggregates, and *Nibbāna*. That is, the three of them are mentality-materiality (See nos. 246). Sorrow, suffering, melancholy, all are grievous feeling, belong to feeling faculties (See nos. 248). Despair, foundations of mindfulness, and right strivings belong to volitive formation (See nos. 249). Basis of psychic accomplishment belongs to consciousness while *Jhāna* belong to feeling, and both are partially associated with volitive formation (See nos. 250, 251). The rest of the SOE are accompanied by different cetasikas (see Table 1.6b) but all of them come under volitive formation. These 16 subject matters of enquiry are associated with 4 mental aggregates, mind-base, and mind-consciousness element. Thus, each of the first three SOE is dissociated from gross matters. Each of of the other 13 SOE is dissociated from 28 matters and *Nibbāna*.

These dissociated states in turn are dissociated from 4 aggregates (4 mental aggregates), 1 base (mind-base), and 1 element (mind-consciousness element). The latter, those dissociated states (B), are in dissociation from 1 aggregate (matter), 10 bases (10 gross bases), and 16 elements (10 gross elements, and the remaining 6 consciousness elements). They are partially dissociated from 1 base (ideation-base), 1 element (ideation-element), subtle matters, and *Nibbāna*.

States of enquiry (SOE):	SOE dissociate from *these* states (A) :	These states (A) dissociate from (B):			Those states, (B), dissociate from:			These states, (B), partially dissociated from:		
		agr	bse	el.	agr	bse	el.	agr	bse	el.
367. Contact; Feeling; Perception; Volition; Consciousness; Attention. (6)	28 matters and *Nibbāna*	4	1	7	1	10	10	-	1	1

Contact, volition, and attention belong to volitive formation aggregate. Feeling is under feeling aggregate, consciousness is under consciousness aggregate. These three SOE are 3 mental aggregates (feeling, volitive formation, consciousness), and each is mutually associated with perception aggregate. Each of these three states is therefore directly dissociated from 28 matters, and *Nibbāna*.

These dissociated states are in turn dissociated from 4 mental aggregates, mind-base, and 7 consciousness-elements. The latter, those dissociated states (B), are in dissociation from 1 aggregate (matter), 10 bases (10 gross bases), and 10 elements (10 gross elements). They are partially dissociated from 1 base (ideation-base), 1 element (ideation-element), subtle matters, and *Nibbāna*.

A Perfect Knowledge of Mind-Body from the Abhidhamma (Dhātukathā)

States of enquiry:	SOE dissociate from *these* states (A) :	These states (A) dissociate from (B):			Those states, (B), dissociate from:			These states, (B), partially dissociated from:		
		agr	bse	el.	agr	bse	el.	agr	bsc	el.
368. Decision. (1)	1 delusion-rooted citta with doubt, 10 viññāṇas; 28 matters and *Nibbāna*	4	1	2	1	10	15	-	1	1

Decision is accompanied by *adhimokkha-cetasika*. It belongs to volitive formation, is mutually associated with the other 3 mental aggregates. Decision is dissociated from 1 delusion-rooted citta associated with doubt and which is accompanied by 15 cetasikas (13 common non-beautiful cetasikas excluding *adhimokkha, pīti, chanda*; 4 common unwholesome cetasikas; and *vicikicchā*, i.e. 10+4+1=15) and 10 fivefold sensory consciousness by class; matters and *Nibbāna* by category. These dissociated states are in turn dissociated from 4 mental aggregates, mind-base, 2 elements (mind-element, mind-consciousness element). The latter, those states (B), are in turn dissociated from 1 aggregate (matter), 10 bases (10 gross bases), and 15 elements (10 gross elements, and the remaining 5 consciousness elements). They are partially dissociated from 1 base (ideation-base), 1 element (ideation-element), 16 subtle matters, *Nibbāna*.

47 states of enquiry from Dhammasaṅgaṇīmātikā triads

States of enquiry:	SOE dissociate from *these* states (A) :	These states (A) dissociate from (B):			Those states, (B), dissociate from:			These states, (B), partially dissociated from:		
		agr	bse	el.	agr	bse	el.	agr	bse	el.
369. Wholesome states; Unwholesome states. (2)	28 matters, *Nibbāna*; resultant states and functional states,	4	1	1	1	10	16	-	1	1

Wholesome states are the 21 mundane wholesome cittas, accompanied by 38 cetasikas. Unwholesome states sprung from the 12 unwholesome cittas, accompanied by 27 cetasikas. The two states of enquiry belong to 4 mental aggregates. They are hence dissociated from all materiality and *Nibbāna* by category, and dissociated from indeterminate resultant states and functional states by class. The latter, these states (A), are in turn dissociated from 4 mental aggregates, mind-base, and mind-consciousness element. These dissociated states (B) are in dissociation from 1 aggregate (matter), 10 bases (10 gross bases), and 16 elements (10 gross elements, and the remaining 6 consciousness

X. Dissociated and Dissociated

elements). They are partially dissociated from 1 base (ideation-base), 1 element (ideation-element), subtle matters, and *Nibbāna*.

States of enquiry (SOE):	SOE dissociate from *these* states (A) :	These states (A) dissociate from (B):			Those states, (B), dissociate from:			These states, (B), partially dissociated from:		
		agr	bse	el.	agr	bse	el.	agr	bse	el.
370. States associated with happy feeling; States associated with painful feeling. (2)	28 matters, 5 cons. elements	4	1	2	1	10	15	-	1	1

States associated with happy feeling consist of 63 cittas, accompanied by 46 cetasikas. States associated with painful feeling consist of 3 cittas accompanied by displeasure, having 21 cetasikas. Both states come under perception, volitive formation, and consciousness. (See nos. 258). These states are dissociated from materiality, and 5 consciousness elements (eye-cons. element, ear-cons. element, nose-cons. element, tongue-cons. element, and mind-element). The latter, these states (A), are in turn dissociated by category from 4 mental aggregates, mind-base, and 2 elements (body-consciousness element, mind-consciousness element). The latter, those states (B), are in turn dissociated from 1 aggregate (matter), 10 bases (10 gross bases), and 15 elements (10 gross elements, and the aforesaid 5 consciousness elements). They are partially dissociated from 1 base (ideation-base), 1 element (ideation-element), 16 subtle matters, and *Nibbāna*.

States of enquiry (SOE):	SOE dissociate from *these* states (A) :	These states (A) dissociate from (B):			Those states, (B), dissociate from:			These states, (B), partially dissociated from:		
		agr	bse	el.	agr	bse	el.	agr	bse	el.
371. States associated with neither happy feeling nor suffering feeling. (1)	28 matters, body-cons. element	4	1	6	1	10	11	-	1	1

These states are 55 cittas accompanied by equanimity, with 46 cetasikas. They are classified under the aggregates of perception, volitive formation, and consciousness (See nos. 259). These equanimous states are dissociated from 28 matters, and body-consciousness element. The latter, these states (A), are in turn dissociated by category from 4 aggregates (4 mental aggregates), 1 base (mind-base) 6 elements (7 consciousness elements excluding body-consciousness element). The latter, those states (B), are dissociated from 1 aggregate (matter), 10 bases (10 gross bases), and 11 elements (10 gross elements, and body-

A Perfect Knowledge of Mind-Body from the Abhidhamma (Dhātukathā)

consciousness element). They are partially dissociated from 1 base (ideation-base), 1 element (ideation-element), 16 subtle matters, and *Nibbāna*.

States of enquiry:	SOE dissociate from *these* states (A) :	These states (A) dissociate from (B):			Those states, (B), dissociate from:			These states, (B), partially dissociated from:		
		agr	bse	el.	agr	bse	el.	agr	bse	el.
372. Resultant states. (1)	28 matters, *Nibbāna*	4	1	7	1	10	10	-	1	1

Resultant states are referring to 36 resultant cittas, accompanied by 38 cetasikas (13+25=38). They belong to 4 mental aggregates which have no associations. Resultant states are indeterminate states, are neither 21 wholesome states, nor 12 unwholesome states, nor 20 functional states. They are hence dissociated from 28 matters and *Nibbāna*. These dissociated states are in turn dissociated from 4 mental aggregates, mind-base, and 7 consciousness-elements. The latter, those dissociated states (B), are in dissociation from 1 aggregate (matter), 10 bases (10 gross bases), and 10 elements (10 gross elements). They are partially dissociated from 1 base (ideation-base), 1 element (ideation-element), subtle matters, and *Nibbāna*.

States of enquiry (SOE):	SOE dissociate from *these* states (A) :	These states (A) dissociate from (B):			Those states, (B), dissociate from:			These states, (B), partially dissociated from:		
		agr	bse	el.	agr	bse	el.	agr	bse	el.
373. States which produce resultants; States which are corrupted and are objects of corruption (*saṃkiliṭṭha-saṃkilesikā*) (2)	28 matters, *Nibbāna*	4	1	1	1	10	16	-	1	1

States which produce resultants consist of 21 wholesome cittas, 12 unwholesome cittas, and 52 cetasikas. States which are corrupted and are objects of corruption are the 12 unwholesome cittas, and 27 cetasikas (13+14). They are separate from the indeterminate states of 36 resultant cittas and 20 functional cittas. They should not be said to be dissociated, for indeterminate cittas are neither associated with, nor dissociated from wholesome and unwholesome states. These two SOE belong to 4 mental aggregates which have no associations. So, each of them is dissociated from 28 matters and *Nibbāna*.

The latter, these states (A), are in turn dissociated from 4 mental aggregates, mind-base, and mind-consciousness element. These dissociated states (B) are in dissociation from 1 aggregate (matter), 10 bases (10 gross bases), and 16 elements (10 gross elements, and the remaining 6 consciousness elements). They

X. Dissociated and Dissociated

are partially dissociated from 1 base (ideation-base), 1 element (ideation-element), subtle matters, and *Nibbāna*.

States of enquiry (SOE):	SOE dissociate from *these* states (A):	These states (A) dissociate from (B):			Those states, (B), dissociate from:			These states, (B), partially dissociated from:		
		agr	bse	el.	agr	bse	el.	agr	bse	el.
374. States which neither are resultants nor are causing resultants; States which are not the result of clinging but are objects of clinging. (2)	5 sensory consciousness elements	-	-	2	-	-	5	-	-	-

The 1st SOE consists of the 20 functional cittas (mind-elements and mind-consciousness elements), accompanied by 35 cetasikas (38 excluding the 3 abstinences), 28 matters, and *Nibbāna*.

The 2nd SOE consists of 49 cittas (comprised of 17 wholesome cittas, 12 unwholesome cittas, 20 functional cittas), 52 cetasikas, 17 mind-produced matters, 15 temperature-produced matters, and 14 nutriment-produced matters.

Because the two SOE consist of mentality-materiality phenomena, functional cittas, 28 matters, and *Nibbāna*, they are only dissociated by class from the remaining 5 sensory consciousness elements.

States (A), these dissociated 5 sensory consciousness elements, are in turn dissociated from functional cittas which come under 2 elements (mind-element, and mind-consciousness element). In turn, those dissociated functional states (B), are in direct dissociation from 5 elements (eye-cons. element, ear-cons. element, nose-cons. element, tongue-cons. element, and body-cons. element). There are no more possible dissociations from the aggregates and bases, nor are there other possible partial dissociations, for the 5 aggregates and *Nibbāna* are all already included in the two SOE.

States of enquiry (SOE):	SOE dissociate from *these* states (A):	These states (A) dissociate from (B):			Those states, (B), dissociate from:			These states, (B), partially dissociated from:		
		agr	bse	el.	agr	bse	el.	agr	bse	el.
375. States neither are the result of clinging nor are the objects of clinging; States which are not corrupted and not favourable to corruptions. (*asaṃkiliṭṭha asaṃkilesikā*). (2)	81 mundane cittas, 52 cetasikas	-	-	1	-	-	6	-	-	-

A Perfect Knowledge of Mind-Body from the Abhidhamma (Dhātukathā)

These two states belong to the 8 supramundane cittas, accompanied by 36 cetasikas (38 excluding the 2 Illimitables), and *Nibbāna*. They belong to 4 mental aggregates and *Nibbāna*, and so they have no associations. Because these two states are supramundane, they are dissociated by category from materiality, dissociated by class from 81 mundane cittas and 52 cetasikas. These dissociated states are in turn dissociated from 8 supramundane cittas which fall in with mind-consciousness element. The latter is in turn dissociated from the remaining 6 consciousness elements. The supramundane mind-consciousness element also has no other possible dissociations from aggregates and bases, nor possible partial dissociations.

States of enquiry (SOE):	SOE dissociate from *these* states (A) :	These states (A) dissociate from (B):			Those states, (B), dissociate from:			These states, (B), partially dissociated from:		
		agr	bse	el.	agr	bse	el.	agr	bse	el.
376. States with both initial application and sustained application. (1)	28 matters, 5 cons. elements	4	1	2	1	10	15	-	1	1

These states consist of 55 cittas accompanied by 50 cetasikas. They belong to 4 mental aggregates, and are bound up with mind-consciousness element and mind-element. They are dissociated from 28 matters and the remaining 5 sensory consciousness elements. The latter, these states (A), are in turn dissociated from 4 mental aggregates, mind-base, and 2 elements (body-consciousness element, mind-element). The latter, those states (B), are dissociated from 1 aggregate (matter), 10 bases (10 gross bases), and 15 elements (10 gross elements and the 5 sensory consciousness elements). They are partially dissociated from 1 base (ideation-base), 1 element (ideation-element), 16 subtle matters, and *Nibbāna*.

States of enquiry (SOE):	SOE dissociate from *these* states (A) :	These states (A) dissociate from (B):			Those states, (B), dissociate from:			These states, (B), partially dissociated from:		
		agr	bse	el.	agr	bse	el.	agr	bse	el.
377. States without initial application but with sustained application; States accompanied by zest. (2)	28 matters, 6 cons. elements	4	1	1	1	10	16	-	1	1

States without initial application but with sustained application are 11 Second-*Jhāna* cittas (i.e. 8+3=11. See Appendix VI, Chart 4 & 5), 66 cittas with

X. Dissociated and Dissociated

sustained application, accompanied by 36 cetasikas (38 excluding *vitakka*, *vicāra*). States accompanied by zest are 51 associated cittas, accompanied by 46 cetasikas (52 excluding zest, hatred, envy, avarice, worry, and doubt). Both SOE belong to 4 mental aggregates. Both states are bound up with mind-consciousness element. They are dissociated from the remaining 6 consciousness elements, and 28 matters.

The latter, these states (A), are in turn dissociated from 4 mental aggregates, mind-base, and mind-consciousness element. The latter, those states (B), are dissociated from 1 aggregate (matter), 10 bases (10 gross bases), and 16 elements (10 gross elements, and the remaining 6 consciousness elements). They are partially dissociated from 1 base (ideation-base), 1 element (ideation-element), 16 subtle matters, and *Nibbāna*.

States of enquiry (SOE):	SOE dissociate from *these* states (A) :	These states (A) dissociate from (B):			Those states, (B), dissociate from:			These states, (B), partially dissociated from:		
		agr	bse	el.	agr	bse	el.	agr	bse	el.
378. States without initial application and without sustained application. (1)	first *jhāna*, sensuous cittas, mind-element	-	-	6	-	-	1	-	-	-

These states consist of 11 Second-*Jhāna* cittas (8+3=11), 55 cittas arisen with 36 cetasikas (38 excluding *vitakka* and *vicāra*), 28 matters, and *Nibbāna*. They possess the characteristics of mentality-materiality and *Nibbāna*, are bound up with 6 consciousness elements (without the presence of mind-element). They are dissociated from part of the triad mentioned in nos. 376 and 377. These dissociated states (A) are dissociated from the 6 consciousness elements. The latter are dissociated from 1 element (mind-element). They have no other possible dissociations from aggregates and bases, nor possible partial dissociations.

States of enquiry (SOE):	SOE dissociate from *these* states (A) :	These states (A) dissociate from (B):			Those states, (B), dissociate from:			These states, (B), partially dissociated from:		
		agr	bse	el.	agr	bse	el.	agr	bse	el.
379. States accompanied by happiness (1)	28 matters, 5 cons. elements	4	1	2	1	10	15	-	1	1

These states consist of 63 cittas, accompanied by 46 cetasikas. They belong to perception, volitive formation, and consciousness aggregates. These states are

A Perfect Knowledge of Mind-Body from the Abhidhamma (Dhātukathā)

dissociated from 28 matters and 5 consciousness elements (eye-cons. element, ear-cons. element, nose-cons. element, tongue-cons. element, and mind-element). The latter, dissociated states (A), are in turn dissociated from 4 mental aggregates, mind-base, and 2 elements (body-consciousness element and mind-consciousness element). The latter, those states (B), are dissociated from 1 aggregate (matter), 10 bases (10 gross bases), and 15 elements (10 gross elements and the remaining 5 consciousness elements). They are partially dissociated from 1 base (ideation-base), 1 element (ideation-element), 16 subtle matters, and *Nibbāna*.

States of enquiry:	SOE dissociate from *these* states (A) :	These states (A) dissociate from (B):			Those states, (B), dissociate from:			These states, (B), partially dissociated from:		
		agr	bse	el.	agr	bse	el.	agr	bse	el.
380. States accompanied by equanimity, i.e. indifferent to states of happiness. (1)	28 matters; states accompanied by happiness.	4	1	6	1	10	11	-	1	1

These are states which are neither happy nor painful feeling. They consist of 55 cittas accompanied by equanimity, followed by 46 cetasikas (52 excluding feeling, zest, hatred, envy, avarice, worry). They belong to perception, volitive formation, and consciousness aggregates. They are dissociated from 28 matters and body-consciousness element. The latter, dissociated states (A), are in turn dissociated from 4 mental aggregates, mind-base, and 6 elements (7 excluding body-consciousness element). The latter, those states (B), are dissociated from 1 aggregate (matter), 10 bases (10 gross bases), and 11 elements (10 gross elements, and body-consciousness element). They are partially dissociated from 1 base (ideation-base), 1 element (ideation-element), 16 subtle matters, and *Nibbāna*.

X. Dissociated and Dissociated

381. States of enquiry (SOE):	SOE dissociate from *these* states (A) :	These states (A) dissociate from (B):			Those states, (B), dissociate from:			These states, (B), partially dissociated from:		
		agr	bse	el.	agr	bse	el.	agr	bse	el.
1. States eliminated by first Path.										
2. States eliminated by the higher three Paths.										
3. States with root causes eliminated by first Path.										
4. States with root causes eliminated by higher three Paths										
5. States which make for the continuance of death and rebirth. (*ācayagāmino*)	28 matters, *Nibbāna*	4	1	1	1	10	16	-	1	1
6. States which make for the discontinuity of rebirth, i.e. leading out to *Nibbāna* (*apacayagāmino*).										
7. States appertaining to Learners (*sekhā*).										
8. States appertaining to *Arahatta* (*asekhā*)										
9. Sublime states.										

The first 4 SOE are states eliminated by the 4 supramundane Paths, include the 12 unwholesome cittas, accompanied by different cetasikas [7]. The 5th SOE are referred to the 17 mundane wholesome cittas, 12 unwholesome cittas, and 52 cetasikas. The 6th SOE are referred to the 4 supramundane path-cittas with 36 cetasikas. The 7th SOE are referred to the 7 supramundane cittas (without the *Arahatta* fruition) with 36 cetasikas. The 8th SOE are states belong to *Arahatta* fruition-cittas with 36 cetasikas. Sublime states are the 27 *Mahaggatacittāni* with 35 cetasikas. These nine subject matters of enquiry are bound up with mind-consciousness element. each of them is dissociated from 28 matters and *Nibbāna*. These dissociated states (A), are in turn dissociated from these states (B), namely, 4 mental aggregates, mind-base, and mind-consciousness element.

The latter, those states (B), are in dissociation from 1 aggregate (matter), 10 bases (10 gross bases), and 16 elements (10 gross elements, and 6 consciousness-elements having excluded mind-consciousness element). They are partially dissociated from 1 base (ideation-base), 1 element (ideation-element), 16 subtle matters, *Nibbāna*.

A Perfect Knowledge of Mind-Body from the Abhidhamma (Dhātukathā)

States of enquiry:	SOE dissociate from *these* states (A) :	These states (A) dissociate from (B):			Those states, (B), dissociate from:			These states, (B), partially dissociated from:		
		agr	bse	el.	agr	bse	el.	agr	bse	el.
382. Immeasurable states; Superior states. (2)	Limited and sublime states; Inferior and medium states; 6 cons. elements	-	-	1	-	-	6	-	-	-

Both immeasurable and superior states consist of 8 supramundane cittas, accompanied by 36 cetasikas (38 excluding 2 Illimitables). They belong to 4 mental aggregates and *Nibbāna*. These states are bound up with mind-consciousness element. Immeasurable states are dissociated by class from limited states and sublime states. Superior states are dissociated by class from inferior and medium-worth states. Dissociation from matter aggregate is not being considered here. These lowly dissociated states are in turn dissociated from mind-consciousness element. The latter is in dissociation from the remaining 6 consciousness-elements. The dissociated mind-consciousness element has no other possible dissociations and partial dissociations from elements.

States of enquiry:	SOE dissociate from *these* states (A) :	These states (A) dissociate from (B):			Those states, (B), dissociate from:			These states, (B), partially dissociated from:		
		agr	bse	el.	agr	bse	el.	agr	bse	el.
383. States with limited objects. (1)	states with sublime and immeasurable objects; 28 matters, *Nibbāna*	4	1	7	1	10	10	-	1	1

States with limited object are a part of the 54 sensuous cittas and 52 cetasikas. They belong to 4 mental aggregates, and they have no associations. They are dissociated by category from matters and *Nibbāna*, dissociated by class from states with sublime objects and states with immeasurable objects. The latter, dissociated states (A), are in turn dissociated from 4 mental aggregates, mind-base, and 7 consciousness-elements. Those dissociated states (B) are in dissociation from 1 aggregate (matter), 10 bases (10 gross bases), and 10 elements (10 gross elements). They are partially dissociated from 1 base (ideation-base), 1 element (ideation-element), subtle matters and *Nibbāna*.

X. Dissociated and Dissociated

384. States of enquiry (SOE):	SOE dissociate from *these* states (A) :	These states (A) dissociate from (B): agr / bse / el.	Those states, (B), dissociate from: agr / bse / el.	These states, (B), partially dissociated from: agr / bse / el.
1. States with sublime object.				
2. States with immeasurable object				
3. Inferior states.				
4. States fixed as to destinies due to wrong views.				
5. States with fixed destinies due to right views.	28 matters, *Nibbāna*	4 / 1 / 1	1 / 10 / 16	- / 1 / 1
6. States having Path as its object.				
7. States conditioned by Path.				
8. States having Path as the most predominant factor.				

These eight subject matters of enquiry contain varied cittas and cetasikas, characteristic of the three mundane spheres and supramundane sphere. (See Table 1.7). All of them belong to 4 mental aggregates. They are dissociated from materiality and *Nibbāna*. The latter are dissociated from 4 mental aggregates, mind-base, and mind-consciousness element. Those dissociated states (B) are in dissociation from 1 aggregate (matter), 10 bases (10 gross bases), and 16 elements (10 gross elements, and 6 consciousness-elements having excluded mind-consciousness element). They are partially dissociated from 1 base (ideation-base), 1 element (ideation-element), 16 subtle matters, and *Nibbāna*.

States of enquiry	SOE dissociate from *these* states (A) :	These states (A) dissociate from (B): agr / bse / el.	Those states, (B), dissociate from: agr / bse / el.	These states, (B), partially dissociated from: agr / bse / el.
385. States not arisen.	5 consciousness elements	- / - / 2	- / - / 5	- / - / -

States not arisen are the absence of 53 cittas which have not yet occurred which are: the 12 unwholesome cittas, 21 wholesome cittas, and 20 functional cittas. They include also the non-arising of 52 cetasikas, and materiality which are produced by action (17), by temperature (15), and by nutriments (14). States not arisen are characteristic of both materiality and 4 mental aggregates. States not arisen are bound up with 8 elements (vision-element, sound-element, odour-element, taste-element, touch-element, mind-element (of *manodvārāvajjana*), ideation-element, and mind-consciousness element).

A Perfect Knowledge of Mind-Body from the Abhidhamma (Dhātukathā)

So, states not arisen are only dissociated from the remaining 5 consciousness elements. The latter are directly dissociated from 2 elements (mind-element, and mind-consciousness element). The latter, those 2 elements, are dissociated from the remaining 5 sense consciousness elements (eye-consciousness, element, ear-consciousness element, nose-consciousness element, tongue-consciousness element, and body-consciousness element). Those 2 elements have no other possible dissociations from the aggregates and bases, nor partial dissociations.

States of enquiry (SOE):	SOE dissociate from *these* states (A) :	These states (A) dissociate from (B):			Those states, (B), dissociate from:			These states, (B), partially dissociated from:		
		agr	bse	el.	agr	bse	el.	agr	bse	el.
386. States with past object; States with future object (2)	28 matters, *Nibbāna*	4	1	1	1	10	16	-	1	1

These two states belong to 4 mental aggregates. States with past object are accompanied by 47 cetasikas. The other are accompanied by 50 cetasikas. These states are dissociated from materiality and *Nibbāna*, which in turn are dissociated from 4 mental aggregates, mind-base, and mind-consciousness element. The latter are in dissociation from 1 aggregate (matter), 10 bases (10 gross bases), and 16 elements (10 gross elements, and the remaining 6 consciousness-elements). They are partially dissociated from 1 base (ideation-base), 1 element (ideation-element), 16 subtle matters, and *Nibbāna*.

States of enquiry (SOE):	SOE dissociate from *these* states (A) :	These states (A) dissociate from (B):			Those states, (B), dissociate from:			These states, (B), partially dissociated from:		
		agr	bse	el.	agr	bse	el.	agr	bse	el.
387. States with present object; States with internal object; States with external object; States with both internal and external objects. (4)	28 matters, *Nibbāna*	4	1	7	1	10	10	-	1	1

States with present object consist of 43 cittas and 50 cetasikas. The rest three SOE consist of 54 sensuous cittas, different rūpajhānas and arūpajhānas, accompanied by 49 cetasikas, 51 cetasikas, and 48 cetasikas, respectively (See explanatory notes in nos. 210). All these states belong to 4 mental aggregates.

These states are dissociated from materiality and *Nibbāna*. The latter are in turn dissociated from 4 mental aggregates, mind-base, and 7 consciousness-

X. Dissociated and Dissociated

elements. The latter, those dissociated states (B), are in dissociation from 1 aggregate (matter), 10 bases (10 gross bases), and 10 elements (10 gross elements). They are partially dissociated from 1 base (ideation-base), 1 element (ideation-element), 16 subtle matters, and *Nibbāna*.

States of enquiry (SOE):	SOE dissociate from *these* states (A) :	These states (A) dissociate from (B):			Those states, (B), dissociate from:			These states, (B), partially dissociated from:		
		agr	bse	el.	agr	bse	el.	agr	bse	el.
388. States which are visible and impinging; States invisible but impinging. (2)	4 mentalities, subtle matters	1	10	10	4	1	7	-	1	1

States which are visible and impinging is referred to the twofold eye-consciousness and visible object. States which are invisible but impinging is referred to the absence of visible object from the 10 gross bases, and absence of sensitive eye from the 12 gross matters (i.e. remaining with 9 gross bases and 11 gross matters that are still impinging). Both states belong to gross matters. These states are dissociated from 12 subtle matters and 4 mental aggregates which are in turn dissociated from 1 aggregate (matter), 10 bases (10 gross bases), and 10 elements (10 gross elements). The latter, those states (B), are in dissociation from 4 mental aggregates (feeling, perception, volitive formation, and consciousness), 1 base (mind-base), and 7 elements (7 consciousness-elements). They are partially dissociated from 1 base (ideation-base), 1 element (ideation-element), 16 subtle matters, and *Nibbāna*.

111 states of enquiry from Dhammasaṅgaṇīmātikā dyads

389. States of enquiry (SOE):	SOE dissociate from *these* states (A) :	These states (A) dissociate from (B):			Those states, (B), dissociate from:			These states, (B), partially dissociated from:		
		agr	bse	el.	agr	bse	el.	agr	bse	el.
1. States which are root causes. 2. States which have root causes (or accompanied by root causes). 3. States which are associated with root causes. 4. States which are root causes and also having root causes. 5. States which are not root causes but having root causes.	28 matters, *Nibbāna*	4	1	1	1	10	16	-	1	1

A Perfect Knowledge of Mind-Body from the Abhidhamma (Dhātukathā)

6. States which are root causes and also associated with root causes.
7. States which are not root causes but are associated with root causes.
8. States which are not root causes but have associated root causes.

The following biefly explain with regard to the above eight states.

1. referring to greed, hatred, delusion, absence of greed, absence of hatred, absence of delusion — these 6 root causes belong to volitive formation.
2. consist of 71 cittas with associated roots, accompanied by 50 cetasikas (excluded delusion, non-delusion) — belong to 4 mental aggregates.
3. same as no. 2. above.
4. referring to the aforesaid 6 root causes, and excluding delusion present at the 2 delusion-rooted cittas — belong to volitive formation.
5. consist of 71 cittas with associated roots, accompanied by 46 cetasikas (excluded the 6 roots causes — belong to 4 mental aggregates.
6. same as no. 4. above.
7. same as no. 5. above.
8. same as no. 5. above.

These eight states come under mentalities and commonly share the aggregate of volitive formation. Each of them is dissociated from materiality and *Nibbāna*. The latter are in turn dissociated from 4 mental aggregates, mind-base, and mind-consciousness element. The latter, those dissociated states (B), are in dissociation from 1 aggregate (matter), 10 bases (10 gross bases), and 16 elements (10 gross elements, and 6 consciousness-elements having excluded mind-consciousness element). They are partially dissociated from 1 base (ideation-base), 1 element (ideation-element), 16 subtle matters, and *Nibbāna*.

States of enquiry (SOE):	SOE dissociate from *these* states (A) :	These states (A) dissociate from (B):			Those states, (B), dissociate from:			These states, (B), partially dissociated from:		
		agr	bse	el.	agr	bse	el.	agr	bse	el.
390. States not arisen from causes; States not conditioned by causes; States with visibility; States with impinging; States with corporeal change. (5)	89 cittas, 52 cetasikas	1	10	10	4	1	7	-	1	1

265

X. Dissociated and Dissociated

The 1st and 2nd SOE belong to *Nibbāna*. States with visibility are because of gross visible object which causes eye-consciousness. States with impinging are the 12 gross matters. States with corporeal change are referred to the 28 matters. So, these five states belong to pure materiality and *Nibbāna*.

Thus, they are dissociated from 89 cittas and 52 cetasikas, i.e. the 4 mental aggregates. The latter are in turn dissociated from 1 aggregate (matter), 10 bases (10 gross bases), and 10 elements (10 gross elements). The latter, those dissociated states (B), are dissociated from 4 mental aggregates (feeling, perception, volitive formation, consciousness), 1 base (mind-base), and 7 elements (7 consciousness-elements). They are partially dissociated from 1 base (ideation-base), 1 element (ideation-element), and 16 subtle matters.

States of enquiry (SOE):	SOE dissociate from *these* states (A) :	These states (A) dissociate from (B):			Those states, (B), dissociate from:			These states, (B), partially dissociated from:		
		agr	bse	el.	agr	bse	el.	agr	bse	el.
391. Supramundane states. (1)	mundane states, all corporeality	-	-	1	-	-	6	-	-	-

These states consist of 8 supramundane cittas accompanied by 36 cetasikas (38 having excluded 2 Illimitables). They belong to the 4 mentalities and *Nibbāna*. They are dissociated by class from mundane states, dissociated by category from materiality. Because supramundane cittas are essentially mind-consciousness element, they are in directly dissociation from the other 6 consciousness elements (eye-cons. element, ear-cons. element, nose-cons. element, tongue-cons. element, body-cons. element, and mind-element). Matter aggregate is not being considered in this context. Supramundane mind-consciousness element has no other possible dissociations from the aggregates and bases, nor are there possible partial dissociations.

A Perfect Knowledge of Mind-Body from the Abhidhamma (Dhātukathā)

392. States of enquiry (SOE):	SOE dissociate from *these* states (A) :	These states (A) dissociate from (B):			Those states, (B), dissociate from:			These states, (B), partially dissociated from:		
		agr	bsc	el.	agr	bse	el.	agr	bse	el.
1. States which are defilement (*Āsavā*). 2. States which are associated with defilement. 3. States as both defilement and objects of defilement. 4. States which are both defilement and associated with defilement. 5. States associated with defilement but are not defilement.	28 matters and *Nibbāna*; resultant cittas, functional cittas, 8 supramundane cittas, 25 beautiful cetasikas	4	1	1	1	10	16	-	1	1

The following briefly describes each of these five states.

1. They consist of the 3 factors of greed (or sensual desire), wrong view, and delusion, present at the 12 unwholesome cittas — they belong to volitive formation.
2. They consist of 12 unwholesome cittas, accompanied by 26 cetasikas (27 excluding delusion-*cetasika*, present at the 2 hate-rooted cittas and 2 delusion-rooted cittas) — they belong to volitive formation.
3. Same as no. 1 above.
4. Same as no. 1 above.
5. They consist of the 12 unwholesome cittas accompanied by 24 cetasikas (27 excluding the 3 defilement factors) — belong to 4 mental aggregates.

These five states come under mentalities and commonly ascribed to volitive formation. Each of them is dissociated from matters and *Nibbāna* by category. Each is dissociated by class from resultant cittas, functional cittas, 8 supramundane cittas, and 25 beautiful cetasikas. The latter are in turn dissociated by category from 4 mental aggregates, 1 base (mind-base), and 1 element (mind-consciousness element). The latter, those dissociated states (B), are in dissociation from 1 aggregate (matter), 10 bases (10 gross bases), and 16 elements (10 gross elements, and 6 consciousness-elements having excluded mind-consciousness element). They are partially dissociated from 1 base (ideation-base), 1 element (ideation-element), 16 subtle matters, and *Nibbāna*.

X. Dissociated and Dissociated

393. States of enquiry (SOE):	SOE dissociate from *these* states (A) :	These states (A) dissociate from (B):			Those states, (B), dissociate from:			These states, (B), partially dissociated from:		
		agr	bse	el.	agr	bse	el.	agr	bse	el.
1. States which are not the objects of defilement.	28 matters, 81 mundane cittas, 14 unwholesome cetasikas	-	-	1	-	-	6	-	-	-
2. States which are dissociated from defilement and also not objects of defilement.										

The two subject matters of enquiry belong to the 8 supramundane cittas, accompanied by 36 cetasikas (38 excluding the 2 Illimitables). These two states belong to 4 mental aggregates and *Nibbāna*, are bound up with mind-consciousness element. They are dissociated by category from matters, are dissociated by class from 81 mundane state of consciousness, 14 unwholesome cetasikas, and the 2 Appamaññas. These dissociated states (A) are in turn dissociated from 1 element (mind-consciousness element) which is dissociated directly from the other 6 consciousness elements (eye-cons. element, ear-cons. element, nose-cons. element, tongue-cons. element, body-cons. element, mind-element). This supramundane mind-consciousness element has no more other possible dissociations from the aggregates and bases, nor are there any other possible partial dissociations.

A Perfect Knowledge of Mind-Body from the Abhidhamma (Dhātukathā)

394. States of enquiry (SOE):	SOE dissociate from *these* states (A) :	These states (A) dissociate from (B):			Those states, (B), dissociate from:			These states, (B), partially dissociated from:		
		agr	bse	el.	agr	bse	el.	agr	bse	el.
Repeats the same from preceding *Āsavā* cluster for *Saṃyojana, Gantha, Ogha, Yoga, Nīvaraṇa* following nos. 392. Altogether 5 x 5 =25. (1 to 25)	same as in nos. 392	4	1	1	1	10	16	-	1	1
Repeats the same from preceding *Āsavā* cluster for *Saṃyojana, Gantha, Ogha, Yoga, Nīvaraṇa* following nos. 393. Altogether 5 x 2 =10. (26 to 35)	same as in nos. 393	-	-	1	-	-	6	-	-	-
36. States which are attachment (*Parāmāsa*).	same as in nos. 392	4	1	1	1	10	16	-	1	1
37. States associated with attachment.										
38. States which are both attachment and objects of attachment.										

Those 28 states (no. 1 to 25, 36 to 38) have similar answers as in nos. 392 as shown in the chart above. They belong to volitive formation aggregate. The five states from each of the five clusters consist of different made-up factors and cetasikas. Each of them is dissociated from materiality and *Nibbāna*. The latter are in turn dissociated from 4 mental aggregates, mind-base, and mind-consciousness element. The latter, those dissociated states (B), are in dissociation from 1 aggregate (matter), 10 bases (10 gross bases), and 16 elements (10 gross elements, and 6 consciousness-elements without mind-consciousness element). They are partially dissociated from 1 base (ideation-base), 1 element (ideation-element), 16 subtle matters, and *Nibbāna*.

Those 10 states (no. 26 to 35) have similar answers as in nos. 393. They similarly consist of 8 supramundane cittas, accompanied by 36 cetasikas (38 excluding the 2 Illimitables). They belong to 4 mental aggregates and *Nibbāna*, and are bound up with mind-consciousness element. Please refer to nos. 393 for the detailed answers.

X. Dissociated and Dissociated

395. States of enquiry (SOE):	SOE dissociate from *these* states (A):	*These* states (A) dissociate from (B):			*Those* states, (B), dissociate from:			*These* states, (B), partially dissociated from:		
		agr	bse	el.	agr	bse	el.	agr	bse	el.
1. States which are not objects of attachment.	28 matters, 81 mundane cittas, 14 unwholesome cetasikas, *Nibbāna*	-	-	1	-	-	6	-	-	-
2. States dissociated from attachment and are not objects of attachment.										

The analysis and answers for these two states of enquiry are the same as in nos. 393.

396. States of enquiry (SOE):	SOE dissociate from *these* states (A):	*These* states (A) dissociate from (B):			*Those* states, (B), dissociate from:			*These* states, (B), partially dissociated from:		
		agr	bse	el.	agr	bse	el.	agr	bse	el.
1. States which attend to objects.	28 matters, *Nibbāna*	4	1	7	1	10	10	-	1	1
2. States which are consciousness.										
3. States which are mental factors.										
4. States associated with cons.										
5. States conjoined with cons.										
6. States both conjoined with and originated from cons.										
7. States conjoined with, originated from, and arise concurrently with cons.										
8. States conjoined with, originated from, and arise consecutively with cons.										

The 1st and 2nd SOE consist of 89 cittas, accompanied by 52 cetasikas. These two states are consciousness, are mutually associated with the other 3 mental aggregates. The other six of them are the 52 cetasikas. These eight states of enquiry belong to 4 mental aggregates.

These states are dissociated from materiality and *Nibbāna*. The latter are in turn dissociated from 4 mental aggregates, mind-base, and 7 consciousness-elements. The latter, those dissociated states (B), are in dissociation from 1 aggregate (matter), 10 bases (10 gross bases), and 10 elements (10 gross elements). They are partially dissociated from 1 base (ideation-base), 1 element (ideation-element), 16 subtle matters, and *Nibbāna*.

A Perfect Knowledge of Mind-Body from the Abhidhamma (Dhātukathā)

States of enquiry (SOE):	SOE dissociate from *these* states (A) :	These states (A) dissociate from (B):			Those states, (B), dissociate from:			These states, (B), partially dissociated from:		
		agr	bse	el.	agr	bse	el.	agr	bse	el.
397. 1. States which do not have objects. 2. States which are dissociated from consciousness. 3. States which are not conjoined with consciousness. 4. States which are derived.	4 mental aggregates	1	10	10	4	1	7	-	1	1

The 1st, 2nd, 3rd SOE belong to 28 matters and *Nibbāna*. States which are derived are 24 matters (28 excluding the four great elements). Thus, these states are dissociated from 4 mental aggregates. The latter are in turn dissociated from 1 aggregate (28 matters), 10 bases (10 gross bases), 10 elements (10 gross elements), and *Nibbāna*. The latter, those states (B) are in dissociation from 4 mental aggregates (feeling, perception, volitive formation, and consciousness), 1 base (mind-base), and 7 elements (7 consciousness-elements). They are partially dissociated from 1 base (ideation-base), 1 element (ideation-element), and subtle matters.

States of enquiry:	SOE dissociate from *these* states (A) :	These states (A) dissociate from (B):			Those states, (B), dissociate from:			These states, (B), partially dissociated from:		
		agr	bse	el.	agr	bse	el.	agr	bse	el.
398. States which are not the result of clinging (*anupādinnehi dhammehi*) (1)	5 cons. elements, 10 viññāṇas	-	-	2	-	-	5	-	-	-

States which are not the result of clinging (i.e. not acquired by clinging) consist of 57 cittas (comprised of 21 wholesome cittas, 12 unwholesome cittas, 20 functional cittas, 4 supramundane fruition-cittas), arisen with 52 cetasikas; also, 17 mind-produced matters, 15 temperature-produced matters, 14 nutriment-produced matters, and *Nibbāna*. These states come within the whole measures of materiality, mentality and *Nibbāna*. Thus, they are only dissociated from the pairs of fivefold sense consciousness which are also the 5 consciousness elements (eye-cons. element, ear-cons. element, nose-cons. element, tongue-cons. element, and body-cons. element).

The latter are in turn dissociated from 2 elements (mind-element, and mind-consciousness element). The 2 elements are dissociated from the remaining 5 consciousness elements as mentioned above. The 2 elements have no other possible dissociations from aggregates and bases, nor partial dissociations.

X. Dissociated and Dissociated

399. States of enquiry (SOE):	SOE dissociate from *these* states (A) :	*These* states (A) dissociate from (B):			*Those* states, (B), dissociate from:			*These* states, (B), partially dissociated from:		
		agr	bse	el.	agr	bse	el.	agr	bse	el.
1. States which are clinging.										
2. States which are both clinging and objects of clinging.	28 matters	4	1	1	1	10	16	-	1	1
3. States which are both clinging and associated with clinging.										
4. States which are not objects of clinging.	28 matters, 81 mundane cittas, 14 unwholesome cetasikas	-	-	1	-	-	6	-	-	-
5. States dissociated from clinging and are not objects of clinging.										
6. States associated with clinging.										
7. States associated with clinging but are not clinging.										
8. States which are corruptions.										
9. States which are corrupted.										
10. States which are associated with corruptions.										
11. States which are both corruptions and objects of corruptions.		4	1	1	1	10	16	-	1	1
12. States which are both corruptions and are corrupted.	28 matters									
13. States which are corrupted but are not corruptions.										
14. States which are both corruptions and associated with corruptions.										
15. States which are associated with corruptions but are not corruptions.										

These fifteen states above are each summarised as below.

1. They are due to sensual desires and wrong view, present at the 4 greed-rooted cittas accompanied by greed and associated with wrong view — belong to volitive formation.
2. Same as in no. 1 above.

A Perfect Knowledge of Mind-Body from the Abhidhamma (Dhātukathā)

3. Same as in no. 1 above.
4. They are from the 8 supramundane cittas, accompanied by 36 cetasikas (38 having excluded the 2 Illimitables) and *Nibbāna* — belong to 4 mental aggregates and *Nibbāna*.
5. Same as in no. 4 above.
6. They are from the 8 greed-rooted cittas accompanied by 22 cetasikas (27 excluding hatred, envy, avarice, worry, doubt) — belong to 4 mental aggregates.
7. They are from 8 greed-rooted cittas accompanied by 20 cetasikas (27 excluding hatred, envy, avarice, worry, doubt, and the 2 factors of clinging) — belong to 4 mental aggregates.
8. They are from the 10 states of corruptions (the cetasikas of greed, hatred, delusion, conceit, wrong view, doubt, sloth, restlessness, shamelessness, guiltlessness of conscience) — all belong to volitive formation.
9. They are from the 12 mundane unwholesome cittas, accompanied by 27 cetasikas — belong to 4 mental aggregates.
10. Same as in no. 9 above.
11. Same as in no. 8 above.
12. Same as in no. 8 above.
13. They are from the 12 unwholesome cittas, accompanied by 17 cetasikas (27 excluding the 10 factors of corruptions) — belong to 4 mental aggregates.
14. Same as in no. 8 above.
15. Same as in no. 13 above.

The 4th & 5th SOE belong to pure mentality and *Nibbāna*, are bound up with mind-consciousness element. They are dissociated from matters by category, and dissociated by class from 81 mundane cittas, 14 unwholesome cetasikas, and 2 Illimitables. The latter, which have included all 5 aggregates and 12 bases, are dissociated from only 1 element (mind-consciousness element). The latter in turn is dissociated from the remaining 6 consciousness elements. The supramundane mind-consciousness element hence has no dissociations from the aggregates and bases, nor any partial dissociation.

The other 13 SOE are all mentalities. They are dissociated from materiality. 28 matters are in turn dissociated from 4 aggregates (4 mental aggregates), 1 base (mind-base), and 1 element (mind-consciousness element). The latter, those dissociated states (B), are in dissociation from 1 aggregate (matter), 10 bases (10 gross bases), and 16 elements (10 gross elements, and 6 consciousness-elements having excluded mind-consciousness element). They are partially dissociated from 1 base (ideation-base), 1 element (ideation-element), 16 subtle matters, and *Nibbāna*.

X. Dissociated and Dissociated

States of enquiry (SOE):	SOE dissociate from *these* states (A) :	These states (A) dissociate from (B):			Those states, (B), dissociate from:			These states, (B) partially dissociated from:		
		agr	bse	el.	agr	bse	el.	agr	bse	el.
400. States which are not objects of corruptions; States which are dissociated from corruptions and are not objects of corruptions. (2)	81 mundane states, all materiality	-	-	1	-	-	6	-	-	-

Both these two states belong to 8 supramundane cittas, arisen with 36 cetasikas (38 excluding the 2 Illimitables). They belong to 4 mental aggregates and *Nibbāna*. They are hence dissociated by class from all mundane states, 14 unwholesome cetasikas, the 2 Illimitables; and by category from 28 matters. These two states of enquiry are bound up with supramundane mind-consciousness element, and are in dissociation from all mundane states and materiality. Thus, mind-consciousness element is dissociated from the remaining 6 consciousness elements (eye-cons. element, ear-cons. element, nose-cons. element, tongue-cons. element, body-cons. element, and mind-element). There are no more other possible dissociations from the aggregates and bases, nor any other possible partial dissociations, for the 81 mundane cittas and materiality are already covered 5 aggregates and *Nibbāna* in the first case of dissociation.

States of enquiry (SOE):	SOE dissociate from *these* states (A) :	These states (A) dissociate from (B):			Those states, (B), dissociate from:			These states, (B) partially dissociated from:		
		agr	bse	el.	agr	bse	el.	agr	bse	el.
401. States eliminated by first Path; States eliminated by higher three Paths; States with root causes eliminated by the first Path; States with root causes eliminated by the higher three Paths. (4)	all that is corporeality	4	1	1	1	10	16	-	1	1

Answers for these four states of enquiry are the same as in nos. 381.

A Perfect Knowledge of Mind-Body from the Abhidhamma (Dhātukathā)

States of enquiry (SOE):	SOE dissociate from *these* states (A) :	These states (A) dissociate from (B):			Those states, (B), dissociate from:			These states, (B), partially dissociated from:		
		agr	bse	el.	agr	bse	el.	agr	bse	el.
402. States with initial application; States with sustained application. (2)	28 matters, 5 cons. elements	4	1	2	1	10	15	-	1	1

These states correspond to the 55 cittas accompanied by 50 cetasikas. They belong to 4 mental aggregates. The answers follow the same as in nos. 376.

States of enquiry (SOE):	SOE dissociate from *these* states (A) :	These states (A) dissociate from (B):			Those states, (B), dissociate from:			These states, (B), partially dissociated from:		
		agr	bse	el.	agr	bse	el.	agr	bse	el.
403. States without initial application; States without sustained application. (2)	first *jhāna*, sensuous cittas, mind-element	-	-	6	-	-	1	-	-	-

These stwo tates consist of 11 Second-*Jhāna* cittas, 55 cittas accompanied by 36 cetasikas (38 excluding *vitakka* and *vicāra*), 28 matters, and *Nibbāna*. They belong to mentality-materiality, and *Nibbāna*, are bound up with 6 consciousness elements (without the presence of mind-element). Answers are the same as in nos. 378.

States of enquiry (SOE):	SOE dissociate from *these* states (A) :	These states (A) dissociate from (B):			Those states, (B), dissociate from:			These states, (B), partially dissociated from:		
		agr	bse	el.	agr	bse	el.	agr	bse	el.
404. States with zest; States accompanied by zest. (2)	28 matters, 6 cons. elements	4	1	1	1	10	16	-	1	1

Both these states comprise 51 cittas, accompanied by 45 cetasikas (52 excluding hatred, envy, avarice, worry, sloth, torpor, and doubt). Both states belong to 4 mental aggregates, are closely bound up with mind-consciousness element. They are dissociated from the remaining 6 consciousness elements, and 28 matters. The answers are the same as in nos. 377.

X. Dissociated and Dissociated

	SOE dissociate from *these* states (A) :	These states (A) dissociate from (B):			Those states, (B), dissociate from:			These states, (B), partially dissociated from:		
States of enquiry (SOE):		agr	bse	el.	agr	bse	el.	agr	bse	el.
405. States accompanied by happiness. (1)	28 matters, 5 cons. elements	4	1	2	1	10	15	-	1	1

These are the same states as in nos. 379, with similar answers.

	SOE dissociate from *these* states (A) :	These states (A) dissociate from (B):			Those states, (B), dissociate from:			These states, (B), partially dissociated from:		
States of enquiry:		agr	bse	el.	agr	bse	el.	agr	bse	el.
406. States accompanied by equanimity. (1)	28 matters; states accompanied by zest, and by happiness.	4	1	6	1	10	11	-	1	1

These are the same states as in preceding nos. 380, with similar answers.

	SOE dissociate from *these* states (A) :	These states (A) dissociate from (B):			Those states, (B), dissociate from:			These states, (B), partially dissociated from:		
States of enquiry (SOE):		agr	bse	el.	agr	bse	el.	agr	bse	el.
407. States which do not belong to sensuous sphere; States which are not included (in round of rebirths); States which are unsurpassable (3)	54 sensuous cittas (by sphere); 28 matters	-	-	1	-	-	6	-	-	-

States not belonging to sensuous sphere consist of 27 sublime cittas (*mahaggatacittāni*), 8 supramundane cittas accompanied by 38 cetasikas, but not necessarily including *Nibbāna* if states are from the other two mundane spheres. The other two SOE are 8 supramundane cittas, accompanied by 36 cetasikas (38 excluding the 2 Illimitables), and including *Nibbāna*. All these states of enquiry belong to 4 mental aggregates and *Nibbāna*.. These states are essentially mind-consciousness element, dissociated by sphere from 54 sensuous cittas. These dissociated states are in direct dissociation from the other 6 consciousness elements (eye-cons. element, ear-cons. element, nose-cons. element, tongue-cons. element, body-cons. element, and mind-element). Matters are dissociated

A Perfect Knowledge of Mind-Body from the Abhidhamma (Dhātukathā)

by category which is disregarded here. There are no more possible dissociations from the aggregates and bases, nor any other possible partial dissociations.

408. States of enquiry (SOE):	SOE dissociate from *these* states (A) :	*These* states (A) dissociate from (B):			*Those* states, (B), dissociate from:			*These* states, (B), partially dissociated from:		
		agr	bse	el.	agr	bse	el.	agr	bse	el.
1. States belong to form sphere.										
2. States belong to formless sphere.										
3. States which lead out (from cycle of death and rebirth).	28 matters	4	1	7	1	10	10	-	1	1
4. States fixed as to their future destinies.										
5. States which are at odds with supramundane Path.										

The 1st SOE consist of 15 fine-material cittas, accompanied by 35 cetasikas. The 2nd SOE are the 12 immaterial sublime cittas, accompanied by 30 cetasikas. The 3rd are the 4 supramundane path-cittas, and accompanied by 36 cetasikas. The 4th SOE has the same as in the 3rd SOE but including the 7th sensuous *javana* present at the greed-rooted cittas associated with wrong view, and also at the 2 delusion-rooted cittas. The 5th SOE are the 12 mundane unwholesome cittas, accompanied by 27 cetasikas. All these states of enquires come under 4 mental aggregates.

They are dissociated from materiality and *Nibbāna* which in turn is dissociated from 4 mental aggregates, mind-base, and the 7 consciousness-elements. The latter, those states (B), are in dissociation from 1 aggregate (matter), 10 bases (10 gross bases), and 10 elements (10 gross elements). They are partially dissociated from 1 base (ideation-base), 1 element (ideation-element), 16 subtle matters, and *Nibbāna*.

Key points from the text :

Ideation-base, ideation-element, origin-truth and path-truth, vitality-faculty, six bases, mentality-materiality, four greater becomings (fine-material becoming, immaterial-becoming, neither perception nor non-perception becoming, four-aggregate becoming), birth, ageing, death, 19 triplets included in 47 states of enquiry of tikas, 111 states of enquiry of dukas (50 groups, 6 from the shorter clusters, 13 from the intermediate dyads-cluster, and 20 from the last dyads-cluster).

X. Dissociated and Dissociated

In regard to the following two summary tables, the number in the brackets represents the number of enquiries belong to the associated text paragraph nos.

Table 10.1 Summary of the 250 states of enquiry by subject matters

Text's paragraph nos. (with numbers of enquiries):		Subject matter:
353 (1), 354 (4)	5	Aggregates
354 (1), 355 (10)	11	Bases
355 (10), 356 (7)	17	Elements
356 (2), 357 (1)	3	Truths
357 (7), 358 (1), 359 (4), 358 (4), 360 (1), 361 (8)	21	Faculties
361 (2), 362 (3), 363 (3), 364 (1), 365 (3), 366 (7)	19	Dependent Originations
366 (9), 367 (6), 368 (1)	16	Others
369 (2), 370 (2), 371 (1), 372 (1), 373 (2), 374 (2), 375 (2), 376 (1), 377 (2), 378 (1), 379 (1), 380 (1), 381 (9), 382 (2), 383 (1), 384 (8), 385 (1), 386 (2), 387 (4), 388 (2)	47	Triads
389 (8), 392 (5), 393 (2), 394 (38), 395 (2), 399 (15), 400 (2)	72	Dyad-clusters
390 (5), 391 (1)	6	Shorter dyads
396 (8), 397 (4), 398 (1)	13	Intermediate dyads
401 (4), 402 (2), 403 (2), 404 (2), 405 (1), 406 (1), 407 (1), 408 (5)	20	Last dyads

Total = 250 states

Table 10.2 Summary of the 250 states of enquiry by answers

Text's paragraph nos. (with numbers of enquiries):		Dissociated from			Partially dissociated from		
		agr	bse	el.	agr	bse	el.
353 (1), 355 (20), 357 (8), 365 (3), 388 (2), 390 (5), 397 (4)	43	4	1	7	-	1	1
354 (5), 358 (1), 362 (3), 367 (6), 372 (1), 383 (1), 387 (4), 396 (8), 408 (5)	34	1	10	10	-	1	1
356 (9), 359 (4), 361 (10), 363 (3), 366 (16), 369 (2), 373 (2), 377 (2), 381 (9), 384 (8), 386 (2), 389 (8), 392 (5), 394 (28), 399 (13), 401 (4), 404 (2)	127	1	10	16	-	1	1
360 (1), 371 (1), 380 (1), 406 (1)	4	1	10	11	-	1	1
364 (1)	1	-	-	3	-	-	-
368 (1), 370 (2), 376 (1), 379 (1), 402 (2), 405 (1)	8	1	10	15	-	1	1
374 (2), 385 (1), 398 (1)	4	-	-	5	-	-	-
375 (2), 382 (2), 391 (1), 393 (2), 394 (10), 395 (2), 399 (2), 400 (2), 407 (3)	26	-	-	6	-	-	-
378 (1), 403 (2)	3	-	-	1	-	-	-

Total = 250 states in 9 kinds of answer

CHAPTER 11

XI. Associated and Dissociated from the Aggrouped
(*Saṅgahitenasampayuttavippayutta*)

Analysis of 69 states from 8 catechism

The 69 states of enquiry in this chapter are the same states as mentioned in Chapter 4. Of these 69 states, 39 are internal states, 30 states are from the dyads. The rule for this chapter follows the same as in Chapter 4, which requires the states of enquiry to be classifiable with those remaining states such that they can be aggrouped under the same aggregate, under same base, and under same element. With that common basis of comparison, the two antithetical sides of states are permitted to correlate and compare freely with one another.

Note that those remaining states of comparison exclude gross matters and consciousness aggregate. The reason is because they contain different bases and different elements which can not be classified under the same aggregate, under the same base, and under the same element. Those remaining states are then taken up for further enquiry as to which aggregates, bases and elements they are associated with and partially associated with, as well as dissociated from and partially dissociated from. This is association and dissociation as in Chapter 6. A simple diagram is provided below to demonstrate these kinds of relationship.

Diagram 11.1. Associated states and dissociated states from aggrouped

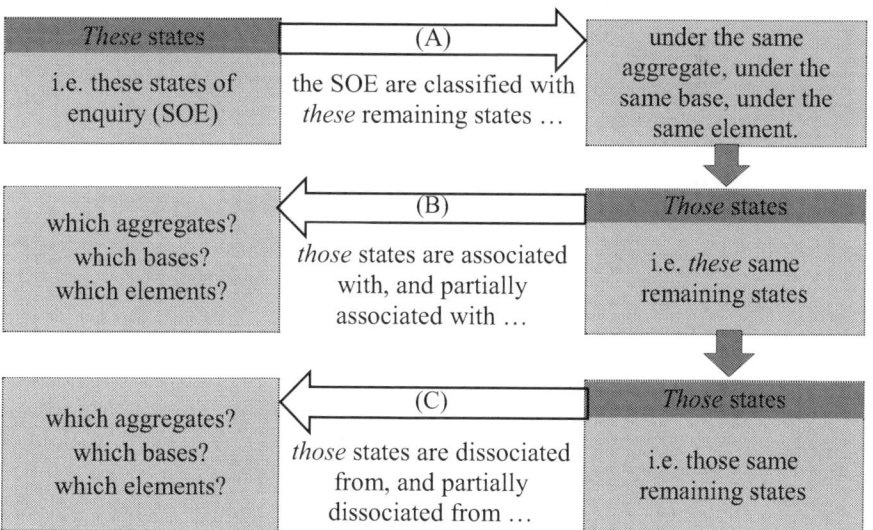

XI. Associated and Dissociated from the Aggrouped

The following abbreviations will be used in the charts and tables throughout this Chapter.

SOE	: States of enquiry
S.	: Subtle matters
F.	: Feeling aggregate
P.	: Perception aggregate
V.	: Volitive formation aggregate
N.	: *Nibbāna*
cons.	: consciousness
agr	: aggregate
As	: Associated
Pas	: Partially associated
Ds	: Dissociated
Pds	: Partially dissociated

The symbol † used in all the following charts denotes that the states of enquiry are classified with the remaining states under the same aggregate, under the same base, and under the same element.

39 internal states of enquiry

		† Those remaining states					Aggregate				Base				Element			
409.	States of enquiry :	S.	F.	P.	V.	N.	As	Pas	Ds	Pds	As	Pas	Ds	Pds	As	Pas	Ds	Pds
1.	Origin-truth				49		3	1	1	-	1	1	10	1	7	1	10	1
2.	Path-truth				50													

These two truths belong to volitive formation aggregate. Origin-truth is bound by greed-cetasika and thus the remaining states are 49 mental factors (50 ' excluding greed). Path-truth has 50 mental factors as its remaining states. Both the two truths are bound up with mind-consciousness element under consciousness aggregate, but which is excluded as per rule. Each of these two truths is classified with the respective remaining states and taken as aggrouped under same aggregate (volitive formation), under same base (ideation-base), and under same element (ideation-element). As just mentioned, the 12 gross matters and consciousness aggregate can not be unclassified on such similar condition.

Those aggrouped remaining states are associated with 3 aggregates (feeling, perception, consciousness), 1 base (mind-base), and 7 elements (7 consciousness elements). They are partially associated with 1 aggregate (volitive formation), 1 base (ideation-base), and 1 element (ideation-element). Those aggrouped remaining states are dissociated from 1 aggregate (matter), with 10 bases (10 gross bases), with 10 elements (10 gross elements). They are also partially

A Perfect Knowledge of Mind-Body from the Abhidhamma (Dhātukathā)

dissociated from 1 base (ideation-base), 1 element (ideation-element), subtle matters, and *Nibbāna*.

410. States of enquiry :	† Those remaining states					Aggregate				Base				Element			
	S.	F.	P.	V.	N.	As	Pas	Ds	Pds	As	Pas	Ds	Pds	As	Pas	Ds	Pds
1. Femininity-faculty. 2. Masculinity-faculty.	15	-	-	-	-	-	-	4	-	-	-	1	1	-	-	7	1

These two states belong to subtle matters. Thus, 15 subtle matters (16-1=15) become the remaining physical states. When either SOE is dealt with these remaining states, they can be aggrouped under 1 aggregate (subtle matters), 1 base (ideation-base), and 1 element (ideation-element).

Because these states of enquiry are both materiality, there are no associated states nor partially associated states. Reason is that they do not conform with the four characteristics of association as mentioned in Chapter 6. The 15 subtle matters are in dissociation from 4 aggregates (4 mental aggregates), 1 base (mind-base), and 7 elements (7 consciousness-elements). Because subtle matters are part of matter aggregate but which come under ideation-base and ideation-element, these remaining states are thus partially dissociated from 1 base (ideation-base), and 1 element (ideation-element), and 52 cetasikas. Matters are never ever partially associated with, nor partially dissociated from *Nibbāna*. So, *Nibbāna* is hereby ignored.

States of enquiry :	† Those remaining states					Aggregate				Base				Element			
	S.	F.	P.	V.	N.	As	Pas	Ds	Pds	As	Pas	Ds	Pds	As	Pas	Ds	Pds
411. Carnal pleasure-faculty; Carnal pain-faculty; Joy-faculty; Melancholy-faculty. (4)	4					3	-	1	-	1	1	10	1	7	1	10	1

These are feeling faculties, belong to feeling aggregate. When each SOE is enquired, the other remaining 4 faculties (faculties of bodily pain, joy, melancholy and equanimity) are taken as its remaining states so that they can be classified under the same aggregate (feeling), under the same base (ideation-base), and under the same element (ideation-element).

Those states, the remaining 4 faculties, which come under feeling aggregate, are associated with 3 aggregates (perception, volitive formation, consciousness), 1 base (mind-base), and 7 elements (7 consciousness elements, because equanimity-faculty is among the remaining states). They are partially associated with 1 base (ideation-base), 1 element (ideation-element), and 51 cetasikas (52 excluding feeling-*cetasika*). It is not 6 cetasikas (7 - feeling-*cetasika*) because

XI. Associated and Dissociated from the Aggrouped

remaining states are confined to feeling aggregate. Those aggrouped remaining states are dissociated from 1 aggregate (matter), 10 bases (10 gross bases), 10 elements (10 gross elements). They are also partially dissociated from 1 base (ideation-base), 1 element (ideation-element), subtle matters, and *Nibbāna*.

States of enquiry :	† Those remaining states					Aggregate				Base				Element			
	S.	F.	P.	V.	N.	As	Pas	Ds	Pds	As	Pas	Ds	Pds	As	Pas	Ds	Pds
412. Equanimity-faculty		4				3	-	1	-	1	1	10	1	2	1	15	1

Equanimity-faculty, like the four faculties in nos. 412, comes under the feeling aggregate. Herein, it is accompanied by 50 cetasikas (52 excluding feeling, and also doubt) based on its remaining 4 faculties (faculties of bodily pleasure, bodily pain, mental joy, and melancholy). These 4 faculties are taken as its remaining states so that they can be classified under the same aggregate (feeling), under same base (ideation-base), and under same element (ideation-element).

Those remaining 4 states (remaining 4 faculties) under feeling aggregate are associated with 3 aggregates (perception, volitive formation, consciousness), with 1 base (mind-base), with 2 elements (body-consciousness element, mind-consciousness element). They are partially associated with 1 base (ideation-base), 1 element (ideation-element), and 50 cetasikas. They are dissociated from 1 aggregate (matter), with 10 bases (10 gross bases), with 15 elements (10 gross elements, and eye-cons. element, ear-cons. element, nose-cons. element, tongue-cons. element, and mind element). They are also in partial dissociation from 1 base (ideation-base), 1 element (ideation-element), subtle matters, and *Nibbāna*.

413. States of enquiry :	† Those remaining states					Aggregate				Base				Element			
	S.	F.	P.	V.	N.	As	Pas	Ds	Pds	As	Pas	Ds	Pds	As	Pas	Ds	Pds
Confidence-faculty; Effort-faculty; Mindfulness-faculty; Concentration-faculty; Wisdom-faculty; "I-shall-comprehend-the-unknown" faculty; Higher knowledge faculty; "Final knower" faculty; Ignorance; conditioned by ignorance is Volitive formation; conditioned by the six bases is Contact; conditioned by feeling is Craving; conditioned by craving is Clinging; Action-becoming (14)				48 & 49		3	1	1	-	1	1	10	1	7	1	10	1

A Perfect Knowledge of Mind-Body from the Abhidhamma (Dhātukathā)

These 14 SOE all come under voilitive formation aggregate. Confidence faculty contains faith-*cetasika*; effort faculty contains energy-*cetasika*; mindfulness faculty contains mindfulness-*cetasika*; concentration faculty contains one-pointedness-*cetasika*; wisdom-faculty and the other 3 facutlies each contain wisdom-*cetasika*; ignorance contains delusion-*cetasika*; volitive formation contains volition-*cetasika*; contact includes contact-*cetasika*; craving includes greed-*cetasika*; clinging includes greed-*cetasika* and wrong view-*cetasika*; action-becoming (*kammabhava*) includes volition-*cetasika*. Thus, clinging is accompanied by 48 cetasikas (50 excluding greed and wrong view). The rest 13 SOE are accompanied by 49 cetasikas (50 excluding their respective cetasika).

When each of these 14 states is dealt with its remaining 48 or 49 states of mental factors, they can be classified under the same aggregate (volitive formation), under the same base (ideation-base), and under the same element (ideation-element). And thereby, those aggrouped remaining states are associated with 3 aggregates (feeling, perception, consciousness), 1 base (mind-base), and 7 elements (7 consciousness elements). They are partially associated with 1 aggregate (volitive formation), 1 base (ideation-base), 1 element (ideation-element) and 49 cetasikas, or 48 cetasikas if clinging is being enquired at the time. Those aggrouped remaining states are dissociated from 1 aggregate (matter), with 10 bases (10 gross bases), with 10 elements (10 gross elements). They are also partially dissociated from 1 base (ideation-base), 1 element (ideation-element), subtle matters, and *Nibbāna*.

States of enquiry :	† Those remaining states					Aggregate				Base				Element			
	S.	F.	P.	V.	N.	As	Pas	Ds	Pds	As	Pas	Ds	Pds	As	Pas	Ds	Pds
414. Lamentation	1	-	-	-	-	-	-	4	-	-	-	1	1	-	-	7	1

Lamentation is treated as sound because of wailing. It belongs to gross matter. Note that 4 mentalities, subtle matters and *Nibbāna* are not taken as its remaining states in this regard. The reason is, as mentioned earlier, these states are not aggroupable with SOE in conformity with the classification rule. Audible object base and audible object element are not the remaining states either, because of homogeneity of the same kind. Thus, two audible objects — of a non-lamented kind (gross), and of temperature-born (subtle) — become its remaining states.

Because both the state of enquiry and remaining states come under matter aggregate, there are no associated states nor any partially associated states. The remaining states are dissociated from 4 aggregates (4 mental aggregates), 1 base (mind-base), and 7 elements (7 consciousness-elements). The remaining state are partially dissociated from 1 base (ideation-base), 1 element (ideation-element), and 52 cetasikas. Matters are never partially associated with, nor partially

XI. Associated and Dissociated from the Aggrouped

dissociated from *Nibbāna*. And so, *Nibbāna* is hereby ignored. Subtle matters are ignored because they are part of those remaining states.

States of enquiry :	† Those remaining states					Aggregate				Base				Element			
	S.	F.	P.	V.	N.	As	Pas	Ds	Pds	As	Pas	Ds	Pds	As	Pas	Ds	Pds
415. Sorrow; Suffering; Melancholy. (3)				49		3	-	1	-	1	1	10	1	7	1	10	1

Sorrow, suffering, and melancholy belong to the feeling faculty. They contain hatred-*cetasika*, present at the two hatred-rooted cittas. Thus, by taking 49 states of mental factors (50 excluding hatred-*cetasika*) as the remaining states, each of these SOE can be classified with these remaining states under the same aggregate (feeling), under the same base (ideation-base), and under the same element (ideation-element). In this respect, SOE and the remaining 3 mental aggregates can not be classified in such similar manner.

Having this classified, those aggrouped remaining states are associated with 3 aggregates (feeling, perception, consciousness), 1 base (mind-base), and 7 elements (7 consciousness elements). They are partially associated with 1 base (ideation-base), 1 element (ideation-element), and 49 cetasikas. Those aggrouped remaining states are dissociated from 1 aggregate (matter), 10 bases (10 gross bases), 10 elements (10 gross elements). They are also partially dissociated from 1 base (ideation-base), 1 element (ideation-element), subtle matters, and *Nibbāna*.

416. States of enquiry :	† Those remaining states (cetasikas in Volition F. agr.)	Aggregate				Base				Element			
		As	Pas	Ds	Pds	As	Pas	Ds	Pds	As	Pas	Ds	Pds
1. Despair.	49												
2. Application of Mindfulness.	49												
3. Right Striving.	49												
4. The Illimitables.	48												
5. The 5 Faculties.	45												
6. The 5 Powers.	45	3	1	1	-	1	1	10	1	7	1	10	1
7. 7 Factors of Enlightenment.	43												
8. Noble Eightfold Path.	42												
9. Contact.	49												
10. Volition.	49												
11. Decision.	49												
12. Attention.	49												

A Perfect Knowledge of Mind-Body from the Abhidhamma (Dhātukathā)

These 12 states of enquiry come under voilitive formation aggregate, with associated cetasikas as shown below.

- despair contains, occasionally, hatred-*cetasika*;
- the four application/foundation of mindfulness contain mindfulness-*cetasika*;
- the four right strivings contain energy-*cetasika*;
- 2 Illimitables contain the 2 cetasikas of compassion (*karunā*) and altruistic joy (*muditā*);
- 5 faculties contain the 5 cetasikas of faith, effort, mindfulness, one-pointedness, and non-delusion;
- 5 powers contain the same 5 cetasikas as in the 5 faculties;
- 7 factors of enlightenment contain the 7 cetasikas of mindfulness, non-delusion, effort, zest, calmness, one-pointedness, and equanimity;
- noble eightfold path contains the 8 cetasikas of mindfulness, non-delusion, 3 abstinences, effort, mindfulness, and one-pointedness;
- contact contains contact-*cetasika*, volition contains volition-*cetasika*;
- decision contains decision-*cetasika*; attention contains decision–*cetasika*.

Their respective remaining states of mental factors are shown in chart above. (50 in volitive formation aggregate excluding the respective number of cetasikas corresponding to each SOE). When each of these 12 states is dealt with its remaining states of mental factors, they can be classified under the same aggregate (volitive formation), under the same base (ideation-base), and under the same element (ideation-element).

Those aggrouped remaining states are associated with 3 aggregates (feeling, perception, consciousness), 1 base (mind-base), and 7 elements (7 consciousness elements). They are partially associated with 1 aggregate (volitive formation), 1 base (ideation-base), 1 element (ideation-element), and the cetasikas proper to each state of enquiry. Those aggrouped remaining states are dissociated from 1 aggregate (matter), 10 bases (10 gross bases), and 10 elements (10 gross elements). They are partially dissociated from 1 base (ideation-base), 1 element (ideation-element), subtle matters, and *Nibbāna*.

XI. Associated and Dissociated from the Aggrouped

30 states of enquiry from Dhammasaṅgaṇīmātikā dyads

416. States of enquiry :	† Those remaining states (cetasikas in Volition agr.)	Aggregate				Base				Element			
		As	Pas	Ds	Pds	As	Pas	Ds	Pds	As	Pas	Ds	Pds
13. States which are root causes.	44												
14. States which are root causes and having root causes.	44												
15. States which are root causes and also associated with them.	44												
16. States which are *defilement*.	47												
17. States which are both defilement and objects of defilement.	47												
18. States which are both defilement and associated with defilement	47												
Repeats step 16,17,18 for *Fetters* (3).	42, 42, 42												
Repeats step 16,17,18 for *Bonds* (3).	47, 47, 48												
Repeats step 16,17,18 for *Raging current* (3).	47, 47, 47	3	1	1	-	1	1	10	1	7	1	10	1
Repeats step 16,17,18 for *Yokes* (3).	47, 47, 47												
Repeats step 16,17,18 for *Hindrances* (3).	42, 42, 42												
Repeats step 16,17 for *Attachment* (2).	49, 49												
Repeats step 16,17,18 for *Clinging* (3).	48, 48, 48												
39. States which are corruptions.	40												
40. States which are both corruptions and objects of corruptions.	40												
41. States which are corruptions and are corrupted.	40												
42. States which are both corruptions and associated with corruptions.	40												

A Perfect Knowledge of Mind-Body from the Abhidhamma (Dhātukathā)

The following describes the specific cetasikas and the remaining states of mental factors with regard to the above 30 states, all of which belong to volitive formation aggregate.

13. States which are root causes — include the 6 cetasikas of greed, hatred, delusion, non-greed, non-hatred, non-delusion. Thus, there are remaining 44 states of mental factors. (50-6=44).
14. States which are root causes and having root causes — include 6 roots causes (excluding delusion present only at the 2 delusion-rooted cittas). Thus, there are remaining 44 states of mental factors.
15. States which are root causes and also associated with them — same as in nos. 14 above.
16. States which are defilement — include the 3 cetasikas of greed (or sensual desire), wrong view, and delusion, present at the 12 unwholesome cittas. Thus, the other 47 mental factors become remaining states.
17. States which are both defilement and objects of defilement — same as in nos. 16 above.
18. States which are both defilement and associated with defilement — same as in nos. 16 above.
19. States which are fetters — include the 8 states of fetters (8 as in Dhammasaṅgaṇi), namely, greed, ill-will, conceit, wrong view, doubt, envy, avarice, ignorance. Thus, the other 42 cetasikas become the remaining states.
20. States which are both fetters and objects of fetters — same as in 19. above.
21. States which are both fetters and associated with fetters — same as in nos. 19 above.
22. States which are bonds — include the 3 states of bonds, namely, greed, hatred, and wrong view. Thus, 47 cetasikas become the remaining states.
23. States which are both bonds and objects of bonds — same as in 22. above.
24. States which are both bonds and associated with bonds — include the 2 states of bonds (excluding greed and wrong view present only at the 4 greed-rooted cittas associated with wrong view). Thus, giving 48 cetasikas as the remaining states.
25. States which are raging current — same as defilement in nos. 16 above.
26. States which are both raging current and objects of raging current — same as defilement in nos. 17 above.
27. States which are both raging current and associated with raging current — same as defilement in nos. 18 above.
28. States which are yokes — same as defilement in 16. above.
29. States which are both yokes and objects of yokes — same as defilement in nos. 17 above.
30. States which are both yokes and associated with yokes — same as defilement in nos. 18 above.

XI. Associated and Dissociated from the Aggrouped

31. States which are hindrances — include the 8 states of hindrances, namely, restlessness, greed, hatred, delusion, worry, doubt, sloth, and torpor. Thus, the other 42 cetasikas become the remaining states.
32. States which are both hindrances and objects of hindrances — same as in nos. 31 above.
33. States which are both hindrances and associated with hindrances — same as in nos. 31 above.
34. States which are attachment — include wrong view *cetasika* (*diṭṭhi*), present at the 4 greed-rooted cittas associated with wrong view. Thus, giving 49 cetasikas as the remaining states.
35. States which are both attachment and objects of attachment — same as in nos. 34 above.
36. States which are clinging — include the 2 states of clinging (2, as in Dhammasaṅgaṇi), namely, *kāma* (sensual desire) and *diṭṭhi* (wrong view), as identical to greed-*cetasika* and wrong view-*cetasika*. Thus, the other 48 cetasikas become the remaining states.
37. States which are both clinging and objects of clinging — same as in 63 above.
38. States which are both clinging and associated with clinging — same as in nos. 63 above.
39. States which are corruptions — include the 10 states of corruptions, namely, the 10 cetasikas of greed, hatred, delusion, conceit, wrong view, doubt, sloth, restlessness, shamelessness, and the guiltlessness of conscience. Thus, giving 40 remaining states.
40. States which are both corruptions and objects of corruptions — same as in nos. 39 above.
41. States which are corruptions and are corrupted — same as in nos. 39 above.
42. States which are both corruptions and associated with corruptions — same as in nos. 39 above.

The remaining states of mental factors are shown in chart above. When each of these 30 states is dealt with its remaining states of mental factors, they can be classified under the same aggregate (volitive formation), under the same base (ideation-base), and under the same element (ideation-element).

The analysis and answers for these 30 states of enquiry are the same as the preceding 12 states in nos. 416

Key points from the text :

2 truths, 15 faculties, 11 dependent originations, next 11, 30 kinds from clusters

A Perfect Knowledge of Mind-Body from the Abhidhamma (Dhātukathā)

In the two table below, the number in the brackets represents the number of enquiries which belong to the associated text paragraph nos.

Table 11.1 Summary of the 69 states of enquiry by subject matters

Text's paragraph nos. (with numbers of enquiries):   Subject matter:

Text's paragraph nos.		Subject matter:
419 (2)	2	Truths
410 (2), 411 (4), 412 (1), 413 (8)	15	Faculties
413 (6), 414 (1), 415 (3), 416 (1)	11	Dependent Originations
416 (11)	11	Others
416 (30)	30	Ten dyad-clusters

Total = 69 states

Table 11.2 Summary of the 69 states of enquiry by answers

Text's paragraph nos. (with numbers of enquiries):		Aggregate				Base				Element			
		As	Pas	Ds	Pds	As	Pas	Ds	Pds	As	Pas	Ds	Pds
1. 409 (2), 413 (14), 416 (42)	58	3	1	1	-	1	1	10	1	7	1	10	1
2. 410 (2), 414 (1)	3	-	-	4	-	-	-	1	1	-	-	7	1
3. 411 (4), 415 (3)	7	3	-	1	-	1	1	10	1	7	1	10	1
4. 412 (1)	1	3	-	1	-	1	1	10	1	2	1	15	1

Total = 69 states in 4 kinds of answer   69

CHAPTER 12

XII. Aggrouped and Ungrouped from Associated
(*Sampayuttenasaṅgahitāsaṅgahita*)

Analysis of 120 states from 31 catechism

56 internal states of enquiry

This chapter follows the same 120 states of enquiry from Chapter 9, using the associated states as the basis for classification and unclassification as was first examined in Chapter 1. The guidelines and explanation for association are provided in Chapter 6, while answers can be found in Chapter 9. Note that the text has taken the associations as already included partially associated states. However, I will still include analysis of partially associated states in this chapter.

Matters and *Nibbāna* are excluded from being the states of enquiry in this chapter because the two have no associated states. The states of enquiry are first dealt with to determine the states with which they are associated. The associated states are taken as *these* states. *Those* states (that is, *these* associated states) are then analysed to determine which aggregates, bases and elements they are classified with and not classified with. The answers are categorised as aggrouped and ungrouped, respectively, under the aggregates, bases, and elements. A diagram below describes the flow process and clarifying the relationship between terms like *these* states (1st), *these* states (2nd), and *those* states.

Diagram 12.1. Classification and unclassification based on associated states

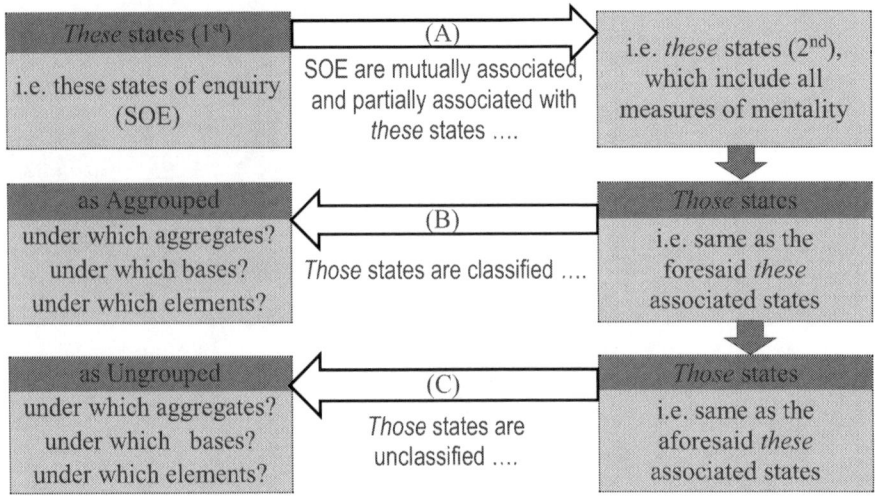

A Perfect Knowledge of Mind-Body from the Abhidhamma (Dhātukathā)

The following abbreviations are used in all the charts and tables throughout this Chapter.

SOE : States of enquiry
cons. : Consciousness
agr. : aggregate
bse : base
el. : element

States of enquiry (SOE):	Associated with *these* states :	Aggrouped agr	bse	el.	Ungrouped agr	bse	el.
417. Feeling aggregate; Perception aggregate; Volitive formation aggregate. (3)	89 cittas, 51 cetasikas	3	2	8	2	10	10

Each of these three states of enquiry is associated with 89 cittas, and 51 cetasikas (52 excluding the respective mental factor of *vedanā, saññā, cetanā*). In another word, each of these mental aggregates is mutually associated with the remaining 3 mental aggregates. The latter, those associated states, are classifiable as aggrouped under 3 aggregates (i.e. the remaining 3 mental aggregates corresponding to each SOE), under 2 bases (ideation-base, mind-base), and under 8 elements (ideation-element, 7 consciousness elements). However, if we were to look at the partially associated states, it would be that each SOE is partially associated with 1 base (ideation-base), with 1 element (ideation-element), and with 51 cetasikas. But in the original text of this chapter, partial association is being combined as one single association. Subtle matters and *Nibbāna* are herein ignored because they are the partially dissociated states.

Thus, those associated states are not classifiable as ungrouped under 2 aggregates (matter, and the respective mental aggregate which is the subject matter in question), under 10 bases (10 gross bases), and under 10 elements (10 gross elements).

Take for example, volitive formation aggregate consists of 50 cetasikas, and together with feeling and perception, these 52 cetasikas accompany the 89 cittas. It is mutually associated with 89 cittas (under consciousness aggregate) and 51 cetasikas (52 excluding volitive-*cetasika*) which also incorporate feeling aggregate and perception aggregate. These associated states are classifiable as aggrouped under 3 aggregates (feeling, perception, consciousness), under 2 bases (ideation-base and mind-base), and under 8 elements (ideation-element and the 7 consciousness elements). Those associated 89 cittas and 52 cetasikas are unclassifiable as ungrouped under 2 aggregates (matter, volitive formation), under 10 bases (10 gross bases), and under 10 elements (10 gross elements).

XII. Aggrouped and Ungrouped from Associated

States of enquiry (SOE):	Associated with *these* states :	Aggrouped agr bse el.			Ungrouped agr bse el.		
418. Consciousness aggregate; Mind base; Eye-consciousness element, Ear-consciousness element; Nose-consciousness element; Tongue-consciousness element; Body-consciousness element; Mind element; Mind consciousness element. (9)	feeling, perception, volitive formation (52 cetasikas)	3	1	1	2	11	17

All these nine subject matters of enquiry come under consciousness aggregate which consists of 89 cittas, accompanied by 52 cetasikas. All these states are taken as under consciousness aggregate so that association can be possible based on aggregates. Herein, consciousness aggregate can not associate with its co-adjunct mind-base and 7 consciousness elements. Consciousness aggregate, or each of these states of enquiry, is thus mutually associated with the remaining 3 mental aggregates, and partially associated with ideation-base, ideation-element, and 52 cetasikas. Those associated states are thus classifiable as aggrouped under 3 aggregates (feeling, perception, volitive formation), under 1 base (ideation-base), and under 1 element (ideation-element). They are unclassifiable as ungrouped under 2 aggregates (matter, consciousness), under 11 bases (10 gross bases, mind-base), and under 17 elements (10 gross elements, 7 consciousness elements).

States of enquiry (SOE):	Associated with *these* states :	Aggrouped agr bse el.			Ungrouped agr bse el.		
419. Origin-truth; Path-truth. (2)	51 and 52 cetasikas	4	2	2	1	10	16

Origin-truth is bound by greed-*cetasika* present at the 8 greed-rooted cittas, and accompanied by the 21 cetasikas (27 excluding feeling, zest, greed, wrong view, conceit, doubt). Path-truth are the 4 supramundane path-consciousness, accompanied by 36 cetasikas. The two truths belong to volitive formation aggregate, are bound up with mind-consciousness element.

Each of these two truths is mutually associated with the remaining 3 mental aggregates, mind-base and mind-consciousness element. Each is partially associated with volitive formation aggregate, ideation-base, ideation-element, and 51 or 52 cetasikas. Those associated states are classifiable as aggrouped under 4 aggregates (4 mental aggregates), under 2 bases (ideation-base, mind-base), and under 2 elements (ideation-element, mind-consciousness element). They are unclassifiable as ungrouped under 1 aggregate (matter), under 10 bases (10 gross bases), and under 16 elements (10 gross elements, eye-cons. element, ear-cons. element, nose-cons. element, tongue-cons. element, body-cons. element, and mind-element).

A Perfect Knowledge of Mind-Body from the Abhidhamma (Dhātukathā)

States of enquiry :	Associated with *these* states :	Aggrouped agr bse el.	Ungrouped agr bse el.
420. Mind-faculty. (1)	feeling, perception, volitive formation	3 1 1	2 11 17

Mind-faculty includes 89 cittas under consciousness aggregate. As the latter can not associate with itself, mind-faculty is thus mutually associated with the other 3 mental aggregates, and partially associated with ideation-base, ideation-element, and 52 cetasikas. Those associated states are classifiable as aggrouped under 3 aggregates (feeling, perception, volitive formation), under 1 base (ideation-base), and under 1 element (ideation-element). They are unclassifiable as ungrouped under 2 aggregates (matter, consciousness), under 11 bases (10 gross bases, mind-base), and under 17 elements (10 gross elements, the 7 consciousness elements).

States of enquiry :	Associated with *these* states :	Aggrouped agr bse el.	Ungrouped agr bse el.
421. Carnal pleasure faculty, Carnal displeasure faculty, Joy faculty, Melancholy faculty. (4)	perception, volitive formation, and consciousness aggregates	3 2 2	2 10 16

These four faculties, together with equanimity-faculty, form the five feeling faculties. So, these four faculties belong to feeling aggregate. Each of these feeling faculties is mutually associated with the other three mental aggregates, mind-base, and body-consciousness-element, while partially associated with feeling aggregate, ideation-base, ideation-element, and 6 cetasikas (7 excluding feeling).

Those associated states are thus classifiable as aggrouped under 3 aggregates (perception, volitive formation, consciousness), under 2 bases (ideation-base, mind-base), and under 2 elements (ideation-element, body-consciousness element). They are unclassifiable as ungrouped under 2 aggregates (matter, feeling), under 10 bases (10 gross bases), and under 16 elements (10 gross elements, the remaining 6 consciousness elements).

States of enquiry (SOE):	Associated with *these* states :	Aggrouped agr bse el.	Ungrouped agr bse el.
422. Equanimity-faculty. (1)	perception, volitive formation, consciousness, 46 cetasikas	3 2 7	2 10 11

Equanimity-faculty is among the 5 faculties of feeling, belong to feeling aggregate. It is mutually associated with the remaining 3 mental aggregates mind-base, 6 consciousness elements (7 excluding body-consciousness element), and partially associated with ideation-base, ideation-element, and 46 cetasikas (which accompany the 55 cittas). Therefore, those associated states are

XII. Aggrouped and Ungrouped from Associated

classifiable as aggrouped under 3 aggregates (perception, volitive formation, consciousness), under 2 bases (ideation-base, mind-base), and under 7 elements (ideation-element, aforesaid 6 consciousness elements). They are unclassifiable as ungrouped under 2 aggregates (matter, feeling), under 10 bases (10 gross bases), and under 11 elements (10 gross elements, body-consciousness element).

States of enquiry (SOE):	Associated with *these* states :	Aggrouped agr bse el.			Ungrouped agr bse el.		
423. Confidence-faculty; Effort-faculty; Mindfulness-faculty; Concentration-faculty; Wisdom-faculty; "I-shall-comprehend-the-unknown" faculty; Higher knowledge faculty; "Final knower" faculty; Ignorance; conditioned by ignorance, Volitive formation. (10)	51 cetasikas, mind-consciousness element	4	2	2	1	10	16

The first eight SOE are part of the 22 controlling faculties while the last two SOE are dependent originations. All these states of enquiry belong to volitive formation, are accompanied by the different 51 cetasikas. They are all bound up with mind-consciousness element. Each of these SOE is associated with the remaining 3 mental aggregates, mind-base, and mind-consciousness-element. Each is partially associated with volitive formation aggregate, ideation-base, ideation-element, and 51 cetasikas.

Those associated states are classifiable as aggrouped under 4 aggregates (feeling, perception, volitive formation, consciousness), under 2 bases (ideation-base, mind-base), under 2 elements (ideation-element, mind-consciousness element). They are unclassifiable as ungrouped under 1 aggregate (matter), under 10 bases (10 gross bases), and under 16 elements (10 gross elements, eye-cons. element, ear-cons. element, nose-cons. element, tongue-cons. element, body-cons. element, mind-element).

States of enquiry (SOE):	Associated with *these* states :	Aggrouped agr bse el.			Ungrouped agr bse el.		
424. Conditioned by formations, is Consciousness. (1)	89 cittas, 52 cetasikas	3	1	1	2	11	17

Consciousness consists of 89 cittas which come under consciousness aggregate, and accompanied by 52 cetasikas. It is mutually associated with the remaining 3 mental aggregates, and partially associated with ideation-base, ideation-element, and 52 cetasikas. Those associated states are classifiable as aggrouped under 3 aggregates (feeling, perception, volitive formation), under 1 base (ideation-base), and under 1 element (ideation-element). They are unclassifiable as ungrouped under 2 aggregates (matter, consciousness), under

A Perfect Knowledge of Mind-Body from the Abhidhamma (Dhātukathā)

11 bases (10 gross bases, mind-base), and under 17 elements (10 gross elements, 7 consciousness elements).

States of enquiry (SOE):	Associated with *these* states :	Aggrouped agr bse el.			Ungrouped agr bse el.		
425. Conditioned by six bases, is Contact. (1)	89 cittas, 51 cetasikas, 7 consciousness elements	4	2	8	1	10	10

Contact is one of the 7 common non-beautiful cetasikas, belongs to volitive formation aggregate. It is present at 89 cittas, accompanied by 51 cetasikas (52 excluding contact-*cetasika*). Contact is thereby mutually associated with the remaining 3 mental aggregates, mind-base, 7 consciousness-elements, and partially associated with volitive formation aggregate, ideation-base, ideation-element, and 51 cetasikas.

The latter are classifiable as aggrouped under 4 aggregates (4 mental aggregates), under 2 bases (ideation-base, mind-base), under 8 elements (ideation-element, 7 consciousness elements). They are unclassifiable as ungrouped under 1 aggregate (matter), under 10 bases (10 gross bases), and under 10 elements (10 gross elements).

States of enquiry (SOE):	Associated with *these* states :	Aggrouped agr bse el.			Ungrouped agr bse el.		
426. Conditioned by contact, is Feeling. (1)	perception, volitive formation, consciousness, 51 cetasikas	3	2	8	2	10	10

Feeling, as amongst the 7 common non-beautiful cetasikas, is present at the 89 cittas and accompanied by 51 cetasikas (52 excluding feeling-*cetasika*). Feeling belongs to feeling aggregate. Thus, it is associated with the remaining 3 mental aggregates, mind-base, 7 consciousness-elements, and partially associated with ideation-base, ideation-element, and 51 cetasikas.

Those remaining states are classifiable as aggrouped under 3 aggregates (perception, volitive formation, consciousness), under 2 bases (ideation-base, mind-base), under 8 elements (ideation-element, 7 consciousness elements). They are unclassifiable as ungrouped under 2 aggregates (matter, feeling), under 10 bases (10 gross bases), and under 10 elements (10 gross elements).

States of enquiry (SOE):	Associated with *these* states :	Aggrouped agr bse el.			Ungrouped agr bse el.		
427. Conditioned by feeling, Craving; Conditioned by craving, Clinging; Action-becoming. (3)	50 and 51 cetasikas, mind-consciousness element	4	2	2	1	10	16

XII. Aggrouped and Ungrouped from Associated

Craving includes greed-*cetasika*, while clinging includes greed-*cetasika* and wrong view-*cetasika*. Both SOE are present at the 8 greed-rooted cittas. Action-becoming (*kammabhava*) includes volition-*cetasika*, present at 17 wholesome cittas and 12 unwholesome cittas. These three SOE belong to volitive formation aggregate, are bound up with mind-consciousness element.

Each of them is mutually associated with the remaining 3 mental aggregates, mind-base, mind-consciousness element, and partially associated with volitive formation aggregate, ideation-base, ideation-element, and 51 cetasikas (50 in the case of clinging). Those associated states are thus classifiable as aggrouped under 4 aggregates (4 mental aggregates), under 2 bases (ideation-base, mind-base), under 2 elements (ideation-element, mind-consciousness element). They are unclassifiable as ungrouped under 1 aggregate (matter), under 10 bases (10 gross bases), and under 16 elements (10 gross elements, the remaining 6 consciousness elements).

States of enquiry (SOE):	Associated with *these* states :	Aggrouped agr bse el.			Ungrouped agr bse el.		
428. Sorrow; Suffering; Melancholy. (3)	51cetasikas, body-consciousness element	3	2	2	2	10	16

These three SOE are grievous feeling associated with two hatred-rooted cittas. They belong to feeling aggregate. In the feeling-faculties, sorrow and suffering belong to bodily displeasure faculty, while melancholy belongs to melancholy-faculty. Each of these SOE is mutually associated with the remaining 3 mental aggregates, mind-base, body-consciousness element, and partially associated with ideation-base, ideation-element, and 51 cetasikas (52 excluding hatred-*cetasika*).

Those associated states are classifiable as aggrouped under 3 aggregates (perception, volitive formation, consciousness), under 2 bases (ideation-base, mind-base), and under 2 elements (body-consciousness element, ideation-element). They are unclassifiable as ungrouped under 2 aggregates (matter, feeling), under 10 bases (10 gross bases), and under 16 elements (10 gross elements, the remaining 6 consciousness elements).

States of enquiry (SOE):	Associated with *these* states :	Aggrouped agr bse el.			Ungrouped agr bse el.		
429. Despair; Foundations of mindfulness; Right strivings. (3)	51 cetasikas, mind-consciousness element	4	2	2	1	10	16

Despair is accompanied occasionally by hatred-*cetasika*. The four foundations of mindfulness are accompanied by mindfulness-*cetasika*. The four right strivings are accompanied by energy-*cetasika*. These three SOE belong to

A Perfect Knowledge of Mind-Body from the Abhidhamma (Dhātukathā)

volitive formation, are bound up with mind-consciousness element. They are associated with the remaining 3 mental aggregates, mind-base, mind-consciousness element, and partially associated with volitive formation aggregate, ideation-base, ideation-element, and 51 cetasikas.

Those remaining states are classifiable as aggrouped under 4 aggregates (4 mental aggregates), under 2 bases (ideation-base, mind-base), under 2 elements (ideation-element, mind-consciousness element). They are unclassifiable as ungrouped under 1 aggregate (matter), under 10 bases (10 gross bases), and under 16 elements (10 gross elements, the remaining 6 consciousness elements).

States of enquiry (SOE):	Associated with *these* states :	Aggrouped agr bse el.	Ungrouped agr bse el.
430. Basis of Psychic Accomplishment. (1)	feeling, perception, volitive formation, 33 cetasikas	3 1 1	2 11 17

These states, having the same acronym as the Four Means to Accomplishment, contain the three cetasikas of energy, desire, and non-delusion. These states consist of 8 x 5 supramundane cittas, accompanied by 33 associated cetasikas. Although these states are classified as aggrouped under consciousness aggregate and volitive formation aggregate (See preceding nos. 73), they are only in partial association with volitive formation aggregate. And therefore, in this case, consciousness is mutually associated with feeling and perception, while partially associated with volitive formation. There are no associations with base and element for consciousness aggregate can not associated with its co-adjunct bases and elements. The SOE is hence partially associated with volitive formation aggregate, ideation-base, ideation-element, and 33 cetasikas

Those associated states are classifiable as aggrouped under 3 aggregates (feeling, perception, volitive formation), under 1 base (ideation-base), under 1 element (ideation-element). They are unclassifiable as ungrouped under 2 aggregates (matter, consciousness), under 11 bases (10 gross bases, mind-base), and under 17 elements (10 gross elements, 7 consciousness elements).

States of enquiry (SOE):	Associated with *these* states :	Aggrouped agr bse el.	Ungrouped agr bse el.
431. Jhāna. (1)	perception, volitive formation, consciousness, varied cetasikas, mind-consciousness element	3 2 2	2 10 16

Jhāna occurs at the 27 sublime cittas, accompanied by different cetasikas (First-*jhāna* with 35 cetasikas, Second-*jhāna* with 34 cetasikas, Third-*jhāna* with 33 cetasikas, Fourth-*jhāna* with 32 cetasikas, Fifth-*jhāna* with 30 cetasikas), and it also presents at the 8 x 5 supramundane cittas accompanied by varied cetasikas. (See Appendix VI, Chart 11).

XII. Aggrouped and Ungrouped from Associated

Jhāna belongs to feeling, and is partially associated with volitive formation. *Jhāna* is thus mutually associated with aggregates of perception and consciousness, while partially associated with volitive formation aggregate. Those associated states are classifiable as aggrouped under 3 aggregates (perception, volitive formation, consciousness), under 2 bases (ideation-base, mind-base), and under 2 elements (ideation-element, mind-consciousness element). They are unclassifiable as ungrouped under 2 aggregates (matter, feeling), under 10 bases (10 gross bases), and under 16 elements (10 gross elements, and the remaining 6 consciousness elements).

States of enquiry (SOE):	Associated with *these* states :	Aggrouped agr bse el.			Ungrouped agr bse el.		
432. The 2 Illimitables; 5 Faculties; 5 Powers; 7 Enlightenment-Factors; Noble Eightfold Path (5)	varied cetasikas, mind-consciousness element	4	2	2	1	10	16

These five states of enquiry are accompanied by different cetasikas (see Table 1.6b). They are closely identified with mind-consciousness element, and are only partially associated with volitive formation aggregate. Thus, each of these states is mutually associated with the remaining 3 mental aggregates, mind-base, mind-consciousness element, while partially associated with volitive formation aggregate, ideation-base, ideation-element, and the respective cetasikas.

Those associated states are classifiable as aggrouped under 4 aggregates (4 mental aggregates), under 2 bases (ideation-base, mind-base), under 2 elements (ideation-element, mind-consciousness element). They are unclassifiable as ungrouped under 1 aggregate (matter), under 10 bases (10 gross bases), and under 16 elements (10 gross elements, the remaining 6 consciousness elements).

States of enquiry (SOE):	Associated with *these* states :	Aggrouped agr bse el.			Ungrouped agr bse el.		
433. Contact; Volition; Attention. (3)	89 cittas, 51 cetasikas, 4 mentallities	4	2	8	1	10	10

Contact is accompanied by *phasso*-cetasika. Volition is accompanied by *cetanā*-cetasika. Attention is accompanied by *manasikāra*-cetasika. The three states of enquiry are among the 7 common non-beautiful cetasikas, present at 89 cittas, accompanied by 51 cetasikas. They belong to volitive formation. The three states of enquiry are thus mutually associated with the remaining 3 mental aggregates, mind-base, 7 consciousness elements, while partially associated with volitive formation aggregate, ideation-base, ideation-element, and the respective 51 cetasikas.

A Perfect Knowledge of Mind-Body from the Abhidhamma (Dhātukathā)

Those associated states are classifiable as aggrouped under 4 aggregates (4 mental aggregates), under 2 bases (ideation-base, mind-base), under 8 elements (ideation-element, 7 consciousness elements). They are unclassifiable as ungrouped under 1 aggregate (matter), under 10 bases (10 gross bases), and under 10 elements (10 gross elements).

States of enquiry (SOE):	Associated with *these* states :	Aggrouped agr bse el.	Ungrouped agr bse el.
434. Feeling; Perception. (2)	89 cittas, 51 cetasikas	3 2 8	2 10 10

Feeling is accompanied by feeling-*cetasika*. Perception is accompanied by perception-*cetasika*. These two states are among the 7 common non-beautiful cetasikas, present at 89 cittas, each accompanied by 51 cetasikas. For example, when perception as a state of enquiry is dealt with, it is mutually associated with the remaining 3 mental aggregates, mind-base, 7 consciousness elements, while partially associated with perception aggregate, ideation-base, ideation-element, and 51 cetasikas.

Hence, those associated states are classifiable as aggrouped under 3 aggregates (feeling, volitive formation, consciousness), under 2 bases (ideation-base, mind-base), under 8 elements (ideation-element, 7 consciousness elements). They are unclassifiable as ungrouped under 2 aggregates (matter, perception), under 10 bases (10 gross bases), and under 10 elements (10 gross elements). The feeling cetasika is to be analysed in the similar manner.

States of enquiry (SOE):	Associated with *these* states :	Aggrouped agr bse el.	Ungrouped agr bse el.
435. Consciousness. (1)	52 cetasikas, the remaining 3 mentalities	3 1 1	2 11 17

Consciousness consists of 89 cittas, is accompanied by 52 cetasikas. So, it is associated with the remaining 3 mental aggregates. Consciousness can not associate with itself and its own co-adjuncts. Hence, those associated states are classifiable as aggrouped under 3 aggregates (feeling, perception, volitive formation), under 1 base (ideation-base), under 1 element (ideation-element). They are unclassifiable as ungrouped under 2 aggregates (matter, consciousness), under 11 bases (10 gross bases, mind-base), and under 17 elements (10 gross elements, 7 consciousness elements).

States of enquiry (SOE):	Associated with *these* states :	Aggrouped agr bse el.	Ungrouped agr bse el.
436. Decision. (1)	50 cetasikas, 4 mentalities	4 2 3	1 10 15

XII. Aggrouped and Ungrouped from Associated

Decision is contained in 78 cittas (see Appendix VI, Chart 7), and accompanied by 50 cetasikas (52 excluded *vicikicchā* and *adhimokkha*). Decision belongs to volitive formation, is mutually associated with feeling, perception, and consciousness. It is only partially associated with volitive formation. Decision is therefore mutually associated with the remaining 3 mental aggregates, mind-element, mind-consciousness element, and partially associated with volitive formation aggregate, ideation-base, ideation-element, and 50 cetasikas.

Those associated states are classifiable as aggrouped under 4 aggregates (4 mental aggregates), 2 bases (ideation-base, mind-base), and 3 elements (mind-element, ideation-element, mind-consciousness element). They are unclassifiable as ungrouped under 1 aggregate (matter), under 10 bases (10 gross bases), and under 15 elements (10 gross elements, eye-cons. element, ear-cons. element, nose-cons. element, tongue-cons. element, body-cons. element).

8 states of enquiry from Dhammasaṅgaṇīmātikā triads

437. States of enquiry (SOE):	Associated with *these* states :	Aggrouped agr bse el.	Ungrouped agr bse el.
1. States associated with happy feeling.	feeling		
2. States associated with painful feeling.	feeling		
3. States associated with neither happy feeling nor suffering feeling.	feeling		
4. States with initial application and sustained application.	volitive formation	1 1 1	4 11 17
5. States without initial application but with sustained application.	volitive formation		
6. States accompanied by zest.	volitive formation		
7. States accompanied by happiness.	feeling		
8. States accompanied by equanimity.	feeling		

All these 8 states of enquiry are accompanied by varied cetasikas. The 1st, 2nd, 3rd, 7th, and 8th SOE come under perception, volitive formation, and consciousness aggregates. Each of them is associated with feeling aggregate, and partially associated with ideation-base, ideation-element, and the respective cetasikas. Thus, those associated states are classifiable as aggrouped under 1 aggregate (feeling), under 1 base (ideation-base), and under 1 element (ideation-element). They are unclassifiable as ungrouped under 4 aggregates (matter, perception, volitive formation, consciousness), under 11 bases (10 gross bases, mind-base), and under 17 elements (10 gross elements, 7 consciousness elements).

A Perfect Knowledge of Mind-Body from the Abhidhamma (Dhātukathā)

The 4th, 5th, and 6th SOE belong to 4 mental aggregates, and so there are no associations. Because of their associated cetasikas, these three states are partially associated with volitive formation, ideation-base, ideation-element, and the 50, 37, or 46 cetasikas depending on which SOE is under enquiry. Thus, those associated states are classifiable as aggrouped under 1 aggregate (volitive formation), under 1 base (ideation-base), and under 1 element (ideation-element). They are unclassifiable as ungrouped under 4 aggregates (matter, feeling, perception, consciousness), under 11 bases (10 gross bases, mind-base), and under 17 elements (10 gross elements, 7 consciousness elements).

56 states of enquiry from Dhammasaṅgaṇīmātikā dyads

States of enquiry (SOE):	Associated with *these* states :	Aggrouped agr bse el.	Ungrouped agr bse el.
438. States which are root causes (*hetū*); States which are root causes and also having root causes; States which are root causes and also associated with root causes. (3)	4 mentalities, mind-consciousness element	4 2 2	1 10 16

States which are root causes are concerned with the 6 root causes of greed, hatred, delusion, non-greed, non-hatred, non-delusion. The next two SOE are concerned with same 6 root causes, and excluding delusion present only at the 2 delusion-rooted cittas. All three SOE belong to volitive formation. Each of them is mutually associated with the remaining 3 mental aggregates, mind-base, and mind-consciousness element, while partially associated with volitive formation aggregate, ideation-base, and ideation-element.

Those associated states are thus classifiable as aggrouped under 4 aggregates (4 mental aggregates), 2 bases (ideation-base, mind-base), and 2 elements (ideation-element, mind-consciousness element). They are unclassifiable as ungrouped under 1 aggregate (matter), under 10 bases (10 gross bases), and under 16 elements (10 gross elements, and the remaining 6 consciousness elements).

States of enquiry (SOE):	Associated with *these* states :	Aggrouped agr bse el.	Ungrouped agr bse el.
439. States which are not root causes but having root causes; States which are not root causes but are associated with root causes; States which are not root causes but have associated root causes (*na hetusahetukehi*) (3)	volitive formation, 46 cetasikas	1 1 1	4 11 17

301

XII. Aggrouped and Ungrouped from Associated

These three states of enquiry, all of which are not root causes, consist of 71 cittas, accompanied by 46 cetasikas (52 excluding the 6 roots causes). These states belong to 4 mental aggregates, and so there are no direct associations. Because of their associated cetasikas, these three states are partially associated with volitive formation aggregate, ideation-base, ideation-element, and 46 cetasikas.

Thus, those associated states are classifiable as aggrouped under 1 aggregate (volitive formation), under 1 base (ideation-base), and under 1 element (ideation-element). They are unclassifiable as ungrouped under 4 aggregates (matter, feeling, perception, consciousness), under 11 bases (10 gross bases, mind-base), and under 17 elements (10 gross elements, 7 consciousness elements).

States of enquiry (SOE):	Associated with *these* states :	Aggrouped agr bse el.			Ungrouped agr bse el.		
440. States which are defilement (*āsava*); States which are both defilement and objects of defilement; States which are defilement and also associated with defilement. (3)	4 mentalities, mind-consciousness element	4	2	2	1	10	16

These three states of enquiries contain the 3 defilement factors of greed (or sensual desire), wrong view, and delusion, they belong to volitive formation, are bound up with mind-consciousness element. Each of them is mutually associated with the remaining 3 mental aggregates, mind-base, mind-consciousness element, and is partially associated with volitive formation aggregate, ideation-base, ideation-element, and 52 or 26 cetasikas. (States which are objects of defilement contain 52 cetasikas, while states associated with defilement are followed by 26 cetasikas).

Those associated states are classifiable as aggrouped under 4 aggregates (4 mental aggregates), 2 bases (ideation-base, mind-base), and 2 elements (ideation-element, mind-consciousness element). They are unclassifiable as ungrouped under 1 aggregate (matter), under 10 bases (10 gross bases), and under 16 elements (10 gross elements, and remaining 6 consciousness elements).

States of enquiry (SOE):	Associated with *these* states :	Aggrouped agr bse el.			Ungrouped agr bse el.		
441. States which are associated with defilement but are not defilement. (1)	volitive formation in partial association, 24 cetasikas	1	1	1	4	11	17

These states are accompanied by 24 cetasikas (27 excluding 3 factors of defilement, namely, greed or sensual desire, wrong view, and delusion), which are present at the 12 unwholesome cittas. These states belong to 4 mental

A Perfect Knowledge of Mind-Body from the Abhidhamma (Dhātukathā)

aggregates, and so there are no mutual associations. Because of their associated cetasikas, these states are partially associated with volitive formation, ideation-base, ideation-element, and 24 cetasikas.

Those associated states are classifiable as aggrouped under 1 aggregate (volitive formation), under 1 base (ideation-base), and under 1 element (ideation-element). They are unclassifiable as ungrouped under 4 aggregates (matter, feeling, perception, consciousness), under 11 bases (10 gross bases, mind-base), and under 17 elements (10 gross elements, 7 consciousness elements).

442. States of enquiry (SOE):	Associated with *these* states :	Aggrouped agr bse el.			Ungrouped agr bse el.		
Repeats the same from preceding *Defilement* cluster (nos. 440) for *Fetters, Bonds, Raging Current, Yokes,* and *Hindrances.* Altogether 15 SOE (3 x 5 = 15). no. 1. to 15.	4 mentalities, mind-cons. element	4	2	2	1	10	16
Repeats the same from preceding *Defilement* cluster (nos. 441) for *Fetters, Bonds, Raging Current, Yokes,* and *Hindrances.* Altogether 5 SOE (1 x 5 = 5). no. 16. to 20.	volitive formation in partial association	1	1	1	4	11	17
21. States which are *Attachment (parāmāsa).* 22. States which are both attachment and objects of attachment.	4 mentalities, mind-cons. element	4	2	2	1	10	16

Those 17 states (no. 1 to 15, 21, 22 in the above chart) have similar answers as in nos. 440. They all belong to volitive formation aggregate. The three states from each of the five clusters (no. 1 to 15) consist of different cetasikas. Each of these 17 states is mutually associated with the remaining 3 mental aggregates, mind-base, mind-consciousness element, and partially associated with volitive formation aggregate, ideation-base, ideation-element, and the respective cetasikas. (See Table 1.8.4 to Table 1.8.6). Those associated states are classifiable as aggrouped under 4 aggregates (4 mental aggregates), 2 bases (ideation-base, mind-base), and 2 elements (ideation-element, mind-consciousness element). They are unclassifiable as ungrouped under 1 aggregate (matter), under 10 bases (10 gross bases), and under 16 elements (10 gross elements, and the remaining 6 consciousness elements).

Those 5 states (no. 16 to 20 in the above chart) belong to 4 mental aggregates, but each of them has different cetasikas. (See nos. 346, and Table 1.8.4 to Table 1.8.6). They have the same answers as in nos. 441.

XII. Aggrouped and Ungrouped from Associated

States of enquiry (SOE):	Associated with *these* states :	Aggrouped agr bse el.			Ungrouped agr bse el.		
443. States which are associated with attachment. (1)	volitive formation, 20 cetasikas	1	1	1	4	11	17

These states consist of the 4 greed-rooted cittas with wrong view, and 20 cetasikas (27 excluding wrong view, conceit hatred, envy, avarice, worry, doubt). They encompass the 4 mental aggregates, and so there are no direct associations. They are partially associated with volitive formation aggregate, ideation-base, ideation-element, and 20 cetasikas.

Those associated states are classifiable as aggrouped under 1 aggregate (volitive formation), under 1 base (ideation-base), and under 1 element (ideation-element). They are unclassifiable as ungrouped under 4 aggregates (matter, feeling, perception, consciousness), under 11 bases (10 gross bases, mind-base), and under 17 elements (10 gross elements, 7 consciousness elements).

States of enquiry (SOE):	Associated with *these* states :	Aggrouped agr bse el.			Ungrouped agr bse el.		
444. States which are consciousness. (1)	89 cittas, remaining 3 mentalities	3	1	1	2	11	17

Consciousness consists of 89 cittas, is accompanied by 52 cetasikas. It is mutually associated with the remaining 3 mental aggregates, and partially associated with ideation-base, ideation-element, and 52 cetasikas. Those associated states are classifiable as aggrouped under 3 aggregates (feeling, perception, volitive formation), under 1 base (ideation-base), under 1 element (ideation-element). They are unclassifiable as ungrouped under 2 aggregates (matter, consciousness), under 11 bases (10 gross bases, mind-base), and under 17 elements (10 gross elements, 7 consciousness elements).

States of enquiry (SOE):	Associated with *these* states :	Aggrouped agr bse el.			Ungrouped agr bse el.		
445. States which are mental factors; States associated with consciousness; States conjoined with consciousness; States both conjoined with and originated from consciousness; States conjoined with, originated from, and arise concurrently with consciousness; States conjoined with, originated from, and arise consecutively with consciousness. (6)	consciousness	1	1	7	4	11	11

A Perfect Knowledge of Mind-Body from the Abhidhamma (Dhātukathā)

All these states of enquiry are referring to the 52 cetasikas. Thus, these states are in total association with consciousness aggregate. There are no partial associations because the 52 cetasikas are all included as states of enquiry. The associated states are classifiable as aggrouped under 1 aggregates (consciousness), 1 bases (mind-base), and 7 elements (the 7 consciousness elements). They are unclassifiable as ungrouped under 4 aggregates (matter, feeling, perception, volitive formation), under 11 bases (10 gross bases, mind-base), and under 11 elements (10 gross elements, ideation-element).

446.	States of enquiry (SOE):	Associated with *these* states :	Aggrouped agr bse el.			Ungrouped agr bse el.		
1.	States which are clinging (*upādinnā*).							
2.	States which are both clinging and objects of clinging.	4 mentalities, mind-cons. element	4	2	2	1	10	16
3.	States which are both clinging and associated with clinging.							
4.	States which are associated with clinging but are not clinging.	volitive formation in partial association	1	1	1	4	11	17
5.	States which are corruptions.							
6.	States which are both corruptions and objects of corruptions.	4 mentalities, mind-cons. element	4	2	2	1	10	16
7.	States both are corruptions & corrupted.							
8.	States which are both corruptions and associated with corruptions.							

The 1st, 2nd, and 3rd SOE correspond to greed and wrong view (present at the 4 greed-rooted cittas, accompanied by greed and associated with wrong view). The 5th, 6th, 7th, and 8th SOE are the 10 states of corruptions (greed, hatred, delusion, conceit, wrong view, doubt, sloth, restlessness, shamelessness, guiltlessness of conscience). These eight states all belong to volitive formation. These states are either clingings or corruptions per se, are unwholesome states bound up with mind-consciousness element.

Each of these 7 SOE is associated with 3 mental aggregates (feeling, perception, consciousness), mind-base, mind-consciousness element, and is partially associated with volitive formation aggregate, ideation-base, ideation-element, and the respective cetasikas. (See Table 1.8.9 and Table 1.8.10 regarding their associated cetasikas). These associated states are classifiable as aggrouped under 4 aggregates (4 mental aggregates), 2 bases (ideation-base, mind-base), 2 elements (ideation-element, mind-consciousness element).

The 4th SOE consists of 8 greed-rooted cittas, accompanied by 20 cetasikas (27 excluding hatred, envy, avarice, worry, doubt, and the 2 states of clinging,

XII. Aggrouped and Ungrouped from Associated

i.e. sensual desire and wrong view) — it belongs to 4 mental aggregates. As such, there are no direct associations. Because of arisen cetasikas, they are partially associated with volitive formation aggregate, ideation-base, ideation-element, and 20 cetasikas. These associated states are classifiable and taken as aggrouped under 1 aggregate (volitive formation), 1 base (ideation-base), and 1 element (ideation-element). They are unclassifed, and taken as ungrouped under 1 aggregate (matter), under 10 bases (10 gross bases), and under 17 elements (10 gross elements, 7 consciousness elements).

447. States of enquiry (SOE):	Associated with *these* states :	Aggrouped agr bse el.	Ungrouped agr bse el.
1. States which are corrupted but are not corruptions.	volitive formation		
2. States which are associated with corruptions but are not corruptions.	volitive formation		
3. States with initial application.	volitive formation	1 1 1	4 11 17
4. States with sustained application.	volitive formation		
5. States with zest.	volitive formation		
6. States accompanied by zest.	volitive formation		
7. States accompanied by happiness.	feeling		
8. States accompanied by equanimity.	feeling		

The 1st and 2nd SOE are 12 unwholesome cittas, accompanied by 17 cetasikas (27 excluding the 10 factors of corruptions). The 3rd and 4th SOE consist of 55 cittas, accompanied by 50 cetasikas. The 5th and 6th SOE are from 51 cittas, accompanied by 45 cetasikas (excluded hatred, envy, avarice, worry, sloth, torpor, doubt).

These first 6 SOE have no associations because they belong to 4 mental aggregates. Because of their associated cetasikas, they are partially associated with volitive formation aggregate. Thus, the latter are classifiable and taken as aggrouped under 1 aggregate (volitive formation), under 1 base (ideation-base), and under 1 element (ideation-element). They are unclassifiable as ungrouped under 4 aggregates (matter, feeling, perception, consciousness), under 11 bases (10 gross bases, mind-base), and under 17 elements (10 gross elements, 7 consciousness elements).

The 7th SOE contains 63 cittas, accompanied by 46 cetasikas (52 excluding feeling, hatred, envy, avarice, worry, doubt). The states are bound up with body-consciousness element and mind-consciousness element. The 8th SOE consists of 55 cittas accompanied by equanimity, and have 46 cetasikas (52 excluding feeling, zest, hatred, envy, avarice, and worry). The states are bound up with 6 consciousness elements (without body-consciousness element).

The 7th & 8th SOE come under the 3 mental aggregates of perception, volitive formation, and consciousness. Hence, each of these SOE is mutually associated with feeling aggregate, and is only partially associated with ideation-base, ideation-element, and 44 or 46 cetasikas depending which SOE is dealt with. These associated states are classifiable and taken as aggrouped under 1 aggregate (feeling), under 1 base (ideation-base), and under 1 element (ideation-element). They are unclassifiable as ungrouped under 4 aggregates (matter, perception, volitive formation, consciousness), under 11 bases (10 gross bases, mind-base), and under 17 elements (10 gross elements, 7 consciousness elements).

Key points from the text :

4 mental aggregates (ideation-base and mind-base), 7 consciousness elements,
2 Truths, 14 faculties, 12 dependent originations, the next 17;
8 triads, 43 clusters, 7 intermediate dyads, 6 last dyads.

XII. Aggrouped and Ungrouped from Associated

With reference to the following two tables, the numbers in the brackets represent the numbers of enquiries belong to the respective text paragraph nos.

Table 12.1 Total 120 states of enquiry by subject matters

Subject matter:		Text's paragraph nos. (with the numbers of enquiries) :
Mental aggregates	3	417 (3)
Elements	9	418 (9)
Truths	2	419 (2)
Faculties	14	420 (1), 421 (4), 422 (1), 423 (8)
Dependent Originations	11	423 (2), 424 (1), 425 (1), 426 (1), 427 (3), 429 (3)
Miscellaneous	17	429 (3), 430 (1), 431 (1), 432 (5), 433 (3), 434 (2), 435 (1), 436 (1)
Triads	8	437 (8)
Dyad-clusters	41	438 (3), 439 (3), 440 (3), 441 (1), 442 (22), 443 (1), 446 (8)
Intermediate dyads	10	444 (1), 445 (6), 447 (3)
Last dyads	5	447 (5)

Total = 120 states

Table 12.2 Total 120 states of enquiry by answers

Text's paragraph nos. (with numbers of enquiries):		Aggrouped			Ungrouped		
		agr	bse	el.	agr	bse	el.
417 (3), 426 (1), 434 (2)	6	3	2	8	2	10	10
418 (9), 420 (1), 424 (1), 430 (1), 435 (1), 444 (1)	14	3	1	1	2	11	17
419 (2), 423 (10), 427 (3), 429 (3), 432 (5), 438 (3), 440 (3), 442 (17), 446 (7)	53	4	2	2	1	10	16
421 (4), 428 (3), 431 (1)	8	3	2	2	2	10	16
422 (1)	1	3	2	7	2	10	11
425 (1), 433 (3)	4	4	2	8	1	10	10
436 (1)	1	4	2	3	1	10	15
437 (8), 439 (3), 441 (1), 442 (5), 443 (1), 446 (1), 447 (8)	27	1	1	1	4	11	17
445 (6)	6	1	1	7	4	11	11

Total = 120 states in 9 kinds of answer

CHAPTER 13

XIII. Associated and Dissociated from Ungrouped
(*Asaṅgahitenasampayuttavippayutta*)

Analysis of 130 states from 8 catechism

The method in this chapter examines 3 steps. In the first step, each state of enquiry is dealt with the remaining states of comparison, with which they can not be classified under the same aggregate, under the same element, and under the same element as examined in Chapter 5. It is useful at the same time to also ascertain that each state of enquiry with its co-adjunct states are hereby unclassified as ungrouped under which aggregates, bases, and elements, although the text does not specifically mention this. This part was analysed in Chapter 5. The second and third step are the respective association and dissociation of states when those unclassified remaining states are ascertained with respect to each state of enquiry which includes its co-adjunct states and other possible states taken as a whole.

Let's rewind a little to Chapter 5. The states of comparison are "delimited" not only by the states of enquiry, but also by their "co-adjunct states" and "possible states", all of which may be conforming with the aforesaid condition for classification. For instance, matter aggregate as the state of enquiry delimits other states as co-adjuncts and possible states because the 16 subtle matters of 28 matters fall in with ideation-base and ideation-element which can be so classified. Ideation-base and ideation-element encompass 3 mental aggregates which can also be classified, thereby become possible states to matter aggregate. Rules and guidelines as to compliance with association/partial association and dissociation/partial dissociation are explained in Chapter 6.

Total 130 states of enquiry form the subject matters in this chapter. These 130 states are drawn from the 257 in Chapter 5. States which are left out from this chapter include the 10 gross bases, 10 gross elements, 4 mental aggregates, 7 consciousness elements, etc. The reason is that these states consist of various remaining states which fall outside the prescribed condition for classification under the same aggregate, under the same element, and under the same element, and those unclassified remaining states are not in total association with other states nor in total dissociation from other states. States which contain five aggregates like origin-truth, four noble truths, etc. are also excluded.

A simple diagram is drawn below to illustrate these kinds of relationship and the flow process.

XIII. Associated and Dissociated from Ungrouped

Diagram 13.1. Association and dissociation based on ungrouped result

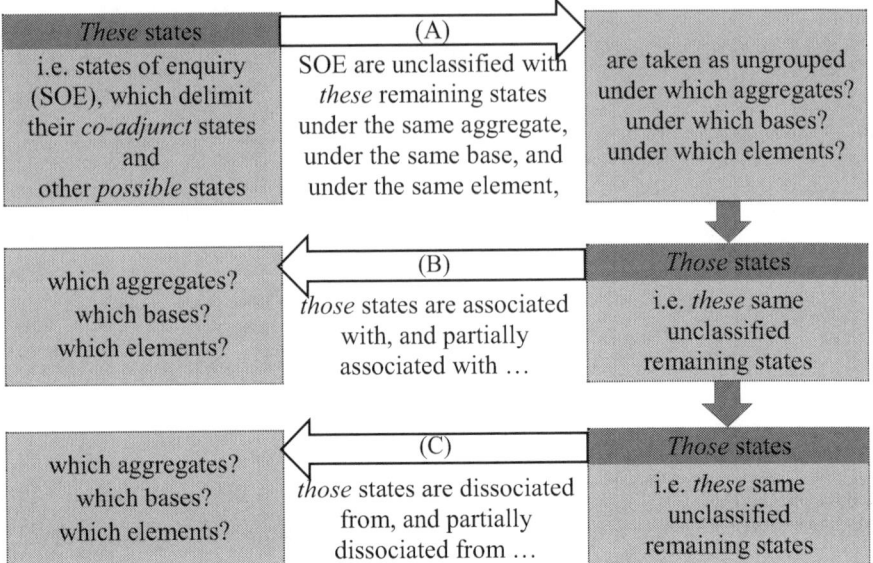

Abbreviations below are used in all the charts and tables in this Chapter.

SOE	: States of enquiry
M.	: Matters
F.	: Feeling aggregate
P.	: Perception aggregate
V.	: Volitive formation aggregate
N.	: *Nibbāna*
Sb	: subtle matters
Gr	: gross matters
cons.	: consciousness
agr	: aggregate
As	: Associated
Pas	: Partially associated
Ds	: Dissociated
Pds	: Partially dissociated

16 internal states of enquiry

This symbol ǂ is used in all the following charts. It denotes that the states of enquiry (SOE) are not classified with the remaining states of comparison under the same aggregate, under the same base, and under the same element.

A Perfect Knowledge of Mind-Body from the Abhidhamma (Dhātukathā)

448. States of enquiry :	‡ Those remaining states						Aggregate				Base				Element			
	M.	F.	P.	V.	N.	C.	As	Pas	Ds	Pds	As	Pas	Ds	Pds	As	Pas	Ds	Pds
Matter aggregate (1)					1		3	-	1	-	-	1	10	1	-	1	10	1

Because subtle matters of 28 matters, and *Nibbāna* are co-adjunct with ideation-base and ideation-element, and the latter contain also the aggregates of feeling, perception and volitive formation which become possible state to matters, the remaining states to matter aggregate therefore come under consciousness aggregate. Matter aggregate can not be classified with these remaining states (consciousness aggregate) under the same aggregate, under the same base, and under the same element. SOE and its co-adjunct states are thereby taken as ungrouped under 1 aggregate (matter), under 11 bases (10 gross bases, ideation-base), and under 11 elements (10 gross elements, ideation-element). Ideation-base and ideation-element are included because they contain 16 subtle matters.

Consciousness aggregate as unclassified remaining states, is mutually associated with the remaining 3 mental aggregates (feeling, perception, and volitive formation). Because consciousness aggregate can not associate with itself, it therefore also can not associate with its co-adjuncts of mind-base and 7 consciousness-elements. Consciousness aggregate is partially associated with 1 base (ideation-base), with 1 element (ideation-element), and with 52 cetasikas. It is dissociated from 1 aggregate (12 gross matters), 10 bases (10 gross bases), and 10 elements (10 gross elements). It is partially dissociated from 1 base (ideation-base), 1 element (ideation-element), 16 subtle matters, and *Nibbāna*.

449. States of enquiry :	‡ Those remaining states						Aggregate				Base				Element			
	M.	F.	P.	V.	N.	C.	As	Pas	Ds	Pds	As	Pas	Ds	Pds	As	Pas	Ds	Pds
1. Ideation-base.						1												
2. Ideation-element.						1												
3. Femininity-faculty.						1												
4. Masculinity-faculty.						1												
5. Vitality-faculty.						1												
6. Conditioned by Cons., is Mind-Matter.						1	3	-	1	-	-	1	10	1	-	1	10	1
7. Non-perception becoming.						1												
8. Single-aggregate becoming.						1												
9. Birth.						1												
10. Ageing.						1												
11. Death.						1												

XIII. Associated and Dissociated from Ungrouped

Both ideation-base and ideation-element include the aggregates of feeling, perception, and volitive formation, also subtle matters and *Nibbāna*. The male and female faculties belong to subtle matters. Vitality-faculty has both physical and mental life, and it comes under subtle matters and volitive formation aggregate. Mind-matter are bound by matters and 3 mental aggregates (without consciousness aggregate). Thus, the remaining states are only the consciousness aggregate. Each of these SOE cannot be classified with consciousness aggregate under the same aggregate, under the same base, and under the same element. For example, each of the first 5 SOE and its co-adjuncts are unclassified, and taken as ungrouped under 4 aggregates (subtle matters, feeling, perception, volitive formation), 1 bases (ideation-base), and 1 elements (ideation-element). Mind-Matter is taken as ungrouped under 4 aggregates (28 matters, feeling, perception, volitive formation), 11 bases (10 gross bases, ideation-base), and 11 elements (10 gross elements, ideation-element).

Non-perception becoming and single-aggregate becoming belong to gross visible object, are associated with the ninefold vitality-group. Vitality consists of subtle matters and volitive formation, is contained by ideation-base. Although birth, ageing and death also contains concretely produced subtle matters and volitive formation, they all come under gross visible object. And so, aggregates of feeling, perception, and volitive formation become possible states which can be so classified. Consciousness aggregate and *Nibbāna* are therefore taken as the classifiable remaining states. Each of these SOE can not be classified with consciousness aggregate under the same aggregate, under the same base, and under the same element. Each of them is taken as ungrouped under 1 aggregate (matter), under 2 bases (eye-base, visible object base), and under 2 elements (eye-element, visible object element).

On the other side, consciousness aggregate is mutually associated with the remaining 3 mental aggregates (feeling, perception, volitive formation). It has no association with base and element for it can not associate with its co-adjunct mind-base and 7 consciousness-elements. Consciousness aggregate is partially associated with 1 base (ideation-base), 1 element (ideation-element), and 52 cetasikas. It is dissociated from 1 aggregate (12 gross matters), 10 bases (10 gross bases), and 10 elements (10 gross elements). It is partially dissociated from 1 base (ideation-base), 1 element (ideation-element), 16 subtle matters, and *Nibbāna*.

A Perfect Knowledge of Mind-Body from the Abhidhamma (Dhātukathā)

450. States of enquiry :	‡ Those remaining states						Aggregate				Base				Element			
	M.	F.	P.	V.	N.	C.	As	Pas	Ds	Pds	As	Pas	Ds	Pds	As	Pas	Ds	Pds
1. Immaterial-becoming.	Gr						-	-	4	-	-	-	1	1	-	-	7	1
2. Neither perception nor non-perception becoming.																		
3. Four-aggregate becoming.																		
4. Four Basis of Psychic Accomplishment.																		

These 4 SOE originate from different cittas and accompanied by different cetasikas. (See Table 1.6a). They are included under subtle matters and 4 mental aggregates. So, gross matters become the only remaining states. These states of enquiry can not be classified with gross matters under the same aggregate, under the same base, and under the same element. The SOE are unclassified, and taken as ungrouped under 4 aggregates excluding *Nibbāna* (feeling, perception, volitive formation, consciousness), under 2 bases (ideation-base, mind-base), and under 2 elements (ideation-element, mind-consciousness element).

Because unclassified remaining states are gross materiality, they have no associations. Gross materiality is dissociated from 4 aggregates (4 mental aggregates), 1 base (mind-base), and 7 elements (7 consciousness-elements). Gross materiality is partially dissociated from 1 base (ideation-base), 1 element (ideation-element), and 52 cetasikas. Subtle matters, being part of materiality, is not herein partially dissociated. *Nibbāna* is ignored because materiality is neither associated with, nor dissociated from *Nibbāna*.

41 states of enquiry from Dhammasaṅgaṇīmātikā triads

451. States of enquiry :	‡ Those remaining states						Aggregate				Base				Element			
	M.	F.	P.	V.	N.	C.	As	Pas	Ds	Pds	As	Pas	Ds	Pds	As	Pas	Ds	Pds
1. Wholesome states.	28				1													
2. Unwholesome states.	28				1													
3. States associated with happy feeling.	28	1			1													
4. States associated with painful feeling.	28	1			1		all with the same answers											
5. States associated with neither happy feeling nor painful feeling.	28	1			1		-	-	4	-	-	-	1	1	-	-	7	1
6. Resultant states.	28				1													
7. Resultant-producing states	28				1													

XIII. Associated and Dissociated from Ungrouped

	‡ Those remaining states					Aggregate				Base				Element			
	M.	F.	P.	V.	N.C.	As	Pas	Ds	Pds	As	Pas	Ds	Pds	As	Pas	Ds	Pds
8. States neither are the result of clinging nor favourable to clinging.	12				1												
9. States which are corrupted and are objects of corruption.	28				1												
10. States which are not corrupted and not objects of corruptions.	28																
11. States with initial application and sustained application.	28				1												
12. States without initial application but with sustained application.	28				1												
13. States accompanied by zest.	28				1												
14. States accompanied by happiness.	28	*1*			1												
15. States accompanied by equanimity.	28	*1*			1				all with the same answers								
16. States eliminated by first Path.	28				1	-	-	4	-	-	-	1	1	-	-	7	1
17. States eliminated by higher three Paths.	28				1												
18. States with root causes eliminated by 1st Path.	28				1												
19. States with root causes eliminated by higher three Paths.	28				1												
20. States which lead to death and rebirth.	28				1												
21. States lead to *Nibbāna*	28				1												
22. States appertaining to Learners (*sekhā*).	28				1												
23. States appertaining to Arahatta (*asekhā*).	28				1												
24. Sublime states.	28				1												
25. Immeasurable states.	28				1												
26. States with limited objects.	28				1												
27. States with sublime objects.	28				1												

A Perfect Knowledge of Mind-Body from the Abhidhamma (Dhātukathā)

	‡ Those remaining states					Aggregate				Base				Element			
	M.	F.	P.	V.	N.C.	As	Pas	Ds	Pds	As	Pas	Ds	Pds	As	Pas	Ds	Pds
28. States with immeasurable objects.	28				1												
29. Inferior states	28				1												
30. Superior states.	28				1												
31. States fixed in destinies because of wrong views.	28				1												
32. States fixed in destinies ... right views	28				1												
33. States with Path object.	28				1												
34. States conditioned by the Path.	28				1			all with the same answers									
35. States having Path as the predominant factor.	28				1	-	-	4	-	-	-	1	1	-	-	7	1
36. States with past object.	28				1												
37. States with future object.	28				1												
38. States with present object.	28				1												
39. States with internal object.	28				1												
40. States with external object.	28				1												
41. States with both internal and external objects.	28				1												

The italicised *1* marked in the chart above is indicated as those possible states of classification under the same aggregate, under the same base, and under the same element.

Each of these 41 SOE can not be classified with the remaining states under the same aggregate, under the same base, and under the same element. Each SOE would be taken as ungrouped under the different aggregates, bases and elements. The analysis and answers to these 41 states of enquiry with regard to unclassification under the three categories are given in Chapter 5. Please refer to the explanatory notes for Chart 5.13 under nos. 210 in Chapter 5 regarding these 41 states of enquiry.

Since all those remaining states are invariably materiality and *Nibbāna*, there are no associations nor partial associations. Those remaining states are dissociated from 4 aggregates (the 4 mental aggregates), 1 base (mind-base), and 7 elements (7 consciousness-elements). They are partially dissociated from 1

XIII. Associated and Dissociated from Ungrouped

base (ideation-base), and 1 element (ideation-element), and 52 cetasikas. The answers are the same for all 41 states.

The following are not from the original text of this chapter, which are the two cases of association and dissociation based on the classification of these 41 states. They have been examined in Chapter 6 but are consolidated into one chart below to assist in comparison and comprehending how these answers correlate with those answers from same 41 states as analysed in nos. 451 above.

States of enquiry (SOE):	Classified under:						Aggregate				Base				Element			
	M.	F.	P.	V.	N.	C.	As	Pas	Ds	Pds	As	Pas	Ds	Pds	As	Pas	Ds	Pds
1. Wholesome states.	•	•	•			•	-	-	1	-	-	-	10	1	-	-	16	1
2. Unwholesome states.	•	•	•			•	-	-	1	-	-	-	10	1	-	-	16	1
3. States associated with happy feeling.			•	•		•	1	-	1	-	-	1	10	1	-	1	15	1
4. States associated with painful feeling.			•	•		•	1	-	1	-	-	1	10	1	-	1	15	1
5. States associated with neither happy feeling nor painful feeling.			•	•		•	1	-	1	-	-	1	10	1	-	1	11	1
6. Resultant states.	•	•	•			•	-	-	1	-	-	-	10	1	-	-	10	1
7. Resultant-producing states	•	•	•			•	-	-	1	-	-	-	10	1	-	-	16	1
8. States neither are the result of clinging nor favourable to clinging.	•	•	•			•	-	-	-	-	-	-	-	-	-	-	6	-
9. States which are corrupted and are objects of corruption.	•	•	•			•	-	-	1	-	-	-	10	1	-	-	16	1
10. States which are not corrupted and not objects of corruptions.	•	•	•	•		•	-	-	-	-	-	-	-	-	-	-	6	-
11. States with initial application and sustained application.	•	•	•			•	-	1	1	-	-	1	10	1	-	1	15	1
12. States without initial application but with sustained application.	•	•	•			•	-	1	1	-	-	1	10	1	-	1	16	1
13. States accompanied by zest.	•	•	•			•	-	1	1	-	-	1	10	1	-	1	16	1
14. States accompanied by happiness.			•	•		•	1	-	1	-	-	1	10	1	-	1	15	1
15. States accompanied by equanimity.			•	•		•	1	-	1	-	-	1	10	1	-	1	11	1

A Perfect Knowledge of Mind-Body from the Abhidhamma (Dhātukathā)

	Classified under:						Aggregate				Base				Element			
	M.	F.	P.	V.	N.	C.	As	Pas	Ds	Pds	As	Pas	Ds	Pds	As	Pas	Ds	Pds
16. States eliminated by first Path.	•	•	•	•			-	-	1	-	-	-	10	1	-	-	16	1
17. States eliminated by higher three Paths.	•	•	•	•			-	-	1	-	-	-	10	1	-	-	16	1
18. States with root causes eliminated by 1st Path.	•	•	•	•			-	-	1	-	-	-	10	1	-	-	16	1
19. States with root causes eliminated by higher three Paths.	•	•	•	•			-	-	1	-	-	-	10	1	-	-	16	1
20. States which lead to death and rebirth.	•	•	•	•			-	-	1	-	-	-	10	1	-	-	16	1
21. States lead to *Nibbāna*	•	•	•	•			-	-	1	-	-	-	10	1	-	-	16	1
22. States appertaining to Learners (*sekha*).	•	•	•	•			-	-	1	-	-	-	10	1	-	-	16	1
23. States appertaining to *Arahatta* (*asekha*).	•	•	•	•			-	-	1	-	-	-	10	1	-	-	16	1
24. Sublime states.	•	•	•	•			-	-	1	-	-	-	10	1	-	-	16	1
25. Immeasurable states.	•	•	•	•			-	-	-	-	-	-	-	-	-	-	6	-
26. States with limited objects.	•	•	•	•			-	-	1	-	-	-	10	1	-	-	10	1
27. States ,, sublime objects	•	•	•	•			-	-	1	-	-	-	10	1	-	-	16	1
28. States ,, immeasurable objects.	•	•	•	•			-	-	1	-	-	-	10	1	-	-	16	1
29. Inferior states	•	•	•	•			-	-	1	-	-	-	10	1	-	-	16	1
30. Superior states.	•	•	•	•			-	-	-	-	-	-	-	-	-	-	6	-
31. States fixed in destinies because of wrong views.	•	•	•	•			-	-	1	-	-	-	10	1	-	-	16	1
32. States fixed in destinies ... right views	•	•	•	•			-	-	1	-	-	-	10	1	-	-	16	1
33. States with Path object.	•	•	•	•			-	-	1	-	-	-	10	1	-	-	16	1
34. States conditioned by the Path.	•	•	•	•			-	-	1	-	-	-	10	1	-	-	16	1
35. States having Path as the predominant factor.	•	•	•	•			-	-	1	-	-	-	10	1	-	-	16	1
36. States with past object.	•	•	•	•			-	-	1	-	-	-	10	1	-	-	16	1
37. States ,, future object.	•	•	•	•			-	-	1	-	-	-	10	1	-	-	16	1
38. States ,, present object.	•	•	•	•			-	-	1	-	-	-	10	1	-	-	10	1
39. States ,, internal object.	•	•	•	•			-	-	1	-	-	-	10	1	-	-	10	1
40. States ,, external object	•	•	•	•			-	-	1	-	-	-	10	1	-	-	10	1
41. States with both internal and external objects.	•	•	•	•			-	-	1	-	-	-	10	1	-	-	10	1

XIII. Associated and Dissociated from Ungrouped

With reference to the chart above, SOE no. 1-2, 7, 9, 16-24, 26-29, 31-37, all belong to 4 mental aggregates. So, matters and *Nibbāna* become the remaining states. When each of these SOE is dealt with those remaining states, they can not be classified under the same aggregate, under the same base, and under the same element. Since all these SOE are pure mentalities, they have no associations. Each of these SOE is dissociated from 1 aggregate (matter), 10 bases (10 gross bases), and 16 elements (10 gross elements, 6 consciousness-elements having excluded mind-consciousness element). Each is partially dissociated from 1 base (ideation-base), 1 element (ideation-element), 16 subtle matters, and *Nibbāna*.

SOE no. 8, 10, 25, 30, all belong to 4 mental aggregates. Because mentality are the states of enquiry, there are no associated states. And because *Nibbāna* is included, there are no partially associated states. These SOE are only dissociated from 6 consciousness elements (eye-cons. element, ear-cons. element, nose-cons. element, tongue-cons. element, body-cons. element, and mind-element).

These five SOE, no. 6, 38-41, belong to 4 mental aggregates. And so, they have no associations with other states. These states are in dissociation from 1 aggregate (matter), 10 bases (10 gross bases), and 10 elements (10 gross elements). They are partially dissociated from 1 base (ideation-base), 1 element (ideation-element), 16 subtle matters, and *Nibbāna*.

SOE no. 3, 4, 14, which are classified under the aggregates of perception, volitive formation and consciousness, are bound up with body-consciousness element. Each of these SOE is associated with only 1 aggregate (feeling). Ideation-base and ideation-element are excluded because they also come under the aggregates of perception and volitive formation. Each is partially associated with 1 base (ideation-base), 1 element (ideation-element), and 46 or 21 cetasikas depending on which SOE is being dealt with at the time. Each of them is dissociated from 1 aggregate (matter), 10 bases (10 gross bases), and 15 elements (10 gross elements, and 5 consciousness-elements having excluded body-cons. element and mind-cons. element). Each is partially dissociated from 1 base (ideation-base), 1 element (ideation-element), 16 subtle matters, and *Nibbāna*.

SOE no. 5, 15, both belong to the aggregates of perception, volitive formation and consciousness. Each of them is associated with 1 aggregate (feeling). It is partially associated with 1 base (ideation-base), 1 element (ideation-element), and 46 cetasikas. Each is dissociated from 1 aggregate (matter), 10 bases (10 gross bases), and 11 elements (10 gross elements, and body-consciousness element). It is partially dissociated from 1 base (ideation-base), 1 element (ideation-element), 16 subtle matters, and *Nibbāna*.

SOE no. 11 are states with initial application and sustained application, belong to 4 mental aggregates. Thus, there are no associations. These states are partially associated with 1 aggregate (volitive formation), 1 base (ideation-base), 1 element (ideation-element), and 50 cetasikas. They are dissociated from 1 aggregate (matter), 10 bases (10 gross bases), and 15 elements (10 gross elements, and 5 sensory consciousness elements having excluded mind-element

A Perfect Knowledge of Mind-Body from the Abhidhamma (Dhātukathā)

and mind-cons. element). They are partially dissociated from 1 base (ideation-base), 1 element (ideation-element), 16 subtle matters, and *Nibbāna*.

SOE no. 12 and 13 also belong to 4 mental aggregates. Thus, there are no associations. Each of them is partially associated with 1 aggregate (volitive formation), 1 base (ideation-base), 1 element (ideation-element), and 37 or 46 cetasikas depending on which SOE is under enquiry at the time. Each of them is dissociated from 1 aggregate (matter), 10 bases (10 gross bases), and 16 elements (10 gross elements, and 6 consciousness-elements having excluded mind-consciousness element). Each is partially dissociated from 1 base (ideation-base), 1 element (ideation-element), 16 subtle matters, and *Nibbāna*.

73 states of enquiry from Dhammasaṅgaṇīmātikā dyads

451. States of enquiry :	‡ Those remaining states						Aggregate				Base				Element			
	M.	F.	P.	V.	N.	C.	As	Pas	Ds	Pds	As	Pas	Ds	Pds	As	Pas	Ds	Pds
42. States which have roots causes.	28				1													
43. States associated with root causes.	28				1													
44. States with root causes but are not root causes.	28				1		all with the same answers											
45. States associated with root causes but are not root causes.	28				1		-	-	4	-	-	-	1	1	-	-	7	1
46. States which are not root causes but have root causes.	28				1													

All these four states of enquiry belong to the aggregates of feeling, perception, volitive formation, and consciousness, leaving 28 matters and *Nibbāna* as the remaining states. When each of these SOE is enquired with the remaining states, they can not be classified under the same aggregate, under the same base, and under the same element. Each SOE is then taken as ungrouped under 4 aggregates (4 mental aggregates), under 2 bases (ideation-base, mind-base), and under 2 elements (ideation-element, mind-consciousness element).

Since all those remaining states are materiality and *Nibbāna*, there are no associations nor partial associations. Those remaining states are dissociated from 4 aggregates (4 mental aggregates), 1 base (mind-base), and 7 elements (7 consciousness-elements). They are partially dissociated from 1 base (ideation-base), 1 element (ideation-element), and 52 cetasikas.

XIII. Associated and Dissociated from Ungrouped

452. States of enquiry :	‡ Those remaining states						Aggregate				Base				Element			
	M.	F.	P.	V.	N.	C.	As	Pas	Ds	Pds	As	Pas	Ds	Pds	As	Pas	Ds	Pds
States with corporeal change. (1)	1	1	1	1	1		3	-	1	-	-	1	10	1	-	1	10	1

These states belong to 28 matters, and so 4 mental aggregates become the remaining states. Mentality and materiality can not be classified under the same aggregate, under the same base, and under the same element. Therefore, this SOE is taken as ungrouped under 1 aggregate (matter), under 11 bases (10 gross bases, ideation-base), under 11 elements (10 gross elements, ideation-element).

Of those remaining 4 mental aggregates, each of them is mutually associated with the other 3 mental aggregates. There are no associations with bases and elements for one can not associate with itself. Those remaining states are dissociated from 1 aggregate (matter), 10 bases (10 gross bases), and 10 elements (10 gross elements). They are partially dissociated from 1 base (ideation-base), 1 element (ideation-element), 16 subtle matters, and *Nibbāna*.

453. States of enquiry :	‡ Those remaining states						Aggregate				Base				Element			
	M.	F.	P.	V.	N.	C.	As	Pas	Ds	Pds	As	Pas	Ds	Pds	As	Pas	Ds	Pds
1. States without corporeal change.	28																	
2. Supramundane states.	28																	
3. States which are not objects of *Defilement*.	28																	
4. States associated with defilement.	28	1					-	-	4	-	-	-	1	1	-	-	7	1
5. States associated with defilement but are not defilement.	28	1																
6. States dissociated from defilement and are not objects of defilement.	28																	

The 1st SOE, states without corporeal change belong *Nibbāna*, 89 cittas, and 52 cetasikas, and which come under 4 mental aggregates and *Nibbāna*. So, matters are the remaining states. Materiality can not be included with these states under the same aggregate, under the same base, and under the same element. The first unclassified SOE thus taken placed as ungrouped under 4 aggregates excluding *Nibbāna* (4 mental aggregates), under 2 bases (ideation-base, mind-base), and under 8 elements (ideation-element, consciousness-elements).

The 2nd to 6th SOE also belong to 4 mental aggregates. The remaining states are 28 matters, except that the 4th and 5th include *Nibbāna*. Even taking in

A Perfect Knowledge of Mind-Body from the Abhidhamma (Dhātukathā)

Nibbāna with the 4 mental aggregates, they can not be classified with 28 matters under the same aggregate, under the same base, and under the same element. Therefore, each of these 5 SOE is taken as ungrouped under 4 aggregates excluding *Nibbāna* (4 mental aggregates), under 2 bases (ideation-base, mind-base), under 2 elements (ideation-element, mind-consciousness element).

For these 6 states, since those remaining states are either pure materiality, with or without *Nibbāna*, they have neither associations nor partial associations. Those remaining states are dissociated from 4 aggregates (4 mental aggregates), 1 base (mind-base), and 7 elements (7 consciousness-elements). They are partially dissociated from 1 base (ideation-base), 1 element (ideation-element), and 52 cetasikas

453. States of enquiry :	‡ Those remaining states M. F. P. V. N. C.	Aggregate As Pas Ds Pds	Base As Pas Ds Pds	Element As Pas Ds Pds
7. States which are not objects of *Fetters*.	28			
8. States associated with fetters.	28 1			
9. States associated with fetters but are not fetters.	28 1			
10. States dissociated from fetters and are not objects of fetters.	28			
Repeats 7. to 10. above for *Bonds, Raging Current, Yokes, Hindrances.* 4 x 4 =16 (i.e. 11. to 26.)	same as in 7. to 10. above	- - 4 -	- - 1 1	- - 7 1
27. States which are not objects of *Attachment*.	28			
28. States associated with attachment.	28 1			
29. States dissociated from attachment and are not objects of attachment.	28			
30. States which attend to objects.	28 1			

All these states belong to 4 mental aggregates, with 12 out of the 30 SOE include also *Nibbāna*. The 4 mental aggregates can not be classified with materiality and *Nibbāna* under the same aggregate, under the same base, and under the same element. Therefore, each of these 30 SOE is taken as ungrouped under 4 aggregates excluding *Nibbāna* (4 mental aggregates), under 2 bases

XIII. Associated and Dissociated from Ungrouped

(ideation-base, mind-base), under 2 elements (ideation-element, mind-consciousness element).

Since those remaining states are either pure materiality, with or without *Nibbāna*, there are no associations and no partial associations. Those remaining states are dissociated from 4 aggregates (4 mental aggregates), 1 base (mind-base), and 7 elements (7 consciousness-elements). They are partially dissociated from 1 base (ideation-base), and 1 element (ideation-element), and 52 cetasikas.

454. States of enquiry :	‡ Those remaining states						Aggregate				Base				Element			
	M.	F.	P.	V.	N.	C.	As	Pas	Ds	Pds	As	Pas	Ds	Pds	As	Pas	Ds	Pds
1. States which do not have objects.		*1*	*1*	*1*		1												
2. States which are not consciousness.						1												
3. States dissociated from consciousness.		*1*	*1*	*1*		1												
4. States not conjoined with consciousness.		*1*	*1*	*1*		1												
5. States produced by consciousness.					1	1	3	-	1	-	-	1	10	1	-	1	10	1
6. States arise together with consciousness.					1	1												
7. States which arise successively with cons.					1	1												
8. States which are external.	5				1	1												
9. States which are derived.	4	*1*	*1*	*1*	1	1												

The italicised *1* in the chart above denotes the possible states of classification.

The following describes the unclassification between these SOE and the remaining states. Note that SOE no. 1, 3, 4 and 9 delimit the 3 mental aggregates (feeling, perception, volitive formation) as possible states of classification (the numbers *1* in italic), thereby making: consciousness as the only remaining states (1st to 4th SOE), consciousness and *Nibbāna* as remaining states (5th to 7th SOE), 23 matters and *Nibbāna* as remaining states (8th SOE), and 4 subtle great elements, consciousness and *Nibbāna* as remaining states (9th SOE).

1. States which have no objects are the 28 matters and *Nibbāna*. The remaining states are those under consciousness aggregate. The unclassified SOE is taken as ungrouped under 1 aggregate (matter), under 11 bases (10 gross bases, ideation-base), under 11 elements (10 gross elements, ideation-element).

A Perfect Knowledge of Mind-Body from the Abhidhamma (Dhātukathā)

2. States which are not consciousness are 28 matters, 52 cetasikas, and *Nibbāna*. The remaining states are those under consciousness aggregate. The SOE is unclassified with consciousness aggregate, and is taken as ungrouped under 4 aggregates (matter, feeling, perception, volitive formation), under 11 bases (10 gross bases, ideation-base), under 11 elements (10 gross elements, ideation-element).
3. Same as no. 1 above.
4. Same as no. 1 above.
5. States which are produced by consciousness are 52 cetasikas, 17 mind-produced matters. The remaining states are *Nibbāna* and consciousness aggregate. Thus, the SOE is unclassified with remaining states and ungrouped with the same answers as in no. 2 above.
6. States which arise together with consciousness are 52 cetasikas, 2 viññatti-rūpas (bodily intimation, vocal intimation). The remaining states are *Nibbāna* and consciousness aggregate. Thus, the SOE is unclassified, and taken as ungrouped with similar answers as in no. 2 above.
7. States which arise successively with consciousness are the same as in 6 above.
8. States which are external are 52 cetasikas and 23 matters (28 excluding 5 *pasāda* rūpas). Thus, remaining states are the 5 gross sensitivities, consciousness aggregate, and *Nibbāna*. The SOE is unclassified with these remaining states, are taken as ungrouped under 4 aggregates (matter, feeling, perception, volitive formation), under 6 bases (5 gross object bases, ideation-base), and under 6 elements (5 gross object elements, ideation-element).
9. States which are derived are 24 derived matters (28 excluding 4 Great Elements). Because SOE delimits the aggregates of feeling, perception, and volitive formation as possible states of classification, and thereby 4 Great Elements, consciousness aggregate and *Nibbāna* become the remaining states. The 24 derived matters are unclassified with consciousness aggregate, are taken as ungrouped with the same answers as in no. 2 above.

For each of these 9 SOE, only consciousness as amongst the remaining states which is mutually associated with the other 3 mental aggregates (feeling, perception, volitive formation). It has no association with its co-adjunct bases and elements. It is partially associated with 1 base (ideation-base), 1 element (ideation-element), and 52 cetasikas.

Consciousness aggregate is dissociated from 1 aggregate (matter), 10 bases (10 gross bases), 10 elements (10 gross elements), and partially dissociated from 1 base (ideation-base), 1 element (ideation-element), 16 subtle matters, and *Nibbāna*.

XIII. Associated and Dissociated from Ungrouped

455. States of enquiry:	ǂ Those remaining states						Aggregate				Base				Element			
	M.	F.	P.	V.	N.	C.	As	Pas	Ds	Pds	As	Pas	Ds	Pds	As	Pas	Ds	Pds
1. States which are not the objects of clinging.	28																	
2. States associated with clinging.	28					1												
3. States associated with clinging but are not clinging.	28					1												
4. States dissociated from clinging and are not objects of clinging.	28																	
5. States not the objects of corruptions.	28																	
6. States which are corrupted.[12]	28																	
7. States associated with corruptions.	28					1			all with the same answers									
8. States corrupted but are not corruptions	28					1	-	-	4	-	-	-	1	1	-	-	7	1
9. States associated with corruptions but are not corruptions.	28					1												
10. States dissociated from corruptions and are not objects of corruption.	28																	
11. States eliminated by first Path.	28					1												
12. States eliminated by the higher three Paths.	28					1												
13. States with root causes eliminated by 1st Path.	28					1												
14. States with root causes eliminated by the higher three Paths.	28					1												

---

[12] It is printed as *asaṃkiliṭṭhehi* dhammehi ye dhammā in CTS4, and from other online sources like http://suttacentral.net/ and http://tipitaka.sutta.org/. That means it is states which are not corrupted, which have included the full measure of five aggregates. It should have been *saṃkiliṭṭhehi* dhammehi ye dhammā as archived in http://www.dhammatalks.net/

A Perfect Knowledge of Mind-Body from the Abhidhamma (Dhātukathā)

	‡ Those remaining states						Aggregate				Base				Element			
	M.	F.	P.	V.	N.	C.	As	Pas	Ds	Pds	As	Pas	Ds	Pds	As	Pas	Ds	Pds
15. States with initial application.	28				1													
16. States with sustained application.	28				1													
17. States with zest.	28				1													
18. States which are accompanied by zest.	28				1													
19. States accompanied by happiness.	28	1			1													
20. States accompanied by equanimity.	28	1			1													
21. States not characteristic of the sensuous sphere.	28						all with the same answers											
22. States characteristic of form sphere.	28				1		-	-	4	-	-	-	1	1	-	-	7	1
23. States characteristic of formless sphere.	28				1													
24. States which are not included (in the round of death and rebirth).	28																	
25. States which lead out to *Nibbāna*.	28				1													
26. States which are fixed as to their destinies.	28				1													
27. States which are unsurpassable.	28																	
28. States at odds with the supramundane Path	28				1													

With exception from the 19th and 20th SOE which are classified under the aggregates of perception, volitive formation, and consciousness, the other 26 SOE belong to 4 mental aggregates, of which 7 of them include *Nibbāna* as shown in the chart above.

The 19th SOE can not be classified with their remaining states under the same aggregate, under the same base, and under the same element. Thus, it is taken as ungrouped under 3 aggregates (perception, volitive perception, consciousness), 2 bases (ideation-base, mind-base), and 3 elements (body-consciousness element, ideation-element, and mind-consciousness element).

Likewise, the 20th SOE can not be classified their remaining states, and is taken as ungrouped under 3 aggregates (perception, volitive perception, consciousness), 2 bases (ideation-base, mind-base), and 7 elements (eye-

XIII. Associated and Dissociated from Ungrouped

consciousness element, ear-consciousness element, nose- consciousness element, tongue-consciousness element, mind-element, ideation-element, mind-consciousness element).

The 15th and 16th SOE which come under 4 mental aggregates, can not be classified, are each taken as ungrouped under 4 aggregates (feeling, perception, volitive formation, consciousness), under 2 bases (ideation-base, mind-base), and under 2 elements (mind-element, ideation-element, mind-consciousness element).

Each of the other 24 SOE are similarly unclassified in this manner, and are taken as ungrouped under 4 aggregates (4 mental aggregates), under 2 bases (ideation-base, mind-base), and under 2 elements (ideation-element, mind-consciousness element).

Since all those remaining states are either 28 matters, or 28 matters and *Nibbāna*, there are no associated states, and no partially associated states. Each of those remaining states are dissociated from 4 aggregates (4 mental aggregates), 1 base (mind base), 7 elements (7 consciousness-elements), and partially dissociated from 1 base (ideation-base), 1 element (ideation-element), 16 subtle matters, and *Nibbāna*.

Key points from the text :

Matter aggregate, ideation-base, ideation-element, femininity-faculty, masculinity-faculty, vitality-faculty, mentality-materiality; two becomings, birth, ageing, death; next three becomings, basis of psychic accomplishment; 41 from triads; corporeal states, objectless states, non-consciousness, dissociated from consciousness; not conjoined with consciousness, produced by consciousness, arising together with consciousness, arising consecutively with consciousness; external states, derived states.

A Perfect Knowledge of Mind-Body from the Abhidhamma (Dhātukathā)

Referring to the two summary tables below, the numbers in brackets represent the number of enquiries under each text's paragraph's nos.

Chart 13.1. Total 130 states of enquiry by subject matters

Text paragraph nos.
(with the numbers of enquiries) :   Subject matter:

Paragraph nos.	Count	Subject matter
448 (1)	1	Aggregates
449 (1)	1	Bases
449 (1)	1	Elements
449 (3)	3	Faculties
449 (6), 450 (3)	9	Dependent Originations
450 (1)	1	Others
451 (41)	41	Triads
451 (5), 453 (23), 453 (4), 455 (10)	42	Dyad-clusters
452 (1), 453 (2)	3	Shorter dyads
453 (1), 454 (9)	10	Intermediate dyads
455 (18)	18	Last dyads

Total = 130

Table 13.2 Total 120 states of enquiry by answers

Text's paragraph nos. (with numbers of enquiries):		Aggregate				Base				Element			
		As	Pas	Ds	Pds	As	Pas	Ds	Pds	As	Pas	Ds	Pds
1. 448 (1), 449 (11), 452 (1), 454 (9)	22	3	-	1	-	-	1	10	1	-	1	10	1
2. 450 (4), 451 (46), 453 (30), 455 (28)	108	-	-	4	-	-	-	1	1	-	-	7	1

Total 130 states in 2 kinds of answer   **130**

CHAPTER 14

XIV. Aggrouped and Ungrouped from Dissociated
(*Vippayuttenasaṅgahitāsaṅgahita*)

Analysis of 324 states from 63 catechism

These 324 states of enquiry are the same from the two catechism in Chapter 8. I have not previously analysed the association and dissociation of these states in Chapter. The reason is, as I have mentioned in Chapter 8, the two parts of answers from that chapter actually form the first two of the four parts of answers given for this chapter. The states of enquiry in this chapter are each dealt with in four parts, namely, to determine: (i) dissociation from which states; (ii) association with which states. And, because all these 324 states are similarly associated with no other states, those dissociated states are then ascertained as to: (iii) under which aggregates, under which bases, and under which elements they are classified (as aggrouped); (iv) under which aggregates, under which bases, and under which elements they are not classified (as ungrouped). The classification and unclassification follow the same as in Chapter 1.

As mentioned in Chapter 8, those dissociated states from the 324 states of enquiry are in turn associated with none. The Reason being, after the states of enquiry are first ascertained of their dissociated s and partially dissociated states, there are no other states left to be associated with. In this chapter, the answers given for dissociation have both dissociated states and partially dissociated states combined. The few common points with regard to dissociation are, for example, the state of *Nibbāna* is always dissociated from the 4 mental aggregates and 28 matters. The 4 mental aggregates are always in dissociation from materiality and *Nibbāna*. Also, whenever mental aggregates are the states of enquiry, 16 subtle matters and *Nibbāna* are always the partially dissociated states.

Of these 324 states, 97 are interior states, 227 states belong to triads and dyads, which form the subject matters of this chapter. All these 324 states of enquiries fall in with the four kinds of dissociation as explained in Chapter 6, that is, dissociation by spheres, classes, times, and continuity. The 63 catechism in this chapter have not excluded other kinds of states for analysis. They belong to matters, one or all of the 4 mental aggregates, *Nibbāna*, and states belong to mentality-materiality which are only in dissociation.

A simple process flow diagram below describes the method of analysis used in this chapter.

A Perfect Knowledge of Mind-Body from the Abhidhamma (Dhātukathā)

Diagram 14.1. Aggrouped and ungrouped based on dissociated states

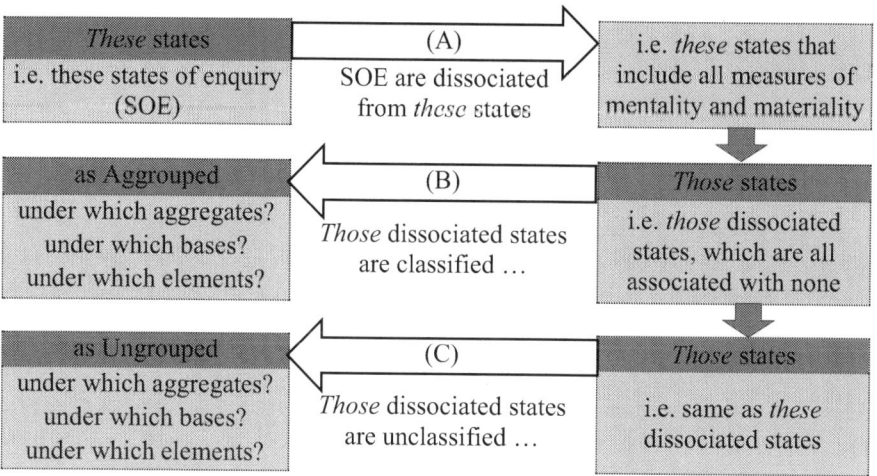

The following abbreviations are used in the charts throughout this Chapter.

SOE	: States of enquiry
Agr	: Aggregate
Bse	: Base
El.	: Element
cons.	: consciousness
P. Dissociated	: Partially dissociated

The symbol ✗ is marked in all the following charts which is used to indicate that those states that are dissociated from the respective states of enquiry are in turn associated with none. The same answer applies to all the 324 states.

97 internal states of enquiry

1. Aggregates, etc. (*Khandhādi*)

			Those dissociated states					
		is dissociated from	Aggrouped			Ungrouped		
456.	States of enquiry (SOE):	*these* states (✗) :	Agr	Bse	El.	Agr	Bse	El.
	Matter aggregate (1)	4 mental aggregates	4	2	8	1	10	10

	Dissociated			P. dissociated		
	Agr	Bse	El.	Agr	Bse	El.
	4	1	7	-	1	1

329

XIV. Aggrouped and Ungrouped from Dissociated

Matter aggregate at all times is dissociated from the 4 mental aggregates, and vice versa. It is dissociated from 4 aggregates (4 mental aggregates), 1 base (mind-base), 7 elements (7 consciousness elements), and partially dissociated from 1 base (ideation-base), 1 element (ideation-element), and 52 cetasikas. In turn, those states are associated with none, as denoted by the symbol ✗ marked in the second column header.

Those dissociated states are classified, and taken as aggrouped under 4 aggregates excluding *Nibbāna* (4 mental aggregates), under 2 bases (ideation-base, mind-base), and under 8 elements (ideation-element, 7 consciousness elements). They are unclassified with materiality, are taken as ungrouped under 1 aggregate (matter), under 10 bases (10 gross bases), and under 10 elements (10 gross elements).

457. States of enquiry (SOE):	is dissociated from *these* states (✗) :	Those dissociated states					
		Aggrouped			Ungrouped		
		Agr	Bse	El.	Agr	Bse	El.
Feeling aggregate; Perception aggregate; Volitive formation aggregate; Consciousness aggregate; Mind-base, Mind-faculty. (6)	28 matters, *Nibbāna*	1	11	11	4	1	7
	Dissociated				P. dissociated		
	Agr	Bse	El.	Agr	Bse	El.	
	1	10	10	-	1	1	

All these states of enquiry are mentality. Each of them is dissociated from matter aggregate, 10 gross bases, 10 gross elements, and partially dissociated from ideation-base, ideation-element, subtle matters, and *Nibbāna*. Those dissociated states are classified, and taken as aggrouped under 1 aggregate (matter), under 11 bases (10 gross matters, ideation-base), and under 11 elements (10 gross elements, ideation-element). They are unclassified and taken as ungrouped under 4 aggregates (4 mental aggregates), under 1 base (mind-base), and under 7 elements (7 consciousness elements).

458. States of enquiry (SOE):	is dissociated from *these* states (✗) :	Those dissociated states					
		Aggrouped			Ungrouped		
		Agr	Bse	El.	Agr	Bse	El.
Eye-base; Ear-base; Nose-base; Tongue-base; Body-base; Vision-base; Sound-base; Odour-base; Taste-base; Tangible-base; Eye-element; Ear-element; Nose-element; Tongue-element; Body-element; Vision-element; Sound-element; Odour-element; Taste-element; Tangible-element (20).	4 mental aggregates	4	2	8	1	10	10

A Perfect Knowledge of Mind-Body from the Abhidhamma (Dhātukathā)

These are the 10 gross bases and 10 gross elements. Each of these 20 gross materiality is dissociated from the 4 mental aggregates, mind base, 7 consciousness-elements, while partially dissociated from ideation-base, ideation-element, and 52 cetasikas.

Those dissociated states are aggrouped under 4 aggregates (feeling, perception, volitive formation, consciousness), under 2 bases (ideation-base, mind base), and under 8 elements (ideation-element, 7 consciousness-elements). They are ungrouped under 1 aggregate (matter), under 10 bases (10 gross bases), and under 10 elements (10 gross elements).

		Those dissociated states					
	is dissociated from	Aggrouped			Ungrouped		
459. States of enquiry (SOE):	*these* states (≭) :	Agr	Bse	El.	Agr	Bse	El.
Eye cons. element, ear cons. element, nose cons. element, tongue cons. element, body cons. element, mind-element, mind-cons. element. (7)	28 matters, 6 remaining cons. elements, 52 cetasikas, *Nibbāna*	5	12	17	-	-	1

These states belong to the group of 7 consciousness-elements which come under mind base and consciousness aggregate. Each of these states is dissociated from the remaining 6 consciousness elements, 52 cetasikas, 28 matters, and *Nibbāna*.

These dissociated states have included the matter aggregate, 52 cetasikas which are essentially the 3 mental aggregates of feeling, perception, and volitive formation, and also the remaining 6 consciousness elements which fall in with consciousness aggregate.

Those dissociated states can thus be classified, are taken as aggrouped under 5 aggregates (matter, feeling, perception, volitive formation, consciousness), under 12 bases (10 gross bases, ideation-base, mind base), and under 17 elements (10 gross elements, ideation-element, and 6 consciousness-elements having excluded the state of enquiry that is being dealt with). Those dissociated states which are not classified, are taken as ungrouped under 1 element (the respective state of enquiry). There are no more states left that are unclassified as ungrouped under aggregates and bases.

XIV. Aggrouped and Ungrouped from Dissociated

2. Truth, etc. (*Saccādi*)

460. States of enquiry (SOE):	is dissociated from *these* states (✗) :	Those dissociated states					
		Aggrouped			Ungrouped		
		Agr	Bse	El.	Agr	Bse	El.
The truth as to suffering. (1)	8 supramundane cittas, 36 cetasikas	4	2	2	1	10	16
	Dissociated						
	Agr	Bse	El.	Agr	Bse	El.	
	4	1	1	-	1	1	

(Note: lower sub-table shows Dissociated / P. dissociated with values 4 | 1 | 1 | - | 1 | 1)

The truth as to suffering is attributed to the pursuance of all that is materiality, 81 mundane cittas accompanied by the 51 cetasikas (52 excluding the greed-cetasika). It is dissociated from the 8 supramundane cittas accompanied by 36 cetasikas, as under 4 aggregates (4 mental aggregates), 1 base (ideation-base), 1 element (mind-consciousness. element), and partially dissociated from 1 base (ideation-base), 1 element (ideation-element), and 52 cetasikas.

Those dissociated states are classified as aggrouped under 4 aggregates excluding *Nibbāna* (4 mental aggregates), under 2 bases (ideation-base, mind-base), under 2 elements (ideation-element, mind-consciousness element). They are not aggrouped under 1 aggregate (matter), under 10 bases (10 gross bases), and under 16 elements (10 gross elements, the remaining 6 consciousness elements).

461. States of enquiry:	is dissociated from *these* states (✗) :	Those dissociated states					
		Aggrouped			Ungrouped		
		Agr	Bse	El.	Agr	Bse	El.
1. Origin-truth.	hate-rooted cittas, delusion-rooted cittas, wholesome cittas, resultant cittas, functional cittas, supramundane cittas, 6 cons. elements, 28 matters, *Nibbāna*	5	12	18	-	-	-
2. Path-truth.	12 unwholesome cittas, resultant cittas, functional cittas, 6 cons. elements, 28 matters, *Nibbāna*						

Origin-truth contains greed-*cetasika* present at the 8 greed-rooted cittas, accompanied by 21 cetasikas. Origin-truth is dissociated from 2 hate-rooted cittas, 2 delusion-rooted cittas, 17 wholesome cittas, 32 resultant cittas, 20 functional cittas, 6 consciousness elements, 28 matters, and *Nibbāna*.

Path-truth corresponds to the 4 supramundane path-consciousness, accompanied by 36 cetasikas. It is dissociated from all mundane cittas, materiality, and *Nibbāna*. The two truths are bound up with mind-consciousness element.

A Perfect Knowledge of Mind-Body from the Abhidhamma (Dhātukathā)

Those dissociated states are classified as aggrouped under 5 aggregates excluding *Nibbāna* (matter, feeling, perception, volitive formation, consciousness), under 12 bases (10 gross bases, ideation-base, mind base), and under 18 elements (10 gross elements, ideation-element, the 7 consciousness-elements). Having all included, there are no more unclassified remaining states.

462. States of enquiry (SOE):	is dissociated from *these* states (✶):						Those dissociated states					
							Aggrouped			Ungrouped		
							Agr	Bse	El.	Agr	Bse	El.
Truth as to the cessation of suffering; Vision-faculty; Hearing-faculty; Smell-faculty; Taste-faculty; Touch-faculty; Femininity-faculty; Masculinity-faculty (8)	4 mental aggregates						4	2	8	1	10	10
	Dissociated			P. dissociated								
	Agr	Bse	El.	Agr	Bse	El.						
	4	1	7	-	1	1						

Cessation-truth comes under *Nibbāna*, is dissociated from 4 mental aggregates. To recall from Chapter 6, when *Nibbāna* is compared with materiality, there are neither associations nor dissociations.

The 5 sense-faculties come under gross matters, is dissociated from 4 mental aggregates. The femininity-faculty and masculinity-faculty come under subtle matters, are dissociated from 4 mental aggregates.

Therefore, each of these states of enquiry is dissociated from 4 mental aggregates, mind base, 7 consciousness-elements, while partially dissociated from ideation-base, ideation-element, and 52 cetasikas. Those dissociated states are classified as aggrouped under 4 aggregates (4 mental aggregates), under 2 bases (ideation-base, mind base), and under 8 elements (ideation-element, 7 consciousness-elements). They are not classified as ungrouped under 1 aggregate (matter), under 10 bases (10 gross bases), and under 10 elements (10 gross elements).

463. States of enquiry (SOE):	is dissociated from *these* states (✶):	Those dissociated states					
		Aggrouped			Ungrouped		
		Agr	Bse	El.	Agr	Bse	El.
Carnal pleasure faculty, carnal displeasure faculty, joy faculty, melancholy faculty (4)	remaining 4 feeling faculties, 45 cetasikas, 6 consciousness elements, 28 matters, *Nibbāna*	5	12	18	-	-	-

These four faculties are 4 out of the 5 feeling faculties, belong to feeling aggregate. These four states are bound up with body-consciousness element. These states are each dissociated from the remaining 4 feeling faculties which include equanimity-faculty, 6 consciousness-elements (7 excluding body-

XIV. Aggrouped and Ungrouped from Dissociated

consciousness element), 28 matters, and *Nibbāna*. They are in partial dissociation from 45 cetasikas (52 excluding the 7 primary, non-beautiful cetasikas)

In this regard, the 8 viññāṇas (excluding the pair of body-consciousness), *manodvārāvajjana* citta (mind-door advertence), 2 *upekkhā-sampaṭicchana* cittas (2 receiving cittas), and remaining 76 cittas under consciousness aggregate, are essentially also those remaining 6 consciousness-elements, and all of them fall in with mind-base. Therefore, matter aggregate, the aggregates of feeling, perception, volitive formation, and consciousness are all considered in dissociation.

Those dissociated states are classified, and taken as aggrouped under 5 aggregates excluding *Nibbāna* (matter, feeling, perception, volitive formation, consciousness), under 12 bases (10 gross bases, ideation-base, mind base), and under 18 elements (10 gross elements, ideation-element, 7 consciousness-elements). There are no other states left for unclassification.

However, it could have been a mistake in the text which may be given the answer as classified under 17 elements (10 gross elements, ideation-element, remaining 6 consciousness-elements), and not classified under 1 element (body-consciousness element). This is because all the subject matters of enquiry are bound up with body-consciousness element, and not the 7 consciousness-elements.

		Those dissociated states					
	is dissociated from	Aggrouped			Ungrouped		
464. States of enquiry :	*these* states (✗) :	Agr	Bse	El.	Agr	Bse	El.
Equanimity-faculty. (1)	remaining 4 feeling faculties, 45 cetasikas, body-consciousness element, 28 matters, *Nibbāna*	5	12	13	-	-	5

Equanimity-faculty is among the 5 feeling faculties, is concerned with 6 consciousness element (excluded body-consciousness element). Equanimity-faculty is dissociated from the remaining 4 feeling faculties, body-consciousness element, 28 matters, and *Nibbāna*. It is in partial dissociation from 45 cetasikas (52 excluding the 7 primary, non-beautiful cetasikas)

Those dissociated states are classified, and taken as aggrouped under 5 aggregates excluding *Nibbāna* (matter, feeling, perception, volitive formation, consciousness), under 12 bases (10 gross bases, ideation-base, mind base), and under 13 elements (10 gross elements, body-consciousness element, ideation-element, mind-consciousness element). They are not classified as ungrouped under 5 elements (eye-consciousness element, ear-consciousness element, nose-consciousness element, tongue-consciousness element, and mind-element).

A Perfect Knowledge of Mind-Body from the Abhidhamma (Dhātukathā)

		Those dissociated states					
	is dissociated from	Aggrouped			Ungrouped		
465. States of enquiry (SOE):	*these* states (✗) :	Agr	Bse	El.	Agr	Bse	El.
Confidence-faculty; Effort-faculty; Mindfulness-faculty; Concentration-faculty; Wisdom-faculty; "I-shall-comprehend-the-unknown" faculty; Higher knowledge faculty; "Final knower" faculty; Ignorance; conditioned by ignorance is Volitive formation (10)	remaining 6 consciousness elements, 51 cetasikas, 28 matters, *Nibbāna*	5	12	18	-	-	-

These 10 states belong to volitive formation and each has its own single cetasika. (See nos. 413). Each of these SOE is dissociated from 6 consciousness elements (7 excluding mind-consciousness element), 51 cetasikas, 28 matters, and *Nibbāna*.

Note that the 10 *viññāṇa* cittas (fivefold pairs of sensory consciousness), *manodvārāvajjana citta* (mind-door advertence) and 2 *upekkhā-sampaṭicchana* cittas (2 receiving cittas) under consciousness aggregate, are essentially also the aforesaid 6 sensory consciousness-elements. Therefore, matter aggregate, the aggregates of feeling, perception, volitive formation, and consciousness are all considered as in dissociation.

Those dissociated states are classified, and taken as aggrouped under 5 aggregates excluding *Nibbāna*, under 12 bases (10 gross bases), and under 18 elements (10 gross elements, ideation-element, 7 consciousness-elements).

		Those dissociated states					
	is dissociated from	Aggrouped			Ungrouped		
466. States of enquiry (SOE):	*these* states (✗) :	Agr	Bse	El.	Agr	Bse	El.
Conditioned by volition, is *Consciousness*; conditioned by the six bases, is *Contact*; conditioned by contact, is *Feeling*. (3)	28 matters, *Nibbāna*	1	11	11	4	1	7

Consciousness is under consciousness aggregate. Contact is contact-*cetasika* from the 7 common mental factors, which accompanies 89 cittas. It belongs to volitive formation. Feeling is also one of the 7 common mental factors, present at 89 cittas, accompanied by 51 cetasikas (52 excluding feeling-*cetasika*). It comes under feeling aggregate. Thus, each of these SOE is dissociated from materiality and *Nibbāna*. Each is dissociated from 1 aggregate (matter), 10 bases (10 gross bases), 10 elements (10 gross elements), and partially dissociated from 1 base (ideation-base), 1 element (ideation-element), subtle matters, *Nibbāna*.

Each of them is classified and taken as aggrouped under 1 aggregate (matter), under 11 bases (10 gross matters, ideation-base), and under 11 elements (10

XIV. Aggrouped and Ungrouped from Dissociated

gross elements, ideation-element). Each is taken as ungrouped under 4 aggregates (4 mental aggregates), under 1 base (mind-base), and under 7 elements (7 consciousness elements).

		Those dissociated states					
	is dissociated from	Aggrouped			Ungrouped		
467. States of enquiry :	*these* states (✗) :	Agr	Bse	El.	Agr	Bse	El.
1. Conditioned by feeling, is *Craving.* *2.* Conditioned by craving, is *Clinging.*	21 wholesome cittas, 38 cetasikas; resultant cittas and functional cittas, 38 cetasikas; supramundane cittas, 36 cetasikas; 28 matters, *Nibbāna*	5	12	18	-	-	-
3. Action-becoming.	resultant cittas, functional cittas, 38 cetasikas; supramundane cittas, 36 cetasikas; 28 matters, *Nibbāna*						

Craving is accompanied by greed-*cetasika*, clinging is accompanied by greed and wrong view cetasikas. Clinging is accompanied by 48 cetasikas (50 excluding greed and wrong view). These two states are present at the 8 greed-rooted cittas. They are dissociated from 21 wholesome cittas, accompanied by 38 cetasikas; resultant cittas and functional cittas, accompanied by 38 cetasikas; supramundane cittas, accompanied by 36 cetasikas; 28 matters and *Nibbāna*.

Action-becoming (*kammabhava*) includes volition-*cetasika*, present at the 17 wholesome cittas and 12 unwholesome cittas. Action-becoming belong to volitive formation aggregate. They are dissociated from resultant states, functional states, accompanied by 38 cetasikas; supramundane states accompanied by 36 cetasikas; 28 matters, and *Nibbāna*.

Those dissociated states are classifiable, and taken as aggrouped under 5 aggregates excluding *Nibbāna*, under 12 bases, and under 18 elements. There are no other remaining states left.

		Those dissociated states					
	is dissociated from	Aggrouped			Ungrouped		
468. States of enquiry (SOE):	*these* states (✗) :	Agr	Bse	El.	Agr	Bse	El.
Resultant-becoming or rebirth-becoming (*upapatti bhava*); Perception-becoming; Five-aggregate becoming. (3)	unwholesome states, wholesome states, functional states, supramundane states, mind-element, mind-cons. element, *Nibbāna.*	4	2	3	1	10	15

Resultant-becoming consists of 20 kamma-produced matters, 32 sensual sphere resultants, and accompanied by 35 cetasikas (38 excluding the 3

A Perfect Knowledge of Mind-Body from the Abhidhamma (Dhātukathā)

abstinence factors). Perception-becoming consists of 31 resultants (32 resultants excluding neither-perception-nor-nonperception resultant citta of the immaterial sphere). Five-aggregate becoming consists of 20 kamma-produced matters, 23 sense-sphere resultants, 5 immaterial resultants, and accompanied by 35 cetasikas. These 3 kinds of dependent origination belong to mentality-materiality.

As these three states of becomings are resultants, they dissociated from wholesome states, unwholesome states, functional states, and supramundane states. The three becomings are bound up with 5 sense-based consciousness elements.

Each of these becomings are dissociated from 4 mental aggregates, mind-base, mind-element, mind-consciousness element, and partially dissociated from ideation-base, ideation-element, and *Nibbāna*.

These dissociated states are classified and aggrouped under 4 aggregates excluding *Nibbāna* (4 mental aggregates), under 2 bases (ideation-base, mind-base), under 3 elements (mind-element, ideation-element, mind-consciousness element). They are not classified as ungrouped under 1 aggregate (matter), under 10 bases (10 gross bases), and under 15 elements (10 gross elements, and the remaining 5 consciousness elements having excluded mind-element and mind-consciousness element).

			Those dissociated states					
	is dissociated from		Aggrouped			Ungrouped		
469. States of enquiry:	*these* states (✗) :		Agr	Bse	El.	Agr	Bse	El.
Sensuous becoming. (1)	fine-material becoming, immaterial-becoming, unwholesome states, wholesome states, functional states, supramundane states, *Nibbāna*.		4	2	5	1	10	13

Sensuous becoming consists of 20 kamma-produced matters, 32 sensual sphere resultants which are accompanied by 33 cetasikas (38 excluding the 3 abstinence factors, and 2 Illimitables). Sensuous becoming belongs to mentality-materiality. It is bound up with mind-element and mind-consciousness element.

As sensuous becomings are sensuous resultants, they are dissociated from fine-material becoming, immaterial-becoming, 5 sensory consciousness elements, 12 unwholesome states, 17 wholesome states, 20 functional states, 8 supramundane states, and *Nibbāna*.

Those dissociated states are classified and aggrouped under 4 aggregates excluding *Nibbāna* (4 mental aggregates), under 2 bases (ideation-base, mind-base), under 5 elements (eye-cons. element, ear-cons. element, nose-cons. element, tongue-cons. element, and body-cons. element). They are not classified and are taken as ungrouped under 1 aggregate (matter), under 10 bases (10 gross bases), and under 13 elements (10 gross elements, mind-element, ideation-element, mind-consciousness element).

XIV. Aggrouped and Ungrouped from Dissociated

470. States of enquiry (SOE):	are dissociated from *these* states (✗) :	Those dissociated states					
		Aggrouped			Ungrouped		
		Agr	Bse	El.	Agr	Bse	El.
Fine-material becoming; Non-perception becoming; Single-aggregate becoming; Lamentation. (4)	4 mental aggregates, *Nibbāna*	4	2	8	1	10	10

Fine-material becoming consists of 5 resultant cittas, 2 eye-cittas, 2 ear-cittas, 2 receiving cittas, 2 investigating cittas, 35 cetasikas (38 excluding 3 Abstinences), and 15 kamma-produced matters (20 excluding femininity, masculinity, nose, tongue, and body, i.e. 20-5=15). It belongs to mentality-materiality. It is dissociated from 3 sense-based consciousness elements, sensuous becoming, immaterial-becoming, supramundane cittas, and *Nibbāna*. These dissociated states span the 4 mental aggregates.

Non-perception becoming and single-aggregate becoming are identical, are both bound by visible object base. Lamentation is taken as audible object base because of wailing. The three SOE belong to gross materiality, are dissociated from the 4 mental aggregates.

Therefore, each of these SOE is dissociated from 4 mental aggregates, mind-base, 7 consciousness-elements, and partially dissociated from ideation-base, ideation-element, and 52 cetasikas. Those dissociated states are classified and aggrouped under 4 aggregates (4 mental aggregates), under 2 bases (ideation-base, mind base), and under 8 elements (ideation-element, 7 consciousness elements). They are taken as ungrouped under 1 aggregate (matter), under 10 bases (10 gross bases), and under 10 elements (10 gross elements).

471. States of enquiry (SOE):	are dissociated from *these* states (✗) :	Those dissociated states					
		Aggrouped			Ungrouped		
		Agr	Bse	El.	Agr	Bse	El.
Immaterial becoming; Neither perception nor non-perception becoming; Four-aggregate becoming; Sorrow; Suffering; Melancholy; Despair; Foundations of mindfulness; Right strivings; Basis of psychic accomplishment; *Jhāna*; The Illimitables; 5 Faculties; 5 Powers; 7 Enlightenment-Factors; Noble eightfold path. (16)	sensuous becoming, fine-material becoming, 10 gross elements, 6 consciousness-elements, *Nibbāna*	5	12	18	-	-	-

Immaterial-becoming is identical to neither perception nor non-perception becoming and four-aggregate becoming. These three states come under subtle

A Perfect Knowledge of Mind-Body from the Abhidhamma (Dhātukathā)

matters, 4 mental aggregates, and *Nibbāna*. These three states belong to mentality-materiality.

Sorrow, suffering, and melancholy are associated with body-consciousness element. The other 13 states of enquiry are associated with mind-consciousness element. Sorrow, suffering, and melancholy are grievous feeling present at the two hatred-rooted cittas. They belong to feeling faculty.

Despair is bound by occasional hatred-*cetasika*. Four foundations of mindfulness are bound by mindfulness-*cetasika*. Four right strivings are bound by energy-*cetasika*. These three states belong to volitive formation aggregate.

The basis of psychic accomplishment consists of supramundane cittas, accompanied by 33 cetasikas (i.e. 13 common cetasikas excluding effort and desire, and 25 beautiful cetasikas excluding the 2 Illimitables and non-delusion). It is bound by three cetasikas (effort, desire, wisdom). It belongs to consciousness aggregate.

Jhāna is present at the 27 sublime cittas, with the first *jhāna* accompanied by 35 cetasikas (38 excluding excluding the 3 Abstinences). As the concentrative absorption progresses to the second, third, and fourth *jhāna*, the numbers of 35 cetasikas are correspondingly reduced by one mental factor in respect of *jhāna* factor (i.e. 34 at the second *jhāna*, 33 at third *jhāna*, 32. at the fourth *jhāna*). There are 30 cetasikas instead remain at the fifth *jhāna* is because the two Illimitable factors of compassion (*karuṇā*) and altruistic joy (*muditā*) are equated with the *jhāna* factor of happiness (*sukha*) which is replaced by equanimity (*upekkhā*). For the details, refer to the Chart 11 in Appendix VI. At the transcendental sphere, it belongs to the 8 supramundane Fifth-jhānas. The *jhāna*-factor of happiness belong to feeling aggregate, the other 4 *jhāna*-factors belong to volitive formation aggregate. And so *Jhāna* comes under feeling and volitive formation aggregates.

The two or four Illimitables, 5 Faculties, 5 Powers, 7 Factors of Enlightenment, and Noble Eightfold Path, which are accompanied by the different cetasikas (See Table 1.6b), are all belong to volitive formation aggregate.

Overall, these 16 states are dissociated from gross matters, and *Nibbāna*. The 3 states of sorrow, suffering, and melancholy are also dissociated from 6 consciousness-elements (7 excluding body-consciousness element). The other 13 states are also dissociated from 6 consciousness-elements (7 excluding mind-consciousness element). Since the 10 *viññāṇā, manodvārāvajjana* cittas and 2 *upekkhā-sampaṭicchana* cittas under consciousness aggregate are essentially the same as the 6 sensory consciousness-elements, and also, the other 3 mental aggregates have become the possible, classifiable states with reference to each SOE, these dissociated states and possible states now span the 4 mental aggregates. And therefore, those dissociated states and possible states are classified, and taken as aggrouped under 5 aggregates, under 12 bases, and under 18 elements. There are no more other states as unclassified.

XIV. Aggrouped and Ungrouped from Dissociated

3. Group of contact 7 (*Phassādisattakaṃ*)

		Those dissociated states					
	is dissociated from	Aggrouped			Ungrouped		
472. States of enquiry (SOE):	*these* states (✗) :	Agr	Bse	El.	Agr	Bse	El.
Contact; Feeling; Perception; Volition; Consciousness; Attention. (6)	28 matters, *Nibbāna*	1	11	11	4	1	7

Contact is accompanied by the mental factor of *phasso*. Feeling is accompanied by the mental factor of *vedanā*. Perception is accompanied by the mental factor of *saññā*. Volition is accompanied by the mental factor of *cetanā*; Attention is accompanied by the mental factor of *manasikāra*. These six states come under the 4 mental aggregates, are dissociated from 28 matters and *Nibbāna*. Each of them is dissociated from 1 aggregate (matter), 10 bases (10 gross bases), 10 elements (10 gross elements), and partially dissociated from 1 base (ideation-base), 1 element (ideation-element), 16 subtle matters, *Nibbāna*.

Those dissociated states are classifiable and taken as aggrouped under 1 aggregate (matter), under 11 bases (10 gross matters, ideation-base), and under 11 elements (10 gross elements, ideation-element). They are taken as ungrouped under 4 aggregates (the 4 mental aggregates), under 1 base (mind-base), and under 7 elements (the 7 consciousness elements).

		Those dissociated states					
	is dissociated from	Aggrouped			Ungrouped		
473. States of enquiry :	*these* states (✗) :	Agr	Bse	El.	Agr	Bse	El.
Decision. (1)	1 delusion-rooted citta associated with doubt, 15 cetasikas, 10 viññāṇas, 28 matters, *Nibbāna*	5	12	17	-	-	1

Decision is accompanied by the mental factor of *adhimokkha*, belongs to volitive formation aggregate. Decision is dissociated from 1 delusion-rooted citta associated with doubt, arisen with 15 cetasikas (13 excluding *adhimokkha*, *pīti*, *chanda*; 4 common unwholesome cetasikas and *vicikicchā*, i.e. 10+4+1=15); 10 kinds of viññāṇas under consciousness aggregate; 28 matters, and *Nibbāna*.

Decision is dissociated from 1 delusion-rooted unwholesome citta associated with doubt, accompanied by 15 cetasikas; 10 viññāṇas, 28 matters, and *Nibbāna*. The fivefold 10 viññāṇas, mind-door advertence citta and 2 receiving cittas are the same as the 6 sense-based consciousness elements, all come under consciousness aggregate. These dissociated states thus cover matter aggregate, 4 mental aggregates, and *Nibbāna*.

Those dissociated states are classifiable and taken as aggrouped under 5 aggregates excluding *Nibbāna* (matter, feeling, perception, volitive formation, consciousness), under 12 bases (10 gross bases, ideation-base, mind-base), and

A Perfect Knowledge of Mind-Body from the Abhidhamma (Dhātukathā)

under 17 elements (10 gross elements, ideation-element, 6 consciousness-elements without mind-consciousness element). Those dissociated states which are unclassified are taken as ungrouped under 1 element (mind-consciousness element). There are no other unclassified states under bases and elements.

64 states of enquiry from Dhammasaṅgaṇīmātikā triads

4. Triads (*Tikaṃ*)

		Those dissociated states					
	are dissociated from	Aggrouped			Ungrouped		
474. States of enquiry (SOE):	*these* states (≠) :	Agr	Bse	El.	Agr	Bse	El.
Wholesome states; Unwholesome states; States associated with happy feeling; States associated with painful feeling. (4)	28 matters, resultant states, functional states, and *Nibbāna*	5	12	18	-	-	-

Wholesome states are the 21 mundane wholesome cittas, accompanied by 38 cetasikas. Unwholesome states are the 12 unwholesome cittas, accompanied by 27 cetasikas. States associated with happy feeling and with painful feeling consist of 63 cittas, accompanied by 46 cetasikas. States associated with painful feeling consist of 3 cittas accompanied by displeasure, arisen with 21 cetasikas.

These four states are mentality, are dissociated from materiality, resultant states, functional states, and *Nibbāna*. These dissociated states cover 28 matters and the 4 mental aggregates. Thus, those states are classified, and taken as aggrouped under 5 aggregates, under 12 bases, and under 18 elements. There are no more other states as unclassified.

		Those dissociated states					
	are dissociated from	Aggrouped			Ungrouped		
475. States of enquiry (SOE):	*these* states (≠) :	Agr	Bse	El.	Agr	Bse	El.
Indeterminate states. (1)	active wholesome cittas, active unwholesome cittas	4	2	2	1	10	16

Indeterminate states consist of 36 resultant cittas, 20 functional cittas, 38 cetasikas, 28 matters, and *Nibbāna*. They belong to mentality-materiality. Indeterminate states are dissociated from the 17 wholesome cittas and 12 unwholesome cittas. They are bound up with mind-consciousness element.

Those dissociated states span the 4 mental aggregates. They are classified and taken as aggrouped under 4 aggregates excluding *Nibbāna* (4 mental aggregates), under 2 bases (ideation-base, mind-base), under 2 elements (ideation-element,

XIV. Aggrouped and Ungrouped from Dissociated

mind-consciousness element). They are taken as not aggrouped under 1 aggregate (matter), under 10 bases (10 gross bases), and under 16 elements (10 gross elements, and the remaining 6 consciousness elements).

		Those dissociated states					
	are dissociated from	Aggrouped			Ungrouped		
476. States of enquiry (SOE):	these states (✻) :	Agr	Bse	El.	Agr	Bse	El.
States associated with neither happy feeling nor suffering feeling; Resultant states. (2)	28 matters, wholesome states, unwholesome states, functional state, Nibbāna	5	12	13	-	-	5

States associated with neither happy feeling nor suffering feeling are 55 cittas accompanied by equanimity, arisen with 46 cetasikas (52 excluding feeling, zest, hatred, envy, avarice, worry). They are dissociated from materiality, feeling, body-consciousness element, and *Nibbāna*. The SOE belongs to the aggregates of perception, volitive formation, and consciousness.

Resultant states are the 36 resultant cittas, arisen with 38 cetasikas. They belong to 4 mental aggregates, are dissociated from materiality, wholesome states, unwholesome states, functional states, and *Nibbāna*.

Those dissociated states span the 4 mental aggregates. They are classified and taken as aggrouped under 5 aggregates excluding *Nibbāna*, under 12 bases, and under 13 elements (10 gross elements, body-consciousness element, ideation-element, mind-consciousness element). They are taken as ungrouped under 5 elements (eye-cons. element, ear-cons. element, nose-cons. element, tongue-cons. element, and mind-element). There are no more other states as unclassified.

		Those dissociated states					
	are dissociated from	Aggrouped			Ungrouped		
477. States of enquiry (SOE):	these states (✻) :	Agr	Bse	El.	Agr	Bse	El.
States which produce resultants; States which are corrupted and favourable to corruption. (2)	28 matters, resultant cittas, functional cittas, supramundane cittas, Nibbāna	5	12	18	-	-	-

States which produce resultants are 21 wholesome cittas, 12 unwholesome cittas, and 52 cetasikas. States which are both corrupted and objects of corruption are the 12 unwholesome cittas, accompanied by 27 cetasikas. The two states of enquiry belong to 4 mental aggregates, are bound up with mind-consciousness element.

They are dissociated from all materiality, resultant cittas, functional cittas, supramundane cittas, and *Nibbāna*. These dissociated states include all measures of mentality and materiality. They are therefore classified, and taken as

A Perfect Knowledge of Mind-Body from the Abhidhamma (Dhātukathā)

aggrouped under 5 aggregates excluding *Nibbāna*, under 12 bases, and under 18 elements. There are no more states as to unclassification.

			Those dissociated states					
478. States of enquiry (SOE):	are dissociated from *these* states (✗) :		Aggrouped			Ungrouped		
			Agr	Bse	El.	Agr	Bse	El.
1. States which neither are resultants nor causing resultants; 2. States are not the result of clinging but are favourable to clinging; 3. States neither are the result of clinging nor are favourable to clinging; 4. States which are not corrupted nor are favourable to corruptions (*asaṃkiliṭṭha asaṃkilesikā*). (4)	wholesome states, unwholesome states, resultant states		4	2	8	1	10	10

The 1st SOE consists of 20 functional cittas accompanied by 35 cetasikas (38 excluding 3 abstinence factors), 28 matters, and *Nibbāna*. The 2nd SOE consists of 49 cittas (17 wholesome cittas, 12 unwholesome cittas, 20 functional cittas) accompanied by 52 cetasikas, 17 mind-produced matters, 15 temperature-produced matters, and 14 nutriment-produced matters.

The 1st & 2nd SOE are bound up with mind-element and mind-consciousness element. They are characteristic of mentality-materiality.

The 3rd and 4th are 8 supramundane cittas, accompanied by 36 cetasikas (38 excluding the 2 Illimitables), and *Nibbāna*. They belong to 4 mental aggregates and *Nibbāna*, are typical of mind-consciousness element.

As a whole, these four states of enquiry are dissociated from the mundane 17 wholesome cittas, 12 unwholesome cittas, and the 32 resultant cittas. Therefore, those dissociated states are classified, and taken as aggrouped under 4 aggregates (4 mental aggregates), under 2 bases (ideation-base, mind base), and under 8 elements (ideation-element, 7 consciousness-elements). They are taken as ungrouped under 1 aggregate (matter), under 10 bases (10 gross bases), and under 10 elements (10 gross elements).

		Those dissociated states					
479. States of enquiry :	is dissociated from *these* states (✗) :	Aggrouped			Ungrouped		
		Agr	Bse	El.	Agr	Bse	El.
States which are the result of clinging and are favourable to clinging. (1)	sound object, wholesome states, unwholesome states, functional states, supramundane states, *Nibbāna*	4	2	3	1	10	15

The states of enquiry belong to 20 kamma-produced matters, 32 mundane resultant cittas, accompanied by 35 cetasikas (38 excluding 3 abstinence factors).

XIV. Aggrouped and Ungrouped from Dissociated

They consist of 9 gross elements (10 excluding audible object element), ideation-element, 6 consciousness elements (7 excluding ear-consciousness element). These states belong to mentality-materiality.

They are dissociated from sound object, the mundane 17 wholesome states, 12 unwholesome states, 20 functional states, 8 supramundane cittas, and *Nibbāna*. These dissociated states span the 4 mental aggregates. Those dissociated states are therefore classified, and taken as aggrouped under 4 aggregates excluding *Nibbāna* (4 mental aggregates), under 2 bases (sound-base, ideation-base), and under 3 elements (sound-element, ear-consciousness element, ideation-element). They are not aggrouped under 1 aggregate (matter), under 10 bases (9 gross bases without sound-base; mind-base), and under 15 elements (the aforesaid 9 gross elements and 6 consciousness elements).

	are dissociated from *these* states (≠) :	Those dissociated states					
		Aggrouped			Ungrouped		
480. States of enquiry (SOE):		Agr	Bse	El.	Agr	Bse	El.
States which are not corrupted but are the objects of corruptions. (1)	unwholesome states, supramundane states, 6 cons. elements, *Nibbāna*	4	2	2	1	10	16

These states include 28 matters, 69 cittas (constitute of 17 wholesome cittas, 32 resultant cittas, 20 functional cittas), arisen with 38 cetasikas. These states of enquiry are characteristic of mentality and materiality. They are linked to mind-consciousness element. They are in dissociation from unwholesome states, supramundane states, and *Nibbāna* which span the 4 mental aggregates.

Those dissociated states are classified, and taken as aggrouped under 4 aggregates excluding *Nibbāna* (4 mental aggregates), under 2 bases (ideation-base, mind-base), and under 2 elements (ideation-element, mind-consciousness element). They are taken as not aggrouped under 1 aggregate (matter), under 10 bases (10 gross bases), and under 16 elements (10 gross elements, and the remaining 6 consciousness elements).

	are dissociated from *these* states (≠) :	Those dissociated states					
		Aggrouped			Ungrouped		
481. States of enquiry (SOE):		Agr	Bse	El.	Agr	Bse	El.
States with initial application and sustained application. (1)	28 matters, 6 consciousness elements, third jhānas, fourth jhānas, immaterial jhānas	5	12	17	-	-	1

These states consist of 55 cittas accompanied by 50 cetasikas (52 excluding *vitakka, vicāra*). They are bound up with mind-consciousness element. These

A Perfect Knowledge of Mind-Body from the Abhidhamma (Dhātukathā)

states are dissociated from materiality, the third to fifth jhānas, and the remaining 6 consciousness elements.

Those dissociated states are classified, and taken as aggrouped under 5 aggregates excluding *Nibbāna*, under 12 bases, and under 17 elements (10 gross elements, ideation-element, 6 consciousness-elements without mind-consciousness element). Those states are ungrouped under 1 element (mind-consciousness element).

		Those dissociated states					
	are dissociated from	Aggrouped			Ungrouped		
482. States of enquiry (SOE):	*these* states (✗) :	Agr	Bse	El.	Agr	Bse	El.
States without initial application but with sustained application; States accompanied by zest; States accompanied by happiness. (3)	28 matters, 5 or 6 cons. elements, sensuous cittas, immaterial cittas	5	12	18	-	-	-

States without initial application but with sustained application are 11 Second-*Jhāna* cittas, 66 cittas with sustained application accompanied by 36 cetasikas. States accompanied by zest are 51 associated cittas, accompanied by 46 cetasikas. Both SOE belong to 4 mental aggregates and are bound up with mind-consciousness element. They are dissociated from 28 matters and the remaining 6 consciousness elements.

States accompanied by happiness consist of 63 cittas, accompanied by 46 cetasikas. They are classified under perception, volitive formation, and consciousness aggregates. These states are bound up with body-consciousness element and mind-consciousness element. They are dissociated from 28 matters and the remaining 5 consciousness elements.

As a whole, these three states of enquiry are dissociated from materiality, sensuous cittas, and immaterial cittas which are all fifth jhānas. These dissociated states cover all 4 mental aggregates.

Therefore, those dissociated states are classified, and taken as aggrouped under 5 aggregates excluding *Nibbāna*, under 12 bases, and under 18 elements. There are no remaining states that are unclassified.

		Those dissociated states					
	are dissociated from	Aggrouped			Ungrouped		
483. States of enquiry (SOE):	*these* states (✗) :	Agr	Bse	El.	Agr	Bse	El.
States without initial application and without sustained application. (1)	sensuous cittas, first jhānas, mind-element	4	2	3	1	10	15

These states consist of 11 Second-*Jhāna* cittas, 55 cittas dissociated from *vitakka* and *vicāra* which are accompanied by 36 cetasikas (38 excluding *vitakka*,

XIV. Aggrouped and Ungrouped from Dissociated

vicāra), 28 matters, and *Nibbāna*. These states are dissociated from sensuous cittas, first jhānas, and partially dissociated from mind-element.

Those dissociated states are thus classified, and taken as aggrouped under 4 aggregates excluding *Nibbāna* (4 mental aggregates), under 2 bases (ideation-base, mind-base), under 3 elements (mind-element, ideation-element, mind-consciousness element). They are not aggrouped under 1 aggregate (matter), under 10 bases (10 gross bases), and under 15 elements (10 gross elements, and the remaining 5 consciousness elements).

		Those dissociated states					
		Aggrouped			Ungrouped		
484. States of enquiry :	are dissociated from *these* states (✗) :	Agr	Bse	El.	Agr	Bse	El.
States accompanied by equanimity. (1)	states accompanied by zest, states accompanied by happiness, body-consciousness element, 28 matters	5	12	13	-	-	5

These are states which are indifferent to happy feeling and painful feeling, consist of 55 cittas accompanied by equanimity, are arisen with 46 cetasikas (52 excluding feeling, zest, hatred, envy, avarice, and worry). They belong to perception, volitive formation, and consciousness. They are dissociated from materiality, feeling, states accompanied by zest, states accompanied by happiness, body-consciousness element, and *Nibbāna*. These dissociated states span 4 mental aggregates.

Thus, those dissociated states are classified, and taken as aggrouped under 5 aggregates excluding *Nibbāna*, under 12 bases (10 gross bases, ideation-base, mind base), and under 13 elements (10 gross elements, body-consciousness element, ideation-element, mind-consciousness element). They are taken as ungrouped under 5 elements (eye-cons. element, ear-cons. element, nose-cons. element, tongue-cons. element, and mind-element). There are no more other states as unclassified.

A Perfect Knowledge of Mind-Body from the Abhidhamma (Dhātukathā)

485. States of enquiry (SOE):	are dissociated from *these* states (≠) :	Those dissociated states Aggrouped Agr Bse El.	Ungrouped Agr Bse El.
States eliminated by first Path; States eliminated by higher three Paths; States with root causes eliminated by first Path; States with root causes eliminated by higher three Paths; States which make for the continuity of death, rebirth (*ācayagāmino*); States which make for the discontinuity of death & rebirth; States leading to *Nibbāna*; States appertaining to Learners; States appertaining to *Arahatta*; States which are sublime. (9)	28 matters, resultant states, functional states, *Nibbāna*	5 12 18	- - -

These nine subject matters of enquiry are essentially a list of wholesome cittas, unwholesome cittas, supramundane path-cittas, supramundane fruition-cittas, which all belong to 4 mental aggregates. All these states are bound up with mind-consciousness-element. They are dissociated from materiality, resultant states, functional states, and *Nibbāna*.

Those dissociated states are classified, and taken as aggrouped under 5 aggregates excluding *Nibbāna*, under 12 bases, and under 18 elements. There are no more other states as to unclassification.

486. States of enquiry (SOE):	are dissociated from *these* states (≠) :	Those dissociated states Aggrouped Agr Bse El.	Ungrouped Agr Bse El.
States neither eliminated by the first Path nor by the higher three paths; States with root causes eliminated neither by the first Path nor by the higher three Paths; States which neither lead to rebirth and death nor to *Nibbāna*; States appertaining to neither Learners nor *Arahatta*; States which are limited. (5)	supramundane cittas (8 for *Arahatta*, 7 for *Sekhā*), 36 cetasikas	4 2 2	1 10 16

These five subject matters of enquiry are a list which contain the full measure of mentality-materiality which include part of 81 mundane cittas, resultant cittas, functional cittas, 28 matters, and *Nibbāna*. For states appertaining to neither *Sekhā* nor *Arahatta*, it contains all 81 mundane cittas and 52 cetasikas. These five states of enquiry are invariably dissociated from supramundane cittas, in which case, only 7 for learners because they are not Arahats.

XIV. Aggrouped and Ungrouped from Dissociated

Those supramundane cittas are classified, and taken as aggrouped under 4 aggregates (4 mental aggregates), under 2 bases (ideation-base, mind-base), under 2 elements (ideation-element, mind-consciousness element). They are taken as not classified and ungrouped under 1 aggregate (matter), under 10 bases (10 gross bases), and under 16 elements (10 gross elements, and the remaining 6 consciousness elements).

		Those dissociated states					
	are dissociated from	Aggrouped			Ungrouped		
487. States of enquiry:	these states (≠) :	Agr	Bse	El.	Agr	Bse	El.
Immeasurable states; Superior states. (2)	limited and sublime states; inferior and medium states; 6 cons. elements	4	2	8	1	10	10

Immeasurable states are the 4 resultant cittas associated with knowledge, 4 functional cittas associated with knowledge, mind-door advertence citta, 2 supernormal power attained from fifth rūpajhānas, and 8 supramundane cittas. Superior states are 8 supramundane cittas and *Nibbāna*.

Immeasurable states are dissociated from limited states and sublime states which have included 54 sensuous cittas, 27 sublime cittas, 52 cetasikas, and *Nibbāna*. In this context, 28 matters are disregarded from limited states.

Superior states are dissociated from inferior and medium-worth states which have included 12 unwholesome cittas, 17 mundane wholesome cittas, 32 resultant cittas, 20 functional cittas. In this context, 28 matters are disregarded from medium-worth states.

Those dissociated states are classified, and taken as aggrouped under 4 aggregates (4 mental aggregates), under 2 bases (ideation-base, mind base), and under 8 elements (ideation-element, the 7 consciousness-elements). They are ungrouped under 1 aggregate (matter), under 10 bases (10 gross bases), and under 10 elements (10 gross elements).

		Those dissociated states					
	are dissociated from	Aggrouped			Ungrouped		
488. States of enquiry (SOE):	these states (≠) :	Agr	Bse	El.	Agr	Bse	El.
States with limited object. (1)	states with sublime and immeasurable objects; 28 matters, *Nibbāna*	5	12	12	-	-	6

States with limited object are 54 sensuous cittas, arisen with 52 cetasikas. They belong to 4 mental aggregates, are bound up closely with 6 sensory consciousness-elements (without the mind-consciousness element). They are dissociated from states with sublime objects, states with immeasurable objects, all materiality, and *Nibbāna*.

A Perfect Knowledge of Mind-Body from the Abhidhamma (Dhātukathā)

States with sublime object consist of 8 great wholesome cittas, 8 great functional cittas, mind-door advertence citta, 2 of the 5 supernormal powers obtained from fifth rūpajhānas, 6 arūpajhānas, 47 cetasikas (52 excluding the 3 *viratī* and 2 *appamaññā*).

States with immeasurable object consist of 4 great wholesome cittas associated with knowledge, 4 great functional cittas associated with knowledge, mind-door advertence citta, 2 supernormal powers, 8 supramundane cittas arisen with 36 cetasikas (38 excluding 2 Illimitables), and *Nibbāna*.

As such, those dissociated states are classified, and taken as aggrouped under 5 aggregates excluding *Nibbāna*, under 12 bases, and under 12 elements (10 gross elements, ideation-element, mind-consciousness element). They are taken as ungrouped under 6 elements (7 excluding mind-consciousness element).

		Those dissociated states					
	are dissociated from	Aggrouped			Ungrouped		
489. States of enquiry (SOE):	*these* states (✗) :	Agr	Bse	El.	Agr	Bse	El.
1. States with sublime object; 2. States with immeasurable object; 3. States which are inferior; 4. States fixed as to their destinies due to wrong views; 5. States fixed as to their destinies due to right views; 6. States having Path as its object; 7. States conditioned by the Path; 8. States having Path as the predominant factor. (8)	states with limited object; states which are superior; states of medium worth; states which not entail fixed future destinies; unconditioned element; 28 matters	5	12	18	-	-	-

Below are the brief summaries with reference to these eight states of enquiry.

1. States with sublime object are the 8 great wholesome cittas, 8 great functional cittas, mind-door advertence citta, 2 of the 5 supernormal powers obtained from fifth rūpajhānas, 6 arūpajhānas, 47 cetasikas. They are dissociated from states with limited objects and immeasurable objects.
2. States with immeasurable object are the 4 great wholesome cittas associated with knowledge, 4 great functional cittas associated with knowledge, mind-door advertence citta, 2 supernormal powers, 8 supramundane cittas arisen with 36 cetasikas. They are dissociated from states with limited objects and sublime objects.
3. States which are inferior are the 12 unwholesome cittas, accompanied by 27 cetasikas. They are dissociated from states of medium worth and states which are superior.
4. States fixed as to their destinies due to wrong views are the 7th sensuous *javana* (impulsion) present at the 4 greed-rooted cittas associated with

XIV. Aggrouped and Ungrouped from Dissociated

wrong view, and at the 2 hatred-rooted cittas; 25 cetasikas. They are dissociated from states which are fixed to future destinies as a result of right views, and states which do not entail fixed future destinies.

5. States fixed as to their destinies due to right views are the 4 supramundane path-cittas, arisen with 36 cetasikas. They are dissociated from states which are fixed to future destinies as a result of wrong views, and states which do not entail fixed future destinies.
6. States having Path as the object are the 4 great wholesome cittas associated with knowledge, 4 great functional cittas associated with knowledge, mind-door advertence citta, 2 supernormal powers, 33 cetasikas. They are dissociated from states which are conditioned by Path, and states which are dominated by Path.
7. States conditioned by the Path are the 4 supramundane path-cittas, arisen with 36 cetasikas. They are dissociated from states which having Path as the object, and states which are dominated by Path.
8. States are dominated by Path are 4 great wholesome cittas associated with knowledge, 4 functional cittas associated with knowledge, 4 supramundane path-cittas arisen with 36 cetasikas. They are dissociated from states which are conditioned by Path, and states which have Path as the object.

All those dissociated states are classified, and taken as aggrouped under 5 aggregates excluding *Nibbāna*, under 12 bases, and under 18 elements. There are no more other states as to unclassification.

		Those dissociated states					
	are dissociated from	Aggrouped			Ungrouped		
490. States of enquiry (SOE):	*these* states (✗) :	Agr	Bse	El.	Agr	Bse	El.
States of medium worth; States which do not entail fixed destiny. (2)	supramundane 4 path- and 4 fruition-cittas	4	2	2	1	10	16

States of medium worth consist of the mundane 69 cittas arisen with 38 cetasikas, and 28 matters. States which do not entail fixed future destinies consist of 4 greed-rooted cittas dissociated from wrong view, 2 delusion-rooted cittas, 17 mundane wholesome cittas, 32 resultant cittas, 20 functional cittas, 52 cetasikas, 28 Matters, and *Nibbāna*.

These two states of enquiry are dissociated from the 8 supramundane cittas. They are therefore classified, and taken as aggrouped under 4 aggregates (4 mental aggregates), under 2 bases (ideation-base, mind-base), under 2 elements (ideation-element, mind-consciousness element). They are taken as ungrouped under 1 aggregate (matter), under 10 bases (10 gross bases), and under 16 elements (10 gross elements, and the remaining 6 consciousness elements).

A Perfect Knowledge of Mind-Body from the Abhidhamma (Dhātukathā)

491. States of enquiry (SOE):	are dissociated from *these* states (✗) :	Those dissociated states					
		Aggrouped			Ungrouped		
		Agr	Bse	El.	Agr	Bse	El.
Arisen states; Non-arisen states; States which bound to arise; Past states; Future states; Present states; Internal states; External states; States which are visible and impinging; States not visible but are impinging. (10)	wholesome cittas, unwholesome cittas, functional cittas, supramundane cittas, *Nibbāna*.	4	2	8	1	10	10

States arisen, past states, future states, present states, and internal states are referred to 89 cittas, 52 cetasikas, and all corporeality. External states consist of the same but including *Nibbāna*. External states have included all possible states and hence there are no dissociations. The other five states are dissociated from *Nibbāna*.

States not arisen are states not yet occurred with respect to 53 cittas (comprised of 12 unwholesome cittas, 21 wholesome cittas, 20 functional cittas), 52 cetasikas, 17 action-produced matters, 15 temperature-produced matters, and 14 nutriment-produced matters. They are dissociated from 8 supramundane cittas arisen with 36 cetasikas, and *Nibbāna*.

States which are bound to arise consist of 20 kamma-produced matters, 36 resultant cittas arisen with 38 cetasikas. They are dissociated from 21 wholesome cittas, 12 unwholesome cittas, 20 functional cittas, and *Nibbāna*.

States which are visible and impinging consist of the 2 eye-consciousness, and gross visible object. States which are not visible but impinging consist of 11 gross matters having excluded gross visible object. They both are dissociated from 12 subtle matters and 4 mental aggregates.

On the whole, these ten subject matters of enquiry are dissociated from 4 mental aggregates and *Nibbāna*. These dissociated states are classified, and taken as aggrouped under 4 aggregates (4 mental aggregates), under 2 bases (ideation-base, mind base), and under 8 elements (ideation-element, the 7 consciousness-elements). They are unclassified and taken ungrouped under 1 aggregate (matter), under 10 bases (10 gross bases), and under 10 elements (10 gross elements).

492. States of enquiry (SOE):	are dissociated from *these* states (✗) :	Those dissociated states					
		Aggrouped			Ungrouped		
		Agr	Bse	El.	Agr	Bse	El.
States having past object; States having future object; States having internal object; States having external object. (4)	8 supramundane cittas (except for states having external object), 28 matters, *Nibbāna*	5	12	18	-	-	-

XIV. Aggrouped and Ungrouped from Dissociated

States with past object consist of mind-door advertence citta, 29 sensuous javanas (17 wholesome and 12 unwholesome cittas of *kammabhava*), 11 Registering cittas (3 Investigating cittas, 8 *mahāvipāka* cittas), 2 of the 5 *abhiññā* powers obtained from fifth rūpajhānas, 6 arūpajhānas (3 cittas of perceived Infinity, 3 cittas of neither-perception-nor-non-perception) arisen with 47 cetasikas (52 excluding 3 Abstinences and 2 Illimitables). They are dissociated from 8 supramundane cittas, 28 matters, and *Nibbāna*.

States having future object consist of mind-door advertence citta, 29 sensuous javanas, 11 Registering cittas, 2 supernormal powers attained from fifth rūpajhānas, and 50 cetasikas (52 excluding 2 Illimitables). They are dissociated from 8 supramundane cittas, 28 matters, and *Nibbāna*.

States with internal object comprise 54 sensuous cittas, 2 of the 5 *abhiññā* powers from fifth rūpajhānas, 3 arūpajhānas of the base of neither perception-nor-non-perception, arisen with 49 cetasikas (52 excluding envy and 2 Illimitables). They are dissociated from 8 supramundane cittas, 28 matters, and *Nibbāna*.

States with external object include 54 sensuous cittas, 15 rūpajhāna cittas but excluding the 3 fifth jhānas (that produce the 2 *abhiññā* powers), 3 arūpajhāna cittas on the base of Infinity, 8 supramundane cittas, 51 cetasikas having excluded avarice. They are dissociated from 28 matters.

Those dissociated states therefore are 8 supramundane cittas (except for states having external object), 28 matters, and *Nibbāna*. They are classified, and taken as aggrouped under 5 aggregates excluding *Nibbāna*, under 12 bases, and under 18 elements. There are no more states for unclassification.

		Those dissociated states	
	are dissociated from	Aggrouped	Ungrouped
493. States of enquiry (SOE):	*these* states (✗) :	Agr Bse El.	Agr Bse El.
States having present object; States having both internal and external objects. (2)	8 supramundane cittas, 36 cetasikas, 28 matters, *Nibbāna*	5 12 12	- - 6

States having present object consist of 43 cittas (from 10 viññāṇas, 3 mind-elements, 1 mind-door advertence citta, 29 sensuous javanas), 11 registering cittas, 2 *abhiññā* powers, and 50 cetasikas (without 2 Illimitables). They are dissociated from 8 supramundane cittas, 36 cetasikas, 28 matters, and *Nibbāna*.

States having both internal and external objects consist of 89 cittas, 52 cetasikas, 28 matters. They are dissociated from *Nibbāna*.

Thus, those dissociated states have included matter aggregate, 4 mental aggregates, and *Nibbāna*. They are classified, and taken as aggrouped under 5 aggregates excluding *Nibbāna*, under 12 bases, and under 12 elements (10 gross

A Perfect Knowledge of Mind-Body from the Abhidhamma (Dhātukathā)

elements, ideation-element, mind-consciousness element). They are taken as ungrouped under 6 elements (the remaining 6 consciousness elements).

163 states of enquiry from Dhammasaṅgaṇīmātikā dyads

5. Dyads (*Dukaṃ*)

494. States of enquiry (SOE):	are dissociated from *these* states (✗) :	Those dissociated states					
		Aggrouped			Ungrouped		
		Agr	Bse	El.	Agr	Bse	El.
States which are root causes; States which have root causes (i.e. accompanied by root causes); States which are associated with root causes; States which are root causes and also having root causes; States which are not root causes but having root causes; States which are root causes and also associated with root causes; States which are not root causes but are associated with root causes; States which are not root causes but have associated root causes. (8)	supramundane cittas, 36 cetasikas, 28 matters, *Nibbāna*	5	12	18	-	-	-

The following briefly describes regarding these eight states.

1. States which are root causes (attributed to having greed, hatred, delusion, absence of greed, absence of hatred, absence of delusion) — belong to volitive formation.
2. States which have root causes (attributed to having 4 root causes without delusion and non-delusion), consist of 71 cittas with associated roots, accompanied by 50 cetasikas — belong to 4 mental aggregates.
3. States which are associated with root causes — same as in no. 2 above, belong to 4 mental aggregates.
4. States which are root causes and also having root causes (attributed to the same 6 root causes, and excluding delusion present at the 2 delusion-rooted cittas) — belong to volitive formation.
5. States which are not root causes but having associated root causes (are attributed to having the 6 roots causes) consist of 71 cittas with associated roots, accompanied by 46 cetasikas (52-6=46) — belong to 4 mental aggregates.
6. States which are root causes and also associated with root causes — same as in no. 4 above, belong to volitive formation.

XIV. Aggrouped and Ungrouped from Dissociated

7. States which are not root causes but are associated with root causes — same as in no. 5 above, belong to 4 mental aggregates.
8. States which are not root causes but have associated root causes — same as in no. 5 above, belong to 4 mental aggregates.

These eight states of enquiry belong to the all 81 mundane cittas, are hence dissociated from 8 supramundane states, 28 matters, and *Nibbāna*. These dissociated states are classified, and taken as aggrouped under 5 aggregates excluding *Nibbāna*, under 12 bases, and under 18 elements. There are no more states for unclassification.

		Those dissociated states	
	are dissociated from	Aggrouped	Ungrouped
495. States of enquiry (SOE):	*these* states (✗) :	Agr Bse El.	Agr Bse El.
States which have no root causes (i.e. not accompanied by root causes); States which are dissociated from root causes; States which are neither root causes nor having root causes. (3)	the remaining 71 cittas with roots, 52 cetasikas	4 2 2	1 10 16

These three states consist of 18 cittas without root causes (15 from resultant cittas, 3 from functional cittas), arisen with 11 cetasikas (13 common cetasikas excluding *adhimokkha, vicikicchā*), 28 matters, and *Nibbāna*. The remaining 71 cittas with root causes are hence the dissociated states. They are classified, and taken as aggrouped under 4 aggregates (4 mental aggregates), under 2 bases (ideation-base, mind-base), under 2 elements (ideation-element, mind-consciousness element). They are unclassified and taken as ungrouped under 1 aggregate (matter), under 10 bases (10 gross bases), and under 16 elements (10 gross elements, and the remaining 6 consciousness elements).

		Those dissociated states	
	are dissociated from	Aggrouped	Ungrouped
496. States of enquiry (SOE):	*these* states (✗) :	Agr Bse El.	Agr Bse El.
States not arisen from causes; States unconditioned by causes; States with visibility; States with impinging; States with physical change; States which are supramundane. (6)	81 mundane cittas, 52 cetasikas	4 2 8	1 10 10

States which are not arisen from causes, and states unconditioned by causes are referring to *Nibbāna*. They are dissociated from 4 mental aggregates.

A Perfect Knowledge of Mind-Body from the Abhidhamma (Dhātukathā)

States with visibility refer to the 2 eye-consciousness and gross visible object. They are dissociated from 12 subtle matters, and 4 mental aggregates.

States with impinging refer to gross materiality. States with physical change refer to all matters. They are dissociated from 4 mental aggregates.

States which are supramundane are *Nibbāna* by way of 8 x 5 supramundane cittas, accompanied by 36 cetasikas (38 excluding 2 Illimitables). They are dissociated from 81 mundane cittas.

Thus, those dissociated states as a whole are 81 mundane cittas (17 wholesome cittas, 12 unwholesome cittas, 32 resultant cittas, and 20 functional cittas). They are classified, and taken as aggrouped under 4 aggregates (4 mental aggregates), under 2 bases (ideation-base, mind base), and under 8 elements (ideation-element, 7 consciousness-elements). They are unclassified and taken as ungrouped under 1 aggregate (matter), under 10 bases (10 gross bases), and under 10 elements (10 gross elements).

		Those dissociated states					
	are dissociated from	Aggrouped			Ungrouped		
497. States of enquiry (SOE):	*these* states (≠) :	Agr	Bse	El.	Agr	Bse	El.
States which are mundane. (1)	8 supramundane states, 36 cetasikas *Nibbāna*	4	2	2	1	10	16

All 81 mundane cittas are bound up with 6 sensory consciousness-elements, and parting from supramundane states. Those dissociated states, 8 supramundane states and *Nibbāna* are classified, and taken as aggrouped under 4 aggregates excluding *Nibbāna* (4 mental aggregates), under 2 bases (ideation-base, mind-base), and under 2 elements (ideation-element, mind-consciousness element). They are not aggrouped under 1 aggregate (matter), under 10 bases (10 gross bases), and under 16 elements (10 gross elements, remaining 6 consciousness elements).

		Those dissociated states					
	are dissociated from	Aggrouped			Ungrouped		
498. States of enquiry (SOE):	*these* states (≠) :	Agr	Bse	El.	Agr	Bse	El.
States which are defilement; States which are associated with defilement; States which are both defilement and objects of defilement; States which are both defilement and associated with defilement; States associated with defilement but are not defilement. (5)	wholesome cittas, resultant cittas, functional cittas, supramundane cittas, beautiful cetasikas, all matters, *Nibbāna*	5	12	18	-	-	-

XIV. Aggrouped and Ungrouped from Dissociated

The following briefly explains regarding these five states above.

1. States which are defilement (attributed to the 3 factors of greed (or sensual desire), wrong view, and delusion, present at the 12 unwholesome cittas) — belong to volitive formation.
2. States which are associated with defilement (attributed to 12 unwholesome cittas, accompanied by 26 cetasikas (27 excluding delusion-*cetasika*, present at the 2 hate-rooted cittas and 2 delusion-rooted cittas) — belong to unwholesome cittas.
3. States which are both defilement and objects of defilement — same as no. 1 above, belong to volitive formation.
4. States which are both defilement and associated with defilement — same as no. 1 above, belong to volitive formation.
5. States associated with defilement but are not defilement (attributed to 12 unwholesome cittas, accompanied by 24 cetasikas (27 excluding the aforesaid 3 root causes) — belong to unwholesome cittas.

These four states of enquiry belong to the 12 unwholesome cittas, are hence dissociated from 21 wholesome states, 36 resultant states, 20 functional states, 8 supramundane states, 28 matters, and *Nibbāna*. These dissociated states are classified, and taken as aggrouped under 5 aggregates excluding *Nibbāna*, under 12 bases, and under 18 elements. There are no more states for unclassification.

		Those dissociated states					
	are dissociated from	Aggrouped			Ungrouped		
499. States of enquiry (SOE):	*these* states (≠) :	Agr	Bse	El.	Agr	Bse	El.
States which are objects of defilement; States which are dissociated from defilement; States which are objects of defilement but are not defilement; States which are dissociated from defilement but still are objects of defilement. (4)	supramundane cittas, 36 cetasikas, *Nibbāna*	4	2	2	1	10	16

The following briefly explains regarding these four states of enquiry.

1. States which are objects of defilement (attributed to 81 mundane cittas, 52 cetasikas, and all that is materiality) — belong to 28 matters and mundane cittas.
2. States which are dissociated from defilement (attributed to 77 cittas constituted of 21 wholesome cittas, 36 resultant cittas, and 20 functional cittas, arisen with 38 cetasikas (13+25); the 2 delusion-rooted cittas, all materiality, and *Nibbāna*) — belong to 28 matters and mundane cittas.

A Perfect Knowledge of Mind-Body from the Abhidhamma (Dhātukathā)

3. States which are objects of defilement but are not defilement (attributed to all that is materiality, 81 mundane cittas arisen with the 49 cetasikas having excluded 3 root causes of greed, wrong view, and delusion) — belong to 28 matters and mundane cittas.

4. States which are dissociated from defilement but still are the objects of defilement (attributed to 69 cittas comprised of the active 17 mundane wholesome cittas, 32 resultant cittas, and 20 functional cittas, all accompanied by 38 cetasikas (13+25=38); the 2 delusion-rooted cittas; 2 hatred-rooted cittas; as well as materiality — belong to 28 matters and mundane cittas.

These four states of enquiry belong to materiality and 4 mentalities appertaining to the 81 mundane cittas. They are dissociated from the 8 supramundane cittas and *Nibbāna*. These dissociated states are classified, and taken as aggrouped under 4 aggregates excluding *Nibbāna* (4 mental aggregates), under 2 bases (ideation-base, mind-base), and under 2 elements (ideation-element, mind-consciousness element). They are not classified and taken as ungrouped under 1 aggregate (matter), under 10 bases (10 gross bases), and under 16 elements (10 gross elements, remaining 6 consciousness elements).

		Those dissociated states					
	are dissociated from	Aggrouped			Ungrouped		
500. States of enquiry (SOE):	*these* states (✗) :	Agr	Bse	El.	Agr	Bse	El.
States which are not objects of defilement; States which are both dissociated from defilement and not objects of defilement. (2)	81 mundane cittas, 52 cetasikas	4	2	8	1	10	10

States which are not objects of defilement belong to the 8 supramundane cittas, accompanied by 36 cetasikas (38 excluding 2 Illimitables), and *Nibbāna*.

States which are both dissociated from defilement and not objects of defilement have the same constituent states as above.

The two states of enquiry are supramundane cittas, dissociated from 81 mundane cittas cittas (17 wholesome cittas, 12 unwholesome cittas, 32 resultant cittas, and 20 functional cittas) which also encompass all 7 consciousness elements.

Those dissociated 81 mundane states are classified, and taken as aggrouped under 4 aggregates (feeling, perception, volitive formation, consciousness), under 2 bases (ideation-base, mind base), and under 8 elements (ideation-element, the 7 consciousness-elements). They are ungrouped under 1 aggregate (matter), under 10 bases (10 gross bases), and under 10 elements (10 gross elements).

XIV. Aggrouped and Ungrouped from Dissociated

501. States of enquiry (SOE):	are dissociated from *these* states (≠) :	*Those* dissociated states					
		Aggrouped			Ungrouped		
		Agr	Bse	El.	Agr	Bse	El.
1. States which are fetters (*Saṃyojana*).	wholesome cittas, resultant cittas, functional cittas, supramundane cittas, beautiful cetasikas, all matters, *Nibbāna*	5	12	18	-	-	-
2. States which are associated with fetters.							
3. States which are both fetters and objects of fetters.							
4. States which are both fetters and associated with fetters.							
5. States which are associated with fetters but are not fetters.							
6. States which are objects of fetters.	supramundane cittas, 36 cetasikas, *Nibbāna*	4	2	2	1	10	16
7. States which are dissociated from fetters.							
8. States which are objects of fetters but are not fetters.							
9. States which are dissociated from fetters but are objects of fetters.							
10. States which are not objects of fetters.	81 mundane cittas, 52 cetasikas	4	2	8	1	10	10
11. States which are both dissociated from fetters and not objects of fetters.							
(repeat the above 11 states for *Gantha, Ogha, Yoga,* and *Nīvaraṇa*. Thus, giving 11 x 4 =44)	follows the same answers as in no. 1 to 11 above.						
56. States which are attachment (*Parāmāsa*).	wholesome cittas, resultant cittas, functional cittas, supramundane cittas, 28 matters, *Nibbāna*	5	12	18	-	-	-
57. States associated with attachment.							
58. States which are both attachment and objects of attachment.							

The following briefly describes regarding these 58 states of enquiry.

1. States which are fetters (*saṃyojana*) are the 8 states of fetters (according to Dhammasaṅgaṇi), viz. 8 cetasikas of greed, ill-will, conceit, wrong view, doubt, envy, avarice, ignorance — they belong to volitive formation.
2. States which are associated with fetters are attributed to the 12 unwholesome cittas, accompanied by 26 cetasikas (27 excluding restlessness-*cetasika*) — belong to 4 mental aggregates.
3. States which are fetters and also objects of fetters — same as no. 1 above, belong to volitive formation.

A Perfect Knowledge of Mind-Body from the Abhidhamma (Dhātukathā)

4. States which are both fetters and associated with fetters — same as no. 1 above, belong to volitive formation.
5. States which are associated with fetters but are not fetters — are attributed to the 12 unwholesome cittas, arisen with 19 cetasikas (27 excluding the 8 states of fetters) — belong to 4 mental aggregates.
6. States which are objects of fetters are attributed to 81 mundane cittas, 52 cetasikas, all materiality) — belong to 28 matters and 4 mental aggregates.
7. States which are dissociated from fetters are attributed to 77 cittas (21 mundane wholesome cittas, 36 resultant cittas, 20 functional cittas), arisen with 38 cetasikas (13+25); 1 delusion-rooted citta associated with restlessness, arisen with 15 cetasikas (13 common non-beautiful factors excluding *pīti* and *chanda*; 4 common unwholesome factors, i.e. 11+4=15); all materiality; *Nibbāna*) — belong to 28 matters and 4 mental aggregates.
8. States which are objects of fetters but are not fetters per se are attributed to the 81 mundane cittas, arisen with 44 cetasikas (52 excluding the 8 states of fetters), and all materiality — belong to 28 matters and 4 mental aggregates.
9. States which are dissociated from fetters but are objects of fetters — are attributed to 69 cittas (17 mundane wholesome cittas, 32 resultant cittas, and 20 functional cittas), accompanied by 38 cetasikas (13+25=38); 1 delusion-rooted citta associated with restlessness, accompanied by 15 cetasikas; and materiality — belong to 28 matters and 4 mental aggregates.
10. States which are not objects of fetters are attributed to the 8 supramundane cittas accompanied by 36 cetasikas (38 excluding 2 Illimitables), and *Nibbāna* — belong to 4 mental aggregates and *Nibbāna*.
11. States which are both dissociated from fetters and not objects of fetters — same as no. 10 above, belong to 4 mental aggregates and *Nibbāna*.
12. to 55. Repeats the above 11 states for *Gantha* (See Table 1.8.5), *Ogha* (same as *Āsava*. See Table 1.8.3), *Yoga* (same as *Āsava*. See Table 1.8.3), and *Nīvaraṇa* (See Table 1.8.6).
56. States which are attachment (*parāmāsa*) are due to one's misapprehension owing to 'wrong view' (*diṭṭhi*) — belong to volitive formation.
57. States associated with attachment are attributed to the 4 greed-rooted cittas associated with wrong view, arisen with 20 cetasikas (27 excluding wrong view, conceit hatred, envy, avarice, worry, doubt) — belong to 4 mental aggregates.
58. States which are both attachment and objects of attachment — same as no. 56 above, belong to volitive formation.

The answers for SOE no. 1 to 5 are the same as in nos. 498.
The answers for SOE no. 6 to 9 are the same as in nos. 499.
The answers for SOE no. 10 to 11 are the same as in nos. 500.
The answers for SOE no. 12 to 55 (11 x 4 for *Gantha*, *Ogha*, *Yoga*, and *Nīvaraṇa*) are obtained in the same manner as in SOE no. 1 to 11.

XIV. Aggrouped and Ungrouped from Dissociated

SOE 56, 57 and 58 are dissociated from wholesome cittas, resultant cittas, functional cittas, supramundane cittas, 28 matters, and *Nibbāna*. Thus, those dissociated states are aggrouped under 5 aggregates excluding *Nibbāna*, under 12 bases, and under 18 elements. There are no more states that unclassified.

			Those dissociated states					
		are dissociated from	Aggrouped			Ungrouped		
502.	States of enquiry (SOE):	*these* states (✗) :	Agr	Bse	El.	Agr	Bse	El.
1.	States which are not objects of attachment.	81 mundane cittas, 52 cetasikas	4	2	2	1	10	16
2.	States which are dissociated from attachment.	8 supramundane cittas, 36 cetasikas	4	2	2	1	10	16
3.	States which are objects of attachment but are not attachment.							
4.	States which are dissociated from attachment but are objects of attachment.							

These four states of enquiry are explained as follows:

1. States which are not objects of attachment are attributed to the 8 supramundane cittas accompanied by 36 cetasikas (38 excluding 2 Illimitables), and *Nibbāna* — belong to supramundane cittas and *Nibbāna*.
2. States which are dissociated from attachment are attributed to 85 cittas (comprised of the 21 mundane wholesome cittas, 36 resultant cittas, 20 functional cittas, 4 greed-rooted cittas dissociated from wrong view, 2 hatred-rooted cittas, 2 delusion-rooted cittas) accompanied by 51 cetasikas (52 excluding wrong view), also 28 matters, *Nibbāna* — belong to 28 matters, mundane cittas, and *Nibbāna*.
3. States which are objects of attachment but are not attachment are attributed to the 81 mundane cittas accompanied by 51 cetasikas (52 excluding wrong view), and all materiality — belong to 28 matters and mundane cittas.
4. States which are dissociated from attachment but still are objects of attachment are attributed to the 77 cittas (constitute of the 4 greed-rooted cittas dissociated from wrong view, 2 hatred-rooted cittas, 2 delusion-rooted cittas, 17 mundane wholesome cittas, 32 resultant cittas, 20 functional cittas) accompanied by 51 cetasikas (52 excluding wrong view), and also all materiality — belong to 28 matters and mundane cittas.

Those dissociated states are 81 mundane cittas and 8 supramundane cittas which encompass the 4 mentalities and 52 cetasikas. Those dissociated states are classified, and taken as aggrouped under 4 aggregates excluding *Nibbāna* (4 mental aggregates), under 2 bases (ideation-base, mind-base), and under 2

A Perfect Knowledge of Mind-Body from the Abhidhamma (Dhātukathā)

elements (ideation-element, mind-consciousness element). They are not classified and taken as ungrouped under 1 aggregate (matter), under 10 bases (10 gross bases), and under 16 elements (10 gross elements, and remaining 6 consciousness elements).

			Those dissociated states	
		are dissociated from	Aggrouped	Ungrouped
503.	States of enquiry (SOE):	*these* states (✗) :	Agr Bse El.	Agr Bse El.
States which are not objects of attachment; States which are both dissociated from attachment and not objects of attachment. (2)		81 mundane cittas, 52 cetasikas	4 2 8	1 10 10

These two states of enquiry are both attributed to the 8 supramundane cittas accompanied by 36 cetasikas (38 excluding 2 Illimitables), and *Nibbāna*. These states are directly dissociated from 81 mundane cittas.

Those dissociated states are classified, and taken as aggrouped under 4 aggregates (4 mental aggregates), under 2 bases (ideation-base, mind base), and under 8 elements (ideation-element, 7 consciousness-elements). They are not classified and taken as ungrouped under 1 aggregate (matter), under 10 bases (10 gross bases), and under 10 elements (10 gross elements).

			Those dissociated states	
		are dissociated from	Aggrouped	Ungrouped
504.	States of enquiry (SOE):	*these* states (✗) :	Agr Bse El.	Agr Bse El.
States which attend to objects; States which are consciousness; States which are mental factors; States associated with consciousness; States conjoined with consciousness; States both conjoined with and originated from consciousness; States conjoined with, originated from, and arise concurrently with consciousness; States conjoined with, originated from, and arise consecutively with consciousness. (8)		28 matters, *Nibbāna*	1 11 11	4 1 7

States which attend to objects (or which have objects) consist of 89 cittas, accompanied by 52 cetasikas. States which are consciousness are 89 cittas. The other six states all referring to mental factors.

These eight states of enquiry come under 52 cetasikas and consciousness aggregate, are dissociated from matter aggregate and *Nibbāna*. The latter are classified, and taken as aggrouped under 1 aggregate (matter), under 11 bases (10 gross matters, ideation-base), and under 11 elements (10 gross elements, ideation-element). They are not classified and taken as ungrouped under 4

XIV. Aggrouped and Ungrouped from Dissociated

aggregates (4 mental aggregates), under 1 base (mind-base), and under 7 elements (7 consciousness elements).

		Those dissociated states					
	are dissociated from	Aggrouped			Ungrouped		
505. States of enquiry (SOE):	*these* states (✗) :	Agr	Bse	El.	Agr	Bse	El.
1. States which do not have objects.							
2. States dissociated from consciousness.	4 mental aggregates						
3. States not conjoined with consciousness.		4	2	8	1	10	10
4. States which are derived.							
5. States which are not the result of clinging (not obtained by clinging) (*anupādinnehi dhammehi*)	10 viññāṇas						

The 1st, 2nd, 3rd SOE all belong to materiality and *Nibbāna*. States which are derived are the 24 matters (28 excluding 4 great elements). These three SOE are dissociated from 4 mental aggregates.

States which are not the result of clinging are 57 cittas (21 wholesome cittas, 12 unwholesome cittas, 20 functional cittas, 4 supramundane fruition-cittas), arisen with 52 cetasikas; 17 mind-produced matters, 15 temperature-produced matters, 14 nutriment-produced matters, and *Nibbāna*. They are dissociated from fivefold 10 pairs of sense-consciousness, or the 5 sensory consciousness elements.

These five subject matters of enquiry are therefore dissociated from the 4 mentalities. These dissociated states are classified, and taken as aggrouped under 4 aggregates (4 mental aggregates), under 2 bases (ideation-base, mind base), and under 8 elements (ideation-element, 7 consciousness-elements). They are not classified as ungrouped under 1 aggregate (matter), under 10 bases (10 gross bases), and under 10 elements (10 gross elements).

		Those dissociated states					
	are dissociated from	Aggrouped			Ungrouped		
506. States of enquiry:	*these* states (✗) :	Agr	Bse	El.	Agr	Bse	El.
States which are the result of clinging (i.e. acquired by clinging) (*upādinnehi dhammehi*) (1)	mind-element, mind-consciousness element	4	2	3	1	10	15

These states consist of the 32 mundane resultant cittas, accompanied by 35 cetasikas (38 excluding 3 abstinences), and 20 kamma-produced matters. They are bound up with the 10 sensory viññāṇas. They are thus dissociated from mind-element and mind-consciousness element. These dissociated states are classified,

A Perfect Knowledge of Mind-Body from the Abhidhamma (Dhātukathā)

and taken as aggrouped under 4 aggregates excluding *Nibbāna* (4 mental aggregates), under 2 bases (ideation-base, mind-base), under 3 elements (mind-element, ideation-element, mind-consciousness element). They are unclassified and ungrouped under 1 aggregate (matter), under 10 bases (10 gross bases), and under 15 elements (10 gross elements, and remaining 5 consciousness elements).

		Those dissociated states					
	are dissociated from	Aggrouped			Ungrouped		
507. States of enquiry (SOE):	*these* states (≠) :	Agr	Bse	El.	Agr	Bse	El.
1. States which are clinging (*Upādinnā*).	wholesome cittas, resultant cittas, functional cittas, supramundane cittas, beautiful cetasikas, 28 matters, *Nibbāna*	5	12	18	-	-	-
2. States which are associated with clinging.							
3. States which are both clinging and objects of clinging.							
4. States which are both clinging and associated with clinging.							
5. States which are associated with clinging but are not clinging.							
6. States which are objects of clinging.	8 supramundane cittas, 36 cetasikas	4	2	2	1	10	16
7. States which are dissociated from clinging.							
8. States which are objects of clinging but are not clinging.							
9. States which are dissociated from clinging but are objects of clinging.							
10. States which are not objects of clinging.	81 mundane cittas, 16 cetasikas	4	2	8	1	10	10
11. States which are dissociated from clinging as well as are not objects of clinging.							
States which are corruptions (*Kilesa*); States which are corrupt; States which are associated with corruptions; States which are both corruptions and objects of corruptions; States which are both corruptions and are corrupt; States which are corrupt but are not corruptions; States which are both corruptions and associated with corruptions; States associated with corruptions but are not corruptions. (12-19)	wholesome cittas, resultant cittas, functional cittas, supramundane cittas, beautiful cetasikas, 28 matters, *Nibbāna*	5	12	18	-	-	-

These eighteen states of enquiry are briefly explained as below.

XIV. Aggrouped and Ungrouped from Dissociated

1. States which are clinging are attributed to the 2 states of clinging which sprung from sensual desire and wrong view, or 4 kinds which include ceremonial observances (*sīlabbata*), mind-matter as soul (*attavāda*). It is reduced to 2 kinds because *sīlabbata* and *attavāda* are considered as wrong view present at 14 unwholesome cetasikas — belong to volitive formation.
2. States which are associated with clinging are attributed to the 8 greed-rooted cittas, accompanied by 22 cetasikas (27 excluding hatred, envy, avarice, worry, and doubt) — belong to unwholesome cittas.
3. States which are both clinging and objects of clinging are the 2 states of clinging as to sensual desire and wrong view, which present at the 4 greed-rooted cittas associated with wrong view — belong to volitive formation.
4. States which are both clinging and associated with clinging are attributed to are the same as in no. 3 above — belong to volitive formation.
5. States which are associated with clinging but are not clinging are attributed to the 8 greed-rooted cittas, accompanied by 20 cetasikas (27 excluding hatred, envy, avarice, worry, doubt, and the 2 states of clinging (greed as sensual desires, and wrong view) — belong to unwholesome cittas.

> These five states above are dissociated from wholesome cittas, resultant cittas, functional cittas, supramundane cittas, beautiful cetasikas, 28 matters, and *Nibbāna*. These states span the whole measures of mentality and materiality.

6. States which are objects of clinging are attributed to 81 mundane cittas accompanied by 52 cetasikas, and all materiality — belong to 28 matters and 81 mundane cittas.
7. States which are dissociated from clinging are attributed to 81 cittas (2 hatred-rooted cittas, 2 delusion-rooted cittas, 21 mundane wholesome cittas, 36 resultant cittas, 20 functional cittas) accompanied by 49 cetasikas (52 excluding greed, wrong view, conceit), 28 matters, and *Nibbāna* — belong to mundane cittas, 28 matters, and *Nibbāna*.
8. States which are objects of clinging but are not clinging are attributed to materiality, 81 mundane cittas accompanied by 50 cetasikas (52 excluding greed and wrong view) — belong to 28 matters and 81 mundane cittas.
9. States which are dissociated from clinging but are objects of clinging are attributed to 73 cittas (2 hatred-rooted cittas, 2 delusion-rooted cittas, 17 mundane wholesome cittas, 32 resultant cittas, 20 functional cittas) arisen with 49 cetasikas (52 excluding greed, wrong view, and conceit), and materiality — belong to 28 matters and 73 mundane cittas.

> These four states above are dissociated from the 4 supramundane path-cittas, 4 supramundane fruition-cittas, and 36 cetasikas.

A Perfect Knowledge of Mind-Body from the Abhidhamma (Dhātukathā)

10. States which are not objects of clinging are attributed to 8 supramundane cittas, accompanied by 36 cetasikas (38 excluding 2 Illimitables), and *Nibbāna*.

11. States which are dissociated from clinging as well as are not objects of clinging are attributed to the same as in no. 10 above.

These two states above are dissociated from 81 mundane cittas, and 16 cetasikas (14 unwholesome cetasikas + 2 Illimitables).

Answers for SOE no. 1 to 5 are obtained in the same way as in nos. 498.
Answers for SOE no. 6 to 9 are obtained in the same way as in nos. 499.
Answers for SOE no. 10 to 11 are obtained in the same way as in nos. 500.

12. States which are corruptions are attributed to the 10 states of corruptions, namely, the mental factors of greed, hatred, delusion, conceit, wrong view, doubt, sloth, restlessness, shamelessness, and the guiltlessness of conscience — belong to volitive formation.

13. States which are corrupted are attributed to 12 unwholesome cittas, accompanied by 27 cetasikas (13+14) — belong to unwholesome cittas.

14. States which are associated with corruptions are attributed to the same as in no. 13 above, belong to unwholesome cittas.

15. States which are both corruptions and objects of corruptions are attributed to the same aforesaid 10 states of corruptions — belong to volitive formation.

16. States which are both corruptions and are corrupted are attributed to the same aforesaid 10 states of corruptions — belong to volitive formation.

17. States which are corrupted but are not corruptions are attributed to 12 unwholesome cittas, accompanied by 17 cetasikas (27 excluding the aforementioned 10 states of corruption — belong to unwholesome cittas.

18. States which are both corruptions and associated with corruptions are attributed to the same aforesaid 10 states of corruptions — belong to volitive formation.

19. States associated with corruptions but are not corruptions are attributed to the same as in no. 17. above — belong to unwholesome cittas.

SOE 12 to 19 are 12 unwholesome cittas, are dissociated from wholesome cittas, resultant cittas, functional cittas, supramundane cittas, 28 matters, and *Nibbāna*. Thus, these dissociated states are classified, and taken as aggrouped under 5 aggregates excluding *Nibbāna*, under 12 bases, and under 18 elements.

XIV. Aggrouped and Ungrouped from Dissociated

508. States of enquiry (SOE):	are dissociated from *these* states (≠) :	Those dissociated states					
		Aggrouped			Ungrouped		
		Agr	Bse	El.	Agr	Bse	El.
States which are objects of corruptions; States which are not corrupted; States dissociated from corruptions; States which are not corruptions but are objects of corruptions but; States dissociated from corruptions, but are objects of corruptions. (5)	supramundane cittas, 36 cetasikas	4	2	2	1	10	16

These five states of enquiry are briefly explained as follows:

1. States which are objects of corruptions are attributed to materiality, 81 mundane cittas accompanied by 52 cetasikas.
2. States which are not corrupted are attributed to 77 cittas (21 mundane wholesome cittas, 36 resultant cittas, 20 functional cittas) accompanied by 38 cetasikas (13+25), 28 matters, and *Nibbāna*.
3. States which are dissociated from corruptions are the same as in no. 2 above.
4. States which are not corruptions but are objects of corruptions are attributed to 81 mundane cittas, accompanied by 42 cetasikas (52 excluding the 10 states of corruptions as mentioned in nos. 507, 12.), and 28 matters.
5. States which are dissociated from corruptions but are objects of corruptions are attributed to 69 cittas (17 mundane wholesome cittas, 32 resultant cittas, 20 functional cittas) accompanied by 38 cetasikas (13+25), and 28 matters.

These four states of enquiry are mundane cittas dissociated from the 8 supramundane cittas and 36 cetasikas. These dissociated states are classified, and taken as aggrouped under 4 aggregates excluding *Nibbāna* (4 mental aggregates), under 2 bases (ideation-base, mind-base), and under 2 elements (ideation-element, mind-consciousness element). They are not aggrouped under 1 aggregate (matter), under 10 bases (10 gross bases), and under 16 elements (10 gross elements, and the remaining 6 consciousness elements).

509. States of enquiry (SOE):	are dissociated from *these* states (≠) :	Those dissociated states					
		Aggrouped			Ungrouped		
		Agr	Bse	El.	Agr	Bse	El.
States which are not objects of corruptions; States dissociated from corruptions and are not objects of corruptions. (2)	81 mundane cittas, 16 cetasikas	4	2	8	1	10	10

A Perfect Knowledge of Mind-Body from the Abhidhamma (Dhātukathā)

These two states of enquiry are the 8 supramundane cittas, accompanied by 36 cetasikas (38 excluding 2 Illimitables), and *Nibbāna*. They are dissociated from 81 mundane cittas, and 16 cetasikas (14 unwholesome cetasikas and 2 Illimitables). All matters are herein ignored. Thus, those dissociated states are are classified and taken as aggrouped under 4 aggregates (the 4 mental aggregates), under 2 bases (ideation-base, mind base), and under 8 elements (ideation-element, the 7 consciousness-elements). They are ungrouped under 1 aggregate (matter), under 10 bases (10 gross bases), and under 10 elements (10 gross elements).

			Those dissociated states	
		are dissociated from	Aggrouped	Ungrouped
510.	States of enquiry (SOE):	*these* states (≠) :	Agr Bse El.	Agr Bse El.
States eliminated by first Path; States eliminated by the higher 3 Paths; States with root causes eliminated by first Path; States with root causes eliminated by the higher 3 Paths. (4)		wholesome cittas, resultant cittas, functional cittas, supramundane cittas, 28 matters, *Nibbāna*	5 12 18	- - -

These four states of enquiry are briefly explained as below.

1. States eliminated by first Path [7, 11] are the 3 fetters as to wrong view in the theory of soul over the truth in respect of five aggregates, doubt or perplexity, and wrong view as to the observances of rites and rituals (*sakkāyadiṭṭhi, vicikicchā, sīlabbataparāmāsa*). In another word, the states eradicated are the 4 greed-rooted cittas associated with wrong view, 1 delusion-rooted citta associated with doubt, accompanied by 22 cetasikas.
2. States eliminated by the higher three Paths [7, 11] are better to look at them individually. The Second Path (*Sakadāgāmimagga*) only attenuated the remaining 7 unwholesome cittas (12-5=7) accompanied by 25 cetasikas (27 excluding wrong view and doubt). The Third Path (*Anāgāmimagga*) eliminated the 2 hatred-rooted cittas associated with aversion, accompanied by 25 cetasikas (27 excluding wrong view and doubt). The Final Path (*Arahattamagga*) eliminated the remaining 4 greed-rooted cittas dissociated from wrong view, and 1 delusion-rooted citta associated with restlessness, accompanied by 21 cetasikas. When measured by the elimination of 10 Fetters, the second Path only attenuated the remaining 7 of the 10 Fetters; the third Path eradicated the 5 Fetters of the 'Lower region' (*sakkāyadiṭṭhi, vicikicchā, sīlabbataparāmāsa, kāmarāga*—attenuated from *kāmacchandā*, and *paṭigha*—attenuated from *byāpāda*); the fourth Path eradicated the five Fetters of the 'upper region' (*rūparāga, arūparāga, māna, uddhacca, avijjā*).
3. States with root causes eliminated by first Path are the 4 greed-rooted cittas associated with wrong view, 1 delusion-rooted citta associated with doubt, accompanied by 22 cetasikas.

XIV. Aggrouped and Ungrouped from Dissociated

4. States with root causes eliminated by the higher three Paths are the 4 greed-rooted cittas dissociated from wrong view, 2 hatred-rooted cittas, 1 delusion-rooted citta associated with restlessness, accompanied by 25 cetasikas (second Path and third Path), 21 cetasikas (the final Path).

These four states of enquiry are dissociated from 17 wholesome cittas, 32 resultant cittas, 20 functional cittas, 8 supramundane cittas, 28 matters, and *Nibbāna*. Those dissociated states are classified, and taken as aggrouped under 5 aggregates excluding *Nibbāna*, under 12 bases, and under 18 elements. There are no more remaining states that are unclassified.

		Those dissociated states					
		Aggrouped			Ungrouped		
511. States of enquiry (SOE):	are dissociated from *these* states (✗) :	Agr	Bse	El.	Agr	Bse	El.
States not eliminated by the first Path; States not eliminated by the higher 3 Paths; States with root causes not eliminated by the first Path; States with root causes not eliminated by the higher 3 Paths. (4)	wholesome cittas, indeterminate cittas, and 38 cetasikas; supramundane cittas and 36 cetasikas	4	2	2	1	10	16

Below are brief descriptions with regard to these four states of enquiry.

1. States not eliminated by the first Path consist of 4 greed-rooted cittas dissociated from wrong view, 2 hatred-rooted cittas, 1 delusion-rooted citta associated with restlessness; 21 mundane wholesome cittas, 36 resultant cittas, 20 functional cittas, 50 cetasikas (52 excluding wrong view and doubt), 28 matters, and *Nibbāna*.
2. States not eliminated by the higher three Paths consist of 4 greed-rooted cittas associated with wrong view, 1 delusion-rooted citta associated with doubt (which are eliminated by the first Path), 21 mundane wholesome cittas, 36 resultant cittas, 20 functional cittas, 50 cetasikas (52 excluding hatred and restlessness), 28 matters, *Nibbāna*.
3. Same as in no. 1 above.
4. Same as in no. 2 above.

These four states of enquiry consist of the 12 unwholesome cittas and 27 cetasikas. They are dissociated from 21 wholesome cittas, 36 resultant cittas, 20 functional cittas, which are all accompanied by 38 cetasikas (13+25=38); supramundane cittas accompanied by 36 cetasikas (38 excluding 2 Illimitables).

Those dissociated states are classified, and taken as aggrouped under 4 aggregates (4 mental aggregates), under 2 bases (ideation-base, mind-base), and under 2 elements (ideation-element, mind-consciousness element). They are not

A Perfect Knowledge of Mind-Body from the Abhidhamma (Dhātukathā)

aggrouped under 1 aggregate (matter), under 10 bases (10 gross bases), and under 16 elements (10 gross elements, remaining 6 consciousness elements).

512. States of enquiry (SOE):	are dissociated from *these* states (✗) :	Those dissociated states					
		Aggrouped			Ungrouped		
		Agr	Bse	El.	Agr	Bse	El.
States with initial application; States with sustained application. (2)	28 matters, 6 consciousness elements, third jhānas, fourth jhānas, immaterial jhānas	5	12	17	-	-	1

Answers are the same in preceding nos. 481.

513. States of enquiry (SOE):	are dissociated from *these* states (✗) :	Those dissociated states					
		Aggrouped			Ungrouped		
		Agr	Bse	El.	Agr	Bse	El.
States with zest; States which are accompanied by zest; States accompanied by happiness. (3)	sensuous cittas, immaterial jhānas, supramundane jhānas, matters, *Nibbāna*.	5	12	18	-	-	-

States with zest and states which are accompanied by zest are 51 cittas (see Chart 7 in Appendix VI), accompanied by 46 cetasikas (52 excluding zest, hatred, envy, avarice, worry and doubt).

States accompanied by happiness are 63 cittas including with both *somanassa* and *sukha* (see Chart 18 in Appendix VI), accompanied by 46 cetasikas (52 excluding feeling, hatred, envy, avarice, worry and doubt). These states are bound up with body-consciousness element and mind-consciousness element.

These three states are dissociated from 54 sensuous cittas, 12 immaterial cittas, 8 supramundane cittas, 28 matters, and *Nibbāna*. These dissociated states are classified, and taken as aggrouped under 5 aggregates excluding *Nibbāna*, under 12 bases, and under 18 elements. There are no more remaining states that are unclassified.

514. States of enquiry :	are dissociated from *these* states (✗) :	Those dissociated states					
		Aggrouped			Ungrouped		
		Agr	Bse	El.	Agr	Bse	El.
States accompanied by equanimity. (1)	states accompanied by zest, states accompanied by happiness, body-consciousness element, 28 matters	5	12	13	-	-	5

Answers are the same as in preceding nos. 484.

XIV. Aggrouped and Ungrouped from Dissociated

515. States of enquiry (SOE):	are dissociated from these states (≠) :	Those dissociated states					
		Aggrouped			Ungrouped		
		Agr	Bse	El.	Agr	Bse	El.
1. States which are characteristic of the sensuous sphere.	27 sublime states and 35 cetasikas; 8 supramundane cittas and 36 cetasikas; *Nibbāna*	4	2	2	1	10	16
2. States which are included (in round of deaths and rebirths)	8 supramundane cittas and 36 cetasikas; *Nibbāna*	4	2	2	1	10	16
3. States which lead out (from round of deaths and rebirths).	81 mundane cittas, 52 cetasikas	4	2	2	1	10	16

These three states of enquiry are briefly explained as below.

1. States which belong to sensuous sphere are the 54 sensuous cittas, 52 cetasikas, 28 matters — are dissociated from the 27 sublime states, 8 supramundane cittas, and *Nibbāna*.
2. States which are "included" are 81 mundane cittas, 52 cetasikas, 28 matters — are dissociated from 8 supramundane cittas, and *Nibbāna*.
3. States which lead out to *Nibbāna* are 4 supramundane path-cittas, accompanied by 38 cetasikas — are dissociated from 81 mundane cittas.

All those dissociated states belong to 4 mental aggregates. They are classified, and are taken as aggrouped under 4 aggregates excluding *Nibbāna* (4 mental aggregates), under 2 bases (ideation-base, mind-base), and under 2 elements (ideation-element, mind-consciousness element). They are not classified and ungrouped under 1 aggregate (matter), under 10 bases (10 gross bases), and under 16 elements (10 gross elements, the remaining 6 consciousness elements).

516. States of enquiry (SOE):	are dissociated from these states (≠) :	Those dissociated states					
		Aggrouped			Ungrouped		
		Agr	Bse	El.	Agr	Bse	El.
1. States not characteristic of the sensuous sphere.	54 sensuous cittas, 52 cetasikas	4	2	8	1	10	10
2. States which are not included (in round of existence).	81 mundane cittas, 52 cetasikas	4	2	8	1	10	10
3. States which do not lead out (from round of existence).	4 supramundane path-cittas, 36 cetasikas	4	2	8	1	10	10

These three states of enquiry are briefly explained as below.

A Perfect Knowledge of Mind-Body from the Abhidhamma (Dhātukathā)

1. States which do not belong to the sensuous sphere are 27 sublime states (*Mahaggatacittāni*) of fine-material and immaterial spheres, 8 supramundane cittas, and *Nibbāna* — are dissociated from 54 sensuous cittas.
2. States which are not included are 8 supramundane cittas accompanied by 36 cetasikas, and *Nibbāna* — are dissociated from 81 mundane cittas.
3. States which do not lead out (to *Nibbāna*) are 85 cittas (4 supramundane fruition-cittas, 81 mundane cittas), 52 cetasikas, 28 matters, and *Nibbāna* — are dissociated from the 4 supramundane path-cittas.

Those dissociated states are under the ambit of 4 mental aggregates and 7 consciousness elements. Thus, they are classified, and are taken as aggrouped under 4 aggregates (4 mental aggregates), under 2 bases (ideation-base, mind base), and under 8 elements (ideation-element, 7 consciousness-elements). They are ungrouped under 1 aggregate (matter), under 10 bases (10 gross bases), and under 10 elements (10 gross elements).

		Those dissociated states					
	are dissociated from	Aggrouped			Ungrouped		
517. States of enquiry :	*these* states (✗) :	Agr	Bse	El.	Agr	Bse	El.
1. States which are characteristic of the fine-material sphere;	54 sensuous cittas & 52 cetasikas; 27 sublime cittas & 35 cetasikas; 8 supramundane cittas & 36 cetasikas; 28 matters; *Nibbāna*.	5	12	18	-	-	-
2. States which are characteristic of the immaterial sphere.	54 sensuous cittas & 52 cetasikas; 15 fine-material cittas & 35 cetasikas; 28 matter, *Nibbāna*.	5	12	18	-	-	-
3. States which lead out (from round of existence)	4 supramundane fruition-cittas & 36 cetasikas; 28 matter; *Nibbāna*.	5	12	18	-	-	-
4. States which are fixed as to their future destinies	4 supramundane fruition-cittas & 36 cetasikas; 28 matters; *Nibbāna*.	5	12	18	-	-	-
5. States at odds (*saraṇā*) with supramundane Path.	21 wholesome cittas, 36 resultant cittas, 20 functional cittas, and 38 cetasikas; 28 matters; *Nibbāna*	5	12	18	-	-	-

Brief explanations are given below in respect of these five states.

1. States belong to fine-material sphere are 15 rūpajhānas, accompanied by 35 cetasikas (38 excluding 3 abstinence factors) — are dissociated from 54 sensuous cittas, 12 immaterial cittas, supramundane 4 path-cittas and 4 fruition-cittas, 28 matters, and *Nibbāna*.
2. States belong to immaterial sphere are 12 arūpajhānas, accompanied by 30 cetasikas (13 excluding *vitakka*, *vicāra*, and *pīti*; 25 excluding 3 abstinence factors and 2 Illimitables) — are dissociated from 54 sensuous cittas, 15

XIV. Aggrouped and Ungrouped from Dissociated

fine-material cittas, supramundane 4 path-cittas and 4 fruition-cittas, 28 matters, and *Nibbāna*.

3. States which lead out (from round of existence) are the 4 supramundane path-cittas, accompanied by 36 cetasikas — are dissociated from 4 supramundane fruition-cittas, 28 matters, and *Nibbāna*.
4. States which are fixed as to their future destinies are the 4 supramundane path-cittas accompanied by 36 cetasikas, and the 7th sensuous impulsion (*javana*) present both at the 4 greed-rooted cittas associated with wrong view and the 2 delusion-rooted cittas — are dissociated from 4 supramundane fruition-cittas, 28 matters, and *Nibbāna*.
5. States at odds (*saraṇā*) (departing from supramundane Path) are 12 unwholesome cittas, accompanied by 27 cetasikas — are dissociated from 21 wholesome cittas, 36 resultant cittas, 20 functional cittas, 28 matters, and *Nibbāna*.

Those dissociated states cover the full ambit of matter aggregate, 4 mental aggregates, and *Nibbāna*. Hence those dissociated states are are classified, and are taken as aggrouped under 5 aggregates excluding *Nibbāna*, under 12 bases, and under 18 elements. There are no more other states that are unclassified.

		Those dissociated states					
	are dissociated from	Aggrouped			Ungrouped		
518. States of enquiry (SOE):	*these* states (✗) :	Agr	Bse	El.	Agr	Bse	El.
1. States which are not characteristic of the fine-material sphere.	15 rūpajhānas, 35 cetasikas.	4	2	2	1	10	16
2. States which are not characteristic of the immaterial sphere;	12 arūpajhānas, 30 cetasikas.	4	2	2	1	10	16
3. States which do not lead out (from round of existence).	4 supramundane path-cittas, 36 cetasikas.	4	2	2	1	10	16
4. States which are not fixed in future destinies.	4 supramundane fruition-cittas, 36 cetasikas.	4	2	2	1	10	16
5. States which are not at odds (*araṇā*) with the supramundane Path.	12 unwholesome cittas, 27 cetasikas	4	2	2	1	10	16

Brief explanations are given below in respect of these five states.

1. States which are not characteristic of the fine-material sphere are referred to the 74 cittas (54 sensuous cittas, 12 immaterial cittas, supramundane 4 path-

A Perfect Knowledge of Mind-Body from the Abhidhamma (Dhātukathā)

cittas and 4 fruition-cittas, 52 cetasikas, 28 matters, and *Nibbāna* — they are dissociated from the 15 rūpajhānas.

2. States which are not characteristic of the immaterial sphere are referred to the 54 sensuous cittas, 15 fine-material cittas, supramundane 4 path-cittas and 4 fruition-cittas, 52 cetasikas, 28 matters, and *Nibbāna* — they are dissociated from the 12 arūpajhānas.

3. States which do not lead out (from round of existence) are referred to the 85 cittas (4 supramundane fruition, 81 mundane cittas), 52 cetasikas, 28 matters, and *Nibbāna* (because fruition-cittas and *Nibbāna* are not noble path) — they are dissociated from the 4 supramundane path-cittas, accompanied by 36 cetasikas.

4. States which are not fixed as to future destinies are referred to 79 cittas (17 wholesome cittas, 36 resultant cittas, 20 functional cittas, the 7th sensuous javanas present at the 4 greed-rooted cittas associated with wrong view and with the 2 delusion-rooted cittas, i.e. 17+36+20+4+2=79), 52 cetasikas, 28 matters, and *Nibbāna* — they are dissociated from the 4 supramundane fruition-cittas. (for it is the 4 supramundane path-cittas which are states which are fixed as to future destinies).

5. States which are not at odds (*araṇā*) with supramundane Path are referred to the 77 cittas (21 wholesome cittas, 36 resultant cittas, and 20 functional cittas) accompanied by 38 cetasikas, 28 matters, and *Nibbāna* — they are dissociated from the 12 unwholesome cittas.

Those dissociated states all belong to 4 mental aggregates. They are thus classified, and taken as aggrouped under 4 aggregates excluding *Nibbāna* (4 mental aggregates), under 2 bases (ideation-base, mind-base), and under 2 elements (ideation-element, mind-consciousness element). They are not classified and taken as ungrouped under 1 aggregate (matter), under 10 bases (10 gross bases), and under 16 elements (10 gross elements, the remaining 6 consciousness elements).

Key points from the text :

Ideation-base, ideation-element, faculties, mentality-materiality, six bases, birth, ageing, death.

63 states from triplets, 7 states from the shorter dyads, 10 dyad-clusters, 14 intermediate dyads, 6 from final dyads.

XIV. Aggrouped and Ungrouped from Dissociated

In the following tables, the number in the brackets represents the number of enquiries relative to the associated text paragraph nos.

Table 14.1 Total 324 states of enquiry by subject matters

Text's paragraph nos. (with numbers of enquiries):		Subject matter:
456 (1), 457 (4)	5	Aggregates
457 (1), 458 (10)	11	Bases
458 (10), 459 (7),	17	Elements
460 (1), 461 (2), 462 (1)	4	Truths
457 (1), 462 (7), 463 (4), 464 (1), 465 (8)	21	Faculties
465 (2), 466 (3), 467 (3), 468 (3), 469 (1), 470 (4), 471 (7)	23	Dependent Originations
471 (9), 472 (6), 473 (1)	16	Others
474 (4), 475 (1), 476 (2), 477 (2), 478 (4), 479 (1), 480 (1), 481 (1), 482 (3), 483 (1), 484 (1), 485 (9), 486 (5), 487 (2), 488 (1), 489 (8), 490 (2), 491 (10), 492 (4), 493 (2)	64	Triads
494 (8), 495 (3), 498 (5), 499 (4), 500 (2), 501 (58), 502 (4), 503 (2), 507 (19), 508 (5), 509 (2)	112	Ten dyad-clusters
496 (6), 497 (1)	7	Shorter dyads
504 (8), 505 (5), 506 (1)	14	Intermediate dyads
510 (4), 511 (4), 512 (2), 513 (3), 514 (1), 515 (3), 516 (3), 517 (5), 518 (5)	30	Last dyads

Total = 324 states

Table 14.2 Total 324 states of enquiry by answers

Text's paragraph nos. (with numbers of enquiries in brackets):	Total 324	Dissociated states :					
		Aggrouped			Ungrouped		
		agr	bse	el.	agr	bse	el.
456 (1), 458 (20), 462 (8), 470 (4), 478 (4), 487 (2), 491 (10), 496 (6), 500 (2), 501 (10), 503 (2), 505 (5), 507 (2), 509 (2), 516 (3)	81	4	2	8	1	10	10
457 (6), 466 (3), 472 (6), 504 (8)	23	1	11	11	4	1	7
459 (7), 473 (1), 481 (1), 512 (2)	11	5	12	17	-	-	1
460 (1), 475 (1), 480 (1), 486 (5), 490 (2), 495 (3), 497 (1), 499 (4), 501 (20), 502 (4), 507 (4), 508 (5), 511 (4), 515 (3), 518 (5)	63	4	2	2	1	10	16
461 (2), 463 (4), 465 (10), 467 (3), 471 (16), 474 (4), 477 (2), 482 (3), 485 (9), 489 (8), 492 (4), 494 (8), 498 (5), 501 (28), 507 (13), 510 (4), 513 (3), 517 (5)	131	5	12	18	-	-	-
464 (1), 476 (2), 484 (1), 514 (1)	5	5	12	13	-	-	5
468 (3), 479 (1), 483 (1), 506 (1)	6	4	2	3	1	10	15
469 (1)	1	4	2	5	1	10	13
488 (1), 493 (2)	3	5	12	12	-	-	6

A Perfect Knowledge of Mind-Body from the Abhidhamma (Dhātukathā)

Here ends the analysis for Dhātukathā

Conclusion

It is only at this point that I have come to the idea of using Chart 1 for the front cover of this book. There are indeed people who can memorise the dhammasaṅgaṇī mātikā with ease, and after reading this book for quite some times, may be able to recall the answers for all those combinations of the 371 states by just looking at the front cover of the book. The chart is an effective reference source which can help us to reflect on whatsoever dhammas that we have read from books by the different authors, from online media, or what we have heard from others; and to also mirror on what we are doing, saying, and thinking every day, to reinforce and improve our practice of consistent mindfulness. This chart is the blueprint which guides our logical thought and penetrative insight on the core concepts and practical applications of the Buddha's teaching, by considering all conceivable phenomena which ends with 2453 states of enquiry in total, through fourteen methods. Some detailed interpretation with regard to Chart 1 have already been provided on few pages immediately after Chart 1 in Chapter 1.

Realities are not really the reality if we interpret them through our five aggregates, in the same way what quantum mechanics has revealed to us. There is no such thing as pure five aggregates. For as long as we are using five aggregates in dealing our everyday life with the mundane world, looking for true happiness, we will always be clinging to the view of individuality and covetousness as a result of our six subjective cognitions experiencing with the six sense objects. We should understand realities as just the eighteen elements, as is with *Nibbāna* but an element unconditioned, having the five aggregates and twelve bases functioning as mere support base. If we do not comprehend the co-relations and interdependence between these three categories and the four ultimate realities, and not able to adapt it positively to making necessary changes within our life, we will forever remain a bondage to our greed, lust, ill-will, aversion, and all worldly attachments. These whole exercises from the book is designed for only one purpose, which is to tell us that there is nothing that is truly reality as to self and individual substantiality.

Now we have examined all the exercises, we understand that states pertaining to past, future, and present; states as to internal, external, or both; states which do not lead us out from the round of existence and all mundane states, are subject to the encumbrance and full measure of the five aggregates, twelve bases and eighteen elements. There is really nothing in the five aggregates which can co-relates with leading a life of nobility. But *Nibbāna*, unconditioned by any causes, is included only in ideation-base and ideation-element, which is why volitive activities and consciousness cease altogether with the cessation of perception and feeling, thenceforth one begins with practising supramundane cittas.

Without the unshaken faith and gratitude in the Buddha's teaching, made complete by the literal works and analytical comprehensiveness of Abhidhamma, I can not imagine how I could have carried on with this truly tough work of Dāthukathā. I hope you will benefit from reading this book.

Appendix I: 28 Types of Material Phenomena

Concretely Produced Matter (18) (*nipphanna-rūpā*)			Non-Concrete Matter (10) (*anipphanna-rūpā*)		
I. Four Great Essentials (4 *mahābhūtā*)	1. Earth element 2. Water element 3. Heat element 4. Air element		VIII. Limiting Phenomenon (*pariccheda-rūpa*)	19. Space element (*ākāsa dhātu*)	
II. Sensitive Phenomena (5 *pasāda-rūpā*)	5. Sensitive eye 6. Sensitive ear 7. Sensitive nose 8. Sensitive tongue 9. Sensitive body	12 Gross Matters (*oḷārika-rūpā*)	IX. Communicating Phenomena (2 *viññatti-rūpā*)	20. Bodily intimation (*kaya viññatti-rūpa*) 21. Vocal intimation (*vāci viññatti-rūpa*)	10 Suble Matters (*sukhuma-rūpā*)
III. Objective Phenomena (7 *gocara-rūpā*)	10. Visual 11. Sound 12. Odour 13 Taste *Gross Tangibility (includes the 3 elements of earth, heat, air)		X. Mutable Phenomena (3 *lahutadi-rūpā*)	22. Lightness (*lahutā*) 23. Malleability (*mudutā*) 24. Wieldiness (*kammaññatā*)	
	Subtle Tangibility: fuild (element of cohesion)	6 Suble Matters (*sukhuma-rūpā*)	XI. Characteristics of Matter (4 *lakkhaṇa-rūpā*)	25. Accumulation (*upacāya-rūpā*) 26. Continuity (*santati-rūpā*) 27. Decay (*jaratā-rūpā*) 28. Impermanence (*aniccatā-rūpā*)	
IV. Sexual Phenomena (2 *bhāva-rūpā*)	14. Femininity 15. Masculinity				
V. Heart Phenomenon (*hadaya-vatthu*)	16. Heart-base				
VI. Vitality Phenomenon (*jīvitindriya-rūpa*)	17. Vitality faculty				
VII. Nutritional Phenomenon (*āhāra-rūpa*)	18. Body nutriment				

* fluid (element of cohesion) is excluded from gross tangibility and is classified under subtle matter.

Appendix II: 89 States of Consciousness

Wholesome States (*Kusalacittāni*) (21)	Unwholesome States (*Akusalacittāni*) (12)	Indeterminate States (*abyākata*) (56)	
		Resultants (*Vipākacittāni*) (36)	Functionals (*Kiriyācittāni*) (20)
THE SENSUOUS SPHERE (54)			
8 wholesome, beautiful cittas with cause: *(mind-consciousness-elements)*	12 unwholesome, non-beautiful cittas with cause: *(mind-consciousness-elements)*	8 wholesome resultant cittas without cause:	3 functional cittas without cause:
(1) Accompanied by joy, associated with knowledge, unpremeditated.	8 greed-rooted cittas	(34) Eye-consciousness accompanied by equanimity.	(70) Five-sense-doors 'adverting' citta accompanied by equanimity. *(mind-element)*
(2) Accompanied by joy, associated with knowledge, premeditated.	(22) Accompanied by joy, associated with fallacy, unpremeditated.	(35) Ear-consciousness accompanied by equanimity.	(71) Mind-door 'adverting' citta accompanied by equanimity. *(mind-consciousness-element)*
(3) Accompanied by joy, dissociated from knowledge, unpremeditated.	(23) Accompanied by joy, associated with fallacy, premeditated.	(36) Nose-consciousness accompanied by equanimity.	(72) 'Smile-producing' citta accompanied by joy. *(mind-consciousness-element)*
(4) Accompanied by joy, dissociated from knowledge, premeditated.	(24) Accompanied by joy, dissociated from fallacy, unpremeditated.	(37) Tongue-consciousness accompanied by equanimity.	
(5) Accompanied by equanimity, associated with knowledge, unpremeditated.	(25) Accompanied by joy, dissociated from fallacy, premeditated.	(38) Body-consciousness accompanied by pleasure/happiness.	8 functional beautiful cittas with cause: *(mind-consciousness-elements)*
(6) Accompanied by equanimity, associated with knowledge, premeditated.	(26) Accompanied by equanimity, associated with fallacy, unpremeditated.	(39) Receiving citta accompanied by equanimity. *(mind-element)*	(73) Accompanied by joy, associated with knowledge, unpremeditated.
(7) Accompanied by equanimity, dissociated from knowledge, unpremeditated.	(27) Accompanied by equanimity, associated with fallacy, premeditated.	(40) Investigating citta accompanied by joy. *(mind-consciousness-element)*	(74) Accompanied by joy, associated with knowledge, premeditated.
(8) Accompanied by equanimity, dissociated from knowledge, premeditated.	(28) Accompanied by equanimity, dissociated from fallacy, unpremeditated.	(41) Investigating citta accompanied by equanimity. (*mind-consciousness-element*)	(75) Accompanied by joy, dissociated from knowledge, unpremeditated.
	(29) Accompanied by equanimity, dissociated from		

A Perfect Knowledge of Mind-Body from the Abhidhamma (Dhātukathā)

fallacy, premeditated. 2 hatred-rooted cittas : (30) Accompanied by displeasure, associated with aversion (*paṭigha*), unpremeditated. (31) Accompanied by displeasure, associated with aversion (*paṭigha*), premeditated. 2 delusion-rooted cittas (32) Accompanied by equanimity, associated with doubt. (33) Accompanied by equanimity, associated with restlessness.	8 wholesome, beautiful resultant cittas with cause: *(mind-consciousness -elements)* (42) Accompanied by joy, associated with knowledge, unpremeditated. (43) Accompanied by joy, associated with knowledge, premeditated. (44) Accompanied by joy, dissociated from knowledge, unpremeditated. (45) Accompanied by joy, dissociated from knowledge, premeditated. (46) Accompanied by equanimity, associated with knowledge, unpremeditated. (47) Accompanied by equanimity, associated with knowledge, premeditated. (48) Accompanied by equanimity, dissociated from knowledge, unpremeditated. (49) Accompanied by equanimity, dissociated from knowledge, premeditated. 7 unwholesome resultant cittas without cause: (50) Eye-consciousness accompanied by equanimity.	(76) Accompanied by joy, dissociated from knowledge, premeditated. (77) Accompanied by equanimity, associated with knowledge, unpremeditated. (78) Accompanied by equanimity, associated with knowledge, premeditated. (79) Accompanied by equanimity, dissociated from knowledge, unpremeditated. (80) Accompanied by equanimity, dissociated from knowledge, premeditated.

Appendix II: 89 States of Consciousness

		(51) Ear-consciousness accompanied by equanimity. (52) Nose-consciousness accompanied by equanimity. (53) Tongue-consciousness accompanied by equanimity. (54) Body-consciousness accompanied by pain/suffering. (55) Receiving citta accompanied by equanimity. *(mind-element)* (56) Investigating citta accompanied by equanimity. *(mind-consciousness-element)*	
THE FINE—MATERIAL SPHERE (15)			
(mind-consciousness-elements) (9) First Jhāna together with initial application, sustained application, zest, happiness, one-pointedness. (10) Second Jhāna together with sustained application, zest, happiness, one-pointedness. (11) Third Jhāna together with zest, happiness, one-pointedness. (12) Fourth Jhāna together with happiness and one-		*(mind-consciousness-elements)* (57) First Jhāna together with initial application, sustained application, zest, happiness, one-pointedness. (58) Second Jhāna together with sustained application, zest, happiness, one-pointedness. (59) Third Jhāna together with zest, happiness, one-pointedness. (60) Fourth Jhāna together with happiness, and one-	*(mind-consciousness-elements)* (81) First Jhāna together with initial application, sustained application, zest, happiness, one-pointedness. (82) Second Jhāna together with sustained application, zest, happiness, one-pointedness. (83) Third Jhāna together with zest, happiness, one-pointedness. (84 Fourth Jhāna together with

A Perfect Knowledge of Mind-Body from the Abhidhamma (Dhātukathā)

pointedness. (13) Fifth Jhāna together with equanimity, and one-pointedness.	pointedness. (61) Fifth Jhāna together with equanimity, and one-pointedness.	happiness, and one-pointedness. (85) Fifth Jhāna together with equanimity, and one-pointedness.
THE IMMATERIAL SPHERE (12)		
(mind-consciousness -elements) (14) Pertain to the base of infinite space. (15) Pertain to the base of infinite consciousness. (16) Pertain to the base of nothingness. (17) Pertain to the base of neither perception nor non-perception.	*(mind-consciousness -elements)* (62) Pertain to the base of infinite space. (63) Pertain to the base of infinite consciousness. (64) Pertain to the base of nothingness. (65) Pertain to the base of neither perception nor non-perception.	*(mind-consciousness -elements)* (86) Pertain to the base of infinite space. (87) Pertain to the base of infinite consciousness. (88) Pertain to the base of nothingness. (89) Pertain to the base of neither perception nor non-perception.
THE SUPRAMUNDANE SPHERE (8)		
(mind-consciousness -elements) (18) Path-citta of Stream-Entry. (19) Path-citta of Once-Returning. (20) Path-citta of Non-Returning. (21) Path-citta of Arāhantship.	*(mind-consciousness -elements)* (66) Fruition-citta of Stream-Entry. (67) Fruition-citta of Once-Returning. (68) Fruition-citta of Non-Returning. (69) Fruition-citta of Arāhantship.	

Appendix III: Summarised tables of the 89 (121) cittas

	Active States		Indeterminate States		
	Wholesome States	Unwholesome States	Resultant States	Functional States	
Sensuous Sphere	8	12	23	11	54
Fine-Material Sphere	5		5	5	15
Immaterial Sphere	4		4	4	12
	(17)	*(12)*	*(32)*	*(20)*	
Supramundane Sphere	4		4		8
Total:	21	12	36	20	89

Note: the 81 *Lokiyacittāni* of the three mundane spheres (54+15+12 =81) are 'mundane states'; the 27 *Mahaggatacittāni* of the fine-material and immaterial sphere (15+12=27) are the 'sublime states'.

		Uyyutta		Abyākata		
		kusala	akusala	vipāka	kiriyā	
Kāmāvacara	sahetuka sobhana-kusala	8				
	sahetuka *lobhamūla*		8			
	sahetuka *dosamūla*		2			
	sahetuka *mohamūla*		2			54
	ahetuka-kusala			8		
	ahetuka-akusala			7		
	sahetuka-sobhana-kusala			8		
	ahetuka				3	
	sahetuka-sobhana				8	
Rūpāvacara	First-jhāna	1		1	1	
	Second-jhāna	1		1	1	
	Third-jhāna	1		1	1	15
	Fourth-jhāna	1		1	1	
	Fifth-jhāna	1		1	1	
Arūpāvacara	Ākāsānañca āyatana	1		1	1	
	Viññāṇañca āyatana	1		1	1	12
	Ākiñcañña āyatana	1		1	1	
	Nevasaññā-nāsaññā āyatana	1		1	1	
Lokuttara		4 x 5		4 x 5		40
Total:		37	12	52	20	121

Appendix IV: 52 Mental Factors (*Cetasikā*)

THE 52 MENTAL FACTORS (*CETASIKĀ*)	
COMMON, NON-BEAUTIFUL FACTORS - 13 (*asobhaṇa sādhāraṇā*)	**BEAUTIFUL FACTORS - 25** (*sobhaṇa*)
Universals -7 (*Aññasamāna*) Contact (*phassa*) Feeling (*vedanā*) Perception (*saññā*) Volition/ Intentive thought (*cetanā*) One-pointedness (*ekaggatā*) Vitality-faculty (*jīvitindriya*) Attention (*manasikāra*)	**Beautiful Universals - 19** (*Sobhanāññasamāna*) Faith (*saddhā*) Mindfulness (*sati*) Discreet shamefulness (*hirī*) Guilt-conscience (*ottappa*) Non-greed (*alobha*) Non-hatred (*adosa*) Neutrality of mind (*tatramajjhattatā*) Calmness of mental body (*kāyapassaddhi*)
Occasionals (*Pakiṇṇakā*) - 6 Initial application (*vitakka*) Sustained application (*vicāra*) Decision (*adhimokkha*) Energy/ Effort (*viriya*) Zest (*pīti*) Desire (*chanda*)	Calmness of consciousness (*cittapassaddhi*) Lightness of mental body (*kāyalahutā*) Lightness of consciousness (*cittalahutā*) Malleability of mental body (*kāyamudutā*) Malleability of consciousness (*cittamudutā*) Wieldiness of mental body (*kāyakammaññatā*) Wieldiness of consciousness (*cittakammaññatā*) Proficiency of mental body (*kāyapāguññatā*) Proficiency of consciousness (*cittapāguññatā*)
UNWHOLESOME FACTORS-14 (*Akusala*)	Rectitude of mental body (*kāyujjukatā*) Rectitude of consciousness (*cittujjukatā*)
Unwholesome Universals - 4 (*Akusalasādhāraṇā*) Delusion (*moha*) Shamelessness (*ahirīka*) Unconscientiousnes (*anottappa*) Restlessness (*uddhacca*)	**Abstinences (*Virati*) - 3** Right speech (*vaciduccarita virati*) Right action (*kāyaduccarita virati*) Right livelihood (*ājīvaduccarita virati*)
Unwholesome Occasionals - 10 (*Akusalapakiṇṇakā*) Greed (*lobha*) Wrong view (*diṭṭhi*) Conceit (*māna*) Hatred (*dosa*) Envy (*Issā*) Avarice (*macchariya*) Worry (*kukkucca*) Sloth (*thīna*) Torpor (*middha*) Doubt (*vicikicchā*)	**Illimitables (*Appamaññā*) - 2** Compassion (*karuṇā*) Altruistic or Appreciative joy (*muditā*) **Non-Delusion (*Amoha*) - 1** Wisdom faculty (*paññindriya*)

Appendix V. 52 cetasikas in relation to the 89 (or 121) cittas

52 Cetasikas \ 89 (or 121) Cittas	(1-7. Universals)	8. Initial application	9. Sustained application	10. Decision	11. V Effort	12. Zest	13. Desire	(14-17. Universals)	18. Greed	19. Fallacy	20. Conceit	21. Hatred; 22. I Envy	23. Avarice; 24. Worry	25. Sloth; 26. Torpor	27. Doubt	(28-46. Universals)	47. Right speech; 48. Right action; 49. Right livelihood	50. Compassion; 51. Altruistic joy	52. Non-Delusional (Wisdom faculty)	Sub-Total Cittas
Mental Factors Total:	7	1	1	1	1	1	1	4	1	1	1	2	2	2	1	19	3	2	1	52
1. greed-rooted, accompanied by joy, associated with fallacy	7	1	1	1	1	1	1	4	1	1										19
3. greed-rooted, accompanied by joy, dissociated from fallacy	7	1	1	1	1	1	1	4	1		1									19
5. greed-rooted, accompanied by equanimity, associated with fallacy	7	1	1	1	1		1	4	1	1										18
7. greed-rooted, accompanied by equanimity, dissociated from fallacy	7	1	1	1	1		1	4	1		1									18

12 Sensuous Sphere Unwholesome Cittas — 5 Unpremeditated

A Perfect Knowledge of Mind-Body from the Abhidhamma (Dhātukathā)

	Consciousness														Total
	9. hatred-rooted, accompanied by displeasure, associated with aversion	1	7	1	1	1	1		1	4			2	2			20
5 Premeditated	2. greed-rooted, accompanied by joy, associated with fallacy	1	7	1	1	1	1	1	1	4	1	1		2			21
	4. greed-rooted, accompanied by joy, dissociated from fallacy	1	7	1	1	1	1	1	1	4	1		1	2			21
	6. greed-rooted, accompanied by equanimity, associated with fallacy	1	7	1	1	1	1		1	4	1	1		2			20
	8. greed-rooted, accompanied by equanimity, dissociated from fallacy	1	7	1	1	1	1		1	4	1		1	2			20
	10. hate-rooted, accompanied by displeasure, associated with aversion	1	7	1	1	1	1		1	4			2	2	2		22
2 Delusion-rooted	11. delusion-rooted, accompanied by equanimity, associated with doubt	1	7	1	1		1			4					1		15
	12. delusion-rooted, accompanied by equanimity, associated with restlessness	1	7	1	1	1	1			4							15

Appendix V. 52 Mental Factors in relation to 89 States of Consciousness

18 Sensuous Sphere Rootless Cittas

8 Wholesome Resultants

Citta								Total
1-4. cittas accompanied by equanimity (eye, ear, nose, and tongue cognitions)	4	7						7
5. body-consciousness accompanied by pleasure	1	7						7
6. receiving citta accompanied by equanimity	1	7	1	1	1			10
7. investigating citta accompanied by joy	1	7	1	1	1	1		11
8. investigating citta accompanied by equanimity	1	7	1	1	1			10

7 Unwholesome Resultants

Citta							Total
1-4. cittas accompanied by equanimity (eye, ear, nose, and tongue cognitions)	4	7					10
5. body-consciousness accompanied by displeasure	1	7					10
6. receiving citta accompanied by equanimity	1	7	1	1	1		10
7. investigating citta accompanied by equanimity	1	7	1	1	1		10

A Perfect Knowledge of Mind-Body from the Abhidhamma (Dhātukathā)

																	Total
3 Functionals		1. five-sense-doors advertence citta accompanied by equanimity	1	7	1	1	1										10
		2. mind-door advertence citta accompanied by equanimity	1	7	1	1	1	1									11
		3. 'smile-producing' citta accompanied by joy	1	7	1	1	1	1	1								12
24 Sensuous Sphere Rooted Cittas	8 Great Wholesome-Beautifuls	4 Unpremeditated															
		1. accompanied by joy, associated with knowledge	1	7	1	1	1	1		1				19	3	2	1	38
		3. accompanied by joy, dissociated from knowledge	1	7	1	1	1	1		1				19	3	2		37
		5. accompanied by equanimity, associated with knowledge	1	7	1	1	1	1		1				19	3	2	1	37
		7. accompanied by equanimity, dissociated from knowledge	1	7	1	1	1	1		1				19	3	2		36
		4 Premeditated															
		2. accompanied by joy, associated with knowledge	1	7	1	1	1	1	1	1				19	3	2	1	38
		4. accompanied by joy, dissociated from knowledge	1	7	1	1	1	1	1	1				19	3	2		37
		6. accompanied by equanimity, associated with knowledge	1	7	1	1	1	1		1				19	3	2	1	37

Appendix V. 52 Mental Factors in relation to 89 States of Consciousness

8 Great Wholesome-Beautiful Resultants	4 Unpremeditated	8.accompanied by equanimity, dissociated from knowledge	1	7	1	1	1	1		1					19	3	2		36
		1.accompanied by joy, associated with knowledge	1	7	1	1	1	1		1					19			1	33
		3.accompanied by joy, dissociated from knowledge	1	7	1	1	1	1		1					19				32
		5.accompanied by equanimity, associated with knowledge	1	7	1	1	1	1		1					19			1	32
		7.accompanied by equanimity, dissociated from knowledge	1	7	1	1	1	1		1					19				31
	4 Premeditated	2.accompanied by joy, associated with knowledge	1	7	1	1	1	1	1	1					19			1	33
		4.accompanied by joy, dissociated from knowledge	1	7	1	1	1	1	1	1					19				32
		6.accompanied by equanimity, associated with knowledge	1	7	1	1	1	1		1					19			1	32
		8.accompanied by equanimity, dissociated from knowledge	1	7	1	1	1	1		1					19				31

A Perfect Knowledge of Mind-Body from the Abhidhamma (Dhātukathā)

8 Great Beautiful Functionals	4 Unpremeditated	1. accompanied by joy, associated with knowledge	1	7	1	1	1	1		1					19		2	1	35
		3. accompanied by joy, dissociated from knowledge	1	7	1	1	1	1		1					19		2		34
		5. accompanied by equanimity, associated with knowledge	1	7	1	1	1	1		1					19		2	1	34
		7. accompanied by equanimity, dissociated from knowledge	1	7	1	1	1	1		1					19		2		33
	4 Premeditated	2. accompanied by joy, associated with knowledge	1	7	1	1	1	1	1	1					19		2	1	35
		4. accompanied by joy, dissociated from knowledge	1	7	1	1	1	1	1	1					19		2		34
		6. accompanied by equanimity, associated with knowledge	1	7	1	1	1	1		1					19		2	1	34
		8. accompanied by equanimity, dissociated from knowledge	1	7	1	1	1	1		1					19		2		33

Appendix V. 52 Mental Factors in relation to 89 States of Consciousness

15 Fine-Material Sphere Cittas	First Jhāna together with initial application, sustained application, zest, happiness, one-pointedness (wholesome [01], resultant [06], functional [11])	3	7	1	1	1	1	1	1				19	2	1	35
	Second Jhāna together with sustained application, zest, happiness, one-pointedness (wholesome [02], resultant [07], functional [12])	3	7		1	1	1	1	1				19	2	1	34
	Third Jhāna together with zest, happiness, one-pointedness (wholesome [03], resultant [08], functional [13])	3	7			1	1	1	1				19	2	1	33
	Fourth Jhāna together with happiness, and one-pointedness (wholesome [04], resultant [09], functional [14])	3	7			1	1		1				19	2	1	32
	Fifth Jhāna together with equanimity, and one-pointedness (wholesome [05], resultant [10], functional [15])	3	7			1	1		1				19		1	30

A Perfect Knowledge of Mind-Body from the Abhidhamma (Dhātukathā)

	Citta type		7															19			Total
12 - Immaterial Sphere Cittas	Pertaining to base of infinite space (wholesome [01], resultant [05], functional [09])	3	7			1	1	1										19		1	30
	Pertaining to base of infinite consciousness (wholesome [02], resultant [06], functional [10])	3	7			1	1	1										19		1	30
	Pertaining to base of nothingness (wholesome [03], resultant [07], functional [11])	3	7			1	1	1										19		1	30
	Pertaining to the base of neither perception nor non-perception (wholesome [04], resultant [08], functional [12])	3	7			1	1	1										19		1	30
40 Supramundane Cittas	1—8. 1st Jhāna	8	7	1	1	1	1	1	1									19	3	1	36
	1–8. 2nd Jhāna	8	7		1	1	1	1	1									19	3	1	35
	1–8. 3rd Jhāna	8	7			1	1	1	1									19	3	1	34
	1–8. 4th Jhāna	8	7			1	1		1									19	3	1	33
	1–8. 5th Jhāna	8	7			1	1											19	3	1	33
Total (according to 89 cittas)		89	55	58	78	73	35	69	12	8	4	4	2	2	5	1		59	16	28	47
Total (according to 121 cittas)		121	55	66	110	105	51	101										91	48		79

Denotation of the Mental Factors:

The 7 Common Non-Beautiful Universals:
01. Contact, 02. Feeling, 03. Perception, 04. Volition, 05. One-pointedness, 06. Vitality faculty, 07. Attention.

The 4 Common Unwholesome Universals:
14. Delusion, 15. Shamelessness, 16. Unconscientiousness, 17. Restlessness.

The 19 Common Beautiful Universals:
28. Faith, 29. Mindfulness, 30. Shame, 31. Fear of wrong or Conscience, 32. Non-greed, 33. Non-hatred, 34. Neutrality of mind, 35. Tranquility of mental structure, 36. Tranquility of consciousness, 37. Lightness of mental structure, 38. Lightness of consciousness, 39. Malleability of mental structure, 40. Malleability of consciousness, 41. Wieldiness of mental structure, 42. Wieldiness of consciousness, 43. Proficiency of mental structure, 44. Proficiency of consciousness, 45. Rectitude of mental structure, 46. Rectitude of consciousness.

Appendix VI. Other classifications by types

Chart 1. The 72 ultimate dhammas

Ultimate dhammas :	
Matter (*rūpa*)	18
Mental factors (*cetasikā*)	52
State of consciousness (*citta*)	1
Unconditioned element (*nibbāna*)	1
	72

Note:
There are only 18 concretely created matters (*nipphanna-rūpā*), the other 10 are not real matters. Each of 52 mental factors has its own characteristic while the 89 or 121 cittas must eventually come down to 1, true and only ultimate characteristic, similar to *nibbāna* which is without conditions.

Chart 2. Sensuous-sphere cittas by types

The Sensual-Sphere (total 54)	12 Akusala (unwholesome, with root)	24 Sobhana (beautiful, with root)	18 Ahetuka (rootless)
	Greed-Based (8)	Wholesomes (8)	Resultants - wholesome (8)
	Hatred-Based (2)	Resultants (8)	Resultants - unwholesome (7)
	Delusion-Based (2)	Functionals (8)	Functionals (3)

Chart 3. Sensuous-sphere cittas classification by 'feeling'

Sensuous cittas classified according to 'feelng':	Kāmakusala	Kāmākusala	Vipāka	Kriya	Total
cittas associated with joy (*somanassa*)	4	4	5	5	18
cittas associated with happiness/pleasure (*sukha*)			1		1
cittas associated with melancholy/displeasure (*domanassa*)		2			2
cittas associated with pain/suffering (*dukkha*)			1		1
cittas associated with equanimity (*upekkhā*)	4	6	16	6	32
Total:					54

A Perfect Knowledge of Mind-Body from the Abhidhamma (Dhātukathā)

Chart 4. Cittas classification base on the 5 Jhānas

	Classification of the 5 jhānas:	Kāmakusala	Kāmakusala	Vipāka	Kriya	Total
Rūpāvacara	First-jhāna	1		1	1	3
	Second-jhāna	1		1	1	3
	Third-jhāna	1		1	1	3
	Fourth-jhāna	1		1	1	3
	Fifth-jhāna	1		1	1	3
	Sub-total:					**15**
Arūpāvacara	Fifth-jhāna at the base of infinity	1		1	1	3
	Fifth-jhāna at the consciousness of infinity	1		1	1	3
	Fifth-jhāna at the base of nothingness	1		1	1	3
	Fifth-jhāna at the base of neither perception nor non-perception	1		1	1	3
	Sub-total:					**12**
Lokuttara	5 jhānā of the supramundane 1st stage Path- and Fruition-cittāni	5		5		10
	5 jhānā of the supramundane 2nd stage Path- Fruition- cittāni	5		5		10
	5 jhānā of the supramundane 3rd stage Path- Fruition- cittāni	5		5		10
	5 jhānā of the supramundane final stage Path- Fruition- cittāni	5		5		10
	Sub-total:					**40**
	Gross total:					**67**

Chart 5. Cittas classification base on the 5 Jhānas

	First-jhāna	Second-jhāna	Third-jhāna	Fourth-jhāna	Fifth-jhāna	
Fine-material sphere	3	3	3	3	3	**15**
Immaterial sphere					12	**12**
Supramundane sphere	8	8	8	8	8	**40**
	11	11	11	11	23	**67**

Appendix VI. Miscellaneous classifications

Chart 6. Classifying 14 unwholesome cetasikas with the 9 clusters

	Āsava	Saṃyojana	Gantha	Ogha	Yoga	Nīvaraṇa	Upādāna	Kilesa	Anusaya
Classification :	4	10	4	4	4	6	4	10	7
Component factors :	3	9	3	3	3	8	2	10	6
14 Unwholesome Cetasikas									
Delusion (*moha*)	•	•	•	•	•	•		•	•
Shamelessness (*ahirīka*)			•					•	
Unconscientiousnes (*anottappa*)								•	
Restlessness (*uddhacca*)		•				•		•	
Greed (*lobha*)	•	•		•	•	•	•	•	•
Wrong view (*diṭṭhi*)	•	•		•	•		•	•	•
Conceit (*māna*)		•						•	•
Hatred (*dosa*)		•	•			•		•	•
Envy (*Issā*)		•							
Avarice (*macchariya*)		•							
Worry (*kukkucca*)						•			
Sloth (*thīna*)						•		•	
Torpor (*middha*)						•			
Doubt (*vicikicchā*)		•				•		•	•

Denotation: *āsava* (outflow, defilement), *saṃyojana* (fetter), *gantha* (bond, knot), *ogha* (ranging current), *yoga* (yoke), *nīvaraṇa* (hindrance), *upādāna* (clinging), *kilesa* (corruption), *anusaya* (latent tendency).

Chart 7. Classifying cittas base on the 52 cetasikas

Mental Factors	Associated with		Dissociated from	
	89 cittas	121 cittas	89 cittas	121 cittas
Common non-beautiful factors - 13				
7 Universals (aññasamāna) :				
Contact (phassa)	89	121	-	-
Feeling (vedanā)	89	121	-	-
Perception (saññā)	89	121	-	-
Volition/ Intentive thought (cetanā)	89	121	-	-
One-pointedness (ekaggatā)	89	121	-	-
Vitality-faculty (jīvitindriya)	89	121	-	-
Attention (manasikāra)	89	121	-	-
6 Occasionals (pakiṇṇaka) :				
Initial application (vitakka)	55	55	34	66
Sustained application (vicāra)	58	66	31	55
Decision (adhimokkha)	78	110	11	11
Energy/ Effort (viriya)	73	105	16	16
Zest (pīti)	35	51	54	70
Desire (chanda)	69	101	20	20
Unwholesome factors – 14				
4 Unwholesome universals (aññasamāna) :				
Delusion (moha)	12	-	77	-
Shamelessness (ahirīka)	12	-	77	-
Unconscientiousnes (anottappa)	12	-	77	-
Restlessness (uddhacca)	12	-	77	-
10 Unwholesome occasionals (pakiṇṇakā) :				
Greed (lobha)	8	-	81	-
Wrong view (diṭṭhi)	4	-	85	-
Conceit (māna)	4	-	85	-
Hatred (dosa)	2	-	87	-
Envy (Issā)	2	-	87	-
Avarice (macchariya)	2	-	87	-
Worry (kukkucca)	2	-	87	-
Sloth (thīna)	5	-	84	-
Torpor (middha)	5	-	84	-
Doubt (vicikicchā)	1	-	88	-

Appendix VI. Miscellaneous classifications

	Associated		Dissociated	
	89	121	89	121
Beautiful factors - 25				
19 Beautiful universals (*sobhanāññasamāna*) :	59		30	
3 Abstinences (*virati*) :	16		73	
2 Illimitables (*appamaññā*) :	28		61	
1 Non-Delusion/ Wisdom (*amoha*) :	47		42	

Chart 8. Classifying the twelve evil-rooted unwhomesome cittas base on 52 cetasikas

Lobhamūla cittāni :		Associated cetasikas
		composition :
1st greed-rooted citta (accompanied by joy, associated with fallacy, unpremeditated)	19	13 common non-beautiful factors, 4 unwholesome universal factors, lobha, and diṭṭhi (13+4+2=19).
2nd greed-rooted citta (accompanied by joy, associated with fallacy, premeditated)	21	13 common non-beautiful factors, 4 unwholesome universal factors, lobha, diṭṭhi, thīna, and middha. (13+4+4=21).
3rd greed-rooted citta (accompanied by joy, dissociated from fallacy, unpremeditated)	19	13 common non-beautiful factors, 4 unwholesome universal factors, lobha and māna (13+4+2=19).
4th greed-rooted citta. (accompanied by joy, dissociated from fallacy, premeditated)	21	13 common non-beautiful factors, 4 unwholesome universal factors, lobha, māna, thīna, and middha. (13+4+4=21).
5th greed-rooted citta (accompanied by equanimity, associated with fallacy, unpremeditated)	18	7 common and non-beautiful universal factors; vitakka, vicāra, adhimokkha, viriya, chanda; 4 unwholesome universal factors; lobha, and diṭṭhi (7+5+4+2=18).
6th greed-rooted citta (accompanied by equanimity, associated with fallacy, premeditated)	20	7 common and non-beautiful universal factors; vitakka, vicāra, adhimokkha, viriya, chanda; 4 unwholesome universal factors; lobha, diṭṭhi, thīna, and middha. (7+5+4+4=20).
7th greed-rooted citta (accompanied by equanimity, dissociated from fallacy, unpremeditated)	18	7 common and non-beautiful universal factors; vitakka, vicāra, adhimokkha, viriya, chanda; 4 unwholesome universal factors; lobha, and māna (7+5+4+2=18).

A Perfect Knowledge of Mind-Body from the Abhidhamma (Dhātukathā)

Lobhamūla cittāni :	Associated cetasikas	
	composition :	
8th greed-rooted citta (accompanied by equanimity, dissociated from fallacy, premeditated)	20	7 common and non-beautiful universal factors; vitakka, vicāra, adhimokkha, viriya, chanda; 4 unwholesome universal factors; lobha, māna, thīna, and middha. (7+5+4+4=20).
Dosamūla cittāni :	composition :	
1st hatred-rooted citta (accompanied by displeasure, associated with aversion, unpremeditated)	20	7 common and non-beautiful universal factors; vitakka, vicāra, adhimokkha, viriya, chanda; 4 unwholesome universal factors; dosa, issā, macchariya, and kukkucca. (7+5+4+4=20).
2nd hatred-rooted citta (accompanied by displeasure, associated with aversion, premeditated)	22	7 common and non-beautiful universal factors; vitakka, vicāra, adhimokkha, viriya, chanda; 4 unwholesome universal factors; dosa, issā, macchariya, kukkucca, thīna, and middha. (7+5+4+6=22).
Mohamūla cittāni :	composition :	
1st delusion-rooted citta (accompanied by equanimity, associated with doubt)	15	7 common and non-beautiful universal factors; 4 unwholesome universal factors; vitakka, vicāra, viriya; vicikicchā. (7+4+3+1=15).
2nd delusion-rooted citta (accompanied by equanimity, associated with restlessness)	15	7 common and non-beautiful universal factors; 4 unwholesome universal factors; vitakka, vicāra, adhimokkha, viriya. (7+4+3+1=15).

Appendix VI. Miscellaneous classifications

Chart 9. Classifying the sensuous sphere 24 beautiful cittas base on 52 cetasikas

24 *Hetuka sobhanacittāni* (with root, beautiful cittas)	Mahākriyacittāni	Mahāvipākacittāni	Mahākusalacittāni		Associated cetasikas
1st citta (accompanied by joy, associated with knowledge, unprompted)	●			38	13 common, non-beautiful factors (7+6); 25 beautiful factors. i.e. (13+25=38).
2nd citta (accompanied by joy, associated with knowledge, prompted)	●			38	
3rd citta (accompanied by joy, dissociated from knowledge, unprompted)	●			37	13 common, non-beautiful factors (7+6); 25 beautiful factors excluding amoha i.e. (13+(25-1)=38).
4th citta (accompanied by joy, dissociated from knowledge, prompted)	●			37	
5th citta (accompanied by equanimity, associated with knowledge, unprompted)	●			37	7 common, non-beautiful universal factors; vitakka, vicāra, adhimokkha, viriya, and chanda; 25 beautiful factors. i.e. (7+5+25=37).
6th citta (accompanied by equanimity, associated with knowledge, prompted)	●			37	
7th citta (accompanied by equanimity, dissociated from knowledge, unprompted)	●			36	7 common, non-beautiful universal factors; vitakka, vicāra, adhimokkha, viriya, and chanda; 25 beautiful factors excluding amoha. i.e. (7+5+(25-1)=36).
8th citta (accompanied by equanimity, dissociated from knowledge, prompted)	●			36	
1st citta (accompanied by joy, associated with knowledge, unprompted)		●		33	13 common, non-beautiful factors (7+6); 25 beautiful factors excluding the 3 Abstinences and 2 Illimitables. i.e. (13+(25-3-2)=33).
2nd citta (accompanied by joy, associated with knowledge, prompted)		●		33	
3rd citta (accompanied by joy, dissociated from knowledge, unprompted)		●		32	13 common, non-beautiful factors (7+6); 25 beautiful factors excluding the 3 Abstinences, 2 Illimitables and Amoha. i.e. (13+(25-3-2-1)=32)
4th citta (accompanied by joy, dissociated from knowledge, prompted)		●		32	

A Perfect Knowledge of Mind-Body from the Abhidhamma (Dhātukathā)

24 *Hetuka sobhanacittāni* (beautiful, with root cittas)	Mahākriyacittāni	Mahāvipākacittāni	Mahākusalacittāni		Associated cetasikas
5th citta (accompanied by equanimity, associated with knowledge, unprompted)	•			32	7 common, non-beautiful universal factors; vitakka, vicāra, adhimokkha, viriya, and chanda; 25 beautiful factors excluding the 3 Abstinences and 2 Illimitables. i.e. (7+5+(25-3-2)=32).
6th citta (accompanied by equanimity, associated with knowledge, prompted)	•			32	
7th citta (accompanied by equanimity, dissociated from knowledge, unprompted)	•			31	7 common, non-beautiful universal factors; vitakka, vicāra, adhimokkha, viriya, and chanda; 25 beautiful factors excluding the 3 Abstinences, 2 Illimitables, and Amoha. i.e. (7+5+(25-3-2-1)=31).
8th citta (accompanied by equanimity, dissociated from knowledge, prompted)	•			31	
1st citta (accompanied by joy, associated with knowledge, unprompted)			•	35	13 common, non-beautiful factors (7+6); 25 beautiful factors excluding the 3 Abstinences. i.e. (13+(25-3)=35).
2nd citta (accompanied by joy, associated with knowledge, prompted)			•	35	
3rd citta (accompanied by joy, dissociated from knowledge, unprompted)			•	34	13 common, non-beautiful factors (7+6); 25 beautiful factors excluding the 3 Abstinences and Amoha. i.e. (13+(25-3-1)=34).
4th citta (accompanied by joy, dissociated from knowledge, prompted)			•	34	
5th citta (accompanied by equanimity, associated with knowledge, unprompted)			•	34	7 common, non-beautiful universal factors; vitakka, vicāra, adhimokkha, viriya, and chanda; 25 beautiful factors excluding the 3 Abstinences. i.e. (13+(25-3)=34).
6th citta (accompanied by equanimity, associated with knowledge, prompted)			•	34	
7th citta (accompanied by equanimity, dissociated from knowledge, unprompted)			•	33	7 common, non-beautiful universal factors; vitakka, vicāra, adhimokkha, viriya, and chanda; 25 beautiful factors excluding 3 Abstinences and Amoha. i.e. (7+5+(25-3-1)=33)
8th citta (accompanied by equanimity, dissociated from knowledge, prompted)			•	33	

Appendix VI. Miscellaneous classifications

Chart 10. Classifying the 18 rootless cittas base on 52 cetasikas

18 *Ahetukacittāni* (rootless cittas)	Kriyacittāni	Vipākacittāni		Associated cetasikas
10 *Viññāṇa* cittas (2 sets of the fivefold consciousness of eye, ear, nose, tongue, and body)		•	7	the 7 common, non-beautiful universal mental factors.
2 Receiving citta accompanied by equanimity (*upekkhā-sampaṭicchana*)		•	10	the 7 common, non-beautiful universal mental factors; vitakka, vicāra, and adhimokkha. i.e. (7+3=10).
2 Investigating citta accompanied by equanimity (*upekkhā-santīraṇa*)		•	10	
1 Five-doors advertence citta accompanied by equanimity (*upekkhā-pañcadvārāvajjana*)	•		10	
1 Investigating citta accompanied by joy (*somanassa-santīraṇa*)		•	11	the 7 common, non-beautiful universal mental factors; vitakka, vicāra, adhimokkha, and pīti. i.e. (7+4=11).
1 Mind-door 'adverting' citta accompanied by equanimity (*upekkhā-manodvārāvajjana*)	•		11	the 7 common, non-beautiful universal mental factors; vitakka, vicāra, adhimokkha, and viriya. i.e. (7+4=11).
1 'Smile-producing' citta accompanied by joy (*somanassa-hasituppāda*)	•		12	the 7 common, non-beautiful universal mental factors; vitakka, vicāra, adhimokkha, viriya, and pīti. i.e. (7+5=12).

Chart 11. Classifying the 5 Jhānas based on 52 cetasikas

Fine-material sphere:	Immaterial sphere:		Associated cetasikas :
First-jhāna	3		35	13 common, non-beautiful factors (7+6); and 25 beautiful factors excluding 3 Abstinences. i.e. (13+(25-3)=35).
Second-jhāna	3		34	7 common, non-beautiful universal factors; 6 common occasional factors excluding vitakka; 25 beautiful factors excluding the 3 Abstinences. i.e. (7+(6-1)+(25-3)=34).
Third-jhāna	3		33	7 common, non-beautiful universal factors; 6 common occasional factors excluding vitakka and vicāra; 25 beautiful factors excluding the 3 Abstinences. i.e. (7+(6-2)+(25-3)=33).
Fourth-jhāna	3		32	7 common, non-beautiful universal factors; 6 common occasional factors excluding vitakka, vicāra and pīti; 25 beautiful factors excluding the 3 Abstinences. i.e. (7+(6-3)+(25-3)=32).
Fifth-jhāna	3	12	30	7 common, non-beautiful universal factors; 6 common occasional factors excluding vitakka, vicāra and pīti; 25 beautiful factors excluding the 3 Abstinences and 2 Illimitables. i.e. (7+(6-3)+(25-3-2)=30).

Supremandane sphere:			Associated cetasikas :
First-jhāna	8	36	13 common, non-beautiful factors (7+6); and 25 beautiful factors excluding 2 Illimitables. i.e. (13+(25-2)=36).
Second-jhāna	8	35	7 common, non-beautiful universal factors; 6 common occasional factors excluding vitakka; 25 beautiful factors excluding the 2 Illimitables. i.e. (7+(6-1)+(25-2)=35).
Third-jhāna	8	34	7 common, non-beautiful universal factors; 6 common occasional factors excluding vitakka and vicāra; 25 beautiful factors excluding the 2 Illimitables. i.e. (7+(6-2)+(25-2)=34).
Fourth-jhāna	8	33	7 common, non-beautiful universal factors; 6 common occasional factors excluding vitakka, vicāra and pīti; 25 beautiful factors excluding the 2 Illimitables. i.e. (7+(6-3)+(25-2)=33).
Fifth-jhāna	8	33	

Appendix VI. Miscellaneous classifications

Chart 12. Classification of the 28 matters by characteristics

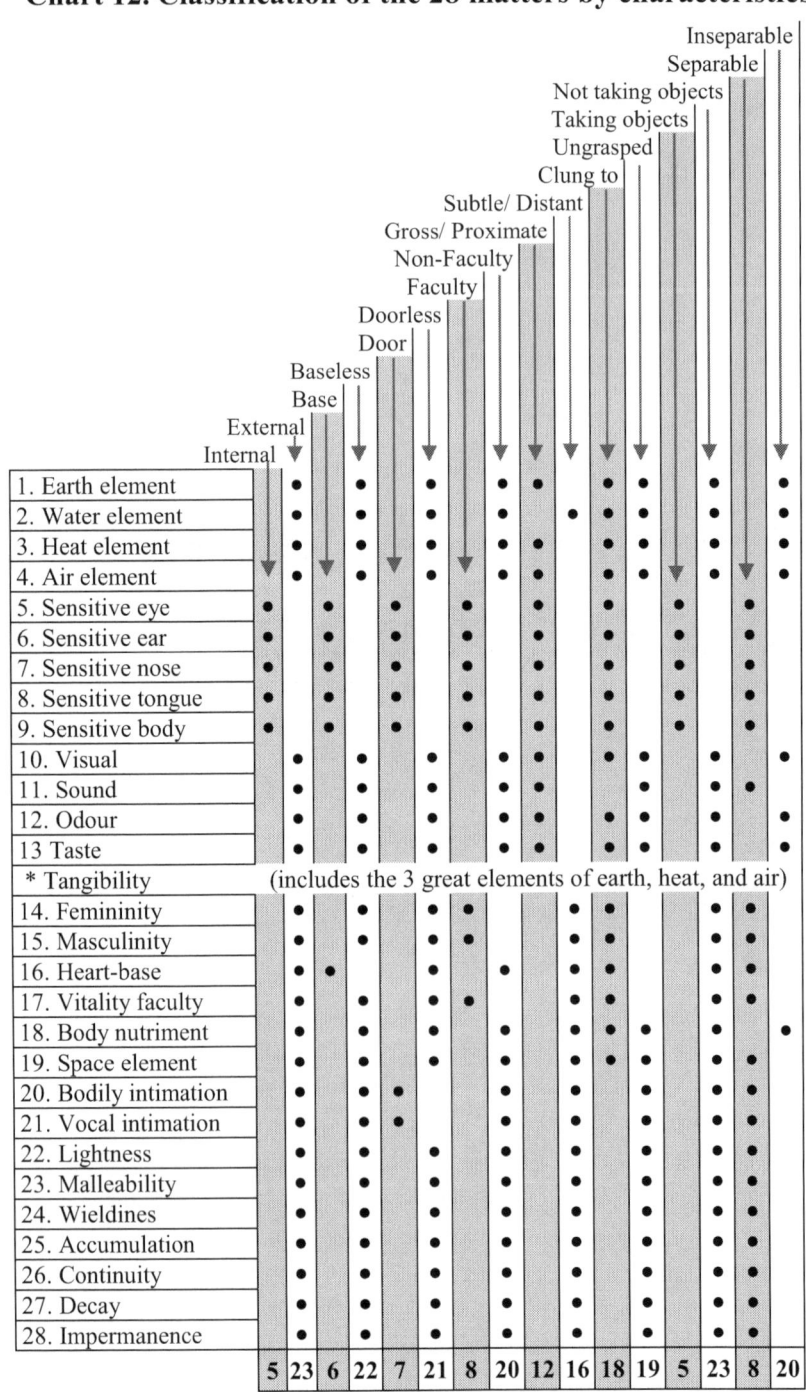

Chart 13. Classification of the 28 types of matters through their characteristics and functions – 12 classes

	Characteristics :		Constituent groups of matter :
1	Concretely-produced (*nipphanna*)	18	4 mahābhūtā, 5 pasāda, 4 gocara (visual, sound, odour, taste), 2 bhāva, hadaya, 1 jīvita, 1 āhāra).
	Non-concrete Matter (*anipphanna*)	10	the remainder of the 28 types of matter. i.e. (28-18=10).
2	Internal/self (*ajjhattika*)	5	the 5 pasāda-rūpas, serve as "doors" to the mind.
	External (*bāhira*)	23	the remainders, i.e. (28-5=23).
3	Base (*vatthu*)	6	regards as "seat" of mind, composed of the 5 pasāda-rūpas, 1 hadaya-vatthu.
	Baseless (*avatthu*)	22	that is, without substance, are the remainders. i.e. (28-6=22)
4	Door (*dvāra*)	7	serve as "doors" to the mind, namely the 5 pasāda-rūpā, 2 viññatti-rūpā (bodily intimation, vocal intimation).
	Doorless (*advāra*)	21	the remainders, i.e. (28-7=21).
5	Faculty (*indriya*)	8	serves as the controlling matter that governs the function, made up of the 5 pasādas, the 2 bhāvas and 1 jīvita.
	Non-faculty (*anindriya*)	20	the remainders, i.e. (28-8=20).
6	Gross (*oḷārika*)	12	the 5 pasādas, and the 7 gocaras.
	Subtle (*sukhuma*)	16	the remainders, i.e. (28-12=16).
7	Proximate (*santike*)	12	same as that of *oḷārika*.
	Distant (*dure*)	16	same as that of *sukhuma*.
8	Impinging (*sappaṭigha*)	12	lit. 'with striking', its matter groups are the same as that for *oḷārika*.
	Non-impinging (*appaṭigha*)	16	same as that of *sukhuma*.
9	Clung-to (*upādinna*)	18	5 pasāda-rūpas, 2 bhāva-rūpas, hadaya-vatthu, jīvita-rūpa, pariccheda-rūpa (referring to space element), and the 8 avinibbhogas.
	Ungrasped (*anupādinna*)	10	the remainders, i.e. (28-18=10).
10	Visible (*sanidassana*)	1	gocara-rūpa, visible matter seen with the eye.
	Invisible (*anidassana*)	27	the remaining matters. (28-1=27).

Appendix VI. Miscellaneous classifications

	Characteristics :		Constituent groups of matter :
11	States of object taken (*gocaraggāhika*)	5	literally, '*gocara*' means object, '*gāhika*' means 'state' that is taken in. *Gocaraggāhika* herein refers to the five sensitivities of the eye, ear, nose, tongue and body (5 pasāda-rūpas).
	States of no object taken (*agocaraggāhika*)	23	the remainders, i.e. (28-5=23)
12	Inseparable (*avinibbhoga*)	8	the 8 Inseparables made of the 8 inanimate things consist of the 4 Great Elements, colour, odour, taste and nutriment. Material life (*jīvita*) as also inanimate, is sometimes included.
	Separable (*vinibbhoga*)	20	the remainders, i.e. (28-8=20)

Chart 14. The five physical effects produced by the mind

	Effects :		Associated cittas :
1	Matter	19	cittas of the 2 Receving, 3 Investigating, 1 'Adverting' at one of the five sense-doors, 8 resultants (hetuka, sobhana-kusala), and the 5 fine-material resultants.
2	Bodily postures	26	the 10 fine-material cittas of the resultants and functionals, the 8 immaterial cittas, and the 8 supramundane cittas — produce matter and sustain bodily postures.
3	Intimation	32	the active 12 unwholesome cittas, 1 'Adverting' at one of the five sense-doors, 1 'smile-producing' functional citta (*hasituppāda*), 8 sensuous sphere active kusalas, 8 kriyas (hetuka- sobhana), 2 of the 5 *abhiññā* powers (viz. reminiscience of past lives, and ability to distinctly reading the mind of others, which can be attained by the 5th rūpajhāna) — produce matter, sustain bodily postures, and bring about intimation (*viññatti*).
4	Laughter	13	pleasant feeling that is associated with joy, coming from the 4 greed-rooted cittas, 1 'smile-producing' citta (*somanassa-hasituppāda*), 4 active wholesome cittas, 4 functional cittas — produce matter, sustain bodily postures, intimation, and bring about laughter.
5	Weeping	2	the 2 hatred-rooted cittas — produce matter, sustain bodily postures, intimation, laughter, and bring about crying.

A Perfect Knowledge of Mind-Body from the Abhidhamma (Dhātukathā)

Chart 15. Four material groups by the 4 conditions of matters

		Rūpa-kalāpā :	Constituents :
Kammaja	1	eye-decad	8 avinibbhoga matters + vitality + eye
	2	ear-decad	8 avinibbhoga matters + vitality + ear
	3	nose-decad	8 avinibbhoga matters + vitality + nose
	4	tongue-decad	8 avinibbhoga matters + vitality + tongue
	5	body-decad	8 avinibbhoga matters + vitality + body
	6	female-decad	8 avinibbhoga matters + vitality + femininity
	7	male-decad	8 avinibbhoga matters + vitality + masculinity
	8	heart-decad	8 avinibbhoga matters + vitality + heart base
	9	vital-nonad	8 avinibbhoga matters + vitality
Cittaja	1	pure octad	8 avinibbhoga matters
	2	bodily intimation-nonad	8 avinibbhoga matters + bodily intimation
	3	vocal intimation-decad	8 avinibbhoga matters + vocal intimation + sound
	4	mutability-undecad	8 avinibbhoga matters + lightness + malleability + wieldiness (3 *lahutadi-rūpā*)
	5	bodily intimation-dodecad	8 avinibbhoga matters + bodily intimation + the 3 *lahutadi-rūpā*
	6	sound-mutability-tridecad	8 avinibbhoga matters + sound + the 3 *lahutadi-rūpā*
Utuja	1	pure octad	8 avinibbhoga matters
	2	sound-nonad	8 avinibbhoga matters + sound
	3	mutability-undecad	8 avinibbhoga matters + the 3 *lahutadi-rūpā*
	4	sound-mutability-dodecad	8 avinibbhoga matters + sound + the 3 *lahutadi-rūpā*
Āhāraja	1	pure octad	8 avinibbhoga matters
	2	mutability-undecad	8 avinibbhoga matters + the 3 *lahutadi-rūpā*

Note:
i. Kammaja-kalāpā (matter group born of kamma) has 9 units, and 18 types of kamma-born matters. The 8 inseparable matters + vitality form one unit (a minimum 9 types of matter to form a single unit of this group). By adding other kamma-born matters to the unit, *Kammaja-kalāpā* has 18 types (9+9=18).
ii. Cittaja-kalāpā (matter group born of mind) has 6 units, 15 types (8+7=15).
iii. Utuja-kalāpā (matter group born of heat) has 4 units, 13 types (8+5=13).
iv. Āhāraja-kalāpā (matter group born of nutriment) has 2 units, 12 types (8+5)

Appendix VI. Miscellaneous classifications

Chart 16. Classification the 28 types of matters by their 4 conditions

28 Matters :	The 4 conditions (causes) of Matters																	
	Kammaja-kalāpā									Cittaja						Utuja				Āharaja	
	eye-decad	ear-decad	nose-decad	tongue-decad	body-decad	female-decad	male-decad	heart-decad	vital-decad	pure octad	bod. Int. nonad	vocal Int. nonad	mut. undecad	bod. Int. dodecad	sound M.ut. tridecad	pure octad	sound-nonad	mut. undecad	sound mut. dodecad	pure octad	mut. undecad
1. Earth element	•	•	•	•	•	•	•	•	•	•	•	•	•	•	•	•	•	•	•	•	•
2. Water element	•	•	•	•	•	•	•	•	•	•	•	•	•	•	•	•	•	•	•	•	•
3. Heat element	•	•	•	•	•	•	•	•	•	•	•	•	•	•	•	•	•	•	•	•	•
4. Air element	•	•	•	•	•	•	•	•	•	•	•	•	•	•	•	•	•	•	•	•	•
5. Sensitive eye	•																				
6. Sensitive ear		•																			
7. Sensitive nose			•																		
8. Sensitive tongue				•																	
9. Sensitive body					•																
10. Visual	•	•	•	•	•	•	•	•	•	•	•	•	•	•	•	•	•	•	•	•	•
11. Sound											•			•			•		•		
12. Odour	•	•	•	•	•	•	•	•	•	•	•	•	•	•	•	•	•	•	•	•	•
13 Taste	•	•	•	•	•	•	•	•	•	•	•	•	•	•	•	•	•	•	•	•	•
* Tangibility	(* includes the 3 great elements of earth, heat, air)																			
14. Femininity						•															
15. Masculinity							•														
16. Heart-base								•													
17. Vitality faculty	•	•	•	•	•	•	•	•	•												
18. Body nutriment	•	•	•	•	•	•	•	•	•	•	•	•	•	•	•	•	•	•	•	•	•
19. Space element																					
20. Bodily intimation											•			•							
21. Vocal intimation												•			•						
22. Lightness													•	•	•			•	•		•
23. Malleability													•	•	•			•	•		•
24. Wieldines													•	•	•			•	•		•
25. Accumulation																					
26. Continuity																					
27. Decay																					
28. Impermanence																					
	10	10	10	10	10	10	10	10	9	8	9	10	11	12	13	8	9	11	12	8	11

A Perfect Knowledge of Mind-Body from the Abhidhamma (Dhātukathā)

Chart 17. The 20 types of matters at the moment of Rebirth (produced by kamma)

	Kamma-born matters arising at moment of rebirth			Matters which do not arise at the moment of rebirth	
1	earth	4 mahābhūta	1	sound	5 vikāra-rūpa
2	liquid		2	bodily intimation (communicating)	
3	heat		3	vocal intimation (communicating)	
4	air/wind		4	lightness (mutable)	
5	sensitive eye	5 pasāda-rūpa	5	malleability (mutable)	
6	sensitive ear		6	wieldines (mutable)	
7	sensitive nose		7	decay (characteristic of matter)	
8	sensitive tongue		8	impermanence (characteristic of matter)	
9	sensitive body				
10	visible object				
11	odour				
12	taste				
13	femininity				
14	masculinity				
15	heart-base				
16	vitality				
17	nutriment				
18	space				
19	accumulation				
20	continuity				

Appendix VI. Miscellaneous classifications

Chart 18. Classification of cittas by types of feeling

Cittas classified by feelng:	Kāmakusala	Kāmakusala	Vipāka	Kriya	1st jhāna	2nd jhāna	3rd jhāna	4th jhāna	5th jhāna	Total	Composition:
Cittas associated with joy (*somanassa*)	4	4	5	5	11	11	11	11		62	4 kāma kusalas, 4 *lobhamūla*, 4 resultants (*hetuka sobhana-somanassa*), 4 functionals (*hetuka sobhana-somanassa*), 1 investigating resultant, 1 'smile-producing' functional (*hasituppāda*), 44 of 1st to 4th jhānas (11x4=44 excluded 5th jhānas). (4+4+4+4+1+1+44=62)
Cittas associated with happiness (*sukha*)			1							1	1 body-consciousness resultant, accompanied by happiness. The 63 cittas have 46 cetasikas.
Cittas associated with displeasure (*domanassa*)		2								2	2 *kāma hetuka-akusala* hatred rooted (*dosamūla*), follows by 21 cetasikas.
Cittas associated with suffering (*dukkha*)			1							1	1 body-consciousness resultant with pain or suffering, follows by 21 cetasikas.
Cittas associated with equanimity (*upekkhā*)	4	6	16	6					23	55	4 kāma kusalas, 6 kāma akusalas (4 *lobhamūla*, 2 *mohamūla*), 16 resultants (10 kusalas, 6 akussla), 6 functionals (2 rootless, 4 beautiful), 23 Fifth-jhānas (3 of rūpavacara, 12 of rūpavacara, 8 of lokuttara). Total 55 cittas are accompanied by 46 cetasikas.
									Total:	121	

Note:

i. cittas accompanied by joy are treated as 63 types as joy (*somanassa*) and pleasure/ happiness (*sukha*) are taken together as a group. (62+1=63).

ii. cittas accompanied by pain are treated as 3 types as displeasure (*domanassa*) and suffering (*dukkha*) are grouped as one. (2+1=3).

A Perfect Knowledge of Mind-Body from the Abhidhamma (Dhātukathā)

Chart 19. Classification of the types of feeling by spheres

Sphere	Sub-group	Type	joyful feeling	pleasurable feeling	displeasing feeling	painful feeling	equanimous feeling
Sensuous sphere	With root, Beautiful	Active wholesome	4				4
		Resultant	4				4
		Functional	4				4
	Rootless	Wholesome resultant	1	1			6
		Unwholesome resultant				1	6
		Functional	1				2
		Active unwholesome	4		2		6
Fine-material sphere		Wholesome	4				1
		Resultant	4				1
		Functional	4				1
Immaterial sphere		Wholesome					4
		Resultant					4
		Functional					4
Supramundane sphere	Path	*Sotāpatti*	4				1
		Sakadāgāmi	4				1
		Anāgāmi	4				1
		Arahatta	4				1
	Fruition	*Sotāpatti*	4				1
		Sakadāgāmi	4				1
		Anāgāmi	4				1
		Arahatta	4				1
			62	**1**	**2**	**1**	**55**

Appendix VI. Miscellaneous classifications

Chart 20. Classification of 89 cittas by association with 'roots'

18 cittas without roots	Kāmakusala	Kāmākusala	Vipāka	Kriya	Composition :
Five-sense-doors advertence citta				1	1 functional citta of 5 sense-doors 'adverting' accompanied by equanimity (*upekkhāsahagataṃ pañcadvārāvajjanacittaṃ*)
Sense-consciousness		10	10		10 resultant viññāṇas (fivefold pair of eye, ear, nose, tongue, body cons.)
Receiving cittas			2		2 resultants of 'receiving' cittas accompanied by equanimity
Investigating cittas			3		3 resultants of 'investigating' cittas (1 citta accompanied by joy, 2 cittas accompanied by equanimity).
Determining citta				1	only the one functional mind-door 'adverting' citta which performs the function of determining in five sense door citta and which brings about intellection or thought process.
'Smile-producing' citta				1	1 'smile-producing' functional citta (*somanassa-hasituppāda*)
				18	
71 cittas with roots					**Composition :**
2 cittas associated with 1 root		2			2 delusion-rooted cittas (*mohamūla*)
22 cittas associated with 2 roots	10				8 *lobhamūla*, 2 *mohamūla* (8+2=10), 4 kusala dissociated from knowledge, 4 resultant *hetuka sobhana-kusala* cittas dissociated from knowledge (2 with joy, 2 with equanimity), 4 functional *hetuka-sobhana* cittas dissociated from knowledge (2 with joy, 2 with equanimity)
	4		4	4	
47 cittas associated with 3 roots	4		4	4	12 of *hetuka-sobhana* associated with knowledge (cittas from 4 wholesome, 4 wholesome resultants, 4 beautiful functionals).
Fine-material sphere	5		5	5	1st to 5th jhānas.
Immaterial sphere	4		4	4	5th jhānas.
Supramundane sphere	4		4		cittas with jhānas (4 paths, 4 fruitions)
				71	

Chart 21. The 14 Functions of cittas

	Function:	Definition:
1.	Rebirth-linking or "re-linking" (*paṭisandhi*)	The citta that one experiences at the dying moment of conception, is one which links the past life with present. *Paṭisandhi*, in the same way as *cuti*, arises only once at final moment of death.
2.	Life-continuum (*bhavaṅga*)	*Bhavaṅga* arises and perishes in an infinitesimal part of time and innumerable times in between our occasions of active cognition. It is comparable to a stream-flow without ever remaining static for two consecutive moments. *Bhavaṅga* preserves the continuity of one's life.
3.	Adverting (*āvajjana*)	*Āvajjana* (lit. 'turning towards') corresponds to 3 *bhavaṅga* states: (i) 'past *bhavaṅga*' which is the moment which just passes by its passive state; (ii) 'vibrating *bhavaṅga*' is when an object impinges on the mind, *bhavaṅga* 'vibrates' for one single mind-moment (*cittakhaṇa*); (iii) 'arrest *bhavaṅga*' refers to the flow of *bhavaṅga* thereafter is checked or 'arrested' before the next mind-moment arises to 'advert' the consciousness towards that object.
4.	Seeing (*dassana*)	These five sentivities can be grouped collectively under fivefold sense-impressions (*pañcaviññāṇa*). For external objects, the mind-moment is termed as this fivefold sense-door cognition (*pañcaviññāṇa*), while mental object is functioned under mind-door cognition (*manodvārāvajjana*).
5.	Hearing (*savana*)	
6.	Smelling (*ghāyana*)	
7.	Tasting (*sāyana*)	
8.	Touching (*phusana*)	
9.	Receiving (*sampaṭicchana*)	When an object impinges on a sense faculty at one of the five sense-doors, a single mind-moment arises from that sense-impression. In that sense, the sense-door is said to "receive" the object into contact.
10.	Investigating (*santīraṇa*)	*Santīraṇa* arises immediately after the Receiving citta, which examines the object that had just been cognised.
11.	Determining (*voṭṭhabbana*)	*Voṭṭhabbana*, influenced by one's own past experiences and inclinations, discriminates and determines the thought-process as being moral or immoral.
12.	Impulsion (dynamic) (*javana*)	*Javana* usually lasts for seven mostly identical mind-moments, or five at the moment of death. *Javana* is volitional which explains at this point whether a dream, for example, can be understood as unwholesome or not.
13.	Registering (*tadārammaṇa* or *tadālambana*)	*Tadārammaṇa* (lit. 'having that object') after identifying *javana*, it registers for two mind-moments. After the second registering mind-moment has perished, *bhavaṅga*

Appendix VI. Miscellaneous classifications

		resumes again until it is interrupted by another thought process.
14.	Death (*cuti*)	*Cuti* is of the same type of *paṭisandhi* and *bhavaṅga*, they possess the same object and same mental co-adjuncts. It differs from them only because it marks the exit from an existing life.

Chart 22. Classification of cittas through their functions

	Functions of cittas :		The associated cittas :
1.	Rebirth-linking (*paṭisandhi*)	19	2 investigating cittas (*upekkhā-santīraṇa*), 8 mahāvipākas (8 cittas with roots, beautiful resultants, 5 fine-material resultants, 4 immaterial resultants. (2+8+5+4=19).
2.	Life-continuum (*bhavaṅga*)	19	same as *paṭisandhi*
3.	Adverting (*āvajjana*)	2	1 five-doors 'adverting' citta (*upekkhā-pañcadvārāvajjana*), 1 mind-door 'adverting' citta (*upekkhā-manodvārāvajjana*)
4.	Seeing (*dassana*)	2	2 eye-consciousness (*cakkhuviññāṇa*)
5.	Hearing (*savana*)	2	2 ear-consciousness (*sotaviññāṇa*)
6.	Smelling (*ghāyana*)	2	2 nose-consciousness (*ghānaviññāṇa*)
7.	Tasting (*sāyana*)	2	2 tongue-consciousness (*jivhāviññāṇa*)
8.	Touching (*phusana*)	2	2 body-consciousness (*kāyaviññāṇa*), acompanied by pleasure and by pain.
9.	Receiving (*sampaṭicchana*)	2	2 receiving cittas (*upekkhā-sampaṭicchana*)
10.	Investigating (*santīraṇa*)	3	3 investigating cittas (1 *somanassa- santīraṇa*, 2 *upekkhā-santīraṇa*)
11.	Determining (*voṭṭhabbana*)	1	mind-door 'adverting' citta (*manodvārāvajjana*)
12.	Impulsion (*javana*)	55	12 unwholesome cittas, 21 wholesome cittas; 18 functional cittas (excluded the two 'adverting' cittas (*pañcadvārāvajjana* and *manodvārāvajjana*), and 4 supramundane *phalacittāni*. (12+21+18+4=55)
13.	Registering (*tadārammaṇa*)	11	3 investigating cittas, the 8 mahāvipākas (8 great resultant cittas, with root, beautiful) are following the *javana*-object.
14.	Death (*cuti*)	19	same as *paṭisandhi*

Chart 23. Cittas classification with multiplicity of functions

Function counts:		The associated cittas :
with single function	68	10 viññāṇa cittas (5x2), 1 five-doors 'adverting' citta (*pañcadvārāvajjana*), 2 receiving cittas (*upekkhā-sampaṭicchana*), 55 *javana*-associated cittas (10+1+2+55=68).
with two functions	2	1 investigating citta accompanied by joy (*somanassa-santīraṇa*), 1 mind-door 'adverting' citta (*manodvārāvajjana*).
with three functions	9	5 fine-material resultants, and 4 immaterial resultants.
with four functions	8	8 mahāvipākas (the 8 great resultant cittas, with root, beautiful) [13]
with five functions	2	2 investigating cittas with equanimity (*upekkhā-santīraṇa*). [14]

---

[13] The 8 mahāvipāka cittas are associated with the 4 functions of *paṭisandhi*, *bhavaṅga*, *javana*, *tadārammaṇa*, and *cuti*.

[14] The 2 Investigating cittas accompanied by equanimity present at the 5 functions of *paṭisandhi*, *bhavaṅga*, *santīraṇa*, *tadārammaṇa*, and *cuti*.

Appendix VI. Miscellaneous classifications

Chart 24. Cittas classification base on sense-doors

		Eye-door	Ear-door	Nose-door	Tongue-door	Body-door	Mind-door	Arise without sense-doors
1.	Five-doors adverting citta (*pañcadvārāvajjana*)	1	1	1	1	1		
2.	Sense-based — Eye-consciousness	1						
	Ear-consciousness		1					
	Nose-consciousness			1				
	Tongue-consciousness				1			
	Body-consciousness					1		
3.	2 Receiving cittas (*upekkhā-sampaṭicchana*)	2	2	2	2	2		
4.	3 Investigating cittas (somanassa 1, upekkhā 2)	3	3	3	3	3		
5.	1 Determining mind-door adverting citta (*manodvārāvajjana*)	1	1	1	1	1	1	
6.	29 sensuous javanas (refer to the active side of life consisting of the 17 kusala cittas and 12 akusala cittas, belong to *kammabhava*).	29	29	29	29	29	55	
7.	Registering citta (*tadārammaṇa*) (11-3=8)	8	8	8	8	8	11	
	Cittas that arise through any of the 5 sense-doors:	45	45	45	45	45		
	Cittas that arise through the mind-door:						67	
	Cittas that do not arise through the sense-doors:							19

The 19 types of cittas which arise without sense-doors are associated with the three functions of rebirth-linking, life-continuum, and death.

Chart 25. Cittas classification base on multiplicity of doors

Door counts:		The associated cittas :
By one door	36	the 10 viññāṇa cittas, and 26 appanā javanas (namely the 4 arūpa kusalacittāni, 4 arūpa kriyācittāni, 5 rūpa kusalacittāni, 5 rūpa kriyācittāni, 8 lokuttaracittāni).
By five doors	3	the 2 receiving cittas (*upekkhā-sampaṭicchana*), 1 five-doors 'adverting' citta.
By six doors	31	1 investigating citta accompanied by joy, 1 mind-door 'adverting' citta, 29 sensuous javanas (bound up with the active side of the 17 moral and 12 immoral cittas).
Either by six doors or door-free	10	the 2 investigating cittas (*upekkhā-santīraṇa*), the 8 mahāvipākas (with root, beautiful resultants). Note that investigating cittas present at 5 functions [14] while the 8 mahāvipākas present at 4 functions [13] which both include rebirth-linking, life-continuum, and death, thereby can also be "doors-free" performing cittas.
Ever door-free	9	5 resultants of the fine-material sphere, 4 resultants of the immaterial sphere.

Chart 26. Classification of cittas base on their objects

Types :		Associated cittas :
Sense-sphere objects (*kāmāvacarārammaṇa*)	25	the 10 viññāṇa cittas, the 3 mind-elements (1 *pañcadvārāvajjana*, 2 receiving (*upekkhā-sampaṭicchana*), 1 'smile-producing' citta, 11 remaining resultants (3 Investigating, 8 mahāvipakas).
Sublime objects (*mahaggatārammaṇa*)	6	the 6 jhāna cittas of immaterial sphere (the 2nd and 4th, as the 2nd citta takes the 1st as its 'concept object', and the 4th citta takes the 3rd as its 'concept object')
Concept objects (*paññatti*)	21	the 15 fine-material cittas, and the 6 immaterial cittas (1st and 3rd cittas only, thereby 2x3=6).
Nibbāna objects (*nibbānārammaṇa*)	8	the 8 supramundane cittas.

Appendix VI. Miscellaneous classifications

Chart 27. Classification of the 28 Concept Objects in Jhānas

			First jhāna	Second jhāna	Third jhāna	Fourth jhāna	Fifth jhāna	1st Arūpajhāna	3rd Arūpajhāna
10	undesirableness (*asubha*)		10						
1	bodily mindfulness (*kāyagatasati*)		1						
1	benevolence (*mettā*)		1	1	1	1			
1	compassion (*karunā*)		1	1	1	1			
1	altruistic joy or appreciation (*muditā*)		1	1	1	1			
1	equanimity (*upekkhā*)						1		
10	contemplative object (*kasina*)		10	10	10	10	10		
1	breathing mindfulness (*ānāpānasati*)		1	1	1	1			
1	the infinity of space							1	
1	nothingness								1
28	Combined objects :		25	14	14	14	11	1	1

Chart 28. Classification of cittas according to their Bases

Types:			Associated cittas :	
Eye-base	2		the 2 eye-consciousness	*cakkhuviññāna*
Ear-base	2		the 2 ear-consciousness	*sotaviññāna*
Nose-base	2		the 2 nose-consciousness	*ghānaviññāna*
Tongue-base	2		the 2 tongue-consciousness	*jivhāviññāna*
Body-base	2		the 2 body-consciousness	*kāyaviññāna*
Heart-base (prominent)	33		2 hatred-rooted cittas	*dosamūla*
			2 receiving cittas	*sampaṭicchana*
			3 investigating cittas	*santīraṇa*
			1 five-doors 'adverting' citta	*pañcadvārāvajjana*
			1 'smile-producing' citta	*hasituppada*
			8 resultants (hetuka-sobhana-kusala)	*mahāvipāka*
			15 fine-material sphere cittas	*rūpāvacara*
			1 'Stream-Winning' path-citta	*sotāpattimagga*

(10 *viññānas* bracket on right side for the first five rows)

A Perfect Knowledge of Mind-Body from the Abhidhamma (Dhātukathā)

Types:		Associated cittas :	
Heart-base (occasional)	42	8 greed-rooted cittas	*lobhamūla*
		2 delusion-rooted cittas	*mohamūla*
		1 mind-door 'adverting' citta	*manodvārāvajjana*
		8 sense-sphere great wholesome cittas	*mahākusala*
		8 functional cittas (with root, beautiful)	*mahākriya*
		4 immaterial sphere wholesome cittas	*arūpa kusala*
		4 immaterial sphere functional cittas	*arūpa kriya*
		7 supramundane cittas excluding 1st path	*lokuttara*
Without base	4	the 4 immaterial sphere resultant cittas	*arūpa vipāka*

Chart 29. Classification of cittas according to consciousness, bases, and elements

89 Cittas :	Base :	Consciousness-Elements :
2 Eye-Consciousness	Mind-Base	Eye-Consciousnss Element
2 Ear-Consciousness		Ear-Consciousnss Element
2 Nose-Consciousness		Nose-Consciousnss Element
2 Tongue-Consciousness		Tongue-Consciousnss Element
2 Body-Consciousness		Body-Consciousnss Element
1 Five-doors advertence, 2 Receiving		Mind-Element
76 remaining cittas		Mind-Consciousnss Element

Bibliography

[AN] Aṅguttara-Nikāya

[CTS4] Chaṭṭha Saṅgāyana Tipiṭaka 4

[Dhs] Dhammasaṅgaṇi

[DhsA] Atthasālinī (Dhammasaṅgaṇi-Aṭṭhakathā)

[DN] Dīgha-Nikāya

[KN] Khuddaka-Nikāya

[MN] Majjhima-Nikāya

[PañkA] Pañcappakaraṇa-Aṭṭhakathā

[SN] Saṃyutta-Nikāya

[Vibh] Vibhaṅga

A.P. Buddhadatta Mahāthera. *Concise Pāli-English Dictionary*. Delhi: Motilal Banarsidass, 1997.

Nyanatiloka Mahāthera, Nyanaponika Thera (ed.). *Buddhist Dictionary: Manual of Buddhist Terms and Doctrines*. Kandy: BPS, 1980.

Nyanatiloka Mahāthera. *Guide Through The Abhidhamma Pitaka: A Synopsis of the Philosophical Collection of the Theravada Buddhist Canon*. Sri Lanka: BPS, 1938.

R.C. Childers. *A Dictionary of Pali Language*. London: Trübner & Co, 1875.

T. W. Rhys Davids and William Stede, eds. *The Pali-English Dictionary*. Oxford: PTS, 1921-1925.

U Kyaw Khine (trans). *The Dhammasaṅganī: Enumeration of the Ultimate Realities Vol 1*. Delhi: Sri Satguru Publications, 1999.

U Nārada Mūla Paṭṭhāna Sayadaw. *Discourse On Elements* (*Dhātu-Kathā*): *The Third Book of the Abhidhamma Piṭaka*. Oxford: PTS, 1977.

About The Author

P.B. Tan (隨藏) is from Kuching, a scenic town in a state they called "land of the hornbills". The author is a passionate scholar in the Buddhist studies, with specialisation in Theravada Buddhism. He has been a longtime practitioner of the Buddha's teaching since his youth. He graduated with a Master Degree in Buddhist Philosophy in early 2015, from the International Buddhist College in Thailand. Currently he has returned to his hometown to continue his research in the Theravada Abhidhamma Piṭaka. P.B. Tan has authored the following books on Abhidhamma:

An Anatomy of Mind. Being Essence of the Dhammasangani in Abhidhamma. (2015)

An Analysis of Mind from the Vibhaṅga in Abhidhamma
First Edition, Sept. 2016
Second Edition, Feb. 2017

Essential Teaching of the Dhammasaṅgaṇi from Abhidhamma
First Edition, 2017
Second Edition, Mar. 2019

An Analysis of Individual-Types from the Abhidhamma (Puggalapaññatti). (2016)

A Perfect Knowledge of Mind-Body from the Abhidhamma (Dhātukathā)
First printing: Mar. 2017
Republication: Aug. 2019

An Analytical Study of the Yamaka from Abhidhamma, Volume I
First printing: Nov. 2017
Second Edition: April, 2018
Third Edition: July, 2018

An Analytical Study of the Yamaka from Abhidhamma, Volume II
June, 2018

Made in United States
Orlando, FL
01 May 2025